Obedience and Civilization

Obedience and Civilization
AUTHORIZED CRIME AND THE NORMALITY OF EVIL

Don Mixon

PLUTO  PRESS

London   Winchester, Mass

First published 1989 by Pluto Press
345a Archway Road, London N6 5AA
and 8 Winchester Place, Winchester,
MA 01890, USA

Typesetting: Ransom Electronic Publishing,
Woburn Sands, Bucks

Printed and bound in Hungary by Interpress

British Library Cataloguing in Publication Data

Mixon, Don.
  Obedience and civilization : the origins of
  authorized crime.
  1. Man. Obedience – sociological perspectives
  I. Title
  303.3' 6

  ISBN 0–7453–0331–5

Library of Congress Cataloging-in-Publication Data
Mixon, Don. 1930-
    Obedience and civilization : authorized crime and the normality
    of evil / Don Mixon.
        p. cm.
    Bibliography: p.
    Includes index.
    ISBN 0-7453-0331-5
    1. Authority. 2. Obedience. I. Title.
  HM271.M52   1989
  303.3'6—dc20   89-31926
                                                                 CIP

Contents

For Eloise

Acknowledgements

Mind is so thoroughly social that to adequately acknowledge all those who have contributed to my way of thinking would require an autobiography. Most of the influences specific to the book's subject matter are mentioned in the text. The writers I have found most helpful in understanding obedience and hierarchy are Hannah Arendt, Elias Canetti, Lewis Mumford and Alexander Rüstow. Since Arendt, Canetti, Mumford and Rüstow are not psychologists I would like to thank here four people (among many) who made it possible for me to think that a social psychologist can range as widely as I have done: Paul Secord, Rom Harré, Willard Day and A.R. Louch, who in their writing have opened up the notion of what psychology might be. Whether or not this particular exercise will meet with the approval of any of them I do not know. Paul Secord and later Willard Day supervised the PhD thesis upon which the second chapter is based. Paul showed himself well in advance of psychologists *circa* 1970 in approving and encouraging the thesis.

Bill Noble read an early draft of the book and made invaluable comments and objections. Bill hasn't seen the final manuscript so I do not know what he will think of the way I have dealt with his objections. Siu Chow offered helpful comments on the Preface. In order to get the manuscript typed I had to learn to use a computer. I would like to thank (among others) Lyn Nicholson, Kathy Wilson and Anne Porter for helping me grapple with getting the computer to obey me. The problem, of course, is not in the commanded, but the commander – as it has been for the several millennia since the command hierarchy was invented.

Preface

A year or two before the campus witnessed the longest student strike in history a fellow student at San Francisco State told me about an exciting study that portrayed the ultimate conformity: experimental subjects obediently giving very strong, possibly lethal, shocks to other subjects.

'Why would they do that?'

'Read it.'

So I went to the library, opened Volume 67 of the *Journal of Abnormal and Social Psychology*, and saw something I had never before and never since encountered. The article in question, called 'Behavioral Study of Obedience', had been handled so often that, quite literally, it was in tatters. Bound volumes of psychology journals more commonly appear pristine, as if never touched by student hands.

Why the excitement and interest? Some of the marks left by use may have resulted from frequent classroom assignment, but I suspect, knowing something of the habits of students, that most got to the article in the same way that I did. But why should students at San Francisco State be so eager to read about experimental subjects behaving badly?

In the late 1960s student opposition to the undeclared, but seemingly never-ending, war in Vietnam was very strong. Internal opponents of any war must counter the notion that not only is their country in the right, but their country's people are better than the enemy's people. Historically, American self-righteousness has flourished untroubled by doubt, nourished in the Second World War by the relative ease with which Americans could picture themselves the moral superiors of the unspeakable Nazis.

The study in question, the first in a series on obedience conducted by the social psychologist Stanley Milgram, seemed to provide powerful ammunition for anti-war students wishing to penetrate the armour of American ethical superiority. (My Lai was still in the future.) For Milgram had recruited a cross-section of ordinary American males who seemingly were willing to harm, possibly fatally harm, a fellow subject. What was so fascinatingly horrifying was that subjects did what they did for no discernible reason other than wishing to follow the instructions of the experimenter. Even the abominable Nazis had available the excuse that they *believed* in killing Jews, or if they did not, could claim to fear the consequences of refusing to obey commands. In contrast, Milgram's subjects could suffer no penalty for refusing to obey.

 The study was liberating. People of all countries are brought up believing that fellow-nationals in all sorts of ways are superior to people in other countries. Those who later learn about how naïve nationalism works against international cooperation and peaceful relations often come to consider themselves above the temptations of national prejudice. Nevertheless I would be surprised if all are entirely successful in shaking off their upbringing. At some level even the most sophisticated probably continue to suspect that fellow-nationals probably are just a bit better than people of other countries. Milgram's study helped liberate those who wished to be free from lingering illusions.

I was deeply interested in what I found in San Francisco State's tattered volume and quickly read all that Milgram had subsequently published. When in a graduate seminar in the summer of 1968 the subject of Milgram's studies came up I was well prepared and talked enthusiastically about the findings only to be brought up short by a seemingly simple question asked by the instructor, Harvey Peskin. Would I be willing to conduct such a study myself? The question was difficult because, though I did not doubt the importance of Milgram's work, I did have serious reservations about the ethics of his research procedure. Not only was the research design built on an elaborate deception – a series of lies if you like – but many of the subjects in it had shown alarming signs of emotional disturbance. In other words many were led by lies to experience something extremely disturbing. Could the findings possibly justify the lying and the suffering?

I had no conflict about deception studies in general, for I thought most of them were misconceived, trivial and uninteresting. Findings from such studies could not possibly justify the lies told to subjects. In contrast, Milgram's findings were of vital consequence and seemed to show that experimental social psychology could be an important discipline. If to Peskin's question I replied that I would not conduct such a study, I appeared to be saying that I would be unwilling to undertake research of importance or significance. Since trivial work is at least as unattractive as lying, saying no meant that if I wished to do social psychology I would need to devise a way of doing research that could pose significant questions without lying to research participants. Despite the ubiquity of deception in social psychological research the task didn't seem impossible: after all, experimental psychologists in such areas as perception and learning get along perfectly well without lying to their subjects. I made three separate attempts in graduate seminars and finally put together what I had learned in my PhD research.

Here the story takes a turn. For though I was able to demonstrate that important social questions can be investigated without lying to research participants, I also found that Milgram's findings are not what they appear to be. When examined closely the behaviour of his subjects does *not* provide the powerful lesson that made the findings so attractive and valuable.

At the time I was not particularly concerned about the loss of the lesson. I have long thought that scholars who claim the status of scientist, as do most psychologists, must be able to warrant scientifically the assertions they make on the basis of their research. I became convinced that Milgram, like many social psychologists, could not scientifically warrant the assertions he made about his subjects. No matter how interesting the findings, if the warrant is not there, a study fails as a piece of science. The most important lesson from any failed study is the invitation to find out why it failed and to work on problems of research method so that, in future, assertions can be properly warranted.

I quickly discovered that criticism of Milgram's work was not particularly welcome. Over the years I have had ample opportunity to find out from students and colleagues the pitfalls involved in criticizing, not just Milgram's work, but any study that claims to offer scientific evidence in support of something the student or colleague wants to believe. Criticism of a study's method is taken as criticism of the study's conclusions, whereas in fact criticism of method attacks the warrant, not the conclusion. But, of course, an unwarranted conclusion is stripped of its scientific support. Even so, when writing or talking about obedience it has always seemed obvious to me that if I say that the subjects in Milgram's studies did not do what Milgram claimed, I am *not* saying that the lesson drawn from the studies necessarily is false. If a person makes a true statement and then supports it by evidence which can be shown to be spurious, the evidence's spuriousness does not negate the truth of the statement. As obvious as this may seem, it is not surprising that criticism of a study's method often gets mistaken for an attack on the study's conclusions.

Social and political beliefs can insulate studies from criticism. Siamak Movehedi told me that when he and Ali Banuazzi (1975) published a criticism of the research method used in the Stanford Prison Experiment (Haney, Banks & Zimbardo, 1973) they received impassioned letters, many from prisoners or former prisoners, claiming that their criticism was wrong, that prisons really are as claimed in the study. Movehedi was saddened by the letters for it had been no part of his intention to deny that prisons are as the study describes. A criticism of method simply denies that the study can scientifically warrant the claims. It does not and cannot show that the claims are false.

Milgram's studies seemed to show ordinary Americans behaving far more obediently than anyone thought they would. My demonstration that the ordinary Americans were not behaving as Milgram claimed does not and cannot show that the general lesson is untrue. Americans are indeed far more obedient than they think they are. But then so are citizens of all nominally democratic states. Obedience plays a major role in the everyday life of people who fancy themselves autonomous and independent. How this can be so and how everyday obedience has become partially invisible is a subject of this book.

The late Stanley Milgram deserves credit for calling the attention of a large audience to the seriousness of everyday obedience. That I need to devote a long chapter to showing what Milgram got wrong can be seen as a tribute to how his work has dominated current thought about obedience.

If I believe in the importance of the general social/political lesson taught by Milgram's studies why do I take the trouble, in effect, to discredit the work? Wouldn't it be more socially salutary to let the lesson stand? I could make a long list of reasons, but two stand out. One reason is connected with the fact that statements made in late twentieth century society claiming the authority of science have a credence unmatched by any other form of warrant. Science's authority is so closely bound up with honesty that nothing more seriously threatens scientific credibility than dishonesty. Since self-deception is so easy, those of us who wish to believe in the results of a study have a particular charge to look closely at its warrant. Personal as well as scientific credibility is at issue. Personal credibility cannot be maintained by critically examining only studies with unwanted conclusions.

A second reason comes from seeing that although it is generally salutary to be aware that people are more obedient than they think they are, Milgram's particular lesson actually feeds a dangerous prejudice. Milgram's prototypical situation showed 65 per cent of subjects obeying and 35 per cent defying. Those who take the percentages as a true estimate of what happens when authorities issue commands to harm or kill suffer from a dangerous delusion. The proportion of subordinates who obey authorized criminal commands to harm or kill ordinarily is 100 per cent. The 65/35 split feeds the dangerous fancy that only the mass of conformists obey such commands, whereas I, one of the élite, would be defiant. Milgram failed to describe the command/ obedience relationship accurately.

A psychologist recently remarked that criticism of Milgram is 'old hat' – a solid textbook supported opinion. That most psychologists get much of what they know from textbooks is unsurprising. What goes under the name of 'psychology' is divided into many disciplines and even more subdisciplines. Textbook writers – most of them subdisciplinary specialists who get most of their material from other textbooks – paint an uncomplicated picture of Milgram's work. If they give any hint at all that the studies generated controversy, readers are assured (at least by implication) that everything was properly aired and settled long ago. How could it be otherwise? Psychology is after all a science and in science difficulties are dealt with in open public forum. Or so it is believed.

Psychologists who think that their discipline deals with controversy openly and publicly are mistaken. A detailed rendering of how psychological journals failed to provide a forum for Milgram's critics would make an interesting but long story, a story which I hope one day will tempt an historian of science. For now I will swiftly sketch a few instances.

The story begins rather well with the publication of Diana Baumrind's (1964) ethical critique of Milgram's study in the *American Psychologist*, a genuinely public forum received by all members of the American Psychological Association. Milgram (1964) replied to Baumrind in the same journal. Although his reply by no means satisfactorily answered Baumrind, at least the critique and reply appeared in a place where psychologists were likely to see it. From here on the record is not good. I suspect the reason is that many psychologists, not unlike many other people, are able to separate ethics from fact. The separation of ethical judgement concerning what Milgram did from what Milgram claimed that he found, allows the findings to stand, untouched by whether or not Milgram behaved ethically.

[The story of Baumrind's efforts to publish her critique is not as rosy as I supposed. After type was set I received a letter from

Professor Baumrind informing me that she had considerable difficulty publishing her 1964 paper and no success at all in publishing a rebuttal to Milgram's reply. Baumrind assures me that she has no wish to complain in print about the treatment of her critique and rebuttal. Her reasons for not wishing to complain are based on a clear understanding of why the psychological establishment did not encourage criticism of Milgram, but I think she is both too forgiving and too modest. The unpublished rebuttal, which I have just read for the first time, is not simply an important contribution to ethical issues, but also is a serious challenge to Milgram's interpretation of his findings. I cannot help but think that had the *American Psychologist* been willing to publish the rebuttal in 1964, consequent public perception of Milgram's work would have been considerably different.]

Criticisms based on Milgram's research method and conceptual grasp of what he was doing are another matter, for such criticisms challenge his interpretation of the findings. In 1968 Charles Holland finished a PhD dissertation that raised important methodological questions. I can find no record that Holland ever succeeded in publishing any part of the thesis in a psychological journal. However, he and Martin Orne did publish a jointly written article in that same year (Orne & Holland, 1968). Orne, one of psychology's best known and most important thinkers on questions of method, had published a landmark article (Orne, 1962) in *American Psychologist* only a few years before. However, the critique of Milgram did not appear, as might be expected, in *American Psychologist* or any other APA journal, but in a *psychiatric* journal which was not abstracted by *Psychological Abstracts*. Since searching *Psych Abstracts* was at that time the chief means of finding out what was published, the criticism in effect was out of sight.

A theoretical version of my own PhD dissertation was published in 1972 in a new journal not then abstracted in *Psych Abstracts*. But when I attempted to publish an empirical version where social psychologists would see it, the paper was rejected. Journals, of course, claim that they reject papers on grounds of quality. Yet concurrently with the journal rejections, my dissertation was judged the best of the year in the Measurement and Evaluation field by the American Institutes for Research.

In 1977 I found out from a philosopher colleague about two articles by Steven Patten (1977a, 1977b) in philosophical journals that raise important questions about Milgram's work. It might be too much to expect psychologists to take account of a philosophical argument. But ethical arguments are another matter. When Patten and Baumrind in 1977 tried to raise ethical issues with an APA journal regarding the use of children in a particularly insensitive Milgram-type study, they were rebuffed. The journal gatekeepers no doubt believed that all such issues were 'settled' by the publication of Milgram's reply to Baumrind 13 years earlier. Issues raised by Milgram's studies may be 'old hat' but nothing is settled unless and until the challenges are satisfactorily answered in open, public forum.

In the chapters that follow I make some interrelated assumptions about late twentieth century readers. I assume that most readers endorse what ordinarily are thought of as civilized values, particularly those values so prominent in modern political thought: liberty and equality. I further assume that many readers believe that something is wrong with obeying – that to obey is a sign that a person is not free and equal, is not autonomous. And I assume that many readers believe that they themselves would defy a command that was contrary to civilized values.

I, too, endorse the values of liberty and equality. A major reason for writing this book is to show why their realization has proved so difficult.

1
The Context

... when I speak of the banality of evil, I do so only on the strictly factual level, pointing to a phenomenon which stared one in the face at the trial. Eichmann was not Iago and not Macbeth, and nothing would have been farther from his mind than to determine with Richard III 'to prove a villain.' Except for an extraordinary diligence in looking out for his personal advancement, he had no motives at all. And this diligence in itself was in no way criminal; he certainly would never have murdered his superior in order to inherit his post. He *merely*, to put the matter colloquially, *never realized what he was doing.* (Arendt, 1963, p. 287, emphasis in original)

In *Beyond Freedom and Dignity* (1972) the psychologist B.F. Skinner informed readers that their belief in human freedom and dignity was an illusion. Behaviour, like everything else in the universe, is determined and thus people can take no credit nor need they accept blame for what they do. Since for Skinner the world's difficulties are due to misbehaviour, social problems can be solved by developing a behavioural technology that not only will enable controllers to get people to behave themselves, but to enjoy behaving as they should. For Skinner the chief obstacle standing between the anxious people of the late twentieth century and the better world a behavioural technology can bring is the deluded belief in freedom, in autonomy, in responsibility. People who stubbornly insist on believing in freedom and dignity resist control even when being controlled clearly is to their benefit and for the good of society. By giving up the deluded belief and getting on with developing a behavioural technology the better world waiting and attainable can be claimed.

Skinner's book is unusually consistent and carefully argued. But like any argument it succeeds only if the basic premise is accepted. Skinner's basic premise is that the world is determined; that every movement, every event, every behaviour is determined, or to use his favoured term 'controlled', by something else. In a determinist universe the only thing that can happen is what does happen. Possibility has no place in a determined scheme of things.

Skinner had grounds for hoping that people would accept his premise and be persuaded by his argument. After all science in all its branches bases itself on some form of determinism. And science is the modern world's dominant form of thought and belief. Surely those who believe in science should believe in behavioural determinism. People would have to be inconsistent to believe that everything in the universe is determined except for their own and others' behaviour. Unfortunately for those who wish to save the world with behavioural technology, people are inconsistent: a belief in freedom and the capacity for responsibility seems to be built into the everyday notion of what it is to be human. The customs and laws of all societies are based on a belief in the human capacity for responsibility and on a belief in the coherence of the notions of praise and blame. In fact it can be argued that science makes sense, is possible, only if scientists believe that they themselves, as distinguished from their subject matter, are in some sense free. Or to use Skinner's term, whereas the controlled are determined, the controllers are not. Skinner's book received a great deal of deserved attention, but I doubt if many readers put it down with a new-born conviction that they can have no responsibility for what they do.

In 1974 another psychologist, this time a social psychologist, published a book that seemed to demonstrate, rather than assert, that people are less free than they think they are. But this time the problems identified were due not to people's misbehaviour, but rather to what usually is considered proper behaviour. Or to state the subject matter more exactly, the behaviours addressed are those 'hideous crimes' committed because people behave themselves (obey) when they should misbehave (disobey). Stanley Milgram, in *Obedience to Authority*, described a series of studies in which people, by doing what an 'experimenter' told them to do, behaved in a 'shockingly immoral' fashion. Although neither Milgram's theory nor his argument is as consistent or as elegant as Skinner's I suspect that many more readers have been convinced by Milgram than by Skinner. Milgram's laboratory scenes were vivid and powerful and seemed to explain themselves. Furthermore, because some subjects did *not* behave in a 'shockingly immoral' fashion the reader was left free to believe that although people in general are surprisingly obedient, the reader, of course, would have been one of the exceptions. Obedience is a normal social phenomenon, but normal for all those others. And, unlike Skinner,

Milgram did not frighten readers with calls for a technology of control.

Milgram, like Skinner, is a determinist, but in common with most social scientists, and unlike Skinner, Milgram is an inconsistent determinist. For Skinner, humans are not free – full stop. For Milgram, people are less free than they think: much of the time they must do as they are told because they are in a genetically-based 'agentic state'. Although he grants the role of heredity, Skinner's behavioural technology is based, not on genetics, but on the control of behaviour by environmental contingencies. Behavioural determinists usually choose to emphasize one or the other, either the environment or genetic endowment. Milgram's research, although originally designed to discover the effects of situation (environment) on obedience, ultimately was explained by him in terms of genes, 'a fatal flaw nature has designed into us' (1974, p. 188).

Like Skinner and Milgram I am called a psychologist. And one of my reasons for undertaking this essay is to explore human unfreedom. Unlike Skinner and Milgram I am not a determinist – except in the sense of granting that a great deal of what we do can be understood in terms of environment and heredity. Unlike modern existentialists who tend to write of freedom as something absolute, as a choice people always have, I believe that people have a limited capacity to initiate and to inhibit action and to be responsible for what they do. A related assumption is the belief that the way to increase the limited capacity for action and responsibility is to understand as thoroughly as possible the limits on action.

One obvious limit on action is the obligation people have to do what an authority tells them to do. Like Milgram's studies the chief subject of this book is obedience to authority in general and, in particular, the obedience which results in hideous crimes. I hope that by correcting conceptual and interpretative errors in Milgram's work and by exploring the extent to which hierarchical notions and organization permeate all levels of civilized society I can foreclose the possibility of readers believing that they are exceptions to complicity in hideous crimes. In order to gain understanding of hierarchy's pervasiveness I shall need to enter byways psychologists usually avoid. I hope to show that, whereas people can disobey, for them to do so is far more difficult than they think. And that a chief obstacle to defying authority is becoming convinced that authority should be disobeyed. People who have no difficulty in identifying when someone else should disobey forget that reasons for obedience are far more compelling than they appear from the perspective of those not caught up in the immediacy of a situation.

If the book's message is the familiar one that people are not as free as they think they are, it is conveyed not with the intention of diminishing human stature, but with the belief that, however difficult the path may be, we can become freer than we are. Greater freedom, however, is contingent upon dethroning an idol which has dominated imagination, thought, and practice since the reign of the first Divine King.

Authorized Crime

People, particularly those who live in cities, live in fear of other people. Moved by malice, hatred, greed, jealousy, desperation, fear, madness, a desire for thrills and excitement or the support of a drug habit, people can, and do, kill, maim, rape, rob – harm other people. Fearing harm, vulnerable to media refrains that crime is increasing in quantity and in callousness, people direct anxious gazes to crime on the streets.

From primitive groups to modern municipalities measures are taken in an attempt to control and, if possible, prevent people from doing damage to each other. Customs, rules and laws describe and proscribe types of harmful conduct, and forms of punishment are prescribed for those who ignore or defy the customs and laws. In modern states police are charged with protecting people from each other and, when deterrence fails, with apprehending those who engage in criminal conduct so that they can be suitably punished. In spite of proliferating laws, expanding police ranks, and the enthusiastic assistance of science and technology, criminal conduct thrives and continues to frighten.

Yet people need not be moved by base motives such as malice, hatred, greed or jealousy; need not be seeking thrills or the support of a drug habit to harm other people. Loyalty, fidelity, allegiance, devotion, self-sacrifice, obedience to law and command – some of the most prized virtues – move people to kill and otherwise harm other people. The killing, maiming, raping and rapine done by individual criminals or even by criminal organizations shrink to insignificance when compared with the killing and other hideous acts authorized by political communities or states. Murderers in the United States would need to maintain their current extraordinary rate of killing for over 250 years to 'catch up' with the number of Jewish civilians whose deaths were authorized by the Nazi state in the Second World War. The sheer scale of state-authorized crime far exceeds either the voracity, or indeed, the capacity of individual criminals or of criminal organizations.[1]

Not all crimes committed during a war are authorized. In all wars soldiers are held accountable for atrocities they commit without orders. In contrast, *authorized* crimes are means of carrying out policies of the military and of the state. The words 'authorized crime' contain a paradox, for authorization makes a particular destructive or vicious act no longer a crime. For example, killing, when done for the state, changes from a crime to a duty, a virtue. The notion 'authorized crime' is but the first example of a number of contradictions or paradoxes built into the fabric of civilization.

> War consists largely of acts that would be criminal if performed in time of peace – killing, wounding, kidnapping, destroying or carrying off other people's property. Such conduct is not regarded as criminal if it takes place in the course of war, because the state of war lays a blanket of immunity over the warriors. (Taylor, 1971, p. 19)

The state authorizes criminal conduct either because of its own designs on other states or its fear of the aggressive intentions of other states. Violent conduct is an inevitable part of aggressive warfare and is thought to be a necessary means of defending against aggression. Attitudes differ according to time and place, but generally speaking, pacificists and other eccentrics excepted, people have believed that the wartime enemy gets no more than he deserves. (The use of 'he' is deliberate; the enemy, according to military tradition, is male.) In other words, most people accept the proposition that a criminal act is not a crime when directed at an enemy at the behest of a duly authorized superior.

Authorizing crimes in time of war has posed a problem for religions and ethical systems which proscribe conduct such as killing, wounding, kidnapping, destroying or carrying off other people's property. But the argument that states face certain defeat and enslavement by unscrupulous enemies, unless permitted to engage in violent defence, has proved compelling enough to persuade most believers and most rationalists. Even so, warriors are not given carte blanche; in order to be authorized violent action must be kept within clearly defined limits. For example, according to military tradition crimes can be authorized only so long as the criminal activity is directed at other warriors (prior to surrender) and only so long as civilians are protected from harm. General

Douglas MacArthur, confirming the death sentence imposed by a United States military commission on General Tomayuki Yamashita, expressed a traditional moral principle underlying authorized crime.

> The soldier, be he friend or foe, is charged with the protection of the weak and unarmed. It is the very essence and reason for his being. When he violates this sacred trust, he not only profanes his entire cult but threatens the very fabric of international society. The traditions of fighting men are long and honorable. They are based upon the noblest of human traits – sacrifice. (quoted in Taylor, 1971)

Failure to live up to the military code is not the only threat to the weak and unarmed. Beginning with the French Revolution and the ideological changes that made mass conscription possible, and accelerated by technological improvements that made mass killings ever more efficient, modern warfare has become less and less a clash between warriors and more and more the total engagement of entire populations. The enemy no longer is solely male and the factories and workshops producing military equipment (and the people working in them and living near them) become targets of military destruction. The warrior class itself has greatly expanded as a result of the practice of conscripting large portions of the population. As weapons become more destructively powerful their human 'controllers' lose the capacity to limit destruction to other warriors or even to military targets. Large-scale use of nuclear weapons would make everyone (them and us) and everything (theirs and ours) part of the target.

But it was not nuclear weapons, the enormity of which numbs the imagination, but the cold-blooded use by the Nazi state of other forms of modern bureaucracy and technology against the weak and unarmed that sparked a profound challenge to the general acceptance of authorized crime. The importance of the first Nuremberg trial to modern attitudes toward authorized crime can hardly be overstated. (The Nuremberg trial – 20 November, 1945 – 1 October 1946 – took its name from the location of the trial of major Nazi war criminals conducted by the International Military Tribunal. The procedures of the Tribunal, made up of eight judges, two each from France, Great Britain, Russia and the United States, were governed by a Charter, signed in London on 8 August 1945).

The Nuremberg trial was about the actions and inactions of individual defendants in relation to laws of war. But underlying the legal questions were inescapable moral issues. For example, the trial quickened interest in the part loyalty, fidelity and obedience play in making large-scale atrocity possible. All of the Nuremberg defendants insisted that it was their duty to obey orders, even though the obedience led to hideous death and destruction for millions of people; they insisted that this was the case despite knowing that the court would not accept obedience-to-orders as a defence.

One effect of Nuremberg was to stimulate a particular line of moral thought: since the success of the German Führer's hideous designs depended upon the obedience of a very large number of people, it follows that his subordinates needed only to disobey to bring a halt to the horror. The solution to authorized horror is seductively simple: people obey hideous commands only because they ignore the promptings of conscience; they should instead do as their consciences demand. Indeed, believers in moral autonomy must sicken at the thought of people doing something contrary to deeply held belief – just because someone tells them to. People who obey contrary to conscience are like automata – no, worse than automata – because, unlike machines, people with consciences know better.

Unfortunately for those who like simple solutions, the situation is not as straightforward as it might seem. For one thing, recipients of the hideous commands for the most part are military personnel, and military organizations from the time of civilization's original command hierarchy in the first Divine Kingdom have been organized on a principle directly antithetical to moral autonomy. Military training and discipline are for the purpose of replacing any thought of moral autonomy with the habit of instant and automatic obedience. Automata are what the military wants and what a command hierarchy must have in order to function as designed. Yet military tradition recognizes the cost and pain of surrendering autonomy. For as MacArthur wrote, the traditions of fighting men 'are based upon the noblest of human traits – sacrifice'. The sacrifice is self-sacrifice, the renunciation of one's own judgement, one's own desires, one's own conscience, one's very life, to control by the commands of others. Even so, military personnel are expected to retain enough judgement to be able to recognize and be prepared to disobey unlawful commands.

The generations living in the twentieth century have seen the removal of more and more of the limits that in times past have kept the authorized crimes of war somewhat within bounds. The two World Wars demonstrated the possibility of removing geographical limits, of engaging much of the world in conflict. The wars also introduced innovations in the technology of destruction that not only made possible the killing and maiming of tens of millions, but also foreshadow a war of literally unlimited destruction. Hitler and his collaborators directed their technology of destruction not only outward in conquest, but inward, in a way never seen before, directed at unarmed civilians already under Nazi control. As the century nears its end there seems to be no serious barrier capable of limiting crimes states are willing to authorize and commit. And in the shadows of consciousness, occasionally seen with unwanted vividness, more often than not is a button, a technician and a finger awaiting the command to begin the end. If the picture were not so bleak it might not have occurred to anyone to take seriously the rather astonishing notion that individual disobedience might be a way of limiting authorized crime.

This notion *did* occur to psychologists, and I shall begin my own examination of obedience and authorized crime by looking at Stanley Milgram's studies of obedience, the work upon which psychology's contribution is based. The laboratory scenes Milgram created were vivid, dramatically powerful, and carried (for the most part) a salutary social/political message. For Milgram's work effectively undermined any tendency to attribute Nazi atrocities to something specific in the German character. A cross-section of ordinary male New Englanders appeared in one sense to be behaving in a way that was *worse* than obedient Second World War Germans – for they continued giving shocks to a helpless victim even though there was no penalty for refusal. In contrast, most of those who defied the commands of Hitler's minions might have expected something particularly nasty as a consequence. I think the nature of the lesson Milgram taught *is* salutary if properly understood – ordinary people indeed obey far more frequently than they suppose and probably would obey even in situations in which they fancy themselves refusing. One way of looking at Milgram's first report, which appeared in the same year (1963) as Hannah Arendt's *Eichmann in Jerusalem,* is that it supports her thesis concerning the banality of evil with experimental evidence of the normality of obedience. In a world in which obedience is the norm much evil is bound to be banal. The importance of the political message has served to insulate the studies from criticism; if something is wrong with the studies supporters fear that the lesson may be undermined or even lost. The political message may also be responsible for some of the things said about the studies: 'Milgram's work is the single most important contribution to understanding social behavior that anyone has ever made' (Allen, 1978).[2]

If Milgram began his study with the hope of discovering something about obedience that might help prevent a recurrence of Nazi horrors, he was disappointed. For although people have only to disobey to prevent authorized horrors, Milgram found, or thought he found, that in the situations he created an often large percentage of his subjects could not disobey. Some years after completing his research Milgram constructed a theory in an attempt to explain what he took to be the extraordinary degree of obedience exhibited by his experimental subjects. In summary, he theorized that a 'person entering an authority system no longer views himself as acting out of his own purposes but rather comes to see himself as an agent for executing the wishes of another person' (1974, p. 133).

Milgram goes on to describe the person in 'an authority system' as being in an 'agentic state', a state which presumably prevents that person from acting autonomously. Obedience, in Milgram's view, is biologically based and is not limited to the military, to dogs, or to children. In spite of our dislike for doing-as-we-are-told, all of us in authority systems are likely to find ourselves in an agentic state, a state in which we have no choice but to do as we are told. Since most of us are in authority systems much of the time, we must, if Milgram is correct, spend much of our lives in an agentic state doing what others wish us to do.

Milgram's findings and his theory, if accepted, leave little place for resisting commands to commit authorized crimes and raise troubling moral and legal questions. For example, if the Nazi defendants were in an agentic state when following orders, should they have been found guilty? People in agentic states obey commands because they must. The agentic state is a theoretical construct invented to explain findings that seemed inexplicable. Most psychologists who have commented on Milgram's studies accept his interpretation of the findings. Indeed the laboratory scenes he constructed are dramatic and compelling. But the psychologists and Milgram are wrong. Milgram's study is seriously flawed: he did not find what he thought he found. The behaviour of his subjects is far from inexplicable and requires no special theoretical constructs to be understood. The flaws were due to conceptual inadequacy and, once revealed, show how and why Milgram is wrong, and reopen for discussion the question of the possibility of resisting destructive commands.

If I think that it was socially salutary for people to be jolted out of complacent assumptions by Milgram's experimental scenes, another lesson taken from his work is more dubious. John Laurent has shown how eagerly writers of textbooks on management have fastened on Milgram's work. Why? '... the idea apparently being that management trainees can be reassured that their subordinates will have an inbuilt predisposition to want to comply with their superiors' wishes' (Laurent, in press). Milgram's second lesson gives comfort and encouragement to superiors in hierarachical organizations, including, of course, those superiors who issue inhuman commands. I find the second lesson neither salutary nor true. For even though subordinates ordinarily *do* obey legitimate orders, that is only part of the story. An object in writing is to tell some of the rest of the story.

In a broad sense I think that too many easy political and psychological assumptions have been made about both obedience and the capacity to disobey. The biggest, easiest, and most suspect assumption is that the moral choice is clear in those situations in which people, by obeying, appear to be behaving badly. Milgram, for example, assumed that his subjects believed that it was wrong to continue shocking the 'learner' but, because of their agentic state, obeyed, contrary to conscience. I shall show that in those situations, both experimental and everyday life situations, in which by obeying people appear to be behaving badly, strong grounds exist for both obedience and defiance. Indeed, unless and until the strength of the grounds for obedience is understood there can be little hope of countering them.

Because of Milgram's terminology a note of caution is in order. The usual term used to describe the capacity to act and to be responsible is 'agency'. Milgram has used the somewhat similar term 'agentic state' to mean something quite different. Someone in an agentic state *lacks* agency, and is in fact the agent of another's wishes. In contrast, agents in the usual sense are those who have a capacity to carry out their own wishes, desires, intentions, etc.

Imagining, as I write, an audience made up in part of non-specialists, I might wish to avoid questions of determinism and agency. But when considering obedience such questions are unavoidable. For when one obeys (agentic state or no) one *is* carrying out the wishes, desires and intentions of someone else. If the person carrying out the wishes of another is in an agentic state the behaviour has no moral content, whereas if the person is an agent the action does. For an agent can refuse.

Connected with my assumption of limited agency is the notion that once circumstances are understood, including the grounds or reasons for action, a large proportion of human activity needs no

special explanation, scientific or otherwise. Obedience to authorized commands is an activity that needs no special explanation; this
is transparent once circumstances are understood. Part of my story
will be devoted to showing why obedience ordinarily is understandable, and a greater part will be devoted to exploring the question of
why it is generally believed that in some circumstances people
should refuse to obey.

  Like Milgram and most social psychologists I think, contrary to
assumptions of modern individualism, that much of the time we do
carry out the wishes, desires and intentions of other people. How
can sense be made of people who take pride in their individualism
and autonomy yet spend much of their life doing as others wish? A
consistent determinist such as Skinner can answer the question
quite simply: people who think of themselves as autonomous
individuals are deluded: their behaviour is determined by environmental contingencies (or internal drives, or agentic states, etc.). I
shall undertake to offer another sort of understanding of agents
who spend much of their lives carrying out the wishes of others.
But readers looking for an optimistic counter to Milgram's pessimism
should be forewarned. If the agentic state is dubious conjecture,
the propensity of civilized people to obey is not. I too think that
people are less autonomous than they fancy, not because, in a
determinist sense, they *must* do what they do, but because they
live in a form of social organization that can make independent
thinking and acting extraordinarily difficult. But if there is little
reason for optimism, there is also reason – for anyone who values
the human capacity for responsibility – to look into possibilities for
agency and for disobedience.

2

Obedience Research

'An order is an order.' Commands are by their nature final and categorical, and this may be the reason why so little thought has been given to the subject. They seem to us as natural as they are necessary and we accept them as something which has always existed. From childhood onwards we are accustomed to commands; they make up a good part of what we call education, and the whole of our adult life is permeated with them, whether in the sphere of work, of war, or of religion. Thus the question has scarcely ever been raised of what a command actually is: whether it is really as simple as it appears; whether, in spite of the ease and promptness with which it normally achieves its object – that is, obedience – it does not in fact mark the person who obeys it. (Canetti, 1976, p. 303)

But in matters concerning the disposal of actions and human affairs, a subject is bound to obey his superior within the sphere of his authority; for instance a soldier must obey his general in matters relating to war, a servant his master in matters touching the execution of the duties of his service, a son his father in matters relating to the conduct of his life and the care of the household; and so forth. (Saint Thomas Aquinas)

Obedience brings to mind uniformed soldiers snapping to attention and executing precision, machine-like drill, or dogs being carefully trained to abandon their dog-like ways and do as commanded. At first thought, obedience does not seem to have much to do with civilian – or civil – life. The word, formerly much honoured, seems somewhat old-fashioned for describing even the contemporary relationship of children to parents. The notion that no one tells a free, autonomous person what to do may be behind the surprise and dismay which greeted Stanley Milgram's studies of obedience: the report that 65 per cent of subjects in his first study administered to a fellow subject the highest shock (450 volts) on a particularly lethal-looking shock generator. How could Milgram's subjects behave as they did? Why did they follow instructions? Unlike soldiers they were not trained to obey, were not required to obey, did not have to face punishment for refusing to obey. Yet 65 per cent obeyed.

Obedience, as such, is not often discussed by psychologists and other social scientists – possibly because obedience is not an action, but a reaction: to obey is to react in a particular way to a command. Obedience as a concept seems subordinate to more primary concepts such as 'power' or 'authority', terms that crowd library subject indexes.

Yet I think there are other reasons for the neglect of obedience. We who live in late twentieth century capitalist countries do not much fancy the idea of obeying. We value our independence, autonomy and freedom. When we think of obedience it is likely to be in negative terms. *Dis*obedience attracts us. We may have caught up with the artist's judgement. Oscar Wilde: 'Disobedience, in the eyes of any one who has read history, is man's original virtue. It is through disobedience that progress has been made, through disobedience and through rebellion.'

Had our forebears not exercised the virtues disobedience and rebellion we still would be frozen in some ancient social hierarchy, the lineal descendants of pharaohs, priests and clerks – or, with greater statistical probability, slaves. Unless, as is more likely, the hierarchy simply expired or collapsed of its own rigidity. Yet, civilization began with, was made possible by, the invention of a form of social organization based on the right of authorities to issue commands and the duty of subordinates to obey them. The command/obedience relationship so infuses civilization that it dominates our ways of thinking: the very doctrine of determinism we use to understand the natural world is patterned on and derives from it. Causes work like commands or laws: 'As obedient as the planets to the law of gravitation' is a metaphor whose source is a social invention of great antiquity. There are other more subtle, more equalitarian, ways of coordinating work and activity, but obedience has been the mainstay of civilizations, from their dim beginnings in the fourth millennium BC until the present. The introduction of democratic practices has disguised but not altered the basic form. And we obey every day; we obey far more frequently and in many more ways than we think we do. Each time we obey we are moved by someone else's wish or desire rather than our own. People living today may be as unconscious of the ubiquity and key nature of obedience as former generations were unconscious of the primacy of sexual impulses.

In times past the social necessity of obedience was rather better understood. The problem then was to get people to obey. Now we often see the problem as getting people to disobey. Both obedience and disobedience are necessary for all hierarchically organized groups. Most modern writers could benefit and would gain a valuable perspective by reading the six articles on obedience in the thirteenth century *Summa Theologica*. As might be expected in an organization as clearly and openly hierarchical as the Catholic Church, obedience is seen as a virtue. Aquinas argued for obedience being a special virtue ('a special virtue is assigned to all good deeds that have a special reason for praise'), but argued against the proposition that obedience is the greatest of the virtues. Obedience's virtue did not blind Aquinas to its limits.

> There are two reasons, for which a subject may not be bound to obey his superior in all things. First on account of the command of a higher power . . . Secondly, a subject is not bound to obey his superior, if the latter command him to do something wherein he is not subject to him.

Modern psychological studies of obedience have focused on the first of Aquinas's two reasons for which a subject may not be bound to obey his superior and have characterized the 'command of a higher power' as conscience. When our conscience (a 'higher power') tells us that our superior's command is wrong, we should refuse to obey. The importance of the second of the two reasons has not been appreciated, resulting in serious misunderstanding of the command/obedience relationship.

Stanley Milgram, who is chiefly responsible for the modern psychological study of obedience, did not hide the reasons for his interest in the conflict between conscience and authority. In the opening paragraph of his initial report (1963) Milgram writes:

> Obedience, as a determinant of behavior, is of particular relevance to our time. It has been reliably established that from 1933 to 1945 millions of innocent persons were systematically slaughtered on command. Gas chambers were built, death camps were guarded, daily quotas of corpses were produced with the same efficiency as the manufacture of appliances. These inhumane policies may have originated in the mind of a single person, but they could only have been carried out on a massive scale if a very large number of people obeyed orders.

In other words, if subordinates, whose consciences must have told them the unspeakable commands were wrong, had refused to obey, the innocent persons could not have been slaughtered – at least not on a mass scale.

When obedience was a virtue it was easy to see how it was responsible for the glories of civilization. But civilization and the command/obedience relationship produce horrors as well as splendours, as sages, saints and poets throughout history have testified. Today few can ignore any longer the realization that the advances of civilization bring unimaginable terrors as well as most of the things civil people value. And that the terrors produced are not confined to fascist states. During the period in which Milgram's studies appeared the most powerful democracy in history was engaged in appalling forms of air and land warfare in a small area of southeast Asia. Hundreds of thousands of Americans were faced with deciding between conscience and authority. A single year of the Vietnamese war, it is estimated, saw 100,000 conscientious objectors, 89,088 deserters, and tens of thousands of drug addicts. There is no way of establishing the degree to which conscience was involved in each case, but all were resisting inhumane commands in one way or another. Each, in his own way, resisted the agentic state – the 'state', Milgram conjectured, of one who obeys inhuman commands.

When he began his research in 1960 Milgram could not have foreseen the future horrors of Vietnam; he looked backward to the known horrors of Second World War. His examination of the conflict between conscience and malevolent authority hardly could have been more timely. A handful of minor psychological studies preceded Milgram, three of them done in Nazi Germany. Prior to modern psychology what we knew of obedience came from common knowledge, from observation, and from thought and reflection. The major writers on the subject were philosophers, theologians and other thinkers.[1] We knew a great deal about obedience, but Milgram brought to his study the developing tools of a new experimental social science. Where previous writers had observed or read about people obeying and disobeying, Milgram introduced standardized laboratory settings in which people could be studied in the same situation, over and over again in a way unavailable to earlier writers.

Milgram's work quickly drew a great deal of attention, commentary and controversy, for his subjects appeared to behave so badly that readers were able to drop the modern taboo on passing judgement. 'About nothing does public opinion everywhere seem to be in happier agreement than that no one has the right to judge somebody else' (Arendt, 1963, p. 296). The studies were and are featured in introductory and social psychology textbooks. A film Milgram made of the studies continues to be shown in psychology classrooms. A fictionalized television version was screened nationwide on a United States television network. The series of studies quickly became the best known and most talked about in the field of social psychology.[2]

Milgram in effect constructed a stirring modern morality play that dramatized a failure to affirm one of western civilization's most deeply held beliefs. From at least the time of Luther people have been urged to place personal experience and conscience above the dictates of authorities. The conscience of each of us is deemed a moral sovereign. The morality play showed a large proportion of subjects surrendering their precious moral sovereignty to a 'malevolent authority'. The play, which might be called 'Sovereign Conscience *vs* Authority' is made palatable for modern tastes by showing a minority affirming their moral sovereignty by resolute defiance. Audiences are thus able both to regret and decry the moral lapse of the majority and to assure themselves that in a similar situation they would be one of the splendidly defiant minority.

But Milgram did *not* stage a drama pitting sovereign conscience against authority. The claim that an investigator does not understand his own work is both unusual and serious, but by showing the sort of morality play Milgram *did* stage, neglected issues concerning the nature of obedience and its place in society can be revealed and then discussed.

Obedience in the Laboratory

> Following a rule is analogous to obeying an order. We are trained to do so; we react to an order in a particular way. But what if one person reacts in one way and another in another to the order and the training? Which one is right? (Wittgenstein, 1953, p. 82^e)

When writing of obedience philosophers and theologians deal with topics such as whom or what should be obeyed and whether or not the moral right to rule and to be obeyed can be justified. Milgram's questions and method of enquiry are strikingly different. He assumed that he knew 'which one is right?' when one person 'reacts in one way and another in another' and decided (without arguing for the proposition) that a particular command in a particular situation *should* be defied; and then he put people into the situation to find out whether they would obey or disobey. He also varied the situations. For Milgram used two baseline conditions, the first of which he varied in three different ways, the second in 13 ways. ('Baseline' in this context means simply a basic experimental situation which is modified or varied in subsequent experiments.) In all 'almost a thousand adults were individually studied in the obedience research.' Of these, 636 (596 males; 40 females) took part in the 18 studies described in his book. I shall look initially at Milgram's pilot study and then at the first formal study and the 40 men who took part in it. If what happened in the first study is understood, reinterpretation of the remaining 17 studies becomes relatively straightforward.

Should we accept Milgram's claim that subjects in his study *should* disobey? I pose the question in spite of the fact that most people have assumed that the answer is obvious. Judging from published comments and student reactions most people agree with Milgram that those subjects who obey are 'shockingly immoral', for it seems clear that the obeyed commands are immoral. The situation is not as simple or as straightforward as has been assumed.

Before going further in this examination I think it is important that readers understand points that are *not* at issue. For one, I agree with Milgram that throughout history people have shown themselves all too willing to obey authorities. The comments of C.P. Snow partially quoted in Milgram's 1963 paper set the tone for his studies and will provide a major theme for this work:

> When you think of the long and gloomy history of man, you will find *far more, and far*[3] more hideous crimes have been committed in the name of obedience than have ever been committed in the name of rebellion. If you doubt that, read William Shirer's *Rise and Fall of the Third Reich*. The German Officer Corps were brought up in the most rigorous code of obedience . . . in the name of obedience they were party to, and assisted in, the most wicked large-scale actions in the history of the world. (1961, p. 24)

Also not at issue is what people should do when ordered to do something inhumane: (generally speaking) they should resist. I use the qualification 'generally speaking' because when the significance of *who* gives the command to *whom* is made clear I suspect that most readers will wish to specify circumstances in which an inhumane command should be obeyed rather than resisted. Incidentally, my own position is closer to *always* resist than is Milgram's or the position I imagine most readers are prepared to defend.

I do not quarrel with Milgram's refusal to see a bright side to obedience. Some of Milgram's critics seem exercised by the pessimism of his conclusions concerning our propensity to obey. They would like to think that he is wrong. I cannot say that I am less pessimistic than Milgram, but I do say that he is wrong in his grounds for pessimism. And to the extent that understanding something – in this case the grounds for obedience and resistance – opens possibilities for change, pessimism can become realism.

Another matter not at issue is what happened in Milgram's laboratory exercises. Readers unfamiliar with social psychology may wonder how 'what happened' could possibly be at issue. Put simply, in scientific practice results are so subject to error and artifact that 'what happened' is not decided until outcomes are reliably repeated in other laboratories. Unfortunately, social psychologists are so enamoured of originality that they seldom take the trouble to repeat experiments. As a consequence, strictly speaking, social psychology has few scientific findings. In Milgram's case enough of his work has been repeated, both in his own format and in the form of simulations, that we can be fairly confident of the percentages in his two baseline conditions: 65 per cent of subjects are fully obedient; that is, 65 per cent push the 450 volt lever. Whereas I have no quarrel with the last statement, my analysis centres not on 'what happened' in the physical sense but on the *meaning* of 'what happened' – on the meaning of pushing the 450 volt lever. 'Meaning' in the sense of what subjects might have thought they were doing can be decided by looking carefully at the context in which obedience and disobedience occurred.

I have said that most people familiar with Milgram's study probably agree with him that his obedient subjects behaved in a 'shockingly immoral' way. What did subjects do to be so judged? Although Milgram characterizes his 'experiment' as 'simple', merely to describe clearly what subjects did involves considerable complications. The reason this is so lies in the nature of what he wished to study. Milgram's laboratory exercise was designed to be analogous to situations in Nazi Germany wherein obeyed commands resulted in harm and death. The major obstacle to creating such a laboratory analogue is as simple as it is formidable: harm and death are not allowed in psychology laboratories. Experimenters are not allowed (it is not within their authority) to harm and kill their subjects. If harm and killing are to be part of an experiment they must be simulated somehow. Milgram rejected a straightforward simulation and chose instead a disguised simulation, a simulation that attempts to hide from subjects the fact that it is a simulation, something social psychologists call a 'deception experiment'. Why he chose to deceive is connected with the history of the use of deception in social psychological research and to a profound confusion and misunderstanding surrounding the nature of simulation and of experimentation. I have dealt with these matters at length elsewhere (most recently, Mixon, 1986).[4]

Given the prohibition on harm and killing, the problem was to create a laboratory situation in which subjects would *believe* that obeying a command would result in harm or death. If harm and killing are prohibited, how can people be convinced that harm and killing is going on in the laboratory? Milgram attempted to create the appearance of harm in the laboratory by inventing a bogus learning experiment that purported to investigate the effects of punishment on memorizing a set of word pairs. Punishment for failing to remember the correct word was to be administered in the form of an electric shock, a suitably 'scientific' form of punishment that can be precisely calibrated. Electric shock, as such, is not foreign to the psychology laboratory, for mild electric shocks are not considered harmful. Whereas harm and killing are prohibited in laboratories, a certain amount of harmless pain is thought to be a small price to pay for scientific knowledge.

The dummy shock generator Milgram had constructed is not the sort commonly found in psychology laboratories. According to its labels the shocks it could generate were far from harmless. The control panel consisted of 30 levers ranging in claimed output from 15 volts at one end and progressing in 15 volt increments to 450 volts at the other. Each lever had its voltage output plainly labelled. In addition, seven verbal labels and one symbol described the nature of the shocks, ranging from 'Slight Shock' on the lower end to 'Danger Severe Shock' near the upper end and under the final two levers (435 Volts and 450 Volts) was the ominous symbol 'XXX'. Clearly such a generator appeared capable of more than harmless pain.

So lethal, in fact, did it appear that Milgram assumed that a fairly simple laboratory exercise would convince subjects that harm was occurring. Simple in its procedure, that is, but rather more complicated in its staging. The staging is connected with the bogus learning (memory) experiment, an 'experiment' that must appear as realistic as possible. The 'learning experiment' involved three people, an 'experimenter', a 'teacher' and a 'learner'. The only one of the three that interested Milgram was the person who did the teaching in the bogus learning experiment. The 'experimenter' and the 'learner' were actors employed by Milgram to pretend to be an experimenter and a learner. In order to keep conditions constant the same actors played the 'experimenter' and the 'learner' in all variations of his study. The actors he chose, a high school biology teacher as 'experimenter' and an accountant as 'learner' clocked over 1,000 hours in their roles, equivalent in time to major roles on Broadway in a play with a run of a year and a half.

The 'simple' exercise became a 'pilot study', something social psychologists do to find out how well or poorly their procedures work. Milgram, using undergraduates as subjects, brought them to the laboratory one at a time. There they found another 'subject' (the accountant) and the 'experimenter' (the biology teacher). The 'learning experiment' was explained to them as an experiment designed to find out the effects of punishment on learning. That is, instead of being rewarded for right answers, subjects were to be punished for wrong answers. One subject was to be the teacher, the other the learner. A drawing was held to determine which was to be which, a drawing rigged to ensure that the accountant always became the 'learner' and the naïve subject the 'teacher'. The 'learner' was taken to another room and strapped in a chair wired to deliver shocks. The 'teacher' had the procedure explained to him (all subjects in the pilot study, in the first formal study, and in all but one subsequent study were male), was given a sample shock described as 45 volts to give him an idea of the pain involved, and was given a practice run on the task before beginning the 'experiment'. Experimental procedure involved the 'teacher' reading a list of 25 word pairs over an intercommunication system to the 'learner', who was to attempt to memorize them. Then the 'teacher' was to administer what amounted to an oral multiple choice test on the 25 word pairs. Each time the learner made a mistake he was to be told the correct answer and then punished with a shock, beginning with the 15 volt shock and increasing one step (15 volts) with each further mistake. In other words, 30 mistakes (after reading the 25 mulitple-choice questions the 'teacher' was instructed to begin again at the top of the list) by the 'learner' would see (if the procedure is followed) a progression of shocks from 15 to 450 volts. The 'learner' (unknown to the 'teacher') had been instructed to give a predetermined set of correct and incorrect answers which ensured a fairly swift progression from 15 to 450 volts.

Milgram expected that many of the teachers would refuse to push such obviously harmful levers as those labelled 'Strong Shock', 'Very Strong Shock', 'Intense Shock', 'Extreme Intensity Shock', 'Danger Severe Shock' and 'XXX'. To his surprise the undergraduate 'teachers' pushed all the levers, proceeding 'blithely' to the end of the board. Either they were all incredibly callous, or for some reason the bogus shock generator was not convincing subjects that the shocks were harmful.

The latter is the most probable explanation, but Milgram cannot be expected at that date (*circa* 1960) to have known why. During this same period Martin Orne (who later became one of the most incisive critics of the obedience studies)[5] was beginning his laboratory study of hypnosis and was having great difficulty finding *any* laboratory task that subjects would refuse to carry out. Why was Orne looking for such tasks? One of the beliefs in the folklore of hypnotism is that people who are put in an hypnotic trance can be ordered successfully to do things they would not do in a waking state. They might, should the hypnotist be so evil, even obey a command to commit murder. Clearly, in order to investigate this phenomenon in the laboratory an investigator must first find tasks that ordinary, unhypnotized laboratory subjects will refuse to do. For if an unhypnotized subject will do something on command, you hardly could claim that a hypnotized subject does it because of the trance state.

In 1962 Orne reported to the psychological profession how difficult it was to find such a task. Subjects in psychological studies seemed willing to do just about anything they were told to do, including the most boring and senseless tasks. Why are subjects so obedient in experiments? A number of reasons have been given, not the least of which is the wish to advance science. Subjects assume that their role in an experiment is to do as they are told, even if, as is frequently the case, they do not know why they are doing what they are doing. More relevant to Milgram's puzzlement is something Orne and Evans reported in 1965. In this case the tasks subjects were ordered to carry out involved harm – either to themselves or to someone else. They were ordered in sequence to pick up a venomous snake, thrust their hand into a flask of fuming nitric acid and throw the flask of acid into the face of a laboratory assistant. After the experiment concluded, when asked why they were willing to do such dangerous and anti-social things, subjects replied that they assumed that they were in a reputable experiment and that safeguards would protect them (and the assistant) from harm. Of course they were right – and they had found no evidence to show that they were wrong. When they reached for the snake an invisible glass protected them; a sleight-of-hand switch of flasks kept their hand from burning; and another invisible glass protected the assistant.

There is no record that Milgram asked the Yale undergraduates why they went blithely to the end of the shock panel, but I presume they would have answered much as Orne and Evans's subjects answered. Although the shock generator appeared deadly, there was nothing in the procedure to violate the assumption that safeguards were in place. The chief difference between Orne and Evans's report and Milgram's pilot study is that Orne and Evans's subjects were described as under some strain, they did not perform 'blithely' and one of six subjects refused to go on. The snake and the fuming acid may have been more effective and powerful stage props than the shock generator.

Essential to any understanding of the psychological experiment is a knowledge of the special nature of the laboratory situation. Things in laboratories are not always as they seem. Obeying a command to throw acid in someone's face in a laboratory does not mean the same thing as obeying a command to throw acid in someone's face in everyday life. Pushing a lever marked '450 volts' 'XXX' does not mean the same thing in a psychology laboratory where some inevitable scientific mystification is part of the game as it would in a situation where shocks are known to harm and where safeguards are not part of the game.

Milgram may not have known why his subjects were so blithely obedient, but he did know that he did not have an experiment. There was nothing in the behaviour of his subjects to suggest that they believed the shocks were harmful. Milgram had failed to come up with a laboratory simulation of authentic commands to harm and kill. He could not study what he came to call 'destructive obedience' with the pilot study format.

A small but potent change transformed the pilot exercise into the powerful and arresting scene reported in 1963. In the pilot study, once the bogus learning experiment was under way, the only awareness the 'teacher" had of the 'learner' was when the 'learner's' right or wrong answer appeared on an electronic board. The new study followed the pilot format until the teacher pushed the lever marked '300 volts' 'Extreme Intensity Shock'. At that point a sound of pounding came from the 'learner's' room. Then silence. Nothing more was heard from the 'learner', even in the form of right or wrong answers. What happened? From Milgram's point of view the question is: will the teachers continue to administer 'shock'? If so, how far will they go? The simple change in procedure which made it appear that something ominous had happened to the learner effectively undermined any certainty that safeguards are in effect.

When Milgram described this study (called then the 'remote feedback condition') to advanced psychology students and asked them to predict the behaviour of 100 hypothetical subjects they were of the opinion that most people put into such a situation would refuse at some point to continue giving shock (only 1.27 per cent would push the 450 volt lever). At a later time Milgram described either this study or his voice-feedback study to groups of people, including 39 psychiatrists. They were of the same opinion. When asked to predict their own behaviour, rather than the behaviour of hypothetical subjects, *all* people questioned (110 of them) stated that they would refuse to continue. The predictions of psychiatrists, college students, and middle-class adults laid the groundwork for Milgram's claim that his findings were 'counterintuitive' and therefore a genuine discovery made possible by his empirical laboratory research.

The first formal study incorporated the change in procedure and, instead of students, used as subjects a cross-section of the adult male population. In this and future studies Milgram characterized subjects who broke off at any point prior to the 450 volt lever as 'defiant' and subjects who pushed the 450 volt lever as 'obedient', i.e., they were put into one of only two categories. Sixty-five per cent, 26 of 40 subjects, did not refuse, but, after pushing the 300 volt lever and hearing the pounding on the wall, pushed each of the ten levers remaining, including the 450 volt lever. The large proportion of obedience surprised and dismayed most, gave satisfaction to pessimists, and grabbed the attention of all who heard of the study.

The scene Milgram describes is very dramatic. Why no response? Had the 'learner' decided not to cooperate? Was he unconscious? Dead? Heightening the drama was the behaviour of the naïve subjects. 'Blitheness' no longer characterized them. Many subjects showed striking signs of 'tension and emotional strain': nervous laughter, sweating, stuttering, trembling and groaning. Not the sort of behaviour expected of subjects in psychological experiments. Something extraordinary was going on. The question is: What? Milgram explains the unusual tension and emotional strain as a conflict 'between the deeply ingrained disposition not to harm others and the equally compelling tendency to obey others who are in authority' (1974, pp. 42–3).

Readers need more information before they can begin to judge for themselves. The procedure is straightforward prior to the 300 volt lever. It is a 'learning experiment' as in the pilot study with the wrong answers of the learner feeding the inevitable increase in the severity of the shock to be administered. The procedure specifies that for each wrong answer a shock is given, 15 volts higher than the shock for the previous wrong answer. In other words, prior to pushing the twentieth lever (300 volts) everything is routine. Then comes the pounding on the wall. And the next question. But there is no response to the next question. Typically the 'teacher' will turn to the 'experimenter' with a query, either verbal or nonverbal. The 'experimenter' then tells him to treat the absence of a response as a wrong answer and to continue the procedure as before. Many do, and without further question push the remaining ten levers and stop only when instructed. Others are less trusting and more questioning. In order to keep conditions as constant as possible Milgram instructed the 'experimenter' to respond to questions or objections with what he calls 'prods'. Four of the prods, spoken in sequence were increasingly strong instructions to continue, from Prod 1: 'Please continue' to Prod 4: 'You have no other choice, you *must* go on.' Two special prods dealt with 'teacher' concerns. If a 'teacher' asked about the possibility of injury, the 'experimenter' said: 'Although the shocks may be painful, there is no permanent tissue damage, so please go on.' If a 'teacher' said the *'learner'* did not wish to continue, the 'experimenter' replied: 'Whether the learner likes it or not, you must go on until he has learned all the word pairs correctly. So please go on!'

One reason for the power of Milgram's study is that it has seemed so obvious that subjects *should* refuse to continue giving shocks. If so, how is it that something so obvious to people who hear of or read the study is not obvious to the subjects *in* the study? Why do I assume that what they *should* do was *not* obvious to subjects? Social psychologists believe that people in experiments try to make themselves look good; Milton Rosenberg (1969) called the phenomenon 'evaluation apprehension'. The notion is that people who take part in experiments assume that they are being evaluated in some way and quite naturally wish to appear at their best. A reason frequently given for lying to subjects is that if they know what they should do, they will do it. If it was obvious to Milgram's subjects that they *should* disobey, they would disobey.[6] Why the difference in clarity between those who hear or read a description of the study and those who participate in the study?

One difference has to do with the nature of description. All description is selective. The same situation can be described in countless ways. Our understanding of something depends upon how it is described to us. 'An act viewed in one perspective may seem heinous; the same action viewed in another perspective seems fully warranted' (Milgram, 1974, p. 145). A prosecuting attorney can describe the events surrounding a death in such a way that the defendant seems clearly guilty of murder. The defence attorney can describe the same events so as to make the defendant appear obviously guiltless.

Milgram's study is extremely difficult to describe in such a way that someone hearing or reading it sees the situation from the point of view of the subject (the 'teacher'). Unfortunately, because he kept no record (S. Milgram, personal communication, 23 November 1970), we do not know precisely how Milgram described the study to the 110 people, all of whom said they would refuse to continue. Since I have been unable to find any indication that he ever grasped the subjects' point of view, we can be fairly certain that Milgram's description reflected a conviction expressed in all his writing: that subjects in the experiment believed that they were administering obviously harmful shocks. After describing the experiment in which 'teachers' are delivering obviously harmful shocks and providing a schematic diagram of the shock generator Milgram gave two instructions: 'privately to record how he himself would perform in it' and 'plot the distribution of break off points of one hundred Americans of diverse ages and occupations'. People asked to record where they or others would break off giving harmful shocks are being told that subjects *should* 'break off' at some point. Never in an ordinary psychological experiment is there any question that subjects should 'break off'. Subjects are there to follow procedure. In Milgram's 'learning experiment' everything possible was done to suggest that there was no question but that the subjects should continue.

If people were given an account of Milgram's study that attempted to describe the 'learning experiment' in enough detail that someone hearing it could grasp the subjects' point of view and then were questioned in a way that did not reveal what subjects *should* do, how would they assess the situation? In 1971 I tried out four descriptions which differed only in detail.[7] Contrary to Milgram's descriptions which produced judgements that only a tiny proportion would be obedient, each of my four descriptions produced judgements of obedience ranging from 40 per cent to 80 per cent depending on descriptive detail. The average was 55 per cent. In other words, had Milgram used any of my descriptions rather than his own, he would not have been able to claim that his findings are counterintuitive. Given enough detail, and when care is taken not to point to what should be done, people are quite good at judging what happens in Milgram's study. Judgements based on faithful descriptions show that, at the very least, the obedience study situation is not as unambiguous as has been assumed.

The question of why, using Milgram's description, has it seemed so obvious that subjects *should* refuse to continue giving shocks, still must be answered. Think back for a moment to the dramatic change Milgram made to the pilot study procedure. When the 300 volt lever was pushed a sound of pounding came from the 'learner's' room. From that point on nothing more was heard; the 'learner' no longer responded to questions. The most innocent interpretation of the silence is that the 'learner' is fed up and is refusing to cooperate – not a very plausible interpretation, because one would assume that unless he had somehow freed himself from the straps holding him to the chair he would be protesting the fact that the shocks were continuing even after he quit. More likely interpretations are that he is unconscious or, quite possibly, dead. Certainly it seems that harm of some kind must have come to him. If he were harmed, surely the person administering the shocks should stop and go to his aid. Why?

To my knowledge no one has asked 'why' before. The answer seems so obvious. But consider for a moment other situations in which an authority commands a subordinate to harm or kill another. The first thing that becomes apparent is that not many people have the authority to order a subordinate to harm or kill someone. Most instances are found in the armed forces or police. As Max Weber pointed out: 'a state is a human community that (successfully) claims the monopoly of the *legitimate use of physical force* within a given territory' (1946, p. 78, italics in original). Now if a battle scene were described to us in which an officer ordered his men to fire and we were asked what the men would do, most of us would say that they would fire – unless (and the *unless* is most important) the order clearly violated international law or in some other way went beyond the authority of the officer. If the command was legitimate – and none of the special circumstances surrounding disaffection or revolt were present – people probably would predict that all would obey and further assume that all *should* obey. Few would say that the subordinate should disobey and go to the aid of the enemy.

As Milgram points out, an experimenter in a psychological

experiment is a legitimate authority. If an officer – a legitimate authority – has the right to order a private to kill someone, why do we say that subjects should refuse an experimenter's command to harm or kill the 'learner'? To ask the question is to answer it. A psychologist, unlike an officer, does not have the authority, at any time or place, to harm or kill anyone, nor the authority to command anyone else to harm or kill someone. We are not bound to obey orders that are not legitimate. Or as Aquinas put it 'a subject is not bound to obey his superior, if the latter commands him to do something wherein he is not subject to him.' All authorities, even heads of totalitarian states, are limited in the commands that go with their position. An experimenter can command a subject to throw acid in someone's face only so long as the act can do no harm.

Milgram called his book *Obedience to Authority*. He is studying, not obedience in general, but obedience to authority. An elementary fact about authorities is that they can expect to be obeyed only when they issue legitimate commands. Yet nowhere does Milgram apply the essential notion of 'legitimate command' to the laboratory situation he created. Like any serious student of obedience Milgram has to be aware of the phenomenon. In fact he writes: 'Thus in a military situation, a captain may order a subordinate to perform a highly dangerous action, but he may not order the subordinate to embrace his girlfriend' (1974, p. 141). For some reason it does not occur to Milgram to ask what range of commands an experimenter might legitimately issue. He thus fails to see that his study, no matter how powerful and psychologically interesting, is not, and could not possibly be, an analogue to the conditions in Nazi Germany. Despite the nearly universal postwar opprobrium heaped on the Nazis and in spite of decisions by the postwar war crimes tribunals, within the wartime context the hideous commands so many obeyed were commands authorized by the Nazi state.

Reasons for thinking that Milgram's subjects should disobey commands to harm and kill are not simply humanitarian. Humanitarian reasons do not stop most people from condoning legitimate commands in the armed forces or police to harm and kill. A combination of humanity and an awareness – no matter how dim – that this particular authority, this 'experimenter,' has no right to harm anyone, tells us that disobedience is the only proper response. We might not even get so far as awareness of rights; it might simply seem absurd or grotesque to hurt somebody for the sake of a crude and ill-conceived learning experiment.

If rights and wrongs are so transparent to observers, why not to the subjects? Why didn't they all disobey? Milgram's eventual answer (1974) was that rights and wrongs were transparent, that it was clear the commands should be defied, but that subjects were in an 'agentic state' and so could not disobey. If this is the case why were rights and wrongs not transparent to the people to whom I read my descriptions of the study? They were not in an agentic state; they simply had available to them a detailed description of the study; yet their responses closely matched those of Milgram's subjects.

The answer should become obvious as soon as I add a further item of description. When the pounding on the wall occurred, followed by silence, it seemed clear at the very least that something had gone wrong with the experiment. Yet the 'experimenter' gave no indication, either verbally or nonverbally, that he was surprised or in the least bit concerned about what had happened in the other room. In normal circumstances, how might an experimenter be expected to react if a subject appeared to be unconscious or possibly dead? Even if he were as callous and unfeeling as some stereotypes would lead us to believe, the experimenter might at least be expected to show some concern for himself. After all, experimenters are not authorized to kill or harm subjects. They are responsible for the equipment and what it does to people. Part of the power of the scene Milgram created is due to a careless piece of script writing. The only motivation that would explain the 'experimenter's' composure and lack of interest in what had happened in the other room is certain knowledge on his part that the subject is not harmed. And of course he did have certain knowledge. The shock generator was a fake that delivered no shocks whatsoever to the 'learner'.

Interpreting the Situation

What gets lost in most descriptions of Milgram's study is the part played by the 'experimenter' in the affair. In 1971 I attempted (successfully) to simulate the conditions in the study that led to the extreme tension and stress exhibited by many of Milgram's subjects. In other words, in a role-playing simulation participants showed the same sort of spontaneous laughter, tics, stuttering, etc., as did subjects in the deception study. When I questioned participants after the role play was over, many of them expressed puzzlement and disturbance concerning the 'experimenter's' behaviour. They simply could not understand why he behaved the way he did, how he could *know* without looking that the 'learner' was all right. I owe to 40 participants in my study the explanation for what previously had appeared to be extraordinary obedience.

How does the experimenter's behaviour explain the obedience? Rom Harré (1979) has suggested that the situation Milgram created is a study of trust. For those subjects who trust the experimenter, who believe him when he says that 'although shocks may be painful, there is no permanent tissue damage', who believe that his composure is a sign that he knows the 'learner' is all right, the correct thing to do is to continue. Is it reasonable for subjects to believe the 'experimenter' rather than their own senses? According to no less an authority than Milgram, it may be. Speaking generally, but not applying the wisdom to his own study Milgram claims: *'There is a propensity for people to accept definitions of action provided by legitimate authority.* That is, although the subject performs the action, he allows authority to define its meaning' (his italics, 1974, p. 145). If this is the case, then the 'learner's' definition of pushing the 450 volt lever would be, in Milgram's words, 'that the shocks administered to the subject are painful but not dangerous' (1963, p. 378).

> . . . in the obedience experiment the experimenter explicitly denies the possibility of harm. He states, 'Although the shocks can be extremely painful, they cause no permanent tissue damage.' (The subject also watches, after the electrode is attached to the victim's wrist, the application of a paste 'to avoid blisters and burns.') The indications of harm come from other sources, and the subject must weigh information from his own senses against his trust in and dependence on the experimenter. (Milgram, 1972, p. 146)

Readers may be somewhat puzzled. Each time I make a point critical of Milgram's interpretation of his own experiment, I quote Milgram in my support. Why hasn't Milgram seen how his remarks are relevant to the meaning of pushing the 450 volt lever? I cannot be certain, but I assume that his initial deception is responsible. In order to keep the purposes of his study hidden from his subjects Milgram used two definitions of the laboratory situation and pushing the 450 volt lever, one for himself and his readers, another for his subjects. For himself and his readers Milgram defined the situation as a study of destructive obedience analogous to situations in Nazi Germany, and he defined pushing the 450 volt lever as a 'shockingly immoral' willingness to administer a harmful, possibly lethal, shock to the 'learner'. But for his *subjects* he defined the situation as a learning experiment designed to discover the effects of punishment on learning and the shock delivered by the 450 volt lever as 'painful but not dangerous'. Possibly because, by refusing, defiant subjects showed that they did not believe the 'experimenter', Milgram assumed that pushing the 450 volt lever somehow in the course of the study had become redefined as administering a harmful, possibly lethal shock. He has never explained why, if this happens, 65 per cent of the subjects fail to see that what is needed to put them in a good light is to refuse to obey. At any rate it seems that having defined the action as immoral and harmful, Milgram failed to see that his subjects would take their definition not from him, but from *their* authority, the 'experimenter'. The 'experimenter' defined the action as delivering a 'painful but not dangerous' shock.

'The trouble with lying and deceiving is that their efficiency depends entirely upon a clear notion of the truth that the liar and deceiver wishes to hide' (Arendt, 1972, p. 31). In order to make plausible the assertion that subjects are willing to give harmful, possibly lethal shocks the truth that must at all costs be hidden from subjects is the fact that the shocks are harmless. The 'experimenter's' behaviour gives the truth away. For if the shocks are not harmful (as testified by the experimenter's verbal and nonverbal behaviour) then the experimenter is issuing a legitimate command and obedience is the expected response. In terms of celebrity and 'success' Milgram was fortunate that he did *not* have a clear notion of the truth he wished to hide. For if he had, if he had coached the 'experimenter' to behave as if the shocks were harmful, Milgram, just as in his pilot study, would not have had an experiment. In the pilot study most subjects pushed the 450 volt lever. If the 'experimenter' behaved as if the shocks were harmful, most subjects would refuse to push the 450 volt lever.

How do I know? For one thing, when I altered the earlier mentioned detailed descriptions of the obedience study to make the 'experimenter's' behaviour more believable (chiefly by describing him as surprised, worried and agitated by the 'teacher's' nonresponse) hearers said that subjects would disobey. But just because my descriptions were successful in matching the obedience study outcome does not necessarily mean that they will be equally successful if done as experiments.

Fortunately, experimental evidence concerning what would happen if the 'experimenter's' behaviour indicated harm is provided by Milgram himself. In three of his 18 studies *all* subjects disobeyed, just as you might expect them to do *if* they believed the shocks were harmful. And in all three studies the 'experimenter' – in one case, one of two 'experimenters' – behaved as if the shocks were harmful. Even though each of these experiments was a substantial variation on the scene I have analysed, they all support my interpretation. For in each case the unanimous disobedience suggests that, in Milgram's words, 'he [the subject] allows authority [the 'experimenter'] to define its [the action's] meaning.' When it is clear that the *authority* thinks the shocks are harmful, all subjects disobey. For if the authority thinks the shocks are harmful, his commands are illegitimate.

Common sense – the notion that people should and do defy illegitimate commands – when added to my descriptions and Milgram's three studies should be sufficient support for my interpretation. At any rate, those who believe only in the experimental 'proof' of deception studies are probably doomed to disappointment. For although my descriptions are quite minor variations on the baseline condition and technically would be simple to turn into studies, two reasons combine to make it unlikely that they will ever be done. For one thing ethics committees, rightly, would be difficult to convince. And if in 1971 when I did my role-playing simulations I had some difficulty making certain that all my participants were ignorant of the obedience study, by this time Milgram's studies are so well known that the task of finding ignorant subjects would be formidable. Subject ignorance (or naïveté as psychologists like to call it) is essential, for once you've heard of Milgram's studies you know that he (the *real* authority) and very nearly everyone else defines pushing the 450 volt lever as immoral. Thus, you know that the right thing to do is to disobey.

Milgram has felt free to pass moral judgement on his obedient subjects, using such locutions as 'callous', 'severe', 'shockingly immoral' and 'harshly and inhumanely' to characterize their actions, yet he is quite sensitive to anyone passing moral judgement on his own actions. In 1964 Diana Baumrind in the *American Psychologist* questioned the morality of Milgram's laboratory procedure, being particularly concerned with the severe stress exhibited by many of his subjects. Do psychologists have the right to subject their subjects to such distress? Milgram replied at length in the same journal, and ten years later in his book reprinted the substance of his reply (together with ethical endorsements – one by a former student who worked with him on the obedience studies). Defending his decision to continue putting subjects through extremely stressful moments he writes:

It is true that after a reasonable number of subjects had been exposed to the procedures, it became evident that some would go to the end of the shock board, and some would experience stress. That point, it seems to me, is the first legitimate juncture at which one could even start to wonder whether or not to abandon the study. But momentary excitement is not the same as harm. (1974, p. 194)

In other words Milgram would need to witness scenes like the following a number of times before even thinking about stopping the study:

I observed a mature and initially poised businessman enter the laboratory smiling and confident. Within 20 minutes he was reduced to a twitching, stuttering wreck, who was rapidly approaching a point of nervous collapse. He constantly pulled on his earlobe, and twisted his hands, at one point he pushed his fist into his forehead and muttered: 'Oh God, let's stop it'. (1963, p. 377)

I can stake no claim to moral superiority, for I allowed forty people to take part in my role-playing simulations, many of them exhibiting similar distress, before deciding that I would not do any more. My reason for discussing the matter is to show how easy it is to have one standard for authorities, and another, more severe standard, for subordinates. For couldn't Milgram's obedient subjects, if sophisticated enough, have used the same sort of argument as Milgram's to justify their own continuation in the study? Couldn't they claim that the 'learner's' momentary excitement is not the same as harm? Each of Milgram's 'shockingly immoral' obedient subjects continued only once; Milgram himself continued 'nearly a thousand' times.

Steven Patten has looked in detail at Milgram's claim that there was nothing immoral in carrying out the obedience experiments. He concludes in part:

In this paper I have endeavored to establish a pair of connected hypotheticals. First, that if Milgram's proposed defenses are as efficacious as he takes them to be, then the subjects of his experiments are equally entitled to their protection. Second, that if the subjects can justify their actions by these defenses, then the experiments fail to establish anything about unethical obedience. (1977a, pp. 363–4)

But, of course, the subjects do not need the justification. Milgram claimed 'The aim of this investigation is to find out when and how people would defy authority in the face of a clear moral imperative' (1974, p.4). Milgram's subjects were not given a clear moral imperative. We cannot know the moral content of their actions because we cannot know what they believed. Pushing the 450 volt lever is shockingly immoral only if they believed the shock was harmful. Subjects were given abundant reason to believe the shocks were not harmful. The laboratory situation was anything but clear. The two actors were conveying opposite information. The dramatic behaviour of the 'learner' was clearly saying that something terribly wrong was going on. The behaviour of the 'experimenter' was just as clearly demonstrating the harmless nature of the shocks. No wonder many subjects showed such stress. What to believe? The right thing to do depends on which actor is believed.

On the final page of the Epilogue to his book Milgram writes:

> The results, as seen and felt in the laboratory, are to this author disturbing. They raise the possibility that human nature, or – more specifically – the kind of character produced in American democratic society, cannot be counted on to insulate its citizens from brutality and inhumane treatment at the direction of malevolent authority. A substantial proportion of people do what they are told to do, irrespective of the content of the act and without limitations of conscience, so long as they perceive that the command comes from a legitimate authority. (1974, p. 189)

If by 'malevolent authority' Milgram means those authorities who are authorized to command subordinates to harm and kill, then seldom has human nature, character or conscience insulated sufficient citizens to thwart the designs of authorities. Fear of the enemy, righteousness of the cause, and rigorous training in automatic obedience usually enables authorities to gain their ends. On occasion doubts about whether or not the enemy should be feared, about the righteousness of the cause, and the manner of conducting the war can slow down and even stop war machines, as the experience in Vietnam shows. And we know all this without the benefit of Milgram's studies.

Milgram must be claiming something quite different, something we have not always known, something that makes his findings special and deeply disturbing. He does not put it this way because he lacks the concepts 'legitimate command' and 'illegitimate command', but Milgram must be claiming that 'malevolent authorities' lacking the authority to order subordinates to harm and kill can issue illegitimate commands to harm and kill and expect 'a substantial proportion' of subordinates to obey. This must be what he means because he could not call his obedient subjects 'shockingly immoral' unless he believed that they thought the shocks were harmful and possibly lethal. A command by an experimenter to deliver a harmful or lethal shock clearly is an illegitimate command.

No wonder people were so disturbed and struck by Milgram's 'findings'. For he is saying in effect that authorities no longer need the specific authority to issue lethal commands, that any authority can expect 'a substantial proportion of people' to obey a command to harm or kill – a prospect that might well give us pause. Fortunately, conceptual clarity gives the game away and reveals the absurdity of the claim. For if authorities can expect a substantial proportion of people to obey such commands that means that I, an authority in the lecture hall, could command the students on my right to attack and harm and kill those on my left and expect a substantial proportion to obey. Or that an office manager could order a subordinate preparing the coffee to add an emetic or poison and expect obedience.

To recapitulate: if Milgram is saying that a substantial proportion of people will obey legitimate commands to harm or kill then he is not telling us anything we did not already know – except that he has the proportions wrong. An army officer who could expect only 65 per cent obedience would be in serious trouble. Further, if he is speaking of legitimate commands then to call those who obey them 'shockingly immoral' is an astonishing judgement from anyone but a convinced pacifist or anarchist. Except for an acknowledged debt to an anarchist's book (Milgram, 1974, p. xv) nothing in Milgram's writing suggests that he is sympathetic to either pacifism or anarchism.

If Milgram means that a substantial proportion of people will obey illegitimate commands to harm or kill then the claim, quite simply, is absurd. Absurd, that is, unless modified to state that a substantial proportion of people might possibly be tricked and mystified into obeying illegitimate commands. If people can be deceived into believing that harmful shocks are harmless an experimenter can probably get a substantial proportion of people to obey.

What can be said of the obedience study? Subjects found themselves in a 'learning experiment' which must have seemed, at the very least, a bit peculiar. They were told that its purpose was 'to find out just what effect different people have on each other as teachers and learners, and also what effect *punishment* will have on learning in this situation' (1974, p. 18); yet the experimental procedure was so predetermined that the role of teacher could have been done by machine – with one exception. The 'teachers' were told that they had control of the duration of each shock – but no control over which shock to give or the level or intensity of shock. This is of no consequence as I believe most volunteer subjects do not expect to understand the mysteries of experimentation. Some time after the rather sterile 'learning' routine was well established something seemed to go seriously wrong. The 'learner' pounded on the wall and then stopped responding to the 'learning' task. Stranger still, the 'experimenter' showed no interest or concern about what had happened and calmly urged that the experiment continue. The pounding and subsquent silence surely indicated that something serious, something ominous, had happened. Yet, if so, why isn't the experimenter interested or concerned? Milgram's subjects found themselves in a deeply ambiguous, mysterious, and disturbing situation. No wonder many of them showed signs of severe stress. What to do?

We know what they did. What should they have done? They should have defied his 'experimenter'. If the world were just and modern experts were not minor deities they would have defied him and told him in no uncertain terms where to put his 'experiment'. And my actors should have defied me when I did my active role-playing simulation. Authorities and experts have no right to mystify and distress those upon whom their work depends. If I as subject think that something serious has happened and the expert gives no satisfaction, rather than suffering agonies myself and possibly harming someone else (for, after all, the expert may be incompetent or even insane), I should defy the expert. But I say this rather in sorrow than in condemnation of those who continued. Most of us, as Milgram points out, do indeed learn that we should not harm others. But we also learn that increasingly large chunks of the social and physical world that we live in can be understood only by experts and that we are dependent upon these experts; that in matters scientific our senses and judgement can deceive us. The more we depend upon experts the more our knowledge of the world rests upon faith and trust.

Faith and trust, the spectacle of subject after subject trusting the expert, even when such trust means great distress to themselves and possible harm to another, gives the studies much of their morbid fascination. A poignant scene in Milgram's film (1965) involves a middle-aged man, a 'teacher', who becomes painfully concerned about the 'learner's wellbeing. He fears that something terrible has happened and pleads with the 'experimenter' to call a halt. The 'experimenter', of course, does nothing of the kind, but instead issues his prods and assurances. If the 'teacher' believes his actions are harming the 'learner' why does he continue to plead? Why not simply stop? I cannot know, but judging from his attitude toward the 'experimenter', the 'teacher' continues because he cannot simultaneously believe that the 'learner' is being harmed *and* that the expert is lying to him. He could not put his judgement above the expert's concerning what is happening, what is going on. For an act of defiance would be a declaration that he believes the 'experimenter' is mistaken or is lying. The 'teacher' could only plead, not defy.

I suppose that what I mean when I say that Milgram's subjects should be defiant is that I *wish*, I think it would be good if, people were less trusting, less respectful of experts. My wish is neither profound nor original, but needs stating nonetheless. Part of my own distrust of experts comes from knowledge of my own field of study. For by society's measure, I am an expert who can certify my expertise (an ugly word) by appropriate academic degrees, postdoctoral study, publications, etc. But what I have learned is how little of substance can be found in my discipline. In fact I am far from certain that social psychologists know anything that is superior to common sense or common knowledge. Stripped of its mystification and jargon much of what we know – like information based on Milgram's studies – is plainly wrong, is *mis*information: not common sense, but uncommon nonsense.

Readers may protest that social psychology is an exception, that surely other fields must possess substantial knowledge. Look at what we can *do* that we could not do prior to modern science. Yes, the social and behavioural sciences may be an exception in that sense, but there is a second reason to urge a healthy scepticism, even disrespect of experts. This has to do with experts' proneness to self-mystification and self-deception. Experts, of course, are not the only prey of self-deception. Few are immune. But the jargon and the perceived importance of what they do make experts particularly prone to self-deception and particularly likely to succumb to moral sophistry. Scientific experts in a number of fields have justified the most cruel practices on animal and human subjects by asserting the importance of their task, the importance of their charge to seek the 'truth'.[8] And, fearful that if we abandon such means of seeking the 'truth' we will be more unhealthy or unhappy than we already are, we respectfully accept the blanket justification. Yet no expert can demonstrate that such means are the only or even the best means of seeking scientific truth, or whether in the long run the results of any particular research programme will make us healthier and happier or more sick and miserable. One thing that no expert knows or can know is the moral, social, or political consequences of any bit of knowledge or truth. Except for present-day descendants of Dr Pangloss that part of the scientific creed which assumes that all knowledge must benefit society has become transformed from a noble dream into a tragic joke.

My discussion has been limited to Milgram's pilot study and to the study reported in 1963. In Milgram's book the 1963 study is called Remote-Victim (Experiment 1). He describes it as his first baseline condition. Most of Milgram's reported experiments are variations on Experiment 5: New Base Line. Readers may wonder why I have chosen to focus on a less familiar and less representative study. The reason is simple: Experiment 1 is the better study, has fewer interpretive problems.

In the New Base Line the 'learner' protests vocally 18 times (if the 'teacher' continues that long). The protests begin with 'Ugh!' after the 75 volt shock and continue until after the 330 volt shock.

> (*Intense and prolonged agonized scream.*) Let me out of here. Let me out of here. My heart's bothering me. Let me out, I tell you. (*Hysterically*) Let me out of here. Let me out of here. You have no right to hold me here. Let me out! Let me out! Let me out! Let me out of here! Let me out! Let me out! (1974, p. 57)

The 330 volt shock is not the first time the 'learner' calls attention to his heart condition; he mentions the heart problem to the 'experimenter' and 'teacher' before the experiment begins and also protests after the 150 and 195 volt shock that his heart is bothering him.

There is reason to suppose that hearing the 'learner' protest would make the consequences of this shock more clear and thus reduce some of the ambiguity of the situation and increase the disobedience. But the proportion of disobedience remained the same as in the Remote-Victim condition – 35 per cent. I think that one reason for the 'learner's' protests failing to increase disobedience is that the late James McDonough, who played the part of the learner, was not a very good actor. (Experimental procedure prevented him from improving, for his protests were recorded at the beginning of his long run – before he had any experience.) An 'intense and prolonged agonized scream' can be so effective as to chill the heart of a 'teacher'. Or it can be so unmoving, so unconvincing that it can be ignored, not taken seriously. Mr McDonough's protests are featured in the film Milgram made and I have heard them countless times. The screams and protests do not chill the heart; they are neither convincing nor moving.

Readers are not bound to accept my opinion regarding the quality of the 'learner's' protests. Nor, after what I said about experts, should they react with anything but hearty scepticism when I assure them that I trained for the theatre, was an actor myself, and that I know unconvincing acting when I hear it. The point is that the vocal feedback inevitably makes acting an issue and creates more difficulties for anyone trying to answer questions about what the 'teacher' might or might not believe. And if acting is a problem when recorded vocal feedback is used, it is an even bigger problem when the actor/learner is brought into the room with the 'teacher' (Proximity condition) and has to perform 'live'. And when brought even closer in the Touch-Proximity condition the actor/learner had to be convincing to a 'teacher' who was holding the actor/learner's hand on the shock plate. Milgram created an acting challenge for the accountant few actors ever have had to face: to express truly, to be believable, not just with body and voice, but through the skin, through touch.

Believability is not an issue when feedback consists of pounding on the wall; it *is* an issue when the feedback is vocal protests. Thus the Voice-Feedback exercise does nothing to resolve the unclarity and ambiguity of the Remote condition. If anything it adds further ambiguity. And the basic problem of the Remote condition – the 'experimenter's' assurances – continues to be the basic problem in the Voice-Feedback condition.

The title of a paper Milgram published in 1965 – 'Some conditions of obedience and disobedience to authority' – describes his research method. By systematically introducing changes in his baseline studies Milgram hoped to be able to specify the degree of obedience to be expected in situations of various sorts. What seems like a sensible and potentially valuable procedure becomes less so as soon as one realizes that changes in situation should have little or no effect on the degree of obedience of those charged with carrying out an authorized criminal command. In contrast to those at the bottom of a chain of command, as will be seen in the next chapter, those high in a command hierarchy have considerable latitude in avoiding, evading or misdirecting commands. Command hierarchies are structured in such a way that the latitude near the top is absent at the bottom.

⌐Because in the baseline studies the legitimacy of the commands was unclear the remaining experimental variations must be interpreted with caution⌐ One thing that must be understood is the effect of each experimental manipulation on the relationship between the authority and the subordinate, for whether or not a subordinate obeys depends on the relationship. If the authority gives a clearly legitimate command the subordinate is obliged by the terms of the relationship to obey. If the command for whatever reason appears of doubtful legitimacy then in order to exact obedience the authority must be able to convince subordinates of the command's rightfulness. Understood in these terms, the variations in context rung by Milgram serve either to strengthen or weaken the experimenter's case for legitimacy.⌐

It seems clear from the way Milgram writes about Nazi atrocities that by using the developing tools of a young experimental discipline he hoped to find out something about obedience that would help prevent a recurrence of the Second World War scenes that haunt our imaginations. Few investigators can have had a better reason for a research programme. Judging from his sombre and pessimistic conclusion (quoted on p. 33) the likelihood is that Milgram came to think that he failed to find anything useful to impede the course of what he calls 'destructive obedience'.

Ironically, given Milgram's purpose, it is fortunate that he failed. His experimental design sought to produce a situational anatomy of obedience and to establish the degree of obedience that might be expected in a range of situations. Had Milgram been able to identify with any degree of certainty the sorts of situations in which obedience can be expected, the knowledge would benefit commanders far more than the commanded. For it is the commanders, not the commanded, who have the power to control situations. A successful situational anatomy would benefit, not deter, future Hitlers.

I have examined 'Milgram's shocking experiments' (Patten, 1977b) from a number of angles and run a risk of obscuring the basic argument. The obedience study results were counterintuitive, surprising, dismaying, and seemed to offer a new and grim view of human nature, because Milgram failed to ask himself, and his large audience failed to wonder, what sort of command the subjects were obeying and defying. Was it a legitimate command or was it an illegitimate command? When, throughout his research papers and his book, Milgram makes generalizations about obedience to authority, is he talking about obedience to legitimate commands or obedience to illegitimate commands? If he is referring to legitimate commands he is wrong in his conclusions (65 per cent obedience is much too low), for the relatively small number of authorities who are empowered to give commands to harm or kill attempt by rigorous training and selection to ensure that all such commands are obeyed. If Milgram is talking about illegitimate commands, once again he is wrong. The number of authorities who issue illegitimate commands to harm and kill (for example, the number of lecturers who command students to harm and kill) is probably very small both because of the slim likelihood of being obeyed and the certainty of being prosecuted if obeyed. The use of deception and mystification might produce some success – that is, an authority who used deception to convince subordinates that something harmful was harmless, might well be obeyed. But I can think of no general statement relating to illegitimate commands that can be warranted by Milgram's studies. To suppose that in ordinary circumstances 65 per cent of the population can be expected to obey an illegitimate command to harm and kill is quite simply a delusion.

Milgram's lack of clarity was built into the laboratory scenes he wrote and produced – which ensured that his subjects could not be certain about the nature of the command or of what they should do. Hence the deep distress many of them showed.

Milgram's topic of study is rich with psychological interest; his hope of solving some of the grave issues of destructive obedience with the application of experimental methods is understandable. His considerable professional and popular success gave wide currency to the notion of the normality of obedience. Yet because Milgram misinterpreted his own study he left a legacy of misunderstanding and confusion, and at least one important delusion. Since a fair proportion (35 per cent) of subjects disobeyed, readers were left with the comforting thought that the normality thesis applies, not to themselves, but to all those others: others more compliant and less ethically sensitive.

The state of affairs in the ongoing struggle between sovereign conscience and authority is both not as bad and considerably worse than suggested in Milgram's morality play: not as bad, because people ordinarily *do* resist *un*authorized criminal commands; considerably worse, because in relation to authorized criminal commands conscience is sovereign for only a tiny minority.

Grounds for Obedience and Resistance

'Convention' embraces a number of other concepts, among them status and role. They have in common the sense of carrying out instructions, doing assigned tasks, and playing one's part. If behaviour is seen as a performance, it is automatically explained in a certain way. A priest celebrating mass, a merchant bargaining in the market-place, a Park Avenue heiress walking her poodle, are, among hosts of others, events or actions which do not need explaining. This is not because they are difficult, opaque, or too unique to afford the accommodation of general theory, but because they are transparent. (Louch, 1966, p. 163)

My duty is to obey orders. (General Thomas Jonathan 'Stonewall' Jackson)

Milgram's scenes disturbed us because his subjects seemed to have no good reason for obeying and every reason for defying. I have argued that so long as they could trust the 'experimenter's' words and attitude subjects did have reason to obey. Readers may agree with me in wishing that all subjects had disobeyed: for trust in the 'experimenter' does not seem a good enough reason to obey. But before judging Milgram's subjects ask yourself whether or not in fact the trust was justified. Were the aspects of the scene that contributed to trust – the 'experimenter's' attitude, his 'prods' and assurances – true or false? Strictly speaking they were both true and false: in general they were true, but the truth was mixed. For example, the last half of: 'Although the shocks may be painful, there is no permanent tissue damage' is true, the first half false. Nonexistent shocks can cause no tissue damage, permanent or otherwise. But then nonexistent shocks cannot be painful either. Cutting through the interpretative uncertainties built into the scene by deception and lying, ultimately the obedient subjects were right to trust the experimenter when he claimed that the 'learner' was not being harmed. The 'learner' in truth was not being harmed.

Properly understood Milgram's study remains a powerful modern morality play. We see subject after subject placing faith in the expert, even though they cannot be sure the expert is telling the truth, indeed, even though there is strong evidence the expert is lying. That ultimately they were right to trust the expert does not negate the fact that they could not know he was telling the truth.

Imagine that a scientific purist decides that simulation, even disguised simulation, is not good enough, that the importance of the subject matter demands a series of *real* experiments on obedience. So the purist decides to replicate Milgram's simulation of destructive obedience by substituting a genuine subject for the actor/learner, a genuine experimenter for the actor/experimenter, and a genuine shock generator for the fake, but otherwise following Milgram's procedure exactly. In the resulting *real* experiment, *if* she or he could persuade a teacher that the shocks are not harmful, the genuine experimenter no doubt could get a genuine teacher to harm or kill the genuine learner. But the purist would have data on one, not 1,000 subjects. For the purist's first 'success' would be followed by his (or her) arrest, charge, trial, conviction and sentence. If she or he came to trial, the subject who obeyed the command to harm or kill would probably be found innocent, for her/his lawyer could show that the history of psychological experimentation gave the accused every reason to believe an experimenter who assured him that the shocks would cause no harm. The publicity from the trial might ensure that no future psychological subject would trust an experimenter who claimed a treatment was painful but not harmful.

Milgram's results were surprising because his experimental scene is unlike any commonly occurring situation in the social world. The essential unreality of the simulations should be clear. However, there is nothing unreal about the scenes that prompted Milgram's studies. The hideous crimes of history involved all-too-real harm and death. Hitler's death camps involved death and other all-too-real unspeakable actions directed at inmates. If Milgram's subjects had reason to obey because they could believe they were not harming the 'learner', surely the instruments of history's hideous crimes had no such reason.

Those who obeyed the hideous commands that crowd the historical record knew that they were harming and killing: their job, their role, was harming and killing. But just because they knew what they were doing does not mean that they had no reason to obey the hideous commands. Milgram set up a situation that seemed to pit no reason to obey against every reason to disobey.

Those who obeyed in the collective situations which make up history's hideous crimes had reasons to obey as well as reasons to disobey.[1]

Grounds for Obeying and for Defying Authorized Criminal Commands

Obedience means doing things, not because of personal desire, wish, or motive, but because someone tells us to. It means doing what someone tells us to do, not because of a personal relationship, but because of a status relationship – a relationship of subordination to a superior status with the authority of command. When we do not wish to do as commanded awareness of our obedience and our subordination is unavoidable. But obedience, more commonly, can be invisible or difficult to see – as when we have learned to wish and desire to do those things our status demands us to do and thus experience the status demands and commands as personal wishes or desires. Such invisible obedience can even seem compatible with what commonly is thought of as 'freedom'.

Doing something because we are told to do it is such a common part of everyday life that, unless the command in some way is strange or unusual, we commonly are unaware that someone else's wish is moving us. Yet if what we are moved to do is a crime, in most cases we are held responsible for the action. If I kill a person, for example, and claim innocence because someone told me to do it, ordinarily such an excuse will fail to impress the authorities. A court of law will determine my degree of responsiblility for the crime and sentence me accordingly – unless, that is, the killing was authorized. But even killings done by military personnel can be subject to court proceedings, for not all wartime crimes are authorized. 'I was only obeying orders' is or is not an acceptable plea depending on circumstance.

Although science as ordinarily conceived offers no starting point for examining the morality of obedient acts, the law does and will serve here as a rough guide for evaluating obedience to criminal commands. The legal tradition, in contrast to conventional social scientific belief, assumes a degree of human agency. As a consequence such concepts as reasons, grounds and responsibility are essential parts of legal thought.

Authorizing crime in times of war is a serious matter and the military has long been aware of an obligation to try to keep destruction within bounds. The destructive forces unleashed by the authorization are so great that efforts must be made to ensure that crimes committed by military personnel are in fact authorized. Broadly speaking two types of unlawful acts can be committed by military personnel: (1) crime done without orders or contrary to orders; and (2) crime resulting from obeying unlawful orders. Soldiers who rape, loot or kill on their own initiative are subject to court martial and punishment, for they must limit their crimes to those they are authorized to commit. Soldiers are not given a personal licence to misbehave. Crime done without orders or contrary to orders closely resembles ordinary, civilian crime and a military court dealing with such crime faces issues of grounds and responsibility similar to those faced by civilian courts. Destructive acts done by military personnel without orders or contrary to orders ordinarily are deplored, condemned, and categorized as criminal.

The question of who is responsible for an action done at someone else's command becomes important in the second type of unlawful military act: crime resulting from obeying unlawful orders. Those authorized to issue destructive commands do not have authority to issue any command they choose and sometimes issue orders that, in one way or another, are unlawful. Unlawful commands are a possibility in any command hierarchy – officers can be incompetent, lose control of themselves, be traitorous, etc. Military organizations all must find ways of dealing with such situations when they occur. According to Telford Taylor (1971) the German Military Penal Code of 1872 contained the earliest statement of a general, governing rule:

> If execution of an order given in line of duty violates a statute of the penal code, the superior giving the order is alone responsible. However, the subordinate obeying the order is liable to punishment as an accomplice if ... he knew that the order involved an act the commission of which constituted a civil or military crime or offense. (quoted in Taylor, 1971, p. 47)

The statement clearly defines one type of unlawful military command (an order that violates a statute of the penal code) and gives clear guidelines for assigning responsibility (the superior who gives the order has major responsibility). Since the crimes in question are unlawful according to national (German) law, offenders could expect to be tried by German military courts.

A second type of unlawful command is unlawful according to international law. Violators of international law can be tried by national courts, but also can be tried by the victor in a war or by an international court. Thus far in the history of warfare international tribunals empowered to punish have been the courts of victors. Developments since 1872 in international law have greatly expanded the notion of what constitutes an unlawful military command. The current status of unlawful military commands takes its form from the series of postwar trials of German and Japanese war criminals that began with the first Nuremberg trial.

> a ... remarkable feature of the trials was that they brought about a great expansion of the principle that individuals may be held criminally liable under international law, even though their conduct was valid under, or even required by, domestic law. (Taylor, 1971, p. 82)

A crime authorized by domestic authorities is of course not a crime under domestic (national) law. If I am given a lawful command to kill and I do so the question of my legal responsibility for the murder does not arise because I have broken no law. Legal responsibility does not arise, that is, unless what I have done violates international law – and I am brought before an international tribunal. The potential legal importance of the Nuremberg trials is enormous, for there exist to a far greater extent than ever before identified crimes against peace, war crimes and crimes against humanity that, according to international precedent and law, cannot be authorized by domestic authority. The precedent and law, however, have not been tested, for no international court has been set up to try individuals for nationally authorized, but internationally proscribed, crimes committed in the wars since the Second World War.

Both in the Charter of the International Military Tribunal that governed the first Nuremberg trial and in the trial's conduct great care was taken to link the acts named as crimes to military custom and to legal precedent. Even so the links to custom and to past cases were not and are not without controversy and in a number of important ways the Nuremberg trial set new legal precedents and is a major milestone in international law.

The initial Nuremberg trial assessed the individual guilt of 22 prominent party, government and military leaders of the Third Reich. Twenty-one defendants were in the dock and one, Martin Bormann, was tried *in absentia*. The prosecutors drew up a four-count indictment: (1) Conspiracy to Wage Aggressive War; (2) Crimes Against the Peace; (3) War Crimes; (4) Crimes Against Humanity. More than sufficient documentary evidence that the crimes named had been committed was introduced by the prosecution. The task of the court was to decide each defendant's responsibility for the documented crimes. Twelve of the defendants were charged on all four counts in the indictment, six were charged on three counts, and four on two counts.

Of the 12 defendants charged on all four counts six were found guilty on all four; five of the guilty six were sentenced to hanging (Goering, Von Ribbontrop, Keitel, Rosenberg and Jodl), and one to 15 years' imprisonment (Von Neurath). Three of the remaining six defendants charged on four counts were found guilty on three of the counts; two were sentenced to hanging (Frick and Seyss-Inquart) and one to life imprisonment (Funk). The three remaining defendants charged on four counts were found guilty on two counts; one was sentenced to hanging (Sauckel), one was sentenced to life imprisonment (Hess), and one to 20 years' imprisonment (Speer).

Of the six defendants charged on three counts one was found guilty on all three and was sentenced to life imprisonment (Raeder). Four of the remaining five defendants charged on three counts were found guilty on two counts; three were sentenced to hanging (Kaltenbrunner, Frank and Bormann) and one to ten years' imprisonment (Doenitz). The other defendant charged on three counts was found innocent on all three and acquitted (Fritzsche).

Of the four defendants charged on two counts two were found guilty on one of the counts; one was sentenced to hanging (Streicher) and one to 20 years' imprisonment (Von Schirach). The two remaining defendants charged on two counts were found innocent of both and acquitted (Schacht and Von Papen).

The Nuremberg tribunal, like other courts of law, tried individual defendants for specific crimes. As can be seen from the verdicts and the sentencing the judges made careful discriminations in assessing degrees of guilt and innocence. Although all of the defendants made important contributions to the Nazi capacity to commit crimes, they were not all judged equally responsible for the crimes. A law court's charge to determine whether or not a defendant is guilty and, if guilty, the degree of guilt, should be kept in mind when thinking about the moral, as opposed to legal, questions which have been stimulated by Nazi atrocities.

Those Nazis found guilty were guilty because of their responsibility for crimes which, though authorized by the German state, were judged unlawful according to international custom and law. 'The laws of war remain a body of what lawyers call 'customary' laws – that is to say, laws that are not created by statutes enacted by legislatures, but develop from societal custom and practice' (Taylor, 1971, pp. 28, 29). Most people today, including many living in the former Axis states, have little difficulty in agreeing with the Nuremberg judges concerning the wrongness of the guilty defendants' actions. The same actions were judged differently during the war. In time of war people undoubtedly look to their own nation state as the font of authority, the arbiter or judge of what is and is not permitted. If nationally authorized, but internationally proscribed, criminal commands are to be disobeyed, grounds must be found for resistance.

Legal and moral grounds for obedience and resistance to authorized criminal commands share basic features in all cases, yet differ in important ways according to the nature of the command and to time and circumstance. In order to establish general grounds for obedience and resistance I shall begin with an example that lumps together all authorized criminal commands and then go on to discuss four historical examples. These will bring out some of the legal and moral complexities involved in deciding the rightness or wrongness of obeying or resisting authorized criminal commands. I shall try to capture the type of command involved in each historical case. The historical examples all concern obedient actions judged illegal and immoral by some commentators.

The broadest possible example comes from looking at history as a whole, as did C. P. Snow in the comments quoted earlier. Arthur Koestler provides an alternative statement:

> Even a cursory glance at history should convince one that individual crimes committed for selfish motives play a quite insignificant part in the human tragedy, compared to the numbers massacred in unselfish loyalty to one's tribe, nation, dynasty, church, or political ideology, *ad majorem glorian dei.* (1978, p. 14)

The massacres mentioned by Koestler are only the most prominent of the hideous crimes referred to by Snow. History's authorized crimes include the enormous variety and range of crimes inflicted by warriors upon the bodies of other people. Generally speaking, on what legal grounds do warriors obey such commands? They have a legal obligation or duty to obey and often face severe penalties for disobedience. The disobedient are commonly called 'traitors' and charged with treason to the state. On what legal grounds might warriors resist or disobey commands to commit hideous crimes? If they knew a command was unlawful or if they believed the government itself was unlawful they might feel they had sufficient grounds to risk resistance or disobedience. In fairly recent times some governments have made legal provisions to exempt from military duty those men who can convince a court that their religious beliefs forbid killing under any circumstances. Ordinarily only members of religious groups which openly and consistently espouse such beliefs (for example, the Society of Friends, the Mennonites and the Brethren) are successful in pleading grounds of conscience. Once in the military, however, lawful orders must be obeyed.

Moral grounds for obeying authorized criminal commands include virtues which cluster around a quality most groups cannot do without: loyalty, a wish to be faithful, true, steadfast, devoted and trustworthy. Obedience itself, of course, is a fundamental group virtue. Moral grounds for resisting or disobeying authorized criminal commands are similar to, but considerably broader than, legal grounds. Not all governments recognize conscientious objection as legal grounds for refusing military duty and those governments severely limit who can qualify. Anyone who believes a command, legal or not legal, is wrong or immoral has reason to resist, defy or evade such a command. The grounds may come from any number of religions, from moral philosophy, or from human feeling and sentiment.

The hideous crimes of history frequently seem like senseless, stupid carnage. Removed politically and psychologically from the quarrels that prompted the butchery, moral grounds for disobedience can seem overwhelming. We may be genuinely puzzled as to how people could obey commands that seem both bloodthirsty and stupid. Puzzlement can vanish when we realize that in the eyes of their perpetrators the hideous crimes of history are not hideous crimes at all, but acts of loyalty, patriotism and duty. From the vantage point of the present we can see them as hideous crimes, but ordinarily from that same vantage point we cannot see the crimes of our own governments as hideous or even as crimes. We can see the crimes of the *enemy* as hideously criminal, but such always has been the case. Although the differences that roused passion in Romans and Carthaginians, for example, no longer move us, in most times and in most places, from the perspective of the warriors, the legal and moral grounds for obedience far outweighed the legal and moral grounds for resistance or disobedience.

The general grounds or reasons for obeying and for disobeying history's hideous commands hold true for specific historical examples, but the special circumstances of each case can augment or diminish their force. The first historical example I shall discuss – the hideous crimes of Nazi Germany – stimulated Snow's remarks about 'the long and gloomy history of man'.

> The German officer corps were brought up in the most rigorous code of obedience. To themselves, no more honorable and God-fearing body of men could conceivably exist. Yet in the name of obedience they were party to, and assisted in, the most wicked large-scale actions in the history of the world. (1961, p. 24)

Enemies had been mistreated and conquered peoples abused in past wars, but the technological competence of Nazi mistreatment and abuse, including the killing of millions and the enslavement of millions more, was so chillingly applied and so bureaucratically systematic as to numb the imagination. Prior to Nazi aggression eastern Europe had a miserable tradition of officially encouraged persecutions and massacres (pogroms) directed against minorities, but the Nazis escalated persecution to routine, systematic genocide by deciding that the 'Reich with all of its incorporated territories was to be cleared of Jews, Poles, and Gypsies alike' (Hilberg, 1985, p. 206). 'Clearing' originally meant 'clearing-by-deporting' but quickly came to mean 'clearing-by-killing'. Many people continue to find obedience to such wicked commands inconceivable.

Legal grounds for obedience to authorized criminal commands were the same in Nazi Germany as in the general case: the duty of a warrior is to obey lawful commands. Some of the commands were unlike commands in any previous war, but as a result of a decree entitled 'Law relating to national emergency defence measures' passed by cabinet on 3 July 1934, the law in Germany was 'whatever Hitler said it to be. He could do nothing wrong, for he could legalize – before or after – any action he might take' (Conot, 1983, p. 129).

Had they cared to look, Nazi officials could have found legal grounds for resisting or disobeying hideous commands both in the largely unwritten tradition of the laws of war and, more specifically, in the series of treaties known today as the Hague and Geneva Conventions (Taylor, 1971). That the legal grounds were there to be found was demonstrated at the Nuremberg trial, but in wartime Germany I suspect few in either the civilian or military bureaucracy believed that military tradition and international treaties took precedence over German domestic law.

Just as in the general case, the moral grounds for obeying the hideous commands can be found in moral virtues such as loyalty, faithfulness and trustworthinesss. A special moral ground for obedience specific to the Nazi situation is often overlooked, forgotten or denied – possibly because of an unwillingness to face squarely the fact that a state that almost made itself Master of Europe preached the rightness of killing 'undesirables'. Like it or not, those actions we call atrocities were positive virtues in the Nazi moral code. For Hitler the war was an ideological crusade, a crusade against a Jewish-Bolshevik and (to some extent) Christian conspiracy. Nazi values were not values to stand in the way of anyone who was ordered to murder Jews and other ideological enemies. The success of the Nazi crusade depended on the elimination of Jews and Bolsheviks (and Gypsies, Poles and others). For a loyal member of the Führer state murdering ideological enemies was a positive virtue. 'Conscience is a Jewish invention. It is a blemish, like circumcision ... Providence has ordained that I should be the greatest liberator of humanity. I am freeing men from the dirty and degrading self-mortification of a chimera called conscience and morality' (Adolf Hitler, quoted in Conot, 1983, pp. 11–12). 'The purification of the German race was a holy duty: the lowest Nazi beating a Jew to his knees in the streets acted under the hierarchical glamor of a party that was "cleansing" the community of its evils' (Duncan, 1962, p. 134).

Moral grounds for resisting or disobeying hideous commands can be found in most religious and ethical codes and in ordinary human compassion. Nazi crimes were so grave that many commentators have believed that moral grounds for resistance can be found in anyone's conscience.

In summary the hideous commands of Nazi Germany which brought so much terror, death and suffering may be typified or categorized as *unlawful* (according to international custom and law) *nationally authorized criminal commands*.

The second historical example occurred over 20 years after the Nuremberg verdicts.

During the period 16–19 March 1968, US Army troops of TF Barker, 11th Brigade, American Division, massacred a large number of noncombatants in two hamlets of Son My Village, Quang Ngai Province, Republic of Vietnam. The precise number of Vietnamese killed cannot be determined but was at least 175 and may exceed 400. (Goldstein, Marshall & Schwartz, 1976, p. 314)

The massacre at Son My (known as My Lai) looks like a straightforward case of officers issuing unlawful commands and so belongs in the category of crime that everyone deplores and opposes. However, the public outcry over the trial and sentencing of Lt. William L. Calley suggests that many people saw the massacre in a different light. Although the slaughter of defenceless men, women, children and babies is atrocious and clearly contrary to the international laws of war, to a public unsophisticated in legal and moral distinctions the crime might appear to differ neither in intent nor result from official United States policies. Standard everyday procedures such as 'free-fire zones', 'free-strike zones', aerial bombing with anti-personnel weapons, and the use of 'body counts' as a measure of military success resulted in the indiscriminate killing of civilians – men, women, children, and babies. *'The ultimate question of "guilt" in the trial of the Son My troops is how far what they did departed from general American military practice as they had witnessed it'* (Taylor, 1971, p. 160, his italics).

Had the soldiers of TF Barker been properly trained in the areas of '(1) provisions of the Geneva Conventions (2) handling and safeguarding of noncombatants, and (3) rules of engagement' (Goldstein, Marshall & Schwartz, 1976, p. 204) and had US policies not condoned indiscriminate killing, Calley's command no doubt would have appeared clearly illegitimate to his subordinates. But then had *Calley* been properly trained, and had US policies been different he might never have issued the terrible commands.

Legal and moral grounds for obeying or resisting are much the same as in the general case. The chief difference is that the post-Second World War war crimes trials greatly clarified and strengthened both legal and moral grounds for resistance and disobedience. Ironically, grounds for obedience were strengthened too, strengthened by the way in which the war in Vietnam was fought. The enemy was not a clearly identifiable uniformed warrior. Children and other civilians, or warriors dressed as civilians, sometimes acted as death-dealing enemies. A concern that seemingly unarmed and innocent civilians might be dangerous served to strengthen loyalty to comrades at the expense of compassion for the ordinarily helpless.

In summary, Lt. Calley's commands at My Lai may be categorized as *unlawful* (by nationally recognized international law), *but implicitly authorized* (by national policy) *criminal commands*.

The third historical example comes from a trial conducted by the victorious Union Army which took place in Washington, DC in the summer of 1865, 80 years before Nuremberg. Confederate Major Henry Wirz, formerly commander of the prison camp at Andersonville, Georgia, was tried before a Union military commission for his responsibility in the death by exposure, starvation and disease of over 13,000 of the Union prisoners in his care. Prisoners were not sent to Andersonville to be killed as in a Nazi death camp, but died in great numbers because of the conditions at the prison, which basically was an open stockade without shelter from winter cold or summer heat. The only drinking water came from a stream running through the enclosure, a stream fouled with human waste and dead bodies. Food was totally inadequate. Yet when neighbouring farmers who had heard of the hunger and starvation arrived at the camp with wagonloads of food, they were turned away by Wirz. The trial is of interest here both because of the nature and magnitude of the crime and because of the failure of the defence argument that Wirz was only obeying the directives of his superior, General John H. Winder. Wirz was found guilty of 'conspiring to destroy the lives of Union soldiers and of murder in violation of the laws and customs of war' (Taylor, 1971, p. 46) and was hanged on 10 November 1865.

Legal grounds for obeying are the same as in the general case: obedience to superior commands is a basic, if not *the* basic military duty. Wirz was able to show in the trial that he indeed did faithfully carry out the directives of Winder, the officer in charge of all the Confederate prison camps. Legal grounds for resisting or disobeying are stronger than in the general case. Incentives for complying with the longstanding customs and laws of war which deal with the good treatment of prisoners stem not only from humanitarian motives but from self-interest. All officers would be aware of the reprisals which threaten combatants who mistreat prisoners. Thus, any state that wishes the enemy to treat prisoners well must themselves treat captured enemies in a proper fashion. Moral grounds for obeying and for resisting are the same as in the general case.

The Andersonville trial and the Nuremberg trial were similar in the sense that both were trials conducted by victors. I include it as an example because of what I see as an important difference. The Nazis at Nuremberg were tried for crimes that resulted from policies of the German state. In spite of their marked failure at the trial to affirm Hitler's crusade the Nazi defendants when obeying his orders no doubt agreed with Hitler's criminal policies. Wirz dutifully carried out his superior's directives, but I find it difficult to believe that he did so thinking that he was carrying out a policy of the Confederate government. So important is the treatment of prisoners in the laws and customs of war that it might be argued that Wirz had a duty to defy Winder by going over his head – or at least to resist or evade the directives in some way.

In summary, Winder's directives may be categorized as *unlawful* (by international custom) *and possibly unauthorized* (by national policy) *criminal commands*.

I include the final historical case, the destruction of the Japanese city Hiroshima on 6 August 1945 by a nuclear weapon, as an example of a problem created for the customs and laws of war by modern technology. Modern wars have marched ever closer to the condition of a 'total war' – total both in the sense of mobilizing an entire population and also in the sense of having the capacity to destroy an entire population. Today obedience to a command to launch a large-scale nuclear attack not only could destroy the enemy's nation state and its people, but the attacker's state and people and eventually, by some estimates, human life on this planet.

All states have customs, rules and laws declaring criminal those actions that harm and kill. In times of war, in order to prevent the enemy's warriors from harming and killing, a state authorizes its own warriors to harm and kill the enemy. In its clearest, ideal form the only ones authorized to harm and kill are the warriors and the only ones who can be killed are the enemy's warriors. That is why MacArthur could say: 'The soldier, be he friend or foe, is charged with the protection of the weak and unarmed. It is the very essence and reason for his being.' In relation to grounds or justifications for authorized crime MacArthur must be right. The moral injunction *Thou Shalt Not Kill* is so strong that one of few justifications sufficiently powerful to waive it is the protection of the weak and unarmed. The customs and laws of war can be interpreted as having evolved in an attempt to keep the waging of wars as near as possible to the ideal form of a clash between warriors whose duty it is to protect the weak and unarmed.

Finding a precise historical beginning for anything is often impossible. But from about the time of the American Civil War the 'improvement' of existing weapons and the invention of increasingly destructive new ones has made confining a war to a clash between warriors ever more difficult. Some weapons are so powerful and indiscriminate in their effects that using them, no matter what the intent, means that the weak and unarmed, rather than being protected, are harmed and killed. When international law permits the use of such weapons the 'very essence and reason' for a soldier's being, the ground and justification for authorizing crime, is seriously undermined if not destroyed altogether.

Powerful and indiscriminate weapons existed and were used prior to Hiroshima. I chose as an example the dropping of the first nuclear weapon not because the destruction caused was unprecedented (it was not), but because of the technology of destruction it foreshadowed. The legal ground for obeying a command to drop a nuclear bomb on Hiroshima is familiar and straightforward: military duty. Legal grounds for resisting such a command are less clear. The postwar military tribunals conducted by the victorious allies, including the Nuremberg tribunal, were silent on the subject of aerial bombardment. Only former enemies have suggested that legal grounds exist for resisting a command to destroy a city and its people.

> In 1963, a Tokyo civil court rendered judgment in a suit for damages brought by survivors of the Hiroshima and Nagasaki bombings. The court denied recovery, but characterized the atomic bombings as 'contrary to the fundamental principles of the laws of war'. (Taylor, 1971, p. 141).

And complaining about Allied 'terror fliers' the Nazi minister for public enlightenment and propaganda Dr Joseph Goebbels, claimed:

> It is not provided in any military law that a soldier in the case of a despicable crime is exempt from punishment because he passes the responsibility to his superior, especially if the orders of the latter are in evident contradiction to all human morality and every international usage of warfare. (quoted in Conot, 1983, p. 513)

The moral ground for obeying a command to bomb Hiroshima is the familiar one of loyalty. Moral grounds for resisting or disobeying are beliefs about the wrongness of indiscriminate killing and destruction. Since the bomb was novel and its effect on a populated area unknown, moral grounds specific to the bomb's horrors were not available prior to the bombing. The effects of nuclear weapons, both short-term and long-term, are better understood today. If the ground for authorizing crime is the protection of the weak and unarmed, then the use of nuclear weapons cannot be justified and so cannot be authorized. Nuclear warfare cannot protect the weak and unarmed, it can only disfigure, disable or destroy them.

In summary, the command to drop a nuclear bomb on Hiroshima may be categorized as a *lawful* (according to the victors) *or unlawful* (according to the defeated) *authorized criminal command.*

I have discussed briefly a number of examples in order to make a simple but essential point. All nationally authorized criminal commands are not the same and grounds, both legal and moral, for obeying and disobeying have different weight according to circumstance. The point which may seem obvious nevertheless needs stating, since much of the writing on obedience makes the rather simple-minded assumption that when given a criminal command conscience offers an infallible guide to behaviour. Conscience may supply the grounds for obedience and disobedience, but it cannot offer surety, for grounds in conscience can be found for both.

The Nuremberg Principle and Responsibility

The Nuremberg trial may have had an even greater influence on moral thought than on international law. One vehicle of influence is what is called the Nuremberg principle or precedent. Article 8 of the Charter of the International Military Tribunal, which forms the basis of the Nuremberg principle or precedent, reads in full: 'The fact that the defendant acted pursuant to order of his Government or of a superior shall not free him from responsibility, but may be considered in mitigation of punishment if the Tribunal determine that justice so requires.' The Nuremberg principle denies that a person can escape responsibility by pleading superior orders. The principle was applied in a particular way in the course of the trials. Telford Taylor has discussed the diverse and contradictory interpretations read into the principle during the Vietnam war, but states: 'beneath ... wildly divergent views of the Nuremberg precedent there is a common denominator: that there are some universal standards of human behaviour that transcend the duty of obedience to national laws' (1971, p. 16).

One interpretation of the Nuremberg precedent goes something like this: the atrocities committed in the name of the Nazi state which took the form of highly organized authorized crimes manifestly violated universal standards of human behaviour. The atrocities were possible only so long as the German people as a whole signified their consent by obeying the laws and commands of the state. How, possibly excepting those who actively and consistently opposed the state, can *any* German escape responsibility for the atrocities? In contrast to the careful legal assessment of individual guilt and innocence, moral reasoning can and sometimes does lead to an overall indictment of universal guilt.

The ability to see individual responsibility based on the interdependence of all citizens of a modern state is an important capacity, especially when contrasted to the protestations of innocence from all of the Nuremberg defendants on grounds of only obeying orders' or 'only doing my duty'. 'All the defendants, without exception, accepted the evidence they had heard, and never denied that "these things" had happened. But they could not accept that the evidence implicated themselves, not just legally, but even more clearly morally' (Tusa & Tusa, 1983, pp. 239–40).

Both those who claim universal guilt and those who plead individual innocence ultimately base their claim on the same state of affairs: that the agency of destruction was not an individual or even an agglomeration of individuals but a civilian/military bureaucratic apparatus. Those who plead innocent affirm their obligation to uphold the apparatus and to obey the commands of superiors. Believers in universal guilt claim that when the state apparatus engages in evil it is the duty of every citizen to withdraw consent and actively to oppose (defy, disobey) the apparatus. Thus if *all* are innocent (except possibly Hitler and Himmler), no one is responsible for the atrocities. And if *all* are guilty (except possibly a handful of heroes), everyone is responsible for the atrocities. Our inescapable enmeshment in the modern state means that there is a psychological and moral sense in which *no one* and *everyone* is responsible for the atrocities. But each moral claim posits an equally inert German people: a nation of innocents, helplessly manipulated by a couple of super-evil and super-powerful leaders, or a nation of guilty souls helplessly loyal, faithful and obedient, uninfluenced by the example of a few heroes. If all are innocent or all are guilty then no one is responsible.

Sorting out legal responsibility may help with moral responsibility. In the ordinary course of civilian life a person who commits a crime is legally responsible for the act. Since in the armed forces criminal actions are authorized, the question of the responsibility of those committing them is of no legal interest. Legally, authorized crimes are not crimes. 'I obeyed orders' explains and justifies the actions. The question of legal responsibility arises when a soldier obeys a command that is proscribed by international law and precedent (an unlawful authorized crime). Who then is responsible – the person issuing the command or the person carrying out the command? The answer given by Article 7 of the Charter of the International

Military Tribunal: 'The official position of defendants, whether as Heads of State or responsible officials in Government departments, shall not be considered as freeing them from responsibility or mitigating punishment', while not answering the question directly, when combined with Article 8: 'The fact that the defendant acted pursuant to order of his Government or of a superior shall not free him from responsibility, but may be considered in mitigation of punishment if the Tribunal determine that justice so requires' forms the basis of the Tribunal's judgment. Obedience is a military necessity, but shall not free anyone from responsibility. Even so, responsibility increases as one goes up a command hierarchy. Taylor describes the military reality of those at the bottom of a command hierarchy.

> The military service is based on obedience to orders passed down through the chain of command, and the success of military operations often depends on the speed and precision with which orders are executed. Especially in the lower ranks, virtually unquestioning obedience to orders, other than those that are palpably vicious, is a necessary feature of military life. If the subordinate is expected to give such obedience, he should also be entitled to rely on the order as a full and complete defense to any charge that his act was unlawful. (1971, p. 50)

In other words if anyone is protected by the defence 'I obeyed orders', it is the warrior at the bottom end of the chain of command. Following the logic of hierarchical organization, responsibility for the act shifts upward in the chain of command. The closer to the top of the hierarchy, the greater the responsibility. The persons initiating and giving the criminal commands bear greater responsibility than those carrying out the commands. That is why top Nazis sat in the dock at Nuremberg.

It seems only reasonable and just that those giving commands bear greater responsibility than those obeying. Given the creed of hierarchical organization those giving commands are superior to those obeying – are granted greater power, status, intelligence and moral sensitivity – more of everything that makes agency and responsibility possible. Those at the higher level of a command hierarchy have the capacity, should they so wish, to modify, change, misplace and misdirect orders. For example, when defining punishment for the criminal act of cohabitation between a German man and a Jewish woman, Hitler, the *Führer* of a totalitarian state, decided that the German man, but not the Jewish woman, was to be punished. 'Gruppenführer Heydrich of the Security Police on his part decided that a Jewish woman could not remain free if her German partner went to jail. Such an arrangement went against his grain, Hitler order or no Hitler order' (Hilberg, 1985, p. 160). So Heydrich and like-minded others found ways of evading the Hitler order.

Raul Hilberg, who devoted 36 years of his life to studying the administrative apparatus that destroyed over 5 million European Jews comments:

> Every bureaucrat knows, of course, that open defiance of orders is serious business, but he also knows that there are many ingenious ways of evading orders. In fact, the opportunities for evading them increase as one ascends in the hierarchy. (1985, p. 1024)

Despite the undoubtedly greater discretionary power at the top levels of a command hierarchy psychological studies of obedience have looked only at people at the very bottom of a chain of command. Milgram, for example, showed interest chiefly in those who actually carry out commands, rather than in those who give them. As can be observed in his film (Milgram, 1965), after the experiment ended Milgram sometimes went to great lengths to persuade reluctant subjects to admit responsibility for 'harming' the 'learner', ignoring the objections of those who tried to point out that the 'experimenter' had some responsibility for what happened. Unlike the military, Milgram saw no mitigation for those at the bottom of a command hierarchy.

I think one reason moralists can be so severe with people at the bottom of a hierarchy is that, unlike in a court of law, grounds need not be examined. The guilt of the person who actually does the criminal act appears obvious. Involved in moral censure is the notion that an action, the slaughter of defenceless Jews, for example, is so clearly wrong that the consciences of, say, Einsatzgruppe members would have told them that the command to slaughter was clearly wrong, and the privates in the Einsatzgruppe are culpable for choosing obedience over conscience. (The Einsatzgruppen were Security Police Units charged with liquidating designated categories of conquered peoples.)   No doubt many, possibly most, Einsatzgruppen, despite military training, Nazi indoctrination and other influences, knew that human compassion called for defiance and that by obeying they betrayed themselves and in a sense were damned. But if their consciences gave them grounds for disobedience, they failed to find there sufficient grounds for putting human compassion clearly above those other conscience-based grounds for obedience – loyalty to their country, and more particularly, loyalty to their immediate group of comrades.

In an attempt to save themselves, the prominent Nazis on trial at Nuremberg adopted a defence that both shifted responsibility down the hierarchy and obscured the ideological content of the Nazi conquests. Had they remained true to their Führer's crusade they would have proudly accepted responsibility for the crimes documented by the prosecution. Instead of saying 'Yes, I played a key role on our near-success in ridding Europe of its Jewish plague,' each denied that at the time he had direct knowledge of the Final Solution and denied any personal responsibility for crimes against the Jews or any other crimes.

Judging from their behaviour at Nuremberg Hitler may have liberated his top followers from the 'blemish' of conscience, but he failed further down the hierarchy. For had Hitler succeeded in freeing Germans from the 'blemish' of conscience they could have carried out his projects without conflict. He must have known that he failed, because Hitler took great care to keep secret from the larger German public the crimes against Jews, Poles, Russians, Gypsies, political prisoners, etc. And because Hitler had not freed them from the blemish of conscience those who had to carry out the commands often did so at great personal cost. Compassion, while not preventing obedience, was by no means dead.

I have read nothing to suggest that Hitler himself ever personally witnessed his handiwork being carried out. Himmler did. On one occasion Himmler was present when an Einsatzgruppe liquidated 100 people. Their commander, Obergruppenführer von dem Bach-Zelewski, said to Himmler, 'Look at the eyes of the men in this Kommando, how deeply shaken they are! These men are finished [*fertig*] for the rest of their lives. What kind of followers are we training here? Either neurotics or savages!' (quoted in Hilberg, 1985, p. 332).

Himmler was unsettled by what he saw and decided to make a speech to the men.

He pointed out that the Einsatzgruppe were called upon to fulfil a repulsive (*widerliche*) duty. He would not like it if Germans did such a thing gladly. But their conscience was in no way impaired, for they were soldiers who had to carry out every order unconditionally. He alone had responsibility before God and Hitler for everything that was happening. They had undoubtedly noticed that he hated this bloody business (*dass ihm das blutige Hanwerk zuwider wäre*) and that he had been aroused to the depth of his soul. But he too was obeying the highest law by doing his duty, and he was acting from a deep understanding of the necessity for this operation. (summary taken from Hilberg, 1985, pp. 332, 333)

Those who believe that conscience is unitary and specific against authorized criminal commands would say that if the Kommando had heeded conscience and defied their orders they would not be deeply shaken. Perhaps not. What is often ignored is that military discipline and training, any country's military discipline and training, is designed to exact automatic compliance with orders to do things that go against civilian conscience. All authorized criminal commands, not just the particularly revolting commands of Nazi Germany, are contrary to 'conscience' as ordinarily conceived. Fulfilling military duty, that sovereign virtue, by definition is going to be painful. A very large component of military duty is the moral obligation to violate civilian conscience.

Himmler's injunctions to his audience follow a form that must have existed since the early days of military organizations: the actions do not compromise conscience; if God or Hitler should become displeased Himmler alone is responsible; all are obeying a higher law – military necessity.

Having attempted to satisfy God and Hitler Himmler squared everything with nature by delivering a 'sociobiological' homily that included a lesson in dehumanization. Himmler claimed that from primitive times the human being has designated 'what is useful to him as good and what is harmful as bad. Didn't bedbugs and rats have a life purpose also? Yes, but this has never meant that man could not defend himself against vermin' (summary from Hilberg, 1985, p. 333).

The responsibility of those who carry out criminal commands can seem glaringly obvious. For example, if my town is occupied by enemy soldiers and I see one of them obey a command to kill someone I love, that soldier's face will be etched in my memory. *He* killed her, *he* is the monster who took the life I cherished, *he* is responsible for my loss. Of course, I am right. My beloved would not be dead had the soldier not fired the shot that killed her. Military tradition and the Charter of the Nuremberg Tribunal are also correct to look for responsibility, not at the killer, but at the top of a command hierarchy. After all, the soldier might not have fired except that he was ordered to; he wouldn't be in my town had he not been ordered to go there; he wouldn't even be in the army had he not been conscripted. Except for the orders of superiors, the monster who took the life I cherished would be in his home town working at whatever he does, no doubt cherishing those *he* loves.

People at the bottom of a command hierarchy are the ones who actually do what is commanded. In the case of authorized crimes, those at the bottom do the dirty work. Kings, presidents and dictators can order hideous crimes in part because to them the crimes are abstract. Those at the top do not have to hear, see, feel, touch, taste and smell the consequences of their commands. The question of the responsibility of people at the bottom is interesting and vital, but cannot be decided in the absence of a clear grasp of the reality of an entire command hierarchy. The moral position of those at the bottom cannot be grasped unless it is clearly understood that the power of the state to conscript is the power to require the conscripted to violate their civilian consciences.

Since 'conscience' is a term that can take a number of meanings the psychological issue can be better understood by redescribing the conflict between civilian conscience and a duty to obey as a conflict between two types of commands: a general negative command of the thou-shalt-not variety conflicting with a positive command to violate the negative. The discussion until now has focused on obedience or resistance to positive commands: obedience or resistance, that is, to commands to do something. Negative commands, commands *not* to do something, play an important role in human communities and make up a large part of what ordinarily is called 'conscience'. I suspect that most of the laws in every society are prohibitions of some sort. Eight of the Ten Commandments Moses brought down the mountain were of the thou-shalt-not variety. Because, given encouragement and opportunity, people will engage in almost endless kinds of actions, all societies put a limit on the sorts of actions that will be tolerated. The thou-shalt-nots – the negative commands or laws – define those actions harmful to the social group. Snow's phrase 'far more, and far more hideous, crimes have been committed in the name of obedience than have ever been committed in the name of rebellion' can be restated to read: far more, and far more hideous, crimes have been committed in the course of dutifully obeying positive authorized commands than have ever been committed by rebelliously disobeying negative commands or laws. Far more of history's hideous crimes have been committed by obedient citizens than by criminals or rebels.

The situation is not as simple as the last two sentences suggest. A 'hideous crime' is not a hideous crime unless it violates some law or commandment. The most common hideous crime occurs when, in the course of obeying an authorized criminal command, a person at the same time violates the Sixth Commandment. Authorized commands to kill are in clear violation of the unambiguous command 'Thou shalt not kill.' (Killing is not the only crime involving harm and the Ten Commandments deal with three others: adultery, stealing and false witness.)

General commandments capable of guiding daily behaviour play a prominent part in the history of ethics, but each society finds that over time commandments become less general and more conditional. Killing is generally forbidden, but the circumstances in which killing occurs affect the seriousness with which society views the action. A killing may in fact be justified (justifiable homicide), completely unjustified (first degree murder) or not a crime at all (authorized crime).

General prohibitions such as eight of the Ten Commandments are often believed to be commands of God (or a god) and can be taken to be absolute. If 'thou-shalt-not-kill' is believed to be an absolute law, what does a believer do when an authority issues a legitimate command to kill? Because early rulers were gods themselves or God's chief deputy, the Divine Kings of the first civilizations had an advantage over latter-day secular rulers. The authority ordering the believer to kill is simply the channel for God's commands. The Divine King, who at one time may have said: 'thou shalt not kill', has a right to change His mind and issue new commands through His chain of command. The believer has only to obey the most recent command. If the command is to kill, killing is the Divine King's will.

When kings lost their divinity absolute negative commands became a problem. Three broad ways have been developed for dealing with the conflict that can arise when the absolute negative command is from a religious authority and the contrary or countermanding positive order is from a civil authority. One method grants authority to religion in some situations and to earthly rulers in others. This solution is most memorably summarized with the words 'Render therefore unto Caesar the things which are Caesar's; and unto God the things that are God's.' So long as there is no difficulty in deciding which things are whose, there is no problem about knowing when to obey and when to disobey.

A minority solution, followed by a few small religious groups and some individuals, is to allow no exceptions to general commandments or laws. For example, when members of the Society of Friends, the Mennonites or the Brethren are ordered to report for military service they simply refuse to serve. They refuse to put themselves under those who can command them to violate the general commandments or laws. What then is done to them for their disobedience depends upon the times and on the nature of the government they have defied.

A third solution is related to the first and will be discussed more fully in a later chapter. It involves the practice, consistent throughout history, of denying that the general laws apply to everyone. The denial takes the form of: 'Thou shalt not kill' applies to *us*, not to *them*. *Them* in each case is defined as anyone who is not *us*. In other words, we shall not kill each other, but we shall surely do our best to kill all of *them* when the command is given. The solution is helped along if you can believe those you are ordered to kill are 'vermin' which need extermination, or 'gooks', 'dinks', 'slopes' and 'slants' which make up the body count.

The third solution, then, to the conflict between positive authorized commands and negative moral commands is to deny the conflict. They do not conflict because the negative moral commands apply only to *us* – those who are human; the positive authorized commands are directed against *them* – those who are not fully human. The solution is so ancient that it taps a process older than civilization's commands. Conflicting commands are an issue only for those who cannot view the enemy as less than human. Those who believe one of the less-than-human stories no doubt think that anyone who is bothered by an absolute negative command is making a category error.

Dehumanization as I discuss it here is an enabling process: by taking a group out of the category 'human' things can be done to them that cannot be done to human beings. Because taking away another's humanity can make killing easier, dehumanizing the enemy is an enabling process soldiers often invoke to help them carry out commands to kill. Although a frequent accompaniment, dehumanization is not a necessary part of authorized crime. Features of some civil wars, for example, make dehumanizing the enemy difficult. If members of the same family are on opposing sides *they* cannot be dehumanized without in some way dehumanizing *us*.

Removing people from the category 'human being' is a psychological process that, though clearly demanding careful study, until recently has received little attention from social scientists.[2]

Dehumanizing helps to justify acts that would be criminal if done to humans.

In this chapter I have tried to confine the discussion to legal and moral grounds available to those who must decide whether to obey or resist an authorized criminal command. Some of the same or similar grounds will be discussed again in a later chapter on the subject of justifications for issuing criminal commands.

In Chapter 2 I attempted to show that Milgram was wrong to suppose that a special theory of obedience was needed to explain his findings: that when seen from the subject's point of view obedience becomes understandable. In this chapter I have examined actual hideous crimes, crimes that came about as a result of obeying inhuman commands. Once again, seen from the point of view of the commanded, obedience becomes understandable. No matter how horrible the command, how contrary to conscience, grounds for obedience can be found. Obedience that occurs in a hierarchical social structure in response to lawful commands needs no special explanation. However, disobedience in the same circumstances does need explaining.

Also in need of explanation is why the chief organizing principle in those modern democracies which put great value on liberty and equality should violate both. Although most clearly visible in the military, hierarchical organization is found throughout civilian life. Modern societies, whether democratic or totalitarian, like all of history's civilized societies, are organized hierarchically. Hierarchies are made up of superiors and inferiors – a state of affairs that contradicts equality. And inferiors are bound to obey lawful commands from superiors – a condition that violates liberty.

4

The Original Sin of Superstratification

> Psychologists who study only the working of the mind of the individual and pay no attention to its relation to the totality of the social process are apt to forget that the decisive fact is not that the sadistic element is latent in the human psyche, but that the organization of society has, from nomadic times till our own day, given this irrationality an objective function. (Karl Mannheim, quoted in Rüstow, 1980, p. 8)

The transformation wrought by language enables us to imagine things which are not now here and provides an alternative here and now. There is something magical, marvellous and deeply satisfying about being able to get someone to do as you wish with just a word, even a glance. And something maddening, and mad, about someone who always does as you wish. The determinist dream of being able to predict and control human behaviour, stripped of its value-free guise, is a totalitarian nightmare, a dream of a well-oiled, perfectly functioning machine. Humans are defined by their defiance, their disobedience, even of God, who is alleged to be omnipotent. In the Judeo-Christian tradition, the very first man disobeyed God, as did God's first angel. Beings who must obey the reinforcers or treatments of determinists would not be human beings, but beings of some other sort. Along with its other virtues language, the great enabler, makes it possible to get others to do things for us.

Language is the prototype of magic: a sound ('abracadabra') issues from my lips and another, or others, may – subject to a complex set of conditions – do as I wish. The sound can take one of the three forms Hugh Dalziel Duncan (1962) has identified as the basic modes of interpersonal communication. People can communicate as superior to inferior, as inferior to superior, as equal to equal. Thus, if I am a superior I can command, order, bid, enjoin, direct, instruct or charge an inferior to do as I wish. As an inferior I might beg, crave, beseech, implore, entreat or importune a superior to carry out my wishes. Or talking with an equal I might ask, request, desire, advise, tell, or even demand, that something be done. An inferior hearing the command of a superior can obey, can disobey or can attempt to evade the command. A superior being importuned by an inferior can consent or not consent – or can ignore or evade. Similarly, an equal being asked by an equal can consent or not consent – or can evade. Obedience, the subject of my story, takes place in relationships between inferiors and superiors.

That relationship, of inferior and superior, is not a personal relationship, but a relationship between positions (or roles, or ranks or statuses). The difficulty in choosing a word, I think, is due to modern democratic sensibility – the wish to deny inequality. We shy away from words that too obviously point to the fact that what is being discussed is the relationship between inferiors and superiors. The term 'role' has become quite popular in recent years, in part because we can think of roles without being reminded of inequality. Since my purpose is to remind readers of inequality I shall use 'role' sparingly. 'Rank' would serve, for not only does its first meaning refer to relative social position, but it is the term commonly used when describing relative position in avowedly hierarchical organizations such as the military or the aristocracy. But 'rank' today is usually applied only to acknowledged hierarchies. For that and other reasons that will become apparent, in most instances I shall use the term 'status' to refer to the relative position or standing of those who can be identified as inferiors and superiors.

Each status (except the bottom status) has its inferior and each (except for a Divine King or any other single ruler) its superior statuses. Each has a limited authority of command over particular other statuses and a limited obligation to obey others. The obedience that needs no explanation is obedience in response to a command from a status with the authority to issue such a command. Obedience by a cog to a lawful command in a status hierarchy needs no explanation because obedience is the proper function of the cog. As with any machine the proper functioning of a command hierarchy is explained in terms of the machine's design. Explanations are needed only when machines malfunction, do things they are not designed to do.

Obedience can occur in other sorts of relationships and when it does may need explaining. As everyone knows, people with no authority over us, equals or even inferiors, can tell us what to do – and sometimes we do it. Because obedience is not confined to relationships between statuses a certain amount of confusion has arisen, a confusion resulting from a failure to distinguish consistently between *having* status and *playing* status. Except when specifically noted the obedience which is the subject of this book is in response to commands of those who *have* status.

Keith Johnstone's (1979) discussion of playing status is the most stimulating and perceptive I have seen. As might be expected from the term *playing* Johnstone's book is about theatre. Johnstone found when training actors that student scenes were lifeless until he hit upon giving the actors instructions concerning status, instructions such as 'Try to get your status just a little above or below your partner's' (1979, p. 33). The direction to *play* status brought the scenes to life. Johnstone's instruction to play status is independent of the actual relative status of the role being played: an actor playing a servant might be instructed to get his status a bit above his master's or vice versa. According to Johnstone, moment by moment status shifts and struggles bring theatrical scenes to life in the same way such shifts and struggles inject drama into everyday social intercourse. If all social actors simply played the status they *have*, social life would have the lifeless characteristics of a well-oiled machine or a mechanically-acted play. Johnstone makes the provocative claim that *all* social interaction is in terms of playing up or down, that there is no such thing as a simple interaction between equals with neither partner playing high or low.

Playing status, that is, a status interaction independent of actual status, is a powerful notion and I suspect that we will not get very far in our understanding of everyday social transactions until we give considerably more attention to it. However, I have introduced the notion not to explore it but in order to clarify the subject matter. My story is about *having* status, about hierarchy or social stratification, and accompanying rights to command and obligations to obey. In civilized states the statuses people have are prior to and set the stage for the status dramas people play.

In societies organized on status differences relative status is the most important measure of any person. What more interesting game can social actors play than attempting to move status in everyday transactions? Johnstone may be right about the ubiquity of *playing* status. In fact once the importance of status is grasped it would be curious if he were not. How did having status and playing status become so important? How did status become the chief organizing principle of human societies? Why, given the modern insistence on equality, do we treat one another as superiors and inferiors? Given the other possible forms of address, why would anyone want to issue commands? Given the relationship it implies, why should anyone obey?

A favoured way to understand a present-day practice is to look to the past to try to identify its origin and development. Acceptance of evolutionary theory has added a new twist to historical explanation. For if humans have evolved from animal ancestors then in a sense historical explanation can be sought in the present. For living animal species are thought to be representative of our animal ancestors. If this is the case our sociobiological history can be inferred by studying living species. Explanations of human practices based on ethological or sociobiological study of living animals have attracted considerable attention in recent years.

Relationships between superiors and inferiors bear some resemblance to relations observed in animal groups. In fact, a number of commentators are convinced that the resemblance is so strong, that hierarchical organization is so universal, that it is inevitable that human societies be so ordered. If this is the case, if hierarchy is inescapable, then the wish for human liberty and equality must remain nothing more than a pipe dream. For the only thing attainable would be more liberty and more equality within a superstructure composed of superiors and inferiors.

Although extremely popular in the late twentieth century general statements about humans based on animal observation sometimes fail to stand up to even casual scrutiny. The reasoning used to support claims often goes from observations on one or two animal groups to statements about the inevitability of such behaviour in human society. The variety of animal societies and behaviour is so great that with enough ingenuity and industry all researchers can find species suitable to their purposes, making the game wide open for moralists to discover empirical generalities for anything they wish to prohibit or endorse. Sociobiologists and others engage in the game of selective selection of empirical generalizations which, to no one's surprise, supports their conservative political yearnings. The following sentence is an example of the worst of the literature and only slightly overstates some of the best: baboons are fiercely territorial and since territoriality has been observed in other species also, human societies court disaster unless they organize themselves on the basis of private property.

One example of animal behaviour, relevant to obedience, looks like an exception to the game of selective selection. A claim has been made (Maclay & Knipe, 1972) that not simply all mammal societies, but all vertebrate societies are organized in dominance hierarchies. All *vertebrates* – hardly a matter of selective selection.

If ever there was a case for generalization from animal to human, surely this is it.

But there is more. Maclay and Knipe's statement about vertebrates seems modest when compared to a claim by Arthur Koestler: *'All complex structures and processes of a relatively stable character display hierarchic organization*, regardless of whether we consider galactic systems, living organisms and their activities, or social organizations' (his italics, 1978, p. 31).

If Koestler and Maclay and Knipe are correct it seems that hierarchy is an inevitable and unavoidable form of social organization and that obedience to commands in some sense must be inevitable too. But if this is so, why should nature enforce a form of social organization that human beings so often find unsatisfactory? Should not a form of social relationship so universal, so ubiquitous, so longstanding be, if not deeply satisfying, at least satisfactory? But the very period in which Milgram and Maclay and Knipe wrote was marked by revolt, turmoil and outrageous displays of public disobedience. 'The defiance of established authority, religious and secular, social and political, as a worldwide phenomenon may well one day be accounted the outstanding event of the last decade' (Arendt, 1972, p. 69). To make sense of the seeming coexistence of necessity for hierarchy and, over and over again throughout history, disgust with and defiance of hierarchy it is necessary to distinguish forms of animal dominance hierarchies from human command hierarchies and both from a form of human social organization that preceded civilization.

First of all, what is meant by a dominance hierarchy? The words chosen to describe animal social order are taken from human social organization: *dominance* from the Latin *dominus*, master, lord; and *hierarchy* from the Greek *hierarkhes*, rule of a priest. Used together the two words seem redundant, unless they are meant to suggest that animal social organization is both secular (dominance) and religious (hierarchy). The richness of cultural association is there because in the first instance human social organization was the model that inspired the categorization of animal social organization: conceptually and linguistically, human social orders are models for animal social order – a Divine King, who combined secular and religious authority, the model for a top ape. It could not be otherwise. We were familiar with our own ways of social organization long before the attempt, from the standpoint of modern science, to carefully observe, describe, and classify animal social organization. What could observers do other than try to understand animal order in terms of well understood human social organization? It is unwise to discount the part conceptual spectacles play in finding hierarchy everywhere.

Psychologists and biologists usually take great care to avoid the error of anthropomorphism: attributing human characteristics to animals. Usually this means avoiding descriptions of animals that suggest thought processes or purpose. It seems not to have occurred to observers to be similarly alert to the care needed to avoid attributing human social organization to animals. Rank is particularly prone to misuse: as an organizing principle, rank can be applied to anything except absolutely identical objects. Thus virtually anything which can be observed can be ranked. If an observer believes that a social group can be described in terms of rank it will be impossible to look for and not see a rank order. Whether or not the rank order 'seen' and described at any moment in time has much bearing on the continuing social life of the group is another question. If in Koestler's statement the word 'display' is dropped and 'can be described in the language of' is substituted we will be nearer the truth. 'All complex structures and processes of a relatively stable character *can be described in the language of* hierarchical organization.' Whether such a description is or is not a key to understanding is another matter.

As do many others, I enjoy reading ethological literature and greatly admire some of those that Tinbergen calls 'animal watchers' (1974). But precisely because the work is so full of interest and delight, care must be taken to draw the right lessons from it. Popularizers of animal studies often do them disservice. Certainly the study of animals offers better lessons than solemn injunctions slavishly to imitate. Differences, differences found even in group behaviour considered similar, can throw into relief what some of the problems are.

Critics of biological determinism often go too far in emphasizing human flexibility, human unformedness. Humans without doubt are born with more possibility in them than other animals. The helplessness of human infants, the long period of dependency, the lack of specific instincts to perform particular behaviours combine to make humans especially malleable and teachable. But at the same time there is a human nature that both differs from and is similar to gorilla nature, for one example, or chimp nature, for another. But since so much of what humans are and do comes from living in already formed societies, the argument goes that a clear-eyed grasp of human nature is gained if we study non-human social groups. A knowledge of similar but less culture-formed creatures can provide the needed comparisons. Without serious comparative study we are prone to endorse either the extreme of a genetically programmed nature or the opposite extreme of no nature at all – a blank slate.

The two active terms used to describe what happens in an animal dominance hierarchy are 'dominance' and 'submission'; the two active terms in a study of obedience are 'command' and 'obedience'. Is submission to the threat of a higher ranking ape a good analogy for obeying the command of a superior? Only in a rough and incomplete way. But it does seem a rather good analogy for Johnstone's 'playing status'. Status playing is chiefly a nonverbal phenomenon: actors play up or down by the way they do things and the way they say things: 'every inflection and movement implies a status' (1979, p. 33). Language, of course, makes playing status a richer and more complex game than the dominance and submission of animal groups. In order to get an idea of what I mean, think of the small number of things that an animal can command nonverbally. (Except for Washoe and a few other linguistically trained apes, vocal and bodily nonverbal expression is the only way an ape can 'command.') Essentially nonverbal expression can 'command' immediate wants: wants for that banana right there, for the female presenting just there, for more space, and for other immediate concerns. The range of nonverbal commands available to animals is limited to the 'here and now'. Although issuing a command is a form of dominance and obeying a form of submission, language – which makes command possible – adds a dimension which transforms the relationship.

The game also is transformed by *having* status. Playing status, like animal dominance, depends upon a moment by moment ability to get on top. The status player or the dominant animal can fail at any time and lose the game. In contrast a person who *has* status, even if interpersonally ineffectual, can exact obedience solely because of the status. The statused person can fail, but the status cannot fail unless displaced or overthrown by revolution. One of the oldest and most persistent characteristics of *having* status is the determination to make the status permanent. Not only must I have my status for life, but my heirs must have the status (or a higher one) forever.

An authorized command carries a quality not found in the nonverbal 'commands' within animal groups. If Elias Canetti (1978) is correct this is because commands originate, not within animal societies, but *between* animal species. For Canetti, describing a relationship between species, 'The original command results in *flight*. Flight is dictated to one animal by another stronger animal, by something *outside* itself' (1978, p. 303, Canetti's emphasis).

> All command derives from this *flight-command*, as I propose to call it. In its original form the command is something enacted between two animals of different species, one of which threatens the other. The great difference in strength between the two, the fact that one of them is habitually preyed on by the other, the unalterable nature of the relationship, which is felt to have existed for ever – all this makes what happens seem absolute and irrevocable. Flight is the final and only appeal against a death sentence. For the roar of a lion *is* a death sentence. It is the one sound in its language which all its victims understand; this threat may be the only thing they have in common, widely different as they otherwise are. The oldest command – and it is far older than man – is a death sentence, and it compels the victim to flee. We should remember this when we come to discuss human commands. Beneath *all* commands glints the harshness of the death sentence. Amongst men they have become so systematized that death is normally avoided, but the threat and the fear of it is always contained in them; and the continued pronouncement and execution of real death sentences keeps alive the fear of every individual command and of commands in general. (Canetti, 1978, pp. 303-4, his italics)

Canetti's story of the origin of command is strikingly original, provocative, *and* unprovable. Its great virtue is its psychological plausibility. An arresting feature of command hierarchies, especially when compared to either animal dominance 'hierarchies' or precivilized groups, is that those of lower rank or status are believed to be unlike the commander and are treated as inferior. Commands in a command hierarchy, like flight-commands, are directed at what amounts to another species.

Pre-history

According to Canetti's story the origin of the flight-command is indeed ancient, occurring when one species first preyed on another. When did characteristics of the terrible inter-species flight command make their intra-species appearance within a human group? Command hierarchy, the form of secular/religious social organization which appeared with the first civilizations, makes use of the distinctive characteristics of the flight-command. The distance between ape societies and civilization is a long one. What comes in between?

Much of what is known of precivilized societies is inferred from knowledge of the small-scale groups which, until recent times, lived relatively free from civilization's incursions. The physical remains of precivilized groups provide the other major source of inference. The variety of small-scale human social organization is great and differs, as might be expected, from both animal societies and large-scale human social organization. Is there some way of characterizing precivilized societies that captures some characteristic that underlies their variety? A number of writers have been struck by the equalitarian nature of primitive societies. Andrew Schmookler, for example, cited four authorities to support his claim:

> In the beginning, human society was essentially egalitarian. No one was subject to the power of another. Activity was coordinated through spontaneous cooperation, and what leadership there was was granted on the basis of respect and exercised without power of command. (1984, p. 277)

To what extent can any human society be egalitarian? Certainly equality cannot mean that all members of a group are the same or that they necessarily do the same things. No human society is made up of undifferentiated components. For one thing, as Schmookler notes, groups have leaders and to the civilized mind leadership is strongly associated with hierarchy. Indeed, given the ubiquity of social stratification, it is difficult to view something like leadership except through hierarchical glasses. I shall attempt to look at some of the features of precivilized societies that appear similar to hierarchical counterparts in order to arrive at a clearer idea of what early egalitarianism looked like.

Tribal societies and village communities often have a head or chief, but his role in group life bears more resemblance to a top ape than a Divine King. What appear to be status differences are more in the realm of *playing* than of *having* status. That is, should a chief (or top ape) appear to be exercising dominance, it is gained, as in *playing* status, without the power of command. The chief typically is described as a first among equals. Care must be taken not to idealize the Neolithic village, but the relations between the head and fellow villagers is more likely to take the form of asking, desiring, advising, telling and demanding than commanding, bidding, directing, instructing and charging. And the response of villagers commonly involves consent or dissent rather than obedience or disobedience. That communication resembles more the transactions of equals than the relations of superiors and inferiors should come as no surprise: the terms 'inferior' and 'superior' take their full meaning, become understandable, only with the sharp divisions and social stratification characteristic of large-scale social organization, that is, of civilization. If members of hunting-and-gathering bands, tribes and village societies are not equals in a modern, idealized sense of the word, they are equals when compared either to modern reality or to the early civilized command hierarchies upon which modern reality rests.

By emphasizing the difference between primitive societies of equals and command hierarchies I run the risk of seeming to ignore similarities to civilized societies. It would be strange if the ancient flight-command, for example, did not figure at all in primitive communal life. For although the command hierarchy was a human invention that probably appeared in the valleys of the Jordan, the Euphrates, the Tigris, the Nile and the Indus (Mumford, 1967), it must have had its precursors or models. Something like the command/obedience relationship no doubt was known to tribes and villages. Who in a society of equals can command with any expectation of being obeyed?

Every human group, no matter how organized, has one category of dependants: children. Primitive societies have been much praised for their easy, non-authoritarian ways with children. Even so, children are dependent and helpless; they must be nurtured, socialized and brought into the social group. Learning the ways of a group requires instruction. Giving instruction is a command of sorts, and receiving instruction a kind of obedience. In addition the deference shown to elders and leaders can involve a form of consent bordering on obedience. Hunting groups often involve a quite precise and prompt coordination orchestrated by signals that can be likened to commands. Customs can be described in terms of injunctions which are to be obeyed. Gods and spirits have been known to command and issue injunctions, which, if they carry the fear of death, means the flight-command has been introduced into group life.

Another possible user of the flight-command is the tribal bully. Any group may have to contend with bullies – social equals who attempt to exact obedience by arousing fear and engaging submission. The fear can be aroused with physical force, by psychological means, or both. Bullies, of course, ordinarily *play* rather than *have* status. (Incidentally, judging from descriptions of animal watchers, psychological bluff rather than brute force is the chief animal means of gaining dominance – something that makes good evolutionary sense. The group would suffer if males engaging in dominance contests seriously injured each other.)

Civilization

The existence in precivilized groups of relationships somewhat similar to the command/obedience relationship takes nothing from the dramatically different form of social organization that appeared with the first civilizations. Erich Fromm distinguishes precivilized social organization from civilized command hierarchies in terms of what he calls rational and irrational authority:

> While in the Neolithic village, as well as among primitive hunters, leaders guided and counselled the people and did not exploit them, and while their leadership was accepted voluntarily or, to use another term, while prehistoric authority was 'rational' authority resting on competence, the authority of the new patriarchal system was based on force and power; it was exploitative and mediated by the physical mechanism of fear, 'awe', and submission. It was 'irrational authority'. (1973, p. 165)

The fear, awe and submission associated with Fromm's 'irrational authority' signals the unmistakable employment of Canetti's flight-command within a human social group. The aspect Fromm highlights is the difference between acting after taking council and doing what you are told because of the status occupied by the person giving the command. The one is a relationship of equals; the other of inferiors and superiors. The psychological and social distance between the two forms of relationship is immense.

If Neolithic villages cannot boast of civilization's irrational authority, also missing are projects carried out by the able-bodied that are the will of one person or a small class of persons. Village 'commands' (except for those of a bully) are to do what the community wishes, not, as in command hierarchies, to do as the Divine King wishes, or the ruling class wishes, or as the boss wishes. It would be difficult for a command hierarchy to arise in a small group protected and nourished by custom and tradition. It is more likely that the first command hierarchies were formed when one group conquered and enslaved another. Civilization began when one group forced another to do its will. 'Primitive man could be transformed, in one small step, from a rich creator of meaning in a society of equals to a mechanical thing' (Becker, 1975, p. 97). How did the transformation come about?

Imagine a hot river valley populated with numerous villages and small towns, each with its own land, its own customs, its own language or dialect. The land is fertile and agricultural arts produce a surplus of food for each village. Disputes, raiding parties or armed conflict are not unknown to the neighbouring groups. But once a conflict is ended each village returns, however damaged or diminished, to its own way of life.

Suppose an inventive village chieftain (or, as some believe, the leader of an invading nomadic tribe) gets an inspiration and thinks: why let these villagers we have just defeated return to their old ways? Why not demand that they pay us a tribute each year? Why not, indeed? But to turn the demand into a command something is needed to gain continuing submission. The most likely model ready to hand is the coercive practices of tribal bullies. The defeated village must be frightened into obedience. Once one village can be dominated, why not another? And another, and another, until the whole valley pays its annual tribute? In order for a single chieftain to hold a number of villages in thrall those villages would need to be convinced that resistance was useless. Needed is a military force obviously superior to anything put together by the combined villages. A new sort of military force, the model for all succeeding armies and all civilized social organizations was the answer. The first command hierarchy in all likelihood was a military organization put together in one of the cradles of civilization. Called the military machine by Lewis Mumford, this new form of social organization was designed to enable one man to issue a command that would be carried out quickly and precisely by scores, by hundreds, even thousands of soldiers 'under his command'. Since it is unlikely that one man's voice could be heard, much less obeyed, by hundreds, let alone thousands of soldiers, a 'chain of command' was devised – levels of superiors, each officer in descending rank commanding ever smaller numbers of inferiors. The common soldiers at the end of the command chain were, of course, by far the most numerous rank, greatly outnumbering their superiors.

Why should a great mass of armed men at the bottom of a chain-of-command do what a small number of officers tell them to do? From the whips of early days to the verbal scourges of master sergeants the methods of the bully have always played a central role in military discipline. But the other tool of the bully, known in rudimentary form to small groups, played a major role in establishing the first kingdoms. Physical coercion can be magnified several fold by bluff if inferiors can be persuaded that superiors are indeed superior, more grand, possessors of powers unknown to base people. At the head of the first civilizations were kings who were also gods, or in some cases, god's chief steward. The fear which produced obedience in the base was produced by brute force magnified several fold by psychological force.

A collection of villages and towns headed by a Divine King in command of a military machine still does not constitute a civilization. One of the hallmarks of civilization is its works – its roads, its irrigation projects, its monuments and its architecture. The works of the first kingdoms were accomplished by what Mumford calls the labour machine. The labour machine was organized hierarchically just as the military machine and proved itself capable of projects far beyond the capacity of any prior form of social organization.

The remarkable products which survived the Egyptian kingdoms – the pyramids – are at once physical evidence of the power of the command/obedience relationship and the continuing symbol of hierarchy. A pyramid still serves as a graphic representation of a social hierarchy with its levels of command. Imagine for purposes of simplified illustration that the pyramid is divided horizontally into five sections or levels. The Divine King (I) at the pinnacle can command anyone below, but usually commands through those on the level immediately beneath Him(II). The II's, more numerous than the single Divine King, can command the III's, IV's and V's, but usually issue orders to the III's who are more numerous than II's, but less numerous than IV's. And so on down the social pyramid until at the base level (V) are found the by far most numerous class – those who obey, but do not command. Although those at the base of a hierarchy do not issue commands *within the command hierarchy*, it is important to keep in mind that once command hierarchies were introduced into society they were recapitulated in societal sub-groups. For example, though the common soldier within his command hierarchy could only obey, he could command his wife and children. And the wife, subject to her husband's commands, could in turn command her children. And an elder child, a younger. Even authorized crimes appear within the family. Assault against a woman or child is a crime – unless the person assaulted is the aggressor's wife or child. The right to beat family subordinates, so long enshrined in law, is still taken as a customary right, mocking efforts to understand the problem of battered wives and children in terms of personal psychopathology.

In an ideal-typical command hierarchy responses to commands would be immediate and mechanical. Lewis Mumford makes an interesting and persuasive case that the social organization invented in the great river valleys took the form of an 'archetypal

machine composed of human parts' (1967, p. 11). The intricate
mechanical functioning of the human parts of the military machine
and the labour machine became the model or prototype of the
nonhuman machines imagined, invented and constructed later.
'This was an invisible structure composed of living, but rigid, human
parts, each assigned to his special office, role, and task, to make
possible the immense work-output and grand designs of this great
collective organization' (Mumford, 1967, p. 189).

Command hierarchies are so much a part of the fabric of
civilization that it is difficult to imagine social life in their absence.
Also difficult to imagine is the capacity of the early labour machines
which functioned without the nonhuman mechanical devices we
take for granted. The only two mechanical aids available to the
labour machine which built the Great Pyramid at Giza were the
inclined plane and the lever; even such basic mechanical devices as
the pulley and the screw were still to be invented. Yet the labour
machine was able to construct a geometrically precise mountain of
stone, encasing a complex interior. A single slab weighed 50 tons
and the precision of joinery remains a marvel today: stones of
considerable length show joints of one-ten-thousandth of an inch.

A modern head of state – or corporate head – who desired a tomb
that matched the Great Pyramid in size, interior complexity,
precision and splendour, given enough financial resources, could
order and pay for a pyramid, and a modern construction firm could
build it. Whether or not modern techniques are capable of the
same precision of joinery is questionable, but a fair facsimile no
doubt could be built. The idea, the wish, and the command to build
are open to anyone. Getting the command obeyed, however,
depends upon whether or not the commander can engage the
obedience of people capable of fulfilling the wish.

'I had this great idea. There, just there above the river. It'll be
pretty heavy so the sand will have to be dug out and a stone
foundation filled in. I want it big. Big. The base about 755 x 755
feet. Then with an angle of 51° 52" you should get the apex
about 482 feet above the base. I'll want passages inside, and face
the whole thing with dressed limestone, of course. It will be like
nothing anybody's ever seen.'
'Sounds pretty impressive. Come back to bed.'
'I will not come back to bed. You're not taking me seriously. I
command you to build it for me.'
'Don't be daft. How could I build it?'

How indeed? With language we can imagine and describe the most fantastic things. And we can command people to build, embody, and manifest our fantasies. But getting them to do it, getting them to obey, is another matter. The early kings, by subduing and enslaving previously autonomous groups with the help of command hierarchies, found out how.

> ...as wounds healed, masters and slaves intermingled and grew together into a single social body with the same language and the same religion, and the earlier, externally forced obedience of the subject people gradually became a duty of conscience, with all the sanctions of religion and morality. Thus, the bloody deed of superstratification played a role in the real social fall of man: as a hereditary curse and original sin, it burdens, however covertly, everything that has sprung from it. (Rüstow, 1980, pp. 37, 38)

Alexander Rüstow's interpretation of original sin and the Fall is sharply at odds with the story usually heard. According to the Old Testament account passed on by Christian churches, the original sin was the sin of disobedience and the Fall was man and woman's falling away from God and His blissful garden because of their own curiosity and wilfulness. In contrast, Rüstow's original sinner was not man or woman, not Eve or Adam, but a man who claimed to be a Divine King. The sin was not disobedience but the forceful and bloody imposition of hierarchical rule on formerly independent communities. Man and woman did not fall away from God, but were pushed by the Divine King, pushed into their 'place' – pushed into servitude from a previous condition of autonomy and community.

Many cultures have their own version of the Garden of Eden, a story of a time in the past when things were better, when people lived in harmony with each other and the rest of creation. That better time is often called the golden age. If the accounts I have followed in my brief reconstruction are even roughly correct, that dimly remembered past age was the tribal and village life that preceded civilization.

Psychologically, it is of considerable interest that according to the Hebrew and Christian story the Fall was the fault of a woman and a man. If Adam and Eve had done as they were told we all would be living today in the Garden of Eden. For a people who could still remember a better time, such an attribution of blame would have fitted precisely the needs of a Divine King. If His priests could get the enslaved people to believe that bondage was their own fault, the Divine King's capacity to rule would be considerably augmented. Those present at civilization's beginnings saw not just the first military machine and labour machine, but heard the first big lie.

There are then two sharply differing versions of the Fall: in one it was due to something disobedient or sinful in the nature of those who fell; in the other, it was because of submission to physical and psychological force. In one version Adam and Eve were expelled from their garden because of their sinful nature; in the other Eve and Adam were expelled from their garden because of the Divine King's wish to command, because of his introduction of the flight-command into human society. Social science has its analogues of the rival accounts. Biological or genetic reductionism assigns responsibility to something in an organism's makeup or nature. In contrast, environmental explanations seek responsibility in external events or social structures which impinge on the organism.

I think that some version of the story of subjection and enslavement by early Kings plausibly accounts for what must have happened. Acknowledging the 'bloody deed of superstratification' is central to any understanding of the origin and development of civilization. After millennia of church-instigated guilt it would be most satisfying to say simply that they got the story precisely backwards and then to persuade people that the original sin was superstratification, not disobedience, and so ease some of the guilt that continues to burden. But, much as I would like to tell the story of inversion by the original big lie, I think it is not quite that simple.

I can believe the story of tribal and village societies being subdued and enslaved by physical and psychological force and still see that human nature is implicated in the Fall. Something in the nature of those who survived prefers enslavement to death. Whatever it is that places survival above conditions of survival had to be part of the human makeup or I would not be here writing these words. We might, because of our values, wish that humans would be willing to die rather than submit to slavery. Just as some animals cannot be domesticated, some people like many New World Indians, cannot be enslaved and chose death over survival. But enough of our ancestors preferred a life of servitude to ensure that the race continued.

Our cravenness is not simply a matter of physical survival. Disobedience, that is, resistance to hierarchy's commands, risks our place in the hierarchy, our place in society. Once the bloody deed of superstratification took place, everyone, even those at the very bottom, has had something, in addition to their life, to lose by defiance. 'You have nothing to lose but your chains' is a brave untruth, unless one does not count livelihood, family, home or health – just about everything valued.[1]

The original sin of superstratification introduced into the world the possibility that one man's fantasies might be given concrete form. An embittered ex-corporal, wounded and gassed in the Great War, might imagine that Germany's postwar economic and social problems were due to the plotting of non-Germanic people, of Jews in particular. With all his heart he might believe that a Germany, a Europe, cleansed of Jews and other 'sub-human' conspirators could build a shining new Aryan Kulture, stronger, more beautiful than any previous culture. In a fit of enthusiasm he might even command similar-thinking followers to rid Germany and Europe of Jews and their fellow-travellers. But ridding Europe of many millions of people is a far more difficult and complex fantasy to make actual than building the Great Pyramid at Giza. In the twentieth century only a highly efficient bureaucracy would have any chance of succeeding. For such a command to be carried out the person issuing it would have to be at the top of a large and efficient command hierarchy. In order to understand human obedience we need to understand the context in which it works, the machine obedience fuels. Mumford has described those aspects of civilized institutions, of command hierarchies, most relevant to my concerns.

> I use the term 'civilization' ... to denote the group of institutions that first took form under kingship. Its chief features, constant in varying proportions throughout history, are the centralization of political power, the separation of classes, the lifetime division of labor, the mechanization of production, the magnification of military power, the economic exploitation of the weak, and the universal introduction of slavery and forced labor for both industrial and military purposes. (1967, p. 186)

These seven features, found in various guises throughout history, are some of the darker aspects of civilization we prefer not to think about. Civilization's positive features hardly need elaboration: since the term 'civilization' is synonymous with all that we value, songs of praise to civilization have seldom stopped over the past 5,000 years. Anyone who reads, sees or listens to the daily news is so familiar with their tune that reminders of civilization's triumphs are hardly necessary. But lest even one reader imagine that I wish to ignore civilization's virtues, the following sentences complete Mumford's paragraph.

These institutions would have completely discredited both the primal myth of divine kingship and the derivative myth of the machine had they not been accompanied by another set of collective traits that deservedly claim admiration: the invention and keeping of the written record, the growth of visual and musical arts, the effort to widen the circle of communication and economic intercourse far beyond the range of any local community: ultimately the purpose to make available to all men the discoveries and inventions and creations, the works of art and thought, the values and purposes that any single group has discovered. (1967, p. 186)

A state command hierarchy, a human machine and accompanying institutions had to be in place for obedient citizens to carry out the 'inhumane policies [which] may have originated in the mind of a single person'. The people who carried out (obeyed) the commands were not simply individuals with consciences, but components, parts of a modern, impersonal and bureaucratic human machine with its institutional and psychological means for exacting obedience.

Clearly, the Divine King's command hierarchy differs in detail from the command hierarchy characterizing a modern democracy – just as a democracy's command hierarchy differs markedly from Hitler's Führer state. The importance of such differences for the people who are parts of command hierarchies, particularly for those at the base, cannot be overemphasized. But before looking for the source of differences I wish to show how the command hierarchy is not simply the basis for social, political, military and economic organization, but for vital aspects of human thought and human values as well.

5

The Command Hierarchy

If one stops to consider the matter, is there not something strange in the fact that men should consider loyalty to 'laws,' principles, standards, ideals to be an inherent virtue, accounted unto them for righteousness? (Dewey, 1929/1980, p. 278)

The myth (and reality) of the Divine King dominates some of our most important ways of thinking and valuing. Indeed, so habitual is hierarchical thinking that like all habits (Mixon, 1980), it seems so natural and unavoidable that it goes unnoticed and unremarked. Chiefly, I aim to draw attention to the unremarked, and only secondarily to suggest some of the implications of the Divine King's dominance. For it is far from clear to what extent matters could be otherwise.

A command hierarchy is a human machine designed to carry out the will of a single person. The design, on the whole, has worked wonders: those collective projects which comprise much of the glory that was Rome – and every other civilization – were produced by command hierarchies. But even the best of designs do not always work as intended. If what happens is supposed to be the result of a command from the apex, no occupant of the top job has been able to get a human machine to work perfectly. If Divine Kings had succeeded, history and biography would hold little of interest. A perfect machine, even a perfect human machine, is completely predictable – a form of life too dull to tempt an historian or a biographer.

A human machine is a less than perfect machine. To get it to run at all always has depended on rewards, threats, bluffs, punishments and physical coercion. The invention of nonhuman machines is not simply a rational effort to 'save' labour. Indeed, Mumford (1967) observes that the earliest machines were 'labor-using devices'. Whatever the motive for their invention, nonhuman machines can be more perfect (for 'perfect' read 'controllable' or 'obedient') than humans, can provide a more reliable, less fractious, less unruly means of carrying out commands. But alas for dreams of control, even machines have been known to disappoint. Machines may have the virtue of being unable to disobey, but they can misperform – and the more sophisticated they are, the more prone to misadventure. When they do malfunction (and so seem to demonstrate an engagingly human imperfection) machines often are cursed and beaten, as if they were disobedient slaves.

The workings of a command hierarchy are seen most clearly when the hierarchy is uncomplicated, is perfect – when it appears in its ideal-typical form. In order to understand something it can be helpful to look at how it functions ideally, how it is intended to function. Then it becomes possible to examine measures taken to get it to function as intended and to understand why, despite such measures, it can fail to function as its designers wish.

In order to be certain that all commands are obeyed promptly and fully a Divine King would need extraordinary powers. A Divine King first of all would require the power of life and death over all His subjects. No competing powers can be tolerated, for if power existed elsewhere in the kingdom it could be used to resist commands. The Divine King must be all-powerful, omnipotent. But power, even supreme power, is not enough. Unwilling subjects might privately or secretly evade, sabotage or avoid commands. As a countermeasure the Divine King would need spies and informants everywhere. But then, even spies and informants are not immune from temptations secretly to engage in projects of their own. Ideally the Divine King would need the power to see into the hearts and minds of all His subjects, including His chain of command, His spies, and His informants. The Divine King would need to be all-seeing or omniscient.

Gods, of course, are frequently described as being both omniscient and omnipotent. And it is not difficult to see why. If believers can be brought truly to believe that their God can see into their minds and hearts and to believe that He will punish them severely if He glimpses the slightest disloyalty, they may be persuaded to change their thinking and their feeling and become, internally and externally, more compliant and more obedient. For what must be overcome, the chief obstacle in the way of command hierarchies reaching their ideal-typical form, is the human power to lie, pretend and dissimulate. Citizens who have the ability to pretend loyalty and love while plotting disobedience and treason are serious threats to the security of any power-that-be. Only if people can be persuaded that their efforts to lie and pretend are rendered fruitless by an all-seeing eye, can pliability and obedience become assured.

No earthly Divine King has managed to become omnipotent or omniscient, nor is it likely that any Divine King has ever managed to persuade all subjects that their efforts to lie and pretend are fruitless. But so powerfully has the notion of a perfect Divine Kingdom worked on the human imagination that ideal-typical command hierarchies do exist – but they exist not as earthly kingdoms, but as kingdoms of the mind, as forms of thought. The command hierarchy has come to serve not simply as the basic form of human social order, but also as the dominant model of natural order, as a model of causation.

Since the first kingdoms were Divine Kingdoms it is not difficult to see why religious explanation takes the form of a command hierarchy. The greater a Divine King's success in persuading His subjects of His omnipotence and omniscience, the more perfectly His human machines will function. But no matter how terrible or awesome, the Divine Kings that we can see are less than all-powerful and all-seeing and less than perfect in exercising their wills. Perhaps a God that we cannot see, except in imagination, may be able to command belief in His all-powerful and all-seeing nature. An invisible God at the apex of the universe is so powerful that He issues commands not just to human subjects, but to all His creatures. God's Word, we are told, created everything. If we wish to understand the doings of any of His creatures at the base of the pyramid we can do so by tracing back and up step by step to the origin, to the first Creation and Commandments. Thus we are told: *In the beginning was the Word, and the Word was with God, and the Word was God.* God's Word (Divine Logos) is best understood as God's Command.

Nonetheless, even when constructed in thought and belief, ideal-typical command hierarchies have difficulties. If God is indeed all-powerful, how can anyone fail to do His will? Are not people always behaving badly, displaying a disobedience no all-powerful God would tolerate? No matter, to preserve God's power and the ideal-typical command hierarchy it is necessary to deny that anyone *can* fail to do His will and to explain human misbehaviour in another way. God's command hierarchy takes its purest form in the extreme version of the doctrine of predestination. For a predestinarian an act of God foreordained all things. In other words, in its extreme form the doctrine of predestination posits a perfect ideal-typical command hierarchy. God's original command set into motion everything and everybody in the universe, then, now and forever. All things that happen from the time the command was issued (including of course, the writing of this sentence) happen in obedience to the command. No creature or physical object can do anything other than obey. Should they appear to be disobeying, the appearance is but appearance, for the disobedient actions are in fact the will of God.

The secular account of the universe modelled on God's command hierarchy maps almost perfectly on to the doctrine of predestination. Those who hold to the philosophic creed of determinism are certain that all that can happen is what does happen (including, of course, the writing of this sentence). But instead of following the causal sequence up to God as do the predestinarians, determinists have turned the pyramid on its side and trace the causal sequence of anything that happens back in time (a direction usually imagined as horizontal movement) to an origin – an original impetus. They can't always agree on what to call the origin (was it a big bang?), but the movement of thought is backward and convergent as with a horizontal pyramid. The determinist universe is as fully predetermined as the predestinarian universe. There is no possibility in it. That is why Laplace believed that with sufficient knowledge of initial conditions every thing and every event can be predicted. All creatures and physical objects must be forever obedient to the original impetus.

Modern determinists, forswearing any interest in values, have a distinct advantage over predestinarians who would like to believe that God not only is all-powerful and all-seeing, but also possessed of unlimited goodness. God's goodness, of course, raises questions about why He permits so much suffering and evil on His earth. Believers have written a great many words trying to reconcile God's goodness with His all-powerful and all-seeing nature. By denying interest in goodness or any other value determinists are able to maintain their ideal type and its accompanying certainty – and are able, too, to avoid a thorny problem.

Reductionism, a belief which often accompanies scientific determinism, employs the same mode of thought but turns the model upside down and stands the pyramid on its apex. Reductionism is not a belief about origins and cause but a belief about rank. (To assign rank, of course, is to value. But since rank is a hierarchical value, I suspect that it is a value invisible to scientific determinists.) Reductionists rank the various types of scientific explanations according to which account is imagined to be most powerful, most satisfactory, most basic. With pyramids that which is highest in rank is at the apex and the apex, of course, is at the top. But with reductionism that which is highest in rank is also the most basic and that which is basic or fundamental is thought to be at the bottom of things. Therefore to visualize how reductionism works the pyramid must be stood on its apex so that the highest in rank which commands all other ranks, can also be at the bottom of things. The lowest ranked explanation at the base of the upside down pyramid (Level V – sociology?) can be reduced down to, is obedient to, the next lowest in rank (Level IV – psychology?), which in turn can be reduced to, is obedient to, the next lowest rank (Level III – biology?), in turn reduced to, obedient to, the next lowest (Level II – chemistry?), which is reduced to, obedient to, that which is at the bottom of things, the highest-ranked form of explanation at the apex of the upside down pyramid – Level I – physics: a mode of explanation which does not reduce, which is obedient to nothing, and which can command (and thus explain) everything.

The most striking feature of the form of thought associated with hierarchy is the conviction that the power to do anything, to act, is found only at the apex. Hierarchical thought always looks toward the apex for the source of power and movement. Excepting the source nothing in the universe has the power to move itself. Each thing is moved by something else, which in turn is moved by something else. And so on until the original impetus is reached. The original impetus can move itself and, by command, set everything subservient to it into motion. This mode of thought reflects what is so in an ideal-typical command hierarchy. Language may give us the capacity to imagine that which is not, but the only person with the power to make fantasy real is the Divine King. Everyone else in the kingdom must do only what the Divine King commands.

Human thought depends upon analogy – seeing correspondences in otherwise dissimilar things. We come to understand things or events we do not understand by seeking correspondences to things we do understand. In science that part of the analogy we do understand is called a model. Clearly, the better we understand the model, the more useful the analogy. An ideal-typical command hierarchy has served as a master model of how the universe and everything in it works. The more specialized models that scientists use are based on the assumption that the master model is in place. One reason for the ubiquity of the master model is that it is something we all can easily understand. In that sense it is a marvellous model. Everyone lives in, has grown up in, some sort of command hierarchy, so that everyone has an understanding of how hierarchy works. Since the social world works that way, why not the natural world?

The master model served science very well for several hundred years. Twentieth century physics, however, is said by some (such as Capra, 1983) to require another set of assumptions, another sort of model. Rom Harré and Paul Secord (1972) place a radical change in the conceptual basis of modern science at a much earlier date – in the late eighteenth and early nineteenth centuries. However, changes in the conceptual basis of science have not affected most current discussions in the social sciences, discussions which assume that the master model is still in place. In fact, Rüstow (1980) implies that though seen most obviously in mechanics the master model still can be discerned in modern physics. He also notes how appropriate and indispensable 'a sharp and ruthless absolutist centralism, a rigid and unconditional systematic super- and subordination' (p. 297) is not only to theoretical physics, but to mathematics as well.

A list of hierarchical ways of thinking, though finite, must be very long. One of the most influential instances has dominated capitalist thought for over 200 years and has thus affected the lives and fortunes, both positively and negatively, of countless millions. The notion goes something like this: if everyone devoutly obeys the commands of the Divine King's invisible hand everyone in His earthly kingdom will prosper. Obedience in this case means doing nothing to interfere with the divine hand's control of the market. Since disobedience is possible, the invisible hand clearly is less powerful than the predestinarian God.

Our very notions of self are dominated by the master model. Since commanding oneself, telling oneself what to do, is something everyone does, nothing could be more everyday-run-of-the-mill ordinary. Even so, is it not strange? Given the fact that language enables us to address ourselves, is it not, if not strange, significant that, of all possible forms of address, we should use the command? The command, of course, is the form of address superiors use to inferiors. 'The man-made distinction between those who give orders and those who have to obey them implies that they have no common language between them' (Canetti, 1978, p. 294). Surely we should be able to find a form of common language to talk to ourselves.

Most psychologists are unhappy with any form of mind–body dualism and typically blame the philosopher Descartes and sometimes Plato for advocating dualism. But the mind–body problem is not simply a problem invented by philosophers. Being both the commander and commanded is part of the everyday experience of all people living in hierarchical societies. If the full introduction of the flight-command into the fabric of society can be attributed to the first Divine King, I assume that the introduction of the sting of command into intra-psychic life took place at much the same time.

So common is the self-command that I suppose most readers will find it difficult even to imagine another state of psychic affairs. Even so I do find it significant that self-command seems so 'natural'. The words Rüstow applied to theoretical physics and mathematics also describe intra-psychic life: 'a sharp and ruthless centralism, a rigid and unconditional systematic super- and subordination'. I am not saying that I find psychic division, inner conflict or a plurality of selves exceptional or puzzling. What I find significant is the assumption that we must all have an interior little Divine King to bring order to division and conflict and to put the plurality of selves at His service. James Ogilvy (1979), from another point of view, discusses ways of decentralizing not only self, but society, and the sacred too.

The Command Hierarchy as a Way of Valuing

The distribution of power in an ideal-typical command hierarchy could not be more obvious. The Divine King at the apex is all-powerful and at each step down the pyramid or chain of command is a rank with less power than the rank above. The same ranking decides questions of value: the Divine King is most highly valued and each succeeding subordinate rank is progressively less valued. The spatial metaphor we use in valuing anything fits that mountain of stone, the pyramid: at the top is found the best, at the bottom, the worst. The valuing is reflected in the English language in both the form used by the working class (Anglo-Saxon) and the form favoured by the upper class (Graeco-Latin) (Corson, 1986). Top is best whether we use the Anglo-Saxon word 'high' – which can be used in a purely spatial sense and also can mean such things as pre-eminent in rank or standing, lofty or exalted in quality, character or style; or we can use a more culturally sophisticated Graeco-Latin word such as 'superior' – which can be used in a spatial sense (e.g., above) or to mean such things as higher in rank, station, authority and of great value or excellence. The Anglo-Saxon word 'low' can be used in a spatial sense or can mean of inferior quality or character, morally base, having inferior social, moral or cultural status. The Graeco-Latin word 'inferior' also can be used in a spatial sense (e.g., below or beneath) and can mean low in order, degree or rank; low or lower in quality, status, or estimation. Spatial reference also appears in definitions of the basic moral terms 'good' (superior) and 'bad' (inferior).

That in civilizations based on command hierarchies the chief way of valuing takes hierarchical form is not surprising. Also unremarkable is the observation that what our betters do and what they possess is the standard of excellence, the object of imitation, emulation and envy for all social classes. 'The rich are mythic figures who motivate action because, like all such figures, they *are* the principle, the ultimate value, which shapes the dramatic struggle' (Duncan, 1962, p. 366). In times past the lower orders often had little contact and thus little direct knowledge of the higher orders. Certainly only servants or house slaves could look closely at how their betters lived. And few had any prospect, even in imagination, of living like their lords and masters. In modern times imitation and envy have been stimulated and facilitated by mass media and mass production. The twentieth century has seen a joint flourishing of word and photographic industries whose chief purpose is to write about and picture the activities and nonactivities of the rich and powerful, as well as mass production industries whose chief purpose is to make less expensive imitations of the clothes and other possessions of the rich and powerful. Television and print industries, feeding a seemingly insatiable curiosity, spend much of their resources producing fiction and fact about the top people. If the female élite, the 'best' females, wear exclusive gowns purchased from Parisian couturiers, in a very short time mass produced imitations will be on department store racks. If eminent people live in Tudor mansions with acres of rolling lawns, then less eminent people (who can afford the cost) will live in mock-Tudor subdivisions with spacious lawns, and very nearly everyone else with a few square feet of ground will have grass of some sort. If notables drive largely hand-made luxury cars, mass-produced mock-luxury is available to the less-notable who can be persuaded to indebt themselves to money lenders. If the beautiful rich spend winters on exclusive sunny beaches, sun tan lamps and tanning chemicals can be sold to those who cannot. The list can go on and on – and does in the form of shelves of books. Rather than trying to condense or update Veblen, I will discuss one form of value-emulation that has received too little attention: the value-emulation of 'value-free' science.

'To conceive of the world as value-free is a task which men set themselves on account of a value: the vital value of mastery and power over things' (Max Scheler, quoted in Leiss, 1972, p. 109). In practice a value-free science means that the objects studied have no value in themselves; their only value is in serving the masters who study them. Early theoreticians and boosters of modern science such as Francis Bacon (1561–1626) and René Descartes (1596–1650) were perfectly open about the reasons and justifications for science: successful scientific knowledge would lead to the domination and control of nature. Descartes, for example, claimed that the aim of science is 'to make us masters and possessors of nature'. Few seventeenth century mechanists can have thought that dominating nature was anything other than a good thing. Nature would be commanded like serfs or slaves. A properly submissive nature could lead to untold power and unimagined wealth.

To this day the popular press treats science's encounter with nature, frequently quoting scientists themselves, in terms of domination and control. Military imagery is fashionable: the battle with nature can be seen as a religious or holy war, the favoured term being 'crusade'. Scientists frequently find themselves engaged in a crusade against some aspect of the natural world that we think ought to be other than it is, or, if time seems short, they mount a *battle* against something we fear or find inconvenient.

So clear, so obvious is the nature, intent and project of modern science that making a case would be unnecessary except for the fact that some scientists and philosophers deny that science is about domination and control. The denial usually takes the form of insisting on the long-standing distinction between science's theoretical (pure) and practical (technological) arms. Practical science or technology can hardly hide its ambition to command nature. The technician's business is to get some part of nature to do as someone wishes. The theoretical or pure sciences, on the other hand, have produced some of history's greatest intellectual triumphs, often mathematical in form and, in appearance, abstract and disinterested. And pure scientists, with truth, can often say of themselves that they have no interest in dominating and controlling anything. A pure scientist can be a good, gentle and unworldly creature – prototypically represented by Albert Einstein.

Yet the nature of a project is not belied by the motives or characters of those who make up part of the project. An army is designed to be a killing machine and remains a killing machine even if all of its officers are gentlemen and all of its fighters are conscripts who would rather be doing anything than risking death. Another reason that pure science cannot be anything but part of the domination/control project is that scientific determinism is a form of hierarchical thought that by its nature must produce domination/control knowledge. The cause of something is its command. Pure science discovers or works out how nature's chain of command functions; practical science or technology puts the chain of command to work. Governments and private funding agencies understand the connection between pure and applied science, indeed acknowledge technology's dependence on pure science. Otherwise lavishly funded pure scientists could count themselves – would rank with – those other pure, but fund-poor, scholars in the humanities.

For as long as hierarchy has been the chief form of social organization one of humanity's headiest dreams has taken the form of a two-sided wish: to command everyone and to be obedient to no one. Such a desire is inevitable, for in hierarchical terms to command is a sign of superiority and to obey a sign of inferiority. Unfortunately for wish-fulfilment the only position from which anyone can command everyone and obey no one is the top, the apex of the command hierarchy. There is room at the top for only one. For most people living in command hierarchies, particularly for the slaves at the bottom, the dream was and is just that. In practical terms most members of hierarchies can hope at best to command a few more and obey a few less people.

In early modern times the dream took on what appears to be a more realistic form: a two-sided wish to command (control) every *thing* and to be obedient to (controlled by) no *thing*. The wish appears more realistic because whereas it is clear that only the one at the top could command every *one*, it seemed that humanity as a whole might be able to gain control of every *thing*. Whereas a situation in which everyone can command everyone is out of the question, the dream of every one commanding every thing might come true if science succeeded in its project to dominate and control nature.

Science and technology – or Techne, to use Jacques Barzun's (1964) term for the fusion of science and technology that has been the rule since the nineteenth century – has succeeded in dominating nature, succeeded beyond the wildest imaginings of seventeenth century enthusiasts. Techne's inventiveness has been prodigal – much of it lavished on machines or appliances that enable those without slaves or servants to live like their masters. How do masters live? For most of humanity masters live magical lives, lives without labour. Slaves, servants, or 'employees' do everything for them. Masters are those who can do as they wish. One master-wish can be traced back to early Divine Kings and their pyramidal monuments to themselves. Masters wish to live forever. Techne has not yet managed to grant that wish but can provide deep-freeze facilities for those with faith in Techne's inevitable triumph. Techne seeks to bring master-magic to everyone.

Despite Techne's successes and promises, for most of humanity the magical wish remains a dream. The reason why humanity as a whole has not shared equally in the fruits of nature's conquest is found in the words 'equally' and 'fruits'. Humanity as a whole shares in some of the consequences, intended and unintended, of Techne's projects because, living on this planet, we cannot escape the consequences. But not all of the consequences are 'fruits'. We do not share equally for the simple reason that we live in hierarchies which ensure that the fruits are not shared equally. Nor do we share equally the unintended negative consequences of science's conquests. People, if high enough in the economic hierarchies, can buy, or, if high in political hierarchies, can arrange, safeguards and other hedges against the various forms of social and environmental degradation that distinguish modern life.

It might be objected that no one possessed of the least political realism would ever have dreamed that science would put everyone in command of nature. Science in its beginnings was an activity of gentlemen and the fruits of science would of course go to the class that did science. Everyone else at best might get what managed to trickle down. If the words of Bacon and Descartes for example, seem to include everyone it is only because 'everyone' in most times and places means 'everyone who counts'. Science was originally an occupation of gentlemen and later of the rather small educated classes; today it is an occupation that employs distinguished practitioners from all social classes. Yet the fruits of science still go chiefly to 'everyone who counts'. Or as C.S. Lewis put it: 'what we call Man's power over Nature turns out to be a power exercised by some men over other men with Nature as its instrument' (1943/1978, p. 35).

Fearing nature and her cruelties and desiring to take command, moderns set out to dominate and subdue her. The greater the successes of the domination project, the more completely feared nature is turned into an obedient slave, the more we have to fear human dominators, human authorities. For the power gained by enslaving nature goes not equally to everyone, to every human, but, unequally, to dominators and authorities. The power goes to those who authorize criminal commands.

6

Justifying Criminal Commands

It should be emphasized that psychological justifications were an essential part of the killing operations. If a proposed action could not be justified, it did not take place. (Hilberg, 1985, p. 331)

Men use thought only to justify their wrongdoings. (Voltaire)

Milgram ended his book, as he had an earlier paper, with selections from an article called 'The dangers of obedience' by Harold J. Laski (1929).

> ... civilization means, above all, an unwillingness to inflict unnecessary pain. Within the ambit of that definition, those of us who heedlessly accept the commands of authority cannot yet claim to be civilized men (p. 5) ...
> Our business, if we desire to live a life not utterly devoid of meaning and significance, is to accept nothing which contradicts our basic experience merely because it comes to us from tradition or convention or authority. It may well be that we shall be wrong; but our self-expression is thwarted at the root unless the certainties we are asked to accept coincide with the certainties we experience. That is why the condition of freedom in any state is always a widespread and consistent skepticism of the canons upon which power insists. (p. 10)

The whole of Laski's article is an eloquent expression of the liberal-democratic attitudes toward civilization and individual responsibility that mark the psychological study of obedience. A civilized person will refuse to inflict unnecessary pain. But Laski is clear that this is not only a matter of refusing direct commands: a citizen of a democracy has an obligation to speak out against and combat all examples of injustice, all of society's stultifying conformities, everything that violates conscience. For 'when we surrender the truth we see, by that betrayal we betray also the future of civilization. For the triumphs of a free conscience are the landmarks on the road to the ideal' (Laski, 1929, p. 10).

Most people reading this essay I suspect agree with Laski that civilization means, among other things, an unwillingness to inflict unnecessary pain. To be civilized is to be sensitive to suffering and pain. To deal with something in a civilized manner means to behave politely, gently and agreeably. To be civilized is to obey the canons of civility. Yet much of our 'long and gloomy history' is, as Snow observed, a story of hideous crimes. Hideous crimes inflict pain. The hideous crimes 'committed in the name of obedience' were committed at the command of civilized states, at the command of civilized religions, at the command of the guardians of civility. The authorities Laski warns us of are those charged with running and preserving civilized states. The guardians of civility must have their reasons for ordering their subordinates to commit hideous crimes.

Civilization, the home of civility, began with conquest, subjugation and enslavement. Civilization was made possible by hideous crimes against the autonomy of formerly independent communities. The history of civilization until this day is a history of conquest, subjugation and enslavement. A cynic, wishing to reconcile Laski's statement with Snow's, might say that conquest, subjugation and enslavement are the infliction of *necessary* pain, pain necessary to civilization's functioning and mission. And the cynic would be partly right. Authorizing crime, in a sense to be discussed at a later point, has been a necessary component of civilization.

The contradiction is made bearable for some by hierarchy's division of labour. For if to be civilized means an unwillingness to inflict unnecessary pain, then to save my civility I simply make certain that I am never in a position in which an authority can command me to inflict unnecessary pain. This is the move that keeps the contradiction alive, but out of sight: a manoeuvre typical of and open to civilization's élite. I can lead my courteous, genteel, and *civilized* life and leave civilization's dirty work to surrogates – to the coarser, more brutal and *less* civilized types. (The hangman who carries out civilization's judgments and inflicts the necessary pain of death traditionally was a pariah.) The military, police, and prison work can be left to those whose sensibilities are not offended by a little (or a great deal of) necessary pain. An image sharply etched into western consciousness is of the cultivated, civilized Roman governor, Pontius Pilate, washing his hands of an affair involving a particularly brutal and agonizingly painful form of execution.

I can retain my civilized sensibilities by dissociating myself from military, police or prison work. Or, if the life attracts me, I must see to it that I am in a position of command, for generals and admirals have often been polished, civil and sensitive men. I, civilized person that I am, would never issue a command to cause *un*necessary pain. If the command is to drop napalm which will cling to and sear the flesh of any body it touches – babies, women, the old and infirm – the command can be justified as inflicting *necessary* pain. 'You see, we had reliable reports of Viet Cong in the vicinity.'

The civilized virtues are real and we have reason to be proud of them. Over the millennia since civilization began civilized ways of doing things have become more and more widespread among the population (Elias, 1978). Civility is no longer a monopoly of those at the top. Most people, I suspect, would be genuinely distressed at the prospect of inflicting unnecessary pain. At the same time there seems no lessening of the human capacity to justify inflicted pain as *necessary* pain. The most hideous crimes of modern times have been and are justified as necessary.

In ordinary circumstances a civilized person would have difficulty imagining a more senseless and hideous crime than dropping on a populated rural village a substance that attaches indiscriminately to flesh and burns and sears and burns... Yet, not long ago, intelligent, civilized people, without blushing, accepted the justification: military necessity. Historically, military necessity has offered a blanket justification peculiarly immune to 'scepticism of the canons upon which power insists'. It is as if once the words 'military necessity' are pronounced nothing more needs to be said.

Sceptic: Even if you can be sure your intelligence is correct and Viet Cong are in the vicinity, why is it necessary to drop napalm on the village?
Justifier: It's the most effective thing we have.
S: Effective for what? Suppose it is 100 per cent effective and effectively kills all the Viet Cong and every other living creature in the village, why is that necessary?
J: They've got to be stopped. If we don't stop them now Vietnam will become communist. Then the communists will take all of southeast Asia. Everything will start falling like dominoes. And then they'll join up with the Chinese Communists and invade the United States. We've got to defend our democracy in Vietnam or soon we'll fighting in California.
S: Never mind whether or not the Communist Conspiracy exists

or, if it does, that the conspirators might be stopped by other means than napalm, or that the more honourable and courageous course would be to protect our country in our own country, aren't you being a bit overanxious? Even if they want to conquer the United States, how are they going to get there? What are they going to travel in? How will they get past the US Navy and Air Force?

J: Don't worry, they'll find a way. Look at how many of them there are.

The sceptic (who seems easily diverted and a bit long-winded) cannot get the justifier to consider the means used (napalm) in a single action (bombing a village) of an extended war. The justifier believes that the war itself is necessary and that questioning the means used to fight the war can only hinder the war effort. It seems not to matter that the beliefs about the enemy which are used to justify the war's necessity have crossed the border dividing reality from fantasy. I recall with pain how many versions of the 'Chinese-junks-are-going-to-land-en-masse-in-California' scenario were seriously proposed to me by all classes of people in the 1960s as justification for hideous crimes committed by the world's richest, most powerful and most secure democracy.

People who are ordered to commit hideous crimes can find grounds for obedience. Superiors who give the orders to commit hideous crimes can find grounds to justify their commands. Justifications, of course, can be more coherent and less fantastic than visions of all-conquering junks crossing the Pacific. Milgram, for example, justified inflicting extreme distress on many of his subjects by claiming that the stress was an unintentional, indeed unexpected, byproduct of 'scientific inquiry'. Since for most people scientific enquiry is as immune from scepticism as a war then the subject's distress, by definition, is necessary distress. Research scientists who commit hideous crimes against their animal subjects offer justifications employing similar logic. Scientific enquiry is an unassailable end and the pain, harm, terror and death of the animals an unfortunate but necessary byproduct of the experimental design. The justifiers also play on our fear by warning that if not allowed to continue torturing animals they will be unable to find the cure that will save us and our loved ones from disease and death. Those engaged in the business of raising animals for human consumption justify keeping their charges in unspeakably confined conditions by the efficiency of their methods. Since 'efficiency' is an unassailable idol of today's marketplace the unconscionably confined conditions are necessary if (heaven forbid) people are not to pay more money for their 'necessary' meat. Similar arguments were offered by the slavers who transported Africans to the New World in such incredibly confined conditions that over one-half of the 'cargo' died. Simply substitute for 'our necessary meat' 'our necessary workers'.

The justifications convince only so long as the idols cited are immune to 'consistent scepticism'. Indeed, those offering the justifications must assume that the idols are unquestionable, for if the idols are in any sense discredited the justifications collapse. As long as idols remain immune to question, civilized people will continue to commit hideous crimes in the name of civilization. Untold 'necessary' pain will continue to be part of the everyday world.

I have been writing of justification, using examples from military, police, prison, research work, farming and the slave trade. The discussion was of justifying a deed or practice, not, as in Chapter 3, of justifying an act of obedience. Although discussed in separate chapters, commands and obedient acts have the same or similar justifications. For once a deed or practice has been justified, then obeying a legitimate command to do it can be readily justified. Reasons for obeying can be drawn from the reasons used to justify the act.

A striking feature of Milgram's study of obedience is that both the stimulus for the study (the Holocaust) and the deed featured in the study (electric shock-delivery) seemed clearly unjustifiable. I have shown that 'shocking' the 'learner' lacks justification only if the 'learner' is being harmed – something that was far from clear to participants. In contrast to Milgram's mock learning experiment where all was pretence, there is no doubt about the horrible reality of the Holocaust and other hideous Nazi crimes, no doubt, that is, except in the minds of the excited few who insist that the Holocaust was a hoax, a hoax perpetrated by a conspiracy involving thousands, possibly, millions of conspirators.

Justification by Inferiority

State crimes, no matter how hideous, are justified in some manner. To claim that the crimes of the Third Reich or that the hideous crimes of history were (and are) justified is not, of course, to claim that they are justifiable. My object is to show how the Third Reich's policies and history's hideous crimes were justified and how, being justified, they could thus appear justifiable to the perpetrators.

The crimes of the Third Reich, while having their own uniquely terrible aspects, have features in common with all of history's hideous crimes. The deeds are similar and the justifications are similar. What do the deeds have in common? What *are* hideous crimes? What *is* unnecessary pain?

At this point I think it essential to distinguish between two kinds of war actions. In both a warrior killed is just as dead and a warrior maimed is just as maimed. Each of the war actions is an authorized crime, yet I think one type of action more than the other can be justly called a hideous crime. The type of action I wish for the moment to exclude from discussion is a particular sort of conflict between warriors. History has seen conflicts that in some ways resemble sporting events: call them 'death contests'. The warriors on each side treat one another as respected opponents, fight more or less according to the rules, but unlike most sporting events those engaged in death contests frequently die. We might call their deaths 'tragic', or 'a waste', or even 'stupid butchery', but I would like to limit the term 'hideous crime' to a conflict of a second sort, a type of conflict that can be clearly distinguished, psychologically, from the first.

Force is involved in both death contests and hideous crimes, but whereas in death contests force is used against a respected opponent, hideous crimes involve using force to treat people as if their pain, their bodily and mental integrity and their very life are of no importance or account. People so treated are seen as objects, but objects of a particular sort – objects that are known to be sentient. These sentient objects can be treated cruelly (cruelty is their due) in ways that, by common agreement, cannot be justified when done to people of our own kind. The last three words – 'our own kind' – hold the key to a form of justification that goes back beyond history, a justification endemic even before the first Divine Kingdom. 'Our own kind' maps, of course, on to the concept discussed earlier: 'everyone who counts'. The hideous crimes of history and of prehistory were and are done to people not of our own kind – to those who do not count.

Those not of our own kind can be identified in a number of ways. Groups with a common language and a common culture seem always to have considered other groups – groups with a different language or dialect, a different culture – as inferior, less than human, not of their own kind.

... ruthless brutality and violence had been applied only outwardly against beasts and against alien human beings, the latter being viewed not as humans but as a species of especially repulsive and dangerous monkey. This outlook finds its most significant expression in the fact that many primitive peoples use the word that means 'human being' in their language as the distinguishing designation reserved exclusively for their own tribe and its members. Those not belonging to the tribe are not considered human beings. (Rüstow, 1980, p. 35)

The attitude, however deplorable it may seem, is not difficult to understand. Contrary to Rüstow, ruthless brutality and violence at times are applied to tribal members – those tribal members who violate tribal ways. The thinking or reasoning must go something like this: our tribal customs and laws show the right way to live and behave. Since a member of my own tribe who breaks tribal laws or fails to observe our customs is wrong, is a bad person, is base, then members of other tribes who fail to observe our tribal laws and customs must also be wrong, bad or base. The attitude, like it or not, has a moral logic: if our ways are good, then people who do not observe our ways must be bad. If it is wrong for us to drink alcohol, then it is wrong for *them* to drink alcohol.

Members of my tribe who violate tribal custom or law thereby set themselves apart. They are no longer fully one of our own kind and so must no longer be treated like one of us. They can be punished harshly, cruelly; they can even be killed. In the same way members of other tribes who do not observe our ways are not of our kind; they are different, wrong, bad and inferior, can be treated harshly, cruelly, and can be killed.

Human groups then create two categories: 'us' (humans) and 'those who are not us' (not-humans). Humans are treated like one of our own kind, treatment which includes positive prohibitions against harm. The prohibitions against harm do not apply to not-humans. Not only is there no obligation to treat not-humans like humans, often there is an implied obligation to treat not-humans badly. Otherwise they might forget themselves – forget their place.

The situation with precivilized communities was quite straightforward: our own kind, human beings, are the law abiding members of our group, our tribal or village community. The coming of civilization complicated things. Civilization, which in the long run did so much to sensitize people to suffering and pain, invented entire new categories of people not of 'our own kind'. The new categories were made up, not of lawbreakers or foreigners, but of classes, statuses or ranks in the command hierarchy itself. In other words citizens of a civilized state, unlike members of a tribe, do not have to break a law or custom to be considered 'not of our own kind'; they have only to be members of a particular class, rank or status. Typical of civilizations from the beginning is the practice of categorizing groups of their own citizens, particularly that most numerous class at the base of the pyramid, as inferior and thus fit subjects for harsh and cruel treatment. Typically those at the base were slaves and could be treated as slaves, as less than human. In terms of common treatment 'our own kind' was no longer all members of the social unit minus the law breakers, but members of a particular rank or class within a command hierarchy.

Since all who read this have lived in hierarchies all their lives, I feel no need to offer extensive examples of the broad and subtle differences in the kind of treatment people of different statuses can expect and demand. Graded differences in respect and treatment are characteristic of all hierarchies from Divine Kingdoms to modern corporations. Just as only nobles of sufficient rank are allowed in the king's bedroom, only executives of sufficient rank are given keys to the executive washroom. Even convicted law breakers of high rank when imprisoned often are treated more like one of us than one of them.

History's hideous crimes were facilitated by that innovation of civilization: categorizing people by what they are, by the status they *have*, rather than by what they do. Tribal antipathies can be traced to disapproval of what people do. Lawbreakers act different-ly, behave badly – and so can be treated cruelly. Members of other tribes speak and act differently and so are wrong and bad and can be treated cruelly. With the coming of civilization people no longer had to do anything to be subject to cruel treatment, they had only to be born to parents of a particular rank. Justifications for cruel treatment, whether of the Divine King's slaves or of blacks living today in South Africa all take the same form: they are not exempt from cruel treatment, they are not one of us, because of who they are. Inferiority is theirs by birth, or can come from something that happens to them, for example, physical or mental disability. The logic has remained the same over the millennia: all inferior people can be treated as not human (major premise); people in category X are inferior (minor premise); therefore people in category X can be treated as not-human (conclusion). The universal hierarchical justification of cruel treatment is justification-by-inferiority.

Although bad treatment based on justification-by-inferiority continues to be common, twentieth century states progressively have taken away legal support for the practice. For example, laws enshrining and supporting racial discrimination in the United States were declared unconstitutional over 30 years ago. However, *de facto* segregation and discrimination continues in both south and north USA. South Africa has become a pariah state, not because it practises racial discrimination, but because it insists on continuing to legalize racist practices.

Hideous crimes, then, are justified by the victims' inferiority. Victims are inferior because of who they are. Atrocities are often given an added justification: Jews are not only Jews but are plotting to undermine the state; Vietnamese are not just Gooks, but are part of a Communist conspiracy to enslave the Free World. But the added justification is just that: added, not essential.

Scientific Determination of Inferiority

For most people living today the hideous crimes of the Nazi state are clearly unjustifiable. Most, with good reason, might well protest that 'unjustifiable' is far too mild a word. The policies resulted in such incredible inhumanity that planners and perpetrators must have been out of their minds, insane – or, if not insane, moral monsters. Forgotten, or not known, are the years of scientific work that helped to justify the policy; forgotten, or not known, is the degree of serious intellectual support for the sort of genetic theories the Nazis used to justify their policies. Nazi policy and practice was an extreme but logical extension of hierarchical thinking.

For all hierarchies the people at the base are not 'us' and so can be treated cruelly. But for the Divine King and most succeeding hierarchies those at the base are not only useful, but essential: the base people do the work, do the fighting – make the good life possible for their betters. Thus much of the cruelty inflicted on the base was part of an effort to increase their usefulness. Cruelty was often connected with modifying behaviour in the direction of exacting more perfect obedience and submission. In modern times theories clustering around notions of biological determinism have identified categories of people as not simply inferior, but as either useless or as an active hindrance to the good society. Now if someone is useless or harmful to the state it can be very expensive and frequently fruitless to apply cruelty, which hierarchically is their due, to change their behaviour. The cruelty can be more efficiently applied to diminish or remove the useless or harmful category from society.

Prior to Nazi policy most of the suggestions of eugenicists and other biological determinists were confined to the comparatively mild cruelty of sterilization. If categories of people are believed to be genetically inferior then the simple and 'humane' solution is to remove such categories from society by preventing them from reproducing. Sterilization programmes were carried out in many of the countries, including the United States, which later became prosecutors of Nazi war criminals.

With clear-eyed Aryan logic Nazi politicians, physicians, scientists, and theoreticians saw that the crusade for a thousand year Reich, a crusade which put the existence of the Fatherland at risk, demanded an extension of the 'humane solution'. If it is justifiable over time to 'cleanse' the state of useless and harmful categories of people, then in war it is justifiable to cleanse the state of such 'elements' as quickly as possible. Otherwise the crusade might fail. Not only is such a policy logical and hierarchically justifiable, but surely it is the duty of every patriotic citizen to assist in the policy's execution.

The good scientists and physicians began with inmates of mental institutions – people who were not only inferior but were clearly 'useless eaters'. The efficient factory-like liquidation by gas chamber was tried out and perfected on those diagnosed 'mentally ill'. From there it was only one step further to eliminate other inferior and useless people and people thought to be an active cancer on the state. This last category included but was not limited to the millions of Jews who became objects of the logical Final Solution.

Stephen Chorover has traced the contributions made by psychologists, biologists and other genetic determinists to Nazi practice.

> In the last analysis, it was sociobiological scholarship, claiming to be scientifically objective, morally neutral, and ethically free, that provided the conceptual framework by which eugenic theory was transformed into genocidal practice while garnering support, or at least not rousing opposition, among the German people as a whole. (1979, p. 109)

Biological determinists and their sympathizers will be swift to claim that Chorover is wrong, to protest that all they do is use objective, scientific means to determine who is inferior. Politicians determine what to do to or with inferiors. Chorover, however, has shown in considerable detail how in the United States and elsewhere biological determinists have been prominent in actively recommending and pushing for solutions – for policies such as immigration exclusion, sterilization and brain surgery. In fact the scientific determination of inferiority, historically and logically, is a programme pursued in order to solve perceived social problems. In its most common form it takes certain categories of people to be a drain on social resources and a threat to national breeding stock. Ethical neutrality in principle is impossible. In hierarchical societies the only reason for determining who is inferior is in order to know who to treat as inferior. The Nazis carried hierarchical thinking to its logical – its hier-logical – Final Conclusion.

Books continue to be written, and movies made, that agonize over the very disturbing question: how could good, ordinary people have cooperated with the Final Solution? The question *is* disturbing, but also is an extreme example of something characteristic of many, if not most civilized groups. The mass of people at the bottom of hierarchies are often good, kind, decent people, and often live by more rigorous moral standards than their betters. Why do not such people follow their own decent impulses and defy the evil policies of their betters?

Of course, not all commoners are good, kind and decent. Many of them are vicious and base. But there would be no question to agonize over if most are not thought to be good, kind and decent. For it is hardly puzzling why vicious and base people cooperated with the Final Solution.

Along with being good, kind and decent commoners are often modest. They have accepted their position of inferiority and often even believe that their betters know best. If their betters have decided that particular categories of people are threats to the state then they should know. I must presume that a large proportion of good, kind, decent people were persuaded by the propaganda machine, driven by the Minister for Propaganda and Enlightenment, that the Jews and other 'sub-humans' were a threat to German society. (That same propaganda machine did its best to keep secret the terrible details of the Final Solution.) If persuasion failed, then what could they do? Except what some of them did: behave heroically. Or, what others did – give assistance and act kindly when they had a chance. Or do what most of them probably did – go on as usual and hope that the rumours about the killing centres were not true.

Heroic behaviour in Nazi Germany depended not simply on the sort of courage ordinarily associated with heroes, but also on the confidence that the designs of superiors were wrong – so wrong that death became preferable to complicity. Historically heroes with such confidence and courage have been rare. Why were Germans expected to be exceptions?

The obedience study's central question: Why do people obey commands that must clearly conflict with human feeling and moral conscience? – may be a final, deeply felt, romantic *cri du coeur*. From at least the time of Rousseau intellectuals have sensed a strength, a decency, in the commons that was lacking in the higher circles. Intellectuals have looked to the commons to revitalize, to save, to transform society – or as in the case of Germany, to defy a Führer state. Such hopes have been repeatedly dashed. Workers' and peasants' revolutions have succeeded in overthrowing effete, corrupt masters only to put in their place workers' and peasants' states with new hierarchies, headed by new Divine Kings who demand obedience and submission in the name of the workers and peasants.

The qualities in the commons seen and admired by intellectuals are no doubt there. But intellectuals can expect such qualities to revitalize and transform society only by ignoring two things. One is the day-to-day life experience of commoners (Laski's 'basic experience'). Most commoners in the wealthier states are no longer brutalized in the same way as the nineteenth century proletariat. But conditions of work, for those fortunate enough to have work, no matter how improved relatively, continue, if not to brutalize, to stupify, leaving little inclination for anything but various forms of mindless or semi-mindless diversion. Having little experience of work, intellectuals may not realize the stifling boredom that can descend once a routine mechanical job is 'mastered'. Few jobs, whether factory, office or service jobs demand anything more than the willingness and ability to follow instructions – to do as you are told. As that is what is wanted of them, as that is their *function*, the most pervasive, most basic experience for anyone near the bottom of a hierarchy is the habit of obedience.

The second thing intellectuals ignore is the inseparability of hierarchy and civilization. Civilization's chief form of social organization is and always has been a command/obedience hierarchy. Hierarchy is the only form of social organization most people have experienced. If, as Laski urges, we are 'to accept nothing which contradicts our basic experience', the most basic experience of the million is obedience and submission. Even if the commons were all that Romantics imagine, even if their chief yearning were for liberty and equality, a revolution by the commons can succeed only in replacing one hierarchy with another of a different kind. To expect otherwise is to engage in magical thinking.

All states and civilizations have withered away or have suffered some other form of demise. But states do not wither into conditions of freedom and equality. Nor will they, unless in the time left before the nuclear warriors write their end to civilization we have the wit or the luck to invent alternative forms of social organization that can supplant hierarchy: alternatives to obedience and submission, alternatives to civilization.

7

Reactions and Counteractions

He could not deny that the law of the new multiverse explained much that had been most obscure, especially the persistently fiendish treatment of man by man; the perpetual effort of society to establish law, and the perpetual revolt of society against the law it had established; the perpetual building up of authority by force, and the perpetual appeal to force to overcome it; the perpetual symbolism of a higher law, and the perpetual relapse to a lower one; the perpetual victory of the principles of freedom, and their perpetual conversion into the principles of power. (Adams, 1918/1933, p. 458)

We were before ruled by King, Lords and Commons; now by a General, a Court Martial and House of Commons; and we pray you what is the difference? (The Levellers, quoted in Hill, 1972, p. 87)

Usually I refer to the form of social organization which not only was the origin of civilization, but has remained as civilization's organizing principle, as a 'command hierarchy'. I use that particular term because of a desire to discuss superstratification's simplest form, its ideal type. The use of an ideal type is not meant to imply that modifications and alterations make no difference. An oligarchy differs from a command hierarchy, an aristocracy from an oligarchy, a plutocracy from an aristocracy, and a democracy from all of them. The most obvious difference can be seen by looking at the meaning of the terms: the difference is in the answer to the question: who rules? Is it a single commander? (a Divine King), the few? (an oligarchy), the best? (an aristocracy), the wealthy? (a plutocracy), the common people? (a democracy). All the variations listed put a group, rather than a single person at the top of a stratified pyramid. But democracy puts such a large group (the common people) on top that it seems either to turn the pyramid upside down or dissolve it altogether. Democracy has been the most important political variation on the command hierarchy. Democratic changes in hierarchy's brutal rigidity are of supreme importance to those people who live in democracies. Nevertheless, I shall argue that even the best of democracies continue to be organized as multiple command hierarchies and continue to live by hierarchical values. The only reason an argument is needed is that devotion to the ideals of liberty and equality blinds many moderns to the fundamentally hierarchical nature of political, economic and social reality.

Command hierarchies are machines for dominating and controlling, if necessary by force, coercion or compulsion. In the course of domination the obedient cogs which make up command hierarchies have carried out the hideous crimes that mark civilization's long and gloomy history. Hopes for a less gloomy future depend upon doing something about command hierarchies. Since history can be read as a story of doing things about command hierarchies, continued hope may depend on doing something new about them.

Command hierarchies are at once superb instruments for carrying out the wishes of the person or group on top and the instrumentality which eventually produces a more or less acute sense of enslavement for everyone except the top strata. The humiliation (from the Latin *humilis*, low, lowly, base) of submission can be relieved by the dignity (from the Latin *dignus*, worthy) of command. To go from commanded to commander is a matter of changing rank in a hierarchy. People change their place or status in hierarchies either via individual (selfish) ambition or through political reform, or by a combination of the two.

Individual hierarchical advancement is less important to this story than hierarchical reform. The one rests on ambition, the other on a perception that something is wrong with obedience and with command. Those who try to scale the heights of hierarchy are not hostile to hierarchical values. The route of individual advancement endorses, indeed embraces, the values of superstratification – for why bother to get on top if not to command and be obeyed? Political reform sometimes, but not always, includes endorsement of values that counter or in some way oppose hierarchical values.

Success in hierarchical advancement depends in part on the fortunes of the ambitious and in part on the nature and permeability of the hierarchy. The ambitious can advance by hard work or luck, guile, generosity or bribery, friendship or sycophancy, marriage or sex. The means for advancement are as endless as ambition and have been part of social drama for as long as people have been wounded by the contempt of superiors and flattered by the abasement of inferiors.

It should be kept in mind that historical attempts to modify hierarchy do not confront perfect or ideal-typical command hierarchies. What they have to work on are concrete human institutions and organizations far from the perfection of an ideal type. Even those that appear close to perfection depart from the ideal type in various ways. For example, prior to the coming of National Socialism, even the Wehrmacht, that modern model of military efficiency, was a less than perfect machine. We know this because the Führer found ways to make it even more machine-like. Alexander Rüstow (1980) quotes a German officer: 'Earlier the German soldier had been accustomed to act independently, but the spirit of independence was broken by Hitler's system of regulating to the minutest detail and enforcing these regulations on pain of death or court martial' (p. 628).

Before looking at historical challenges to hierarchy, consideration of that aspect of hierarchy identified by Rüstow's officer can throw light on the staying power of hierarchical organization. Hierarchies all eventually collapse, but some last for a considerable time. What keeps the mass submissive? The position of those at the bottom is just that: they are at the bottom in relation to every measure of worth. Given the relative conditions of those at the bottom, why is revolt not more common? Of course, the part played by force and by belief in forestalling collapse or rebellion cannot be overestimated. In addition life at the bottom can be bearable because most hierarchies limit what they attempt to regulate or command. As every draftee discovers, military machines regulate and command parts of a warrior's life ignored by civilian hierarchies. But even within a military machine many aspects of warriors' lives are their own, untouched by regulation or command. And ordinarily, even in those areas where commands rule, some discretion or independence is allowed and often encouraged. Artists and social scientists have long been aware that alongside their formal command structure hierarchies often have informal networks of power and influence. An entertaining example can be found in Bernard Shaw's *Too True to be Good* with its story of a private (based loosely on T.E. Lawrence) who runs what passes for a regiment, nominally commanded by a colonel.

That it was Hitler who extended regulation and control in the Wehrmacht is not without significance. One of the horrors of modern totalitarianism is the thought that political hierarchies now have the will, the intent, and possibly even the means, to establish total control of all aspects of a person's life: every movement can be observed and regulated, possibly every thought as well. The means of control, to the extent they exist, come from modern science and technology and from my own profession: psychology. In times past commanders may have wished to know and control all, but the wish lacked credible means. Command hierarchies have been civilization's chief form of organization, but typically regulation came from multiple hierarchies and each hierarchy was limited in what its members could be commanded to do.

Axial Teachings

The story of the varying fortunes of hierarchy from the brutal reigns of Divine Kings to the nightmare vision of modern totalitarianism is long and complex and I shall limit myself to noting and discussing a few of the most central challenges to hierarchical values and political organization. An early challenge from religion and philosophy involved a radical transformation, indeed in many cases, a reversal, of hierarchical values. Without such a value transformation no one would ever think it wrong to obey an authorized command since obedience to such a command is a hierarchical virtue. The value transformation began slowly, according to Mumford, between the ninth and sixth century BC with the earliest universal religions, Buddhism and Zoroastrianism. Mumford names (as did Karl Jaspars) the new religions and philosophies 'axial' with the intention of trading on a dual sense of value (Greek *axios*, worth) and centrality (Latin *axis*, hub, axis, axle). If Islam is taken to be the last of the great axial faiths (along with Buddhism, Confucianism and Christianity) the movement continued generating new forms until the seventh century AD.

> This revolt began in the mind, and it proceeded quietly to deny the materialistic assumptions that equated human welfare and the will of the gods with centralized political power, military dominance and increasing economic exploitation – symbolized as these were in the walls, towers, palaces, temples of the great urban centers. All over Europe, the Middle East and Asia – and notably out of the villages rather than the cities – new voices arose, those of an Amos, a Hesiod, a Lao-tzu, deriding the cult of power, pronouncing it iniquitous, futile, and anti-human, and proclaiming a new set of values, the antithesis of those upon which the myth of the megamachine had been built. Not power but righteousness, these prophets said, was the basis of human society: not snatching, seizing and fighting, but sharing,

cooperating, even loving: not pride, but humility: not limitless wealth, but a noble self-restricting poverty and chastity. (Mumford, 1967, p. 258)

Two things stand out. On the one hand thinkers, speakers and writers in the axial tradition have had a profound, indeed dominant, effect on the human spirit, on culture in all its forms. They continue to be read, talked about, admired, emulated and, in some cases, worshipped. On the other hand, despite a softening, modifying and humanizing of hierarchy's brutal arrogance, hierarchy with all its pomps and vanities continues to be civilization's chief form of social organization. If, when compared to early Divine Kingdoms whose slaves were cruelly controlled by whips, truncheons and shackles, modern democracies seem like gentle and humane states, then modern totalitarian states (and some agencies of democratic states) use means of control that make whips, truncheons and shackles look like mild amusements.

The axial revolt both succeeded and profoundly failed. For if most people today have been affected by and indeed endorse axial values, the same people continue to be affected by and to endorse hierarchical values. The moral economy of the million has ample room for both axial and hierarchical values. The same person can believe that 'It is easier for a camel to go through the eye of a needle, than for a rich man to enter into the kingdom of God' *and* believe that to be as rich as possible is the greatest of earthly blessings. Although many axial values are diametrically opposed to hierarchical values, hierarchy has managed to absorb them. In many cases axial values help hierarchy work better. For example: sharing, cooperating and loving are not incompatible with submission and can help make even slavery more bearable.

Axial values can also strengthen hierarchical organization by making it more intelligent. For all its unrivalled coercive power a command hierarchy can be profoundly stupid – as all who have suffered unintelligent commands or bureaucratic rules can attest. For example, hierarchical organization depends upon people doing as they are told. In order for such organization to be stable and peaceful two conditions must be met: (1) people must be content to do as they are told; and (2) superiors must issue commands which, if obeyed, will result in a stable and peaceful society. When things go wrong superiors typically blame inferiors, but by so doing contradict the logic of hierarchical organization. Since superiors usually get their commands obeyed, the fault is not in the subordinate, but in the command. Just as when the good fairy grants a wish, obeyed stupid commands bring misfortune rather than fortune.

Comprehensively intelligent commands cannot be expected from a single intelligence. By loosening hierarchy, by making it more flexible, axial values inject intelligence and so strengthen hierarchical organization. The quality of command is both the strength and the weakness of command hierarchies.

A number of interconnected reasons can be given for hierarchy's successful incorporation or cooptation of axial values. For example, the teachings of some of the major axial prophets became institutionalized and the teachers themselves became gods. A god, of course, is a prototypical hierarch and the worshipper is a model servant. The earthly institutions which were established to serve God and to promote His interests often took the form of a hierarchy. An example, both familiar and extreme, is the Catholic Church, the Church of Rome: a hierarchic structure of bishops and priests dedicated to the glory of God, headed through grace of apostolic succession by God's sometimes infallible representative, the Pope. Anti-hierarchical teachings when spoken by a God through a Pope and glorified and propagated by a churchly hierarchy whose walls, towers, palaces, and temples rival those of ancient Divine Kings have little power to loosen hierarchy's hold.

Another reason has to do with the otherworldly nature of much of the axial teaching. Despairing of reforming this world the kingdom of righteousness is moved to another time, another place, another world. This world, dedicated to the pomp, power and glory of our superiors is an inferior world, a place of sin and a vale of tears. Those who believe in God and in His axial values will have their reward in another world, in a place more splendid than any earthly realm, the Kingdom of Heaven. This world of necessity is doomed or damned to be dominated by hierarchical values and good men and women can only do their best to live as they should and wait for their just reward which will come in the fullness of time.

The language of otherworldliness contains a clue to yet another reason for the failure to unseat hierarchy. Ordinary thought and language is so saturated with hierarchical images, concepts and words that much of the revolt against hierarchy is couched in hierarchical terms. The righteousness which is to supplant power becomes the kingdom of righteousness. The society of the meek and just becomes the Kingdom of Heaven. Language that can be interpreted as a call for a caring, cooperative, loving community can also be read as a description of an alternative form of hierarchy.

Matthew, for example, reports Jesus as saying:

> And call no *man* your father upon the earth: for one is your
> Father which is in heaven. Neither be ye called masters: for one
> is your Master, *even* Christ. But he that is greatest among you
> shall be your servant. And whosoever shall exalt himself shall be
> abased; and he that shall humble himself shall be exalted. (23:
> 9-12, emphasis in original)

And Mark:

> And Jesus answered and said, Verily I say unto you, There is no
> man that hath left house, or brethren, or sisters, or father, or
> mother, or wife, or children, or lands, for my sake, and the
> gospel's, but he shall receive an hundredfold now in this time,
> houses, and brethren, and sisters, and mothers, and children, and
> lands, with persecutions; and in the world to come eternal life.
> But many *that are* first shall be last; and the last first. (10: 29-31,
> emphasis in original)

Matthew uses almost identical words to describe what seems to be
not a society of equals but a turning of the tables, a reversed
hierarchy: 'But many *that are* first shall be last; and the last *shall be*
first' (19: 30, emphasis in original).

Although many of the values of axial religions and philosophies
(such as brotherhood, love, humility) seem incompatible with
hierarchical values anchored as they are in power, axial values had
to become incorporated or lose influence entirely. For the axial
prophets offered no viable political or secular alternative to
hierarchy. Small groups more or less successfully based on axial
values have been tolerated from time to time within hierarchical
states. But the chief legacy of axial values, for those who take them
seriously, is a moral imperative to *believe* in axial values and a
concrete necessity to *live by* hierachical rules and commands.

Democracy

What looks like an exception is democracy, a form of government
which takes seriously some strands of axial thinking. Surely in a
democracy people *live by,* not hierarchical rules, but axial values. I
shall argue that democracy in most cases has proven to be, not an
alternative to hierarchy, but an alternative form of hierarchical
organization.

Democracy – from Greek *demokratia: demos*, common people + -*kratia*, from *kratos*, strength, power. A form of government that gives strength and power, or, as it is sometimes translated, 'rule' to the common people is based on values antithetical to hierarchy. Democracy in modern times has taken many forms. However, the type of democracy that offers the clearest counter to hierarchy is the form it first took in ancient Greece. Some of the Greek city states, most notably Athens, practised a kind of direct democracy in which all citizens participated in the affairs of state. That is, all citizens were eligible to attend and to vote in an assembly empowered to act in executive and judicial as well as legislative affairs. Public offices, for which all citizens were eligible, were decided in some cases by election and in others by the casting or drawing of lots. (Although seldom used then and rarely even considered today, alternating leadership decided by random selection probably is the most democratic means of choosing leaders.)

In his account of democracy in *Politics* Aristotle, no lover of democracy, emphasizes equality:

> The most pure democracy is that which is so called principally from that equality which prevails in it; for this is what the law in that state directs; that the poor shall be in no greater subjection than the rich; nor that the supreme power shall be lodged in either of these, but that both shall share it. For if liberty and equality, as some persons suppose, are chiefly to be found in a democracy, it must be so by every department of government being alike open to all; but as the people are the majority, and what they vote is law, it follows that such a state must be a democracy. (Book iv, Ch. 4, 1290b, 1291b)

In a Greek democratic city state liberty and equality were not enjoyed by all, but only by all citizens. Women were not eligible for citizenship, nor were resident aliens, nor others who failed to satisfy descent criteria – and slaves, more numerous than the free population, had no rights at all.

Direct democracy was possible in ancient Greece because the state, made up of a city and its surrounds, ordinarily had 10,000 or fewer citizens. In other words the number of citizens was small enough for all citizens who so wished periodically to gather together in a single assembly for legislative, judicial and executive purposes.

The direct democracy of the ancient Greeks granted citizens

political power to an extent no modern democracy can hope to match. But, as I have noted, those who qualified for citizenship were only a fraction of the population. Ironically, without the contribution of non-citizens direct democracy would have been impossible: the labour of women and slaves gave their husbands and masters leisure for public affairs. And had women and slaves been citizens the multiplied population would have made government-by-assembly-of-all-citizens unworkable except in very small city states.

Direct democracy in ancient Greece successfully deformed the ideal-typical stratified pyramid. Although some of the greatest of Greek writers had little good to say about democracy, the freedom of interchange characteristic of democratic manners must have had something to do with the extraordinarily creative performance of the tiny city states. Greek architecture, sculpture, poetry, philosophy and drama continue to exercise a profound influence after the passage of more than 2,000 years. Nevertheless, even if all of the accomplishments of the city states are credited to democracy, the seven essential features of hierarchy identified by Mumford continued as characteristics of the city states, most prominently the sixth and seventh: 'the economic exploitation of the weak, and the universal introduction of slavery and forced labor for both industrial and military purposes' (1967, p. 186).

The strength of direct democracy in ancient Greece is that political equality for citizens attained a reality seldom matched; one weakness was that the possibility of citizenship was limited both by notions of who *should* be citizens and by the numbers of citizens who could participate in face-to-face assemblies. In addition the relatively small size of the city states made them vulnerable to the designs of large states. Athens overcame this limitation by organizing a league of free cities under Athenian leadership, but over time methods of voluntary cooperation broke down and Athens behaved less and less like a member of a confederacy of equals and more and more like the head of an empire. The victory of the oligarchic state Sparta in the Peloponnesian War brought an end to the empire and hastened the decline of Athenian democracy – and Athenian creativity.

The democratic challenge to political hierarchy occurred early in the history of civilizations. Greek direct democracy was at its most successful and vigorous in the fifth century BC and continued in some form until the Roman conquest. Democracy then disappeared as a challenge to political hierarchy for nearly 2,000 years, or until interest was rekindled during the religious, political and intellectual ferment of sixteenth and seventeenth century Europe.

Because for centuries it had been the centre of religious, intellectual and even political life, the Church of Rome became the focus of reform. Groups that left the Roman Catholic Church each had different reasons for dissatisfaction, differing attitudes toward hierarchy and individual notions of how to organize a church. The Church of England, for example, except for the absence of a Pope and College of Cardinals, continued Roman Catholic hierarchical practice with archbishops, bishops and priests. The hierarchic structure deriving from Calvinist doctrine stressed the equality of Church members and their right to choose who should govern them. Dissenters such as the Baptists insisted that each congregation must govern itself, choose its own minister, and be subject to no higher body. The Society of Friends, with no formulated creed, liturgy nor separated priesthood (Friends believe in the priesthood of all believers) and no outward sacrament, adopted a consistently non-hierarchical attitude. In the early years the attitude extended to manners (including a refusal to remove the hat as a sign of submission) and to forms of speech (a refusal to use pronouns which distinguished rank).

Religious groups proved easier to reorganize than states. States, whatever else they do, protect the interests of established classes and groups. In times of dissatisfaction and revolt many of those opposing established authority have their own class and individual interests they want to preserve and thus resist calls for thoroughgoing reform even when the calls come from their own ranks. For example, had the Levellers been successful in persuading the New Model Army to support their demands, democracy would have come to England and the modern world over a century earlier than its eventual appearance in North America. The list of Leveller demands was long and included matters of basic rights and economics as well as political reforms. Among the latter were demands for a sovereign house of commons (withdrawing sovereignty from the King and Lords), manhood suffrage, and other electoral reforms designed to make the commons truly representative. As it happened, although popular in London, the Levellers failed to persuade the army as a whole. The Leveller leaders were arrested, the radical regiments provoked into unsuccessful mutiny, which was crushed at Burford in May 1649. Army democracy was finished. So, effectively were the Levellers' (Hill, 1972, p. 56).

The first modern democracy was established by 13 former British colonies after their successful war for independence (1776–81) formally initiated by a Declaration of Independence. Largely written by Thomas Jefferson and a model for the French Declaration of the Rights of Man (1791), the Declaration of Independence contains the memorable sentence, 'We hold these truths to be self-evident, that all men are created equal, that they are endowed by their Creator with certain unalienable Rights, that among these are Life, Liberty and the pursuit of Happiness.' The French Declaration also affirmed liberty and equality and laid down in addition the right of every citizen to property and security. George Washington, the first president of the United States of America was inaugurated on 30 April 1789. A few days later on 5 May occurred the event – the first meeting of the estates-general since 1614 – that marked the beginning of the French Revolution.

Modern democracy has succeeded in modifying political hierarchy in two ways. The first, the franchise, or power to choose representatives to sit in legislative assembly, is the feature most often used to distinguish a democracy from other forms of governance. Yet 'free elections' do not guarantee a non-repressive government. Majorities can oppress minorities and legislators can oppress the very people they are supposed to represent. Governments, even 'democratic' governments, if unchecked, can abuse the power they are entrusted to exercise.

A second, and possibly more important, modification in hierarchy associated with democracy takes the form of various limitations on governmental power that either are written into a constitution or are found in governmental and common law tradition. The framers of the US constitution, for example, took care to attempt to balance the three centres of governmental power – the legislature, the judiciary and executive – in such a way that none would have ascendancy. The first ten amendments to the US constitution are called the Bill of Rights. When combined with latter amendments and the guarantees and limitations written into the body of the constitution there are in all some 40 guarantees of individual rights and limitations on state and federal governmental power.

Just as Greek democracies excluded over half of their populations from citizenship, so most modern democracies began with groups of people excluded from the franchise and unprotected by the rights of citizenship. In the United States all men may have been created equal, but male Indians did not qualify as 'men', nor did males who failed to meet certain property qualifications, nor did male slaves. And women, red or white, poor or rich, slave or free, failed to qualify as 'men'. Such exclusions could not be forever rationalized and gradually those excluded have become included – or partially included. But inclusion still is not complete. For example, efforts to amend the United States constitution so as to guarantee that women have rights equal to men have failed.

Although demands for liberty and equality are central to the push for modern democracies, hierarchy is deformed but not replaced by more equal and free social and political arrangements. The biggest failures are in the realm of the original machines – the military machine and the labour machine. The French, for example, appeared to believe that if a revolution is undertaken for the people, then the people must defend it whether they wish to or not. The Jacobean government in 1793 attempted the compulsory enlistment of all Frenchmen between the ages of 18 and 25 and succeeded in fielding 13 armies totalling about 750,000 men. In 1798 the Directory passed the first conscription law, used later by the Emperor Napoleon between the years 1800 and 1812 to bring 2,613,000 men into his armies. Although conscription is contrary to US democratic ideals it was introduced during the Civil War (1861–5) and has been used in most wars since. Divine Kings employed a relatively small proportion of their subjects in military machines. There seems no limit to the proportion of citizens a modern democracy can draft as cogs in its military machine.

Economic Equality

The labour machine is the other major bulwark of hierarchy in modern democracies. The difficulty was anticipated at the time of the English Civil War by the Diggers (who also called themselves the 'True Levellers'). In 1649 the Diggers, whose theoretician was Gerrard Winstanley, attempted to establish a number of agrarian communities, the best known a colony on common ground at St George's Hill near Cobham in Surrey. Winstanley held that the rich were rich because of the labour of the poor, that buying and selling was the cause of oppression, that private property in land should be abolished, and that a cooperative society should be established.

> The poorest man hath as true a title and just right to the land as the richest man ... If the common people have no more freedom in England but only to live among their elder brothers and work for them for hire, what freedom then have they in England more than we can have in Turkey or France? (Winstanley, quoted in Hill, 1972, p.106)

In the mid-seventeenth century thoughts of revolution were couched in the language of religion. Religious life was still at the centre of things and one of the aims of revolution was to break churchly power: the power to collect compulsory tithes, the power of the Church and its courts to regulate daily life, the power to prohibit any but approved preachers, etc. The language of religion gave to revolutionaries a directness of speech seldom possible in our more complicated age. Winstanley, for example, stated that the Diggers' aim was 'to restore the pure law or righteousness before the Fall' (quoted in Hill, 1972, p. 107). And a bishop, of all people, wrote:

> At the beginning (say they), when God had first made the world, all men were alike, there was no principality, then was no bondage or villeinage: that grew afterwards by violence and cruelty. Therefore why should we live in this miserable slavery under those proud lords and crafty lawyers, etc.? (Bishop Cooper, quoted in Hill, 1972, p. 92)

The Diggers, the Fifth Monarchists, the Seekers, the Ranters and the Quakers were not talking about a better life in the hereafter, but a more just and righteous life here on earth. Christopher Hill has commented on the relationship of revolutionary expectations to the dreams of Francis Bacon concerning the project of science.

> Bacon extracted from the magical-alchemical tradition the novel idea that men could help themselves – mankind, not merely favoured individuals. This together with the dramatic events of the English Revolution helped to transform the backward look to a golden age, a Paradise Lost, into a hope for a better life here on earth, attainable by human effort. (Hill, 1972, p. 132)

The human effort of the Diggers has left little behind except for Winstanley's words. The Diggers were suppressed and dispersed but the contradiction they saw and dramatized, the contradiction between political democracy and economic hierarchy, was not forgotten. The several varieties of nineteenth century communism, socialism and anarchism are theoretical and sometimes practical attempts to get rid of or modify those hierarchies based on and sustained by the private accumulation and possession of wealth in its many forms. The power of communist/socialist/anarchist theories rests on the incontrovertible observation that those who must work for hire do not cease being wage slaves by gaining the vote. The vote in some instances may make the social and economic hierarchy more open to climbers, but the class stratification remains.

The term 'wage slavery' has become a cliché and the condition it describes is universal. If a person who works for hire does not feel like a slave, to what can the term refer? It refers to the simple fact that if in order to live people have to hire themselves to others, they must do as their employers say or starve. Welfare practices in some states have changed the 'starve' to 'go on welfare' or 'go on the dole', but I suspect that, despite occasional rightist claims to envy the unemployed, few would be willing to defend the proposition that people on the dole live in a condition of freedom and equality.

The liberty and autonomy so prized by moderns is largely a delusion based on a confusion between what is valued and what is. Louis Dumont, who identifies liberty and equality as the cardinal virtues of the modern age, describes the confusion:

> The ideal of the autonomy of each person became established among men who were dependent on one another for material things to a much greater extent than all their predecessors. Still more paradoxically, these men ended up by reifying their belief and imagining that the whole of *society* functioned in fact as they thought the *political* domain they had created ought to function. (his italics, 1972, p. 45)

Anyone as dependent upon bosses for material things as are most moderns cannot be free. Just as few whose life is spent subject to society's hierarchies can even imagine a society of equals. In fact our two cardinal values have taken on a distinctly hierarchical gloss: *liberty* has come to mean the freedom to move up in hierarchies, whereas *equality* in modern times has been redefined as 'equality of opportunity', which, like liberty, means the freedom to move up in hierarchies.

Most political debate in the closing years of the twentieth century is based on the assumption that people today must choose between two types of political and economic organization: the Free World or Communism. The Free World is represented by capitalist countries like the United States with its constitutional guarantees of political freedom and its highly stratified economic and social pyramids. Also included are democratic socialist states and welfare states which affirm democracy and political freedom, but whose programme for modifying economic hierarchy is aimed at amelioration, not equality. Communism is seen as some form of Marxist dictatorship dedicated to ending private property and to bringing forward the day when the state will cease to be. Twentieth century experience has confirmed the nineteenth century anarchist judgement that states do not wither away. Marxist dictatorships ruling in the name of the proletariat not only fail to grant equal incomes, but in the name of economic equality have created states in which highly stratified military and civil bureaucracies rule a mass of state slaves.

One way of interpreting nineteenth century political theorists is in terms of axial and hierarchical values. The theoreticians hoped to end the conflict between axial and hierarchical values by creating an axial society, not in the world beyond, but here on earth. With the exception of some anarchists, theorists failed to imagine what an axial society would look like, failed to see that a society of equals could not resemble any previous civilization – that the very forms and structures of civilization both symbolize and constitute hierarchy. They wished to keep some of the features of civilization while discarding others. Taking the seven features listed by Mumford as a guide: (1) the centralization of political power; (2) the separation of the classes; (3) the lifetime division of labour; (4) the mechanization of production; (5) the magnification of military power; (6) the economic exploitation of the weak; and (7) the universal introduction of slavery and forced labour for both military and industrial purposes, most communist and socialist theorists were for ending the separation of classes and the economic exploitation of the weak. Most would oppose, at least in theory, forced labour for industrial purposes, but would be ambivalent at best about forced labour for military purposes. Theorists seem to imagine that a 'communist' or 'socialist' society which retains the centralization of power, the lifetime division of labour, the mechanization of production and the magnification of military power can end the separation of classes and the economic exploitation of the weak. The examples of failed revolutions suggest that societies which retain these elements in order to end the separation of classes and the economic exploitation of the weak in fact retain, if in altered forms, the very oppression it was their mission to end.

The seven features of hierarchical organization are all of a piece and by looking at the purpose of hierarchy it is not difficult to see why. Hierarchy is a machine designed to carry out the interests of an individual or a small class. Free World democracy leaves the social hierarchies and their economic supports intact and (technically) puts representatives of the common people in political command. But who do the representatives represent? Since the hierarchies and their economic supports remain in place, in practice they represent the hierarchical interests of the various classes and groups that make up the hierarchies. Modern democratic politics typically attempt to balance the demands of competing interest groups. Technically, everyone can be heard by a representative, but anyone who believes that representatives can hear the angry shouts of assembly line workers or miners as clearly as the confident whispers of factory owners can do so only by basing their opinion on ideals at the expense of political reality. Representative democracy has not prevented hierarchy from doing what hierarchy is designed to do: serving the interests of the ruling strata.

Communist revolutions have put at the apex of national pyramids a small and dedicated élite who see themselves as serving the proletariat. The élite's ultimate aim is to oversee the decay of the hierarchy and to foster the emergence of a true society of equals, that is, true communism. The élite is convinced that the only possible way to attain communism is for everyone to do as they are told. Since a command hierarchy is the best machine yet devised to get people to do as they are told, the hierarchical levers in Communist countries are kept well oiled. For Communism to emerge, the ruling bureaucracy, having eliminated all dissenters, class enemies and other opponents, would need to take the unprecedented step of eliminating itself.

Any brief account of attempts to ameliorate or overthrow hierarchy must be incomplete. However, one more movement, remarkable for its successes and failures, must be mentioned. One reason wage slavery was experienced as slavery is that the removal of feudal rights and obligations left the will of the new masters or bosses unchecked. (According to the OED 'boss' in the sense of 'master' is an American term which first appeared in the early nineteenth century and which can be applied to anyone who has a right to give orders.) If the boss said 'jump' you jumped. Or if he said to work 18 hours a day, 6 days a week for 50 cents per day, you worked the commanded hours at the specified wage. If you refused you were fired. Ironically, the term 'wage slavery' may not sufficiently describe the vulnerability of those forced to hire themselves to the new capitalist masters. For slave owners in the same period, unlike capitalist bosses, had certain duties and obligations to the people they owned.

The rise of labour unions has immeasurably softened the sting of wage slavery. The story of the attempts to establish unions of workingmen and women is long, complex and unfinished. Once established and legally recognized unions became a check on the will and wilfulness of bosses. When the boss said 'jump' conditions were specified when a worker could refuse. If workers decided that the rate of 16 hours per day for 50 cents' pay was too many hours for too little pay, the union could attempt to negotiate a contract for fewer hours and more pay. Union successes, despite possessing no power except the possibility of withdrawing labour, have been remarkable. Especially when one considers that the military and police power of the state invariably aligned itself with the owners, the bosses.

Unions have contributed immeasurably to making wage slavery bearable, to ameliorating the sting of subordination. Although some union leaders and some unions have tied their aspirations to the establishment of a cooperative or Communist society, the day-to-day role of unions in capitalist countries of necessity has been to soften hierarchical brutality. In fact many unions have become so hierarchically powerful themselves, so fully a part of the social and economic establishment that they can no longer draw upon the moral credit that was theirs in the days when they courageously stood up to the all-powerful bosses. Big unions (mistakenly in many cases) are seen by some as little different from big corporations.

Why has hierarchy proven so resistant to axial transfomation? Much of this book has been aimed at providing sufficient background to answer the question. Certainly our animal heritage is important, as are the psychological consequences of the exceptional dependency of human children. Elias Canetti (1978) states that every obeyed command leaves behind a *sting* that 'sinks deep into the person who has carried out the command and remains in him unchanged' (p. 305). The most common way of getting rid of the sting is to give the same order to someone else. 'What spurs men on to achievement is the deep urge to be rid of the commands once laid upon them' (p. 306). Thus commands recapitulate themselves: privates become corporals and pass on the sting to other privates; children grow up and rid themselves of the sting left by the commands of their parents by repeating the commands to their own children.[1]

Some of our most influential modes of thinking are strongly dependent on analogy with hierarchy. Hierarchical values are potent sources of motivation. Furthermore, with the exception of the few who belong to non-hierarchical groups, humans live their lives in hierarchies of one sort or another. The command/obedience relationship is so ubiquitous that much of the time we are, without knowing it, moved by the explicit or implicit commands of others.

Yet the attraction of axial values remains strong and, if anything, continues to grow. The millions who espouse axial values, who yearn for liberty and equality, for a society of equals, may be dreamers, but most, I am confident, are not hypocrites. Even those who turned autocratic Czarist Russia into an even more bloody totalitarian nightmare typically did so because they believed that their actions would lead to a future society of equals.

All of the background factors are important: biological, psychological, philosophical, moral. But I think that the single most important factor to explain hierarchy's continued dominance is the same factor that made possible its original success. Hierarchical organization was and still is the most powerful and successful engine of coercion ever devised. Since people assume that a military machine can annihilate or conquer a non-hierarchical organization one of two things would have to happen to bring hierarchical organization to an end. Either all groups must agree to organize themselves without hierarchy and to eschew coercion or some non-hierarchical way of defending against hierarchical coercion must be developed.

The Parable of the Tribes

Andrew Schmookler recently (1984) took the notion of the power of coercion and developed it into a theoretical explanation for the course of civilization. His explanation takes the form of evolutionary theory and is based on what he calls the Parable of the Tribes, the lesson of which is: *'no one is free to choose peace, but anyone can impose upon all the necessity for power'* (p. 21, Schmookler's italics).

Imagine a group of tribes living within reach of one another. If all choose the way of peace, then all may live in peace. But what if all but one choose peace, and that one is ambitious for expansion and conquest? What can happen to the others when confronted by an ambitious and potent neighbor? Perhaps one tribe is attacked and defeated, and its people destroyed and its lands seized for the use of the victors. Another is defeated, but this one is not exterminated; rather, it is subjugated and transformed to serve the conqueror. A third seeking to avoid such disaster flees from the area into some inaccessible (and undesirable) place, and its former homeland becomes part of the growing empire of the power-seeking tribe. Let us suppose that others observing these developments decide to defend themselves in order to preserve themselves and their autonomy. But the irony is that successful defense against a power-maximizing aggressor requires a society to become more like the society that threatens it. Power can be stopped only by power, and if the threatening society has discovered ways to magnify its power through innovations in organization or technology (or whatever), the defensive society will have to transform itself into something more like its foe in order to resist the external force. (p. 21)

Schmookler identifies the four choices for the threatened tribes as: (1) destruction (2) absorption and transformation (3) withdrawal and (4) imitation. *'In every one of these outcomes the ways of power are spread throughout the system '* (p. 22, his italics).

Schmookler is right to give central place to coercion and the threat of coercion. The fourth alternative, imitation, has recurred time and again throughout history and is of considerable psychological interest. Imitating the enemy seems to guarantee that the most bloodthirsty, the most unscrupulous, is able to dictate the practices of warfare. We needn't go far back in history for an example of how the behaviour of nations can come to resemble that of feared enemies.

During the Spanish Civil War just prior to the Second World War Hitler gave his fliers some living souls to practise on. When German aircraft bombed the undefended Basque town of Guernica on 18 April 1937 cries of outrage came from all parts of the civilized world. Only particularly evil and coarse barbarians would even think of bombing non-military targets. How could anyone possibly justify such a practice? The world hadn't long to wait for an answer, for in a few years' time the airforces of democratic countries were destroying large cities for no discernible military reason. The justification? Psychology: the raids that levelled cities and killed countless civilians were carried out for their presumed effect on civilian morale. The terror bombing did not, as a matter of record, influence morale in the way those who gave the authorization had hoped.

Fearing the enemy and fearing defeat, an antagonist imagines that the enemy's wicked military practices are militarily superior to more civilized ways of waging war. Thus in order to avoid defeat the enemy's practices must be adopted even if by so doing the antagonist comes to resemble the wicked enemy.

Although terror bombing became an authorized practice of democratic nations it is far from certain that the Allies had to become like Hitler in order to defeat him. The terror bombing seemed to harden rather than weaken civilian will to resist. When later the terror bombing was extended to peasant villages in the Vietnam war, the burned, maimed and dead bodies testified to the power to kill, maim and burn; but imitating the former enemy's villainy did not bring victory; the hideous crimes were part of a lost war. The fact that imitation is not necessarily rational serves to underline the strength of the compulsion. Perceived superior power is imitated. The failure to imitate is seen as softness or weakness.

Over and over again in the course of history states have imitated feared and fearsome rivals. According to the Parable imitation occurs because leaders believe it necessary for successful resistance. It makes little difference that leaders in particular instances may be wrong in their belief. A *claim* of 'military necessity' can justify very nearly any practice. If Schmookler has identified the only choices open to a threatened tribe or state, the outlook for the future is gloomy indeed.

8
Conscience

All the serious perplexities of life come back to the genuine difficulty of forming a judgment as to the values of the situation; they come back to a conflict of goods. Only dogmatism can suppose that serious moral conflict is between something clearly bad and something known to be good. (Dewey, 1929/1980, p. 266)

A single command, if obeyed, can send droves of intercontinental ballistic missiles pushing through the sky on their way to annihilate not just the enemy, but civilization. Scientists have argued and will continue to argue about the precise short-term and long-term effects of a large-scale nuclear attack, about how many might survive and for how long. For many years following Hiroshima scientists and politicians complacently discussed civilization's phoenix-like renewal which would begin at the moment the élite emerged from their fallout shelters. But few today believe that those post-holocaust phoenixes who manage to emerge will find themselves in an environment that can nourish and sustain civilized or even primitive life. A single command, if obeyed, can make history's authorized crimes look like childish pranks.

Whose finger is poised over the button, awaiting command? Imagination can populate underground bunkers with all sorts of possible actors. Who might fill the job description, who is cast in the role? A private, bored and restless with his or her four-hour shift? Or, because of the importance of the post, is it an experience-hardened noncommissioned officer? Or, like NASA's astronauts, might it be one of a collection of élite officers with a sprinkling of blacks and women for equal-opportunity's sake? Or, possibly the 'finger' is electronic, the chain-of-command a series of computers. Computers best fill the casting requirement, for, virtue of virtues, unlike humans, computers cannot disobey, they can only malfunction.

At times voices from the world outside make imagination seem actical, even sensible. A US airforce captain at Whitman Base, a launch officer for the Minuteman III, stated to ... interviewer: 'The fact is, it is possible for four officers in a Minuteman Squadron to launch and start World War III without authorization from anyone ... Naturally, this would be illegal, but who would be around to punish them?' (quoted in Zinn, 1980, p. 567).

Another voice from outside makes it abundantly clear that a nuclear attack – or counterattack – is not a matter of a command, a conscience, and a decision to obey or defy. 'There is, of course, no single "button" to push; the term is a caricature, shorthand for an elaborate set of protocols and arrangements that must be followed to launch the missiles (Ford, 1985, p. 45).'

Ford's description of protocols and arrangements hardly reassures. Computers, of course, *are* involved: for example, NORAD alone (the North America Aerospace Defense Command) has 87 computers for processing 'intelligence' information. The complexities, technological and human, and the time pressure – even in the 'best' of circumstances a matter of minutes to evaluate information and make a decision – seem to ensure that conscience will play little part in the final scene. In fact, since it is possible for the nuclear *deus ex machina* to be set in motion without a command being given, conscience may play *no* part in the final scene.

Milgram's story pitted autonomous conscience against what he called 'malevolent authority'. Conscience lost: 65 per cent obeyed. That Milgram's study is flawed can give little comfort to those who see individual conscience as an effective opponent of authority. For if a laboratory situation could be created that incorporated a true analogue to an *authorized* criminal command far more than 65 per cent would obey – those obeying would be close to 100 per cent of those commanded. Milgram favoured a biological explanation for obedience, whereas I have given my attention to a form of social organization that depends upon obedience and makes of it a virtue. Those who receive authorized criminal commands have been trained to obey promptly and automatically, as if they are parts of a machine. Not only do warriors suffer no obloquy for obeying authorized criminal commands, obeying is their duty, their function and their glory.

At the conclusion of his study Milgram stated that his results 'raise the possibility that human nature, or – more specifically – the kind of character produced in American democratic society, cannot be counted on to insulate its citizens from brutality and inhumane treatment at the direction of malevolent authority' (1974, p. 189). Why did Milgram, why did we, why *do* we think that character or conscience *should* be counted on to enable people to resist malevolent authority?

Before attempting to answer the question something must be mentioned that works as an unvoiced counterpoint to any discussion of obedience. Milgram's 'agentic state' theory and my own emphasis on the machine-like nature of command hierarchies seem to leave little or no room for disobedience. Yet people *do* resist authority, people *do* disobey. Rebellion, though under-emphasized and underreported, is one of history's most common stories. Domestic rebellion, even on university campuses, *especially* university campuses, characterized the very period in which Milgram wrote. 'Wildcat strikes, riots, occupations, absenteeism, and indiscipline broke out in a world plague in the late 1960s' (Skillen, 1977, p. 60). The concept 'obedience' would be meaningless without the capacity to disobey.

When conscience is pitted against malevolent authority an assumption made is that conscience will judge the command to be wrong, immoral, evil. Conscience will judge the killing of defenceless civilians, for example, to be wrong, immoral, evil. But, of course, carrying out *any* authorized criminal command would result in an action being judged wrong, immoral, evil – when not authorized. For the most part those who receive authorized criminal commands believe obedience to them is justified, right and proper. The conscience of most, in order to have a chance of standing up to malevolent authority, would need to be confronted with something more than an evil command.

The 'something more' that enables disobedience, I think, in most cases, is a weakening or loss of confidence in the authorities. The resistance that developed to Hitler and his commands was fed by Hitler's miscalculations, bad decisions and losses. During the period in which Hitler's commands led to success after success, when much of Europe was at his feet and the rest of the world seemed prepared to follow, Hitler was thought a genius. When Hitler's decisions started to go wrong, when the Third Reich seemed headed toward inevitable defeat, his commands were no more evil than before, but his authority was weakened and resistance became thinkable.

In 1917 the seemingly spontaneous resistance, rebellion and disaffection which gripped the huge, but ill-equipped, Russian army was made possible by the gross mishandling of the war by corrupt and incompetent Czarist civilian and military bureaucrats. Enormous casualties (1.7 million dead, 4.95 million wounded, 2.5 million prisoners and missing) were being suffered for no clear purpose. If soldiers refused to fight it was not because conscience suddenly saw that wrong and immoral commands were evil but because those issuing the commands lost their authority. Many of the same soldiers later fought bravely and willingly against each other, some under revolutionary leadership, others commanded by counter-revolutionary White Russians.

Much the same can be said about the United States's experience in Vietnam. From early days in the undeclared war the particularly inhumane manner of waging the war provided ample reason to see its commands as evil. But if, as leaders had repeatedly promised, the war had been quickly and cleanly won, with clear military and political outcomes, nothing like the disaffection, rebellion and disobedience that did result would have occurred. Victory enhances the authority of those authorized to issue criminal commands; but perceived muddle, incompetence and defeat, in some, though not all, circumstances, can undermine that authority and make resistance and disobedience possible.

Character or conscience, not just the sort produced in US democratic society, but that produced in all civilized states from the time of the divine kings until the present, can be counted on to choose obedience, not resistance, to authorized criminal commands – unless authority, by its own incompetence, hubris or corruption has undermined itself. In most cases those who courageously, and often desperately, defy undermined and discredited authority are ready and eager to obey postrevolutionary authority.

If history is witness to the million obeying authorized criminal commands, history also testifies to exceptions. If what is wanted is to produce character or conscience that will defy authorized criminal commands examples can be found in small religious groups which have had considerable success in developing such consciences. In a previous chapter I named three of the war resisters: the Society of Friends, the Mennonites and the Brethren. I do not know if accurate assessment is possible, but it seems unlikely that the three groups have managed in every case to train a conscience that will resist authorized criminal commands. In any war even a committed pacifist may find compelling the case for putting aside the unconditional proscription against inflicting injury and killing. When a state is under threat, or seems to be, a decision to refuse to fight is not an easy one, even for someone brought up to believe that no authority can transform a crime, particularly the crime of killing, into a virtue. Given the difficulty of maintaining non-violence under threat the Friends, the Mennonites and the Brethren have a consistent and distinguished record for producing consciences that can resist authorized criminal commands.

If the object is to produce a conscience that will identify authorized criminal commands as wrong then the essential thing to be grasped and believed is that it is always wrong to harm or kill. Most people do not believe that this is so and do not teach it to their children. Exceptions to the injunction that it is always wrong to harm and kill come too easily to mind. Interestingly, the most popular exceptions do not involve the necessity to defend oneself. Since many are able to imagine themselves dying for their beliefs, it is not a simple matter of kill or be killed, harm or be harmed. The exceptions that persuade involve harm to those we love – spouse, children, parents, siblings. Summoned to a tribunal and asked by the military representative, as was Lytton Strachey in 1916: 'What would you do if you saw a German soldier attempting to rape your sister?' and lacking Strachey's wit and sexual inclination it might not occur to you to reply: 'I should try to interpose my own body' (Holroyd, 1968, p. 179). Instead conscience might waver and you might find yourself admitting to a wish to harm and possibly kill the wicked German.

Because the personal examples appear so forceful hierarchies find little difficulty persuading untrained consciences that, since the wicked enemy is raping their beloved country and would rape their wife/sister/mother/grandmother if he had a chance, it is their duty to defend their country by putting themselves under those authorized to issue criminal commands.

When the country is in little discernible danger as was the case when the US entered the First World War (or the Vietnam war for that matter) the hierarchs have a much more difficult time persuading. In order to be an effective partner in the Great War the US needed to supply soldiers, yet only 73,000 volunteered in the six weeks following the declaration of war in April 1917. Congress voted for a draft. In addition Congress passed a measure called the Espionage Act that provided severe penalties (up to 20 years' imprisonment) for anyone speaking or writing against the war.

The land of free speech used the Espionage Act to imprison about 900 people (Zinn, 1980), the most prominent of whom was the socialist Eugene V. Debs who was sentenced to ten years in prison. (In 1920, campaigning for President from his prison cell, Debs polled nearly one million votes.) The most radical US labour union, the Industrial Workers of the World (IWW), was broken by putting on trial and then imprisoning 165 leaders and by fines of $2.5 million. Academics who opposed the war (for example, Scott Nearing, Charles Beard and J. McKeen Cattell) lost their jobs. Conscientious objectors often were treated with sadistic brutality (Zinn, 1980).

When a nation does seem under serious threat the situation, for most consciences, I think, is much as described in Schmookler's Parable. In order to defeat a wicked enemy one must become like the enemy. If the enemy frightens with particularly vicious and efficient forms of war, we must be willing to counter by using the same means, or if possible by inventing even more vicious and efficient means. Of course, we would not characterize our own use of such means as vicious, but simply as more efficient.

Readers hardly need reminding that today's world is an agglomeration of societies lacking a single social or moral order. Even states seldom have a single moral order. Answers to the question: should I do/not-do? or obey/disobey? can come from a wide variety of sources: religion, philosophy, common sense. Knowing the vulnerability of any generalizations about moral reasoning, I will nevertheless hazard. Underlying the usual 'do as the enemy does', that is, obey authorized criminal commands, is an understandable fear of being subjected by the enemy. Common sense tells us that force can only be countered by force, preferably greater and more fearsome force.

In contrast to what appears obvious to most people, a refusal to harm and kill seems utterly and hopelessly impractical. Unless we harm and kill our enemies they will harm and kill us. For most pacifists the impracticality or imagined consequences of their position is of no moment. Calculating consequences has become so common in modern ethical discourse that we forget sometimes that a person can do or refuse to do something simply because not to do or not to refuse would be morally unthinkable. Yet if the imagined evil consequences of an unresisted rampaging enemy fails to sway a committed pacifist another sort of counterintuitive imagined consequence does. I think that those who turn the other cheek believe at some level that their action may change the heart of the one who strikes it.

A similar belief in or hope for imagined consequences can be seen in two modern movements that have applied the ethics of nonviolence to political problems. Mohandas Karamchand Gandhi in South Africa and in India, and Martin Luther King, Jr, in the United States each made nonviolence the central principle around which actions were based. Gandhi found warrant for disobedience and nonviolence in secular and Hindu sources, King in secular and Christian sources. Each saw nonviolence as not simply refraining from doing something evil, but as a positive force for good. Not only is it wrong to harm or kill an opponent, but by remaining nonviolent, by showing that, even when terrified and brutalized, humans can refrain from violence, an opportunity is created for transforming the opponent.

Throughout history the commonsense response to aggression is to respond in like fashion, to give as good as you get. To remain nonviolent or, in New Testament terms, to turn the other cheek, must appear to many to be mad or, at the least, totally impractical. The common response to being attacked requires you, in some respects at least, to become like the enemy. The nonviolent response embodies the hope, in some degree, that the enemy may become like you. The common response offers no hope of ending history's hideous crimes. The nonviolent response offers some hope. Conscience, in order to be an effective barrier to authorized criminal commands, would need to contain an absolute prohibition against harm and killing.

The question: Why did Milgram, why did we, why *do* we think that character or conscience *should* be counted on to enable people to resist malevolent authority? is only partially answered. An answer of sorts is implicit in the examples chosen. Anyone seeing or hearing the received interpretation of Milgram's studies would know, whether thinking in such terms or not, that an experimenter has no right to order a subject to harm someone. Surely the least that can be expected of conscience is the acuity to identify and of character the strength to resist commands we are under no obligation to obey. The crimes of the Third Reich, particularly the attempt to rid Europe of Jews, Gypsies, Slavs, Bolsheviks, mental patients and other 'undesirables' and 'useless eaters', were so monstrous that very nearly everyone agrees as to their nature. Even the small but growing band of zealots who challenge the usual accounts of Germany's crimes stop short at defending the killing of 'undesirables'; instead they attempt to persuade belief in the astonishing thesis that the killing never took place.

One reason that the question of character and conscience remains unanswered is that I began my discussion by removing the ambiguity from Milgram's subject matter – ambiguity which resulted from his failure to declare whether he was studying authorized or unauthorized criminal commands. The preceding chapters are chiefly about obedience to authorized criminal commands, a plausible way of characterizing the studies. The prominence given Snow's quotation, which is clearly directed to authorized criminal commands, and the intent to create a laboratory analogue to Germany's hideous crimes, which were authorized criminal commands, might suggest that the obedience studies were about history's authorized criminal commands. Yet I think ultimately they were not so interpreted by most people. Little in Milgram's writing suggests to me that he believed authorized criminal commands as such are wrong. I think that whether he knew it or not, Milgram addressed a much narrower and far less clearly defined subject: not authorized criminal commands in general, but conscience and character as a defence against a particular class of authorized criminal commands. This can be seen in his use of the term 'malevolent authority'. Conscience and character should be a bulwark against those authorized criminal commands that come from *malevolent* authority. What is 'malevolent authority?' For most people the answer is simple: malevolent authority is the enemy's authority. Milgram's characterization of malevolent authority was less straightforward. Though unclear, Milgram's subject was somewhat similar to the intended subject of the postwar war crimes tribunals: those actions that are contrary to the customs and laws of war; that is, those criminal commands that go beyond what commonly has been authorized.

Universal Standards?

As Taylor points out, interpretations of the Nuremberg precedent are 'wildly divergent', but beneath the divergent views 'is a common denominator: there are some universal standards of human behavior that transcend the duty of obedience to national laws' (Taylor, 1971, p. 16). Although Milgram repeatedly used Snow's striking quotation and wrote of obedience and authority in a broad and general fashion, he showed no interest in the ordinary run of history's hideous crimes. I think that I do him no injustice to say that his ethical concern was directed to those malevolent authorities (or at least some of them) who give commands that violate 'universal standards of human behavior'. In other words, implicit for Milgram, as for most people, is the notion that obedience is the correct response to most authorized criminal commands. But disobedience is the proper response when malevolent authorities issue especially or extraordinarily criminal commands – those which violate 'universal standards of human behavior'. Setting aside for the moment the problem of identifying the 'universal standards', I shall rephrase my question to read: Why do we think that character or conscience should be counted on to enable people to resist malevolent authorities who issue commands that violate universal standards of human behaviour?

At first glance some readers may think the question naïve or simply wrong. History shows that conscience does *not* enable people to resist malevolent authorities even when they give extraordinarily criminal commands. Who then are the *we* who think character and conscience should enable people to resist malevolent authorities? Milgram is one, but if he were the only one his study would have had little impact. Two assumptions seem to underlie most commentary on Hitler's monstrous crimes: (1) that conscience *should* have enabled Germans to resist Hitler's malevolent authority; and (2) that something in the German character made the crimes possible, that by their failure to resist Germans showed that they lacked something other groups have. The guilt experienced by Germans, many of them unborn at the time of the crimes, is inexplicable without the notion that something like character or conscience was at fault. The efforts of various Jewish groups to ensure that the world in general and the German people in particular remember what happened in Nazi Germany make sense only if they believe that something in conscience, something sensitive to 'universal standards', will respond.

Why conscience? If conscience failed in Nazi Germany what grounds are there for thinking that it can be an effective counter to malevolent commands in future? To place trust in conscience means in effect to expect millions of consciences to agree about the wrongness of particular commands, or to agree about the wickedness of particular authorities. If conscience contains an absolute prohibition against harm and killing it can resist criminal commands as Friends, Mennonites and Brethren have shown. But the conscience we are discussing here is a conscience that will obey some authorized criminal commands and not others. Surely what is needed is a social, a political, solution rather than what amounts to an individual and highly particular psychological solution.

Conscience is considered for a number of reasons, one of which is the general disenchantment with political solutions in western cultures following two world wars and numerous twentieth century revolutions. The eighteenth and nineteenth centuries brought trenchant and radical criticism of existing social, political and economic relationships. But they were also centuries of hope: a millenarian religious hope, an optimistic secular-liberal hope in unstoppable progress, and a radical hope that things would improve 'come the revolution'. After two world wars people might still believe 'you can't stop progress', but with sinking hearts, for the steps of progress seem to lead not to Utopia, but to Armageddon. (For many Christian fundamentalists the millenarian hope has become fixed on *welcoming* that very Armageddon.)   And when the revolutions came, they brought not only expected improvements, but also the singular failure to move toward an open society of equals. A counterpoint to the improvement of abolishing wage slavery was the strengthening of bureaucratic hierarchy and political slavery.

A second reason to consider conscience is that it makes intuitive sense to believe that something common in conscience, some common moral sense, must exist. Human beings are recognizably similar in so many ways that the notion of a human nature is compelling (Midgley, 1978). It is plausible to think that part of what people share is a common revulsion for particular types of acts. But with all its intuitive appeal there are serious difficulties connected with the notion of a universal conscience.

Members of an ideal-typical command hierarchy have no difficulty knowing right from wrong. The commands of authority, malevolent or not, tell them what is right. The font of morality, the standard of right and wrong, is the Divine King. The coming of axial religions provided an alternative source of morality: what are right are the commands of the Prophet or God. But typically, even axial gods did not try to supplant Caesar. God's command might be sovereign in one area of conduct, but in another Caesar's held sway. The situation became more complicated when Church hierarchs, those interpreters of God's commands, became powerful enough to challenge Caesar. In such cases what was right and what was wrong became a matter of dispute among authorities. The million, those not in authority, had to choose which authority, religious or secular, to obey.

An alternative way of determining right from wrong comes from moral philosophy. For over 2,000 years western philosophers have disagreed about how to go about determining the right, but for the most part have agreed that, although it can be done, such determination may be beyond the capacity of untrained thinkers. Thus, for the untrained to know right from wrong philosophers must become the authority, must become philosopher kings.

Medieval life had a remarkable intellectual, moral and spiritual unity (Lewis, 1964), attributable in part to the ascendancy of a universal Church. Learning in general and philosophy in particular was in the hands of clerics and served as a means of helping the Church in its task of interpreting God's will. Philosophy was not an alternative, but rather an aid to authority. The coming of what we now call 'humanism' to fourteenth century Italy was a beginning of the break with the medieval world view. The centre began its shift from God to Man. One of the effects of the shift was to raise the possibility of an individual, with the help of philosophy, asking and answering ethical questions. As the individual became the centre of all, authority came more and more to lose its monopoly. Freedom was exalted by humanists; traditional hierarchical orders which limited freedom became a humanist target.

Traditional hierarchical authority also was a target of Church reformers. In times of medieval unity right and wrong was determined by the churchly authority and (with the guidance of the Church) by the nobility. One of the most important targets of Reformation thought was the monopoly claimed by the Church hierarchy to interpret the scripture and God's will. If the fathoming of God's will is not left to specially trained and endowed authorities, then in some degree or another it must be left to the individual Christian.

Conscience, though exalted, could not be left completely free. If the individual, rather than an authority, is to determine God's will then some assumption must be made that individuals who fulfil certain conditions (purity of heart, humility, election by God, or whatever) will come up with the same answer. Congregations and denominations are distinguished by common belief systems, by agreeing about what is right and what is wrong. But even if Lutheran consciences, for example, can agree with each other, no one has found a way to get all protestant consciences to agree with one another – as attested by the continuing existence of numberless sects and denominations.

The history of science is a story of successfully challenged received authorities. All of the sciences, as a substitute for authority's pronouncements, have worked out ways of interpreting their bit of the world. Scientists may sometimes behave as if *they* are authorities, but are such only to the extent of having a greater trained capacity to use scientific means of interpretation than the nonscientist. Anyone similarly trained can be that sort of authority too. In place of authority the sciences have invented public, agreed upon, repeatable and reliable methods of determining what is. In other words, in place of gods or rulers, science enthroned its authority: method or methods.

A part of the world that scientists place outside their ken is ethics, for they like to think of scientific work as having nothing to do with ethics, as being value-free.[1] In other words science is often characterized as being free of values and, further, to have no means or method of determining value, of determining right and wrong. Science's non-authoritarian ways of determining what is cannot be used to determine what should be. In other words science has successfully undermined authority as a means of identifying right and wrong, but is believed to have no alternative to put in the place of moral authority.

Does any other discipline offer a way or method of determining right and wrong? In so far as the modern world rejects ethical authority philosophy and religion cannot be or become authorities, but at best can show how individuals who wish to know what is right might be expected to come up with identical answers. Alasdair MacIntyre has argued that a crucial Enlightenment project was to provide a rational vindication for just such a morality. And that despite the efforts of philosophers of the stature of Hume and Kant the project failed. '... and from henceforward the morality of our predecessor culture – and subsequently of our own – lacked any public, shared rationale or justification. In a world of secular rationality religion could no longer provide such a shared background and foundation for moral discourse and action' (MacIntyre, 1985, p. 50).

Philosophers may wish to dispute the details of MacIntyre's analysis, but his conclusion can hardly be denied. One of the most striking features of modern life is that people living today have no 'public, shared rationale or justification' for morality. The non-religious are not all Humeans, or Kantians, or Benthamites; the religious are not all Mahayana Buddhists, or Sunni Muslims, or Lutheran Christians. Lacking a shared justification how can the consciences of the million be expected to identify the universal standards that will tell them when to defy malevolent authority? This is not to say that standards cannot be identified, but only that, lacking a shared rationale, people cannot be expected to use the same standards.

At one level rationality and philosophy are not needed to identify universal standards. In spite of the emphasis in both psychology and in fiction (particularly in movies and television) on the pleasure people can take in harming, torturing and killing others, most people seem to feel a physical revulsion at the prospect. Military recruits require rigorous training before showing proper enthusiasm for hand-to-hand combat, even for bayoneting practice dummies. It was clear from accounts that in one way or another the tortured-looking Einsatzsgruppen described in Chapter 3 knew they were doing wrong. Even Himmler was physically moved by the slaughter and had to justify it by invoking a Higher Law. At My Lai, some who obeyed did so under considerable torment.

> Lieutenant Calley and a weeping rifleman named Paul D. Meadlo – the same soldier who had fed candy to the children before shooting them – pushed the prisoners into the ditch ...
> There was an order to shoot by Lieutenant Calley, I can't remember the exact words – it was something like 'start firing.'
> Meadlo turned to me and said: 'Shoot, why don't you shoot?'
> He was crying.
> I said, 'I can't. I won't.'
> Then Lieutenant Calley and Meadlo pointed their rifles into the ditch and fired.
> People were diving on top of each other; mothers were trying to protect their children... (James Dursi, reported in Zinn, 1980, p. 469)

It may be that those who believe that conscience should be able to identify malevolent commands are trusting in human feeling, a natural revulsion against harm and killing. If so, feeling cannot be counted on. For one thing, when successful, military training overrides natural feelings of revulsion. For another, the revulsion is at the prospect of harm and killing, not simply harm and killing in those cases that overstep the limits – that are done at the command of malevolent authorities. A natural revulsion against harm and killing is no help when it comes to distinguishing *malevolent* criminal commands from ordinary authorized criminal commands.

The post Second World War war crimes tribunals made an attempt to draw such a distinction by legal means. The accomplishments of the tribunals were considerable, but they failed in one important respect. The tribunals were victors' courts that established limits for the defeated, but left untouched actions of their own armed forces that might also have violated the unwritten customs of war. An obvious case concerns aerial bombardment. Allied air attacks inflicted far more damage, particularly on civilians (at Dresden, Tokyo, Hiroshima and Nagasaki, for example) than any of the air attacks of the Axis powers. Unchallenged by the tribunals, the terror bombing of civilians for psychological reasons, for the purpose of lowering morale and the will to fight, has become an ordinary, condoned, everyday practice of modern warfare – a common authorized criminal command, not in the special category of malevolent authorized criminal commands. By dealing only with the monstrous aberrations of the enemy, the war crimes tribunals ensured that their own monstrous practices would become common practice in future wars. I fear that Nuremberg's 'universal standards of human behavior that transcend the duty of obedience to national laws' were in fact not universal but, ultimately, the *victor's* standards.

The notion that conscience should be able to identify malevolent authorized criminal commands is based on the assumption that some criminal commands are clearly worse than others. The assumption, I think, is correct: some criminal commands *are* worse than others. In fact some criminal commands (for example, dropping napalm on a peasant village) appear to me so terrible that I have difficulty taking seriously the justifications offered. Which brings us back to the earlier statement of the difficulty: that today we lack a shared rationale or justification for morality. We may all agree that some crimes are worse than others, yet fail to identify the same crimes as overstepping the limits.

An example of differing judgements of the same action can be seen in the case of the former nuclear technician, Mordecai Vanunu, who was charged by the state of Israel with espionage and treason for providing details of Israel's nuclear capabilities to the *Sunday Times*. The state of Israel clearly believes that Vanunu's actions are criminal. In contrast the same actions have prompted the Bertrand Russell Peace Foundation to nominate Vanunu for the Nobel Peace Prize. It is not surprising that a state wishes to punish someone it believes has committed a crime. But the Reverend John McKnight, who in 1986 converted Vanunu to Christianity, has claimed that Israel is in a moral bind. For Israel had executed Eichmann for obeying orders rather than acting on conscience, but now condemns Vanunu for acting on conscience rather than obeying orders.

When questioned about the case, Vanunu's former philosophy lecturer at Ben Gurion University, Dr Haim Marantz, claimed that McKnight's analogy was not logical.

Eichmann was not punished for just following orders; he was punished for following particular orders and Morde (Mr Vanunu) is not simply being punished for what his conscience told him to do but the particular thing his conscience told him to do. (quoted in *The Australian*, Wednesday 12 August 1987)

Marantz went on to say to the *Australian*'s reporter that Vanunu had acted 'immorally'. 'He knew he was working at a place where he had to simply keep his mouth shut.'

McKnight, those at the Bertrand Russell Peace Foundation and Marantz presumably could agree on what Eichmann's conscience should have told him to do, but they sharply disagree concerning Vanunu's conscience. Marantz could call the Eichmann analogy 'not logical' only because he differed with McKnight about the nature of Israel's secret nuclear project. What should a young technician do who finds himself engaged in a project secretly to assemble as many as 200 nuclear weapons? Since the weapons were being assembled in secret the state of Israel cannot offer the usual justification of a need for 'deterrence'. Weapons no one knows you possess cannot deter anything or anyone. For each side the answer is clear but opposite. Israeli officials seem to think they have only to pronounce the word 'traitor' to end the argument, ignoring the fact that had Eichmann's conscience led him to publicize details of the Final Solution he too would have been a traitor.

The history of post-medieval civilizations can be read as the progressive stripping away of oppressive authority. In the field of morality what has replaced authority is 'the individual moral agent [who], freed from hierarchy and teleology, conceives of himself and is conceived by moral philosophers as sovereign in his moral authority' (MacIntyre, 1985, p. 62). One reason conscience is invoked is that individual conscience *is* today's moral authority. The reason conscience ultimately fails as a defence against malevolent authority can be seen in the Vanunu example. If I should say to my fellow moral sovereigns that they should refuse to engage in the assembly of or in any way support the assembly or existence of nuclear weapons and they should answer: 'why'?, I can point to no shared standard or justification that would compel agreement. Unlike the mature sciences, which have a number of generally agreed upon ways of determining what is, where methods have replaced authorities, moral philosophies have various ways, but no generally agreed upon ways or methods – no 'public, shared rationale or justification'.

Responsibility

The drama of conscience vs. criminal command has featured two characters: the person commanded and the authority commanding. Yet, however dramatic, this is not the stage on which conscience ordinarily operates. In the everyday world malevolent authority is opposed, but ordinarily not by direct confrontation or disobedience. James Dursi who refused Calley's criminal command finds himself in a class of heroes whose number is small. The reasons why so few disobey criminal commands are by now familiar and will not be repeated. Conscience, when it takes a stand, ordinarily does so by refusing to occupy the position or status of warrior. Conscientious objectors ordinarily do not join the military and then refuse to obey a criminal command; they refuse to become part of an organization whose purpose is to engage in criminal actions. On the stage of history, for every James Dursi there must be tens of thousands who resisted criminal commands by refusing conscription, by hiding, running away or somehow avoiding becoming an obedient cog in a military machine.

Even the discussion here, focused deliberately on the commanded and commander, of necessity has included other actors. Few of the Nuremberg defendants either issued or obeyed a direct command to kill another. In a command hierarchy the commands from the top make possible the crimes committed by those at bottom, but ordinarily are not themselves direct commands to kill. Yet the courts and common sense can agree that those policy-makers at the top are more responsible than the commander and the commanded. Since conscience is concerned with responsibility it is not difficult to see why a person who believes that killing is wrong cannot in conscience become part of a organization whose purpose is to kill.

Conscience can spread an even wider net. The collective guilt that many Germans feel and many others think they ought to feel is based on the notion that all members of a state bear responsibility for what the state does. Vanunu, for example, was not ordered to harm or kill anyone, nor was he part of an organization which was engaged in harm and killing. His organization was involved in secretly assembling weapons that can harm and kill on an incalculable scale. Since no state can be counted on not to fire its weapons Vanunu no doubt felt responsible for the indiscriminate devastation the nuclear weapons are designed to bring.

It is easy enough to agree that in some sense each member of a state is responsible for what the government does. Even so I must admit that such responsibility seems more plausible in a representative democracy than in a fascist state, for after all, most people believe (however wrongly) that the vote is supposed to result in governments responsive to the wishes of citizens. However, most of those believing in representative government would hold that democratic responsibility is limited to trying to vote into political office representatives who will stop the offending practices. (I suppose those who hold citizens of fascist states responsible would claim that such citizens should work toward ending the dictatorship and instituting representative democracy.) Participating in the electoral process is not nearly enough for some consciences. Approximately 143 years ago the case for sovereign conscience was stated clearly and powerfully in language that influenced (among others) Tolstoy and Gandhi and continues to persuade today.

In 1845 or 1846 (depending on the source consulted) Henry David Thoreau was arrested and imprisoned for refusing to pay his poll tax. The date is important only as a clue to why Thoreau refused. If 1845, it was because of slavery; if 1846, it was because of slavery and the war with Mexico. Because an aunt paid his tax Thoreau was released from jail after an overnight stay. Though brief, his stay in jail produced powerful fruit. In 1848 Thoreau wrote an essay originally called 'Resistance to Civil Government'. In 1849 the essay was printed as 'Civil Disobedience'.

> Must the citizen ever for a moment, or in the least degree, resign his conscience to the legislator? Why has every man a conscience, then? I think that we should be men first, and subjects afterward. It is not desirable to cultivate a respect for the law, so much as for the right. The only obligation which I have a right to assume is to do at any time what I think right. (p. 252)

The final sentence, for me, sums up precisely the assumption behind the belief that people should refuse commands that go against conscience. But more than commands are at issue. In order to always do 'what I think right' I must not undertake the obligation of any status relationship that requires me to do otherwise. In the mid 1800s independence for people in general and Thoreau in particular was more common than today. Thoreau did not undertake any status relationship that required him to violate what he thought right. But no matter how otherwise independent, Thoreau was required by law to associate with the state in one important transaction: the payment of taxes.

I have heard some of my townsmen say, 'I should like to have them order me out to help put down an insurrection of the slaves, or to march to Mexico; see if I would go;' and yet these very men have each, directly by their allegiance, and so indirectly, at least, by their money, furnished a substitute. The soldier is applauded who refuses to serve in an unjust war by those who do not refuse to sustain the unjust government which makes the war. (p. 257)

Thoreau saw clearly how powerfully affected the state would be if a substantial minority withdrew from it their allegiance and denied it their money. But he also saw more clearly than most how difficult such a course would be. Even the minimal state of Thoreau's time made withdrawal a formidable undertaking.

When I converse with the freest of my neighbors, I perceive that, whatever they may say about the magnitude and seriousness of the question, and their regard for the public tranquillity, the long and the short of the matter is, that they cannot spare the protection of the existing government, and they dread the consequences to their property and families of disobedience to it. For my own part, I should not like to think that I ever rely on the protection of the state. But, if I deny the authority of the state when it presents its tax-bill, it will soon take and waste all my property, and so harass me and my children without end. This is hard. This makes it impossible for a man to live honestly, and at the same time comfortably, in outward respects. It will not be worth the while to accumulate property; that would be sure to go again. You must hire or squat somewhere, and raise but a small crop, and eat that soon. You must live within yourself, and depend upon yourself always tucked up and ready for a start, and not have many affairs. (p. 262)

Anyone today who wishes to withdraw allegiance from the state by denying it money faces even greater difficulties. In most cases the state removes its toll from your pay packet before you ever see it. Try and get it back. Nevertheless, considerable consistency is possible even in the days of withholding tax as demonstrated by Ammon Hennacy,[2] an American Catholic Anarchist who openly and successfully refused to pay income tax. With the exception of sales taxes and such like, which cannot be avoided unless one manages to live without purchasing anything, Hennacy lived his life consistently with the principle of nonsupport of the state. But in order to be consistent his life bore a striking resemblance to the life described above by Thoreau. Unless like Hennacy you are willing to own nothing, move often, and work only at jobs that involve no withholding tax your money will support the state whether you like it or not. If that state engages in activity that violates your conscience your monetary support helps provide the substitutes who make that violation possible.

Few people have shown Hennacy's conviction or consistency. Who then has the right to condemn those who obey malevolent commands without at the same time condemning themselves? For if I condemn those who obeyed Calley's command, for example, I am saying that even though, knowing the kind of war being waged, I find it too difficult or inconvenient to avoid paying for my substitute to go to Vietnam, nevertheless I have a right to expect the substitute to defy those commands of which my conscience disapproves.

Why do we think that conscience should be counted on to resist malevolent authority? If we do think so, it is probably because we have not thought or have not given enough thought. It is comforting to think that conscience should be counted on to resist malevolent authority. For what we are saying is that our own consciences can be counted on to resist malevolent authority and that our substitute's conscience should be counted on to resist. Forgotten is that once you are in a rank or status that receives commands to commit hideous crimes the authorities have worked on your conscience. Your conscience has been 'adjusted'.

> Men arrive at basic training with their moral autonomy intact, including the deeply rooted belief that it is wrong to kill one's fellow human beings. That belief is incompatible with warfare. So the Army's solution is 'treatment for an unadjusted conscience,' as a military psychology text once termed it. Each soldier, trained for duty in Vietnam, heard the words of war crimes regulations in one hour of basic training amidst hundreds of hours of instruction on how to obey and how to kill. The method used to train them was simple enough: Don't think, just do what you're told. In bayonet drill when you thrust your weapon forward to impale your imaginary enemy, yell 'Kill!' at the top of your lungs when your left foot hits the ground. Don't think about it, do it. (Goldstein, Marshall & Schwartz, 1976, p. 8)

Believing that conscience should be counted on to resist malevolent authority makes it easier to live a comfortable life, to accumulate property, to raise a family, to be an important citizen.

Then if conscience does not resist malevolent authority it is the substitute's fault. For, of course, the consciences of the upright, good-hearted citizen would have resisted. By all means we must avoid acknowledging the nature of civilization, for a clear-eyed, unfanciful view of the Divine Kingdom we inhabit might lead us to believe that if we are to be consistent we might have to give up our comfortable lives, our property, our families, our status, and exercise our consciences like Ammon Hennacy. Or if consistency does not carry us that far, at least to live like the Friends, the Mennonites or the Brethren.

I have tried to find something in Milgram's term 'malevolent authority' that will explain why he and most commentators have believed that conscience should enable people to resist such authority. The term has no single meaning. I can think of only two clearly defined instances in which conscience can be expected to resist, when people will agree that an authority is malevolent.

The first situation is the one Milgram and his readers thought he had created, a situation in which an authority appeared to be giving a clearly unauthorized command to harm another. In situations in which authorities in fact give such commands, it is hardly surprising that nearly everyone can agree that the commands should be resisted, that the authority is 'malevolent'.

The second situation is one in which an authority gives a command to kill 'one of us'. Who counts as 'one of us' depends on individual conscience. Hitler's minions behaved with exceptional malevolence to a fairly extensive list of enemies. Judging from the literature on the Second World War not all of Hitler's enemies are equally judged 'one of us'. The degree of indignation at the systematic killings depends upon who happens to be the victim. Generally speaking malevolent authorities are the enemy's authorities, but not all of the enemy's commands will be seen as equally malevolent.

Unlike the first situation in which people can be expected to resist malevolent authority, it is unreasonable to expect resistance to a malevolent authority's command to harm 'one of us'. For to the person so commanded the 'one of us' is 'one of them'. And it always has been not only permissible, but obligatory to harm and kill 'one of them'.

9
Conclusion

The system of command is acknowledged everywhere. It is perhaps most articulate in armies, but there is scarcely any sphere of civilized life where commands do not reach and none of us they do not mark. Their threat of death is the coin of power, and here it is all too easy to add coin to coin and amass wealth. If we would master power we must face command openly and boldly, and search for means to deprive it of its sting. (Canetti, 1978, p. 470)

Milgram's scenarios were powerful because we saw, or thought we saw, people engaging in a serious violation of conscience: subjects doing wrong because an experimenter told them to. Although we were *not* seeing what we thought we saw, some version of doing wrong because a superior tells us to is one of history's most common stories. In the late twentieth century, when belief proclaims that conscience should reign, the story takes on particular poignancy. People today are, in MacIntyre's words, moral sovereigns. Quite literally no one has the authority to tell us what is right and what is wrong. Never in the history of the world has moral sovereignty been invested in each individual. Never before have people been so free to decide right from wrong.

Each of us may have responsibility for distinguishing right from wrong, but the world's social and economic hierarchies remain with their superiors and inferiors, their commanders and commanded. In each of the hierarchies in which we find ourselves we are obliged to do what our superiors tell us to do or face the consequences of refusal. We are sovereign in assessing the moral content of what we are told to do, but not sovereign when it comes to doing or not doing as we are told. We are sovereigns in our heads, cognitive sovereigns.

But, you may counter, modern moral sovereigns are free to refuse to do as they are told. True enough, but that is so of anyone, at any time, moral sovereign or not. The contrast I wish to make is between sovereignty in the realm of judgement and of thought and servitude in the realm of practice or action. Without doubt sovereignty in the realm of judgement is better than subordination. In the days before becoming moral sovereigns it may seldom have occurred to anyone that they could disobey a command that went against conscience. Despite the ethical advance, today's sovereignty of people who must do as they are told or face the consequences is hollow and can be acutely painful. True sovereigns are free to do as they wish. For instance, the necessary link between freedom and immunity from consequences is recognized in the practice of academic tenure. Scholars who can be fired for speaking their minds cannot be said to possess free speech, just as sovereigns who can be punished for doing as they think right hardly are sovereign. Such 'sovereigns' can determine what is right but lack even the possibility of backing up their judgements with a shared rationale or justification. People today are cognitive sovereigns who rule only in the kingdom of their own minds.

Milgram's modern morality play at one and the same time confirmed the normality of evil *and* depicted a substantial minority exercising their moral sovereignty. The dramatic scene feeds the illusion that 35 per cent of the population can resist commands to do evil. I have tried to convince readers that, with rare exceptions, they are *not* innocent of complicity in hideous crimes, that the evil made possible by obedience not only is normal, but is an inevitable component of command hierarchies.

I am not denying the possibility of acting according to conscience. Indeed, *individual* solutions to the problem of resisting criminal commands are not arcane, are not hidden from view. We need only follow the time-honoured example of war resisters and refuse to become warriors, refuse to take on a status that can be commanded to harm or kill. If we wish to go further and avoid consenting to substitute warriors taking our place, we can listen to Thoreau and withdraw all support, including monetary support, from the state. In practice, the proportion of the populace willing to take either step has been small. Command hierarchies ordinarily can attract allegiance and when they cannot, they punish those who attempt to exercise moral sovereignty.

If the consciences of modern women and men are at best fragile barriers to authorized criminal commands, can humankind look forward to anything except a future featuring more extensive and more efficient state-authorized hideous crimes? A key to confusions that led me to write this book is that people today, without sense of contradiction, can call state-authorized butchery a crime. At most times in our 'long and gloomy history' Snow's observation that 'far more, and far more hideous crimes have been committed in the name of obedience than have ever been committed in the name of rebellion' would have occasioned little remark or interest – except for his choice of words. Why call necessary carnage 'hideous crimes'? The state must be protected against grasping rivals. Less civilized peoples must be brought under state control. Traitorous groups must be punished. Obedient and skilled warriors are the state's greatest treasure. The patriotic actions of obedient warriors are normal – of course they are normal. But few until modern times would call such patriotic obedience 'evil'.

At most periods in our long and gloomy history a book which attempted to convince readers that obeying authorized criminal commands is a necessary aspect of civilized life would be greeted with puzzlement. For until fairly recently the normality of obedience was obvious to all. It simply is the way things are, the way society works. In hierarchically organized states, in civilizations, the normality of obedience is beyond question.

Only a reader who entertains the possibility that state-authorized carnage can be classified as hideous and criminal will find Snow's observation in any way remarkable. But once state-authorized slaughter is considered evil, then the normality of evil is beyond question. This book is needed only because moderns appear to believe (somehow) that obedience to authorized commands, no matter how hideous or criminal, is not normal practice in all states. If, as in former times, the workings of hierarchy and command were obvious to all, both 'normality theses' – the normality of obedience and the normality of evil – would appear commonplace, even banal. That it is not obvious points to a widespread collective confusion which serves to mask the everyday reality of unfreedom and absence of equality. The Divine King's rule is not obvious because of a confusion between what-ought-to-be and what-is.

Moderns believe (about themselves, but not their enemies) something like: both what-ought-to-be and what-is is a society of individuals freely acting on the basis of conscience who are members of a rational, peace-loving state organized on the basis of liberty and equality. I have attempted to show that the world moderns inhabit is made up of cognitive moral sovereigns free to imagine and (sometimes) to speak as they like who are members of states organized on the basis of obedience to command and inequality.

Good intentions and propaganda have contributed to confusing what-ought-to-be and what-is. For several hundred years people have engaged in a collective project to create a new age of peace and plenty, liberty and equality. The modern age (beginning with the early humanists and Church reformers) set out to install a society based on axial values. Prior to modern times people hardly could mistake the nature of the social world they inhabited. The home of axial values was not in this corrupt world but was believed to be either in a past golden age or in a future other world. In early modern times a new-found confidence in human powers served to shift the location of value away from God and the past and future to Man (more recently to Man and Woman) and the present. The activities set in motion in a number of fields – religious, political, economic, technological – have produced rapid, undigested and continuing change. And, while all was changing, we have been told and have told ourselves, over and over again, that such changes are progressive and lead inevitably in the direction we intend. When unintended consequences come to our attention they are defined as temporary, sure to be overcome in the march of progress and science.

Confidence can distract us, belief and hubris make us blind. How else can we explain the failure to see the obvious – that the two great values of modern times cannot be shifted out of the realm of what-ought-to-be into the hierarchically organized world of what-is? How can we explain the failure to see that equality and hierarchy are not only incompatible, but antithetical? Or that liberty too is incompatible with and antithetical to hierarchy? Anyone obliged to obey the commands of another is hardly free. Progress within the context of hierarchically organized societies can modify the structure and change the content of status obligations, but cannot deliver a condition of freedom and equality, cannot deliver us from the flight command.

In the confident surge toward an earthly paradise something else overlooked (something which continues to be ignored or denied) is the nature of the means being used. The means to earthly paradise are, as might be expected, the Divine King's. The new age of ease, peace and plenty was and is to be brought about by subduing, controlling and *commanding* nature – just as the early Divine Kings installed their personal paradise by subduing, controlling and commanding people.

The conditions of human life have changed drastically over the past few centuries, largely because of the potency of the idea of power. We continue to worship the principle that has brought us to this pass, without considering the nature of the pass. We seek solutions in the very mode of thinking/acting that has caused the problems. (French, 1986, p. 556)[1]

The Divine King's means, the ways of command, are so firmly embedded, seem so obvious and reasonable, that when they go wrong, when, for example, the use of technology to command nature bids fair to turn the planet into a desert or an ever-rising sea, the cry goes up for more power and more technology to solve the problem. Even though greater command over nature brought about the problem, the difficulties can be solved only by continuing to increase power over nature. Or if another of Techne's triumphs – nuclear weaponry – threatens to bring an end to nature and to civilization, then civilization (or one corner of it) will be saved by a super-technological shield.

Examples are too common to warrant iteration. The noble dream of the scientific and technological/industrial revolution was to install a new world of peace and plenty that was believed to be axial in nature. For the benefits brought by command over nature were intended for everyone. But, of course, even with the best will and intentions, that is not the way things work in hierarchical societies. Power and benefits in hierarchies are not distributed equally to everyone. The conquest and subjugation of nature, even if successful, at best can have mixed benefits.

> There neither is nor can be any simple increase of power on Man's side. Each new power won *by* man is a power *over* man as well. Each advance leaves him weaker as well as stronger. In every victory, besides being the general who triumphs, he is also the prisoner who follows the triumphal car. (Lewis, 1943/1978, p. 36, his italics)

Dethroning the Divine King

A basic, indeed necessary, requirement for an axial society, for freedom and equality, is giving up the ways of power, the use of the flight-command. An axial society would not resemble and could not resemble any known state or civilization. If I am right about the necessary requirement most people will conclude, on the basis of history and personal experience, that an axial society is impossible. For how can hierarchy be persuaded to relinquish power and command except by taking it away? Any revolutionist will tell you that states can be overthrown only with power. Revolutionists may be right, but each successful use of power to seize power – even when done in the name of liberty and equality – has installed a new and typically more powerful hierarchy. Even when, as in

India, the old hierarchy was persuaded to withdraw largely through nonviolent means new hierarchies were immediately installed. Of course, sensible readers might interject, if instead of new hierarchies India had established a community of axial villages, how could they possibly defend themselves against other states that continue with the ways of command? Even supposing all of the world's states could be persuaded to give way to axial communities, what could prevent those who continue to love command from subduing the axial communities and establishing new Divine Kingdoms? What can possibly withstand force except stronger force?

I do not know the answers to the three questions. The questions, which have been there in some form since the first military machine and the first Divine Kingdom, suggest two ways of responding, the first of which is to assume, as 'realists' have done throughout history, that the questions are unanswerable. The normality of evil is a necessary evil. Liberty and equality simply must flourish as best they can (and when they can) within the context of hierarchy, of civilization. The second way of responding, which is to look for answers to the questions, may turn out to be less unrealistic than it sounds. Two changes which have occurred over the past 300 years suggest that, as hopelessly unanswerable as the questions sound, intelligible answers to them may nevertheless be possible.

The first change is the failed good intention described earlier: that in recent centuries thinkers from a number of viewpoints have believed and argued that we *should* and can have an earthly equalitarian society. Whereas some in the course of the centuries actually have acted on principles of freedom and equality, most of those advocating an equalitarian society have *not* believed that in order to achieve such a society the ways of command must be forsworn. Usually they have held that power could be contained or balanced in a society of free and equal citizens. Marx was even able to persuade himself that the state and its control somehow would manage magically to wither away. And some anarchists who saw the state as the enemy of freedom and equality thought that the state could be removed only by force and violence. But a few thinkers have been able to avoid confusing what-ought-to-be with what-is. For example, Winstanley over 300 years ago consistently held that power cannot be removed from social life with power. Some people (Tolstoy, for one) have attempted as individuals to act in ways consistent with renouncing force. From as early as the sixteenth century people have joined together in attempts to establish equalitarian communities within hierarchical states. In the twentieth century large-scale movements led by Gandhi and King, by abjuring power, have acted from the principle of nonviolence to bring about changes in the hierarchical state. A few scholars have begun to give nonviolent action serious attention, Gene Sharp going so far as detailing a way of *Making Europe Unconquerable* (1985) through cooperative, nonviolent means.

Imagining, desiring and attempting equalitarian community is a necessary step toward the realization of such community. Even so the distance to cover between that step and giving up the ways of power is great. A second change in the world makes giving up the ways of command less unthinkable than it was in the past. The ways of hierarchy have literally reached a dead end. Apologists for hierarchy and its power to command always have thought of themselves as hard-headed, realistic and tough – particularly compared to the soft, idealistic types who insist on such unrealistic things as community, freedom and equality. Yet history contains no more striking example of blindly wishful thinking than the assertion of today's apologists that the destructive power at the command of modern-day Divine Kings will not be used. Power, as always, is there for Divine Kings to use and it will be used if for no other reason than the modern substitute for disobedience – 'computer error'. Only if a Divine King's wish can be fulfilled without resorting to the destructive power at his or her command will that power not be used – except by mistake. The great Satan probably had no wish to blow an Iranian civilian airliner out of the sky, but all died nonetheless.

The possibility of a less gloomy future depends in the first instance on acknowledging that, with rare exceptions, we are *not* innocent of complicity in hideous crimes, that the evil contingent upon obedience indeed is normal – an inescapable component of command hierarchies. I have written, in the literal meaning of the word, as an iconoclast. Knowing how resistant even insignificant local idols are to breakage I cannot hope to have done more than point to the identity and areas of command of the most powerful of idols. I cannot tell readers how the icon can be broken, but I can hope that those convinced of the extent to which the myth of the Divine King has dominated human thought, imagination and practice will contribute to the conjoint task of discovering ways of dethroning the idol-of-idols.

Searching for alternative ways of thinking and living together must seem like a forlorn, utopian hope. It is. But if my reading of the logic of hierarchy is only roughly correct the hope not only is more attractive but also is less forlorn or utopian than the hope that modern-day Divine Kings will not use their nuclear weapons. Or that the drive to enslave nature will not make the planet uninhabitable.

What began with reflections on obedience concludes with musings on the future. It will be obvious to anyone who has read this far that I see little hope for the future – unless somehow we can break the Divine King's hold on our imagination, thought and practice. His hold can be broken only if we believe that it must be broken. I have written hoping to convince that only by breaking, and breaking with, the idol can we begin to create a society in which evil is not normal and liberty and equality are more than words used to describe degrees of bondage.

Elias Canetti ended *Crowds and Power* with the sentence: 'If we would master power we must face command openly and boldly, and search for means to deprive it of its sting.' 'Master' is the wrong word. The means when found will not be the Divine King's.

Notes

Chapter 1

1. The state, of course, also authorizes police and other authorities to use force against those of their own citizens called 'criminals' or 'suspected criminals', to harm and kill them, if necessary, in the 'line of duty'. Most of what I have to say about military authorized criminal commands is relevant to the police and similar authorities.

2. The political messsage is connected with what Arthur Miller calls the 'normality thesis': 'that people who would not ordinarily be described as unusual, deviant, sick, mentally ill, or pathological are capable of committing acts of unrestrained violence and evil' (1986, p. 184). The normality thesis is compatible with a theoretical assumption held by a large percentage of social scientists: that social environment or circumstance determines (is responsible for) what people do. Miller seems to think that critics of Milgram reject the normality thesis for some version of the 'pathology thesis'. The pathology thesis, for example, would account for the monstrous behaviour of the Nazis and those under their command in terms of personal pathology. Those who hold one of the various forms of the pathology thesis can believe that vile behaviour is limited to vile people. Believers in the pathology thesis will find no support for their theories in this book.

Chapter 2

1. The most original and perceptive modern discussion of obedience I have found is by novelist and playwright Elias Canetti in his nonfiction masterwork *Crowds and Power*. Originally published as *Masse und macht* by Classen Verlag, Hamburg, in 1960, the book first appeared in English in 1962. Elias Canetti was awarded the Nobel Prize for Literature in 1981.

2. Arthur G. Miller (1986) has attempted to describe and evaluate the popular and scholarly reactions to Milgram's simulations. His bibliography is an invaluable resource for the curious.

3. Each time Milgram quoted Snow he omitted, without ellipsis, the words in italics. Since the words add power to the passage I assume error best explains their omission.

4. Defenders of deception like to engage in obfuscation – usually by claiming that it is deceptive to withhold information and that all experimenters withhold information. Information, of course, can be withheld for all sorts of reasons. What usually is objectionable about 'deception experiments' is the attempt to get people to believe something that is not true. Diana Baumrind (1985) has done a great deal to straighten out the issues. See also Noble (1984) and Mixon (1977).

5. My debt to Orne's work (particularly to the 1962 paper and to Orne and Evans, 1965) is great: Orne has identified the essential ingredients for understanding the special nature of the social psychological laboratory. Lacking knowledge of Orne's work I doubt if I could have understood Milgram's scenes. In addition, the PhD dissertation of Orne's collaborator, Charles Holland (1968), provided me with a script of Milgram's study that made my own simulations possible. At the time I wrote my dissertation in 1971 I had a copy of Holland's thesis, but was unaware of Orne & Holland's critical work on Milgram's studies (Orne and Holland, 1968). As might be expected considering my debt to them, their analysis of the situation anticipates mine in many respects. For example, we point to the importance of many of the same situational clues and cues. However, we draw different conclusions. Orne and Holland claim that the conflicting clues and cues lead to suspicion, whereas I think that the essential result of the ambiguity is contrasting definitions of the situation: if you can believe the experimenter you can continue; if not, you must defy him. Holland's dissertation research was able to identify suspicious subjects. Unfortunately for explanation in terms of suspicion the suspicious subjects obeyed and defied in the same proportions as non-suspicious subjects. In other words, suspicion seems not to affect behaviour, does not tell subjects what they ought to do.

6. Readers familiar with Milgram's theory might counter my conclusion with a claim that the agentic state prevented them from disobeying. But an agentic state that powerful would also negate the need for deceiving the subjects in the first place. Lying is necessary only if an experimenter believes that knowledge of what should be done enables some (or all) subjects to do it. Milgram and his supporters seem to simultaneously believe that knowledge enables moral action *and* that an agentic state prevents moral action.

7. The curious can find the complete text of all the descriptions I used in the Appendix of my dissertation (Mixon, 1971).

8. 'Free World' writers who see the dangers of the supposedly 'Communist' belief that 'the end justifies the means' usually fail to

see that precisely the same justification is used by scientists of all persuasions – and by others whose ends they approve.

Chapter 3
1. Two ways of explaining the unexplainable are in contention: reasons and causes. When faced with the baffling willingness of so many subjects to follow instructions that clearly seemed to involve harm and killing, Milgram did what he was trained to do: he administered tests that might point to a cause or to causes. Perhaps something in the personality of subjects caused some to obey and others to defy. Of tests administered only the California F Scale (authoritarianism) gave promising results. But although taken as a group the obedient subjects tested scored higher on the trait 'authoritarianism' than defiant subjects, the test could not distinguish individuals who obeyed from individuals who defied (Elms and Milgram, 1966). Only after the failure of efforts to explain by personality characteristics did Milgram attempt to do the job with a state theory. But since the state that allegedly causes the obedience cannot be identified independently of whether or not the subject obeys, the state theory provides a less than satisfactory explanation.

In contrast to Milgram's state explanation my own account is in terms of reasons or grounds, not of causes. The reason that some participants obeyed and some defied is that some trusted the 'experimenter' sufficiently to stay in the experiment, whereas others did not. An explanation based on reasons or grounds depends on plausibility, not upon independently identifying an alleged cause. Although they did not deal with reasons or grounds, my early papers (Mixon, 1971, 1972, 1974, 1976, 1979) laid the groundwork for such an account. The work was a purely contextual analysis designed to offer a thorough understanding of the situation Milgram created. Fortunately such understanding is precisely what is needed to establish plausibility for a reasoned account. Trust and lack-of-trust is a plausible explanation if readers believe that the situation offered good grounds to either trust or mistrust the 'experimenter'. Rom Harré must be given credit for interpretation in terms of trust. Not until I read his account of Milgram's work in *Social Being* (1979) did I realize how central was the notion of trust to understanding why some participants obeyed and some defied. Even though I appreciated Harré's account it did not occur to me to use it until I read A. R. Louch's *Explanation and Human Action* and decided that action simply cannot be understood unless such things as reasons, grounds and justifications are examined.

Although reasons, grounds and justifications are not what

orthodox social psychologists look for, like everybody else they manage implicitly to use them. The reason Milgram thought he had created a situation that called for a causal explanation was that there did not appear to be any good reason for subjects to obey. Lacking a reason he looked for a cause.

2. An exception is PhD work currently in progress by Debra Keenahan of the University of Wollongong. I have benefited from discussing dehumanization and related concepts with Ms Keenahan and by reading drafts of her thesis.

Chapter 4

1. Bill Noble pointed out to me the following passage from *Gorky Park* (written by M.C. Smith and published by Collins in 1981).

'If I follow orders, then you call me a killer. What did I care about those prisoners from Vladimir Prison? There was nothing personal – I didn't even know them. All they were to me were enemies of the state, and I had the job of getting rid of them. Not everything in the world can be done with perfect legality – that's why we are given intelligence. You must have figured out I had orders. But on a whim, out of some hypocritical superiority, you want to bring a case against me – in other words, to kill me for doing my duty. So you're worse than a killer; you're a snob. Go ahead, laugh, but admit there's a difference between duty and sheer egotism.'

'You have a point,' Arkady conceded.

'Aha! Then you knew I was following orders – '

'Whispers,' Arkady said, 'you were following whispers.'

'Whispers, then – so what? What happens to me if I hadn't done it?'

'You leave the KGB, your family doesn't talk to you, you're an embarrassment to your friends, you can't go to special stores anymore, you're moved to a smaller apartment, your children lose their tutors and fail the university examinations, you drop off the rolls for cars, you're never trusted in any new job you're given – and, besides, if you hadn't killed them, someone else would. I had a lousy marriage, no kids, and I didn't especially care if I had a car.'

'My point exactly!'

Chapter 7

1. Canetti's discussion of the command (1978, pp. 303–33) is richly psychological and offers a complementary counterpoint to my own discussion of obedience which concentrates on context.

Chapter 8

1. Max Scheler claimed that the scientist's belief in value freedom is a delusion. 'To conceive the world as value-free is a task which men set themselves on account of a value: the vital value of mastery and power over things' (quoted in Leiss, 1972, p. 109). Many scientists and some philosophers of science show considerable sensitivity to this issue. They would like to believe and like us to believe that whereas technicians are engaged in attaining mastery and power over things scientists confine themselves to something more abstract: truth or knowledge perhaps. I think it clear that whereas scientists are in search of knowledge, they value knowledge of a particular sort. And I think it hardly accidental that the sort of knowledge scientists value and produce is knowledge that enables mastery and power over things.

2. Hennacy's story can be found in *The Book of Ammon* by Ammon Hennacy. The edition I own was privately printed and bears no date. 'A final word from the author' locates Hennacy at 1131 South 1st West, Salt Lake City, Utah and is dated 11 December 1964. My use of the past tense in the text is an inference only. Hennacy was born in 1893.

Chapter 9

1. I read Marilyn French's brilliant *Beyond Power* after completing this book. It is a thorough, far-seeing and readable anatomy of hierarchy in which French writes convincingly of the need for wholly new ways of thinking, imagining and living together. She usually refers to what I call 'command hierarchy' as 'patriarchy' – an entirely apt usage.

References

Adams, H. (1919/1931). *The education of Henry Adams*. New York: Modern Library.

Allen, B.P. (1978). *Social behavior: Fact and falsehood*. Chicago: Nelson-Hall.

Arendt, H. (1964). *Eichmann in Jerusalem: A report on the banality of evil*. New York: Viking.

—— (1972). *Crises of the republic*. New York: Harcourt Brace Jovanovich.

—— (1978). *The life of the mind: Willing*. London: Secker & Warburg.

Banuazizi, A., & Movahedi, S. (1975). 'Interpersonal dynamics in a simulated prison: A methodological analysis.' *American Psychologist, 30*, 152–60.

Barzun, J. (1964). *Science: The glorious entertainment*. New York: Harper & Row.

Baumrind, D. (1964). 'Some thoughts on the ethics of research: After reading Milgram's "Behavioral study of obedience".' *American Psychologist, 19*, 421-3.

—— (1985). 'Research using intentional deception: Ethical issues revisited.' *American Psychologist, 40*, 165–74.

Becker, E. (1975). *Escape from evil*. New York: Free Press.

Canetti, E. (1978). *Crowds and power*. New York: Seabury.

Capra, F. (1983). *The turning point: Science, society, and the rising culture*. New York: Bantam Books.

Chorover, S.I. (1979). *From Genesis to genocide*. Cambridge, Mass.: MIT Press.

Conot, R.E. (1983). *Justice at Nuremberg*. London: Weidenfeld & Nicolson.

Dewey, J. (1929/1980). *The quest for certainty*. New York: Perigee Books.

Corson, D. (1986). *The lexical bar*. Oxford: Pergamon.

Dumont, L. (1972). *Homo hierarchus*. London: Paladin.

Duncan, H.D. (1962). *Communication and social order*. London: Oxford University Press.

Elias, N. (1978). *The civilizing process*. New York: Urizen Books.

Elms, A. & Milgram, S. (1966). 'Personality characteristics associated with obedience and defiance toward authoritative command.' *Journal of Experimental Research in Personality, 1*, 282–9.

Ford, D. (1985). 'The button.' *The New Yorker,* 1 April, 43–91.

French, M. (1986). *Beyond Power: on women, men and morals.* London: Abacus.

Fromm, E. (1973). *The anatomy of human destructiveness.* New York: Holt, Rinehart & Winston.

Goldstein, J., Marshall, B., & Schwartz, J. (1976). *The My Lai massacre and its cover-up: Beyond the reach of law?* New York: Free Press.

Haney, C., Banks, W.C. & Zimbardo, P.G. (1973). 'Interpersonal dynamics in a simulated prison'. *International Journal of Criminology and Penology, 1,* 69–97.

Harré, R. (1979). *Social being: A theory for social psychology.* Oxford: Basil Blackwell.

—— & Secord, P.F. (1972). *The explanation of social behaviour.* Oxford: Basil Blackwell.

Hilberg, R. (1985). *The destruction of the European Jews.* 2nd ed. New York: Holmes & Meier.

Hill, C. (1972). *The world turned upside down.* New York: Viking.

Holland, C.H. (1968). *Sources of variance in the experimental investigation of behavioral obedience.* (Doctoral dissertation, University of Connecticut) Ann Arbor, Mich.: University Microfilms. No. 69–2146.

Holroyd, M. (1968). *Lytton Strachey: A critical biography.* Vol. II. New York: Holt, Rinehart & Winston.

Johnstone, K. (1979). *Impro: Improvisation and the theatre.* New York: Theatre Arts Books.

Koestler, A. (1978). *Janus.* London: Hutchinson.

Laski, H.J. (1929). 'The dangers of obedience'. *Harpers Magazine, 159,* 1–10.

Laurent, J. (in press). Milgram's shocking experiments: A case in the social construction of 'science'. *Indian Journal of History of Science.*

Leiss, W. (1972). *The domination of nature.* New York: George Braziller.

Lewis, C.S. (1943/1978). *The abolition of man.* Glasgow: Collins.

—— (1964). *The discarded image.* Cambridge: Cambridge University Press.

Louch, A.R. (1966). *Explanation and human action.* Oxford: Basil Blackwell.

MacIntyre, A. (1985). *After virtue.* 2nd ed. London: Duckworth.

Maclay, G. & Knipe, H. (1972). *The dominant man.* New York: Dell.

Midgley, M. (1978). *Beast and Man.* Ithaca, N.Y.: Cornell University Press.

Milgram, S. (1963). 'Behavioral study of obedience'. *Journal of Abnormal and Social Psychology, 67,* 371–8.

—— (Producer) (1965). *Obedience* (Film). New York: New York University Film Library.

—— (1972). 'Interpreting obedience: Error and evidence: A reply to Orne and Holland'. In A.G. Miller (Ed.), *The social psychology of psychological research.* New York: The Free Press.

—— (1974). *Obedience to authority.* New York: Harper & Row.

Miller, A.G. (1986). *The obedience experiments; A case study of controversy in social science.* New York: Praeger.

Mixon, D. (1971). *Further conditions of obedience and disobedience to authority.* (Doctoral dissertation, University of Nevada) Ann Arbor, Mich.: University Microfilms, No. 72–6477.

—— (1972). 'Instead of deception'. *Journal for the Theory of Social Behaviour, 2,* 145–77.

—— (1974). 'If you won't deceive, what can you do?' In N. Armistead (ed.) *Reconstructing social psychology.* London: Penguin Education.

—— (1976). 'Studying feignable behaviour'. *Representative Research in Social Psychology, 7,* 89-104.

—— (1977). 'Why pretend to deceive?' *Personality and Social Psychology Bulletin, 3,* 647-53.

—— (1979). 'Understanding shocking and puzzling conduct.' In G.P. Ginsburg (ed.) *Emerging strategies in social psychological research.* New York: Wiley.

—— (1980). The place of habit in the control of action. *Journal for the Theory of Social Behaviour, 10,* 169-86.

—— (1986). The place of behaviour in psychological experiments. *Journal for the Theory of Social Behaviour, 16,* 123–37.

Mumford, L. (1967). *The myth of the machine: I. Technics and human development.* New York: Harcourt Brace Jovanovich.

Noble, W.G. (1984). 'Ethics, psychologists' practices, and psychological theory'. In M. Nixon (ed.) *Issues in psychological practice.* Melbourne: Longman Cheshire.

Ogilvy, J. (1979). *Many dimensional man: Decentralizing self, society, and the sacred.* New York: Harper & Row.

Orne, M.T. (1962). 'On the social psychology of the psychological experiment. With particular reference to demand characteristics and their implications.' *American Psychologist, 17,* 776–83.

—— & Evans, F.J. (1965). 'Social control in the psychological experiment: Antisocial behavior and hypnosis.' *Journal of Personality and Social Psychology, 1,* 189–200.

—— & Holland, C.H. (1968). On the ecological validity of laboratory deceptions. *International Journal of Psychiatry, 6,* 282–93.

Patten, S.C. (1977a). 'The case that Milgram makes.' *Philosophical Review, 86,* 350–64.

—— (1977b). 'Milgram's shocking experiments.' *Philosophy, 52,* 425–40.

Rosenberg, M.J. (1969). 'The conditions and consequences of evaluation apprehension.' In R. Rosenthal & R.L. Rosnow (eds.) *Artifact in behavioral research.* New York: Academic Press.

Rüstow, A. (1980). *Freedom and domination: A historical critique of civilization.* Princeton, N.J.: Princeton University Press.

Schmookler, A.B. (1984). *The parable of the tribes: The problem of power in social evolution.* Berkeley: University of California Press.

Sharp, G. (1985). *Making Europe unconquerable.* Cambridge, Mass.: Ballinger.

Skillen, A. (1977). *Ruling illusions.* Hassocks, Sussex: Harvester.

Skinner, B.F. (1972). *Beyond freedom and dignity.* London: Jonathan Cape.

Snow, C.P. (1961). 'Either-or.' *Progressive,* February 1961, 24–5.

Taylor, T. (1971). *Nuremberg and Vietnam.* New York: Bantam.

Thoreau, H.D. (1965). *Walden and On the duty of civil disobedience.* New York: Harper & Row.

Tinbergen, N. (1974). Ethology and stress diseases. *Science, 185,* 20–7.

Tusa, A. & Tusa, J. (1984). *The Nuremberg trial.* New York: Atheneum.

Weber, M. (1946). 'Politics as a vocation.' In H.H. Gerth & C.W. Mills (eds.) *From Max Weber: Essays in sociology.* New York: Oxford University Press.

Wittgenstein, L. (1953). *Philosophical investigations.* Oxford: Basil Blackwell.

Zinn, H. (1980). *A people's history of the United States.* New York: Harper Colophon Books.

Index

Representing the king's splendour

Manchester University Press

STUDIES IN EARLY MODERN
EUROPEAN HISTORY

This series aims to publish
challenging and innovative research in all areas
of early modern continental history.
The editors are committed to encouraging work
that engages with current historiographical
debates, adopts an interdisciplinary
approach, or makes an original contribution
to our understanding of the period.

SERIES EDITORS
Joseph Bergin, William G. Naphy, Penny Roberts and Paolo Rossi

Representing
the king's splendour

Communication and reception of symbolic
forms of power in viceregal Naples

GABRIEL GUARINO

Manchester University Press

Manchester and New York

distributed exclusively in the USA by Palgrave Macmillan

Published by Manchester University Press
Oxford Road, Manchester M13 9NR, UK
and Room 400, 175 Fifth Avenue, New York, NY 10010, USA
www.manchesteruniversitypress.co.uk

Distributed exclusively in the USA by
Palgrave Macmillan, 175 Fifth Avenue, New York,
NY 10010, USA

Distributed exclusively in Canada by
UBC Press, University of British Columbia, 2029 West Mall,
Vancouver, BC, Canada V6T 1Z2

British Library Cataloguing-in-Publication Data
A catalogue record for this book is available from the British Library

Library of Congress Cataloging-in-Publication Data applied for

ISBN 978 0 7190 7822 4 *hardback*

First published 2010

Typeset in Perpetua with Albertus display
by Koinonia, Manchester
Printed in Great Britain
by TJ International

For Ayala, of course

Contents

Figures

Acknowledgements

I am indebted to a number of people and institutions for their help and support during the writing of this book. First of all, I would like to thank Peter Burke for his comprehensive and caring supervision throughout the dissertation on which this book is based. The careful and patient reading and correcting of the various drafts, his invaluable suggestions, and his natural warmth and humorous disposition, make him nothing less than an impeccable supervisor. Some of my teachers and friends deserve a special recognition. First of all, Myriam Yardeni for functioning as an infallible and most caring advisor throughout my entire academic career. I cherish the precious support of John Marino, who has been very generous with suggestions, references, and materials. Miri Rubin has been a radiating source of positive energy to which I often turned for treasured advice and friendship. I am grateful to the ever helpful advice and generous support of Melissa Calaresu. My thanks go to David Abulafia and John Robertson for the scrupulous assessment of the work in progress. Thanks are due to Tom Willette, for many helpful references which set me on the right track in the earlier stages of the project, like the pioneering and inspirational works of Benedetto Croce, Franco Mancini, and Adelaide Cirillo Mastrocinque. Mechal Sobel, Amos Megged, and Fania Oz-Salzberger have offered help and support with an unbounded amount of commitment and attention. I would like to thank people who offered guidance and support at various stages of the manuscript preparation: Yossi Ben-Artzi, Giuseppe Cascione, Carmel Cassar, Alejandro Cañeque, José Luis Colomer, Sabina De Cavi, Francesco Di Donato, Gad Gilbar, Arik Kochavi, Sagrario López Poza, Donato Mansueto, Giovanni Muto, Aurelio Musi, Nick Napoli, Alejandra Osorio, Raimondo Pinna, Pier Luigi Rovito, Renato Ruotolo, Haia Shpayer-Makov, Jelena Todorović, Piero Ventura, and Ilana Zinguer. A special thanks is due to Silvana Musella Guida, Ermanno Guida and Sonia Scognamiglio Cestaro for all their advice regarding Neapolitan fashion, and for all of their warmth and hospitality. My gratitude goes to Valerio Filoso and Stefania Ecchia, for their friendship, generosity, and for opening their house to me. To my colleagues at the University of Ulster, many thanks for kindly giving me the precious time needed to complete the book. The generous financial support of the University of Haifa, the University of Cambridge, Churchill College, and the University of Ulster, made it all possible. Thanks are due to Emma Brennan, Reena Jugnarain, Monica Kendall, and the rest of the staff at Manchester University Press for their careful and diligent work. Thanks are due to: Rachel Guarino and the late Saul Agrari for carefully reading and correcting the linguistic aspects of

earlier drafts, and for all of their support along the way; to Michele Guarino for teaching me the art of dream weaving; to Daniel Guarino, for always being a rock of fortitude. To Mary and Moty Shmaia, I wish to express my deepest appreciation for their unending support, now as ever. To the following clans: Harel, Carbonara, and Agrari, thank you for always being there for me. Finally, to my wife Ayala Shmaia-Guarino, as much as it is possible to express gratitude in words, I want to thank her for being the heart and soul of my existence. Nothing would have been possible without her endless support, patience, help, and love. Last but not least, special thanks to my children Eden and Auriel who have provided many hours of joy and laughter, and have helped me focus on what is really important in life.

Abbreviations

ASNA	Archivio di Stato, Naples
ASPN	*Archivio Storico per le Province Napoletane*
BNN	Biblioteca Nazionale, Naples
Codice	*Codice delle leggi del Regno di Napoli*
Nuova collezione	*Nuova collezione delle prammatiche del Regno di Napoli*
Raccolta	*Raccolta di tutti i più rinomati scrittori dell'istoria generale del Regno di Napoli*
SNSP	Società Napoletana di Storia Patria, Naples

Spanish viceroys of Naples

Gonzalo Fernández de Córdoba, Duke of Sessa and Terranova (1503–7)
Juan de Aragón, Count of Ribagorza (1507–9)
Antonio de Guevara, Count of Potenza (1509)
Ramón de Cardona, Count of Albento (1509–22)
Charles de Lannoy (1522–23) (first term)
Andrea Carafa, Count of Santa Severina (1523–26)
Charles de Lannoy (1526–27) (second term)
Hugo de Moncada (1527–28)
Philibert of Châlon, Prince of Orange (1528–30)
Pompeo Colonna, Cardinal (1530–32)
Pedro Álvarez de Toledo, Marquis of Villafranca (1532–53)
Luis de Toledo (1553)
Pedro Pacheco Ladrón de Guevara, Bishop of Jaén (1553–56)
Bernardino de Mendoza (1555)
Fernando Álvarez de Toledo, Duke of Alba (1556–58)
Juan Manrique de Lara (1558)
Pedro Afán de Ribera, Duke of Alcalá (1559–71)
Antoine Perrenot de Granvelle, Cardinal (1571–75)
Íñigo López de Hurtado de Mendoza, Marquis of Mondéjar (1575–79)
Juan de Zúñiga y Requesens, Prince of Pietrapersia (1579–82)
Pedro Téllez-Girón y de la Cueva, Duke of Osuna (1582–86)
Juan de Zúñiga y Avellaneda, Count of Miranda (1586–95)
Enrique de Guzmán, Count of Olivares (1595–99)
Fernando Ruiz de Castro, Count of Lemos (1599–1601)
Francisco de Castro, Count of Lemos (1601–3)
Juan Alonso Pimentel de Herrera, Count of Benavente (1603–10)
Pedro Fernández de Castro, Count of Lemos (1610–16)
Pedro Téllez-Girón, Duke of Osuna (1616–20)
Gaspar de Borja y Velasco, Cardinal (1620)
Antonio Zapata y Cisneros, Cardinal (1620–22)
Antonio Álvarez de Toledo y Beaumont de Navarra, Duke of Alba (1622–29)
Fernando Afán de Ribera y Enríquez, Duke of Alcalá (1629–31)
Manuel de Acevedo y Zúñiga, Count of Monterrey (1631–37)

Ramiro Núñez de Guzmán, Duke of Medina de las Torres (1637–44)

Juan Alfonso Enríquez de Cabrera, Almirant of Castile (1644–46)

Rodrigo Ponce de León, Duke of Arcos (1646–48)

Juan José de Austria (1648)

Íñigo Vélez de Guevara, Count of Oñate and Villamediana (1648–53)

García de Haro y Avellaneda, Count of Castrillo (1653–58)

Gaspar de Bracamonte y Guzmán, Count of Peñaranda (1658–64)

Pascual de Aragón, Cardinal (1664–66)

Pedro Antonio de Aragón, Duke of Segorbe and of Cardona (1666–71)

Fadrique de Toledo y Osorio, Marquis of Villafranca (1671–72)

Antonio Álvarez Osorio, Marquis of Astorga (1672–75)

Fernando Fajardo y Álvarez de Toledo, Marquis of Los Vélez (1675–83)

Gaspar Mendez de Haro, Marquis of Carpio (1683–87)

Francisco de Benavides, Count of Santisteban (1687–96)

Luis Francisco de la Cerda y Aragón, Duke of Medinaceli (1696–1702)

Juan Manuel Fernández Pacheco Cabrera, Duke of Escalona (1702–7)

Introduction

Various studies have traced the Spanish cultural model and its global success in different parts of the Spanish Empire, from the Netherlands to the Americas, and still more widely, in other parts of Europe which were not under direct Spanish rule. However, this topic has been largely neglected in Naples, the capital of southern Italy, where the Spaniards dominated from 1503 to 1707. The purpose of this book is to fill this gap, by concentrating on the main agent of Spanish acculturation, the viceregal court. This line of investigation is concomitant with the recent return of the European princely court to the centre stage of historical writing, redefined, after a long period of scholarly neglect, as one of the most politically, socially, and culturally influential institutions of the early modern era.[1]

In fact, Naples presented itself as a singularly attractive stage for an early modern princely court. Encompassing three millennia as a dynamic port city, Naples was founded by the Achaean Greeks in the ninth century BC. In subsequent centuries, establishing itself as a significant centre of Mediterranean trade, it was taken over by the Romans (328 BC), the Byzantines (325–568), the Lombards (568–1130), the Normans (1137–94), the Germanic house of Hohenstaufen (1194–1266), the Angevin (1266–1442), the Aragonese (1442–95), and finally by the Spaniards (1503–1707). This historical legacy resulted in a rich cultural heritage which turned Naples into a popular destination of the European Grand Tour.[2] The main tourist attractions around the city included Mt Vesuvius, the ancient ruins of Pozzuoli, the Flegrean Fields, and the islands of Capri, Procida, and Ischia. In the city itself, the greatest praise went to the Royal Palace, to the major Neapolitan castles – Castel dell'Ovo, Castel Capuano, Castel Nuovo (also known as Maschio Angioino), and Castel St Elmo – and to a great number of churches and monasteries, many of which displayed precious relics and splendid works of art. Unanimous admiration was solicited by the spectacular vistas of the Neapolitan Bay facing Mt Vesuvius, the great number of historical landmarks and natural curiosities, the delightful all-year-round mild and pleasant climate, and Naples' vibrant city life. Both locals and foreigners paid tribute to Naples with the highest of superlatives. For example, the local chronicler Domenico Antonio Parrino portrayed Naples as 'the

prettiest and noblest city in Europe and probably the entire world',[3] followed closely by the British traveller George Sandys, who dubbed it as 'the pleasantest of cities, if not the most beautiful'.[4] Similarly, the French traveller, Jean-Jacques Bouchard claimed not to have seen a more superb and noble city, outside of Paris,[5] and John Evelyn crowned it as 'the *non ultra*' of his travels.[6]

The city's intrinsic appeal, coupled with the commercial possibilities and the presence of the viceregal and judicial courts, attracted great numbers of merchants, businessmen, nobles, jurists, notaries, courtiers, and diplomats from the entire Italian peninsula, as well as the rest of Europe. Accordingly, in addition to the predominant Italian and Spanish groups, a variety of ethnicities resided in Naples, including Flemish, French, Austrians, Greeks, Muslims, and Jews.[7] Naples also proved to be a pool of attraction to southerners living in the countryside, owing to its employment potential, and to the many privileges and fiscal concessions given to its residents by the Spanish rulers. As a result, the city underwent an exponential growth in the sixteenth and seventeenth centuries. From 150,000 inhabitants at the beginning of the sixteenth century it reached almost half a million inhabitants at its peak, prior to the plague eruption of 1656 which halved its population, thus becoming one of the most densely populated cities of early modern Europe.[8]

Naples' unrestrained process of urbanization turned it also into one of the most crowded, chaotic, noisy, polluted, unhealthy, and crime-ridden cities in the Spanish world. These dire conditions reflected on the Neapolitan populace, earning itself a notorious reputation for disorder and unruliness. This contradiction between a heavenly site and its supposedly wicked people earned Naples its infamous epithet of 'a paradise inhabited by Devils'.[9] All of these multifaceted attributes of Naples turned it into a place that was, at the same time, coveted by Spanish nobles and diplomats looking for a high-ranking position in the Spanish monarchy's machinery of power, but also extremely challenging, as the following pages will illustrate in great detail.

Before starting any discussion of the Neapolitan viceregal court it is necessary to identify the nature of the juridical arrangements binding the Kingdom of Naples to the Spanish monarchy, and to illustrate the relationship between the various political forces that claimed their share of the power over the kingdom. According to Giuseppe Galasso, the Spanish monarchy has been inadequately described as: 'empire', 'commonwealth', 'federation' or 'confederation of states' because such definitions imply a unified juridical reality. In fact, the monarchy was substantially a conglomerate of states, each autonomous and juridically independent in respect to the others, bound to the personal rule of a king, or rather the Habsburg dynasty.[10] Similarly, the conglomerate of Habsburg patrimonial territories has been defined as a 'composite monarchy' in which, according to the seventeenth-century jurist Juan de Solórzano Pereira, there were two kinds of ways to be united to the system of Habsburg states. One was the 'accessory' union, in which a territory, once united to another, was regarded juridically as an integral part

of it. Such was the incorporation of the Spanish Indies into the Kingdom of Castile. According to the second form of union, known as the *aeque principaliter*, the newly acquired territory preserved its own laws, and privileges, and continued to be regarded as a distinct entity.[11] Besides the Kingdoms of Naples and Sicily, one can find under this category most of the kingdoms and provinces of the Spanish monarchy, such as Aragón and Valencia, within the Iberian Peninsula, or the provinces of the Netherlands.[12]

The form of union to each other *aeque principaliter* fit well to the needs of the time given the European profound respect for traditional rights, law, and customs. Moreover, according to John Elliott, 'the very looseness of its association was in a sense its greater strength'.[13] Such a union allowed the continuation of local self-government at a time when monarchs were unable to bring their possessions under tight royal control, and at the same time it ensured local elites the preservation of their existing privileges together with the potential benefits deriving from participation in such a strong and prestigious association as that of the Spanish monarchy. In Helmut Koenigsberger's words: 'The Gonzaga, the Pescara, the Del Vasto preferred the role of an imperial viceroy or captain general to that of a provincial *condottiere*.'[14] Indeed, with a few exceptions, the relationship between Spain and Naples, from the visit of Ferdinand the Catholic in 1506 onwards, was characterized by the maintenance of a delicate balance between keeping the autonomy of Neapolitans and ensuring the collaboration of the viceroys with the local pressure groups to advance the monarchy's goals. The success in maintaining this balance was the key to the relatively stable and rarely disputed Spanish rule in southern Italy during two centuries.[15]

It might be because they were so ready to accommodate local elites that the Habsburgs so easily extracted the kingdom's wealth. The ruler of a composite monarchy, in an emergency, could draw on extra resources.[16] Naples lacked constitutional safeguards, and few opposed Spain's financial demands. The cleavages that fragmented Neapolitan society let the Habsburgs extract huge sums through ever-rising taxes. These were used not only for the defence of the Mediterranean shores to protect the lives of Italians, or for the aid of other Spanish territories like Sicily and Milan, but also, especially after the 1580s, for the support of Spanish commitments in the Netherlands. In this sense, the importance of the Kingdom of Naples within the entire system of Habsburg states is emphasized by Galasso's assessment that it came right after Castile in the hierarchy of states on which the Spanish monarchy could rely on for its existence in the form of resources for military defence and taxation.[17]

Clearly, such a position, just as in Castile's case, would have a detrimental effect in the long run because of the disproportional toll required from its subjects. So much so, that often viceroys had to reject royal requests for more money, assessing that it was simply impossible to wring any more from taxpayers. Obviously, the Spanish composite system had its own disadvantages as well. The problematic task of holding under personal rule such vast possessions, and with so disparate juridical arrangements, can be discerned by the flattering attitude adopted by the Habsburgs towards particular

territories. For example, even such a mighty ruler as Charles V felt the need to tell his Catalan subjects that he valued more his title of Count of Barcelona than that of King of the Romans, and in a similar instance explained to the Castilians that his use of the title Emperor first did not diminish from the importance of the kingdoms of the Crown of Castile.[18] A similar kind of praise is made explicit in the letter of appointment issued in 1599 by Philip III to the future Viceroy of Naples, the Count of Lemos:

> By acknowledging the importance and quality of my loyalest Kingdom of Naples ... being unable [to rule it] with my own person as I would want to ... I chose you for this post, which is the greatest and of most trust I could have given you ... I am convinced that you will rule it according to my will, because you have to fill my place, representing my own person in such a great and principal kingdom placed at the centre of the world, which is Italy, therefore contributing much to your honour and to mine.[19]

Such an unambiguous display of appreciation of the kingdom's first-rank importance within the Habsburg European possessions would also strengthen Neapolitans' feelings of self-worth, and would make of the viceregal appointment one of the most coveted offices available for a Spanish grandee. As stated by Hernando Sánchez, the appointment of an influential string of Castilian viceroys, throughout the seventeenth century, like the Count of Lemos, the Count of Oñate, the Marquis of Carpio or the Duke of Medinaceli, would contribute to the consolidation of Naples as the principal viceregal court of the monarchy.[20] Obviously, these eminent appointments tried to compensate for one of the greatest limitations of the system: the king's absence. In this respect, with the passage of the Kingdom of Naples from the Aragonese to Spanish rule the local elites expressed their resentment at the departure of the royal court and the replacement of the monarch by a governor or a viceroy, who could not possibly compensate for the absence of a monarch.[21] It was not until the beginning of the regency of the viceroy the Count of Ribagorza in 1507, after the visit of Ferdinand the Catholic to Naples, that the local nobility finally gave up the illusion of the transference of the Ferdinandean court to Naples.[22]

Although the local elites of the kingdom perceived the new form of annexation to the Spanish monarchy as the denial of its role as economic, political, and cultural centre of patronage and personal promotion, as embodied by the Aragonese royal court, Galasso stresses that it would be misleading, in juridical and political terms, to rely on Croce's assertion according to which the 'Kingdom of Naples sunk to the status of a "viceroyalty" of Spain'.[23] First, there was no such decline in juridical terms, as the introduction of the viceregal institution to the Kingdom of Naples did not supplant the king's status or the status of the kingdom. The king remained the legal ruler of the Kingdom of Naples, with the formal title of King of Naples, except that he was represented there by a viceroy. This is corroborated in the official contemporary documents and writings, as in all other literature for that matter, where the expression 'viceroyalty' is only used to indicate the viceroy's office whereas the territorial entity is invariably

identified as 'Kingdom of Naples'. Similarly, one should refute the common assertion, which relies on the traditional Italian nationalistic bias against the Spanish rule, that 'viceregal Naples' was treated as if it were one of the conquered viceroyalties in the New World. First, the Spanish kings based their legitimacy of rule on dynastic succession, and not on discovery or conquest. Despite the fact that the Kingdom of Naples was conquered by force from the French, Ferdinand the Catholic based the rights of his conquest on his dynastic rights as heir of Alfonso the Magnanimus, and so did his Habsburg heirs after him. Second, based on the aforementioned union of the Kingdom of Naples to the Habsburg monarchy as *aeque principaliter*, it was regarded as an autonomous entity, enjoying its own laws and privileges, which were reasserted every time a viceroy took office, and every time a king succeeded to the Spanish monarchy. Thus, the relationship between Spaniards and Neapolitans was one of *inter pares* and not the one of blatant disparity that existed between 'indigenous people' and 'colonists'.[24] This point is reinforced by the bitter comment of Milan's governor to Philip II in a letter from 1570: 'for these Italians, though they are not Indians, have to be treated as such, so that they understand that we are in charge of them and not they in charge of us'.[25] More than a serious recommendation, such a comment illustrates the frustration of a Spanish functionary vis-à-vis the Italians' ability to maintain a considerable degree of independence and autonomy under Spanish rule.

This study will rely on the historiography of Spanish Italy and the historiography of princely courts – two traditions which were kept apart until the last decades of the twentieth century. Court historians have worked extensively on the various dynastic courts of Europe, but have neglected those courts that were part of vast territorial empires, where the absence of a resident dynastic sovereign created peculiar political entities, headed by vicarious rulers, as in Naples. Similarly, this lack of an indigenous peninsular monarchy coupled with a generally negative overview of Spanish rule in Italy has probably been a major reason for specialists of southern Italy to generally avoid court studies. In fact, negative epithets, like 'bad government', 'decadence', 'dreary times', have been the leitmotif of most Italian authors assessing the Spanish presence in early modern Italy. Eighteenth- and nineteenth-century interpretations, like the ones of Paolo Mattia Doria, Pietro Giannone, Ferdinando Galiani, Giuseppe Maria Galanti, and Pietro Napoli-Signorelli, blamed fiercely the 200 years of Spanish 'bad government' for the 'decline' of Italy during the seventeenth century.[26]

A meaningful revision of such accounts was first offered in the last decades of the nineteenth century by one of Italy's most prominent historians, Benedetto Croce, who dealt with the relationship of Spain and Italy in a series of studies, setting the Spanish influence in a broad chronological and spatial context, together with relatively mild views of its effects. A large part of these studies was collected in *La Spagna nella vita italiana durante la Rinascenza*.[27] Still today, in the most recent historiography, this volume is cited as a critical reference work on the cultural influence of Spain on Italy. It

does not mean that Croce's work is exhaustive, definitive, or faultless, but it reveals the relative neglect of this subject since.

Croce showed a long-lasting relationship that started in the middle ages with the exchanges of the Italian maritime powers with their Catalan rivals, through the Aragonese domination of the south during the high middle ages, and finally the 200 years of Spanish (or more precisely Castilian) preponderance in the peninsula during the sixteenth and seventeenth centuries.[28] Nevertheless, Croce's revision was only partial. On the one hand, contrary to post-unification nationalist Italians who blamed foreign forces for the delay in Italy's unification and independence, Croce claimed that Spain 'with its dominion, with its hegemony, even with the opposition that it stirred, began to form or prepare certain sentiments of devotion towards the king and the state, which were not without consequence for the civil and political future'.[29] On the other hand, he admitted that between the peace of Cateau-Cambrésis (1559), which signalled the start of full Spanish hegemony on the peninsula at the expense of French claims, and the end of the seventeenth century, 'Italy lacked any political life and national senti-ment, culture impoverished ... the figurative and architectonic arts chose the Baroque style', while Spain's 'malign influence' on all aspects of life was condemned.[30] In sum, according to Croce, Italy showed a true state of decadence in the seventeenth century, but rather than seeking the explanation in Spanish influences alone, one should realize that Italy was internally corrupt just as Spain was at the time. In his own words: 'it was one decadence that embraced another decadence'.[31] However, Croce limited himself to speak of a general, abstract 'decadence', lumping together economy, society, politics, and culture, and so leaving the issues confused, without offering a satisfying explanation.[32]

In the early 1930s, Fausto Nicolini provided a collection of essays that dealt with daily life in Spanish Italy.[33] He took from Croce the need to relinquish the dogmatic negative position against Spain, but, much like him, limited himself to cultural issues, in a descriptive, erudite, and antiquarian fashion. Accordingly, he left at the margins of his explanation the social context in which culture is created. One interesting excep-tion is his interpretation of the hunger revolt in Milan in 1629. Anticipating Villari's introspective interpretation of Naples' revolt of 1647–48,[34] Nicolini placed the blame for Milan's forceful repression on the local patriciate, which influenced the Spanish governor to use force, in spite of the Spaniard's peaceful inclination to seek a compro-mise with the rebels.[35] Another innovation with respect to Croce was the incorpora-tion of the state of Milan alongside the realm of Naples in Nicolini's description of Spanish Italy. However, Naples and Milan were described in separate essays, without showing the important connection, not to say interdependence, between them inside the Spanish system of Italian states.[36] This problem of discontinuity is symptomatic to the whole volume which, contrary to Croce, fails to give a general, chronologically and thematically structured overview of the Spanish influence. Only after the Second World War would the Italian academy offer a serious alternative to Croce's formulations of the Spanish domination.

Italian historiography changed significantly during the 1950s owing to the ideological implementations of Marxist theory and the methodological influences of the Annales School.[37] The explanation for 'Italian decadence' shifted from the ethical-political grounds that it used to rely on, to 'structures' and institutions – the state, society, and so forth – and to the dynamic exchanges between them. Accordingly, the view of Spain as the fundamental cause for so many Italian misfortunes was relinquished. The first important exponent of this new historiography, in relation to the Hispano-Italian relationship, was Federico Chabod. Focusing on Spanish Lombardy, he emphasized the political interaction within the state apparatus that the Spaniards created in the newly acquired territory, from 1535 onwards. Previous nationalistic interpretations scolded the Milanese for accepting the 'Spanish yoke' without serious opposition. However, according to Chabod, they did not have a good reason to oppose. He showed that the strategic importance of Milan as a bridge between southern Italy and the Netherlands prevented the Spanish monarchs from 'rocking the boat'. Accordingly, they tended to maintain traditional privileges, they left the city councils in the entire region untouched, and allowed the local Senate to function as a check to overambitious Spanish governors.[38] In sum, Chabod exposed the relationship between macro-political organisms, such as the Habsburg Empire in Europe, and micro-organisms, such as the Duchy of Milan, and revealed the related strategies employed by Spaniards to run their complicated empire. Even more important was his focus on Milanese society and the exploration of local political institutions, which encouraged similar investigations in other Spanish dominions of Italy.

One such significant contribution was Rosario Villari's book, *La rivolta antispagnola a Napoli* (*The Anti-Spanish Revolt in Naples*), which acknowledged the importance of Chabod's influence among other scholars who had investigated the Spanish state administration. He proposed to do for Naples what Chabod had done for Milan, giving a special emphasis to the autonomy of the kingdom.[39] Villari used the period between two revolts – from the relatively minor one of 1585 to the celebrated revolt of 1647–48 – to describe the change in the relations of power between the Spanish state and the local political and social forces. In a nutshell, he argued that the monarchical government, entering a period of mounting economic and political crisis due to the simultaneous and extended wars it had to contend with, allowed the aristocratic elite to increase its pressure on the lower strata of the population, in a process which he labelled 'refeudalization'. Eventually, the concerted 'oppression' of the landed aristocracy and the state exploded in a large-scale revolt that affected not only the city of Naples and its surrounding countryside, but the entire urban and rural south.[40]

Villari's Marxist perspective enabled him to incorporate large segments of the population in his analysis, and to show the class conflict in both the rural and the urban Mezzogiorno. Despite the author's ideological preferences, the book does not suffer from the reductive socio-economic perspective that characterizes many of Villari's Marxist colleagues. In fact, it abounds with cultural issues alongside the social ones. For instance, we are presented with the account of an urban lynching, full of symbolic

meaning, followed by an equally symbolic repression. Those events are interpreted in an anthropological key, little different from similar accounts of cultural historians.[41] Villari also dedicates a few interesting pages to the cultural values of the Neapolitan ruling class.[42] Unfortunately, in matters of Spanish cultural influences he leaves a complete void. Obviously, such interests are secondary to his thesis which focuses on the relative autonomy and the internal conflicts of southern society.

In years to come, the pioneering work of Chabod and Villari will lead to an increasing interest in Italian society, at the expense of Spanish historical agency. Rather than Villari's cultural insights, it was his 'refeudalization' theory that aroused a vivid debate ever since his work was first published. From Giuseppe Galasso and Guido Quazza, immediately after its publication, to Domenico Sella, Enrico Stumpo, and Tommaso Astarita, just to mention a few of the more recent interventions, all contributed to the increasing knowledge and deepening analysis of the internal factors which brought about the 'Italian decadence'.[43] However, on the rare occasions that Spaniards are mentioned it is always on economic, social, or political issues, rather than in that cultural role that Croce assigned them about a century ago.

This point was reinforced by Eric Cochrane's review article on the historiography of the early modern south of the 1970s and 1980s, where he noted that 'by far the greatest number of ... titles ... fall into two or three major categories, roughly corresponding to the division of historical studies among the university faculties of political science, law and economics'.[44] In other words, these intellectual preferences leave no room for cultural interpretations. Moreover, he emphasized the resistance against interdisciplinary work inside the field of history itself where 'historians of art, literature and politics scrupulously avoid transgressing the boundaries of their respective disciplines'.[45]

Since then, meaningful changes were promoted by that historiographical trend which has started to shift scholars' interest to the cultural aspects of princely courts. Owing especially to the adoption of more qualitative aspects of the social sciences, it brought about an alternative to the dominant quantitative methods and long-term chronologies. Anthropology affected the field through analytical concepts such as ritual and patronage, and historical sociology exerted its influence through specific theories pertaining to the court. The seminal formulations and models of renowned sociologist Norbert Elias, even if they have been heavily criticized over the years, are regarded as the starting point for any discussion on the early modern court.[46] One such major contribution was the establishment of the Centro di studi 'Europa delle Corti', a misleading name for a project that concentrates almost exclusively on early modern courts of central and northern Italy. The Centro's many publications, concentrating on literary and artistic evidence, have widely contributed to the revival of cultural history in the peninsula. However, according to Sergio Bertelli – head of the rival research group on Italian courts, Laboratorio di Storia – 'it seems as if ... the exponents of the Centro Studi have a radical allergy for new methodological approaches ... This can be deducted from their chilly (tardy) reception of Elias' sociological approach to court society'.[47] Indeed,

many of the *Centro's* compilations are oriented towards literary criticism. Some of these explore, for example, the intertextual relations between contemporary manuals for courtiers rather than analysing with sociological tools the environments described in them. However, there are some new inspiring exceptions.[48] As for the *Laboratorio di Storia*, it has contributed a number of interesting publications, drawing heavily on Elias' formulations as is implied by one of the titles: *Rituale, cerimoniale, ettichetta* (*Ritual, Ceremonial, Etiquette*).[49]

The renewed interest in the court, the elites, and international relations has finally caught up with the historiography of southern Italy. Giuseppe Galasso has had a significant role in leading the way. His main contribution is situating Naples within the Spanish imperial system of states and linking its development to the greater historical trends of the early modern period.[50] Abundant research following his lead has been done along these lines, primarily by such scholars as Giovanni Muto, Aurelio Musi, Maria Antonietta Visceglia, and Angelantonio Spagnoletti.[51] Their work has fortunately coincided with that of Spanish historians, like Carlos José Hernando Sánchez, José Martínez Millán, and Antonio Álvarez-Ossorio Alvariño, just to name a few, whose interest in the Spanish monarchy brought them to focus their attention on specific Italian case studies.[52] Ever since the 1980s, Italian and Spanish scholars have cooperated in numerous conferences on the subject, and most recently in some of the various volumes published for the commemorations of the fifth centenary of Charles V's birth, and the fourth centenary of Philip II's death.[53]

Despite this growing interest in Spanish Italy only a very small number of studies focus specifically on the viceregal court, or on the Spanish viceroys of Naples. For example, perhaps taking a cue from the contemporary oeuvre of Domenico Antonio Parrino, Giuseppe Coniglio wrote a collection of short biographical sketches of the numerous viceroys who ruled from 1503 to 1707.[54] Unfortunately, the book lacks a guiding synthetic approach concerning the viceregal office, and fails to address the court *per se* as a subject matter for analysis. Quite a different approach was adopted by Hernando Sánchez, who produced a thorough illustration of the impact of the most influential of Spanish viceroys – Don Pedro de Toledo (1532–52) – on Neapolitan society and culture.[55] Similar recent accounts of the courts of specific viceroys, like the Count of Lemos (1610–16), the Count of Oñate (1648–53), and the brothers Pascual and Pedro Antonio de Aragón (respectively 1664–66, 1666–71), have also enriched the field.[56] Finally, the latest studies on viceroyalties in the Spanish world, dealing with the general aspects of administration, government, and, above all, the various forms of viceregal representation, are particularly relevant to this book.[57]

The following study will rely on the vast aforementioned corpus of work, attempting to fill its lacunae, and trying to provide a fresh depiction of the viceregal court during the seventeenth century. Instead of the conventional negative image of Spanish rule, best illustrated by the popular revolt of 1647 and its charismatic leader Masaniello

— undoubtedly the most exploited historical topic of seventeenth-century Naples[58] — this study will offer a closer analysis of the viceregal court and the ways by which the viceroys attempted to establish and extend their authority to the wider populace by means of various forms of political communication. Indeed, focusing on the seventeenth century is particularly fruitful for such an investigation because it is in this century that European rulers, and in this sense the viceroys of Naples were no exception, reached the apex of courtly magnificence. Elaborate rituals and ceremonies which emphasized the grandeur of their authority at court, and splendid public celebrations that projected it to the general public, served in tandem to forward ideas of cosmic order and transcendental hierarchy that were used as a means of upholding their power. The successful persuasion of different groups of spectators by manipulating symbols from various cultural repertories depended mostly on the effects achieved on the eye. This is why, among the various cultural phenomena that characterized the Spanish presence in Naples, I have chosen to focus my attention on what may be called 'the politics of appearance'.

The seventeenth century also offers a greater interest for this study, which seeks to explore the limits of Spanish influence, because it is a period when Spain's cultural hegemony is continuously questioned and challenged. Spain reached the peak of its power and established itself as the world's superpower after the first quarter of the sixteenth century. But starting from the last two decades of that century onwards, its power progressively declined. In this sense, France will become its greatest rival as a cultural model for Europe, most distinctively in matters of appearance and style. Towards the close of the seventeenth century and during the entire span of the eighteenth century, French hegemony will be completed and consolidated. Obviously, the contest between these two superpowers, which spanned the entire continent and beyond, was felt in such a vast and densely populated European metropolis as Naples.

The first chapter will deal with courtly ceremonial. By presenting the institutional functions of the viceregal court, I will assess the legal contours of the viceroys' political might, as they were defined by the king, and to understand how ceremonial served to sublimate that power in the eyes of Neapolitans. The emphasis will be on the ambiguity of the viceroys' position, who, on the one hand, were vicarious rulers appointed ad hoc by the King of Spain to be their stand-ins, but on the other hand, were elevated to supreme heights by ritual means. Thus, the main concern will be to assess the efficacy of ceremonial mechanisms. This will be done by investigating the way in which Neapolitans of all social denominations addressed, treated, and perceived their Spanish rulers. The overall evaluation of the viceregal image will be achieved also by drawing comparisons between the viceroys and other early modern rulers, which derived, to a large extent, from the models of kingship professed in the leading princely courts of Spain and France. My contention is that the implementation of ceremonial was not enough to maintain the viceregal status intact in times of crisis, especially from the 1620s to the 1650s when Spain was involved in numerous armed conflicts

throughout its widespread territories.

The second chapter will introduce the main forces of Neapolitan society, as they were represented in a hierarchically structured, visible, and symbolic continuum – the cavalcade. The most important public events were celebrated with a religious procession or its secular analogy, the civic cavalcade, which paraded through the various quarters of the city before the eyes of all Neapolitan citizens. It is hard to imagine a better tangible manifestation of the distribution of power in society than on such solemn occasions. However, one needs to ask some cardinal questions concerning this matter: who was in charge of allocating the places of the various groups in the cavalcade? What were the criteria for such distribution? How stable was this structure over time? In other words, was there a possibility of mobility that allowed changing places from time to time? In order to answer these questions I will carefully separate each group in the cavalcade, trying to measure its social and political status in general, and checking how its rank was reflected in the cavalcade. Next, by examining specific cavalcades chronologically I will be able to find out if the order kept was indeed the same through time. For this purpose, the cavalcades chosen are those that took place during royal visits, because the eminent presence of royalty naturally triggered the ambitions of individuals and groups to push the limits of the rules of precedence in order to improve their position on such special occasions. My main argument is that the Neapolitan cavalcade in the seventeenth century reflected noble status well, but failed to make room for the new hierarchies of power represented by arriviste groups of non-noble origin.

The third chapter is concerned with various kinds of festivities. The main emphasis is on those celebrations promoted by the viceroys on special occasions which were related to the Spanish Empire or to the viceroys themselves – births, weddings, funerals, Habsburg military victories, and so forth – although some attention will be given to religious festivities as well, especially when they involved the Spanish authorities. After presenting the system of festivities in early modern Naples, I will emphasize the organizational aspect of celebrations. I will consider the role of sponsorship and organization by the court, as well as parallel efforts displayed by the nobility, the Neapolitan *popolo*,[59] and even the plebs. Next, trying to assess the success of Spanish forms of celebrations, I will concentrate on such Spanish tournaments as bullfights, reed spears, and carousels, which were displayed in Naples for various occasions of merry-making. So far, little attention has been given to these cultural imports, dubbed to be insignificant to Neapolitans, although the historical documents clearly prove their massive popularity in the city among local citizens from all social denominations.

The fourth chapter will deal with fashion, which will be explored in a broad cultural perspective, including, among other things: changes in sartorial trends, cultural clashes between different models of style, and social, economic, and moral considerations related to clothes. First, I will describe the reasons for the success of the Spanish style in Europe, in general, and in Italy and Naples in particular, mainly attributing the reason to the affinity of some of its austere characteristics to the ideas of the

Catholic Reformation. Next, returning to the cultural role of the viceregal court I will describe both its ability to diffuse fashionable garments through personal example and its attempts to impose its ideas of social and moral standards via sumptuary laws.

Finally, the fifth chapter will be dedicated to one of the most persuasive means of political art, the *impresa*. To start with, I will define the origins and various applications of the *impresa*, putting a special accent on its propagandistic usage in public, following its effective structure that combines a suggestive visual image with a didactic motto. Since their most important utilization was at funerals, in which there is a natural inclination, not to say mandatory obligation in the case of absolutist rulers, of eulogizing the deceased, I will describe how these *imprese* functioned in some of the most splendid services of monarchical obsequies in early modern Naples.

Copious primary sources deal with the Kingdom of Naples, and with the Spanish–Italian interaction during this period. Throughout the book I will discuss the various documents thoroughly and critically, placing them in their historical context. At this point, I will limit myself to describing them briefly. Local official and unofficial histories, diaries, letters, festival books, chronicles, and financial records, often show the relationship of the local population with the Spanish administration. In addition, there are official reports by outsiders, in the form of letters from papal nuncios, agents, and ambassadors from other Italian states, and the myriad writings of foreign travellers and ambassadors who visited Naples during this period. Out of these records two of the more important sources for this research ought to be emphasized, the local diaries and the festival books.

The diaries were written by such bourgeois intellectuals as Innocenzo Fuidoro, Domenico Confuorto, Antonio Bulifon, Scipione Guerra, and others, each covering several decades of seventeenth-century Naples.[60] Although not matching an author of the calibre of Versailles' Duke of Saint-Simon, these are extremely interesting writings, portraying everyday life and important events in the city. One can find in them news concerning: official and informal actions of Spanish functionaries, noteworthy foreign personalities, events and gossip related to noble families, festivals and celebrations, the latest fashionable garments worn by the 'celebrities' of the time, and much more. Based on personal impressions, newspapers, rumours and gossip, they provide an invaluable source of data. According to Giuseppe Galasso, historians' rejection of these diaries in the past as unreliable sources has been a mistake. Not only do they represent precious eyewitness accounts, but also many of the historical facts and the quantitative evidence they deliver are corroborated by archival documents.[61]

The festival books present precious testimonies for the official programmes that the rulers aspired to achieve. These products have been evaluated by Helen Watanabe O'Kelly as 'not so much a report *of* the festival but simply another aspect of it, like the triumphal architecture or the firework display. It is as magnificent *as* them without always claiming to be a picture of them' (emphasis in the original).[62] Thus, the credibility

of what is reported in such books should be taken with a pinch of salt, remembering that they always tend to eulogize the sponsor of the event and to overstate its success through the exaggerated enthusiasm of the participants. Nevertheless, lengthy descriptions of the visual effects achieved by the combination of various artistic forms of spectacle, splendid costumes, and such visual and rhetorical devices as the *imprese*, bring to life vivid and tangible snapshots of a reality, whatever its degree of idealization, that would be forever lost without them. Moreover, Naples has been privileged with some of the most exquisite festival books of the time, including abundant descriptions enriched with numerous engravings. Thus, it supplies the researcher with a rich legacy of visual evidence on top of the written reports.

Such themes as ceremonial, festivals, fashion, and the others described above, all deal, on different levels, with representations of the self or of groups, and the display of political and social values through the visual manipulation of symbols. These topics are potentially open to quite a few theoretical frameworks – symbolic and political trends of sociology and anthropology, semiotics, iconography, and more.[63] Alongside some of these theoretical insights, in the work ahead I will orient myself with the following set of questions: what was idiosyncratically Spanish about the cultural phenomena studied? What were the means and practices of Spanish cultural diffusion? How were these perceived and received by the local population?

These questions point in the direction this study is headed: the assessment of the court of Naples within the sphere of Spanish cultural influence. In this sense, it will provide a balanced synthesis between the two underlying approaches: a predominantly negative or neglectful perspective of the Spanish presence, usually adopted by Italian scholars, as opposed to the one promoted by some Spanish historians, which has put too much emphasis on the Spanish preponderance. Thus, in this study, Spain's successes in promoting its culture and values will be featured alongside instances of Neapolitan resistance or rejection, questioning the extent of Neapolitans' proverbial sense of loyalty to their Spanish rulers.[64]

Notes

1 See especially the reviews of John Adamson, 'The Making of the Ancien-Régime Court 1500–1700', in *The Princely Courts of Europe: Ritual, Politics and Culture under the Ancien Régime, 1500–1750*, ed. John Adamson (London, 1999), 7–41; and Hannah Smith, 'Court Studies and the Courts of Early Modern Europe', *The Historical Journal*, 49 (2006), 1229–338.

2 For the Grand Tour in Naples, see Atanasio Mozzillo, *Passaggio a Mezzogiorno. Napoli e il Sud nell'immaginario barocco e illuminista europeo* (Milan, 1993); Jeanne Chenault Porter, 'Reflections of the Golden Age: The Visitor's Account of Naples', in *Parthenope's Splendor: Art of the Golden Age in Naples* (Papers in Art History from The Pennsylvania State University, vol. VII), ed. Jeanne Chenault Porter and Susan Scott Munshower (University Park, Pa., 1993), 11–48; and the collection of essays, *Napoli e il regno dei grandi viaggiatori*, ed. Emanuele Kanceff and Franco Paloscia (Rome, 1994).

3 Domenico Antonio Parrino, *Napoli città nobilissima, antica e fedelissima, esposta agli occhi et alla*

mente de' curiosi, divisa in due parti ... (2 vols., Naples, 1700), I, 3.

4   George Sandys, *A Relation of a Journey Begun Ann: Dom: 1610* (3ʳᵈ ed., London, 1627), 222. Hereafter, any quoted translations from non-English sources are my sole responsibility, unless stated otherwise.

5   Jean-Jacques Bouchard, *Voyage dans le Royaume de Naples. Voyage dans le campagne de Rome*, ed. Emanuele Kanceff (2 vols., Turin, 1976), II, 234.

6   John Evelyn, *John Evelyn in Naples, 1645*, ed. H. Maynard Smith (Oxford, 1914), 56.

7   For a general review of ethnic minorities in the Kingdom of Naples, see Vincenzo Giura, *Storie di minoranze. Ebrei, greci, albanesi nel Regno di Napoli* (Naples, 1984).

8   For the urban development of Naples see Franco Strazzullo, *Edilizia e urbanistica a Napoli dal '500 al '700* (Naples, 1968); Cesare de Seta, *Napoli* (Rome and Bari, 1981); and by the same, *Napoli fra Rinascimento e Illuminismo* (Naples, 1991). For this process from an aristocratic perspective see Gérard Labrot, *Baroni in città. Residenze e comportamenti dell'aristocrazia napoletana, 1530–1734* (Naples, 1979), of which a revised and enlarged edition has appeared as *Palazzi napoletani. Storie di nobili e corteggiani, 1520–1750* (Naples, 1997).

9   The recent title by Jennifer Selwyn, *A Paradise Inhabited by Devils: The Jesuits' Civilizing Mission in Early Modern Naples* (Aldershot, 2004), evokes this established, almost ineradicable, stereotype of Neapolitan citizens to this day. On this topic see also Benedetto Croce, 'Il "paradiso abitato da diavoli"', in his *Uomini e cose della vecchia Italia* (2 vols., Bari, 1927), 68–86; Giuseppe Galasso, 'Lo stereotipo del napoletano e le sue variazioni regionali', in his *L'altra Europa. Per un antropologia storica del Mezzogiorno d'Italia* (Milan, 1982), 143–90; and Mozzillo, *Passaggio a Mezzogiorno*, 148–216.

10 Giuseppe Galasso, 'La Spagna imperiale e il Mezzogiorno', in his *Alla periferia dell'impero. Il Regno di Napoli nel periodo spagnolo (secoli XIV–XVII)* (Turin, 1994), 9.

11 See John H. Elliott, 'A Europe of Composite Monarchies', *Past and Present*, 137 (1992), 52–3. For Elliott's earlier discussions concerning the composite nature of the Spanish monarchy see his *Imperial Spain, 1469–1716* (London, 1963), especially 156–8, 242–78.

12 Aurelio Musi suggests an elaboration and sophistication of the model, calling for a deeper study of the formal and informal relations between the various 'parts' of the 'system'. Hence, focusing on the Italian early modern states under direct or indirect Habsburg control, he claims that they should be considered as a 'sub-system' of the Spanish monarchy. See 'Il Regno di Napoli e il sistema imperiale spagnolo', in his *L'Italia dei Viceré. Integrazione e resistenza nel sistema imperiale spagnolo* (Cava de' Tirreni, 2000), 23–35. See also in *ibid.*, 'Napoli e la Spagna tra XVI e XVII secolo. Studi ed orientamenti storiografici recenti', 46–7.

13 Elliott, 'Composite Monarchies', 68.

14 Helmut G. Koenigsberger, *The Habsburgs and Europe, 1516–1660* (Ithaca, NY, and London, 1971), 26.

15 See *ibid.*, 47; and Guido D'Agostino, 'Il governo spagnolo nell'Italia meridionale (1503–1580)', in *Storia di Napoli*, vol. 5.1: *Il viceregno*, ed. Ernesto Pontieri (Naples, 1970), 14.

16 Elliott, 'Composite Monarchies', 69.

17 Galasso, 'La Spagna imperiale', 23.

18 J. M. Batista y Roca, 'Foreword', in Helmut Koenigsberger's *The Government of Sicily under Philip II of Spain: A Study in the Practice of Empire* (London, 1951), 11.

19 'Istruzioni di Filippo III al vicere Conte di Lemos', Archivo de Simancas, Valladolid, Secretarías provinciales, Nápoles, 634, fol. 135r–135v, appears in the collection of documents by Giuseppe Coniglio, *Declino del viceregno di Napoli (1599–1689)* (4 vols., Naples, 1990–91), I, 69–70.

20 Carlos José Hernando Sánchez, 'Los virreyes de la Monarquía Española en Italia. Evolución y práctica de un oficio de gobierno', *Studia Historica. Historia Moderna*, 26 (2004), 50.

21 For the origin of the use of viceroys in Spain, see Elliott, *Imperial Spain*, 18–19.

22 D'Agostino, 'Il governo spagnolo', 15.

23 Benedetto Croce, *History of the Kingdom of Naples*, trans. Frances Frenaye (Chicago, 1970), 94.

24 Galasso, 'La Spagna imperiale', 14–16.

25 Quoted in Koenigsberger, *Habsburgs and Europe*, 70.

26 These are studied by Gabriele Pepe, *Il Mezzogiorno d'Italia sotto gli Spagnoli. La tradizione storio-grafica* (Florence, 1952).

27 Benedetto Croce, *La Spagna nella vita italiana durante la Rinascenza* (Bari, 1917).

28 For each phase see, respectively, *ibid.*, 1–31, 32–74, 98 ff.

29 *Ibid.*, 238–9.

30 *Ibid.*, 240.

31 *Ibid.*, 251.

32 Croce produced various other works of relevance for the seventeenth century. For the present, I will limit myself to mention two collections of essays: *Saggi sulla letteratura Italiana del Seicento* (Bari, 1911); and *Storia della età Barocca in Italia* (Bari, 1929).

33 Fausto Nicolini, *Aspetti della vita italo-spagnuola nel Cinque e Seicento* (Naples, 1934).

34 See Rosario Villari, *La rivolta antispagnola a Napoli. Le origini (1585–1647)* (Bari, 1967). (See note 39 below.)

35 See Fausto Nicolini, 'Il tumulto di San Martino e la carestia del 1629', in his *Vita italo-spagnuola*, 127–288.

36 For the reconstruction of Spanish Naples in Nicolini's work see *ibid.*, 243–337. For recent evaluations of the interdependence of Naples and Milan see the collection of essays edited by Aurelio Musi, *Nel sistema imperiale. L'Italia spagnola* (Naples, 1994); and Giuseppe Galasso, 'Milano spagnola nella prospettiva napoletana', in his *Alla periferia dell'impero*, 301–33.

37 Guido Quazza, *La decadenza italiana nella storia europea. Saggi sul Sei-Settecento* (Turin, 1971), 15–16.

38 See especially Federico Chabod, *Storia di Milano nell'epoca di Carlo V* (Turin, 1961).

39 See the English translation by James Newell and John A. Marino, *The Revolt of Naples* (Cambridge, 1993), x–xi, 7.

40 On the building of tension towards the revolutionary crisis see especially *ibid.*, 135–52.

41 See *ibid.*, 19–33. Many examples could be brought for comparison. Especially relevant are two historical-anthropological essays which deal with the enactment of subversive rituals: Peter Burke, 'The Virgin of the Carmine and the Revolt of Masaniello', in his *The Historical Anthropology of Early Modern Italy: Essays on Perception And Communication* (Cambridge, 1987), 191–206; and Robert Darnton, 'The Great Cat Massacre at Rue San-Severine', in his *The Great Cat Massacre and Other Episodes in French Cultural History* (London, 1984), 107–44.

42 Villari, *The Revolt of Naples*, especially 115–22.

43 Giuseppe Galasso, *Economia e società nella Calabria del Cinquecento* (Naples, 1967), 44–5, 53–5; Quazza, *La decadenza*, 70–1; Domenico Sella, *Italy in the Seventeenth Century* (London, 1997), 63–9; Enrico Stumpo, 'La crisi del Seicento in Italia', in *La storia. I grandi problemi dal medioevo all'età contemporanea*, vol. 5, ed. Nicola Tranfaglia and Massimo Firpo (Turin, 1986), 313–37; Tommaso Astarita, *The Continuity of Feudal Power: The Caracciolo of Brienza in Spanish Naples* (Cambridge, 1992). Large sections of the book touch on the issue, but strictly on the debate see 204–5.

44 Eric Cochrane, 'southern Italy in the Age of the Spanish Viceroys: Some Recent Titles', *Journal of Modern History*, 58 (1986), 198–9.

45 *Ibid.*, 204.

46 Norbert Elias' principal works on the court are: *The Court Society*, trans. Edmund Jephcott (Oxford, 1983); and *The Civilizing Process*, trans. Edmund Jephcott (2 vols., Oxford, 1978–82). For an exhaustive discussion of his impact see Jeroen Duindam, *Myths of Power: Norbert Elias and the Early Modern European Court* (Amsterdam, 1999).

47 Sergio Bertelli, 'Il Cinquecento', in *La storiografia italiana degli ultimi vent'anni*, vol. 2, *Età moderna*, ed. Luigi De Rosa (3 vols., Rome and Bari, 1989), II, 32.

48 See, for example, Francesco Erspamer, *La biblioteca di Don Ferrante. Duello e onore nella cultura del Cinquecento* (Rome, 1982); and *Le trame della moda*, ed. Anna Giulia Cavagna and Grazietta Butazzi (Rome, 1995).

49 The complete reference is: Sergio Bertelli and Giuliano Crifò (eds.), *Rituale, cerimoniale,*

ettichetta (Milan, 1986). See also by the *Laboratorio di Storia*, Sergio Bertelli, Franco Cardini, Elvira Gabero Zorzi, *Italian Renaissance Courts* (London, 1986).

50 Of most relevance to our study is Galasso's already cited collection of essays *Alla periferia dell'impero*; his *Napoli spagnola dopo Masaniello. Politica, cultura, società* (2 vols., Florence, 1982); and the recent, *Il Regno di Napoli. Il Mezzogiorno spagnolo ed austriaco (1622–1734)* (Turin, 2006).

51 The numerous individual contributions of these scholars will be listed throughout the book.

52 The work of these authors has been preceded by nationalist Spanish scholars who strongly emphasized the preponderance of Spain in Italy. See especially Felipe Picatoste, *Estudios sobra la grandeza y decadencia de España. Los españoles en Italia* (Madrid, 1887); and Francisco Elias de Tejada, *Nápoles Hispánico* (5 vols., Madrid, 1958–64).

53 Here is just a short sample of this extensive bibliography: Gianvittorio Signorotto (ed.), *L'Italia degli Austrias. Monarchia cattolica e domini italiani nei secoli XVI e XVII*, special issue of *Cheiron*, 17–18 (1992); the already cited Musi (ed.), *Nel sistema imperiale*; Luis Antonio Ribot García and Ernest Belenguer Cebría (eds.), *Las sociedades ibéricas y el mar a fin del siglo XVI* (4 vols., Pabellón de España, 1998); Ernest Belenguer Cebría (ed.), *Felipe II y el Mediterráneo* (4 vols., Barcelona, 1999). For a recent compilation on the subject with a larger representation of international scholars see Thomas Dandelet and John A. Marino (eds.), *Spain in Italy: Politics, Society, and Religion 1500–1700* (Leiden, 2006).

54 For Parrino's work see *Teatro eroico e politico de' governi de' vicerè del Regno di Napoli, dal tempo di Ferdinando il Cattolico fino al presente*, in *Raccolta di tutti i più rinomati scrittori dell'istoria generale del Regno di Napoli* [*Raccolta* hereafter], vols. 9–10, ed. Giovanni Gravier (25 vols., Naples, 1769–77). For Coniglio's see *I vicerè spagnoli di Napoli* (Naples, 1967).

55 Carlos José Hernando Sánchez, *Castilla y Nápoles en el siglo XVI. El virrey Pedro de Toledo. Linaje, estado y cultura (1532–1553)* (Valladolid, 1994).

56 For each of the viceroys mentioned see respectively, Isabel Enciso Alonso-Muñumer, *Nobleza, poder y mecenazgo en tiempos de Felipe III. Nápoles y el Conde de Lemos* (Madrid, 2007); and Sabina De Cavi, *Architecture and Royal Presence: Domenico and Giulio Cesare Fontana in Spanish Naples (1592–1627)* (Newcastle, 2009); Ana Minguito Palomares, 'Linaje, poder y cultura. El gobierno de Íñigo Vélez de Guevara, VII Conde de Oñate en Nápoles (1648–1653)' (PhD dissertation, Universidad Complutense de Madrid, 2002); and Diana Carrió-Invernizzi, 'Entre Nápoles y España. Cultura política y mecenazgo artístico de los virreyes Pascual y Pedro Antonio de Aragón (1611–1672)' (PhD dissertation, Universitat de Barcelona, 2006), recently published as *El gobierno de las imágenes. Ceremonial y mecenazgo en la Italia española del siglo XVII* (Madrid, 2008).

57 For a comparative example see Francesca Cantù (ed.), *Las cortes virreinales de la monarquía española. América e Italia* (Rome, 2008). For two insightful Spanish American case studies see: Alejandro Cañeque, *The King's Living Image: The Culture and Politics of Viceregal Power in Colonial Mexico* (New York, 2004); and Alejandra Osorio, *Inventing Lima: Baroque Modernity in Peru's South Sea Metropolis* (New York, 2008).

58 For the pioneering studies on the events of 1647 see Michelangelo Schipa, *La cosidetta rivolta di Masaniello da memorie contemporanee inedite* (Naples, 1918); and by the same *Masaniello* (Bari and Rome, 1925). An influential socio-economic interpretation is provided by the aforementioned Villari, *The Revolt of Naples*. A more recent contextual political analysis is provided by Aurelio Musi, *La rivolta di Masaniello nella scena politica barocca* (Naples, 1989). For an alternative interpretation see Burke, 'Revolt of Masaniello', 191–206; for Villari's rebuttal of the latter see, 'Masaniello: Contemporary and Recent Interpretations', *Past and Present*, 103 (1985), 117–32; Burke's rejoinder appears in 'Masaniello: A Response', *Past and Present*, 114 (1987), 197–9. For two recent monographs on the topic see Silvana d'Alessio, *Contagi. La rivolta napoletana del 1647–48. Linguaggio e potere politico* (Florence, 2003); and by the same, *Masaniello. La sua vita e il mito in Europa* (Rome and Salerno, 2007).

59 Henceforth I will use the original term *popolo*, as this social group was described by contemporaries. Other possible choices as 'people' – too Republican – 'working class' – too Marxist

- and 'third estate', which is probably the most accurate but invariably associated with France in the *Ancien Régime*, give either a distorted or partial picture, or are loaded with anachronistic social and political meanings.

60 See Antonio Bulifon, *Giornali di Napoli dal MDXLVII al MDCCVI* (Naples, 1932); Domenico Confuorto, *Giornali di Napoli dal MDCLXXIX al MDCIC* (2 vols., Naples, 1930–31); Innocenzo Fuidoro, *Giornali di Napoli dal MDCLX al MDCLXXX* (4 vols., Naples, 1934–39); Francesco Capecelatro, *Degli annali della città di Napoli 1631–1640* (Naples, 1849); Scipione Guerra, *Diurnali di Scipione Guerra*, ed. Giuseppe De Montemayor (Naples, 1891). This is only a partial list. Other diaries used will be cited throughout the book.

61 Galasso, *Napoli spagnola*, I, xxxiii.

62 Helen Watanabe-O'Kelly, 'Festivals Books in Europe from Renaissance to Rococo', *The Seventeenth Century Journal*, 3 (1988), 197.

63 Here are a few syntheses, which contain relevant bibliographies: Peter Burke, *History and Social Theory* (Cambridge, 1992); David Kertzer, *Ritual, Politics, and Power* (New Haven, 1988); Edward Muir, *Ritual in Early Modern Europe* (Cambridge, 1997); and Sergio Bertelli, *Il corpo del re. Sacralità e potere nell'Europa medievale e moderna* (Florence, 1990). For semiotic approaches related to festivities see *Carnival!*, ed. Thomas Sebeok (Berlin, 1984).

64 Here are the key texts that deal with this issue: Rosario Villari, *Per il re o per la patria. La fedeltà nel Seicento* (Rome and Bari, 1994); Aurelio Musi, 'La fedeltà al re nella prima età moderna', in his *L'Italia dei Viceré*, 149–64; Giuseppe Galasso, 'Da "Napoli gentile" a "Napoli fedelissima"', in his *Napoli capitale. Identità politica e identità cittadina. Studi e ricerche 1266–1860* (Naples, 2003), 61–110; Carlos Josè Hernando Sánchez, 'Españoles e italianos. Nación y lealtad en el Reino de Nápoles durante Las Guerras de Italia, in *La monarquía de las naciones. Patria, nación, y naturaleza en la Monarquía de España*, ed. Antonio Álvarez Ossorio-Alvariño and Bernardo J. García y García (Madrid, 2004), 423–81; and in the same volume, Angelantonio Spagnoletti, 'El concepto de naturaleza, nación y patria en Italia y en el Reino de Nápoles con respecto a la Monarquía de los Austrias', 483–503; and Giovanni Muto, 'Fedeltà e patria nel lessico politico napoletano della prima età moderna', in *Storia Sociale e politica. Omaggio a Rosario Villari*, ed. Alberto Merola, Giovanni Muto, Elena Valeri, and Maria Anonietta Visceglia (Milan, 2006), 495–522; and also by the same, 'Fidelildad, política y conflictos urbanos en el Reino de Nápoles (siglos XVI–XVII)', in *Ciudades en conflicto (siglos XVI–XVII)*, ed. Jose I. Portea and Juan E. Gelabert (Junta de Castilla y León, 2008), 370–95. I would like to thank Professor Muto for making the last two items available to me.

1

The ritual power of viceroys

The viceregal institution

The following chapter will discuss the structure, function, and reception of the viceregal institution in early modern Naples. In order to assess the political might of this institution within the local context, the focus will be on the ways in which the court's ceremonial helped to create hierarchies within court society, and to elevate the viceroy's public image.[1]

The Neapolitan case presents itself as especially interesting when compared to other princely courts since it had two leading authorities, the legal ruler – the king – and his designated *alter ego* – the viceroy. The famous bookseller and publisher Domenico Antonio Parrino explains how this duality worked in perfect harmony with a metaphor that can practically be considered a cliché in the political thought of the time, that of the *body politic*:[2] 'thus the monarchies do not feel any damage from the Prince's absence, whom through his prime minister, conducts through the main artery, the blood, and the aliment to the far members; and manoeuvres, and governs them, as an arm under his control, physically divided from the bust, yet morally attached to it.'[3] Giulio Cesare Capaccio adds in his celebrated contemporary guide to Naples, *Il forastiero* (*The Foreigner*),[4] that if it were not for the constraint posed by the king's will, one 'can say that they carry with them in all respect the image, and the royal authority'.[5] Similarly, according to Parrino 'they enjoy the same privileges, and pre-eminences, and they are entitled to the same reverence, that is required to the person of the prince, of whom the viceroys are images'.[6] Similar words, although stated with immoderate vehemence, were expressed by a contemporary sycophantic commentator on the arrival of the viceroy the Duke of Osuna (1582–86) in Naples. He claimed that his 'royal aspect' and the 'majesty of his face' brought great joy to the city after having been denied for too long 'the glow and the splendour of a master or the one who represents him'; and with such a clear radiance that it can only be compared to 'the immortal memory of Charles V'.[7] Doubtless, such a direct association would have been intolerable to the ears of a Spanish king.

What was included in the actual authority of viceroys? Their mandate lasted three years, although it was renewable, and it was normally reconfirmed by the king for at least another term. The viceroys' formal titles were those of *lugarteniente* and *capitan general* – that is the highest political and military representative of the crown.[8] Hence, 'they can do what they want, be soldiers, and legislators; owners of the lives and property of their vassals'.[9] Parrino claims that viceroys concentrate three kinds of powers: legislative, executive-judiciary, and gracious. According to the first, viceroys can legislate new laws or repeal part of those already existing, conforming to their will. According to the second, they exercise supreme jurisdiction over all the inhabitants of the Kingdom of Naples. In case of outlaws, especially if they have committed a crime of state, viceroys do not have to take into consideration the existing laws or the local tribunals, and they can act according to their best knowledge of the administration of justice. Last, by means of their gracious power viceroys can pardon, reduce sentences, and intervene in various feudal issues, unless this intervention is forbidden by the royal pragmatics.[10] In brief, viceroys have the authority to do 'everything that the very person of the king would do, if he were present in this kingdom'.[11] When in the following century Montesquieu will warn in his celebrated *De l'esprit de lois* (*The Spirit of the Laws*) against the concentration of all forms of power in one man, or in one body of magistrates, he will refer precisely to autocratic rulers like the Spanish king, and by extension the Neapolitan viceroy.[12]

Since the king/viceroy duality was harmonious only in theory, it lasted just as long as quarrels did not reach the king's ears.[13] In fact, Philip III made sure to keep the channels of communication unobstructed, ordaining that 'from now on they may freely write me what they want without the viceroys or other ministers being able to stop them. I want, and it is my will, that the said city write to me without trouble'.[14] Negative reports on viceroys, coming either from the ranks of Neapolitan nobles or from state officials, aided the Spanish kings to clip their delegates' wings. The most blatant measure was their deposition before the end of their term. Since this step meant a clear sign of royal disfavour it was met with different degrees of resistance. For example, when in 1653 the Count of Castrillo (1653–59) arrived, somewhat unexpectedly, to replace the Count of Oñate (1648–53), the latter is said to have protested furiously: 'Que he hecho yo al Rey?' (What [harm] have I done to the king?).[15] Equally unable to control his temper, the Marquis of Astorga (1672–75) furiously smashed his spectacles on the floor at hearing the news of the appointment of his successor.[16] Much worse was the not uncommon reaction of viceroys who tried to postpone their departure, giving various excuses to prolong their stay, thus blatantly undermining royal will. Probably the most extreme of these instances was supplied by the Duke of Osuna (1616–20), whose efforts to delay the arrival of his successor, Cardinal Borja, reached new peaks of defiance. If we want to believe one of the many unfavourable vignettes of this controversial viceroy, as described in the generally unflattering *Narrazioni* of Osuna's government by Francesco Zazzera, the duke's boldness can be best portrayed by his conduct during the Carnival season that preceded his removal. Wearing a red cardinal's robe, and

impersonating Borja, he cried: 'I am the Cardinal de Aspettatis,'[17] alluding mockingly to the cardinal's forced waiting. In a desperate attempt to retain power after Philip III had already decided to replace him, Osuna started to make frequent populist excursions in the streets, throwing promises and coins in the air in order to buy the sympathy of the Neapolitan people. In one of these instances, clearly challenging the royal decision, he asked those surrounding him whom they wanted to rule the realm, as if it were up to him to decide or up to them to choose. Some answered: His Excellency 'and many ignorant plebeians [answered]: His Majesty'.[18] The chronicler's scorn towards the 'ignorant plebeians' is well deserved. However confusing such an episode might have been for them they should have known the difference between the king and his stand-in. Furthermore, this was a difference that was waved right in their face because no single dynastic early modern ruler would ever have subjected himself to popular vote. Eventually, Osuna's reluctance to leave his position led to a quasi *coup d'état* on behalf of Borja who entered the city incognito, aided by night and by the local organs of state, and took possession of his office behind Osuna's back.[19] Indeed, Capaccio's Foreigner was right to comment concerning the succession of viceroys: 'It must be a difficult thing for the one leaving, to see the one coming'.[20] Similarly, the viceroy the Count of Olivares (1595–99) is said to have exclaimed just before leaving his office: 'One should not wish to be the Viceroy of Naples, to avoid the displeasure of the departure'.[21]

Various constitutional tools mitigated the viceroys' power, by means of 'privileges, constitutions, pragmatics … and mostly by secret instructions, and royal letters'.[22] Moreover, their actual degree of power diminished throughout the years. Their almost incontestable strength in the Kingdom of Naples, on a local level, which reached its apex during the unparalleled long regency of Pedro de Toledo (1532–53), significantly diminished after the middle of the sixteenth century. Then, the Spanish monarchs – yielding to local political pressures to put a check on overambitious viceroys and to respect the kingdom's privileges – subordinated them to the will of the Collateral Council, the highest local organ of central power that worked at the viceroy's side. In fact, the authority held by the viceroy resided during the time of a viceregal interregnum with the Collateral Council. Even when a viceroy was about to leave his place to his successor there was a ritual void of a few hours in which the Collateral held the viceregal authority. Members of the Collateral were referred to during this time with the title of 'Your Excellency', the same held by the viceroy. After the death of the viceroy Ramón de Cardona, in the absence of an available successor, the Collateral stayed in power from March to July 1522.[23] According to a royal order from 1593, all things concerning 'the state, justice, government, and property' would be decided by the majority of the votes. The viceroy was left with the power of veto, in case he did not concord with the majority, leaving the final decision to the king. As noted by Giovanni Muto, 'this principle legitimized the primacy not only of an institution to the daily practice of government, but also that of a status group, the *togati*, already fully trained for the political direction of the state'.[24] Muto refers to the dramatic rising to power

of the jurists-bureaucrats – the local *noblesse de robe* – who drew their power directly from the Spanish crown and from their studies in law. In the Collateral Council they succeeded in alienating the traditional aristocratic component with which they originally shared the number of seats in the council.[25]

Nevertheless, even if the viceroy was to become nothing more than a minister with limited rule during the seventeenth century, he continued to play the central role in the Spanish rites of power in Naples. As Peter Burke has poignantly remarked in Charles V's case, 'the imperial image may also be said to have been constructed out of people, who were walking "representations" as well as "representatives" of the emperor'.[26] Consequently, as I will try to show next, the court ceremonial that revolved around the viceroy, very much as in the case of the Spanish king, aimed to elevate him to supreme heights.

Court ceremonial

So, what were those ritual instances in which the viceroy played the part of a king by proxy? According to the rules of the Neapolitan court collected by the master of ceremonies Joseph Raneo,[27] the viceroy virtually carried out all the ceremonial duties – ordinary and extraordinary – that were the lot of European royalty and ruling princes.[28] Among the ordinary tasks it is worth to note the ceremonial consumption of daily meals, the holding of public audiences, and the regular participation in the cyclical/religious festivities and related processions. Among the extraordinary – the management of civic festive displays and participation in them as the principal actor; the reception and entertainment of Spanish or foreign personalities; the representation of the Spanish monarch at the Neapolitan parliament, which gathered when the king requested an extraordinary financial contribution; the organization of military parades and their direction, as the supreme commander of the army; and the arrangement of obsequies at the death of a royal person, taking an active part at the funerary rites, and receiving condolences on behalf of the king. Even though a deep analysis of all of these roles is beyond our immediate scope, I would like to linger on the protocol involved in them.

Obviously, when we speak of a state protocol in Naples, it is clear that the cultural model was the court of Madrid. The genealogy of Spanish court behaviour, in its turn, can be traced back to fifteenth-century Burgundy, which had reached such splendour with its festivals, triumphal rites, and artistic patronage, and had crafted such an elaborated protocol that it became a model for later West European courts.[29] The Burgundian influence in the Spanish case was the consequence of a deliberate action. On 15 August 1548, Charles V simply superimposed Burgundian ceremonial at the court of his heir Philip II in Valladolid, and so it was retained during the entire Habsburg regency.[30] Thus, following the Spanish model, according to the master of ceremonies that preceded Joseph Raneo, Miguel Diéz de Aux (who served in this position approximately from the

early 1570s to 1621), all the ceremonies 'in the Royal Palace of the Kingdom of Naples were according to the use and custom of the Royal House of Burgundy'.[31] Apparently, the Burgundian main attribute was an aggregative one. 'There were more people, more courses at the banquets, more festivals, more regulations – a quantitative difference which ultimately produced a qualitative one.'[32] Accordingly, one of the most tangible results in Philip II's reorganized court was that the number of officers in his household doubled in size.[33] This inflation of offices at court reinforced the competition and made Spanish nobles exceptionally punctilious and fanatical in all matters regarding court protocol.[34]

What effect would these Spanish courtly ideals have on Naples? Many examples can be quoted of foreigners visiting the Kingdom of Naples criticizing the local nobility as being excessively ceremonious, a quality that has often been attributed to the imitation of Spanish manners.[35] Even Spaniards could see their own behaviour reflected in their Neapolitan subjects. In the instructions for a new Spanish ambassador, Neapolitan nobles were labelled as 'arrogant, have a reverential and ceremonious behaviour; they appear Spaniards'.[36] However, Benedetto Croce, while mapping the stereotypical images of Neapolitans, claims that the Florentines noted the Neapolitan ceremoniousness long before the advent of the Habsburgs. In the fourteenth century, Florentine merchants received large concessions from the Angevin kings to trade in Naples. The Florentines, belonging to a republican tradition, found in the Neapolitans, who belonged to a rigid feudal tradition, an irritatingly high evaluation of feudal honours and a related characteristic pomposity.[37] This observation should be placed in a larger historical context, as Naples enjoyed one of the richest courtly traditions in the peninsula, serving as a 'model court' for the other Italian states, during Angevin rule, between the thirteenth and the fourteenth centuries, and during the subsequent Aragonese monarchy, in the fifteenth century.[38] We can suppose, then, that when the Castilians arrived they found in Naples a very fertile and receptive ground for ceremonial behaviour. Was this also the case for the ceremonial that was superimposed in the Neapolitan court around the image of the viceroy?

A general definition of ceremonial will be useful to understand its mechanisms in Naples. Foremost, it is important to recognize that it was an elaborated form of non-verbal communication, expressed in the language of ceremony, having mainly a dual function. First, according to Norbert Elias' definition, etiquette was the king's tool to communicate his exclusive rule to his courtiers.[39] Second, etiquette created hierarchies among the courtiers, according to the positions of power that they occupied at court.[40] The anthropologist Carmelo Lisón Tolosana identifies two main principles that guide courtly etiquette: a code of proximity (space, time, place, and distance) and a code of kinetics (corporal movements, mimics, and gestures).[41] To these two one might add a third factor, that usually interacts with one or both of these codes – 'ceremonial objects' (hats, crowns, wands, sceptres, swords, curtains, canopies, and so forth).[42]

The code of proximity enhances the ruler's stand by making him the focal point, the centre, of all the ceremonial activities at court, and at the same time it makes it possible to measure the relative status of courtiers according to their radial position from that core. Daily, routine activities, no less than extraordinary events, were ritualized to convey this ubiquitous message. Good examples of the former are the rites known as *lever* and *coucher* at the court of Louis XIV, which celebrated the rising of the king in the morning and his lying down at night, adhering to the symbolism of the king as sun; a symbolism that reaches a new zenith in the seventeenth century because of the acceptance of the new Copernican astronomy, according to which the sun is the centre of the universe, just as the king is the centre of his court.[43] The *lever* consisted of no less than six different entries of family members, court officials, ministers, courtiers, and foreign visitors, among others, in descending order of importance, who were admitted in varying degrees of physical proximity to witness the rising of the *Roi Soleil*.[44] The binary opposition centre/periphery is only one among various others, such as high/low, right/left, behind/in front, first/second, superior/inferior, in/out, seated/standing, and so forth, that mark the hierarchies constructed by the dynamics of proximity. Obviously, the king's body is the axis around which these oppositions revolve. For example, when the Spanish queen was at the king's side, he stood on the right. During processions he stood in the centre, having the Council of Castile at the right and Aragón at the left. When he was not present, the centre, the right, the front, or the first place belonged to his official representative, or to the next in scale of dignity.[45]

The way ceremonial objects interacted with the spatial paradigm is clarified by the axiomatic higher position assumed by the king, by means of a platform or a throne; and the delimitation of his quasi 'sacred space' by being almost always under a canopy.[46] The same thing happened on a larger scale through the physical layout of the environment. For example, foreign ambassadors at the Spanish court were guided to meet the king through richly decorated rooms, with the sole objective of dazzling the guest.[47] An even better example is the Ambassador's Staircase leading to the audience with Louis XIV. 'The point on the staircase at which the king or his household officer chose to receive the visiting diplomat exactly corresponded to the degree of amity or favour the monarch chose to display towards the foreign power.'[48]

As for the code of kinetics, various gestures and movements expressed the self-depreciation and recognition of the sovereign's superiority. For example, at the Spanish court the king was greeted by his subjects with deep bows, to which he responded with a short nod. Supplicants at royal audiences gave the king a genuflection before he spoke, and kept standing in his presence, with only a privileged few being able to hold their hats on their heads in his presence. Other such practices included: speaking in a low voice in the antechamber, kissing the king's hand, never showing him the back, and more.[49] Ceremonial dining in Spain supplies an excellent example of the way that gestures were expressed via ceremonial objects. These offered an entire choreography, where a multitude of valets, servants, carvers, and royal officials manipulated royal cups,

napkins, and various utensils in a reverential play around the royal diner, who usually consumed the food all alone at his table.[50] Examples of this dynamism could be multiplied *ad nauseam* as the entire court, physically and ideologically, was structured to glorify the idea of the absolutist monarchy.

Some of the same rituals and mechanisms described above were adopted in the Neapolitan court. The viceroy's daily dinner, for example, was celebrated with extreme ceremoniousness. Four halberdiers in front and four behind had to escort it to the table. Contrary to the norms of hygiene, which had little or no impact on a code based on deference, all those involved in the cooking and serving of the food had to be bareheaded. An occasional hair in the soup was a small price to pay for a society that valued honour more than life itself. It goes without saying that valets and servants had to remain standing all through the viceroy's dinner.[51] His physical safety was safeguarded with extra care. A squadron of about a hundred German guards had to escort him at all times when he was outside the city. If he stayed overnight, a force of fifty Spanish musketeers was added to protect him.[52] Every time he mounted a horse he had to be escorted by four German guards, two on each side, preceded by an uncovered lackey in front of him.[53]

The number of personnel at the viceregal household can give us an idea of the court's size, a fact that reflected on the viceroy's public grandeur.[54] He had at his disposal: one confessor, two secretaries of war, and of justice, one head butler, one head servant, one master of the horse, one master of the hall, eight gentlemen, twelve pages, one treasurer and one accountant, one doctor of the chamber, four assistants of the chamber, one master of ceremonies and four porters, twenty-six lackeys, four buglers, thirty master cookers, bottlers, storekeepers, and low servants, twenty-seven coachmen and stable boys. The latter took care of twelve horses that were for the viceroy's personal use, forty-four carriage horses, and twelve mules. In addition, one needs to calculate the people who served directly the vicereine: one master of the horse, one secretary, one head servant (female), eight dames, two hall assistants, four female slaves 'for low tasks', and one elder woman.[55] Totting up we reach the sum of 158 people, and this is without counting the few hundred soldiers who guarded the viceroy's person, and the regal palace, mentioned above.

By early modern European standards this number can be considered as relatively elevated but not exaggerated. It surpassed the *famiglia* of an average Italian cardinal's court,[56] it paralleled what was considered a large aristocratic English household, but it could not rival the conspicuous numbers of servants in royal and papal households. It has been calculated that under the service of the various Spanish kings during the seventeenth century, there were no fewer than 2,000 paid employees at a time.[57] This did not prevent the Spanish king passing a law in 1623 which limited the household of the Spanish *grandes* to eighteen persons alone. Excesses were overlooked, but even then, the largest households did not surpass 100 dependants.[58] In this sense, it is clear that Neapolitan viceroys were regarded as a category apart, closer in their privilege to the

Spanish king than to the highest ranks of Spanish aristocracy. This is exemplified by one of the suggestive comments of the 'Foreigner'. After having heard the dimensions of the viceregal household he exclaims: 'I will tell you the truth that I find this government full of so much majesty ... And it is with much reason, from what I have heard, that an old woman told the emperor, I wish I lived to see you [becoming] Viceroy of Naples.'[59] Is this a Neapolitan anecdote that intends to adulatorily exaggerate the viceroy's power, or to ironically deride it? Perhaps both, depending on the occasion. What is sure is that the irony escaped viceregal censure, which certainly preferred the literal interpretation.[60]

A regal effect was probably achieved by a series of exclusive privileges. The viceroy sat or stood on a platform and was covered by a canopy on various occasions such as courtly banquets, public audiences, and visits to churches. In the latter case, consistent with the code of proximity, the platform had to be placed in the centre right in front of the altar. Raneo noted that great care had to be taken that under no circumstances whatsoever should anyone or anything be situated between the platform and the altar. The viceroy sat on a throne on two occasions: at the general parliament and at the procession of St Januarius. He was the only one allowed to have six horses or mules for his carriages, his coachmen were the only ones to go bareheaded, and his portable chair had to be covered with a canopy as a sign of respect. Every time the viceroy and vicereine left the palace, the flag was lowered.[61] In addition, various exalting ceremonial rules applied for the important religious festivals of the year, like Easter and Christmas.[62]

In sum, the ceremonial revolving around the Neapolitan viceroy resembled that of other absolutist rulers of the period, and it fits well within the contemporary European tradition. However, besides these basic similarities, the various rulers could choose to adopt different models of public self-display in a way that determined their image, as we will now turn to examine.

The viceregal public image

The viceroy's public image can be compared to that of the absolutist monarchs of the seventeenth century by evaluating the ruler's degree of accessibility. After the middle of the sixteenth century, with the strengthening of European monarchs, some major changes shaped the structure of courts and the character of kingship. One such important change was the shift from a peripatetic entourage to a residential court. In France, after the accession of Henri IV (1589–1610), the court came to acquire a permanent base in the Louvre, and later, during the last two decades of the seventeenth century, in Versailles. In Spain, Philip II was responsible for making Madrid the capital of his empire and the centre of his court from 1561 onwards. One of the practical consequences of this shift was the restriction of the royal person to a very specific location. Contemporaneously, in both Spain and France, the court ceremonial was elaborated to regulate

the royal activities in a way that screened the royal person and set him apart from the rest of humanity, including his courtiers. The very architectural structure of the royal residence, besides its function to impose the 'code of proximity', expressed royal remoteness and isolation. 'Palaces consisted of a series of "thresholds", each requiring higher degrees of status (or the monarch's favour) before they could be crossed. Court gate, guard chamber, Presence Chamber: each interposed barriers between the outside world and the court's inner sanctum, the private apartments of the monarch.'[63]

Spanish monarchs cultivated jealously the image of a 'hidden monarchy' throughout the seventeenth century.[64] It was a notoriously known fact that it could take several months or even years to meet the Spanish monarch, and this only after having dealt with an endless series of royal officers. Let us take for example the comments of the secretary of Camillo Borghese, the papal ambassador (*nuncio*) at Philip II's court, in 1594: 'it is a monstrous thing for us Italians the way they negotiate and let you say whatever you want without answering a thing ... And in that court no one keeps track of time, so that it takes years to conclude even a simple negotiation.'[65] The French monarchs were less strict, even though they also employed a segregative etiquette that 'protected the king from the press of the crowd and imposed the stamp of his authority on the court'.[66] However, it was only under Louis XIV that etiquette was exploited to its full by attaining an effective balance between the double function of 'protecting' the king's person, inasmuch as it was 'deliberately used to limit access to the ruler's patronage', and 'projecting' his authority through that permanent royal display that came to be known as 'public' kingship.[67]

According to Peter Burke's tripartite typology of kingship, to the 'private', practically inaccessible Spanish model, and the 'public' style of Versailles, though highly dignified and equally inaccessible to those outside the restricted circle of the court, there should be added the 'demotic' archetype, applicable to the Scandinavian early modern rulers. Their public conduct, whether 'spontaneous', as a result of a relatively egalitarian social order, or 'staged', as an alternative to a 'rhetoric of dignity', was characterized by a conspicuous lack of pomp, simplicity of clothes, and frequent exchanges with subjects of low status, which were conducted on relatively equal terms.[68] The Neapolitan viceroys fall between these categories, not conforming to anyone in particular, although their conduct may at times apply to each one of them. What dictated it was the fact that their role was vicarious and delegated. Their ambivalent status as de facto heads of state, on the one hand, and the dependence of their position on the Spanish king, on the other, is well reflected in Capaccio's 'illuminating' metaphor, so to speak. He likens them to 'mirrors that reflect the rays of the sun'. Hence, 'while the kings are far away, with their presence they participate, and communicate their splendour'.[69]

This status of compromise is well reflected in the ceremony that served to mark the viceroys' accession to their office. Generally exploring the place of ritual in politics, David Kertzer explains the purpose of rites of investiture: 'Political organizations and, more generally, political systems require a division of labour. In all state societies this

entails a hierarchy of status and power. In order to invest a person with authority over others, there must be an effective means for changing the way other people view that person, as well as for changing the person's conception of his right to impose his will on others'.[70] Such a 'functional' definition – in the sense that it is based on the belief that society is a 'consensual' body whose institutions, norms, and values function in harmony to keep intact the social equilibrium – which envisions rites of investiture as a universally accepted stage towards a hierarchical 'division of labour', as it were, is not wholly applicable to the investiture of Neapolitan viceroys.[71] As we shall see, side by side with the 'consensual' ceremony, existed a rite that exposed social tensions and conflicts.

The ceremony had two main parts. The first part consisted of the viceroy's ritual entry to the city. The second part, which was usually celebrated a few days after the first, was his taking of the oath and the formal possession of office. Especially interesting is the entry. It was usually done from the sea and not via a regular cavalcade, because it made it possible to achieve an effect of 'greater pomp'.[72] Here is the most detailed description of the 'ceremonial object' that formed the main *apparato* for this ritual:

> On the dock, where it is easier to descend, a long, wide wooden bridge is prepared, covered with satin drape, usually of yellow and crimson damask, the colours of the device of Naples, which spends for the building of this bridge up to 4,000 *scudi*. Sixteen deputies are elected for this matter, eight nobles, and eight from the *popolo*, without the intervention of others, being their particular jurisdiction as long as it lasts. It is decorated with various ornaments of festoons, statues, epigrams according to the deputies' choice, with two big gates, one at the entrance, the other at the exit, where splendid inscriptions are located to honour the prince.[73]

These two gates, of entrance and exit described above, may have signalled the passage of status, when the person in question supposedly becomes the viceroy of Naples, although formally he was considered as such only after the latter ceremony in which he took the formal oath. This symbolism is in complete concordance with the findings of Arnold Van Gennep, who has shown in his seminal study on rites of passage how, 'the passage from one social position to another is identified with a *territorial passage* … often ritually expressed by a passage under a portal, or by an "opening of the doors"'.[74] Immediately following his passage through the bridge, usually on horseback, accompanied by the deputies, the viceroy encountered the formal delegation that used to assemble for such important state occasions. It was composed of Seven Representatives of the City, known as the *eletti* (six nobles and one commoner), and a *sindico* (or *sindaco*), a noble elected ad hoc for the specific event. The latter used to greet him with the following standardised speech:

> Most Excellent Sir, the most loyal City of Naples is delighted at choosing a mayor … who not only is overjoyed on behalf of everyone for Your Excellency's arrival in this realm, but also must serve you and your most excellent house in everything

that you will command, with the same devotion that ought to be given to the majesty of the king our overlord, and which we owe to a minister of the royal crown, and a lord of such grandeur as Your Excellency.[75]

Following these words, the viceroy and his entourage were escorted to the Royal Palace by all the notables of the city, to the acclamation of the crowds and the thunder of the castles' artillery. At the view of such an enthusiastic reception, the entering viceroy, Pedro Fernández de Castro, Count of Lemos (1610–16), is said to have exclaimed: 'Certainly even the King of Spain has never had a happier day.'[76]

So far for the notables' reception, but of no less ritual importance is a parallel rite performed by the Neapolitan plebs, which was cast in a completely different form. Let us take for example the detailed account of the chronicler Scipione Guerra, describing the entry of Fernando Ruiz de Castro, Count of Lemos (1599–1601) in 1599. The appointed viceroy arrived with six galleons. All the vessels that were present in the port approached him, firing their cannons to greet him. Then, immediately after his passage through the damask bridge it 'was pillaged by his halberdiers and by the *popolo*, as customary … and he like each of his entourage found great satisfaction and pleasure in seeing … the fist fight among these people that pillaged it'.[77]

Why should one fight over shreds of damask, when it is quite obvious that they do not retain a significant commercial value? And what is the reason for the viceroy's 'great satisfaction' when seeing this peculiar act of violence? One plausible explanation could be deduced from the comparison of this phenomenon with something similar to the behaviour of pop fans, tearing the clothes, hair, or any imaginable collectable memorabilia that had been in the possession of their idol. The objects of admiration may criticize these acts, but at the same time, as in the viceroy's case, they may be very flattered as well. Carlo Ginzburg and Sergio Bertelli describe identical instances of ritual pillages happening when the pope took possession of his eminent office.[78] Different objects that were personally used by the pope in his procession, a canopy, a litter, and the caparison of his white mule (*chinea*), were often torn to pieces by the accompanying crowd. Just as in the case of the viceroy's halberdiers, the soldiers who carried the litter used to take part in the pillage. In the case of Innocent VIII, they went so far as to hustle him to the church of St John Lateran, risking dropping their eminent cargo, and having him run over by the pursuing crowd. Then, on their arrival, the soldiers rudely unloaded him in front of the altar, tearing the litter into pieces and claiming for themselves the wooden splints. According to Bertelli, 'there is no venality in such violence, but something profoundly religious'.[79] It is immaterial if the object of reverence almost got killed in the process.

This kind of 'devotional violence' is also known in the case of royal persons. Focusing on Neapolitan examples alone, one can cite French soldiers fighting Neapolitan crowds over Charles VIII's canopy, after the French king had used it in his solemn entrance to the city (1495); the pillage of the canopy that served Ferdinand the Catholic for the same purpose in 1506; and the confiscation of Charles V's horse in 1536.[80] An

interesting parenthesis in this tradition is supplied by Philip IV's sister, Maria of Austria, Queen of Hungary. As she planned to enter the city from the sea, in the same manner as the viceroys, she prevented the pillage of the bridge after her passage, choosing to donate it to charity instead.[81]

'Living saints' obtained a similar treatment, and with their death it was inevitable that crowds of worshippers would hunt for relics, made either of their clothes, or of objects of their possession, and when opportunity knocked, of entire body parts.[82] The latter are described by Parrino as 'the most rich treasures of the Neapolitan churches', which contained *in toto* some 170 bodies of saints, 3,000 pieces of saintly relics, and about 50 bodies of people who died with a reputation of sanctity.[83] In 1612, the death of such a saintly friar from the Capuchin order almost caused a perilous contest among the dwellers living adjacent to the Capuchin Convent who literally prepared to fight over his dead body. According to the chronicler, divine intervention alone prevented a disaster as the contestants' spirits were appeased. The enthusiastic worshippers contented themselves in immersing their handkerchiefs in the cadaver's sweat, which miraculously emanated in such an abundant quantity that it sufficed for all.[84]

These examples suggest that certain authorities were considered as possessing a charismatic, quasi-divine quality that received a physical expression through the ritual pillages of their bodies or their symbolical extensions – clothes, canopies, litters, and so forth. Hence, the pillage of the damask bridge subsequent to the viceroy's passage seems to indicate that, even if by proxy, the viceroy's body was thought to have the same sacredness as the king's.

However, a completely different message might have been carried through the pillage of the bridge. Different kinds of ritual pillages, also known as *allegrezze*, were a common feature of Italian princely courts during intervals of power. In a reverse version of the 'kinetic principle', which sees bodily actions expressing reverence towards the ruler, crowds assaulted the objects that represented the rule of the deceased, mainly his palace, the records of his criminal judgements, and his statues scattered throughout the city.[85] The people could thus let off some steam through the vicarious castigation of the ruler's effigy and his property, but more importantly they conveyed a significant message to the successors – 'that justice derives from the people, and the principle that the people consent to be ruled'.[86] Accordingly, the Neapolitan crowds could have been pillaging the bridge as a sign of warning to the coming viceroy, and not as a sign of devotion.

Such an interpretation of the ritual fits with part of Capaccio's explanation of it. He claims that the viceroy usually ordered the German guards to start the pillage 'in order to avoid the danger that is usually caused by the fury … of the multitude which in order to gain a shred of damask, attacks like wild beasts, and could cause a disaster'.[87] However, it is not very plausible that the viceroys really worried about some plebeians hurting each other, especially in light of the fact that they initiated ritual pillages of cockaignes during Carnival, and enjoyed every moment of it.[88] Besides, had the viceroys

wanted to, they could have stopped the plebs from pillaging the bridge altogether. This was done in the cited example of Queen Maria of Austria, or in the case of the Duke of Alcalà (1629–31), who, astonished by the apparel of the bridge, ordered to have it dispatched to the palace for his own pleasure.[89] Indeed, sometime in the seventeenth century, the pillage of the bridge was discontinued; a fact that probably attests to the authorities' discomfort with the practice.[90] While it lasted, I believe that sending the guards to be at the forefront of the pillage was a later attempt of viceroys to manipulate a popular rite from above, in order to take control over the situation, no matter what message the pillage had to communicate. On the one hand, if indeed the popular pillage was a ritualized sign of warning, then sending the guards ahead meant for the viceroy to dispossess the plebs of the initiative, and to countervail with a threat of his own. On the other hand, if the pillage was perceived as a way to honour the viceroy, as suggested before, then the guards were there to 'warm up' the crowds, and make sure that they did it with all the possible enthusiasm. One way or the other, the viceroy's need to assert his position, and to neutralize and control the potentially disruptive forces inherent in Neapolitan society from the very moment that he set foot into the new role, literally speaking, was symptomatic of the fragility of the office.

The public audience also supplied a clear example of the limitations of the viceroy's might.[91] Consistent with the principle of proximity it included an elaborate order of seating or standing, officers, secretaries, guards, porters, etc., according to rank and importance of duty. The viceroy sat on a chair situated on a platform, under a canopy, just like a royal person. On his front left stood the master of ceremonies with a club in his hand, with which he safeguarded the viceroy's quasi-sacred space by preventing anyone from setting foot on that platform. The audience was divided in two separate rooms, one for high-rank nobles who held the privilege of remaining covered, and another, where 'no living person' could remain with the headgear on. Neverthe-less, despite all these deferential rites that elevated the viceroy to the apex of the local hierarchy, in order to remind everyone who was the ultimate authority, the canopy could not carry any signs '*other than the arms of the king* inasmuch as His Excellency represents the royal person' (emphasis in the original).[92] This is a rare and most impor-tant piece of information, crucial to the understanding of how the viceregal ceremonial was subordinated to royal authority. It is the only evidence that I have found about the canopy's arms and ornaments, but it would seem safe to assume that this rule applied also to the other public instances in which the viceroy appeared under one.[93] In this respect, Capaccio adds a curious detail to Raneo's description of the public audience. The supplicants were given a sign by the master of ceremonies to approach the viceroy, to whom they handed over a petition, usually accompanied by a few words. 'And if someone as a sign of reverence, while talking, should bend his knee, he is promptly raised by the master of ceremonies, to prevent the impression that they require what is proper to the king, hence showing generous humility; although they may well accept this really deserved honour.'[94]

The same 'humility', or rather caution not to usurp a royal prerogative, was shown by the viceroy the Count of Monterrey (1631–37). In February 1637, the viceroy's son, the Marquis of Tarazona, celebrated the birth of a son. Consequently, a friend of the father, the Marquis of Charela, also the commander in charge of the Castle of St Elmo, ordered a few pieces of artillery to be shot to compliment the event. However, the Count of Monterrey, condemning the act, since such a gesture 'was proper only for royal persons', ordered the deduction of the cost of the ammunition from the Marquis' salary, and his arrest for a few days.[95] Similar distinctions were made for celebrative occasions. If for the birth of Spanish *infantes* or regal marriages it was customary to have a standard of three days of festivities throughout the city, which included fireworks and various *apparati*,[96] for corresponding events among the viceregal family only the palace's personnel had the formal obligation of celebrating and wearing festive clothes.[97] Finally, the viceroys publicly showed their direct subordination to the king when they were sworn into office. On that occasion when the Secretary of the Kingdom read the patent of appointment, every time the king was mentioned the viceroys had to take off their hat as a sign of respect.[98]

Besides the problems that could rise from disregard of the exclusive rights of the Spanish kings, viceroys also had to worry about issues of status and precedence with respect to ambassadors, nobles, and princes holding equal or higher rank than their own. Here is a short list of the more important rules of conduct employed by viceroys in such instances: 'His Excellency [the viceroy] does not refer to any ambassador as Your Excellency; except grandees of the crown.'[99] 'The viceroy calls the Grand Crosses Sirs and he accompanies them two steps at their entrance and [two] at their exit, and he observes the same with the General of the Vessels of Malta.'[100] 'When some foreign noble of rank arrives to see the viceroy, he treats him according to his pedigree, but always differentiating him from those who are vassals, by not receiving him standing and accompanying him for a while.'[101] 'The same is done with a gentleman who has no income or return in the realm, whom His Excellency allows to cover his head for not being a vassal or a subject, and many of these are called Illustrious Sirs.'[102]

However, despite what seemed to be a clear codification of the various 'treatments' that each party deserved with respect to the other,[103] disputes and discords were not uncommon. On the occasion of the visit of the Duke of Mantua, in May 1603, the viceroy the Count of Benavente (1603–10) refused to give his guest the title 'Your Highness' (*Vostra Altezza*), 'because of the order of His Majesty that his Viceroys of Naples will have equal standing with the potentates of Italy'.[104] Accordingly, they reached a compromise, whereby they would mutually refer to each other as 'Your Excellency' (*Sua Eccellenza*), whereas all the other nobles would address the guest with the title of Highness.[105] In 1686 an identical quarrel emerged between the current viceroy the Marquis of Carpio (1683–87) and the Duke of Mantua, who came on a visit to Naples. This was despite the fact that this time the viceroy did not have a case for denying a higher title to his guest, because a reversal of the previous levelling policy, in

favour of Italian ruling princes, had taken place. A direct conflict was skilfully avoided by making it impossible for the two contestants to meet each other in public.[106] According to Giuseppe Galasso, the reason for the viceroy's attitude towards the Duke of Mantua was 'more than personal or etiquette; it was political', bearing a grudge for the duke's surrender of Casale Monferrato to Louis XIV.[107] Alternatively, one can also frame this behaviour within a perspective that sees ceremonial itself as a political tool that can serve to mark the relations between states.[108] In other words, in this case the viceroy conveyed his disapproval, which might have been politically motivated as well and could carry political implications, through the symbolic language of etiquette.

Mutual compromises or relatively peaceful solutions to ceremonial disagreement, such as those just cited, had little chance of success among the punctilious and ceremonious Neapolitan nobles. The viceroy the Duke of Osuna (1582–86) had a hard time trying to impose his idea of etiquette on them. Trouble started when he wanted his father-in-law, the Count of Haro, to sit next to him in the chapel, 'a thing that was never attempted, before or after, in this kingdom'. Other instances of 'ceremonial nepotism', in which he had two of his sons sitting on the bench of the highest rank of the Neapolitan nobility, were 'all new things that altered the minds of these gentlemen'. So much so, that they wrote to the king to protest against these abuses. On a second occasion, at the banquet organized by the Duke of Bovino, the master of ceremonies ordered all the nobles present to uncover their heads, by order of the viceroy. Full of indignation, the congregation dissolved to the last man. Osuna apologized for the incident, putting the blame on a misunderstanding by the master of ceremonies, but on a later occasion, at a feast at the Royal Palace, he wished to seat his noble guests on benches instead of the usual chairs. Needless to say, no one stayed at the party to take what was perceived as a serious offence.[109] Similar instances could be found also among the opposite sex. In 1629, the Princess of Bisignano, offended by the new vicereine the Duchess of Alcalá, who belittled her title by calling her *Signoria* instead of *Eccellenza*, left the palace in disgust. 'And it is believed she will not come again to the palace during the present government,' predicted the chronicler of the event.[110] These reactions of the Neapolitan nobility, which were very frequent throughout the entire span of viceregal rule, cast a grim light indeed on the viceroys' public image, especially when compared with the unassailable status of the kings of Spain and France during the same period.

Part of such an animosity between the viceroy and the nobility might have been the result of individual incongruity. For example, particularly adverse to the nobility, especially to the courtly entertainments so coveted by Neapolitans, was the Count of Olivares (1595–99). Due to his austere and stoic temperament he abolished all dances, comedies, and banquets that used to take place in the palace in the times of his predecessors. His time was fully occupied in 'giving audience at all hours, in making calculations for the economy of government, and in the right and rigorous administration of justice'.[111] He also clashed with the nobility because of the rigorous bans and

sumptuary laws that he issued to reform 'the vanity of the titled nobles' and 'the immoderate luxuries introduced in women's attires.[112]

The Duke of Osuna (1616–20), who had the exact opposite character of
Olivares, succeeded in causing serious uproar among his subjects, nobles and others,
for completely different reasons. Girolamo Fracchetta, the agent of the Duke of Urbino
in Naples, described him as 'bizarre in his gestures, his words and his dress; he might be
mistaken for a rude soldier of Flanders. He fights willingly, he gambles, and enjoys the
company of jesters.'[113] Apparently, Fracchetta's description was more than generous to
the bizarre duke. His extravagant conduct brought him almost immediately the censure
of the Church, which certainly did not approve of his affability with 'the twenty-five
most famous courtesans of Naples' at a public banquet in Poggioreale.[114] The nobility
was devastated by the outrageous disregard for etiquette when one Monday morning,
instead of the usual public audience, as described above, he gave it outside the palace,
turning it into a curious promenade. Whatever he did, it seemed that he simply could
not avoid falling into excesses. His mercifulness should probably be better described as
outright irresponsibility, as he chose to pardon dangerous criminals, laughing defiantly
at the protests of his councillors.[115] His frequent habit of throwing gifts to the people,
which rulers used to perform as an act of liberality, resembled the acts of a court jester,
as he enjoyed with particular gusto the mayhem he caused among the crowds gathering
under his balcony with his indiscriminate showers of coins, food, and jewels.[116] Contrary
to Zazzera's unforgiving interpretation, on which the description above relies, Parrino
perceived Osuna as a virtuous ruler. Indulgent towards his excesses, he chose to emphasize what he identified as the positive aspects of his exceptionally authoritative style of
rulership. Diametrically opposed to the Habsburgs' 'hidden' style, Osuna aspired to be
omnipresent and omnipotent via his physical display in public. In his frequent private
walks throughout the city, at all hours, he coupled the rigorousness of a martial court by
sentencing on the spot any criminals caught *in flagrante*, with the attitude of a benevo-
lent and attentive ruler, by listening to the people's pleas and accepting indiscriminately
any petitions that were handed to him.[117]

Nevertheless, more temperate viceroys than Olivares and Osuna did not essentially
succeed in gaining the love or respect of Neapolitans. Adverse external circumstances in
the form of famines, earthquakes, epidemics, and economic recession conspired during
the 'general crisis' of the seventeenth century against the best of efforts.[118] To these we
should add some endemic local problems to which the various viceroys could not or
would not find a comprehensive solution, as exposed in Gunn's comment:

> Ravaged and harassed as the citizens were … by brigandage and the raids of
> corsairs; by taxation, especially the *gabelle* on fruit and flour; by bank failures
> and difficulties of commerce through changes in the value of money brought on
> by clipping, sweating and false coining; by the exactions of government and the
> malversation of officials; by the enforced presence of an ill-disciplined foreign
> soldiery; by the impunity of the nobles, the wirepulling and bribery of judges

– the Neapolitans, indeed, felt that their lives depended … on the whim, the caprice of the one man that had power, the autocratic viceroy.[119]

Accordingly, Capaccio illustrates well the problem of having a ruler who was ultimately perceived as vicarious, temporary, and disposable. 'Each time that we do not get the slightest satisfaction from the prince … we get annoyed with the present government, and we want a successor; … wanting always to have things done our way, having more consideration to our own interest, than to the reputation and to the proper reverence to the ruler.'[120] Hence, even a relatively skilful viceroy like the Count of Lemos – who according to the contemporary Scipione Guerra was a 'man of great enterprising, and excellent mind'[121] – won the scorn of Neapolitan satirists at the occasion of his premature death (1601), when he was still in office.[122] Similar is the judgement of the chronicler Innocenzo Fuidoro, who shrewdly combines a protest against the savage viceregal taxation with a literal reduction of the proportions of the viceroy the Count of Monterrey, when commenting about the birth of an unusually weighty baby: 'It is with good reason that a giant had to be born during the government of a viceroy having the stature of a pigmy. Although the latter has operated as a giant in extracting money from the realm, simulating [military] victories … and while ordering the castles to fire … for the real as for the false victories, he imposed more and more taxes.'[123]

The abhorrence described above did occasionally transgress the limits of verbal criticism, breaking into open rebellion – usually during the peaks of economic crisis. The most celebrated is the episode known as 'the Revolt of Starace' from 1585.[124] Following a precipitous rise in the price of bread, actually caused by the mismanagement of grain by the first Duke of Osuna, the plebs consummated their rage against the Representative of the *popolo* Vincenzo Starace. The man was practically torn to pieces, and his body was dragged to the Royal Palace, as done to criminals after their execution in official public rituals. The bold perpetrators brought Starace's corpse in front of the viceroy, 'who could not hold back his tears, while they forced him to say, "Long live the king, and death to misrule"; and insisting, "Say it Sir, Long live the king."'[125] If it were not for the fact that *The Foreigner* was published in 1634, it would be reasonable to suspect that the words were a fiction of Capaccio, borrowed in retrospect from the famous rallying cry of the Neapolitan revolt of 1647. Apparently, the perception of the viceregal institution as a source of misrule (*malgoverno*) had a notoriously long tradition.

In 1622, the lack of respect towards the current viceroy, Cardinal Zapata, reached new peaks, following a new economic crisis, caused, among other things, by the careless depreciation of the currency. During the mounting crisis the cardinal was insulted and humiliated on three different occasions by the Neapolitan plebs. The third time, some stones were thrown at his carriage, and he was constrained to flee, being in real danger of his life.[126] Shocked by the plebs' indiscipline, 'completely oblivious of the reverence owed to His Majesty … of which person was represented by the cardinal', Capaccio commented with hindsight that they should have known better than to attack the Viceroy of Naples 'who had ample control over their life and death'.[127] In fact, since he

could not get respect from the glamour of his authority alone he would gain it through brute coercion. Although he did not respond on the spot to the various humiliations, he revealed his long and vengeful memory by arresting and torturing more than 300 plebeians who were involved in the various acts, and by executing seven of those more actively involved.[128] This time, resistance was crushed, but not for long. In 1648, the Duke of Arcos (1646–48) was forced to leave his office after having failed to control the rebellion that broke out a few months earlier. At his departure the people 'could not satisfy the need of cursing him'. Ultimately, 'they rejoiced at having got rid of a fierce enemy, a liar, a disparager of faith, a violator of oaths'.[129]

Paradoxically, during the first phase of the rebellion against the royal representative and his administration, it co-existed with cries of loyalty to the king. Aurelio Musi has recently explained the solution of this dilemma via Naples' double identity of kingdom and viceroyalty, at the same time, which had a serious bearing on the collective imagination of Neapolitans. When they thought of themselves as belonging to the Spanish kingdom they beheld a positive, not to say glorifying, image, coloured with the mystic, divine quality of absolutist monarchy.[130] Therefore, as noted by Croce: 'Loyalty to the sovereign, to the King of Spain, became a source of pride, and a point of honour; the word and the image of "rebellion" aroused a shudder of disgust, like the direst of crimes, parricide or impiety.'[131]

On the other hand, the viceregal institution, representing the political and administrative apparatus, became more and more associated during the seventeenth century with the peripheralization of southern Italy within the imperial system, and with the increasingly oppressive fiscal policies of Spain, created by the need to sustain the costs of the empire's numerous wars.[132] Thus, in 1647 the rebels could cry: 'Viva il Re, mora il mal governo!' (Long live the king, death to misrule!), without perceiving it as a contradiction in terms.[133] This is precisely the message brought forward by Fuidoro in the following comment: 'The truth is that this poor kingdom has always been treated as the most inferior of all, and not according to the holy intention of its Austrian rulers, but according to the will, convenience, and whim of the ruling ministers.'[134]

In sum, king and subjects could both play on the ambiguity created by the viceregal institution, and use it as a mediating filter that would absorb all the impurities of the exchange. Just as Neapolitans could rebel against viceregal misrule alone, so the king could notoriously squeeze more and more taxes from Naples, via his representative, without risking a serious diminishing of his mythical standing in the eyes of his Neapolitan subjects. Ultimately, the ceremonial and etiquette revolving around the viceroys, even though they were moulded after the royal Spanish archetype, had a limited effect. In order to be efficacious they needed the support of dynastic legitimation, royal authority, and godly charisma – and these belonged to the king alone.

Notes

An abridged version of this section 'The viceregal public image' was published as '"Miscebis Sacra Profanis": Viceregal Exaltation in Religious Rites and Ceremonies', in *Images of the Body Politic*, ed. Giuseppe Cascione, Donato Mansueto, and Gabriel Guarino (Milan, 2007), 69–80.

1   In this study, I will prefer the term 'ceremonial' over such alternatives used in court scholarship as 'ritual' and 'etiquette'. The attempt to give a neat separation and definition of each of these by Sergio Bertelli and Giulia Calvi seems more confusing and equivocal than explanatory, as each of their three definitions is practically interchangeable with one of the other two. See their 'Rituale, cerimoniale, etichetta nelle corti italiane', in *Rituale*, ed. Sergio Bertelli and Giuliano Crifò, 11. See also the discussion of the terminology revolving around 'ceremonial' and 'etiquette' in Duindam, *Myths of Power*, 102–7. Although incomplete, fragmentary, and partly compiled by anonymous masters of ceremonies, the surviving ceremonial ordinances of the Neapolitan court provide a sufficient documental basis for the exploration of the issue. See Archivio di Stato, Naples (hereafter ASNA), Maggiordomia Maggiore e Sopraindtendenza Generale di Casa Reale, Archivio Amministrativo, Inventario IV, vol. 1489, *Traduzione dei Sei libri di cerimoniale contenenti i fatti De' Secoli Dal Sedicesimo al Decimottavo* [hereafter *Sei libri di cerimoniale*], part I, fols. 1r–156r, part II, fols. 1r–127r; José Raneo, *Etiquetas de la corte de Nápoles (1634)*, ed. Antonio Paz y Mélia, *Revue Hispanique*, 27 (1912), 16–284; and Paolo Cherchi (ed.), 'Juan de Garnica. Un memoriale sul cerimoniale della corte napoletana', *Archivio Storico per le Province Napoletane* [hereafter *ASPN*], 13 (1975), 213–24. Only very recently the issue has started to stir the attention of scholars. See especially Carlos José Hernando Sánchez, 'Teatro del honor y ceremonial de la ausencia. La corte virreinal de Nápoles en el siglo XVII', in *Calderón de la Barca y la España del Barroco*, ed. José Alcalá Zamora and Ernest Belenguer Cebría (2 vols., Madrid, 2001), I, 591–674. For the interaction of ceremonial and architecture see Sabina de Cavi, 'Il palazzo reale di Napoli (1600–1607). Un edificio "spagnolo"?', in *Napoli è tutto il mondo. Neapolitan Art and Culture from Humanism to the Enlightenment*, ed. Livio Pestilli, Ingrid D Rowland, and Sebastian Schütze (Pisa and Rome, 2008), 165–71; and Joan Luís Palos Peñarroya, 'Un escenario italiano para los gobernantes españoles. El nuevo palacio de los virreyes de Nápoles (1599–1653)', *Cuadernos de Historia Moderna*, 30 (2005), 125–50.

2   For a classical study of the subject see Ernst H. Kantorowicz, *The King's Two Bodies: A Study in Medieval Political Theology* (Princeton, 1957). For a study in an Italian state see Paolo Prodi, *The Papal Prince: One Body and Two Souls: The Papal Monarch in Early Modern Europe*, trans. Susan Haskins (Cambridge, 1987).

3   Parrino, *Teatro*, in *Raccolta*, vol. 9, 37. Published towards the end of the seventeenth century, Parrino's oeuvre is one of the most important sources for anyone interested in the viceregal court. Its author covers extensively most of the viceroys' governments in Naples, more precisely from 1503 to 1683. Despite this being the 'authorized version', whose publication was favoured over that of his rival Antonio Bulifon, it is far from being an uncritical account of the Spanish presence in Naples.

4   The full reference is Giulio Cesare Capaccio, *Il forastiero. Dialoghi* (Naples, 1634). This is regarded as one of the best contemporary guides to Naples, written as a fictional dialogue between a Neapolitan citizen and a foreign visitor to the city. Rich in detail and in information, the format of a dialogue enables the Foreigner to ask what is obvious to the Neapolitan, satisfying the curiosity of potential future foreigners. The Foreigner's role is also to make, occasionally, pungent and critical remarks, to which the Neapolitan citizen usually answers defensively. However, suspicious minds may claim that this is a rhetorical device that allows Capaccio to camouflage his grievances towards the establishment, via the voice of the Foreigner, within the texture of a favorable account of the Spanish government. Besides giving a concise and efficient narration of all the viceregal administrations up to his day, Capaccio offers interesting general information about the roles, authority, and stately rituals involved in the office. For a deep contextual analysis of the book see John A. Marino, 'The Foreigner and the Citizen: A Dialogue on Good Government in Spanish Naples', in *Reason and its Others: Italy, Spain and the*

New World (1500s–1700s), ed. David Castillo and Massimo Lollini (Nashville, 2006), 145–64.

5 Capaccio, *Il forastiero*, 391.

6 Parrino, *Teatro*, in *Raccolta*, vol. 9, 35.

7 See Ferrante Carafa, *Memorie*, appendix in Raffaele Ajello, *Una Società anomala. Il programma e la sconfitta della nobiltà napoletana in due memoriali cinquecenteschi* (Naples, 1996), 435–6.

8 For a concise summary of the viceregal institution in Naples see Giovanni Muto, 'Il Regno di Napoli sotto la dominazione spagnola', in *Storia della società italiana*, vol. 11: *La Controriforma e il Seicento*, ed. Giovanni Cherubini, Franco Della Peruta, Ettore Lepore (Milan, 1989), 267–9.

9 Capaccio, *Il forastiero*, 392.

10 Parrino, *Teatro*, in *Raccolta*, vol. 9, 35–6. On important festive occasions it was customary for the viceroys to pardon prisoners. For example, in 1652, to celebrate the quelling of the rebellion in Barcelona, the viceroy released 300 prisoners. See the manuscript diary of Andrea Rubino, conserved in the library of the Società Napoletana di Storia Patria [henceforth SNSP], MS. XVIII. D. 14 [vol. 1], *Notitia di quanto é occorso in Napoli dall'anno 1648 per tutto l'anno 1657* [hereafter, *Notitia*], fol. 79.

11 Parrino, *Teatro*, in *Raccolta*, vol. 9, 37.

12 See Charles de Secondat, Baron de Montesquieu, *The Spirit of the Laws*, trans. and ed. Anne M. Cohler, Basia Carolyn Miller, and Harold Samuel Stone (Cambridge, 1989).

13 Capaccio, *Il forastiero*, 414.

14 Ordinance of Philip III from 1599, reaffirming his father's decree from 1585. Quoted in Eric Cochrane, *Italy, 1530–1630*, ed. Julius Kirshner (London and New York, 1988), 276.

15 Parrino, *Teatro*, in *Raccolta*, vol. 10, 162.

16 Fuidoro, *Giornali*, III, 293–4.

17 Francesco Zazzera, *Narrazioni tratte dai giornali del governo di Don Pietro Girone duca d'Ossuna vicerè di Napoli, scritti da F. Z.*, ed. Francesco Palermo, *Archivio Storico Italiano*, 9 (1846), 568. *Cardinal de aspettatis* is a play on words, which can be loosely translated as *Cardinal of waiting*. For a vivid account of Osuna that relays uncritically on Zazzera, see Peter Gunn, 'Los Caprichos of the Duke of Osuna', in his *Naples: A Palimpsest* (London, 1961), 87–129.

18 Zazzera, *Narrazioni*, 589.

19 *Ibid.*, 597–600; Guerra, *Diurnali*, 102–3.

20 Capaccio, *Il forastiero*, 406.

21 Ferrante Bucca, 'Aggionta alli Diurnali di Scipione Guerra', ed. G. de Blasiis, *ASPN*, 36 (1911), 129.

22 Parrino, *Teatro*, in *Raccolta*, vol. 9, 37.

23 See *ibid.*, 57–8.

24 Muto, 'Il regno di Napoli', 306.

25 For the origins of the Collateral Council and other institutions that were erected during the first years of Habsburgs' rule see Pietro Giannone, *Istoria civile del Regno di Napoli* (3rd edn, 4 vols., Naples, 1762), III, 543–50. For a discussion of these political processes see Pier Luigi Rovito, *Respublica dei togati. Giuristi e società nella Napoli del Seicento* (Naples, 1981); and Ajello, *Società anomala*. See also Aurelio Musi, 'Tra burocrati e notabili. Potere e istituzioni nella Napoli del Seicento', *Bollettino del Centro di Studi Vichiani*, 16 (1986), 165–8; and Aurelio Lepre, *Storia del Mezzogiorno d'Italia*, vol. 1: *La lunga durata e la crisi, 1500–1656* (2 vols., Naples, 1986), I, 139 ff.

26 See Peter Burke, 'Presenting and Re-presenting Charles V', in *Charles V, 1500–1558, and his Time*, ed. Hugo Soly (Antwerp, 1999), 402.

27 Raneo's *Etiquetas* supplies a precious glimpse on the author's first-hand experience derived from his prestigious occupation as master of ceremonies. The modern reader might find this compilation a tedious exposition of the master of ceremonies' main interest – who stands or sits where, on such and such occasion – which usually lacks an explanation of the rituals described. However, in Raneo's defence one can claim that such a mode of description furthers one of the main goals of state rituals, that is to show the taken-for-granted, unshaken, and timeless position of the government in power. Significantly, Raneo deduces this ever-present

reality mainly from his own professional experience at the service of the viceroy, the Count of Monterrey (1631–37), and his comparative perspective is usually limited to one or two viceregal courts preceding Monterrey's time. Despite its shortcomings, it is precisely the ponderousness and punctiliousness of this source that make it so precious for an analysis of ceremonial behaviour.

28   This included the popes, whose rites of power are incisively elucidated in Peter Burke, 'Sacred Rulers, Royal Priests: Rituals of the Early Modern Popes', in his *The Historical Anthropology*, 168–82.

29   The traditional account of courtly etiquette that draws a single line of transmission from Burgundy to Habsburg Vienna and Madrid, and from there to Louis XIV's Versailles, affecting in the process all the other European courts, has been questioned in recent studies. See some of the more recent contributions to the debate in Adamson, 'The Making of the Ancien-Régime Court', 28. For example, it has been claimed that the Spanish case presents a complex process of acculturation that merged the old protocol of Castile and the new Burgundian element. See John H. Elliott, 'The Court of the Spanish Habsburgs: A Peculiar Institution?', in his *Spain and its World: Collected Essays* (New Haven and London, 1989), 153; and Carmelo Lisón Tolosana, *La imagen del rey. Monarquía, realeza y poder ritual en la Casa de los Austrias* (Madrid, 1991), 115–18. Werner Paravicini is even more sceptical about the Burgundian impact in Europe, denying the existence of idiosyncratic traits that characterized the Burgundian ceremonial. See Werner Paravicini, 'The Court of the Dukes of Burgundy: A Model for Europe?', in *Princes, Patronage, and the Nobility: The Court at the Beginning of the Modern Age, c.1450–1650*, ed. Ronald G. Asch and Adolf M. Birke (Oxford, 1991), 89. Glyn Redworth and Fernando Checa agree that the Burgundian rite *per se* did not have in its power to enhance the authority of Philip II more than the previous Castilian-Trastámaran could, as the purpose of all ceremonial, of which-ever provenance, is precisely to augment the king's majesty. See Glyn Redworth and Fernando Checa, 'The Kingdoms of Spain: The Courts of the Spanish Habsburgs 1500–1700', in *The Princely Courts of Europe*, ed. Adamson, 48. Therefore, Redworth and Checa's plausible explana-tion is that Charles V's motivation to impose the new ceremonial must have been to bestow on his heir a 'Burgundian image' in order to win over the affection of his future subjects in the problematic territories of Northern Europe. *Ibid.*, 49. This idea has been put forward before them by Elliott, 'Court of the Spanish Habsburgs', in his *Spain and its World*, 152.

30   For the basic study regarding Spanish ceremonial in Habsburg times see Antonio Rodríguez Villa, 'Etiquetas de la casa de Austria', *Revista Europea*, 5: 75 (1875), 161–8.

31   Quoted in de Cavi, 'Il palazzo reale', 165. I would like to thank Dr de Cavi for calling my atten-tion to Diéz de Aux's writings, which unfortunately I have not been able to study yet.

32   Paravicini, 'The Court of the Dukes of Burgundy', 89.

33   Redworth and Checa, 'The Kingdoms of Spain', 47.

34   Lisón Tolosana, *La imagen del rey*, 118.

35   On the entire range of stereotypical descriptions of the Neapolitan nobility see Mozzillo, *Passaggio a Mezzogiorno*, 232–61. The standard account of Spanish ceremonies in Italy is Croce, *La Spagna*, especially chapter 9, 'Le cerimonie spagnuole in Italia', 172–96.

36   Quoted in Benedetto Croce, 'Il tipo del Napoletano nella commedia', in his *Saggi sulla letter-atura Italiana del Seicento*, 280.

37   *Ibid.*, 275–6.

38   Bertelli and Calvi, 'Rituale, cerimoniale, etichetta', 16. For a description of the monarchical past of Naples before the advent of the Castilians see Alan Ryder, *The Kingdom of Naples Under Alfonso the Magnanimous: The Making of a Modern State* (Oxford, 1976). For the courts of Alfonso and his son Ferdinand in Naples see Croce, *La Spagna*, 31–74. For ceremonial during Aragonese rule see Giuliana Vitale, *Ritualità monarchica, cerimonie e pratiche devozionali nella Napoli aragonese* (Salerno, 2006).

39   'The most visible expression of this total focusing of rule on the king's person and his elevation and distinction, is etiquette.' Elias, *The Court Society*, 118.

40   Bertelli and Calvi, 'Rituale, cerimoniale, etichetta', 16; Lisón Tolosana, *La imagen del rey*, 153.

41 Lisón Tolosana, *La imagen del rey*, 141.

42 See Adamson, 'The Making of the Ancien-Régime Court', 28–30.

43 Agustín González Enciso, 'Del rey ausente al rey distante', in *Imagen del rey, imagen de los reynos. Las ceremonias públicas en la España moderna (1500–1814)*, ed. Agustín González Enciso and Jesús María Usunáriz Garayoa (Pamplona, 1999), 4; Olivier Chaline, 'The Kingdoms of France and Navarre: The Valois and Bourbon Courts, c. 1515–1750', in *The Princely Courts of Europe*, ed. Adamson, 85–8.

44 Bertelli, *Il corpo del re*, 135–7; Chaline, 'The Kingdoms of France', 88.

45 Lisón Tolosana, *La imagen del rey*, 141.

46 Adamson, 'The Making of the Ancien-Régime Court', 29. For the privileged position of the king at courtly performances see James E. Varey, 'The Audience and the Play at Court Spectacles: The Roles of the Kings', *Bulletin of Hispanic Studies*, 61 (1984), 399–406; Kristiaan P. Aercke, *Gods of Play: Baroque Festive Performances as Rhetorical Discourse* (Albany, NY, 1994), 33–4; Yi-Fu Tuan 'Space and Context', in *By Means of Performance: Intercultural Studies of Theatre and Ritual*, ed. Richard Schechner and Willa Appel (Cambridge, 1990), 241.

47 Lisón Tolosana, *La imagen del rey*, 143.

48 Chaline, 'The Kingdoms of France', 87. See also William Roosen, 'Early Modern Diplomatic Ceremonial: A Systems Approach', *The Journal of Modern History*, 52:3 (1980), 467.

49 Lisón Tolosana, *La imagen del rey*, 151.

50 Rodríguez Villa, 'Etiquetas', 162–5.

51 Raneo, *Etiquetas*, 118.

52 See the description of these forces in Scipione Mazzella, *Descrittione del Regno di Napoli. Del signore S. M. napoletano. Aumentata in molti parti dal proprio autore* (Naples, 1601), 325.

53 Raneo, *Etiquetas*, 118.

54 On outward luxury as a form of communication see Peter Burke, 'Conspicuous Consumption in Seventeenth-Century Italy', in his *The Historical Anthropology*, 132–49.

55 Parrino, *Teatro*, in *Raccolta*, vol. 9, 53–4.

56 Gigliola Frangito, 'Cardinals' Courts in Sixteenth-Century Rome', *The Journal of Modern History*, 65:1 (1993), 50.

57 Lisón Tolosana, *La imagen del rey*, 123.

58 See some of these comparative figures in Henry Kamen, *Early Modern European Society* (London and New York, 2000), 83–4.

59 Capaccio, *Il forastiero*, 412.

60 For viceregal censure in the period see Fara Fusco, 'La "legislazione" sulla stampa nella Napoli del Seicento', in *Civiltà del Seicento a Napoli* (2 vols., Naples, 1984), I, 459–80.

61 For these and many others see Raneo, *Etiquetas* in the section called 'Estilo de Palacio y fuera', 117–38.

62 For Easter see ASNA, *Sei libri di cerimoniale*, part I, fols. 3r–19r. For Christmas, see *ibid.*, fols. 29r–32v.

63 Adamson, 'The Making of the Ancien-Régime Court', 13. For the French court see Chaline, 'The Kingdoms of France', 83–8. For the Spanish court see Redworth and Checa, 'The Kingdoms of Spain', 52–9. For a comparison see Elliott, 'Court of the Spanish Habsburgs', in his *Spain and its World*, 149–50; and Duindam, *Myths of Power*, 126–33. For an engaging study of art and ceremony centred on regal architecture see John H. Elliott and Jonathan Brown, *A Palace for a King: The Buen Retiro and the Court of Philip IV* (New Haven and London, 1980).

64 Besides the sources cited in the previous note see also Fernando Checa Cremades, 'Monarchic Liturgies and the "Hidden King": The Function and Meaning of Spanish Royal Portraiture in the Sixteenth and Seventeenth Centuries', in *Iconography, Propaganda, and Legitimation*, ed. Allan Ellenius (Oxford, 1998), especially 97–100.

65 Camillo Borghese, *Diario de la relacion de viaje de Camillo Borghese, auditor de la rev. camara de Roma en España, enviado a la corte como nuncio extraordinario del papa Clemente VIII el año 1594 al rey Felipe II*, in *Viajes de extranjeros por España y Portugal. Desde los tiempos más remotos, hasta fines del siglo XVI*, ed. José García Mercadal (3 vols., Madrid, 1952), I, 1479.

66 Chaline, 'The Kingdoms of France', 88.

67 Duindam, *Myths of Power*, 133.

68 Peter Burke, 'State-Making, King-Making and Image-Making from Renaissance to Baroque: Scandinavia in a European Context', *Scandinavian Journal of History*, 22:1 (1997), 7.

69 Capaccio, *Il forastiero*, 392.

70 Kertzer, *Ritual*, 24–5.

71 For a view of social stratification from the sociological perspective known as 'structural functionalism' see Kingsley Davis and Wilbert Moore 'Some Principles of Stratification', *American Sociological Review* 10 (1945), 242–9. Their work is based on Émile Durkheim's, *The Division of Labour in Society*, trans. George Simpson (New York, 1933).

72 Capaccio, *Il forastiero*, 407.

73 *Ibid.*

74 Arnold Van Gennep, *The Rites of Passage*, trans. Monika B. Vizedom and Gabrielle L. Caffee (London, 1960), 192.

75 Capaccio, *Il forastiero*, 408–9.

76 *Ibid.*, 407.

77 Guerra, *Diurnali*, 74. See also by the same, the entries of other viceroys, 45, 47, 119, 144.

78 Bertelli, *Il corpo del re*, 87 ff.; Carlo Ginzburg, coordinator of the Bologna Seminar, 'Ritual Pillages: A Preface to Research in Progress', in *Microhistory and the Lost Peoples of Europe*, ed. Edward Muir and Guido Ruggiero (Baltimore, 1991), 20–41. On the papal rite of possession see also Bonner Mitchell, *The Majesty of the State: Triumphal Progresses of Foreign Sovereigns in Renaissance Italy (1494–1600)* (Florence, 1986), 22 ff. Generally about the papal rituals see Burke, 'Sacred Rulers'. Of general relevance also two recent collections of essays: *Cérémonial et rituel à Rome: XVIe–XIXe siècle*, ed. Maria Antonietta Visceglia and Catherine Brice (Rome, 1997); and *La corte di Roma tra Cinque e Seicento. 'Teatro' della politica europea*, ed. Gianvittorio Signorotto and Maria Antonietta Visceglia (Rome, 1998).

79 Bertelli, *Il corpo del re*, 89.

80 *Ibid.* For the entries of Ferdinand the Catholic and Charles V in Naples see Mitchell, *The Majesty of the State*, respectively 130–3, 157–8.

81 Raneo, *Etiquetas*, 197. For a detailed visit of the queen see Alessandro Fellecchia, *Viaggio della Maestà della Regina di Bohemia e d'Ungheria da Madrid sino a Napoli. Con la descrittione di Pausillipo, e di molte Dame Napoletane* (Naples, 1630).

82 Katharine Park, 'The Criminal and the Saintly Body: Autopsy and Dissection in Renaissance Italy', *Renaissance Quarterly*, 47:1 (1994), 1–33; Muir, *Ritual*, 234; Bertelli, *Il corpo del re*, 94–6.

83 Parrino, *Teatro*, in *Raccolta*, vol. 9, 24–5.

84 Bulifon, *Giornali*, 92–3.

85 On the genesis of pillages of popes, whose documentation goes back as far as the fifth century, see Ginzburg, 'Ritual Pillages', 22–4.

86 Muir, *Ritual*, 261.

87 Capaccio, *Il forastiero*, 408. See also Osuna giving the same order in Zazzera, *Narrazioni*, 479–80.

88 Cockaignes were ephemeral constructions carrying gifts of food for the people, usually set up by the guilds of butchers, fishmongers, dairy producers, bakers, etc. The etymology of cockaigne comers from the French *pays de cocaigne* – the utopian legendary land of plenty popular since the middle ages. Especially informative are the descriptions of cockaignes in the diaries of Domenico Confuorto, during the Carnival season. See for example his *Giornali*, I, 153, 205, 329–30; II, 291.

89 See Parrino, *Teatro*, in *Raccolta*, vol. 9, 406; and Bucca, 'Aggionta', *ASPN*, 36 (1911), 139.

90 ASNA, *Sei libri di cerimoniale*, part I, fol. 55r: 'Da molto tempo da questa parte non si costruisce piu il ponte ed il viceré si prende l'importo in denaro nella summa di 1500 ducati che li sborsa la città.'

91 Raneo, *Etiquetas*, 48–50.

92 *Ibid.*, 36.

93   It should be noted that there were various ceremonial instances in which the vicereine also
     appeared under a canopy, but the documents do not state the canopy's shape or the arms it
     carried. See, for example, the usual visit of ladies to the vicereine on the day after Christmas,
     ASNA, *Sei libri di cerimoniale*, part I, fol. 30v: 'al dopo pranzo vanno tutte le dame a dar la buona
     festa alla viceregina e la medesima le ricever stando sotto il tosello'. Similarly, she receives them
     under a canopy to accept their condolances at the death of a royal person. See *ibid.*, fol. 144r.
94   Capaccio, *Il forastiero*, 423.
95   Raneo, *Etiquetas*, 137.
96   See various examples in Bulifon, *Giornali*, 44, 46, 70, 82, 87; and in Confuorto, *Giornali*, I, 144,
     212, 293; II, 73.
97   This is according to the prescription of Raneo, *Etiquetas*, 118.
98   ASNA, *Sei libri di cerimoniale*, part II, fol. 84v.
99   Raneo, *Etiquetas*, 128.
100 *Ibid.*, 130.
101 *Ibid.*, 133–4.
102 *Ibid.*, 134. Accordingly, just to sample randomly the application of these rules by viceroys with
     respect to some notable guests to the city: 'A Don Luis de Portugal, el mismo Duque de Alba
     le hospedó en Palaçio y le llamó de Señoria Ilustrísima. A Don Fernando Ursino, Duque de
     Montelibreto, hermano del Duque de Brachiano, llamole de Señoria Ilustrísima y le acompañó
     toda la pieça en que le reciviò. Al hijo del Paladín de Polonia llamó S. E. de Señoria Ilustrísima,
     y lo mismo al hijo del Prinçipe de Massa, saliéndole a reçivir a la mitad de la pieça en que
     estava, acompañándole hasta la puerta de la dicha pieça' *ibid.*, 63–4. Similarly, here are the
     conventional rules for the customary receptions made at the Royal Palace by diplomatic repre-
     sentatives during the various celebrations of Christmas, as they are listed in ASNA, *Sei libri di
     cerimoniale*, part I, fol. 30v: 'Viene il Nunzio a dar le buone festa al Viceré e la Viceregina. Viene
     anche l'internunzio di Polonia e se li deve dare sedia e cappello. Viene il residente di Venezia, a
     chi se li dà sedia e cappello ... Viene il Residente di Parma che si riceverà in piedi, e Sua Eccel-
     lenza [i.e. the Viceroy] lo tratterà da Vostra Signoria ma se sarà Titolato avrà sedia e cappello. Il
     Ricevitore di Malta anche viene e sarà ricevuto in piedi e scoverto, e Sua Eccellenza lo tratterà
     da VS.'
103 See also the detailed list titled: 'Trattamento che deve dare il Viceré a tutti coloro che li
     devono parlare d'affari, secondo il grado che tengono', in ASNA, *Sei libri di cerimoniale*, part II,
     fols. 72v–83r, titled: 'Trattamento che deve dare il Viceré a tutti coloro che li devono parlare
     d'affari, secondo il grado che tengono'.
104 Raneo, *Etiquetas*, 228–9.
105 *Ibid.*, 229.
106 Confuorto, *Giornali*, I, 149.
107 Galasso, *Napoli spagnola*, II, 517.
108 Roosen, 'Early Modern Diplomatic Ceremonial', 471–2.
109 All these incidents appear in Capaccio, *Il forastiero*, 482.
110 Bucca, 'Aggionta', *ASPN*, 36 (1911), 134.
111 Parrino, *Teatro*, in *Raccolta*, vol. 9, 258.
112 *Ibid.*
113 Zazzera, *Narrazioni*, 473.
114 *Ibid.*, 513.
115 This is contrary to the orderly and serious fashion in which prisoners were pardoned by
     the viceroy Pedro Antonio de Aragón in 1671. See ASNA, *Sei libri di cerimoniale*, part I, fols.
     53r–55r. According to Rubino, the Count of Oñate, who on one occasion pardoned some
     criminals who 'have committed enormous crimes', refused to exonerate the following catego-
     ries: 'sodomites, counterfeiters, murderers, and coin clippers'. See SNSP, MS. XVIII. D. 14,
     Notitia, fol. 79. Similarly, following the conquest of Budapest, the viceroy, the Marquis of
     Carpio, wrote a formal request to the criminal court with the intention of pardoning some
     prisoners, asking for a careful assessment of them. See ASNA, *Dispacci della sommaria, Registro*

de Viglietti, 72, 13 September 1686, fol. 2: 'que por el tribunal de la cámara se reconozcan todos los presos, que se hallan en la vicaria y su disposición, y que habiendo reflexión de los que pueden ser capaces de gracia, hagan V.S. relación a S.E. de ellos'.

116   For all of these episodes see Zazzera, *Narrazioni*, 489–533.

117   Parrino, *Teatro*, in *Raccolta*, vol. 9, 334–5.

118   See Giuseppe Galasso, 'Il Mezzogiorno nella "crisi generale" del Seicento', in his *Alla periferia dell'impero*, 217–46.

119   Gunn, 'Los Caprichos', 90–1.

120   Capaccio, *Il forastiero*, 414.

121   Guerra, *Diurnali*, 78.

122   Part of a mordant *sonetto* that was written posthumously reads: In somma il più pezzente / E il più affamato huom di tutta Spagna, / Tu del palaggio un banco, una coccagna. (In sum the most miserable, / And most hungry man in Spain, / You turned the palace into a bank, a cockaigne). *Ibid.*, 78–9.

123   Bucca, 'Aggionta', *ASPN*, 36 (1911), 543.

124   The notorious episode appears in various sources. See, for example, Biblioteca Nazionale, Naples, [hereafter, BNN] MS. XV. G. 23, *Istorico Ragguaglio dell'infelice morte di Gio. Vincenzo Starace Eletto del Fedelis.° Popolo di Nap. nel dì di 8 Magio del 1585*, fols. 91r–117r; and Bulifon, *Giornali*, 54 ff. See also the analysis of Burke, 'The Revolt of Masaniello', 195–6, 204; and Villari, *The Revolt of Naples*, 19–33.

125   Capaccio, *Il forastiero*, 487.

126   See the entire sequence of events in Guerra, *Diurnali*, 130 ff.

127   Capaccio, *Il forastiero*, 539.

128   Guerra, *Diurnali*, 132–5.

129   Parrino, *Teatro*, in *Raccolta*, vol. 10, 116.

130   Aurelio Musi, 'La fedeltà al re nella prima età moderna', in his *L'Italia dei Viceré*, 157–8.

131   Croce, *The Kingdom of Naples*, 100.

132   On some of the disastrous results of these policies see Antonio Calabria, *The Cost of Empire: The Finances of the Kingdom of Naples in the Time of Spanish Rule* (Cambridge, 1992), 50–3, 88–90.

133   Musi, 'La fedeltà', 157–8.

134   Bucca, 'Aggionta', *ASPN*, 36 (1911), 377–8.

2

The power of precedence: social and political hierarchies in civic processions

The hierarchical structure of cavalcades in early modern Naples

In the following pages I will place the viceroys and their court in the larger context of Neapolitan society. My main aim is to explore the social structure of the city through the symbolic communication of ritual and festival by evaluating the guidelines according to which social and political hierarchies were expressed in cavalcades. Based on the various ceremonial instances mentioned earlier, in which nobles received preferential treatment in matters of precedence and personal distinction, my underlying assumption is that, in cavalcades, social status mattered more than political power, especially in those cases where the latter was placed in the hands of the lowly nobility, not to mention officers of non-noble status.

Early modern civic institutions used various forms of ritual and pageantry as effective conveyors of political messages, aiming to unite the diverse social layers of the urban fabric under the shared standard of civic pride. Especially in times of general turmoil, these ritual manifestations aided in putting aside social schisms and internecine political conflicts by fostering ideas of communal order and transcendental hierarchy.[1] This objective was epitomized in a specific form of ritual ubiquitously present on significant public occasions – the civic procession also known as cavalcade – owing to its emphatic display of a hierarchically structured order of various public representatives who rode in tandem, and marked the city's seats of civic power via the chosen itinerary. So far, the attention has been concentrated on royal entries and the political messages of the ephemeral arches and artistic adornments displayed along the designated itinerary, thereby neglecting the meaning of the procession's configuration of the participating groups as a legitimate subject in its own right.[2]

Accordingly, the intention of this chapter is to concentrate exclusively on the procession's socio-political morphology, selecting early modern Naples as a particularly relevant city for this purpose. Its status as the Spanish ruled capital of the Kingdom of Naples made it an ideal platform for the crown and its subjects to ritually reaffirm their mutual loyalties and obligations. In addition, the civic procession could serve as an

adhesive strategy to preserve Naples' fragile and unstable social structure.[3] Nevertheless, scholars have been debating whether the civic procession 'authorized and naturalized the communities' power relationships', hence promoting social harmony, or on the contrary, 'by laying hierarchy bare it could incite the conflict of difference even more powerfully sensed in a concentrated symbolic moment'.[4] Those few scholars who have considered the social effects of civic processions in Naples tend to stress their harmonizing influence, agreeing that: they converged in a common communicative attempt which bonded together various mutually inimical pressure groups; and that the Spanish viceroys, appointed to govern on behalf of the Spanish king, succeeded in projecting through them a unifying elitist and static vision of the social order.[5]

Moreover, according to some of these assessments, the cavalcade not only functioned as a conciliatory device, but was itself a mirror image of society, a neat visual expression of the very clearly defined social stratification of Neapolitan society, perfectly intelligible for the entire population participating in the rite.[6] However, whatever contemporaries might have taken for granted is not that obvious to us because the groups parading at the cavalcades did not represent social categories as such (with the exception of the nobility), but mostly political offices. In other words, if we want to understand the hierarchical significance of the various social groups in the cavalcade, it is necessary to know the social origins of those holding the various public positions. Such an assessment is possible because there were offices restricted to the nobility, and others which required professional skills that the higher strata of the nobility would not 'touch' for fear of being derogated.[7] If this was the case, one should question the criteria for ranking a group at a civic procession. Therefore, the key question is: did the group's position reflect its mere political power, or a combination of political power and social status? In order to answer this question I intend to carefully separate each participating group, trying to measure its social and political status in general, and then ascertain how its rank was reflected in the procession.

In order to define the phenomenon it is important to trace its basic constitutive elements. First, it is essential to differentiate between procession and cavalcade. The former was usually intended to mark a religious event: specific saints' days and the principal holidays of the religious calendar, and occasional circumstances celebrated by the different religious orders. Processions were also recurrent during times of major crises, such as earthquakes, famines, plagues, and revolutions, functioning as expiatory devices. Comparatively, the cavalcade was the civic analogue of the procession. Thus, in the case of Naples, cavalcades were organized by the viceregal court in all those celebrative occasions relevant to the Spanish monarchy. However, since 'church' and 'state' were hardly separate categories during this period, cavalcades were not strictly 'civic', just as processions were not exclusive of the 'religious' sphere. The ecclesiastical hierarchy participated in cavalcades, just as the viceregal court and city officials took part in processions. In addition, processions and cavalcades shared two common features: a discriminative hierarchically structured order of the participant groups,

and a pre-selected itinerary that signalled the values of a power structure expressed through a spatial order.

In order to proceed further into the investigation of the power structure exhibited on these public occasions, we must first take a step back and draw a sketch of the social and political structure of the city itself. According to Carlo Celano, the contemporary writer of one of the most celebrated and comprehensive guides of Naples, the city's population consisted of nobles and commoners. The latter were subdivided into citizens, known as civil people, and plebs, whereas the former were separated into the nobility belonging to the *piazza* (*nobiltà di piazza*), and the one outside the *piazza* (*nobiltà fuori piazza*).[8] Let us take a deeper look into these categories.

The noble *piazze*, also known as *seggi*, consisted of five urban districts: Capuana, Nido, Porto, Portanova, and Montagna, to which was ascribed each noble family belonging to the urban patriciate. At the summit of this group stood the 'titled nobility' – princes, dukes, marquises, counts – who were successful in exerting their power both in the city, by participating in the urban *piazza*, and in the countryside, within the jurisdiction of their feudal territories. This elite group had a high level of cohesiveness; a fact that became especially evident with its concerted efforts to close its ranks to aspiring parvenus after the middle of the sixteenth century. Comparatively, the nobles outside the *piazza* formed a much more heterogeneous group, as it included: Neapolitan nobles of pure aristocratic and feudal origin, nobles from other Italian cities, nobles of Spanish roots, and many 'new nobles' of popular origins. The difference between them and the patriciate was not in the degree of nobility, but in the access to the *piazza*, which enabled participation in the government of the city.[9]

For a detailed description of the city's commoners, the *popolo*, it is safe to rely on Giulio Cesare Capaccio, who despite his acute elitist bias was a most insightful contemporary observer of Neapolitan society. He subdivides into three groups those whom Celano simply calls citizens. The first group is extremely wealthy and lives in grand noble style, intermarrying with the nobility as it aspires to be fully integrated within the noble rank. The second group is constituted by those jurists-bureaucrats, known as *togati*, who were recruited by the crown to serve in the various courts of justice and in the high administrative posts.[10] Their political might was such that, according to Capaccio, they could rule over nobles. The third group of Neapolitan citizenry included retail merchants and traders and those belonging to the more prestigious guilds, among which Capaccio mentions silk workers, jewellers, painters, and architects. Comparatively, Capaccio judges the plebs very harshly. Not only does he not consider them as part of the popular status, but describes them as 'the dregs of the Commonwealth … inclined to conspiracies, revolts, to break rules and customs … almost [functioning as] truncated members … who abuse every small occurrence to turn everything in disarray'.[11] That said, he distinguishes between three groups within the plebs: 'some that live with a certain degree of civility' belonging to the lesser guilds, 'some that are considerably declining from civility, and some that by doing the most lowly tasks are

reduced to such debasement that can by no means rise to a true popular state'.[12] To sum up, seventeenth-century Naples was structured in the typical estates system of the *Ancien Régime*.

As for the distribution of political power, historians of the Italian south generally agree about the existence of three main forces that contested it: the monarchy, the nobility, and the upper strata of the *popolo*. In Spanish Naples, as in other European contexts where the centralist tendencies of kings were pursued – especially so when they had to manage composite state systems as did the Habsburgs – the monarchy sought an alliance with popular elements in order to dismantle the feudal power bases of the nobility, which were rightly perceived as obstacles to an effective central government.[13] This alliance of state and *popolo* would materialize in the growing numbers of commoners being integrated in the high offices of the state apparatus alongside Spanish administrators. They would form a new *political class*, dependent on the monarchy and loyal to it. The nobility, on its side, would try, with an uneven degree of success, to retain its strongholds of power. A periodization of these disputes reveals three broad phases in which the balance of power shifted from one side to the other. The monarchical project of centralization started in the early 1530s, intensified during the times of the viceroy Pedro de Toledo (1532–53), and was at its most successful at the end of the century. Then, for half a century, until the revolt of 1647, there was a 'feudal reaction' of the nobility, at the expense of the state and its dependent bureaucracy. Finally, with the Spanish restoration, under the able hand of the viceroy the Count of Oñate (1648–53), a nobility of the *toga*, something parallel to the French *noblesse de robe*, was formed and consolidated, completely displacing the traditional nobility from political power.[14] Hence, at this point, the relevant question is: would these social and political changes receive a tangible expression in the order of the civic procession?

In order to follow this point more closely, let us use the thorough contemporary systematic description of the standard order of the participant groups in the cavalcade, as they appear in Parrino's magisterial *Teatro eroico*. Teaching us about the political primacy of the civic procession, the following description appears in the introduction alongside other rules of precedence in principal civic and court rituals as: royal obsequies, civic gatherings in the cathedral, viceregal audiences, receptions of foreign dignitaries, and so forth. Significantly, unlike the rare cavalcades that involved royal persons in Naples, the following order of precedence is true for the ever-present principal dignitary of the city, the viceroy:

> Riding at the forefront there is usually some company of cavalry ... Follow the buglers of the city, and of the king, at whose sides ride the ... captains of justice. Next [are] the carriages, chairs, and horses of respect of the viceroy, and of the mayor. Next [is] the nobility; and under this name are included titled [nobles], barons, and knights in disorder, to avoid the quarrels of precedence. Then follows the body of the Representatives of the City, wearing togas, and large barrettes [headgear] in old style of golden cloth, or black, depending on the joy, or on

the mourning, in which the ceremony is celebrated, preceded by twenty-four porters, and many officers with their master of ceremonies. These are followed by the door keepers of the Hall of the Viceroy, with the king of arms, and master of ceremonies. Next, the Seven Offices of the Realm. And finally the viceroy with the mayor on his left, followed by all the ministers of the tribunals: the party ends with more carriages of the viceroy, and companies on horse.[15]

It is clear, then, that rather than being organized in a linear ascending or descending order, the hierarchies start climbing until they reach a peak, from which they start descending. To be more precise, the structure of the procession is defined according to the aforementioned positional principle, the 'code of proximity', according to which, the greater the proximity to the viceroy the better the rank of the group. This rule is universally valid for both religious and civic processions, as exemplified by Miri Rubin's description of the Corpus Christi procession: 'the centre of the procession was the most ornate, the most densely decorated; and it included people whose rank was reflected and enhanced by proximity to the holiest of holies'.[16]

Keeping that in mind, let us examine in detail each of the participating groups mentioned. In order to facilitate the examination I will enumerate the important groups, leaving aside buglers, porters, and other ceremonial officers who are inconsequential to our inquiry:

1. A company of cavalry at the head of the cavalcade.
2. The nobility.
3. The Seven Representatives of the City.
4. The Seven Great Officers of the Realm.
5. Viceroy and 'mayor'[17] (side by side).
6. The tribunals.
7. A company of cavalry closing the cavalcade.

1 (and 7) The cavalry

When Parrino mentions that the procession starts and closes with 'some company of cavalry', he probably means that the sponsors of the parade use some available troops at random. If so, it is quite clear that the army is not an integral part of the city's power structure, but a framing, self-contained, force that directly represents the might of the monarchy. Its essential role in the parade is well exposed by Edward Muir: 'Civic ritual both represented the utopian ideal of a harmonious community and reminded citizens of the possibility of coercion if they failed to accommodate themselves to those in power. The most obvious expressions of force were marching militiamen or soldiers who frequently appeared in civic processions.'[18] Accordingly, it is not surprising that the size of the army should increase at times of social unrest. For example, the usual procession of St John the Baptist, which symbolizes more than any other Neapolitan festival the bond of the *popolo* with the viceroy and the monarchy, was used in 1649 by

the viceroy the Count of Oñate to display a military *tour de force*. Instead of the usual civic cavalcade, the army's part was blown out of proportion as the viceroy appeared in the midst of 1,500 intimidating mercenaries, who were especially hired to guard his body, dressed in black capes, and each one of them carrying 'three pieces of short firearms, sword, and dagger'.[19] Clearly, the message carried by the viceroy was that the monarchy was back on a full scale after the revolt of the previous year, in case anyone among the *fedelissimo popolo* thought of challenging its authority again. The chronicler's testimony to the general unrest that followed the cavalcade shows that the viceroy's goal had been accomplished: 'there were those who estimated His Excellency as very implacable, vengeful, others called him Nero, others [said] that he wanted to hurt both the guilty and the innocent under the pretext of new conspiracies by condemning them to various sentences.'[20]

2 The nobility

The nobility was the only social group represented in the cavalcade as such. Its unchanging position in the cavalcade throughout the 200 years of Spanish dominion is a clue to what I believe consists of a conspicuous gap between the immutable stratification of society in the 'ideal light' of the ritual cavalcade and the dynamic changes in the political power structure of the city. Also, it has to be remembered that an important strategy of early modern monarchs was to invite the nobility to take active part in the honorific and ceremonial sphere of the ruler's household. At its best, as in the case of Louis XIV, the court will serve as a 'golden cage' for the great magnates of the realm, placed under the close supervision of the king and alienated from their feudal bases of power, engaged in a ruinously expensive competition over royal favour, and functioning as essential testimonies of the ruler's greatness at the rituals and festivals of the court. Not dissimilar was the Neapolitan situation with the advent of the Habsburgs. 'The new times demanded that the nobles … would live permanently in the capital, making a circle around the viceroy, and this comported a vertiginous rise in the expenditures of maintenance and representation.'[21] Here is the pertinent comment of the contemporary chronicler Domenico Confuorto, predicting the behaviour of the nobility to the viceroy's invitation to participate in various celebrations honouring the marriage of the Spanish king Charles II: 'These gentlemen, being vainglorious and lured by [external] appearances in their nature, even though being poor, they will not fail, as usual, to jeopardize and indebt themselves in order to appear elegant in such functions.'[22]

According to Parrino, despite the clear gradations of power inside the group, it was normative to parade 'in disorder, to avoid the quarrels of precedence'. This cordial understanding is a sign of a general acknowledgement of an acute, uncompromising, sense of self, prevalent among the Neapolitan aristocracy. All the diaries used in this study reveal scores of violent confrontations between nobles for issues of precedence. Thus, as the chances of peacefully negotiating the place of each noble in a ranking continuum were negligible, it made much more sense to 'agree to disagree' beforehand,

by calling off the ranking principle altogether. The need for this norm can be proved by way of a negative example. In one of the festivities of December 1616, the nobility met to parade 'in order to march (as usual) in confusion.' However, the master of ceremonies thought otherwise, and wanting to order the nobility in ascending order – in such a way that according to the principles of proximity the last group would be closer to the viceroy – he ordered that those without title (*privati*) should go first, and the titled ones after them. The reaction of many was to leave the cavalcade altogether. They returned only after the intervention of the viceroy, who ordered the restoration of the consensual 'levelling order'.[23] This is only one of the groups in which the nobility appeared, although, significantly, the one which represents it as a status *per se*. What is shared by all of the cavalcading nobles is the vital importance given to ceremonial appearance.

3. The Seven Representatives of the City

The political and social dynamics that revolve around the administration of the city, as it is represented by the body of the Seven Representatives (*eletti*), can serve as a microcosm of the aforementioned power contests in Naples. In principle the *popolo civile* and the *nobiltà di piazza* shared the municipal government through the assembled body of the Seven Representatives. Six of these were nominated for the five noble *piazze* (each *piazza* received one representative, except the *piazza* of Montagna which received two, being considered conjoined to the once autonomous *piazza* of Forcella), and one for the popular *piazza*. The clear numerical advantage of the nobility seems to put the joint administration on an unequal ground, a fact that was resented and challenged by the *popolo*, who constantly strove, although unsuccessfully, to equalize the number of popular representatives to the noble number. However, it should be noted that the power and the various prerogatives of the popular representative were indeed equal to those of all the other six noble representatives put together, as the jurisdiction of each noble representative was limited to its specific *piazza* whereas the jurisdiction of the popular representative was extended throughout the city. In addition, the popular *piazza* received an exclusive political weight: the representatives of four *piazze* were enough to assemble and represent the city in municipal manners, but the popular representative could not be spared at any time. Despite the rivalries between nobles and commoners, the Seven Representatives, who regularly met at the Tribunal of St Lorenzo, held various tasks and prerogatives that changed through time, the most important of which, from the middle of the sixteenth century onwards, was the administration of the *annona* – the food supply to the city.[24]

The importance of this task is exemplified in the dialogue between Capaccio's Foreigner and the Neapolitan Citizen: 'F. Do you know what seems to me irksome in the government of Naples? The administration of the *annona*; because I don't hear anything else being discussed by your plebs other than *grassa*, *grassiero* [the chief administrator of food supply], bread, edibles, and it seems to me that they think of nothing else.'[25] Despite the elitist impatience in this comment, it reflects the growing difficulty for the

city to maintain a positive balance in the flow of food supplies for an ever-increasing population of different peoples migrating to the city from the countryside, driven by the royal exemptions from taxes. 'Indeed', the Citizen replies, 'if it were not for the trouble involved in this, to govern Naples would be a joy.'[26] And to reinforce this, he mentions the potential logistical problems: 'How much trouble do you think it is not to have grain, wait for it to arrive from outside, to suffer the arrival of bad weather, send for the ships, and it may be possible that galleons will not be available to do it, be anxious that the *popolo* may riot, not to expect anything other than displeasure?'[27] To which the Foreigner replies: 'For all these reasons it seems to me that the viceroy should be *grassiero*, representative of the city, provider, and that in such occasions will really be the leader that gives vigour to the entire republic.'[28] In other words, the viceroy should take over the major responsibilities that fall upon the Seven Representatives. This entire piece is a crafty apology, perhaps with a slant of well-hidden criticism, for the viceregal attempts to minimize the autonomy of the municipal body. Perhaps the viceroy could not be a representative of the city, as suggested by Capaccio, but he could control the one with most power. In 1548 the viceroy Pedro de Toledo imposed a mechanism according to which the viceroy chose the popular representative out of a list of six names brought forward by the popular *piazza*. The viceroy also decided upon the extension of the office. This dependence of the popular representative on the viceroy was another means by which the central government was able to secure its traditional alliance with the *popolo*. Moreover, between 1560 and 1562, a noble appointed by the viceroy known as *grassiero* presided over the food-supply administration. As his jurisdiction grew he came to be considered 'the head of the tribunal of the city's representatives.'[29] In sum, a shrewd monarchical policy of 'divide and rule', coupled with a strong measure of intervention in the internal management of the city, kept the Neapolitan municipal body weak and unable to challenge the central authority.

In sharp contrast, the Seven Representatives enjoyed prestigious ceremonial privileges, such as: exclusive and immediate access to the viceroy,[30] a privileged position in church during public events,[31] and, of course, a central place in the cavalcade. All the representatives marched in one group, appearing in grand style with the same processional uniform, and accompanied by a large and impressive entourage:

> They wear a cloth of gold and crimson with robes of yellow brocade, in senatorial style, all adorned with rich golden frills, with matching berets of golden cloth; and with saddlecloth of crimson velvet on their horses. Their ministers cavalcade ahead of them, dressed in the same way; but with black drapes lined with velvet. They allow the precedence of a [large] quantity of ushers, carrying half red and half golden batons in their hands, dressed with breeches, sleeves, and berets of crimson damask; and with a cassock and gown of scarlet cloth. And it is really a most rich and majestic view.[32]

However, despite these unifying principles, there were some privileges which created distinctions within the group, between the popular representative and those of the

nobility. For example, much more important than the part of the *eletti* in the cavalcade was their privilege of electing from their midst an eighth person, nominated 'mayor' (*sindaco* or *sindico*), who paraded in a much more dignified position – at the very side of the viceroy. I do not wish to comment further on this ceremonial office before reaching its due place in the order of the cavalcade. At this point it suffices to say that he was elected only from the noble *piazze*. This privilege was matched by the popular *piazza*, although on a smaller scale, during the festivity of St John the Baptist, in which the viceroy rode side by side with the popular representative, 'and the nobility does not have a part in it other than escorting the cavalcade'.[33] Of much importance on this occasion was the itinerary of the cavalcade, which passed exclusively through the popular quarters of the city.[34] A similar popular privilege was given during the first Saturday of May, for the celebration of the miracle of the transmutation of St Januarius' blood, done according to a principle of annual rotation in the various *piazze*. When it was done in the popular *piazza*, the captains of *ottine* – the civic units in which the popular area was subdivided – were allowed to remain covered in the viceroy's presence. Notably, this was a special prerogative for that day only.[35]

These last two privileges mentioned illustrate the relationship, to which I referred at the beginning, between the itinerary and social hierarchies. Even more significant in this respect was the procession of the Corpus Domini.[36] Again, based on a rotational principle, the procession passed through all the six *piazze*. At the core of the procession there was a canopy, called *palio*, carried above the sacred host, that was supported by eight poles: five were carried by representatives of the noble *piazze*, one by the *piazza* of the *popolo*, and the two remaining pole carriers that belonged to the lower nobility (*baronaggio*) and the crown were selected by the viceroy. The carriers of the poles changed places as the procession moved into the different *piazze*, so that at the arrival at each *piazza*, its representative moved to the pole at the front. Hence, as explained by Maria Antonietta Visceglia, the passage served two main functions. First, 'the spatial dimension of the procession illustrated the topography of the *piazze* and marked their borders thereby avoiding conflicts and feuds between factions over the territorial control of the city'. Second, 'it also made explicit elements of distinctions and hierarchies between the *piazze* themselves'.[37] As it happens, besides the traditional rivalry between *popolo* and nobility, the noble *piazze* were afflicted by the pretension of the two larger and richer *piazze* – Capuana and Nido – to outdo the other three.[38] Thus, the dissent that already afflicted the municipal body between nobility and *popolo* was intensified by the internecine ritual rivalries among the noble *piazze*.

4. The Seven Great Officers of the Realm

The next group is composed of the Seven Great Officers of the Realm, which included the following list in a descending hierarchical order, High Constable, High Admiral, Chief Justice, High Chamberlain, Great Protonotary, High Chancellor, and High Steward. It is of great significance that this group, which received the most privileged

position besides the viceroy and the 'mayor', carried no political prerogatives whatsoever. The origin of these offices has been traced back to the Norman kings. In the
past they held vast executive powers, but the Aragonese and Spanish kings had them
distributed to the various tribunals and central organs of government. Accordingly, by
the seventeenth century, these offices were virtually void of real political content and
became merely honorific and representational. It is also extremely revealing that all the
contemporary guides and biographies of the city dedicated large sections to describing
the offices, which are disproportionately longer than the place dedicated to the active
central organs of government.[39] A possible explanation for this is the editorial choice
of the viceroys, who firmly controlled the publishing houses of the realm, which was
concomitant with the lopsided privileged position that the Seven Great Officers got in
the cavalcade. In both cases the goal would be to bestow honours and dignities upon
the holders of the offices, with the expectation that they would like holding on to
the prestige, even without the real power. Needless to say, an obvious reason of the
monarchy to rank this group high was the self-serving fact that the offices actually
represented none other but the monarchy itself. It is also revealing that the Seven
Great Officers were occupied by the highest ranks of the titled nobility. Hence, more
than anything else this group represents the successful monarchical cooptation of the
nobility. Moreover, the price that the nobles were willing to pay for the honorific title
was worth a lucrative revenue to the crown. For example, Parrino informs us that with
the death of the Prince of Conca, Great Admiral of the Realm, the office was transferred
to the Duke of Sessa, 'to whom it was conceded by the king, for all his successors' for
300,000 *ducati*.[40]

5. The viceroy and the 'mayor'

As already stated, at each cavalcade a 'mayor' was elected on a rotational basis among
one of the noble *piazze*. At the first instance, a special decree was issued to the noble
Representatives of the City ordering them to elect a 'mayor' for the special occasion.
On the day of the designated cavalcade, the congregation of all the nobility met at the
'mayor''s house to escort him to the Tribunal of St Lorenzo, where he took possession
of the office with all the honours of a solemn ceremony. From there he was escorted to
the palace of the viceroy, where the general cavalcade would eventually begin.[41] These
excessive honours given to the 'mayor', through the act of possession, coupled with a
preliminary cavalcade exclusive to the nobility, is an unmistakable act of self-congrat-
ulation. Moreover, it is important to note that the central government was more than
willing to play along. First, it appears that the 'mayor' and the viceroy coordinated their
clothes, probably wishing to show the mutual harmony existing between the city and
the government.[42] Moreover, by letting the 'mayor' stay on the viceroy's side, although on
the left, he was being promoted as the second most important person. Even more so, in
the event that the cavalcade was led by a royal person, the 'mayor' kept his pre-eminent
position at the side of the majestic dignitary, while the viceroy was the one who had to

relinquish his position by taking a step forward. At least, that was true in principle. As we shall see later on, the presence of royalty at cavalcades often caused disorders and disputes over precedence, shaking the entire hierarchical structure.

6. The Tribunals

What Parrino sums up with one word – tribunals – included a number of bodies, which appear in the cavalcade in a descending order right after the viceroy. First, the Collateral Council, 'known also as the supreme; formed by the most skilful and expert ministers'.[43] As noted in the previous chapter, after the middle of the sixteenth century, the viceroy became subject to this body, where he functioned as no more than *primus inter pares*. It is between the ministers of this group that it would be more likely to see the viceroy parading, if the cavalcade were to be organized to reflect mere political power. Next followed the Council of St Chiara, a judicial court dealing exclusively with matters concerning the nobility. After that came the Royal Chamber of the Sommaria – the organ responsible for the economic administration of the kingdom. Last, the Great Court of the Vicarage was the judicial court responsible for civil and criminal cases.[44]

It is implicit that many of these offices required a legal education. Many others, though, were simply purchasable. The ministerial offices were a coveted venue for civilians interested in ascending the higher ranks of society, and they were strongly encouraged to do so by the central government. However, they also attracted large sections of the nobility, especially those that were denied access to the *piazze*. What matters is that this became a mixed category that was not exclusively of noble birth. Consequently, it would be ill regarded, or more appropriately a target for snobbery, on the part of the higher nobility. Francesco d'Andrea, one of the most celebrated jurists of early modern Naples, has noted that after the revolt of 1647–48 access to the supreme offices of state was open to anyone, starting from the *popolo* and up to the nobles of the *Piazza*. Especially interesting are the statistics that he produces for the years between 1648 and 1696, about the social classes that took up the positions. Despite the profusion of vacant positions after the revolt only five were taken by nobles of the *piazza*, while the rest were taken by nobles outside the *piazza* and commoners. Concentrating on Collateral Regents alone, out of the twenty-two that were created during these forty-eight years, only four positions were taken by the nobles of the *piazza*.[45] In sum, once the *popolo* 'ritually polluted' those occupations that traditionally belonged to the higher nobility, the latter group drifted away from politics.

Our inquiry has thus far determined that it is critical to differentiate between political power and social status in order to understand the order of the groups in the cavalcade, and that social status is ultimately of greater influence in assigning a more privileged position in the cavalcade. Accordingly, if we eliminate the companies of cavalry at the two extremes of the cavalcade, the groups ascend in importance as they get closer to the viceroy. The first group is the nobility, which includes nobles with and without title, the

only participants representing a social group without holding a particular civic office. Next, in a higher position, we find the Seven Representatives of the City, whose position reflects a combination of social status with concrete political powers. As a rule, the six noble representatives belong to the higher echelon of the city's social stratification as they are titled nobles of the *piazza*, and together with the popular representative hold specific powers and prerogatives concerning the city's administration. As we get close to the core of the cavalcade we need to elaborate on the two groups that are in full propinquity with the viceroy: the Seven Great Officers of the Realm preceding him, and the Regents of the Collateral Council (the more important group of the various tribunals) coming right after the viceroy. Apparently, the Seven Great Officers and the Regents of the Collateral Council are not equivalent in their standing, despite an equal proximity to the viceroy. We can learn this from their actual position that reflects a basic ceremonial principle, in which it is more prestigious to precede (the viceroy, in this case) than to follow. In addition, their ceremonial predominance is exemplified in the rules applied on such solemn occasions as royal obsequies. If one of the Great Officers of the Realm is missing from the city, he is replaced by a Collateral Regent, which signifies that the Seven Great Officers, unlike the Regents, are indispensable. Moreover, if one of the Great Officers is missing, the Collateral's Regent that replaces him will not automatically take the original position of the absent person, but, respecting the internal hierarchical order of the Seven Great Officers, those Officers of the Realm that are present in the cavalcade will occupy the most dignified of the vacant Seven Great Officers, leaving the less prestigious offices to the Collateral Regents.[46] Thus, the ceremonial preference of the Seven Great Officers over the Regents of the Collateral Council is a clear example of how social status outranks political power in the cavalcade. The members of the Collateral belong to the strongest political institution in the kingdom, but their social origins can vary from titled nobility to ignoble status, with a growing popular component through the years. The Seven Great Officers, on the other hand, have no political powers whatsoever, but they represent the highest and oldest noble families of the *piazza*. Similarly, the 'mayor' receives the most dignified position next to the viceroy. Although he is supposed to represent the entire city, it should be remembered that he is strictly chosen out of the six noble Representatives of the City, even though the popular representative, who cannot be elected 'mayor', is politically the most powerful of the group.

Hence, this analysis clarifies the intricacies of the cavalcade's morphological organization, although the ordinary descriptions of cavalcades do not allow us to determine how and when this order came into being. The key to understanding changes through time lies in those instances where the rules of precedence were challenged, opening ritual opportunities for future reorganizations of the cavalcade's structure, as we shall now proceed to examine.

Extraordinary cavalcades and conflicts of precedence

The hierarchical structures of the groups in the cavalcades will be clarified, in the following pages, by tackling those particular instances in which the usual rules of precedence, described above, were not respected by the participants, or were consciously readapted by the organizers if they thought that the occasion so required. Inasmuch as the cavalcade included the usual groups of participants, parading in their predetermined position, it might be expected that no serious issues of precedence would occur. But conflicts were almost inevitable when the cavalcade took place in honour of someone whose supreme status destabilized the entire order. I refer to the entries of various eminent personalities into the city – notably kings, queens, ruling princes, and royal kin. In this respect, triggered by the visits of foreign monarchs during the so-called Italian Wars (1494–1559), Italian city-states functioned as a model for European royal entries from the Renaissance onwards.[47] 'The most successful of these demanded the talents of artists, architects, musicians, Latinists, dramatists, and ceremonial specialists, who created a form of outdoor public theatre, which was witnessed by far more people than any other artistic production of the age.'[48] The ludic and artistic aspects of civic celebrations will be studied in depth in the following chapters; at this point it suffices to say that the capital of the Kingdom of Naples, which has been at the heart of the long contest between France and Spain over the political control of the peninsula, was one of the most privileged destinations of such visits. Let us quickly review them.

An important precedent, since it had few examples on which to rely, was established by the celebrated triumphal entry of Alfonso de Aragón in 1443, after his defeat of the Angevin ruler René. At the turn of the century, the sequence of entries, which also reflects the passage of the kingdom from one royal dynasty to another, started with the accession of the Aragonese Alfonso II in 1494. It continued with the arrival and seizure of the throne by the French monarch Charles VIII in 1495. The next few years saw a short return of the Aragonese, with the entry of Ferrante II (1496), who died the following year, succeeded by his uncle, Frederick (1497–1501). Following the completion of the kingdom's conquest by Gonzalo de Córdoba, the Great Captain (1503), Neapolitans greeted their new Spanish king Ferdinand the Catholic in 1506. Last but not least, Emperor Charles V visited the city in 1535–36, following his victorious campaign in Tunis.[49] Also, it is worth noting a few more entries, which, although being outside this period, are interesting for their conflicts of precedence. Still within the sixteenth century, although after the final defeat of France and the establishment of the Spanish pre-eminence over Italy, Naples saw the entry of Don John of Austria (1571), who was sent by his half-brother Philip II to lead the military campaign against the Turks.[50] The same person re-entered the city in triumph after the victory of Lepanto. During the seventeenth century only two entries of Spanish royal persons are recorded: the entry of Maria of Austria (1630) on her way to marry the King of Hungary, and that of Don John of Austria (1648), the illegitimate son of Philip IV, who was sent to subdue the revolt that had started the previous year.[51]

Even though our main focus is on the seventeenth century, those previous entries where conflicts of precedence arose need to be assessed since the resolution of later quarrels was determined according to these precedents. For this purpose, one needs to note the deep structural changes that occurred in royal entries during the times of the Italian Wars, and that those entries replicated the procession of the Corpus Domini. Two phenomena stand out in this respect: the significant ritual changes made in the procession of the Corpus Domini by the leading authorities in times of political transition, and the rearrangement of royal entries in concordance with those changes.

Ferrante II, who had just returned the Aragonese to power after the withdrawal of the French, made the first meaningful modification on 17 June 1496. When he revoked some of the sanctions administered against the popular *piazza* by Alfonso the Magnanimous, despite the harsh resistance of the nobility, he decided to allocate to the *popolo* one of the poles that sustained the canopy under which the Corpus Domini was carried in procession.[52] His decision was confirmed the following year by his successor Frederick of Altamura, who proclaimed that the six poles of the canopy should be carried by the following authorities: one for the king, one for his heir, one for a popular representative, one for a noble representative, one for the Spanish ambassador, and the last one for the Venetian ambassador.[53] This distribution, besides its obvious favouring of royal authority and the elevation of the international powers significant to the kingdom, signalled a clear monarchical predilection for the *popolo* over the nobility. Not only had the latter to suffer the popular presence under the canopy, but the noble representatives of each *seggio* had also to share the same pole in rotation, as the procession advanced through the various *seggi*. For the subsequent coronation of Frederick, the *popolo* requested the right to assert its new privilege and carry one pole of the canopy, but following the stern opposition of the nobility, and the resulting conflict between the two social groups, the king decided to revoke from both the right of holding a pole on that specific occasion.[54]

For the procession of the Corpus Domini of 1499, in order to put an end to the conflict, Frederick changed the number of poles from six to eight, and had them redistributed in the following order: five for the various noble *seggi*, one for the popular *seggio*, one for himself, and one, at his discretion, for either his successor or for some ambassador. Hence, this new formula tried to convey a message of civic unity, where the city's administrative structure as a whole functioned as a mediator, since the *popolo* and the nobility now shared the poles proportionally to the number of *seggi* owned by each side.[55]

Naturally, with the accession of the Spaniards, the two poles that were carried by the Aragonese monarch and his heir had to be reallocated. The king's pole went to the viceroy, and the other to the *baronaggio* – the noble component that had no representation in the *seggi*.[56] Thus, with the arrival of the viceregal government the nobility as a whole was privileged at the expense of foreign representatives, who were completely cut out of the equation, and if we perceive this as a zero-sum logic, at the expense of

the *popolo* as well. This change is also consistent with my previous assertion regarding the general ritual exaltation of the nobility by the Spaniards. Nevertheless, the latest modification could do little to prevent the refusal of the nobility to let the *popolo* carry a pole at the entry of Ferdinand the Catholic in 1507.[57] Just as at Frederick's coronation, ten years earlier, they were not willing to translate the *popolo*'s concession made for the procession of the Corpus Domini to a different occasion. Clearly, the uncompromising nobility believed that each honorific privilege given to the *popolo* deserved a separate contest.

Finally, with the entry of Charles V in 1536 – which Maria Antonietta Visceglia has identified as the model of future political parades in the city[58] – the nobility seemed to have learned to accept the much-contested popular privilege at both the Corpus Domini procession and the royal entries.[59] Accordingly, the emperor rode under a canopy, held by five nobles, one popular, one baron, and a representative of the viceroy, 'conforming to what is usually done at the festivity of the Sacrament'.[60] However, that dispute was promptly replaced by a different one. For the triumphal entry of an emperor, whose stature reached mythical proportions in his own time, it was obvious that all the groups involved would not want to miss the chance to make their best appearance. Hence, it was almost inevitable that someone would think of trying to improve his position, as the following account reveals. 'The foreign gentlemen … did not get a predetermined place in the cavalcade. Some held the opinion of letting them have the closest spot just before the emperor, to honour them as foreigners. But the Marquis of Vasto thought better of it saying that on that day, the Neapolitan nobles should not be denied their proper place, and so it was done.'[61] Accordingly, foreign dignitaries of high prestige such as the Roman Luigi Farnese, or the Spanish grandees who escorted the emperor, received no fixed place but were allowed to cavalcade wherever they pleased.[62]

Reading between the lines it is clear that a conflict of precedence has arisen, when foreign guests asserted a privileged position for themselves. The surprising element is to find a part of the opposing group ready to concede its own place. How can we explain that, especially at a singular event such as Charles V's entry into Naples? A plausible solution can be found in what Johan Huizinga describes as an inverted competition for honour, by turning it into a contest in politeness. Thus, by yielding to someone else 'one demolishes one's adversary by superior manners, making way for him or giving him precedence'. Consequently, this surprising willingness to relinquish their position to the foreigners can be interpreted as quite the opposite from an altruistic motive 'since the reason for this display of civility to others lies in an intense regard for one's own honour'.[63]

An identical dispute took place at the visit of Don John of Austria in 1571. This time the foreign dignitaries were Alessandro Farnese, Prince of Parma, and Francesco Maria della Rovere, Prince of Urbino. To resolve the conflict, the viceroy, Cardinal de Granvelle, who enjoyed a great degree of prestige and esteem, having functioned for many years as one of the closest advisers of Charles V,[64] took over the situation. He

ordered the Representatives of the City to give up their place to the foreigners, to which they agreed, but not before they made him sign a declaration that this was an isolated gesture, and not a precedent that might serve as a case to challenge their position in the future.[65]

The last two cases mentioned show that conflicts of precedence could occur inside the same status group, just as much as between nobility and *popolo*. True enough, the cases presented show a conflict between Neapolitan nobles and foreign aristocrats, suggesting yet another division between different pressure groups. However, as noted in the previous chapter, not only were disputes within the local noble group quite common, but they were also the ones that had the greatest resonance. Many examples could be cited of nobles quarrelling and killing each other over issues of precedence, occurring in all possible social arenas where they interacted. They fought with the same fervour for a better place in church, a privileged seat at a play, or the right of way in the street. The same happened in cavalcades, especially in those where the aforementioned levelling principle of marching 'in confusion' did not apply. For example, such conflicts occurred in the cavalcade organized to celebrate the birth of Prince Baltassar Carlos (19 December 1629), between the Prince of Bisignano and the Prince of Cariati, and between the Duke of la Rocca and the Marquis of Belmonte. Eventually, these quarrels were resolved quite peacefully. The Prince of Bisignano left the noble group, marching at the back of the cavalcade as an act of protest; whereas the Duke of la Rocca was opportunely requested by the viceroy to stay in the palace to receive the ladies arriving for the banquet that was destined to follow the cavalcade.[66]

These incidents diminish when compared with a relatively rare and acute case of self-assertion, on behalf of the Prince of Paternò, first-born to the Duke of Montalto, who chose that same cavalcade to formulate an unprecedented request. He claimed to go before both the Representatives of the City and the Seven Great Officers of the Realm, basing his claim upon being the son of a Spanish grandee, and especially on being a descendant of the Royal House of Aragón. Of course, no precedents could substantiate these extravagant demands, as the Seven Great Officers were not supposed to give way even to Spanish grandees.[67] As for the city's representatives, as previously seen, they relinquished their place only when forced to do so and even then on very special occasions. Nevertheless, the haughty prince, owing to the aid of his father-in-law, the viceroy, the Duke of Alcalá – whose expected support might have been the reason behind his daring experiment – succeeded in having his way. Alcalá ordered the city's representatives, who threatened to withdraw completely from the cavalcade, to stay in their places, otherwise risking to be fined 6,000 ducats each. 'Thus they had to surrender, after having formally protested, that they were not conceding spontaneously, but that they were being constrained and forced.'[68] As for the two representatives out of the Seven Great Officers who were present on that occasion, each opted for a different strategy. The Prince of Conca simply gave in without a fight – 'a thing which has been criticized by the whole city, because as the High Admiral he should have not allowed

it'.[69] Conversely, the Marquis of Fuscaldo, the Chief Justice, stayed in the cavalcade but turned his back on the pretentious prince, as if ignoring his presence. Thus, his honour remained flawless but he won the disfavour of the viceroy who ordered him to leave the city of Naples immediately for his estates.[70]

Alcalá's arm-twisting was successful this time. Despite a rather severe style of resolving conflicts of precedence, Neapolitan nobles seem to have respected his formal duty as the ultimate arbiter of ceremony. In any case, they always had an option of taking the issue to the highest of instances – the king himself. However, a much greater challenge awaited him, saturated with ceremonial quarrels, which would have a fatal outcome on his viceregal career. I refer to the visit of Maria of Austria, sister of Philip IV, who arrived in Naples in July 1630.[71] Her visit came as a result of unfortunate circumstances. She was on her way from Spain to marry the King of Hungary, but upon arrival at Genoa she was forced to delay the continuation of her voyage because of an outbreak of bubonic plague that was ravaging Lombardy. Thus, the Kingdom of Naples, the greatest Spanish possession in the area, must have seemed an obvious choice where a Spanish royal person could 'kill some time'.[72]

Apparently, the citizens of Naples did their best to honour the royal visitor. Accordingly, the place chosen to host Maria of Austria for the first days of her visit was the impressive palace of Fabio Carafa, Prince of Colobrano, situated on the aristocratic coastal hill of Posillipo. Alessandro Fellecchia, the official chronicler of the visit, assesses the palace as the most beautiful and spacious among the luxurious residences of that coast, and describes in great detail its richly ornate rooms and numerous fountains adorning the surrounding gardens. He also praises the beauties of Posillipo, which 'more properly should be named the Terrestrial Paradise',[73] and eulogizes the Neapolitan nobility, sumptuously dressed in the best possible attire, while attending the various promenades, theatrical representations, and banquets organized in the palace to honour the queen.[74]

The same tone was kept for Maria's subsequent great entry to the city, planned to take place a few days after her arrival. As it was decided that she would make an entry from the sea, in the same style as the viceroys, it had been agreed to build a bridge that would exceed in its magnificence all the previous examples made for royal persons.[75] In like manner, following the order of the viceroy, a 'mayor' was elected – Hettore Capecelatro, 'a noble of much quality', belonging to the *seggio* of Capuana, who had incurred 'great expenditure' on the 'bountiful pomp' for the occasion.[76] To be precise, he spent 8,000 *ducati* that served him to dress thirty-six pages with a livery made of black cloth trimmed with gold. According to a contemporary assessment, which sheds light on the utilitarian aspects of conspicuous consumption rather than just being a superfluous waste of money, this was perceived as a potentially profitable investment. Based on the precedent of the 'mayor' elected for Charles V, who received a prestigious office afterwards, it was expected that this time the 'mayor' should be appointed as a regent of the Collateral Council.[77]

But, alas, as the day of the entry approached it became clear that the 'mayor' was going to be denied his traditional place at the royal person's side. Instead, the queen was accompanied by both the former viceroy, the Duke of Alba, to her right, and the current viceroy, the Duke of Alcalá, to her left. The unanimous reaction of the local elites was a concerted and unprecedented withdrawal of all the key participants. 'The mayor did not appear, nor the Representatives of the City, neither the Seven Officers of the Realm, under the pretext, that they did not want to risk [to lose] the order of their old precedence, that is why they stayed home … and for the same reason many nobles were missing, and this [happened] … only because the right order of things has not been understood.'[78] According to this account of Alessandro Fellecchia, it would seem that such a gross gesture of disrespect towards a royal person was in reality nothing more than a misunderstanding. However, the other sources, which do not suffer from the common laudatory, not to say sycophantic, bias of official chronicles of royal visits, reveal that the order of things had been understood all too well.[79] This time the local elite saw no other way out but to report to the king, denouncing the deliberate revocation of the 'mayor''s place on that special occasion – 'a thing so novel and out of the common usage and propriety, that it is impossible to receive without great disgust, as we saw the city, nobility, and reign, stripped from the honours and privileges bestowed by their kings that were gained with so much sweat and blood'.[80] In addition, their petition contained something more than mere protest, as the Neapolitan nobles demanded their privilege 'to serve that Lady with the proper preparations, which they have already arranged without being able to put them to use'.[81] The king's resolution, which was communicated to Alcalá, is summarized in the following letter sent by the latter to the offended 'mayor':

> To Hettor Capeche Latro Mayor of this most loyal city … His Highness orders that upon the departure of the Most Serene Queen of Hungary to Germany she will be accompanied with the greatest pomp and display possible … he has ordered me to notify Your Lordship [*Vostra Signoria*] that as a mayor you should provide for everything necessary, as it is assumed that the journey [of departure] will take place on Saturday, and His Majesty orders that Your Lordship will march before His Excellency, and the others [will march] in their rightful place, and thus Your Lordship will inviolably act as His Majesty commands.[82]

In a nutshell, from the letter we understand that the king decided to compensate the Neapolitan petitioners and let the 'mayor' accompany the queen at her exit. What the letter does not do is to pinpoint the person responsible for the incident. Significantly, the various sources that cover the story give different interpretations, putting the blame on a variety of people and reasons. As a rule, Bucca and Capaccio justified the queen's rejection of the 'mayor', and held the organizers responsible. According to one view, Queen Maria operated rightfully because it was a mistake altogether to choose a 'mayor' for the occasion since she did not have any jurisdiction over the city, as the 'mayor''s reception was intended for kings or their viceroys only. In a similar vein, others were

of the opinion that at the arrival of royal persons, the viceroy was the proper authority to receive them, and not a 'mayor'. Others still claimed that the mistake was to choose a 'mayor' who did not match the queen's stature, not being a high-ranking noble. Apparently, two viceroys before her visit had also dismissed 'mayors' of relatively humble origins.[83] Similarly, Raneo acquitted Maria from all blame, in order to place it all on the master of ceremonies, who made many mistakes on that visit, 'all of which are not brought here to avoid embarrassment'.[84] Simone Giugni, the agent of the Grand Duke of Tuscany, had a totally different opinion. In his letter to his master, issued a few days after the incident, he claimed that the 'mayor' lost his place, 'because it was impossible to find a way to accommodate the pretensions of the precedence of the Duke of Alba'.[85]

Of all these interpretations, the last is the most plausible, because it fits all too well within the master plan of the Duke of Alba. There is a general agreement between contemporaries that the entire idea of having the Queen of Hungary visit Naples was born out of the malicious intentions of her escort, the previous viceroy, the Duke of Alba (1622–29), who wanted 'to obscure with his presence' the authority of his successor in the office, the Duke of Alcalá, 'with whom he remained in a hateful exchange since his departure'.[86] If indeed the plan was to damage his foe, Alba fully succeeded, because according to Bucca: 'In these days occurred the greatest event, seen or perceived during our age, that the Duke of Alcalá has been summoned to the court by the king before the end of his term, to account for some things attributed to him during the reception, and other circumstances related to the Queen of Hungary during her stay in Naples; all of which has been plotted by the Duke of Alba.'[87]

Besides the incident of the cavalcade, there is plenty of evidence to show that Alba did everything possible to belittle, embarrass, or shed a negative light upon Alcalá's behaviour. For example, he requested his friend, the Prince of Colobrano, to provide the queen with a sumptuous ship for her maritime entrance to Naples. The idea was to supply the queen with an alternative to the royal galleon offered by Alcalá for the same purpose.[88] In the same vein, he shrewdly managed to outdo the viceroy in a common stroll in the city, at which the crowd shouted in praise of the Duke of Alba, leaving Alcalá in great embarrassment. That applause, according to Bucca, 'was not spontaneous but contracted, and arranged by him via some of his confidants, and friends'.[89] Four months later the royal guest was still in the city, a fact 'orchestrated, as it was said, by the Duke of Alba, who made it his purpose to prolong it from one day to the other',[90] hence perpetuating the strain that such a visit inflicted on the viceroy's government. Eventually, giving in to the pressure, 'because indeed as long as this stay continues, he does not seem like a viceroy',[91] he asked the queen to inform him about the date of her departure, supposedly in order to take the proper economic measures. According to Fuidoro, 'these instances ... made to the queen cost him very dearly, to such an extent, that the bad luck inflicted upon him by Alba brought the total destruction of his house, and his wife the vicereine was confined to Caserta, where she died in complete poverty.'[92] According to one chronicle, the feud between the two rivals continued into

the next generation, because following these tragic events Alcalá's nephew challenged Alba's son to a duel.[93]

Alba's intrigues were also aided by Maria's disposition. Not only did she hold him in high esteem and yield to his will, but her punctilious behaviour also functioned as such a prolific and autonomous source of trouble as to keep Alcalá's hands full. Besides being able to alienate the entire city with her controversial entry, whether it was Alba's doing or not, she immediately succeeded in moving on a collision course with the Neapolitan ladies who wished to visit her. Conforming to Spanish etiquette she declared that only the great ladies would be allowed to sit on cushions, whereas all the rest would be sitting on the floor. Accordingly, very few ladies honoured her with a visit.[94] Likewise, she quarrelled with some of the religious authorities, claiming that she was not being treated with proper decorum by their institution.[95]

Alba's malevolence, exercised over the queen's head, is best portrayed in the 'regal treatment' that awaited the Prince of Bisignano Caraffa. The Duke of Alba, who was on bad terms with Caraffa since the days of his viceregal government, 'guiding this Lady at his free will', succeeded in having the queen deny the prince and his consort the treatment they deserved. Accordingly, it was said that the wife died of heartache. Nevertheless, upon the queen's departure Caraffa decided to show his respect and accompany her in the cavalcade of egress. But the unforgiving Alba sent him a message on behalf of the queen to withdraw from the cavalcade, as his services were not welcome. Bucca's reaction to the event reveals a direct injury to his sense of national pride. 'And from this single example alone anyone can deduce in what vile servitude we live, and with how much superciliousness we are being trampled by all Spaniards: as we see the first baron of the kingdom mistreated in such a way, everyone can imagine what can be done to others.'[96] Ultimately, the entire episode of the visit uncovers the pitiful story of a malicious person placed in a position of power, who knew well how to manipulate the sensitivities of the Neapolitan elite and his royal protector to his own advantage. The valuable lesson that it teaches us is the great power inherent in issues of precedence and etiquette.

Such ceremonial conflicts bring additional insight into the procession's morphology discussed in the previous section. In my assessment, such exceptional processions functioned as 'windows of opportunities' for ambitious groups or individuals who felt strong enough to challenge the conventional hierarchical order. In fact, a sporadic victory on a specific day could turn into an abiding precedent thereafter, as eventually happened with the *popolo*'s privilege to hold a pole in royal entries. This is why we encounter formal written protests whenever certain groups were coerced into relinquishing their place, made with the intention of refuting new variations in the status quo. Significantly, these ceremonial contests, much like the notorious phenomenon of duelling, generally involved various noble pressure groups fighting between themselves. In this sense, the nobility's loss of actual political power matched the obsolete hierarchical structure of the cavalcade. This completely conforms to Visceglia's

observation regarding the inherent contradiction characterizing Neapolitan nobility 'between the amplification of representation and the scarce ability of constructing a political project to conduct society'.[97]

This last point can be supported with an anecdote, which shall also serve as a humorous way of conclusion, involving the social group that had no representation at all in the cavalcade, the plebs, which was completely excluded from honorific contests unless it played the part of the 'captivated' audience. I already mentioned, looking at the manipulations of the crafty Duke of Alba, how he shrewdly managed to outdo his rival in a common cavalcade in the city, at which the crowd shouted in praise of Alba, thus bringing about Alcalá's humiliation. A more subversive version of the incident brings a dialogue between two of the plebeians who applauded Alba:

'What did you gain from the times of Don Antonio's [Alba's first name] rule?'
'Nothing!'
'So, help me understand, why did you pull off the skin from your hands when he just passed?'
'Because [I am glad] he left.'[98]

Regardless of the veracity of this dialogue, it shows the vulnerability of authority in such a socially thorny city as early modern Naples, and the serious limitations of such symbolic devices as civic processions to demarcate unambiguous hierarchical positions.

Notes

1 Any discussion of this issue should start from the volumes edited by Jean Jacquot, *Les fêtes de la Renaissance* (3 vols., Paris, 1956–75). For a fundamental comparative study see Roy Strong, *Art and Power: Renaissance Festivals (1450–1650)* (Woodbridge, 1984). For some recent collections of essays see Helen Watanabe-O'Kelly and Pierre Béhar (eds.), *Spectaculum Europaeum: Theatre and Spectacle in Europe (1580–1750)* (Wiesbaden, 1999); J. R. Mulryne and Elizabeth Goldring (eds.), *Court Festivals of the European Renaissance: Art, Politics and Performance* (Aldershot and Burlington, Vt., 2002); J. R. Mulryne, Helen Watanabe-O'Kelly, and Margaret Shewring (eds.), '*Europa Triumphans': Court and Civic Festivals in Early Modern Europe* (2 vols., Aldershot and Burlington, Vt., 2004).

2 For the historical roots of these entries see Gordon Kipling, *Enter the King: Theatre, Liturgy, and Ritual in the Medieval Civic Triumph* (Oxford, 1998). For a general review of early modern entries see Muir, *Ritual*, 239–46; and Strong, *Art and Power*, 7–11. A thorough analysis of the various components of the entry appears in Bertelli, *Il corpo del re*, 62–86. For the definition of Italian entries see Mitchell, *The Majesty of the State*, 1–9; and Paulette Choné, 'Triomphes, entrées, feux d'artifice et fêtes religieuses en Italie', in *Spectaculum Europaeum*, 644–6. For a recent collection of essays on this theme see Kathleen Ashley and Wim Husken (eds.), *Moving Subjects: Processional Performances in the Middle Ages and the Renaissance* (Amsterdam and Atlanta, Ga., 2001). For some inspiring exceptions, where the parade's hierarchical structure is the focus of interest, see Robert Darnton, 'A Bourgeois Puts His World in Order: The City as a Text', in his *The Great Cat Massacre*, 107–44; and Michael P. Breen, 'Addressing La Ville des Dieux: Entry Ceremonies and Urban Audiences in Seventeenth-Century Dijon', *Journal of Social History*, 38:2 (2004), 341–64.

3 It is impossible to list here the vast research done on the social and political issues regarding Naples during Spanish rule, thus it is recommendable to consult the bibliographies of the following general works: Galasso, *Alla periferia dell'impero*; Aurelio Musi, *Mezoggiorno spagnolo. La via napoletana allo Stato moderno* (Naples, 1991); and Antonio Calabria and John A. Marino (eds.) *Good Government in Spanish Naples* (New York, 1990).

4 The quotations are respectively from: C. Clifford Flanigan, 'The Moving Subject: Medieval Liturgical Processions in Semiotic and Cultural Perspective', in *Moving Subjects*, ed. Kathleen Ashley and Wim Husken, 40; and Miri Rubin, *Corpus Christi: The Eucharist in Late Medieval Culture* (Cambridge, 1991), 266.

5 For this view see Franco Mancini, *Feste ed apparati civili e religiosi in Napoli dal viceregno alla capitale* (Naples, 1968); Michele Rak, 'Il sistema delle feste nella Napoli barocca', in *Centri e periferie del Barocco*, vol. 2: *Barocco napoletano*, ed. Gaetana Cantone (Rome, 1992), 304–6; and by the same, 'A dismisura d'uomo. Feste e spettacolo del barocco napoletano', in *Gian Lorenzo Bernini e le arti visive*, ed. Marcello Fagiolo (Rome, 1987), 259–312. A couple of alternative views should be mentioned. First, in his study of royal entries in Italy, Bonner Mitchell describes the ceremonial conflicts between the nobility and the commoners in the Neapolitan entries but he does not pursue a deeper analysis of the argument. See his *The Majesty of the State*, 50. Similarly, Maria Antonietta Visceglia presents a fascinating study of the conflictive nature of Neapolitan religious processions. See her 'Rituali religiosi e gerarchie politiche a Napoli in età moderna', in *Fra storia e storiografia. Scritti in onore di Pasquale Villani*, ed. Paolo Macry and Angelo Massafra (Bologna, 1994), 587–620.

6 Lepre, *Storia del Mezzogiorno d'Italia*, I, 158.

7 The most thorough study on Italian noble values and the related contemporary debate regarding the occupations befitting noble rank is Claudio Donati, *L'idea di nobiltà in Italia. Secoli XIV–XVIII* (Bari, 1988). For a Neapolitan overview see Giovanni Muto, ' "I segni d'honore". Rappresentazioni delle dinamiche nobiliari a Napoli in età moderna', in *Signori, patrizi, cavalieri in Italia centro-meridionale nell'età moderna*, ed. Maria Antonietta Visceglia (Rome, 1992), 171–93.

8 Carlo Celano, *Notizie del bello, dell'antico e del curioso della città di Napoli. Divise dall'autore in dieci giornate per guida e comodo de' viaggiatori*, ed. Atanasio Mozzillo, Alfredo Profeta, and Francesco Paolo Macchia (3 vols., Naples, 1970), I, 16.

9 For the differentiation of the various kinds of nobility see Muto, 'I segni d'honore', 175–7. For a general survey of Neapolitan society see by the same, 'Il Regno di Napoli'; and Galasso, *Napoli spagnola*, I, xi–xxix. For the nobility, see *ibid.*, I, 270–8. For a contemporary description see Camillo Tutini, *Dell'origine e fundation de'seggi di Napoli* (Naples, 1644).

10 The unquestionable political importance of the *togati* is evidenced by the numerous studies it has attracted. Among the more fundamental are: Vittor Ivo Comparato, *Uffici e società a Napoli (1600–1647). Aspetti dell'ideologia del magistrato nell'Età moderna* (Florence, 1974); Rovito, *Respublica dei togati*; Silvio Zotta, *G. F. De Ponte. Il giurista politico* (Naples, 1987).

11 The full description is in Capaccio, *Il forastiero*, 783–5. For the quotation see 784–5.

12 *Ibid.*, 785.

13 For various works on Spanish imperialism in Italy see Rosario Villari, 'La Spagna, l'Italia e l'assolutismo', *Studi Storici*, 18 (1977), 5–22; Koenigsberger, *The Government of Sicily under Philip II of Spain*; Thomas Dandelet, *Spanish Rome, 1500–1700* (New Haven and London, 2001), and the aforementioned collection edited by Musi, *Nel sistema imperiale*. Specifically on Naples see Carlos José Hernando Sanchez, *El reino de Nápoles en el imperio de Carlos V. La consolidación de la conquista* (Madrid, 2001); D'Agostino, 'Il governo spagnolo'; and Musi, 'Il Regno di Napoli e il sistema imperiale', 23–35.

14 See Galasso, 'La Spagna imperiale', in his *Alla periferia dell'impero*, 24–30; and Aurelio Musi, 'Stato e stratificazioni sociali nel Regno di Napoli', in his *L'Italia dei Vicerè*, 171–4.

15 Parrino, *Teatro*, in *Raccolta*, vol. 9, 56–7.

16 Rubin, *Corpus Christi*, 255. For a secular example see James E. Varey, 'Processional Ceremonial of the Spanish Court in the Seventeenth Century', in *Studia Iberica. Festschrift für Hans Flasche*, ed. Karl-Hermann Körner and Klaus Rühl (Bern, 1973), 643–52.

17 Henceforth, mayor will be placed in quotation marks to denote that his position carried no political or municipal power, but he was merely elected as a ceremonial officer for the day of the cavalcade.

18 Muir, *Ritual*, 238.

19 Innocenzo Fuidoro, *Successi del governo del conte d'Oñatte MDCXLVIII–MDCLIII*, ed. Alfredo Parente (Naples, 1932), 101–2.

20 *Ibid.*, 102. However, this evidence is somewhat contradicted by a favourable account of the 1649 celebrations that appears in Rubino's diary, SNSP, MS. XVIII. D. 14, *Notitia*, fol. 25: 'et essensi ancora questa festa tralasciata l'anno 1648 per ritrovarsi la città quasi rovinata dalle passate turbulenze, nell'anno 1649 vedendosi già ravvivata per il buon governo dell'Ecc.mo Sigr. Conte Ognatte vicerè volse ripigliare la festa tralasciata da due anni, et la volse fare sì pomposa, che di molti lustri non si era rammentata la simile'.

21 Galasso, 'La Spagna imperiale', in his *Alla periferia dell'impero*, 28–9.

22 Confuorto, *Giornali*, I, 270.

23 Partino, *Teatro*, in *Raccolta*, vol. 9, 56; Zazzera, *Narrazioni*, 497.

24 Celano, *Notizie*, I, 16–17. Galasso, *Napoli spagnola*, I, xviii–xix.

25 Capaccio, *Il forastiero*, 420. The importance of satisfying the plebs in this respect is evident in one of the first actions of the new viceroy the Count of Castrillo, who 'in order to keep the city of Naples happy with his new government ordered to thicken the bread loaves by two ounces.' SNSP, MS. XVIII. D. 14, Rubino, *Notitia*, fol. 134.

26 Capaccio, *Il forastiero*, 420.

27 *Ibid.*, 422.

28 *Ibid.*

29 Muto, 'Il Regno di Napoli', 278.

30 Parrino, *Teatro*, in *Raccolta*, vol. 9, 58.

31 *Ibid.*, 60.

32 Celano, *Notizie*, I, 18.

33 Capaccio, *Il forastiero*, 786.

34 For a detailed description of the itinerary, and the *apparati* along the way, see Gio. Bernardino Giuliani, *Descrittione dell'Apparato di san Giovanni fatto dal fedelissimo popolo Napolitano All'Illustrissimo, & Eccelentissimo Sig. Duca D'Alba l'anno M.DC.XXVIII* (Naples, 1628), 20.

35 Parrino, *Teatro*, in *Raccolta*, vol. 9, 60; Capaccio, *Il forastiero*, 786.

36 For the best general discussion of the spread of Eucharistic rites during the centuries that preceded the Reformation see Rubin, *Corpus Christi*.

37 Visceglia, 'Rituali religiosi', 597.

38 Muto, 'I segni d'honore', 176.

39 An extreme example of this trend is visible in Scipione Ammirato, *Delle famiglie nobili napolitane* (Florence, 1580), 38–44. For a comprehensive history of the offices see Camillo Tutini, *Discorsi de sette officii ovvero de sette grandi del Regno di Napoli* (Rome, 1666).

40 Parrino, *Teatro*, in *Raccolta*, vol. 9, 412.

41 Raneo, *Etiquetas*, 115.

42 See, for example, SNSP, MS. XXIII. D. 15, Rubino, *Notitia di quanto é occorso in Napoli dall'anno 1658 per tutto l'anno 1661*, fol. 89: 'Il sindico fu il duca de Flumini ... et la sua livrea fu di saia imperiale a color di musco tutta guernita di triene d'oro con penne bianche a cappelli, vestendo esso d'un ricamo di tutt'oro [...] Il viceré poi pure andava con veste ricamata d'oro et i suoi staffieri vestivan di panno che andava pure al color di musco, ma chiaro, con triene d'argento trasposte, e penne bianche a cappelli, freggiato con le stesse triene d'argento.'

43 Celano, *Notizie*, I, 15.

44 For a more detailed description of the functions of these institutions see Capaccio, *Il forastiero*, 561–634; and Gio. Francesco de Leonardis, *Prattica degli officiali del Regno di Napoli* (Naples, 1599).

45 See Nino Cortese, *I ricordi di un avvocato napoletano del Seicento. Francesco d'Andrea* (Naples, 1923), 78.

46 Parrino, *Teatro*, in *Raccolta*, vol. 9, 56.

47 This has been widely acknowledged in the specialized literature. See note 2 above.

48 Muir, *Ritual*, 246.

49 For the entry of Charles VIII see 'Nuovi documenti francesi sulla impresa di Carlo VIII', *ASPN*, 24 (1938), 183–257. For the entry of Ferdinand the Catholic see Giacomo Della Morte (Notar Giacomo), *Cronica di Napoli*, ed. Paolo Garzilli (Naples, 1845), 289–93; and Giovanni Passero, *Storie in forme di Giornali* (Naples, 1785), 146–7. For the entry of Charles V see Gregorio Rosso, *Istoria delle cose di Napoli sotto l'imperio di Carlo V cominciando dall'anno 1526 per insino all'anno 1537, Scritta per modo di giornali*, in *Raccolta* , vol. 8, 60–3; Pietro Summonte, *Dell'istoria di Napoli*, in *ibid.*, 186–220; Antonino Castaldo, *Dell'historia ... libri quattro. Ne' quali si descrivono gli avvenimenti più memorabili succeduti nel Regno di Napoli sotto il governo del viceré D. Pietro di Toledo e de'viceré suoi sucessori fino al Cardinal Granvela*, in *ibid.*, vol. 6, 365–78; and Raneo, *Etiquetas*, 200–11.

50 See Bulifon, *Giornali*, 45–6; and Parrino, *Teatro*, in *Raccolta*, vol. 9, 190.

51 For the entry of Queen Maria of Austria see below. For the entry of the second Don John of Austria see Pablo Antonio de Tarsia, *Tumultos de la ciudad y Reyno de Nápoles en el año de 1647* (Lyon, 1670), 187–91.

52 See Della Morte, *Cronica*, 204; Passero, *Storie*, 101; and Pompeo Sarnelli, *Guida de' Forestieri, Curiosi di vedere, e d'intendere le cose più notabili della Regal Città di Napoli, e del suo amenisimo Distretto* (Naples, 1688), 69.

53 Della Morte, *Cronica*, 215.

54 Passero, *Storie*, 115.

55 Capaccio, *Il forastiero*, 433.

56 Parrino, *Teatro*, in *Raccolta*, vol. 9, 60; and Raneo, *Etiquetas*, 80.

57 Della Morte, *Cronica*, 290.

58 Visceglia, 'Rituali religiosi', 605.

59 Various studies have dealt with this subject. For some recent works see the proceedings of the conference *Carlo V, Napoli e il Mediterraneo*, ed. Giuseppe Galasso and Aurelio Musi, which appeared in *ASPN*, 119 (2001). See in *ibid.*, particularly Carlos José Hernando Sánchez, 'El glorioso triumfo de Carlos V en Nápoles y el humanismo de corte entre Italia y España', 447–521; and Teresa Megale, ' "Sic per te superis gens inimica ruat". L'ingresso trionfale di Carlo V a Napoli (1535)', 587–604.

60 Raneo, *Etiquetas*, 204.

61 *Ibid.*, 202.

62 *Ibid.*

63 Johan Huizinga, *Homo Ludens: A Study of the Play-Element in Culture*, trans. R. F. C. Hull (London, 1998), 66.

64 On the clique of advisers and image-makers of Charles V see Burke, 'Presenting and Re-presenting Charles V', 396.

65 Parrino, *Teatro*, in *Raccolta*, vol. 9, 190.

66 See *ibid.*, 412; and Bucca, 'Aggionta', *ASPN*, 36 (1911), 164–5.

67 See Fuidoro's comment in the footnote marked (e) in Bucca, 'Aggionta', *ASPN*, 36 (1911), 164.

68 Parrino, *Teatro*, in *Raccolta*, vol. 9, 412.

69 Bucca, 'Aggionta', *ASPN*, 36 (1911), 164.

70 Parrino, *Teatro*, in *Raccolta*, vol. 9, 412.

71 The visit of the queen and the numerous ritual disputes that it produced were amply discussed in the following sources: Raneo, *Etiquetas*, 196–200; Capaccio, *Il forastiero*, 954–61, 1020–2; Parrino, *Teatro*, in *Raccolta*, vol. 9, 413–18; and especially in the diary of Ferrante Bucca, which follows in great detail the government of the Duke of Alcalá. The daily account of the four months in which the queen resided in Naples appear in his 'Aggionta', *ASPN*, 36 (1911), 336–82, and *ibid.*, 36 (1911), 507–14.

72 For the official account of the visit see Fellecchia, *Viaggio*.

73 *Ibid.*, 12.

74 For the queen's stay in Posillipo see *ibid.*, 12–37.
75 Capaccio, *Il forastiero*, 954.
76 *Ibid.*, 956.
77 Bucca, 'Aggionta', *ASPN*, 36 (1911), 339.
78 Fellecchia, *Viaggio*, 40.
79 See note 71 above.
80 Quoted in Visceglia, 'Rituali religiosi', 605.
81 Capaccio, *Il forastiero*, 1020.
82 Reproduced in *ibid.*, 1021.
83 For these different opinions see *ibid.*, 957.
84 Raneo, *Etiquetas*, 198.
85 The letter, dated 13 August 1630, appears in 'Documenti sulla storia civile ed economica del regno, cavati dal Carteggio degli Agenti del Granduca di Toscana in Napoli', ed. Francesco Palermo, *Archivio Storico Italiano*, 9 (1846), 306.
86 The quotations, in their respective order, are from Parrino, *Teatro*, in *Raccolta*, vol. 9, 413; and Bucca, 'Aggionta', *ASPN*, 36 (1911), 337. See also Raneo, *Etiquetas*, 196 ff.
87 Bucca, 'Aggionta', *ASPN*, 36 (1911), 536.
88 *Ibid.*, *ASPN*, 36 (1911), 338.
89 *Ibid.*, 344.
90 Parrino, *Teatro*, in *Raccolta*, vol. 9, 417.
91 Bucca, *ASPN*, 36 (1911), 378.
92 See note (x) in *ibid.*, 379.
93 BNN, MS. XV G23, fol. 165r.
94 See the letter dated 7 August 1630, in 'Documenti sulla storia civile', 305.
95 Bucca, *ASPN*, 36 (1911), 356–7.
96 *Ibid.*, *ASPN*, 36 (1911), 513.
97 Maria Antonietta Visceglia in the 'Introduction' of her edited collection, *Signori, patrizi, cavalieri in Italia centro-meridionale nell'età moderna* (Rome, 1992), xiv.
98 Quoted in Mario Forgione, *I Viceré. 1503–1707. Cronache irriverenti di due secoli di dominazione spagnola a Napoli* (Naples, 1998), 285.

3

State celebrations in viceregal Naples

The festive system of early modern Naples

In the following pages, allowing for a wide and composite spectrum of performing actors, I shall consider the complex role played by the Spanish administration while organizing a festive programme, as it had to fulfil both the needs of the monarchy and of the different social groups, which did not essentially coincide. At the same time, I will also explore the other side of the equation, namely the response of these groups while trying to conform to the 'call for celebration' of their Spanish rulers. Next, trying to identify the characteristically Spanish elements in Neapolitan festivities, and understanding their reception among the local population, I will distinguish between the various social classes. Throughout the various sections of this chapter, I will demonstrate why Spanish Naples proves to be ideal for investigating a festive culture flourishing during harsh times, in the midst of a conflictive society. Indeed, a revealing apparent inconsistency of baroque Europe was that while most of the continent was afflicted by a 'general crisis' that included a deep economic recession which was augmented by the Thirty Years' War,[1] festive displays reached the apex of magnificence and extravagance. This supposed paradox may be explained by the fact that splendid public celebrations were used to project the grandeur of the rulers' authority to the general public, with the intention of maintaining their power, particularly in times of social unrest. Accordingly, enthusiastic responses stemming from the various social groups to the rulers' celebrations, as in Naples, need to be assessed carefully. Thus, I will argue that the success of these celebrations, rather than being signs of viceregal strength, exposed the aforementioned inherent fragility of the viceroys.

Following a conventional typology, scholars of Neapolitan festivities differentiate between religious/cyclical festivals and civic/occasional festivals.[2] The first kind forms the rigid structure of the festive cycle, and it includes general religious events like Carnival, Easter, Christmas, New Year, etc., and celebrations with an indigenous mark, such as the anniversaries of the eight patron saints of the city – St Januarius, St Asprenus, St Agnos, St Agrippinus, St Severus, St Attanasius, St Eusebius, and St Thomas Aquinas.[3]

However, this classification is unsatisfactory because, despite its departure from the cyclical schematization, one should add to the religious festivals such occasional events pertaining to the religious sphere, as the election of a high functionary of the Church, a jubilee, or the canonization of a saint. In addition, those festive rituals, usually in the form of processions, performed during and after a catastrophe, such as a volcanic blast of Vesuvius, the outbreak of an epidemic, or a violent revolt, retained a religious character because the rehabilitation of the natural and social order was attributed to divine powers, to which the participants directed their prayers and thanksgiving.[4] All these assorted festive forms were usually directed by the local arm of the Church and the different monastic orders, which during the seventeenth century increased their efforts to sponsor festivals throughout Europe, trying to match the splendour of the parallel actions of the absolutist rulers.

The situation was quite the opposite until the beginning of the early modern era, when religious festivals controlled by the Church were the rule, and served as the model for later developments of pageantry. Only during the sixteenth century, did the great European absolutist ruling dynasties – Habsburg, Valois, Stuart – and the princi-palities of the Holy Roman Empire and Italy learn to employ the best intellectuals and artists available in the 'cultural marketplace' to help them legitimize and consolidate their emerging nation states through new forms of rhetorical propaganda - the stately, civic festivals.[5] Especially after the turn of the sixteenth century, ephemeral forms of art were exuberantly used to enhance the brilliance of public displays. Paintings – made on panels rather than on canvas – decorations, sculptures, and architectonic construc-tions – made of wood or pasteboard rather than marble and granite – were employed so efficaciously that 'the more fragile the materials the more amazing the effects obtained with them'.[6] However, it should be noted that the most expensive of materials, such as silver and gold, were also applied to contribute to the extraordinary splendour of the baroque festival. These, in tandem with allegorical devices, mechanical scenery, elabo-rate costumes, fireworks, and carefully staged rituals and performances, succeeded in creating what has been called 'a liturgy of state' centred on the ruler'.[7]

Accordingly, Naples rejoiced or mourned, not only at hearing the news of politi-cally meaningful life-cycle events of the Habsburgs, such as the birth of royal persons, accessions to the throne, royal marriages, state funerals, and so on, but also for more trivial occasions such as their birthdays, or recoveries from illnesses, as was often the case with the feeble Charles II.[8] The same was true for viceroys, vicereines, and their kin, although on a more moderate scale, lest they demean the royal grandeur.

Other matters of state related to the Habsburg Empire – involving both Spanish and German branches of the dynasty – especially military victories or the signing of peace treaties, also required special attention. The need to exalt Spanish military achievements was triggered by the abundance of uprisings in the Spanish Empire and the serious challenges posed to the military hegemony of Spain during the seventeenth century. Hence, the relatively few significant victories achieved during the century, such

as the quelling of the rebellion of Barcelona (1652), and the reconquest of Buda from the Turks (1686), were awarded outstanding manifestations of joy.[9] Conversely, since keeping a triumphalist spirit was equally needed at the centre of the empire, such an important event as the quelling of the Neapolitan rebellion was awarded a threeday celebration in Madrid.[10] The entry in Bulifon's diary of 7 October 1673, supplies an extreme case in point, as he mentions 'celebrations throughout Naples, with fireworks', for the 103rd anniversary of the victory of Lepanto.[11] How can this be interpreted other than as a nostalgic commemoration of a triumph that glorifies the invincible military might of a Spanish *armada*, whose reality lay in an ideal, remote, forever lost past? Similarly, the Neapolitan celebration of the Hispano-French Treaty of the Pyrenees in 1659, which in fact proclaimed France's victory over Spain in their prolonged war since 1635, marks further the low point reached by the Spanish Habsburgs.[12]

Despite the artificial categorizations that distinguish a religious and a civic celebration, things were not clear-cut, as politics and religion went hand in hand throughout our period.[13] Major civic ceremonies involved a stroll to the cathedral, the blessing of church officials, and the chanting of the *Te Deum Laudamus* by the general public. This is especially true in the case of funerals, where the city's cathedral functioned as the central stage of the event. Likewise, the feast of patron saints also served as a display of patriotic feelings. Just as the centrality of St Ambrose for Milan or St Mark for Venice cannot be overstressed, it would be virtually inconceivable to speak of the civic identity of Naples without taking into consideration the cult of St Januarius.[14] Therefore, as seen in the previous chapter, the viceroy, the nobility, and the tribunals played an integral part in such central religious processions as those of St Januarius and the Corpus Domini.

The same duality is true for festive forms. As already shown, the civic cavalcade can be easily identified as the parallel to the religious procession, if not its imitator, and the spectacular machines and decorations, generally known as *apparati*, employed by secular rulers and civic authorities were assimilated by religious groups, especially during the seventeenth century. For example, José Antonio Maravall describes how the Jesuits throughout the Catholic world used to employ theatrical devices to move the emotions of believers. One such technique was to draw a curtain by surprise in the middle of a sermon, thus disclosing a dramatic religious scene in real life, with the aim of moving the congregation to tears.[15] A similar phenomenon is exemplified through Carnival – the most popular of religious festivals. Peter Burke has identified carnivalesque patterns of ritual celebrations in Europe during religious festivals other than Carnival, such as the twelve days before Christmas, May day, Corpus Christi, and the feast of St John the Baptist, and in other ritualized public manifestations like executions and charivaris.[16] Carnivalesque features can also be found in festive civic displays. In our case, for example, the viceregal court and the Neapolitan nobility paraded in masquerade on different occasions that often involved grotesque characters, like the one organized in honour of the double marriage between the Spanish and French ruling

houses (1612), or offered Gargantuan gifts of food evoking motifs from the world of Cockaigne.[17]

Let us demonstrate the permeability of these categories with some concrete examples. In March 1679, for the recovery of Charles II's health, the city feasted for three consecutive days. Since the king's rehabilitation was gained by divine providence it was only natural that the civic event should be accompanied by religious rites. In a solemn function at the cathedral the viceroy the Marquis of Los Vélez (1675–83) received communion from the Cardinal D. Innico Caracciolo. In addition, as the king reported that his health had been regained by the propitious intervention of St Joseph, the viceroy held a religious function in the homonymous church at Pontecorvo, and instituted the same custom for years to come for the saint's anniversary.[18]

Another telling example is the ritual building of a refuge for virgins, during the pestilence of 1656, following the prophecy of the nun Ursula Buonincasa according to which such a construction would save the city from disaster. The site was inaugurated by the viceroy himself, the Count of Castrillo (1653–58), who, with his bare hands, dug out twelve baskets of earth. He was followed by the Representatives of the City, and Neapolitans from every social denomination, 'who joined not only with their purses, but with their very bodies'. In other words, besides an immense flow of donations made by 'men, and women, young, and old, noble citizens, and plebeians', the most surprising thing was to see the physical participation 'of the most distinguished persons in the city, in the most vile of exercises'. In a religious zeal of holy work, they carried on a curious procession: buckets of nails, ropes, stones, and timber, and all the while they kept 'singing psalms, and reciting Orations and Rosaries'.[19]

The festival of St John the Baptist proves to be an especially interesting case in point, because unlike the other extraordinary examples given, it exhibits a common understanding on a cyclical, yearly basis. One would be misled in thinking that this was a strictly religious festivity, sponsored by the Church, with little or no relevance to the Spanish state. The celebrations started on the eve of the designated day (23 June), with a cavalcade and a series of *apparati*. It was all prepared and funded by the Neapolitan *popolo*, or rather the 'most loyal popolo' (*Fedelissimo Popolo*) as its servile title went (paradoxically, it continued to sustain it proudly even after the break of the revolt of 1647), in order to exhibit its allegiance to the Spanish crown via the glorification of the viceroy.[20]

In addition, the cavalcade's processional path played a role in enhancing the *popolo*'s own status pride by trailing its significant meeting places, displayed along the commoners' city quarters, in the following order: Guardiola, a guarding post of the Spanish troops, by the Royal Palace; Rua Catalana, renowned by its numerous shoemakers' workshops; Dogana, a road filled with cotton-wool merchants, as well as knife and sword makers; Fontana di Porto, a fountain around which were concentrated minor artisanal activities like button making, as well as many fruit stands; Piazza Maio, a square that attracted various economic activities related to the nearby port, as well

as the selling of second-hand clothes; Lanzieri, the road of expensive cloth merchants (golden silk, brocade, wool, etc.); San Pietro Martire, home of the great silk merchants; Piazza Larga, a place crowded with hat makers and hat merchants; Orefici, a road renowned for the workshops of goldsmiths and jewel makers; Loggia dei Genovesi, a place containing a rich variety of merchants and artisans of various goods; Fontana della Pietra del Pesce, a square that functioned as a fish market; Spetiaria Antica, a road named after the spice traders who used to populate it, but in the seventeenth century it served various cloth merchants; Gipponari, a road with a vast presence of tailors; Rua Francesca, a road with wool suppliers for mattresses; Rua Campana, the seat of blacksmiths; Pendino-Sellaria, the most significant place for the Neapolitan *popolo*. In the past, it used to be the seat of the popular *seggio*, which was eventually destroyed by King Alfonso of Aragón in 1456. Nevertheless, it remained the centre of all of the *popolo*'s political and institutional life, and, as such, it was the place where all popular rebellions had started; Armieri, the road was originally named after the weapon makers, who were later replaced by silk merchants; Porta del Caputo-Chiesa di San Giovanni, this was an area characterized mostly by the presence of leather workers, and by St John the Baptist's church, where the cavalcade ended. Significantly, at the various stops of the *apparato*, the ephemeral statues and arches were adorned with a variety of goods produced by the various popular guilds, like precious silks, jewels, or edible delicacies, serving as a showcase for the *popolo*'s manufacturing prowess and economic power.[21]

After the cavalcade, the feast went on into the night, with splendid exhibitions of fireworks and popular rites of representations of baptisms in the sea, and ended the next day (24 June) with the liturgical function of the Church. In other words, religious themes, popular rites of presumed pagan origins, and the secular exaltation of the state combined in a relatively harmonious melange.

Nevertheless, there were instances when the boundaries of good taste between the religious and the secular realms were transgressed. At the feast of St John in 1628 we find a *madrigaletto*, exhibited along the cavalcade, which attempts to harmonize religion and the state somewhat sacrilegiously, as the saint and the viceroy receive equal standing:

> Alba del gran Messia
> Fu' l'Battista sincero;
> Alba di questa via
> Sei tu gran Duce Ibero.
> O mio doppio tesoro,
> L'un Alba riverisco, e l'altro adoro.[22]
> (Dawn of the great Messiah
> Was the sincere Baptist;
> Dawn of this lane
> Are you great Spanish Ruler.
> O my double treasure,
> The first Dawn I revere, the other I adore.)

Likewise, the censorious diarist Ferrante Bucca is more unforgiving than usual when describing the rite celebrated on 8 December 1631, for the Immaculate Conception of the Virgin, known also as the *feast of the four altars* because of the sumptuous shrines that were usually built inside the church to honour the Virgin. He claims that the feast would have been worthy of the sacred occasion 'if it had not been adulterated by that damned adulation so pervasive towards the viceroys, since without using the dictum *Ne miscaris sacra profanis* [don't mix the sacred with the profane], they prepared an additional shrine for the viceroy, inside the church, as if he too were a saintly body in the eyes of God.'[23]

The festivity of St John the Baptist, which clearly identifies the *popolo* as the central actor in the functions, also casts doubt on the validity of another common generalization, according to which the upper layers of society – nobility, state function-aries, and high clergy – played the central role in the civic celebration, leaving the *popolo*, provided it was invited to participate, with the passive role of 'spectator'.[24] In fact, the organizers' choice of venues for the various festivals, which usually determined the inclusion or exclusion of specific social groups, shows a wide range of possibilities. The large square surrounding the new Royal Palace built in 1606, known as the Largo di Palazzo, was the place where great public spectacles were staged by the viceroys, including Spanish tournaments like bullfights and reed spear tournaments. These events were open to the entire population, with the propagandistic purpose of attracting as many people as possible.[25] The spacious Via Toledo, named after its founder the viceroy Pedro Álvarez de Toledo, Marquis of Villafranca (1532–53), had a similar comprehensive communal function, serving as the main route for both civic and religious processions. Contrariwise, to the detriment of commoners, maritime regattas on board splendid crafts along the aristocratic costal areas of Mergellina and Posillipo, the palaces of Neapolitan magnates, and inside the Royal Palace, provided venues for festive events restricted to the Neapolitan nobility and the viceregal court.[26] As already shown in the case of St John the Baptist's festival, those celebrations organized by the people took place in the popular quarters. Often, as in the occasion of parochial festivals related to local protector saints or Madonnas, they only involved the inhabitants of the quarter engaged in celebration. In more public kinds of celebrations, like the one of St John the Baptist, the nobility and the royal court were invited, and they were treated as privi-leged spectators.[27]

One cannot deny that the motive for a civic festivity was usually related to the Habsburg dynasty, that the call for celebration and most of the organization was the responsibility of the viceregal court, and that on certain occasions the participation was restricted to the Neapolitan elite. However, if one turns to observe the various constitutive elements of the celebrations – cavalcades, masquerades, triumphs, court balls, jousts, bullfights, cockaignes, fireworks, pyrotechnic machines, theatrical repre-sentations, and so on – it is clear that the social status of the participants, their relative numbers, and their degree of involvement, varied from event to event. Actually, it is not infrequent to find the various social classes not only taking part in the same celebrations

but also sharing cultural forms that dialectically combined 'aristocratic' and 'popular' elements. Hence, methodologically speaking, such findings reveal the need to question some widely accepted, although one-sided, perspectives, which exaggerate the conflict between 'popular culture' and 'official culture', or those which overemphasize the role of the court.[28]

An alternative view is presented by Mitchell, who illustrates how the entire urban population was in unison on such occasions. 'The civic celebration is a moment when people are invited to show their pride at belonging to the body politic and when they are reassured of its integrity in the handling of their political interests ... Material weaknesses, human failings, and internecine conflicts are glossed over in the conscious, artistic depiction of serenity, wisdom, justice, and strength.'[29] However, to attain these common occasions of celebration it did not essentially mean that the popular masses would have to be completely subjected to the ruler's designs or stripped of any opportunity of self-expression, just as they could not have taken place in a milieu where relations between social groups approximated to total detachment or complete antagonism. In fact, different social groups could participate in the same festive occasion, following a different deportment, while conveying different messages.[30] This may be illustrated by the three floats that moved along Via Toledo on February 1687, as part of the Carnival season. One was made *by* the *popolo* and *for* the *popolo*, more precisely for its lower stratus – the plebs. It represented the *Grassa* – loosely translatable as any kind of foodstuff, whose prices were regulated by special officials who had a precarious relationship with the chronically hungry groups of the city – and it was entirely made of eatable products, which were pillaged by the plebs once it reached the usual designated place under the viceroy's balcony. The second float, embodying the most cherished of aristocratic values, represented the temple of honour, accompanied by five noblemen dressed as virtues. The third float was so large that it 'could hardly fit Via Toledo', and it had to be pulled by sixteen horses. It represented the Greek holy mountain, Mt Athos, which was said to have been designed to be sculpted as the effigy of Alexander the Great. Not surprisingly, the story was adapted to the present, with an immense image of the viceroy made of four noble metals, taking the place of the Macedonian ruler.[31] Clearly then, the same festive occasion could be used for different means by each group. It served to emphasize ideal traits of its image in the case of the nobility and the viceregal court, whereas in the case of the *popolo*, it provided an opportunity to manifest issues close to its heart, or more figuratively speaking one should say close to its stomach, such as the constant threat of hunger. Nevertheless, this temporary cooperation was not taken for granted or static, but it was reached through a continuous dialogue and negotiation between the groups, as already seen in the case of the cavalcade, where the position of a certain group could vary according to its relative power.

Management, patronage, and reception of civic celebrations

Giulio Cesare Capaccio, as if responding to his interlocutor, the Foreigner, seizes the opportunity to give the viceroys some advice concerning their proper attitude towards festivals and various entertainments. 'From time to time I want the prince to indulge in the universal celebrations, and invite to his house, to some comedy when the occasion requires it, and to be present in the public spectacles, and to like the feasts of Carnival, and not to despise all amusing things.' However, perhaps having in mind the buffoonery and wantonness of the likes of the Duke of Osuna, he warns that the viceroy has to show moderation in all these things, 'so that nothing would be diminished from his grandeur, in a way that he will aspire to be an excellent governor of peoples, and principal minister of the royal crown.'[32] Dealing with the issue from a different perspective, a significant passage of Antonio Bulifon describes the many virtues of the viceroy the Marquis of Carpio (1683–87), among which was his ability to 'tame' the masses. Very similar to the ancient Roman idea of drugging the plebs with *Panem et Circenses* (bread and circuses), Bulifon advocated the implementation of 'the carrot or the stick' approach. 'And because he knows a lot about the art of good government of peoples, he has coupled to the severity of justice the joyfulness of many festivities, in order to keep the people festive and happy.'[33] In the eighteenth century the Bourbons would adopt all three means in order to control the Neapolitan masses, notoriously known as the three F's – *feste, farina, e forca* (festivals, flour, and gallows).[34]

Elsewhere, Bulifon praises the Marquis of Carpio, in what we may consider a comprehensive theory of the proper 'art of government', exemplified by that viceroy, in which the political usage of festivals takes a prominent part. Let us follow closely this ideal conduct, according to Bulifon. Some of the greatest afflictions pressing Naples seem to receive the diligent care of Carpio. His many endeavours include: the coinage of a new currency that reinvigorates commerce, investment in the armament and training of troops who, being well paid for once, successfully hunt down the powerful gangs of bandits infesting the countryside, the strenuous persecution of pirates, the ruthless punishment of coiners, the control of contraband, and the issuing of many decrees to limit luxuries.[35] For what might seem severe and rigorous measures he compensated with a great indulgence in festivities of every kind. It is immaterial if Carpio really excelled in his government, and Bulifon's judgement can hardly be objective, as he was promoted by that same viceroy as the city's official bookseller. What matters to us is Bulifon's detailed description of what can be viewed as ideal guidelines for the management and use of festivals, as the Marquis of Carpio allegedly implemented them:

1. A wide involvement of all the social strata in the sponsorship of universal merry-making, alternating between private banquets and feasts in his palace for the nobility, and a myriad of open public demonstrations.
2. A qualitative and quantitative input, adding innovation and magnificence to the celebrations. He inaugurates aquatic festivals and tournaments on large floating

platforms built in the sea; he commissions marvellous *apparati* and fireworks never seen before; and Carnivals in his days reach an unprecedented exuberance.

3. Evidently conscious of the propagandistic value of these efforts, he encourages their publication 'in order to keep the perennial memory of such beautiful marvels'.

4. Stemming from the same propagandistic agenda he makes conspicuous attempts to impress outsiders. Many are attracted to his spectacles 'not only from all over Italy, but from the furthest countries', and all the notable visitors of the kingdom that have been hosted by him 'have been overwhelmed by his magnanimity'.

5. He also sponsors religious festivities, 'celebrating with greater solemnity the feasts of Our Lady and of the saints in the churches, and all over the city the triumphs of Christians ... for all the defeats of the Turks'.[36]

If indeed we are allowed to consider the above as an exemplary prototype of princely festival management, how well did viceroys actually conform to such a checklist? Clearly the personal taste and temperament of the single viceroys had a certain influence on the issue, in the sense that those with a self-indulgent temperament gave a boost to the culture of festivals, whereas those with an ascetic character tended to curb them. In this respect, I have already discussed the two extreme opposite examples of the austere Olivares and the extravagant Osuna. Building on the memory of the proverbial lavishness of the latter, Bucca comments that the viceroy the Count of Monterrey (1631–37) was very fond of frolicsome entertainment 'in imitation of the Ossunian government'. Accordingly, he had introduced a custom never followed before by previous viceroys, at least not openly, which was to go to public plays. 'I am not saying for once, in secret, but having ordered to prepare him a box for the purpose, he goes there publicly very frequently, and stays there as if he were at his home.'[37] Perhaps the most radical example is provided by the Marquis of Astorga (1672–75), whose conduct in the subject contradicted completely the exhortations of Capaccio. His corpulent appearance revealed an extraordinary passion for food and wine, which he supplied abundantly in the many banquets and feasts organized in the palace, in Mergellina and Posillipo. Another testimony to his unrestrained character might be deduced from his frequent organization of comedies in the palace 'without the participation of ladies, but only gentlemen',[38] which may suggest that they were of an improper nature for ladies' eyes. Notably, he succeeded in embarrassing even the notoriously spendthrift Neapolitan nobility who had a hard time keeping up with his unrelenting pace. Even worse, his personal excesses harmed his ability to govern from day to day, as he was too often indisposed after having drunk himself senseless.[39]

Such results contradicted the effective political usage of festivals as advocated by Bulifon, since instead of aiding the task of government they impeded it, by turning the means to an end in itself. Despite these negative examples, the correlation of specific historical events with the rise of festivities, and the introduction or the cessation of certain festive forms in specific historical conjunctures, show that the various viceroys

understood their political importance very well. This can easily be proved by the changes implemented after the two most traumatic events of the century, the revolt of 1647–48, and the fatal plague of 1656.[40]

The viceroy the Count of Oñate, who was entrusted with the complicated task of restoring the Spanish regime after the short yet momentous revolutionary paren- thesis, implemented a mixed policy of repressing certain festive forms and encouraging others according to circumstances. The repressive approach came at the expense of the *popolo*, who were the decisive element in the revolt. I have already mentioned how he sabotaged the usual celebration of the bonding between *popolo* and viceroy during the festival of St John the Baptist, organized in his honour, by showing up surrounded by a disproportionate number of menacing soldiers. Rather than being adulated and revered he chose to be forceful and feared.[41] Similarly, the celebrations of Carnival, with all their inherent subversive elements, were drastically undermined by the viceroy's intol- erance towards any manifestation of social disorder – quite an understandable attitude given the recent historical precedent.[42] Oñate's regulation of Carnival must have had a profound impact, if more than twenty years later the chronicler Innocenzo Fuidoro, complaining about the 'insolences of plebeians' during the Carnival season, claimed that 'everyone misses Oñate's government, because during these times the city of Naples looked like a composed religious congregation; so strongly rooted is the [favourable] opinion of an excellent prince in the mind of the subjects'.[43] But Oñate's most signifi- cant innovation in this respect was the annual commemoration of the city's pacifica- tion by the Spaniards after the revolt, celebrated every 6 April. According to Rubino, this celebration, which included a public cavalcade, thanksgivings at the churches of the Carmine and S. Januarius (significantly, the places of worship most identified with the *popolo*), and fireworks for three consecutive nights, ran regularly for the five years of his rule.[44] Eventually, his successor, the Count of Castrillo, decided to discontinue it. Although no official explanations were given, the rumour was that some concerned citizens 'persuaded him that it was not wise to remind the *popolo* of the past turbu- lences with this commemoration'.[45] Nevertheless, while Oñate's rule lasted, Neapolitans proved to be quite receptive to his restorative messages. This can be exemplified by the customary *apparato* staged by the *popolo* in the viceroy's honour for the celebrations of St John the Baptist in 1650:

> The feast started at the Royal Palace where an arch was erected, through which one entered the *apparato*, on which sides were erected two statues … On the right was the statue of love with a crowned head, holding in its hand a cornu- copia full of riches, signifying the love with which the Spanish monarchy rules over us. On the left was the statue of loyalty with a shield in its hand in which was a depiction of the *popolo*'s coat of arms, under which there was a dog alluding to the Neapolitan loyalty towards his Catholic kings, and this love and loyalty was the subject of the entire celebration … because all of the statues, *imprese*, and scenes, did not allude to anything else but that.[46]

Kristiaan Aercke's definition and differentiation between a 'public festive celebration' and a 'private splendid performance', can explain why the latter form, which includes the *opera*, the *ballet de cour*, and other theatrical representations performed within a privileged noble space, was especially suitable to Oñate's restorative and reactionary political worldview.[47] The discussion is based on the tripartite model of communication of the celebrated linguist Roman Jakobson, which includes: the *sender* (in this case the sponsor of the event), the *creator* (the architect, composer, playwright, etc.), and the *receiver* (the sponsor, the audience, and the recorders of the event). In public festivities the ruler, who usually participated as the protagonist, was seen, and, despite the strict ceremonial barriers, he engaged directly in dialogue with the public. At the same time, the messages created by the artists tried to address both sponsor and public. In sum, all the participants in the communication were engaged in a relatively open and genuine process of communication. Things differed in the case of the private splendid performances, in which the ruler communicated indirectly with the 'carefully screened' spectators. Placed on a privileged high seat, which situated him with his back to the audience, the ruler left the performers on stage to deliver his message to the court. Hence, 'Instead of a communication, there is a *communiqué* which rules out a creative response. The audience could merely interpret, admire and applaud, and all the stage techniques and machinery were directed to achieve precisely that response.'[48] It is clear, then, why an autocratic viceroy such as Oñate would prefer this kind of top-down delivery of messages rather than an open dialogue. In fact, Oñate is known for introducing to Naples such private splendid performances as the musical comedies, forerunners of the *Opera*, seeing in their attributes an efficacious tool of propaganda.[49] A well-known example is the production represented in 1649, *The Triumph of Partenope*, whose title blatantly gives away the political message.[50] Not coincidentally, after the first third of the seventeenth century, when the absolutist regimes reached the summit of their existence, in such courts as those of Madrid, Paris, London, and Vienna, the splendid performance would receive a prominent place in the system of festivities. It is exactly during these years that the palace-theatre of the Buen Retiro was built, in order to put to use, with great effect, the propagandistic aspects of festive performances that were so well comprehended by Philip IV and his favourite, the Count-Duke of Olivares.[51]

However, when from the early 1630s onwards the dynastic rulers withdrew as active participants, in accordance with the decline of great public demonstrations to the advantage of private performances, Naples followed a different pattern. At the beginning of the government of Oñate's successor, the Count of Castrillo, it seemed that Naples was about to follow the continental line, already started with Oñate, of cutting down on public festivities.[52] Wanting to improve the efficiency of the Neapolitan tribunals and administration, Castrillo decided to increase the working days by erasing from the calendar some of the festivities, commonly called festivals of the court. According to Rubino, by these means, no fewer than seventy-one festive days were abolished.[53] This

unpopular decision is laudable because whatever the pretext for celebration, whichever the sponsoring body or its political motivation, it is quite clear that the festive days in early modern Naples followed one another at a vertiginous pace all the year round, hampering any chance to sustain a productive society.[54] So much so, that a Genoese visitor in the seventeenth century repeated what seemed to be already a convention: 'it is very true that in Naples almost every day is a holiday'.[55] However, Castrillo was forewarned that a similar attempt in the past had provoked the wrath of God, when all the councillors of Ferrante I, who suggested the change, found sudden deaths. Ironically, following the unprecedented wave of plague that devastated the city and the subsequent insinuations that the cause had been the abolition of the festivities, the viceroy was forced to reintroduce them, and with an even greater fervour than before.[56] One has to assume that there was also a psychological element to it. For the last year of Castrillo's government, which coincided with the end of the infection, court, nobility, and *popolo* were swept in a wave of various festivities for the birth of the Spanish heir to the crown, but foremost they celebrated the sheer joy of having survived a terrible ordeal in which about half of the population perished.[57] This is plainly declared in one of the various theatrical representations, in which the chorus sang panegyrics lauding the viceroy, 'who having surpassed the horror of the plague, and triumphed over death, had brought Naples back to a theatre of Jubilee'.[58] From then onwards, throughout what was left of the seventeenth century, public festivities in Naples reached new peaks of splendour, which culminated in the aforementioned viceroyalty of the Marquis of Carpio. According to Galasso, the strengthening of public displays in this period was due to an increasing demand that reflected how such manifestations 'expressed and realized, in their essence, the intrinsic nature and the inclination of the country and its civilization'.[59] In other words, the pressure towards their continuation seems to have come from below, and given the relatively volatile position of the viceroys, it is clear that they had to yield to public demand.

Nevertheless, pressure was exerted from above as well, since on the occasions of celebrations directly related to the Spanish crown, the viceregal court made all possible efforts to ensure the wide and active participation of all the social groups. By that I do not mean that the court was worried that no one would turn up to celebrate. Some inherent structural conditions of the city – among others, a mild climate all year round that favoured all kinds of social activities in the open; and an enormous multitude of plebeians, unemployed or underemployed, wandering the streets, longing for any kind of diversion from their wretched existence – ensured mass participation at all times. The court intervention sought to achieve the maximal efficacy on the organizational level, trying to regulate and manipulate public behaviour to achieve the greatest effect, and to encourage the economic investment of the public in the celebration.

Of course, the court built first on its own resources. The money employed in festivities usually originated from a yearly budget of 24,000 *ducati* that was at the viceroy's full disposition, known as 'secret expenditures'. Once the viceroy made up his

mind to uphold a certain festive event, he would order the secretary of state to send an order to the *Reggia Camera della Sommaria*, the body responsible for the financial administration of the kingdom. From the meagre quantitative evidence left in the archives it is impossible to reconstruct the exact trajectory of viceregal festive investments.[60] Yet, the receipts that survived give us an idea of what was under his responsibility. Not surprisingly, these included most of the activities surrounding the Royal Palace.[61]

In comparison to the quantitative data, the qualitative documentation gives us a much better perspective of the formal procedures applied towards the organization of state events. Let us take the detailed prescriptions of Raneo as an illustrative example of the deep involvement of the court in promoting celebrations, and functioning as a ceremonial reference point for all the expected rites at the birth of a royal prince. First, as soon as the viceroy reads the letter proclaiming the birth, he opens the door ceremonially to let everyone in to hear the good news. In concordance with the rigid Spanish ceremonial, the nobles come to congratulate the viceroy, and the ladies go to the vicereine. The elected of the six *piazze* are notified and a *sindico* is nominated to fulfil ceremonial functions in the celebrations. Torches are placed in all the windows of the palace, and candles are burnt at its entrance. Next, the castles are ordered to fire their artillery and to shoot fireworks for three consecutive days, beginning from the first day chosen for the celebrations. During these days the courts of justice are closed. On the first day of the celebrations all the nobles and office-holders go to the cathedral to give thanks, by chanting the *Te Deum Laudamus*. To ensure a full presence there, the royal secretary sends letters to all the state functionaries, and to the great chaplain, who is responsible for summoning the musicians to the cathedral. The viceregal court is also responsible for notifying the other provinces, and making sure that they will celebrate properly. A letter is also sent to the popular representative, who has to make sure that fireworks will fill the streets under his jurisdiction.[62] In other words, any bursts of spontaneous joy for the news will be more than welcome, but this cannot be left to chance.

The last point mentioned is worth pursuing further because it seems to hint at a coercion from above that casts a doubt on the voluntary spirit of participation. Various examples reported by the Neapolitan chroniclers show that the viceroys supported the pressure to financially invest in the celebration with threats, and sometimes even with penalties. For example, the Duke of Osuna ordered a general display of fireworks for the day of the Immaculate Conception of the Virgin, warning those failing to comply that they would incur a fine of twenty-four ducats.[63] Obviously then, the responsibility and expenses for these fireworks fell directly upon the citizens. True enough, those parts of the festivities that were sponsored by the court were in great part subsidized, indirectly, by a deep digging into the pockets of taxpayers as well, but the responsibility for the success of the performance fell upon the viceregal court. Who paid the price for the failure to adhere to the direct call for celebration on the part of the viceroy? In the case of the *popolo*, when the viceroy ordered fireworks in the popular urban habitat,

those entrusted for the execution were the captains of *ottine* – the popular districts of the city. Hence, when the viceroy the Marquis of Los Vélez rode through the city on one of the three standard days of celebration declared for the marriage of Charles II with Mary of Orléans (1679), and found no fireworks in the popular districts of Lanzieri and Porto, the two accountable captains were placed under house arrest and deposed from their offices. He also ordered the nomination of two replacements, 'to compensate the next evening for the faultiness of those'. Apparently, the lesson was learned all too well since the new captains supplied the goods with interest. 'On Tuesday evening they arranged for immense fireworks and feasts with music in those streets, to the great delight of the viceroy and vicereine.'[64] This policy of ensuring the participation of the popular element is also evident in the involvement of the master of ceremonies in the organization of the feast of St John, which was supposedly the exclusive responsibility of the *popolo*. Thus, the viceroy entrusted the master of ceremonies to instruct the popular organizers that fireworks be launched throughout the itinerary of the cavalcade, just before, or, depending on the viceroy's orders, just after, the viceroy's passage.[65]

The viceregal twisting of arms did not make distinction of class and status. For the aforementioned occasion of Charles II's wedding, the Marquis of Los Vélez organized a solemn cavalcade, masks, and various tournaments.[66] In what seems nothing more and nothing less than an imposition, for the planned tournament, he assigned seven of the highest nobles of the realm to lead and sponsor a small group of knights, known as a *quadriglia*.[67] Although one might argue that it was an honour to be elected by the viceroy for such an occasion, it certainly was of no benefit for the Prince of Castiglione. Asking to be dismissed from such a duty because he did not have the aptitude of a fighter, since being a doctor of law he had 'always spent his life in the tribunal', he was granted the dubious honour of appointing someone else, but at his expense.[68] The viceroy displayed a similar attitude to the planned cavalcade. He sent a letter to all the barons and feudal overlords of the realm to 'appear with splendour and make a display of themselves at the said cavalcade'. However, many of these 'being ignoble and of no praise, hence not apt to such a solemn function, exempted themselves from appearing, contenting themselves with being taxed for a certain sum of money, as has already been done: a thing that has been very profitable to the viceroy'.[69] In the last two episodes, besides the obvious viceregal attempts of extortion, there seems to be a subplot, which tells the story of social arrivistes of non-noble origins, promoted and ennobled by the crown, who could not, or would not, integrate into the cultural world of high society. It is unclear if, as hinted by Confuorto, the viceroy has summoned these people just to make a profit from their inability to attend. If on this occasion he might receive the benefit of the doubt, his colleague holding the post ten years later cannot. For the second wedding of Charles II, the Count of Santisteban (1687–96) issued an identical 'invitation', even though, according to the chronicler, he actually hoped for a negative response just to be able to cash the fine.[70]

With the above examples I do not wish to mislead the reader to the conclusion that all the economic investments in the festivities were imposed, and to a large extent unwanted. On the contrary, there are abundant examples of an enthusiastic adherence to the sponsorship of festivals by all social groups. For example, for the birth of the Spanish heir to the throne, Philip Prospero (1657), perhaps as a result of the general euphoria that followed the plague not only did the high nobility not try to eschew the leading and sponsoring of a *quadriglia*, but it was also necessary to draw lots in order to select a privileged group out of the many volunteers.[71] This fact can be taken with a pinch of salt as it is drawn from a festival book, which belongs to a genre one of whose prominent characteristics is to exaggerate the success of the event. Nevertheless, there are abundant testimonies of similar behaviour, some of which have already been discussed in the strong competition to appear well (*far bella figura*), and in a privileged position at the cavalcades. This point has been developed in the poignant comment of Michele Rak: 'The viceregal administration, the nobility and the clergy used to turn to "pomp", to the ostentatious marks that distinguished their position in the social hierarchy: the most sumptuous clothes, the most precious jewels, the most luxurious carriages … This amplified ostentatiousness was one of the most fundamental elements of the celebration.'[72] Nevertheless, it should be mentioned that the nobility very often organized private feasts, whose goal, besides the aforementioned urge to show off, was to make a personal profit of some kind. Just to mention one example, one such noble honoured the viceroy the Marquis of Carpio with a sumptuous reception and banquet. However, according to Confuorto, behind the act was a hidden agenda. 'Some malicious tongues want it that this reception, with all the investment made in it … resulted from his great ambition of receiving with it a *toga* [that is a ministerial job] from His xcellency, but with no avail, and he lost the disbursement.'[73]

A similar generosity to the one displayed by the nobility on such occasions, whether calculated or not, was shown by the *popolo*. Despite the viceroy's superfluous concern of making sure that he got a respectable quantity of fireworks for the procession of St John the Baptist, the *popolo* saw in the success of the festivity a personal badge of honour. Accordingly, as a collective sponsoring body it spared no expense on the sumptuous *apparati*, triumphal arches, statues, various adornments, poetic compositions, and many, many firework displays. All of which were amply described in the festival books that were produced by the *popolo* to commemorate the event.[74] Likewise, St Januarius, the most popular of Naples' saints, was celebrated with three processions a year. Thanks to a precious testimony of Bulifon we know the direct involvement of the citizens in the subsidization of the cult, down to the last penny.[75]

How can one explain this universal compliance for such expenditure, even when it seems to defy common sense, favouring a few instances of pleasure at the expense of basic needs, or simply being well beyond the economic possibilities of the participants? Clearly, among all the partners in the celebration, from the viceroy to the

lowest of plebeians, there was an understanding that the grandeur of the celebration reflected directly on its sponsor, who was usually the protagonist of the event. Hence, in the case of the feast of St John the Baptist, the discrepancy between the sponsor – the *popolo* – and the subject of celebration – the viceroy – must have been the reason for the viceroy's mistrust, reflected in the close monitoring of the preparations. In any case, whether the celebration was sponsored by the court, the nobility, the Church, or the *popolo*, the effect was the same. According to Maravall, 'the fiesta was a diversion that stunned both those who commanded and those who obeyed: it made the latter believe, whereas for the former it created the illusion that wealth and power still remained'.[76]

This view is supported by the testimony of a Spanish soldier who served in Naples, Alonso de Contreras. This is how he describes a Spanish-sponsored celebration made in Rome in 1629. 'So many comedies … so many fireworks, so many rivers of wine … spending during three afternoons, like a flowing river, great quantities of money, gold and silver … it is sufficient to say that we were ill reputed in Rome at that time … but these displays of grandeur forced them to go around Rome exclaiming: "Long live Spain!"'[77] No better defence could be made to rebuff those voices, usually coming from the ranks of the tax-paying middle classes who were scandalized by the enormous budgets, whatever their social provenance, dedicated to merry-making. For example, Fuidoro, criticizing the dissipation of dowries, claimed that this was the reason for the ruin of Naples. He described a wide-ranging rivalry in debauchery where 'the noble competes with the titled, the popular competes with the noble, and the plebeian competes with the popular, which indicates how the Jewellers with their Jewish tricks acquire palaces and carriages'.[78] However, his censorious view was not the prevalent one. One can find the counter-argument in the testimony of another Spanish soldier, who speaks precisely in praise of the dissipation of the dowry of his Neapolitan wife, whom he married in Naples. He proudly recalls that the festivities lasted eight days; a period in which he changed daily into a different suit of a different material. Not surprisingly than, 'the thousand *ducados* received as a present were all spent in clothing'. Here is how he recalls his feelings and longings immediately after the marriage: 'married, rich, and happy, there is nothing more to crave for; I only ask to be left to sleep freely, to travel … to eat and to spend, as long as it lasts'.[79] The last sentence embodies in a nutshell the reason for the success of festivals, and the common justification of fantastic expenditure, in the century of 'general crisis', in which all the social groups and actors preferred illusion and escapism to stark reality.[80]

So far, we have revealed the involvement and the capabilities of the various institutions and social groups in arranging a festival without mentioning the plebs' contribution. Accordingly, it would be appropriate to conclude this part with a unique interpretation of Masaniello's revolt, the one by the contemporary Giuseppe Donzelli, who described it as an organization from below of a conspiracy, which

was misinterpreted, or rather disguised as a festive manifestation that went out of hand. Celebrated examples as Emmanuel Leroy Ladurie's Carnival of Romans, or similar conflictive episodes described by Peter Burke and Edward Muir, show that these were not unusual in early modern Europe.[81] Could this not have happened in Naples too?

Here is the chain of events, as related by Donzelli, which led to the presumably planned revolt of Masaniello. First comes the trigger: the many humiliations he suffered trying to free his wife from imprisonment, after she was accused of smuggling a small sack of flour into the city, disguised as an infant in her hands, while trying to avoid the payment of the tax – notoriously known in early modern Naples as *gabbella*. Thus, 'going over a thousand plans in his mind, he adhered to one in order to free all his people from these insufferable miseries'.[82] The designated date was a festive event - the festivity of the Virgin of the Carmine. Among other things, the celebration included a mock battle, or rather the assault on a wooden castle which was usually constructed for that purpose. Masaniello, who commanded a group of youngsters known as 'the Arabs', who participated in the assault, thought of using that occasion to launch the revolt. According to Donzelli, the young fisherman gathered eight of his friends, a sort of a 'revolutionary vanguard', as Lenin would have put it, and together they agreed to manipulate all the youths who participated at the festivity in to start a riot. Thus, they succeeded in gathering 400 of these adolescents, in advance, and armed them with sticks, which would normally serve them for the regular mock battle. Even the mobilization of the funds to buy the sticks was organized by Masaniello. According to Donzelli, he got the money from a friar sympathetic to his cause, 'although others claimed that he sold his own breeches'.[83] In sum, Masaniello's little army was prepared for action before the events of 7 July took place. At the first instance of friction over the new fruit tax, which took place on Piazza Mercato, Masaniello seized the opportunity to unleash his boys and declare war. The rest belongs to the books of history, even though most of the contemporary accounts describing the revolt differ considerably from Donzelli, as they say nothing about a conspiracy, attributing the causes of the revolt to the government's loss of control over 'wild masses' behaving irrationally.[84]

To account for these discrepancies one has to take into consideration the background of the chronicler.[85] Politically, he belonged to the Pro-French/Anti-Spanish faction and, almost exclusively, he held a positive view of the popular revolt. It is possible that he had access to witnesses and information unavailable to the other elitist or royalist chroniclers or to material that they refused to take seriously. In addition, since Donzelli belonged to the medical profession, it is easy to see why his narration consistently seeks for explanations that are structurally ordered in a sequence of cause and effect – the Spaniards abused the levying of taxes and brought upon themselves the anger of the people. Even more important, Masaniello was abused by the government so he sought revenge by organizing a revolt. In other words, things happen for a

reason. The important conceptual point here is that according to Donzelli the revolt was not a casual conjuncture, as described by the other contemporary witnesses, but a conspiracy *tout court*. This is certainly an interpretation that empowers the perpetrators, and raises the possibility of an effective social organization even among the most wretched of peoples.

Spanish tournaments in Neapolitan state festivities

The main objective of the following pages is to continue the exploration of communication and reception of Neapolitan festivities, but this time the focus will be on those festival practices that were brought directly from Spain. In this context, the most representative forms of Iberian spectacle came in a number of unique tournaments: the reed spear tournament (*juego de cañas*), the carousel (*juego de alcancías*), and what has become one of Spain's main sources of national and cultural identification – the bullfight (*corrida*).

The reed spear tournament, and its cognate carousel, consisted of a 'hit and run' contest in which each team took turns at bombarding the other with either reed spears (*cañas*), or hollow earthenware balls (*alcancías*), while the team on the defensive protected itself with appropriate shields. The origins of the game were Moorish, and it was adopted during the years of the *Reconquista*. During the sixteenth century the tournament spread among the nobility of the Iberian Peninsula as one variation of the so-called 'Games of Moors and Christians'. Even if this tournament usually took place between 'Christian' and 'Moorish' teams, with the latter dressed in a distinctively Muslim style, it was not prearranged for the Christians to win. It was the ability or personal prestige of the participants that eventually determined the outcome. The level of risk for the participants seems to have been relatively low, although there were times when serious injuries and death were caused, usually because of some heated spirits that failed to restrain themselves, causing the game to degenerate into a perilous fight. This game was favoured also by the Habsburgs, and it was under their rule that it became customary to have both bullfights and reed spear tournaments on the occasion of great public events.[86] Eventually, this led to the still existing Spanish expression: 'Habran toros y cañas' (There shall be bulls and reed spears), which means that something spectacular and noteworthy is being prepared.[87]

The origin of the bullfight in Spain can be traced well before the period studied. What matters for us is that it was an extremely popular sport by the sixteenth century, as it was part of every possible kind of festival. The bullfight saw a social transformation during the early modern era.[88] All through the sixteenth century it had a more popular character, since often the fighters were probably of humble origins as they confronted the bulls on foot. It is in the seventeenth century that the bullfight seems to become a more knightly source of entertainment. In this version of the fight, a noble mounted on

horseback usually attacked the bull with a wooden spear with a steel point, known as *rejón*, and planted as many of these as possible on the bull's neck.[89]

However, the mounted aristocrat was not the sole performer. In principle, his lackeys were there to help him finish off the animal, yet their fighting skills and their repertoire in the combat are not to be dismissed as a mere sideshow. According to a seventeenth-century observer: 'there are people of the lower class that are quite daring and quite skilful at sticking a dagger or a javelin between the bull's horns as they run past, and when the beast charges them and puts them in a tight spot, they throw their capes over its head or throw themselves to the ground face down, thereby escaping the fury of the bull'.[90] Actually, it is not hard to see via this description how the aristocratic *rejón* turned into the modern bullfighting on foot. Compared with the reed spear tournament and the carousel, the bullfights were a much more risky business, and they often ended with victims. Despite that, the Habsburgs had a great passion for the game, and some of them, like Charles V, actively participated as bullfighters. Accordingly, there seem to have been as many as 107 royal bullfights in Madrid in the seventeenth century alone.[91] According to Croce, Naples already saw bullfights and reed spear tournaments during the reign of the Aragonese Alfonso V (1442–58).[92] Later, during the sixteenth century, the Neapolitan gentlemen were said to have spent their days as follows: during the morning in tournaments, bullfights, and reed spear tournaments; in the afternoon in literary and musical activities; in the evening, having dinner; and dancing at night.[93] Apparently the example was provided from above, since in those days Naples was privileged not only by the bullfighting skills of the viceroy Pedro of Toledo, but by Charles V in person.[94]

However, scholars who have explored these cultural exports have unanimously denied their widespread success among Neapolitans, labelling them as merely marginal, attributing their existence to the long-standing presence of the Spanish court and the Iberian troops alone.[95] It seems that all have simply followed categorically the pioneering work of Mancini without bothering to revise some of his more problematic views. His authoritative work, whose merit relies on the artistic and scenographic aspects of Neapolitan festivals, was shaped in the late 1960s, when Italian historiography closely followed a Marxist perspective. Accordingly, despite the accurate artistic analysis of the festivities, it presents an irresolvable tension between the forceful authoritative action of the Spanish 'evil empire', and a culturally autonomous *popolo*, unaffected by the hegemonic power. Cast in this frame, Spain could have not influenced Neapolitan culture with its tournaments, or with anything else for that matter.

I will use the following exposition to discuss the general methodological problems of this research beyond the strict subject of tournaments. Generally speaking there are two kinds of sources: the local diaries and the festival books. The first kind is very useful for following the different festivals during the annual cycle, since it is written on a daily basis. Unfortunately, so far as detailed description is concerned, it often proves to be extremely disappointing. At best, the writer might give a brief account of the event. In

the worst case, he can give a laconic account such as 'today the city celebrated the usual festivities' of so and so, or even refer the reader to a festival book especially written for the occasion.[96] Nevertheless, one should not dismiss this source altogether. Cavalcades organized for special occasions have often been discussed in some detail, and so have the celebrations of Carnival, or unusual events that happened during the celebration. The main point is that it does not contain some of the inevitable biases present in the festival book, and in this sense it complements it. Nevertheless, the diaries are very sparing with detail about tournaments and bullfights. The scholars of Neapolitan festivities, who used these sources almost exclusively, have probably based their convictions on such lacunae, interpreting them as a lack of local interest.

As for the festival book, it can be an excellent source if one is interested in the intentions of the festival's sponsor, and in his 'image of power'. The festival book will almost infallibly present the reason for the celebration (usually in the prologue), note some of the preparations and costs, and offer a long description of the appearance of the noble participants, at either cavalcades, masquerades, or tournaments.[97] The reader will hardly miss the names of participants, their rich clothes, the *imprese*, very often engraved in detail, their mottoes, and the accompanying madrigals in their entirety. However, when it comes to the fights themselves, they often fall short at the moment of illustrating the game/combat. The most extreme instance that I know of, although it represents well a common problem, is the tournament of 1612, organized by the viceroy the Count of Lemos. The projected exhibition is preceded by an elaborate description of the preparation of the ring, the rules for the fight, the spectators, and especially the costumes, the devices, and the 'inventions', consisting of a masquerade complemented with spectacular machinery, of the fighters.[98] Paradoxically, only a couple of pages describe the fight itself.[99] Comparatively, the description by Giuseppe Castaldi for a *gioco dei caroselli* (Italian for *juego de alcancías*) organized as part of the celebrations in honour of Charles II's marriage with Marie of Orléans is no less problematic: 'They held in their hands some fine balls of clay shaped as silver apples ... and it can be firmly argued that glory followed with the same pace, both the assailers as the assaulted.'[100] Similarly, Parrino recounted the sequence of events of the same kind of tournament celebrated in honour of the marriage of Charles II to Marianne of Neuburg a decade later: 'the one who had previously fled found himself subsequently chasing the enemy ... and by running and taking cover from those small silvery spheres, almost at the same time the victorious became beaten'.[101] What can we make of these narrations? Despite their efforts to show a real course of action, they are too abstract for one to be able to deduce much. The names of the participants are absent, no special incidents are mentioned, and the partiality with which the authors characterize the game is too convenient. In other words, these are formulaic descriptions that could fit any other *gioco dei caroselli* ever played.

According to the festival expert, Helen Watanabe-O'Kelly, this omission of the combat itself was a common topos in the European festival book.[102] The main reason is

that the book was sometimes printed as a brochure intended to be distributed among the important spectators. For example, a week before the entry of Louis XIV and Maria Theresa in Paris, such a booklet was sold to the public, delineating the itinerary of the procession and describing the allegories of the *apparati*.[103] The authors could therefore inform themselves in advance of all the preparations, important participants, their costumes, and their devices, and narrate them as a *fait accompli*, offering an ideal, programmatic, and propagandistic account rather than a journalistic reportage. This might be the case with Valentini's book, whose format follows precisely a prepackaged version of a tournament yet to be played, but was probably not the case with Castaldi and Parrino, since their books do not record a single event but a series of celebrations that unfolded over various days. Nevertheless, since the festival book was usually commissioned by the sponsors of the festival, it is implicit that the presence of the author was not essentially required at the tournament, as long as the final product presented the required ideal picture. Thus, their *gioco dei caroselli* are too general and dull for the historian to find meaningful clues to a lived cultural phenomenon, but their 'political correctness' reflects precisely what the festival/festival's book patron wanted it to be.

Having said all that, the festival book should not be regarded as a completely unreliable source of information for research on the popularity of Spanish forms of tournament in Naples. Rather, the few descriptions of tournaments that we have should be read very carefully, always bearing in mind the general partiality of all festival books. Perhaps then, instead of searching for a direct answer in the documents themselves one should approach the problem contextually and indirectly. For instance, we could put Naples in a general European context and compare it with other courtly environments.

As already mentioned in the chapter on ceremonial, Spain found a serious rival in France in everything that involved courtly forms of culture. Throughout Europe, but mostly in Italy, where the rivalry of the two powers played an especially marked role, the different states chose their cultural models according to their political allegiances. In Florence, for instance, in October 1579, while the Grand Duchy was still considered as a Spanish satellite, for the marriage of Grand Duke Francesco I de' Medici to the commoner Bianca Cappello, Florentines enjoyed a bullfight, a *juego de cañas*, and a *gioco di caroselli*.[104] On the other hand, after the beginning of the seventeenth century, when the political might of Spain started to decline, the tournaments in Florence followed a pattern which originated in France towards the closure of the sixteenth century – the horse ballet.[105] This was not a contest at all but a spectacle in which a group of horsemen exhibited elaborately choreographed movements riding to the sound of music. Eventually, its widespread success was such that 'by the 1630s fighting in a tournament called more upon a courtier's acting ability than his combative skills'.[106] Hence, 'the required skills to excel in the ballet reflected the change that had occurred in court ceremonial and in the functions of the ruler and the court: elegance and grace, rather than muscular force and dexterity, were now the accoutrements of the courtier'.[107] It is probably not a

coincidence that France produced such a safe spectacle after the tragic death of Henry II (1559) in a tournament. Strong has attributed this development of the more traditional forms of tournament to the consolidation of absolutist courts. 'Whereas the court tournament had been a means of maintaining the abilities of a warlike aristocracy in loyalty, in the absolutist age which followed they were merely deployed as elements in an esoteric allegorical drama, whose cosmic claims for the powers of the prince were as insubstantial as the painted sets on stage.'[108]

However, if something worked well for France it would not do for Spain. The horse ballet had little success in the Iberian Peninsula, as Spaniards preferred the more traditional forms of equestrian tournament. It was not before the close of the century, not coincidentally when Naples seemed to be moving closer to the French orbit of influence, that there was a shift of weight from open tournaments and public festivities to exclusive courtly feasts.[109] During the sixteenth century, Spain's supreme military reputation was boosted by its vast equestrian knowledge and by the exportation of horses to the rest of Europe. Virtually every treatise on horses from the sixteenth and seventeenth centuries emphasizes the superiority of Spanish horses. Owing to this reputation, and of course to its political power, it also exported its equestrian games to other Western European nations. For example, the *juego de alcancías* reached most of the Italian courts, and the courts of Germany and Denmark.[110] Accordingly, in the major stately events that accompanied the Habsburg dynasty, from Charles V to Charles II, it was the bullfights alone or paired with the *juego de cañas* that prevailed. It has been calculated that these were about three times as frequent as other forms of tournament.[111]

Since, as we have seen, early modern Naples was strictly controlled by the viceregal court in all matters concerning the promotion and sponsorship of festivities, it is clear that the Spanish tournaments prevailed there. This is true, at least, for their insertion from above. In other words, feasts and tournaments were carefully planned by a court whose main task was to represent and emulate Madrid and not Paris – never Paris. Accordingly, the viceroys not only staged *toros y cañas* tournaments for great events related to the Habsburgs – the royal weddings in 1680 and 1690, and the birth of the *infante* in 1659 being the more prominent examples – but also for more trivial reasons such as the birthday of the queen mother in 1685. Moreover, this Spanish dominance was felt not only as a mere matter of default, but as a clear-cut hegemony. Let as examine, for instance, some linguistic evidence. The rules of the tournament, which were usually publicized in advance, were often written directly in Spanish.[112] Otherwise, when they were written in the Italian vernacular (or rather in Tuscan), the key words were borrowed from Spanish and directly transliterated into the Italian text. In one such example, instead of using the Italian word *mira* for aim the author uses the Spanish *puntería*, instead of *anello* for ring he writes *sortija*, and instead of *corsa* for run he chooses *carrera*.[113] Further linguistic evidence can be found in the nomenclature of some forms of tournaments that were also popular throughout other parts of Italy and

Europe, such as the running at the ring and the running at the quintain. These were known in Naples by their Spanish names, respectively, *sortija* (or *anello*) and *estafermo* (more commonly Italianized to *stafermo*). Needless to say, Spanish wording prevailed in the case of original Spanish tournaments. For example, unlike the inelegant solution used by Cirino to denominate the bullfighters – *cacciatori del toro* – Castaldi and Parrino preferred to force a new occupation on to the Italian language when they Italianized *toreadores* into *toreadori*.[114]

In order to properly undertake the question of reception, one should separate between nobility and *popolo*. It is well known that those members of the Neapolitan nobility who were engaged in warfare were wholly absorbed in the various Spanish campaigns throughout the globe.[115] Nevertheless, some Neapolitan writers of courtly inclinations emphasized and generalized the inherent belligerent aspect of all the local nobility. For example, towards the end of the sixteenth century, Scipione Mazzella describes the Neapolitan nobility as primarily 'liberal, magnanimous, and warlike'.[116] A few decades later, Neapolitan commentators speaking with a certain degree of truth, translated the Spanish supremacy in horse connoisseurship directly on to Neapolitan soil.[117] He also emphasized 'with how much valour they [Neapolitan nobles] handle arms when they appear in carousels, and how expert they are in running with the javelins in tournaments'.[118] Analogous declarations can be multiplied *ad nauseam*.[119]

However, according to Giovanni Muto, this abundant evidence of a proliferation of chivalric values was inconsistent with the actual Neapolitan presence on the battlefield. After the last French attempt to regain the Kingdom of Naples in 1528, in which many Neapolitan barons joined the French ranks, the Spanish government made sure that the important positions of command would be kept out of Neapolitan hands. Hence, the chivalric ethos was kept only symbolically by means of the schools of riding and fencing, the wide participation in the various tournaments, and a rich autobiographical literature that reflects 'a society that intends to portray itself as chauvinistic and courteous at the same time'.[120] Further evidence of these values can be found in the testimony of the seventeenth-century French noble Jean-Jacques Bouchard, who is amused and at the same time critical of the Neapolitan belletristic taste. Giving us a unique view of the literary marketplace, he claims that chivalry books, such as the classical *Amadis de Gaule*, are all you can find in the bookshops. So much so, that some of them are solely engaged in the daily hire of these texts, 'and in the road of the booksellers nothing else can be seen other than the sign: *Chivalry books inside*'.[121]

Accordingly, these tournaments would serve as the best public platform where they could display their fighting skills and vent their chivalric values. Thus, according to Valentini, 'it is ordinary of these nobles … to attend to ballets, banquets, jousts, quintains, tournaments, and other heroic and generous pursuits'.[122] Indeed, a closer look inside the festival books shows clearly that members of the greatest Neapolitan families such as the Carafa, Caracciolo, Pignatelli, Di Sangro, and Tomacello, just to mention a few, and the highest echelons of Italy's southern titled nobility, filled the ranks

of combatants in those tournaments.[1234] And when they were not active performers, they were there to cheer *en masse*, side by side with the viceroy, including *la crème de la crème* of Neapolitan noble ladies, who received a standard round of refreshments at the expense of the viceroy.[124]

It is much more surprising to find in the festival book precisely what Mancini denies – the success of the tournament among the *popolo*.[125] First, it should be remembered that the Spaniards did not follow the French, more elitist development of the 'staged' tournament, which transferred the spectacle away from the public square and from a more heterogeneous public, into the palace courtyard for the eyes of a strictly selected aristocratic public.[126] In all the Spanish dominions including Naples, the *corrida* and the other equestrian tournaments almost always remained outside, more or less open to all. Interior tournaments were also very rare in the middle of the seventeenth century. Accordingly, our festival books, however incredible the statistics may be, report a fabulous number of spectators belonging to all the layers of the *popolo*.

The most revealing report is one that describes how the *popolo*, or rather the plebs, came to see a *corrida* staged on the seashore. From this report it is clear that what the author describes is a multitude of uninvited guests, literally making every effort to be able to take a peek at the spectacle. 'The plebs, some in the streets, and some in the rocks, some at sea in boats, and skiffs, and some in the gardens, and hills, calculating, that those who run to applaud this feast were slightly less, or maybe more than three hundred and fifty thousand people, such a wonder, that in Italy it is impossible to see other than here, and in Europe in few places it is possible to gather such a numerous people.'[127] The next sentence gives a clue to the reasons for this interest. 'But what was of most surprise is that despite such a multitude there did not occur even a minimal accident … although the occasion … could in itself cause confusions and accidents.'[128] In other words, the bullfight itself was considered as a violent spectacle, and that was precisely the source of its attraction. In fact, it often involved the injury or death of a fighter, and it offered a sheer bloodshed of several, sometimes dozens, of bulls.

Moreover, the festival books show clearly that the *popolo* not only watched passionately but also participated actively in bullfights. Some spectators threw firecrackers, irritating the bulls and preparing them for the fight with the mounted bullfighters. Occasionally, these pyrotechnical devices would lethally strike the bulls, 'throwing the bleeding victims at the bullfighters' feet'.[129] According to Andrea Cirino, on other occasions they formed harnessed groups with harpoons, assailing and maiming passing bulls. As a prize, the crowd of killers would get the carcass.[130] Significantly, in all of the descriptions that we have from seventeenth-century Neapolitan bullfights there are violent additions that were also present elsewhere, but were not essentially standard features.[131] The first is the throwing of enraged mastiffs into the ring, which closed their jaws around the bulls' legs in order to excite them for the fight. The second is the ignition of firecrackers that were placed in saddles on the bulls' backs.[132] According to one of the reports, as a result of these horrifying tactics the bulls would turn completely

wild, 'rousing the people with their jumps, their mooing, and their desperate runs'. As a response, the people 'would not stop praising the viceroy's ingenious inventions … and his good taste for bestowing such a singular, noble and delightful celebration'.[133]

These descriptions are attuned with other violent forms of entertainment appreciated by Neapolitans. The chroniclers tell about deadly fights of cats and dogs, and cockfights organized by the plebs.[134] Similarly, a series of edicts from 1573 to 1643 tried unsuccessfully to forbid the citizens of Naples from engaging in frequent street fights using stones, which caused many serious injuries, and occasionally also deaths. The fact that the edicts threaten also to punish 'the great multitude of spectators' from attending these fights shows that these functioned as some sort of public spectacle.[135] Finally, it is important to note in this context the ritual pillages of the enormous floats of cockaigne (*carri-cuccagna*), which were an essential feature of Neapolitan festivities. Massive floats constructed with such expensive foodstuff as delicate meats, cheeses, cakes, and sweets were pillaged by the plebs under the balcony of the Royal Palace.[136] Meanwhile, the viceroy and the court gazed in amusement from the palace's window, often witnessing injuries and deaths of plebeians, who used their daggers to either cut off pieces of food, or to slaughter ducks and chickens that were amassed on the float, as well as to wound rivals. Thus, it is somewhat myopic of Mancini that he considered the *carri-cuccagna* as the most successful of the festive phenomena among the Neapolitan *popolo*, without seeing how the bullfights were equally sources of excitement, based on the same stimulating features that conform so well to the Neapolitan taste.[137]

That said, I do not want to create the impression that the success of a violent sport, like the bullfight in early modern Naples, testifies to a peculiarly bloodthirstiness of the Neapolitan people, or the Spanish people for that matter. Games involving torment of animals, as well as marginal groups, were very popular throughout Europe, especially during the Carnival season.[138] Aside from the already mentioned bulls, cocks, dogs, and cats, the victims could include more unusual creatures. For example, a local chronicler of the Roman Carnival of 1551 informs us of the killing of a porcupine and a hedgehog by a man mounting a horse with his bare bottom, and a woman with bare legs, exposing - so to speak - clear carnivalesque elements of a world turned upside down.[139] Eventually, with the new sensibilities brought forth by the Enlightenment, European elites would undergo a 'civilizing process' – to use Norbert Elias' term – ultimately rejecting such violent entertainments and influencing later the masses. In fact, according to Laura Barletta, in this sense Naples lagged behind the rest of the continent. Eighteenth-century Neapolitan cockaignes, which included various forms of fowl nailed alive to the festive carts, attracted the censure of foreign visitors, who were 'perplexed by the backwardness of the kingdom and, at the same time, delighted to be able to witness an almost obsolete spectacle, which seemed to invoke a past against which they could weigh with satisfaction their own superiority'.[140] Ultimately, these new attitudes would also affect the knightly version of the Spanish *corrida*. After the dynastic change following the death of Charles II, the last Habsburg of the Spanish

branch, the Spanish Bourbons communicated their aversion towards bullfighting to the nobility, and by that they erased almost completely its aristocratic component, paving the way for the modern bullfight on foot. But all through the Habsburg period, the bullfight was, to quote José Maravall, 'a spectacle of violence, pain, blood, and death — a spectacle that was popularly supported and displayed before the masses — and used by the rulers and their collaborators to terrify people and in this way to succeed more efficiently in subjecting them to their place within the order'.[141] Accordingly, one may conclude that the sponsorship of violent entertainments, which included both cockaignes and bullfights, quelled the viceroys' fears of popular rebellion and disorder as much as they fed popular needs for bread and circuses; and it is in this context of maintaining intact the fragile social balances that we should interpret the ubiquity of violent spectacles in early modern Naples.

Notes

An abstract of this chapter was published as 'Spanish Celebrations in Seventeenth-Century Naples', *The Sixteenth-Century Journal*, 37:1 (2006), 25–41.

1 For a local assessment see: Stumpo, 'La crisi del Seicento'. For a general survey see the collection of essays *The General Crisis of the Seventeenth Century*, ed. Geoffrey Parker and Lesley M. Smith (London, 1978).

2 See, for example, Mancini, *Feste*, 17; Rak, 'Il sistema delle feste', 310; Renata D'Elia, *Vita popolare nella Napoli spagnuola* (Naples, 1971), 83; and Laura Barletta, 'Un esempio di festa. Il Carnevale', in *Capolavori in festa. Effimero barocco a Largo di Palazzo (1683–1759)*, ed. Giuseppe Zampino (Naples, 1997), 92.

3 For the relation of the addition of the eighth patron saint, Thomas Aquinas, see Pietro Roseo da Mandurio, *Breve relatione della solenne processione e de'ricchi, e nobili apparati, fatti nella festa del Glorioso Padre San Thomaso d'Aquino, del Sacro Ordine de Predicatori, celebrata nella città di Napoli alli 20 del mese di gennaio, dell'Anno MDCV* (Naples, 1605). Generally on religious festivities in Naples see Mancini, *Feste*, 87 ff.; Giuseppe Galasso, 'La festa', in his *L'altra Europa. Per un antropologia storica del Mezzogiorno d'Italia* (Milan, 1982), 121–42; Laura Barletta, *Fra regola e licenza. Chiesa e vita religiosa, feste e beneficenza a Napoli e in Campania (secoli XVIII–XX)* (Naples, 2003); and D'Elia, *Vita popolare*, 83–95. For specific studies on religious and popular festivals see Burke, 'Revolt of Masaniello', 191–206; John Marino, 'The Zodiac in the Streets: Inscribing "Buon Governo" in Baroque Naples', in *Embodiments of Power: Building Baroque Cities in Austria and Europe*, ed. Gary B. Cohen and Franz A. J. Szabo (Oxford and New York, 2007), 203–29; Giovanni Muto, 'Spazio urbano e identità sociale. Le feste del popolo napoletano nella prima età moderna', in *Le regole dei mestieri e delle professioni. Secoli XV–XIX*, ed. Marco Meriggi and Alessandro Pastore (Milan, 2001), 305–25; Gina Iannella, 'Les fêtes de la Saint-Jean à Naples (1581–1632)', in *Les fêtes urbaines en Italie à l'époque de la Renaissance. Vérone, Florence, Sienne, Naples*, ed. Françoise Decroisette and Michel Plaisance (Paris, 1993), 131–83; Valerio Petrarca, *La festa di San Giovanni Battista a Napoli nella prima metà del Seicento. Percorso macchine immagini scritture* (Palermo, 1986); and Vittorio Gleijeses, *Piccola storia del Carnevale* (Naples, 1971), 153–78. For a rare example of a study dealing with Neapolitan civic celebrations see John A. Marino, 'Celebrating a Royal Birth in 1639: "The Rape of Europa" in the Neapolitan Viceroy's Court', *Rinascimento*, 43 (2003), 233–47.

4 See for example the following declaration made after the extinction of the harsh wave of plague in 1656: 'Perciò si è Concluso per ordine di questa Illustrissima Deputazione si per dimostrarsi grati a beneficio si grande, havendo isperimentata nei Voti, e Invocazione della

Vergine, di S. Gennaro, S. Francesco Xaverio, e S. Rosolia gli effetti della loro singolare protet-
tione non solo per lo sminuimento, ma per la cessatione del contagio.' *Catalogo delle risoluzioni prese dall'Illustrissima Deputazione della Salute Di questa Fedelissima Città di Napoli* (Naples,
1656), 4. See also Rubino's account, SNSP, MS. XVIII. D. 14, Rubino, *Notitia*, fol. 220: 'Per
tanto non sapendo che fare si ricorse a santi, e dagli eletti della città si fe un voto di dare docati
500 alla Madonna Santissima di Constantinopoli, 300 a S. Gennaro, 300 al Beato Gaetano, 200
a S. Antonio di Padua, e 200 altri a S. Francesco di Paula, acciò detti santi intercedessero la sua
Divina Maestà la salute della città di Napoli.'

5   For general works see note 1 of the previous chapter. For different collections of studies
related to Habsburg celebrations see: *Teatro y fiesta en el Barroco. España e Iberoamerica*, ed. José
María Díez Borque (Barcelona, 1986); *Barroco español y austríaco. Fiesta y teatro en la corte*, ed.
José María Díez Borque and K. F. Rudolf (Madrid, 1994); and *La fiesta en la Europa de Carlos V*
(Sevilla, 2000).

6   José Antonio Maravall, *Culture of the Baroque: Analysis of a Historical Structure*, trans. Terry
Cochran (Manchester, 1986), 245.

7   Strong, *Art and Power*, 19. On the effect of new artifices used in baroque pageantry and the
theatre see Maravall, *Culture of the Baroque*, 233–47.

8   Just to mention a couple of extreme examples: the viceroy the Marquis of Carpio (1683–87)
staged a sumptuous bullfight on the name-day of St Anne in honour of the queen mother,
Marianne of Habsburg. Moreover, as in the case of relatively important events, this celebration was recorded in a festival book: *Relazione della solenne Festa de' Tori e de' Fuochi Artifiziati
fattasi nel mare di Napoli il giorno di S. Anna, del presente Anno 1685. Ordinata da quel Viceré
Marchese del Carpio. Per solennizare il nome della Maestà della Regina Madre N. S.* (Milan, 1685). A
similar instance was recorded fifteen years later for the name day of the queen, Marianne of
Neuburg: *Relazione della famosissima Festa Nel giorno della Gloriosa S. Anna a 26. di Luglio 1699.
Per solennizare il Nome, che ne porta la Maestà della Regina Nostra Signora, M. Anna di Neoburgo.
Fatta celebrare nella Riviera di Chiaja, e nello Scoglio di Mergellina dall'Eccelentissimo Signore D.
Luigi dela Cerda e d'Aragóna, Duca di Medina Celi, d'Alcalà, e Viceré, e Capitan Generale in questo
Regno* (Naples, 1699). For various celebrations for the recovered health of Charles II during
the last year of his life see BNN, MS. XV G30, *Diario ossia Giornale Istorico di quanto piu curioso
e memorabile è accaduto in Napoli dall'anno 1700 per tutto l'anno 1701 in cui accadde il tumulto*,
fols. 20v–23v.

9   For the quelling of Barcelona see Fuidoro, *Conte d'Oñatte*, 186–90. There is also a detailed
description in SNSP, MS. XVIII. D. 14, Rubino, *Notitia*, fols. 72–9. Owing to the importance
of the event, an official festival book was printed: *Breve Ragguaglio delle feste celebrate in Napoli
per la ricuperazione di Barzellona fatta dalle armi di S. M. C.* (Rome, 1653). A similar book was
issued for the celebrations made for the liberation of Budapest: Biagio De Calamo, *I giorni
festivi fatti per la presa di Buda dall'Arme Austriache nella Fedelissima Città di Napoli Dall'Eccelentissimo Signor Marchese del Carpio, Viceré e Capitan Generale della detta e da'suoi Cittadini l'anno
1686* (Naples, 1687). For the same event see also Confuorto, *Giornali*, I, 159–61; and ASNA,
Sei libri di cerimoniale, part I, fol. 103v: 'A due di settembre 1686 dopo 4 mesi d'assedio si rese
Buda all'imperatore … Il Viceré ordinò Cappella reale al Carmine, a San Paolo e San Giuseppe,
Santa Maria la Nova, Arcivescovato, con *Te Deum*, salva, squadroni, nove giorni senza Tribunali,
tre giorni di illuminazioni, fuochi artificiali, cucagne, fontane di vino, e serenata al palazzo.'
This is corroborated in a viceregal letter directed to the lieutenant of the *Real Camera della
Sommaria*. See ASNA, *Dispacci della sommaria, Registro de Viglietti*, 72, 11 September 1686, fol.
1: 'Su excelencia ha resuelto celebrar la feliz nueva de la conquista de Buda por las armas
imperiales … Capilla Real mañana jueves en la Iglesia de Nuestra Señora del Carmen, el
viernes en San Gaetano, y el savado en la parroqia de san Joseph, donde ha venido el mismo
S.E. a la mañana. Lo que me manda participarlo a V.S., para que se halle en ella a las nueve con
los ministros de ese tribunal de la Real Cámara.'

10 Given the importance of the event, the chronicle of the celebrations was printed contemporaneously in both Madrid and Naples, *Relacion del hazimiento de gracias, que hizo el Supremo Consejo*

de Italia en Madrid, por el buen Sucesso de Nápoles, por tres dias sucessivos, que fueron a 8, 9, y 10 de Mayo de 1648 (Madrid and Naples, 1648).

11 Bulifon, *Giornali*, 200.

12 See SNSP, MS. XXIII. D. 15, Rubino, *Notitia di quanto é occorso in Napoli dall'anno 1658 per tutto l'anno 1661*, fols. 196–204.

13 Mitchell presents various Italian examples of these mixed instances of religious and civic forms in Renaissance pageantry. See his *The Majesty of the State*, 2–3. For a detailed exposition of these exchanges in Rome during the seventeenth century see Maurizio Fagiolo dell'Arco, *La festa barocca* (Rome, 1997), 45–52.

14 For a comprehensive contemporary account of St Januarius' life and cult see Camillo Tutini, *Memorie della vita, miracoli, e culto di San Gianuario Martire, Vescovo di Benevento e Principal Protettore della Città di Napoli* (3rd edn, Naples, 1703). See also BNN, MS. Branc. II. A. 10, Gio. Battista Bolvito, *Trattato della translatione del Glorioso San Gianuario vescovo e martire, composto ... nell'Anno 1588*, fols. 106r–110v. For the cult of St Januarius in Aragonese times see Vitale, *Ritualità monarchica*, 160–86. For a general outlook see Luigi Petito, *San Gennaro. Storia, folklore, culto* (Rome and Naples, 1983).

15 Maravall, *Culture of the Baroque*, 239.

16 Peter Burke, *Popular Culture in Early Modern Europe* (London, 1978), 191–9.

17 For that specific masquerade see Francesco Valentini, *Descrittione del sontuoso torneo fatto nella fidelissima città di Napoli l'anno MDCXII. Con la relazione di molt'altre feste Per allegrezza delli Regij accasamenti seguiti fra le Potentissime Corone Spagna, e Francia. Raccolta dal Signor F.V. Anconitano, Dottor di leggi, & Accademico Eccentrico. Dedicata all'illustrissima, & Eccelentissima Signora D. Caterina Sandoval Contessa di Lemos Viceregina del Regno di Napoli* (Naples, 1612), 13–14. Cockaignes were very popular in viceregal Naples. For a thorough analysis of the phenomenon in Naples see Barletta, *Fra regola e licenza*, 354–400.

18 Bulifon, *Giornali*, 223.

19 All quotations in this paragraph are from Parrino, *Teatro*, in *Raccolta*, vol. 10, 193–4. The event is described in detail in Salvatore de Renzi, *Napoli nell'anno 1656* (Naples, 1968), 39–45. Archival records show previous examples of popular devotion to Sor Ursula, supported by the viceregal court. See, for example, ASNA, *Dispacci della sommaria, Registro de Viglietti*, 49, 20 October 1649, fol. 169: 'Por parte de la fidelísima plaza del pueblo se ha suplicado al Conde mi señor, asenso que tiene particular devoción a Sor Ursola cuya felicidad se celebra mañana en la Iglesia de la Anunciada, y los ... della entienden renovar la procesión de su reliquia, fuese ... mandar que sea día feriado y no se vaya a los tribunales, y habiendo venido S. E. en su instancia me ha mandado avisarlos a V. S. para que se lo haga executar de los ministros de esa regia cámara, Dios guarde.'

20 Many festival books remain from this festival. Among the various books authored by Giulio Cesare Capaccio see especially: *Apparato della festività del glorioso S. Giovan Battista fatto dal Fedelissimo Popolo Napolitano nella venuta dell'Eccellenza del Signor D. Antonio Alvarez di Toledo, Viceré del Regno* (Naples, 1623); *Apparato della festività del glorioso S. Giovan Battista fatto dal Fedelissimo Popolo Napolitano à 24 di Giugno 1624, all'Eccellenza del Signor D. Antonio Alvarez di Toledo Duca d'Alba, Viceré del Regno* (Naples, 1624); *Apparato della festività del glorioso S. Gio. Battista fatto dal Fedelissimo Popolo Napolitano à XXIII di Giugno MDCXXVI, all'Eccellenza del Signor D. Antonio Alvarez di Toledo Duca d'Alba, Viceré del Regno di Napoli* (Naples, 1626); and *Apparato della festività del glorioso S. Gio. Battista fatto dal Fedelissimo Popolo Napolitano à XXIII di Giugno MDCXXVII, all'Eccellenza del Signor D. Antonio Alvarez di Toledo, Duca d'Alva, Viceré nel Regno* (Naples, 1627). See also Francesco Orilla, *Il zodiaco over idea di perfetione di Prencipi, Formata Dall' Heroiche Virtù dell' illustriss. ... D. Antonio Alvaros di Toledo Duca D'Alba Viceré di Napoli dal fidelissimo Popolo Napoletano ... Nella Pomposissima Festa di San Gio. Battista, celebrato a 23 di Giugno 1629, per il settimo anno del suo Governo* (Naples, 1630); Giuliani, *Descrittione M.DC. XXVIII*; and Gio. Bernardino Giuliani, *Descrittione dell'Apparato fatto nella Festa di S. Giovanni dal fedelissimo popolo Napolitano all'Illustrissimo et Eccelentissimo Sig. D. Emanuel de Zunica et Fonseca, Conte di Monterrey, Vicere di Napoli l'anno M.DC.XXXI* (Naples, 1631); and Pedro Martinez de

Herrera, *Principe advertido y declaracion de las Epigramas De Napoles la Vispera de S. Juan* (Naples, 1631).

21 See Petrarca, *La festa di San Giovanni Battista a Napoli*, 28–9.

22 The motive behind the choice of the word *dawn* as the harmonizing concept between the saint and the viceroy is the viceroy's name – Duke of *Alba* (Italian for dawn). See Giuliani, *Descrittione … M.DC.XXVIII*, 20.

23 Bucca, 'Aggionta', *ASPN*, 37 (1912), 128. Another such example is provided by Confuorto, who relates about the unprecedented building of a fountain in honour of the viceroy for the procession of the Corpus Christi. See his *Giornali*, II, 224.

24 For Naples see Mancini, *Feste*, 29; and Lepre, *Storia del Mezzogiorno d'Italia*, I, 158, 161. For a more moderate view see Aercke, *Gods of Play*, 20. For an alternative approach see Bertelli, *Il corpo del re*, 58 ff.

25 See the cited collection of essays edited by Zampino, *Capolavori in festa. Effimero barocco a Largo di Palazzo (1683–1759)* (see note 2 above).

26 For Mergellina see Giulio Cesare Capaccio, *Mergellina. Egloghe piscatorie* (Venice, 1598).

27 Muto, 'Spazio urbano e identità sociale'.

28 For the former kind see Mikhail Bakhtin, *Rabelais and his World*, trans. Hélène Iswolsky (Bloomington, Ind., 1984). For the latter, Elias, *The Court Society*.

29 See Mitchell, *The Majesty of the State*, 1.

30 Bertelli and Calvi, 'Rituale, cerimoniale, etichetta', 26.

31 Confuorto, *Giornali*, I, 172–3.

32 Capaccio, *Il forastiero*, 416–17.

33 The passage is from Bulifon's introduction to the *Compendio delle vite dei re di Napoli, aggiuntovi il catalogo de'viceré* (Naples, 1687), reproduced in Nino Cortese's 'Introduction' to Bulifon's, *Giornali*, xlviii.

34 See Vittorio Gleijeses, *Feste, farina, e forca* (Naples, 1972).

35 Letter from 14 October 1685, addressed to Arrigo Gusman, reproduced in Bulifon, *Giornali*, 227.

36 For all of these see *ibid.*, 226–8. Carpio's various celebrations for the various defeats of the Turks by the hand of the German Habsburgs are also reported in ASNA, *Sei libri di cerimoniale*, part I, fols. 102r, 103v–104r.

37 Bucca, 'Aggionta', *ASPN*, 37 (1912), 122.

38 ASNA, *Sei libri di cerimoniale*, part I, fol. 35r.

39 Parrino, *Teatro*, in *Raccolta*, vol. 10, 417–18; and Galasso, *Napoli spagnola*, I, 168–9.

40 See Introduction, note 58 for the relevant bibiliography of the revolt. For the plague of 1656 see: De Renzi, *Napoli*; Franco Strazzullo, *La peste del 1656 a Napoli* (Naples, 1957); and Eduardo Nappi, *Aspetti della società ed economia napoletana durante la peste del 1656. Dai documenti dell'archivio storico del banco di Napoli* (Naples, 1980).

41 Fuidoro, *Conte d'Oñatte*, 101–2.

42 See, for example, SNSP, MS. XXIII. D. 14, Rubino, *Notitia*, fols. 82–3: 'et accio si fussero evitate quelle risse e rumori che sogliono nascere ne tempi carnavaleschi dal tirarsi dall'acque e delle cetrangole, et sogliono d'esser lutto alle allegrezze, si fe banno da S.E. nel primo di febbraio che sotto pena di 3 anni di galera all'ignobile e 300 scudi al nobile che nessuno ardisse buttar acqua dalle finestre o tirar cetrangola a chi fusse persona'.

43 Fuidoro, *Giornali*, II, 135.

44 SNSP, MS. XXIII. D. 14, Rubino, *Notitia*, fols. 23–4, 32–5, 64, 94–5. The importance of this celebration for Oñate is evident in the fact that he did not call it off in 1651, despite being in mourning for the death of his brother, see *ibid.*, fol. 64.

45 *Ibid.*, fol. 135.

46 *Ibid.*, fols. 35–6.

47 See Aercke, *Gods of Play*, 38–9.

48 *Ibid.*, 39.

49 Franco Mancini, ' "L'immaginario di regime". Apparati e scenografie alla corte dei viceré' in

Civiltà del Seicento a Napoli (2 vols., Naples, 1984), II, 27.

50 Ferdinando Bevilacqua, *Racconto della festa fatta nel Reale Palazzo di Napoli dalli gentilhuomini della corte dell'Eccelentissimo Signor Conte di Ognatte Viceré. Per il felice arrivo in Milano della Sposa Reale del Cattolico, e Gran Re' Filippo Quarto Nostro Signore* (Naples, 1649).

51 About the festivities and entertainment in the Buen Retiro see Elliott and Brown, *Palace for a King*, 199–219; José Deleito y Piñuela, *El rey se divierte. Recuerdos de hace tres siglos* (2nd edn, Madrid, 1964), 195 ff.; Aercke, *Gods of Play*, 139 ff.

52 According to Rubino, Oñate ordered the celebration of the feast of St John only on the first year of a viceroy's appointment. SNSP, MS. XVIII. D. 14, *Notitia*, fol. 135.

53 *Ibid.*, fols. 215–17.

54 Mancini, *Feste*, 17.

55 Gian Vincenzo Imperiale, 'De' giornali di Gio. Vincenzo Imperiale', ed. Anton Giulio Barrili, in *Atti della Società Ligure di Storia Patria*, vol. 29 (Genoa, 1908), 332.

56 Parrino, *Teatro*, in *Raccolta*, vol. 10, 190–1.

57 De Renzi, *Napoli*, 150–2. For a regional estimation of the depopulation see Galasso, *Il Regno di Napoli*, 573.

58 Andrea Cirino, *Feste celebrate in Napoli per la nascita del serenis.ᵐᵒ Prencipe di Spagna Nostro Signore dall'ecc.ᵐᵒ Sig.ʳ Conte di Castriglio, Viceré e Lungotenente e Capitan Generale nel Regno di Napoli* (Naples, 1658), 101–2.

59 Galasso, *Napoli spagnola*, I, 57.

60 Most of the receipts of the Aragonese and Spanish courts were destroyed in the Second World War. This was the result of an unfortunate decision made by the directors of the Archivio di Stato of Naples, who decided to move the most important documents in the archive to Villa Montesano for safekeeping, on the outskirts of the city. Regretfully, this new location was set on fire by German troops on 30 September 1943. For a general assessment of the quantitative archival material existing on this subject see Carolina Belli, 'Cerimonie e feste d'antaño. Schegge d'archivio', in *Capolavori in festa*, ed. Zampino, 105–9.

61 Just to give some surviving relevant examples revolving around a specific event, for the birthday of the queen consort Marianne of Neuburg in 1697, 400 *ducati* were paid for the celebrations that took place in front of the Royal Palace, and 133 *ducati* were spent on nineteen barrels of Lacrima wine consumed at the occasion. For these see respectively ASNA, *Cedole di Tesoreria*, 523, 22 July 1697, fol. 245; and *ibid.*, 5 October 1697.

62 Raneo, *Etiquetas*, 105–6.

63 Zazzera, *Narrazioni*, 496. We learn from the archives that similar requests were addressed towards high officials as well. Here are, for example, the instructions made to the ministers of the *Real Camara della Sommaria* for the celebration of the marriage of Charles II with Mary of Orléans: 'Habiendo S. E. resuelto de ejecutar precisamente el domingo catorce del corriente la cavalcata, que se está disponiendo por el feliz matrimonio de la rey nuestro señor [...] Me manda S. E. avisarlos a V. S. y encargarles sumamente que los ministros de este tribunal pongan luminarias, procurando mayor lucimiento de ella.' ASNA, *Dispacci della sommaria, Registro de Viglietti*, 63, 11 January 1680, fol. 66.

64 Confuorto, *Giornali*, I, 21.

65 *Ibid.*, 92.

66 A festival book was issued for the occasion. See Giuseppe Castaldi, *Tributi Ossequiosi della Fedelissima Città di Napoli, Per li Applausi Festivi delle Nozze Reali del Cattolico Monarca Carlo Secondo, Ré delle Spagne con la Serenissima Signora Maria Luisa Borbone. Sotto la direttione dell'Eccellentissimo Signor Marchese de Los Velez Viceré di Napoli* (Naples, 1680).

67 *Quadriglia* translates as quartet, but it could include six or eight knights as well.

68 Confuorto, *Giornali*, I, 24.

69 *Ibid.*, 28.

70 *Ibid.*, 253.

71 Cirino, *Feste*, 68.

72 See Rak, 'A dismisura d'uomo', 280.

73 *Ibid.*, 116.

74 See note 20 above.

75 'Per solennizzare con piú pompa questa festa la cittá paga ogni anno per l'aparamento che si fa, non solo al largo della Guglia, incontro quale si fa la musica, ma ancora in tutta la strada dalla cantonata di sopra fin al Seggio Capuano, scudi cinquecento, oltre quaranta setari d'olio per le luminarie, settanta scudi per la musica di tre sere dalle ventiquattro ore fin tre ore di notte, cento libbre di candele dá ai deputati del Tesoro, cento libbre dá alli canonici per dover accompagnare la statua di S. Gennaro sera e mattina dal Tesoro all'altare maggiore per tutta l'ottava. Oltre di ciò paga la cittá alla detta cappella del Tesoro milleduecento scudi ogni anno per l'ornamenti di detta cappella, e ducati dieci per ogni cappellano, quali sono di Piazza'. Bulifon, *Giornali*, 186.

76 Maravall, *Culture of the Baroque*, 244.

77 Alonso de Contreras, *Discurso de mi vida. Desde que sali a servir al Rey a la edad de catorce anos, en el año de 1595, hasta fin del año 1630, el 1 de octubre, en que comence esta relacion*, in *Autobiografias de soldados (siglo xvii)*, ed. José Cossio, *Biblioteca de autores españoles*, vol. 90 (Madrid, 1956), 138.

78 See Fuidoro's annotation in Bucca, 'Aggionta', *ASPN*, 37 (1912), 273.

79 See Don Diego Duque de Estrada, *Comentarios del desengañado de si mesmo, prueba de todos estados y eleccion del mejor de ellos, o sea Vida del mesmo autor, que lo es Don Diego Duque de Estrada*, in *Autobiografias de soldados*, ed. Cossio, 312. The title of this work rightly suggests that it has a generally religious and moralizing goal. The author writes the work at old age, after embracing the vows of the Church. Nevertheless, according to his own testimony, the experiences of his past genuinely express his previous way of thought.

80 Yet, it should be noted that these stately displays of conspicuous consumption were not wholly unrestrained or unchallenged. For example, in the 1680s, the viceroy the Marquis of Carpio displayed his aforementioned festive enthusiasm through lavish celebrations of St Anne's name day in honour of the queen mother Marie Anne. In 1684 the celebrations included the nobility's formal display of compliments to the viceroy in the Royal Palace, and a splendid promenade at Posillipo. The year after, for the same occasion, Carpio increased his efforts by organizing a magnificent bullfight and fireworks display. The same feat was repeated in 1686. However, in 1687, there were only formal compliments given to the viceroy, and a religious ceremony at the St Maria del Carmine church. For all of these see ASNA, *Sei libri di cerimoniale*, part I, fol. 101r–101v. Significantly, 'there were no ulterior celebrations, by order of the king who did not want to incur such exorbitant expenses and refused to pay for those of the previous year, thus the viceroy was obliged to pay for them by himself.' *Ibid*, fol. 101v. The same process can be seen for the celebrations of the name day (St Louis) of the queen, Marie Louise of Orléans. If in 1685 it was celebrated with a bullfight and fireworks, and in 1686 with a regatta, by the following year the formal compliments alone would have had to suffice. *Ibid*.

81 See Emmanuel Leroy Ladurie, *Carnival in Romans*, trans. Mary Feeney (New York, 1979); Burke, *Popular Culture*, 199–204; and Edward Muir, *Mad Blood Stirring: Vendetta and Factions in Friuli during the Renaissance* (Baltimore, 1993).

82 See the modern edition of Giuseppe Donzelli, *Partenope liberata* (Naples, 1970), 30.

83 *Ibid.*, 31.

84 For an assessment of the contemporary accounts of the revolt see Burke, 'Revolt of Masaniello', 192–4. Musi offers a broad overview of the revolt's literature through the ages, *La rivolta di Masaniello*, 13–31.

85 See the introduction by Antonio Altamura in Donzelli, *Partenope*, 5–9.

86 On the reed spear tournament see José Deleito y Piñuela, … *También se divierte el pueblo* (2nd edn, Madrid, 1954), 92–8; María Soledad Carrasco Urgoiti, 'Aspectos folclóricos y literarios de la fiesta de moros y cristianos en España', in her *El moro retador y el moro amigo. Estudios sobre fiestas y comedias de moros y cristianos* (Granada, 1996), 43 ff.; also in *ibid*. see 'La fiesta de moros y cristianos y la cuestión morisca en la España de los Austrias'.

87 Deleito y Piñuela, *También se divierte el pueblo*, 92.

88 See Bartolomé Bennassar, *The Spanish Character: Attitudes and Mentalities from the Sixteenth to the Eighteenth Century*, trans. Benjamin Keen (Berkeley, 1979), 158 ff.

89 Detailed rules appear in the rare collection of various contemporary guidebooks on mounted bullfighting: *Advertencias y reglas para torear a caballo (Siglos XVII y XVIII)* (Madrid, 1947).

90 Quoted in Timothy Mitchell, *Blood Sport: A Social History of Bullfighting* (Philadelphia, 1991), 50. For a contemporary description of the popular involvement in Spanish bullfights see Antoine de Brunel, excerpts from his *Journal du voyage en Espagne* [1655], in *La sociedad española y los viajeros del siglo XVII*, ed. José María Díez Borque (Madrid, 1975), 128–31.

91 For the great appreciation of the bullfight among Spaniards of every social denomination see Marcelin Defourneaux, *Daily Life in Spain in the Golden Age*, trans. Newton Branch (London, 1970), 133–5; Gary Marvin, *Bullfight* (Oxford and New York, 1988), 53–9; Deleito y Piñuela, *… También se divierte el pueblo*, 97–150; and Bennassar, *The Spanish Character*, 158–60.

92 Croce, *La Spagna*, 43.

93 See Adelaide Cirillo Mastrocinque, 'Cinquecento napoletano', in *Storia di Napoli*, vol. 4, ed. Ernesto Pontieri (2nd edn, Naples, 1976), 540.

94 D'Elia, *Vita popolare*, 96–8. A direct testimony is brought by Rosso, *Istoria delle cose di Napoli*, in *Raccolta*, vol. 8, 48.

95 Mancini, *Feste*, 17. Followed by Rak, 'Il sistema delle feste', 304–5; D'Elia, *Vita popolare*, 98; and most recently Dinko Fabris, who erroneously claims that 'the festivities of 1658 were the only ones at which the viceregal regime succeeded in imposing bullfights in spectacular fashion in Naples', in 'Musical Festivals at a Capital without a Court: Spanish Naples from Charles V (1535) to Philip V (1702)', in *Court Festivals*, ed. Mulryne and Goldring, 280.

96 See one such reference in Confuorto, *Giornali*, I, 28.

97 For entries and cavalcades see for example the series of compositions written by Antonio Bulifon related to the visit of Philip V to Naples at the beginning of the eighteenth century. These do not bear the usual sumptuous format of the festival book, but follow closely the aforementioned stylistic requirements of the genre. *Lettera scritta da A.B. a un suo amico in Francia. Dove gli da ragguaglio delle Feste fatte in Napoli coll'occasione della pubblica entrata fatta in essa Città da Filippo V, Monarca delle Spagne* (Naples, 1702); *Altra lettera scritta da A. B. a un suo amico. Nella quale gli da ragguaglio della Seconda Cavalcata fatta a napoli per la solenne entrata dell'Eminentissimo Sig. Cardinal Carlo Barberini, mandato da Sua Santità in qualità di suo Legato a latere a Filippo V monarca delle Spagne* (Naples, 1702); *Distinta, e sincera relazione della regal cavalcata fatta per il publico ingresso in questa fedelissima città di Napoli del gloriosissimo Nostro monarca Filippo Quinto dà Titolati, cavalieri, e Baroni di questo Regno, trà quali tre cardinali, molti Principi, e Signori Romani. Con tutte le solennità, che in funzioni così grandi accostumansi. Seguita il dì 20 di Maggio 1702* (Naples, 1702); and *Giornale del Viaggio d'Italia Dell'Invittissimo e gloriosissimo Monarca Filippo V Re delle Spagne, e di Napoli, etc. Nel quale si da ragguaglio delle cose dalla M.S. in Italia adoperate dal dì di 6 d'Aprile, nel quale approdò in Napoli, infin'al dì 16 di Novembre 1702 in cui s'imbarcò in Genova, per far ritorno in Ispagna* (Naples, 1703).

98 Valentini, *Sontuoso torneo*, 7–40. On the different forms of tournament in Europe see Helen Watanabe-O'Kelly, 'Tournaments in Europe', in *Spectaculum Europeaum*, ed. Watanabe-O'Kelly and Béhar, 595–720.

99 Valentini, *Sontuoso torneo*, 40–2.

100 Castaldi, *Tributi Ossequiosi*, 39–40.

101 Domenico Antonio Parrino, *Ossequio Tributario della Fedelissima Città di Napoli per le Dimostranze Giulive nei Regii Sponsali del Cattolico, e Invittissimo Monarca Carlo Secondo colla Serenissima Principessa Maria Anna di Neoburgo, Palatina del Reno, Sotto i Felicissimi Auspicii dell'Eccelentissimo Signor D. Francesco de Benavides, Conte di S. Stefano, Viceré, e capitan Generale nel Regno di Napoli. Ragguaglio Historico* (Naples, 1690), 30. An even shorter description of the same event appears in the manuscript chronicle, BNN. MS. XV. G23, *Ragguaglio delle feste celebrate in Napoli in occasione de'Sponsali del Re Cattolico carlo II d'Austria colla Serenissima Mairanna di Neoburgo nel 1690*, fol. 205v.

102   Watanabe-O'Kelly, 'Festivals Books', 194–5.

103   See Marie-Christine Moine, *Les fêtes à la cour du Roi-Soleil, 1653–1715* (Paris, 1984), 14.

104   Raffaele Gualterotti, *Feste nelle nozze del Serenissimo D. Francesco Medici Gran Duca di Toscana, e della Sereniss. sua Consorte la Signora Bianca Cappello. Con particolar Descrizione della Sbarra ...* (Florence, 1579), 6–7.

105   See the survey on the Medicean court by Marcello Fantoni, 'The Grand Duchy of Tuscany: The Courts of the Medici, 1532–1737', in *The Princely Courts of Europe*, ed. Adamson, 255–74.

106   Strong, *Art and Power*, 50.

107   Aercke, *Gods of Play*, 27.

108   Strong, *Art and Power*, 50.

109   See Galasso, *Napoli spagnola*, II, 493–6.

110   For a general description of Spanish tournaments see Watanabe-O'Kelly, 'Tournaments in Europe', 623–7.

111   *Ibid.*, 596, 624.

112   For example, Valentini, *Sontuoso torneo*, 8.

113   Castaldi, *Tributi Ossequiosi*, 29–30.

114   Cirino, *Feste*, 104; Castaldi, *Tributi Ossequiosi*, 20–1; Parrino, *Ossequio Tributario*, 43.

115   For Spanish military values, see Raffaele Puddu, *Il soldato gentiluomo. Autoritratto di una società guerriera. La Spagna del Cinquecento* (Bologna, 1982). For the integration of Neapolitans in the Spanish army see Angelantonio Spagnoletti, *Principi italiani e Spagna nell'età barocca* (Milan, 1996), 179–228; and Gino Doria, 'I soldati napoletani nelle guerre del Brasile contro gli olandesi (1625–1641)', *ASPN*, 57 (1932), 224–50.

116   Mazzella, *Descrittione*, 325.

117   Capaccio, *Il forastiero*, 693. The Neapolitan prominence in horse rearing is evident through the influential manuals authored by Neapolitan equitation masters. The most celebrated are: Federico Grisone, *Ordini di cavalcare, et modi di conoscere le nature de' cavalli, emendare i vitii loro, et ammaestrargli per l'uso della Guerra commodita de gli huomini* (Venice, 1553); and Pirro Antonio Ferraro, *Cavallo frenato ...* (Naples, 1602). On this topic see Carlos José Hernando Sánchez, 'La gloria del caballo. Saber ecuestre y cultura caballeresca en el reino de Napoles durante el siglo XVI', in *Felipe II (1527–1598). Europa y la monarquía católica*, ed. José Martínez Millán (4 vols., Madrid, 1998), IV, 277–310.

118   Capaccio, *Il forastiero*, 742.

119   See, for example, Cirino, *Feste*, 26; and Donzelli, *Partenope*, 26.

120   Giovanni Muto, 'I segni d'honore', 182. See the same argument in Mozzillo, *Passaggio a Mezzogiorno*, 254.

121   Bouchard, *Voyage dans le Royaume de Naples*, II, 276.

122   Valentini, *Sontuoso torneo*, 7. See for example the long description of a rare piece of actual bullfighting, narrating the prominent role taken by Emanuele Carafa in Cirino, *Feste*, 104–6.

123   See their entrances into the arena in Parrino, *Ossequio Tributario*, 44–56; Cirino, *Feste*, 135–48; Valentini, *Sontuoso torneo*, 12 ff; and Castaldi, *Tributi Ossequiosi*, 30–8.

124   Castaldi, *Tributi Ossequiosi*, 20–1; *Relazione della solenne Festa de' Tori* (n.p.); Cirino, *Feste*, 11. The Duke of Estrada describes in his biography his ability to attract all the Neapolitan nobility to the bullfights due to his bold fighting technique, *Comentarios*, 312. See also Raneo, *Etiquetas*, 207.

125   Mancini, *Feste*, 29.

126   Strong, *Art and Power*, 43.

127   *Relazione della solenne Festa de' Tori* (n.p.).

128   *Ibid.*

129   Castaldi, *Tributi Ossequiosi*, 20–1.

130   Cirino, *Feste*, 107.

131   See the various essays dealing with bullfights within the vast sphere of Spanish influence: Annie Molinié-Bertrand, Jean-Paul Duviols, and Araceli Guillaume-Alonso (eds.), *Des taureaux et des*

hommes. Tauromachie et société dans le monde ibérique et ibéro-américain. Actes du colloque interna-tional (Paris, 1999).

132 Cirino, *Feste*,110–11; Castaldi, *Tributi Ossequiosi*, 21; Parrino, *Ossequio Tributario*, 43; *Relazione della solenne Festa de' Tori* (n.p.).

133 *Ibid.*

134 Rak, 'A dismisura d'uomo', 305.

135 For the various edicts see Lorenzo Giustiniani (ed.), *Nuova collezione delle prammatiche del Regno di Napoli* [hereafter *Nuova collezione*] (15 vols., Naples, 1803–8), vol. 7, 1–5.

136 For a few illustrative examples see Confuorto, *Giornali*, I, 160; II, 137, 273.

137 Mancini, *Feste*, 17.

138 See Burke, *Popular Culture*, 187.

139 Martine Boiteux, 'Chasse aux taureaux et jeux romains de la Renaissance', in *Les Jeux à la Renaissance*, ed. Philippe Ariès and Jean-Claude Margolin (Paris, 1982), 41.

140 Barletta, *Fra regola e licenza*, 365.

141 Maravall, *Culture of the Baroque*, 163.

4

Spanish fashion and the governance of appearance in viceregal Naples

The analysis of fashionable garments has the appeal, true for all forms of material culture, of the immediacy of the object studied. It deals with tangible articles, which are more cooperative to the investigation of their diffusion than abstract ideas are. Yet, maybe more than any other item of material culture, clothes give critical clues to the identity of their owners. As Daniel Roche has suggested recently: 'Clothing … has a function of communication because it is through clothing that everyone's relation to the community passes. Costume reveals, in the first place, what sex one belongs to … It reveals one's age group, one's rank, occupation, social position.'[1] But clothes are more than just the mere reflection of the multiple identities of a given individual. 'Connected with religious convictions, faith and powerful symbolic expressions, clothing is a prop to beliefs and observances, as it is to social representations. At every moment clothing expresses links with authority, suggests the sexual hierarchy of roles in the family, points to the power of beliefs both in its details and in its totality.'[2] In concordance with this comprehensive definition of fashion, this chapter will deal both with the power relationships between different political and social groups in early modern Naples, and with the larger institutions involved in the communication of dress.[3] Despite this study's greater interest in the baroque period, since the main focus will be on Spanish fashion in Naples, this chapter will begin with the sixteenth century when the grave Iberian style, kin to the spirit of the Catholic Reformation, was at the height of its success in early modern Europe. After the middle of the seventeenth century, with the waning of the religious movement and the weakening of Spain as a continental power at the expense of France, it will be the liberating and extravagant fashion created at the court of Louis XIV's Versailles that will prevail in Europe. Accordingly, this chapter will map these changes in Naples, highlighting the role of the viceroys, who, on the one hand, contributed to the diffusion of fashionable attire through personal example, and on the other hand, tried to impose their social, moral, and religious standards via sumptuary laws. In other words, the cardinal question asked is: How did clothing reflect the power of authority? Viceregal success will be measured against the response of Neapolitans to their rulers' behaviour and policies concerning dress.

Regulating appearance: Spanish fashion and the Catholic Reformation, 1517–1648

Historians agree that fashion usually follows political power.[4] During the first decades of the sixteenth century, Spain itself was influenced by the 'Emperor's new clothes'. Charles V introduced to his newly adopted Castilian court the vogue for German and Flemish styles.[5] These mainly comprised originally military fashion of slashing the outer garment with puffs of contrasting material pulled through the slashes.[6] The flamboyance of this style was enhanced by the contrasting bright colours chosen to be juxtaposed one upon the other, and by swollen sleeves, for both sexes. The liberating formulas of Northern Europe, and to some extent of the Italian Renaissance, also affected Spanish women. In the second and third decades of the century they adopted a sensual close-to-the-body style that emphasized the waist and the bust.[7] Then, towards the middle of the sixteenth century, Spanish fashion took a different turn. It was boosted by the spirit of the Counter-Reformation that was so dear to the Habsburgs, who resolutely set themselves at the side of the papacy at the forefront of the Catholic cause against Protestantism. The consolidation of Spain's political hegemony over the Italian penin-sula, and a close collaboration to promote the Catholic Reformation, encouraged the identification between Italians and Spaniards. It is perhaps not a coincidence, then, that some kinds of people in both countries shared a taste for a grave and austere style of dress, which is generally identified with the values fostered by the religious spirit of the era. So far, historians have signalled a parallelism between the traditional chronology of the Catholic Reformation and the success of Spanish fashion in Europe, roughly from the middle of the sixteenth century to the middle of the seventeenth century, but there has not been a serious exploration of the subject.[8] The following pages will try to illus-trate some of the relationships.

First, what needs to be answered is how Spanish fashion complied with the taste imposed by the religious rigour of the time. The Council of Trent did not specifically deal with the reformation of adornment and dress within secular society. However, some of the more general resolutions for the reform of morals in the lay domain involved the concern about proper appearance, and it is in this broader context that the moral regulation of clothes should be placed. The major Catholic reformers of the second half of the sixteenth century were active in the discipline of secular society. In Spain, besides the well-known operations of Jesuits, we find Cardinal Gaspar de Quiroga, Archbishop of Toledo (1577–94), who in tandem with Philip II, sought to repress blasphemy and sexually immoral activities of both lay and religious offenders through the unforgiving arm of the Spanish Inquisition.[9] In Italy, among others, we find Carlo Borromeo, the Archbishop of Milan, Gabriele Paleotti, Archbishop of Bologna, and, of course, zealous popes like Paul IV, Pius V, and Sixtus V.[10] All of them had in common an austere perception of life, usually exemplified by their own example, and an intolerant attitude towards issues of morality and groups who did not fit the Reformed Catholic

ethic. Muslims, Jews, heretics, and to some degree also prostitutes fell into a category that had to be expelled from society. If in previous centuries the Church saw prostitution as a necessary 'lesser evil' that was supposed to prevent male sexual behaviour from worse sins, the new Tridentine emphasis on the sanctity of marriage left no place for ambiguity, and rejected all forms of sexual relations outside marriage.[11] During this period prostitutes suffered serious setbacks in their status throughout the continent. When brothels were not officially closed, courtesans were meticulously ghettoized and labelled with conspicuous marks of infamy, imposed by sumptuary laws.[12]

As for those groups viewed as most liable to fall prey to the temptations of the flesh – young men and women – Church and state offered a proper model of conduct based on modesty and gravity, which were the two fundamental values stressed by Counter-Reformation authorities. These were supposed to serve as a vehicle to regain the true faith. Every single religious group during the aftermath of Trent embraced those ideals. The way of reaching them was to discipline body and soul through an ascetic regime, that among other things involved the moderation of gestures and apparel.[13] In Milan, Bologna, Ferrara, and generally the areas in the centre and north of the Italian peninsula, young males were modelled in a new image of Christians by means of schools for catechisms, sermons, and pamphlets distributed in churches. It was an image symmetrically opposed to that of the supercilious and riotous nobles, so typical of Renaissance Italy. For example, a pamphlet of 1575 exhorted: 'You will not wear pompous or slashed vestments, or feathers, or arms, but you will show modesty on the outside as on the inside.'[14] In addition, youngsters were supposed to walk with modesty in public and rush to their destination without delay. It is interesting to compare these instructions to those for nubile laywomen active in the company of St Ursula. In a passage from their formal regulation they are advised that: 'when they are in the street, they should keep their eyes low, heads veiled, and garments honestly tightened, and walk rapidly, without delay … because in every place there are diabolical perils, traps, and conspiracies'.[15] However, it is clear that the advice for the same modest conduct for young males was not meant to protect them from the outside world, but rather the other way round, as they were admonished not to make excessive noise, nor injure anyone on their way.[16] These examples show a general acknowledgement of women being the primary victims of male sexual aggression. But paradoxically, women, much more than men, were those signalled as moral offenders, who needed to be disciplined.

Many Spanish and Italian manuals for the correct 'Christian life', popular in the second half of the sixteenth century and the seventeenth century, could be cited to prove this point. Probably the most important of them, in this matter, is Juan Luis Vives' *De institutione foeminae christianae* (*Moulding of the Christian Woman*). It has been considered as the leading sixteenth-century text for instructing women, it was translated into all the major European vernacular languages, and it functioned as a standard model for sixteenth- and seventeenth-century manuals.[17] A feminist historian summarizes the author's intentions well: 'women were reserved the regime of chastity,

decorum, obedience and silence'.[18] Following Vives' steps these manuals showed a great concern with cosmetics and dress. Deep cleavages, eccentric coiffures, face make-up, and perfumes were condemned as external signs of dishonourable intentions, which invited men to think lascivious thoughts and to act upon them.[19] Erasmus of Rotterdam, who was Vives' friend, was somewhat critical of his views on the subject: 'In matters of marriage you have displayed harshness towards women; I hope you will be milder with your own. And on the issue of cosmetics, you have said too much.'[20]

However, Vives was only one of many similar voices echoing in Spain at the time. In fact, the association of feminine attire with vanity, temptation, and sin was far from being a novelty. They relied on an ancient misogynist tradition that drew on the Old and New Testaments, on the subsequent attacks made by the Fathers of the Church, and more recently on the incendiary sermons of fifteenth-century Franciscan and Dominican friars.[21] Moreover, these claims outlived the period under discussion. For example, a Catholic bishop after an earthquake in Naples commented that it was 'a scourge brandished by the merciful hand of the Almighty because of the present scandalous female fashions'.[22] These words were spoken in 1930. The innovation forwarded by the Counter-Reformation was the intensified attack coming from diverse media of communication. Along with the rhetorical tools already mentioned, extensive use was made of images in churches or in the domestic realm to teach women their expected roles and conduct in society. The Church's stress on Madonnas and female saints painted in decent and simple clothes, like the cloistered settings in which they were placed, carried a crystal-clear message.[23]

Sumptuary laws were the official way of enforcing dress codes. Sumptuary legislation was distinctively secular, as royal courts and city councils were those responsible for issuing and enforcing the laws, and economic and social rationales were probably more important for the legislators than moral transgressions. However, the texts frequently invoked moral rationales expressed in terms of preoccupation with the sin of pride, and religious authorities often influenced the process.[24] Sometimes they were involved directly, as the obvious example of the Papal States suggests. In Spain, the *junta de reformacion* (Committee of Reformation) established by Philip IV in 1623 specifically to suppress luxury, included, besides a few nobles, his Dominican confessor, and other ecclesiastics.[25] In principle, sumptuary law was gender neutral, but it was mostly directed at women. Significantly, Florentine officials who were responsible for enforcing sumptuary law were supposed to prosecute men and women alike but they were called *Ufficiali delle donne* (women's officers).[26] Similarly, in Siena they were called *donnai*.[27]

Sumptuary laws that were directed towards prostitutes show best the ideological link by which moralists tried to associate women with vice and luxurious attire. One aforementioned strategy was to impose on them marks of infamy such as conspicuous headgear. Another was to deny them luxurious clothes, but more commonly they were encouraged to wear whatever they pleased. Thus, legislators hoped to repel 'honest' ladies from sumptuous attire because of its association with sexual immorality.[28] To be sure,

sumptuary laws were problematic. They were in their nature self-defeating because the banishing of one fashion automatically created a new one to avoid prosecution.[29] Alan Hunt suggests that what mattered was not the effectiveness of the law but the mere fact of its existence. Its symbolic presence 'expressed elements of an ideological agenda and generated a sense that "something was being done" about the persistent anxieties and tensions concerning class and gender relations which fuelled the sumptuary impulse.'[30] If we are to accept this position, sumptuary laws could be used to measure the 'index of anxiety'. In Italy, compared with the fifteenth century, they doubled in number during the sixteenth and seventeenth centuries.[31] In Spain, as we will describe shortly, they reached their peak towards the middle of the seventeenth-century, when Spanish fashion started to decline. This same anxiety was evident in seventeenth-century sermons: 'O Spain! … Correct indeed this lascivious vanity of your women … Make laws that will force them not to show the neck, the shoulders and the breast … Try to reform your garments, because if you do not amend yourself, I tell you and warn you that the evils you are suffering, will only be the beginning of worse to come.'[32] But this was already a reaction to the disappearance of the grave and modest features of Spanish fashion that we will now turn to describe.

In the light of this abundant evidence it is clear why some of the features of aristocratic Spanish fashion matched the spirit of the time. For example, the enhancement of virile traits in both men and women's clothing at the expense of feminine features matched the deep suspicion of religious authorities towards female sexual temptations. Following Charles V, after the 1530s, European courtiers changed their looks.[33] If, in the fifteenth century, they generally wore long hair, clean-shaven faces, and long skirts, they now favoured full beards, moustaches, and short haircuts, proclaiming a newly discovered virility.[34] Copiously stuffed mid-thigh-length breeches replaced the skirt.[35] Their Spanish origin was emphasized in Italy where they were generally called *Sevillian breeches* (*braghesse alla sivigliana*).[36] On top they wore a long sleeved blouse covered by a close-fitting doublet, which in its more exuberant version was padded in front, giving a pot-bellied effect. It served as protective clothing, offering defence to vulnerable parts of the body. It was practical, in case of a duel, but it also served aesthetically to construct a martial and heroic male image. The most extreme example of this trend is the growing of the codpiece (*bragueta*) to an erected phallic icon that ultimately emphasized the male organ more than it concealed it.[37]

The rigidity apparent in male clothes was even more pronounced in women's attire.[38] A linen corset was tightly fitted to the waist. Upon that came a confining bodice which flattened the bust. These constrictions were nothing compared with what the English called the *Spanish farthingale* (*verdugado*). It has recently been noted that it was 'perhaps the most cumbersome and uncomfortable device ever incorporated into costume in its entire history'.[39] It consisted of a bulky underskirt constructed by hoops of wood or whalebone, extending towards the bottom of the skirt, which gave their wearers the shape of a bell, whose length extended from the waist down to the feet.

This curious outfit made women 'totally inaccessible, enclosed in a rich shell'.[40] Ironically, access was mostly denied to the wearer's very own body. The enormous volume of the skirt prevented a comfortable proximity to the table, and noble women had to be fed by their servants.[41] The bodice flattened the breasts, the farthingale hid the legs, and the ruff, in its original form, prevented any chance for a cleavage. The effacement of femininity was also practised by the gathering of long hair in high coiffures over the head. Noble ladies also wore a version of the man's brimmed cap. Like its male counterpart, it was usually made of velvet, richly decorated with jewels, badges or colourful feathers. However, the most popular head cover, used by Spanish women of all ranks, was a long black thick veil to be worn outdoors. It was a garment adopted from Moorish women, which served to cover the face and the hair.[42] Of women's attire, this specific item was less successful in spreading to European courts, and was mainly restricted to southern Italy. In sum, the guiding rule seems to have been the total concealment of the feminine body, as if moral integrity could have been gained and preserved by these means.

Another feature was the growing predilection for dark colours, especially black. In the loose-knit confederation of states that formed the Habsburg Empire, especially after the conflicts raised by the Reformation movement, it was paramount to preserve religious uniformity. Church and state cooperated closely to guarantee the continuation of political order and stability.[43] Accordingly, John Harvey, in his intriguing book, *Men in Black*, claims that the popularity of black cloth is completely consistent with a concerted effort to discipline and indoctrinate the masses. 'Black often has been the colour of asceticism, and asceticism is discipline whether it is inflicted by a hermit on himself, or by an overlord on a nation.'[44] Harvey also notes that different European nations have taken black as their fashion at their apex of international power. Such were the cases of Burgundy in the fifteenth century, Venice in the fifteenth and sixteenth centuries, Spain in the sixteenth century, the Dutch republic in the seventeenth century, and England in the nineteenth century. His explanation for the phenomenon is that 'the values of black ... – self-effacement and uniformity, impersonality and authority, discipline and self-discipline, a willingness to be strict and a willingness to die – might assist in maintaining an imperial order'.[45] In fact, black served as the colour of the Dominican habit – the religious order most identified with the Spanish Inquisition – but also characterized the favourite tint of four generations of Spanish monarchs, from Charles V in his mature years, to Philip IV, as shown in their contemporary official portraits.[46] Their example was emulated in Spanish and Italian princely courts. When Castiglione encouraged the model courtier to wear black and grave clothes, accrediting their Spanish origin, he was merely describing a growing convention.[47] The values promoted by black clothing can also explain the apparent paradox of Protestant extremists who adopted the Counter-Reformation's Spanish sobriety of dress, of the black suit and white ruff or collar, and made it into the Puritan uniform.[48] Similarly, Venetian patricians used to wear black togas as a long-standing tradition that preceded the black of

Spain, even though Venetian ambassadors at the Spanish court commented that Charles V dressed too soberly for his status, and they described Philip II wearing a plain black suit 'like a simple merchant'.[49]

To set the record straight, not all features of Spanish fashion implied modesty and gravity. A sweeping passage to dark colours did not necessarily mean a complete moderation of ostentatious appearance. Luxury could still be displayed through such expensive textiles as silk, velvet, and brocade. In addition, black seemed to function better than any other hue as a background to valuable adornments of silver, gold, and precious stones. Spanish fashionable clothes achieved the same effect as a dark velvet jewellery box.[50] Moreover, black clothes functioned as status markers *per se*, because the strenuous and expensive procedure of their dye resulted in elevated prices for consumers.[51] These prices rose further at times of growing demand for black cloth. For example, when a rumour of Philip IV's death reached Naples, the cloth merchants removed all the black cloth from circulation in order to inflate the price once the formal announcement was made.[52]

Another badge of status, typical of Spanish fashion, was the ruff that was worn by both sexes. The distinct shape of this collar is best portrayed by its Spanish appellation, lettuce (*lechugilla*). It restricted head movements and implied the inability for manual work that was so cherished by Spanish aristocrats, who punctiliously avoided any activity leading to *dérogeance*.[53] Curiously, despite the general adoption of Spanish fashion, Englishwomen found a curious way of circumventing the ruff's strictness. 'The Elizabethan compromise', as James Laver put it, was to open the ruff in front in a way that allowed a relatively exposed cleavage.[54] These characteristics of noble aloofness were stressed further by the postures and gestures caused by the rigid clothes. Women encased in a farthingale and corset, and men dressed in cuirass-like clothing, were obliged to advance in a stately dignified manner. This seems to fit well the comment of a fashion theorist: 'different fashions and clothes … determine the movements that they enable us or force us to make that are much the fashion as the garments themselves'.[55] However, a wholly mechanistic explanation of posture seems problematic here. Spanish courtiers and ministers faced a general pan-European censure for having a petrified and affected posture, even when most European courts shared that same style of clothing.[56] In sum, it seems to me that the gravity of Spanish clothes and deportment was shared by both sexes, but on the issue of modesty there was a gender divide. While women usually conformed to it, men carried themselves with an arrogance and superciliousness that was destined to become proverbial.

Nevertheless, outsiders visiting Spain were deeply impressed by the relative frugality of the local attire. The French Madame D'Aulnoy found the black outfit 'indeed so unflattering for a man, however handsome he might be otherwise, that it seems they have chosen the least likeable dress of all, to which the eyes cannot accustom themselves'.[57] Other foreign travellers supplied a very modest and devout portrait of Spanish females, covered with a great veil of black cloth, and showing no more than

their right eye when they walked in the streets, which occured mostly on their way to church.[58] D'Aulnoy added another religious dimension to women's appearance: 'they wear belts full of plaques and reliquaries. Numerous churches do not have so many.' They also wore a cord belt representing one of the religious orders in order to symbolize vows they made to the saints. With a pinch of malice she also adds: 'What is the motive for these vows?'[59] It is indicative that the Milanese archbishop Carlo Borromeo, while describing the appropriate fashion of dress for Ursuline laywomen, names almost the same features. The allowed colours of dress are white, black, or other dark shades. Their bodice has to be closed up to the neck. Out of their house they must wear a veil. At their waists they should wear a string that symbolizes exterior mortification, and perfect internal chastity.[60]

How successful was the Spanish style in Italy? During the first decades following the Council of Trent, especially in Milan and Naples where the Spanish ruled, it played a predominant part with all the features already mentioned. In other places it found only a partial fortune.[61] Vecellio's celebrated costume book that was first published in 1590 shows how well the Spanish fashion succeeded among males. Florentine, Milanese, Neapolitan, and Roman nobles are portrayed wearing the same Spanish fashion. He explains this, claiming that 'almost all Italian gentlemen wear the same dress'.[62] The colour black, at least until the closure of the century, was universally accepted. The farthingale succeeded in Genoa and Venice, but did not make an appeal in Bologna and Rome.[63] The Roman author of a journal in the first half of the seventeenth century described the similarity of appearance between men and women in the capital of Christianity, according to the virile Spanish style. They wore their hair almost identically, long at the sides and shorter at the back, just at the height of the collar, and they also shared a predilection for black cloth. He commented that this similarity was so striking that a person seeing a woman at church, especially if she was kneeling, might have easily mistaken her for a young man without a hat.[64] The ruff was generally accepted by both sexes throughout the Italian peninsula, with the exception of Venetian ladies who clung right through this era to their *décolletage*. The comparison of Vecellio's description of Neapolitan women with Venetians emphasized the differences in moral standards. While the former 'go about … closed and secured in their bosoms', the latter wear such low-cut cleavages 'that it is almost possible to see their entire breasts'.[65] Vecellio was probably exaggerating, but visitors to the city were profoundly scandalized at the ladies' boldness in adding cosmetics to the visible parts of the chest.[66] However, the spirit of moral reform was also felt in Venice after the middle of the sixteenth century. In 1562 the Venetian magistrates promulgated a law against cleavages commenting that it was proper for women to dress parsimoniously, and with the appropriate honesty.[67] However, no serious measures were taken to punish the transgressors, who simply ignored the decree.

In fact, Venice seems to have been unusually liberal in comparison with the rest of Italy in exposing the feminine body, contrary to the Spanish style. A sign of this

liberality might be heard through the voice of Cornelia, one of the interlocutors in Moderata Fonte's book *The Worth of Women: Wherein is Clearly Revealed Their Nobility and Their Superiority to Men*. 'One thing that's certain ... is that Venetian women dress in a more attractive manner than women elsewhere ... Women from outside Venice, on the other hand, often look mannish rather than feminine.'[68] One is tempted to exaggerate Venetian liberality, considering not only that feminine bodies were allowed to be seen, but also that women's voices were allowed to be heard. Fonte together with Lucrezia Marinella and Arcangela Tarabotti made a peculiar group of Venetian extraction, whose works were published between the late sixteenth century and the seventeenth century, where bold accusations were formulated against male despotism over their gender. Concerning the issue of fashion, they vindicated the right of women to embellish themselves and emphasized the existence of male vanity, alongside the female – a fact that had been conveniently omitted by male detractors.[69]

It would be mistaken to think that these single Venetian voices were the only female reactions. Women had a way of fighting back in a subtle way from within the system. Those same garments that were promoted by Counter-Reformation moralists proved to be exploitable for feminine subterfuge. Juan Sempere y Guarinos, an eighteenth-century Spaniard evaluating the phenomenon, illustrates best the ambivalence of the dress of Spanish women, known as *tapadas* (tightly dressed and veiled), which was massively introduced during the reign of Philip II. Apparently, this is a style that moralists would have gladly embraced because 'it invalidated a great part of luxury's appeal, making many adornments void and superfluous, since they could not be seen; it [fostered] a more decent deportment, through the covering of the face, the breasts and the hands; and last because, with such a camouflage one could donate to many charities, and do other good deeds, without showing where they come from'. However, he also warns that 'malice, which is always more pervasive and common than virtue ... effectively abused the same device for other different ends, such as deceiving, cursing, mocking the vigilance and care of fathers'.[70] It is not surprising, then, that the bans promulgated against the use of veils, beginning with Philip II in 1594 and continuing all through the reigns of his Habsburg successors, failed as they encountered a strong resistance.[71] Perhaps the most severe of those decrees was the one of Philip III, issued in 1611. Not only did it forbid women to cover their head and face, in order to be recognizable, it also obliged them to be accompanied, whenever in public, by a male member of their family – husband, father, son, or grandfather – apparently to prevent them from damaging the family's honour.[72] In Italy, Church and state differed on this issue. While the Church would have had women veiled, as symbolizing religious piety and sexual modesty, the secular authorities were concerned that women would abuse anonymity to transgress sumptuary limitations.[73] Likewise, in Venice women were forbidden to put on carnival masks beyond the official festive season to avoid their transgression of sumptuary restrictions.[74]

The same was true for the farthingale. An anonymous Genoese author insinuated with malice that young Genoese males particularly favoured this cumbersome gown.

He claimed that despite its total covering of the legs, it often allowed 'a beautiful sight' when its poor wearer tried to sit, or when her admirers strategically placed themselves at the bottom of a staircase to peek under the bulky skirt.[75] But the main objection to it is evident in the change of its name from *verdugado* to *guardainfante* (*babykeeper*) when towards the 1630s it was reintroduced into Spain and Italy in its exaggerated French version. The implication was that women not only concealed their legs but were also able to hide illegitimate pregnancies. Like the veil it provoked the criticisms of moralists and satirists, and was eventually banned by Philip IV's decree of 1639: 'His Majesty orders that no woman, whatever her quality, shall wear a *guardainfante*; which is a costly, superfluous, painful, ugly, disproportionate, lascivious, indecent article of dress, giving rise to sin on the part of the wearers and on that of men for their sakes. The only exception to this rule shall be public prostitutes.'[76] Playing on a similar theme, in Perugia, as early as 1508, probably referring to some precocious version of Spanish *verdugado*, it was forbidden to carry a circle of iron, wood, or any other thing under the skirt, claiming that it might cause an abortion.[77]

In sum, the self-effacing qualities of Spanish fashion proved to be carriers of freedom, just as they could be symbols of oppression. The laws promulgated against veils and *guardainfantes* were generally ignored, and they only serve to illustrate the men's fear of their women evading patriarchal vigilance. One might add that they fitted well into the atmosphere of simulation and dissimulation that characterized the baroque era. Philip IV can be cast in the same ambivalent role, as he was always described as wearing black and standing as rigid as a statue, apparently a God-ordained source of modesty, gravity, and self-restraint. Nevertheless, his friend the nun María of Agreda used to reprehend him: 'Sir, a king is no king if he cannot rule his self and govern and dominate over his passions and appetites.'[78] His exemplary appearance could not change the fact that he was a notorious womanizer.

The age of Spanish fashion ended with the introduction of French styles. What was the secret of their allure? It is worth quoting Adelaide Cirillo Mastrocinque, the greatest expert on Neapolitan costume, who explains why Neapolitans, along with the rest of the peninsula, simply traded one style for the other: 'to wear French clothes means freeing the neck from the tortures of ruffs, the shoulder from the epaulettes, the body from the corsets. For women it also means to free the tight braids from above the head … into soft rolls; for men to wear long hair … and colour, joy, ribbons, laces and false nonchalance for everyone.'[79] In other words, feminine features relinquished all the previous virile traits, as women started revealing their bodies and their hair, and men started to adopt more soft and feminine clothes and accessories, while the grave qualities were tossed aside by both sexes. The darts of male critics were finally starting to target men alongside women, labelling them effeminate and corrupt, although these charges still point towards the traditional sexist attribution of vanity to women.

I do not think it is a coincidence that the avalanche of sumptuary laws in Spain and Italy, which limited French fashions or tried to superimpose Spanish styles, increased

towards the Peace of Westphalia (1648), which has been marked by traditional historiography as the end of the Counter-Reformation. Part of the reason, at least for Spain,
was a rationale based on economic protectionism that aimed to limit the imports from
a hostile country, whose political and economic ascendancy certainly contributed to
the success of its luxury exports. But the features of French fashions, so antithetical to
their Spanish counterparts, and their subsequent success show a moral laxity that was
initially opposed by the authorities.

Just to mention a few examples: Philip IV banned, together with the *guardainfantes*, dresses with deep cleavages. In the case of men, he imposed the black outfit at
court, a step that suggests the decline of its appeal, he banned the fashion of wearing
long curls hanging from the side of the head, and he replaced the expensive ruff with a
new collar – the *golilla* – which was destined to become a standard requisite of Spanish
courtly dress, together with the black attire.[80] To add to the general new spirit of moral
righteousness, something similar to the example set by Girolamo Savonarola, bonfires
of vanities were made of the forbidden articles confiscated in Madrid.[81] These preoccu-
pations with the introduction of foreign fashions were naturally shared by the Church,
as the themes of overexposing dresses for women, extravagant coiffures for men, and
ostentatious clothes for both sexes, became recurrent in sermons after the middle of
the seventeenth century.[82] In Italy, the decline of black attire was also evident as laws in
Genoa and Venice tried to impose it on patricians, and in Tuscany it was enforced upon
married women. In Naples and Milan French fashions were categorically banned, and
periwigs together with laces and other ornaments associated with the new libertine
style found a general opposition throughout the peninsula.[83] All was in vain. Ultimately,
moralists and conservatives in both countries had to give in to the French style.

This point can be best proved by examining the policy of Pope Innocent XI, facing
the massive introduction of French fashions in Rome. In 1683 he called for a congregation of five churchmen, asking for their opinion concerning the use of excommunica-
tion as a punishment for women infringing sumptuary laws.[84] The advisers suggested
withdrawing this extreme punishment, but their decision was more influenced by the
fear of defeat than by tolerance. A passage from the answer of the Jesuit Father Requesens best formulates the general concern shared by the congregation: 'they will not care
much for this new augmentation of excommunications, and if this happens ... I am
afraid his [Holiness's] law will be mocked ..., and at the same time his authority will
remain spoiled of the most potent arm that the Church uses as a last resort in the most
relevant issues of Christianity.'[85] The Church had to raise the white flag in submission
but it was indeed an ephemeral victory for women. They were able to trade black cloth
for colourful material, the veil for a periwig, the ruff for a *décolletage*, but they remained
strictly cloistered in the roles that the androcentric society had assigned them.

Successes and limitations of Spanish fashion

Having described the specific characteristics of Spanish dress and the reason for its success, we may proceed to highlight its influence in Naples. The purpose of this section will be twofold. First, it will trace the presence of these specific garments in early modern Naples, and the means whereby they were introduced. Second, it will focus on the different forces at play in the communication of dress, and its orchestration by the Spanish authorities.

The costume historian Cirillo Mastrocinque asserts that in the sixteenth century Naples was an uncontested stronghold of Spanish dress. Accordingly, brocades of silver and gold begin to wane after the middle of the century, under 'the dark cloud' of the Counter-Reformation, aided by sumptuary laws and the righteous exempla given by the sovereigns. The standard look for men, which is reflected in contemporary portraits, was a black attire, a shaven head, a neatly trimmed beard, and, of course, ruffs. These 'will become the very symbol of Neapolitan costume'.[86] Indeed, recent quantitative findings uncovered by Sonia Scognamiglio Cestaro and Silvana Musella Guida in sixteenth-century inventories seem to confirm the pervasive use of black.[87] This tenebrous style drove the mordacious and melancholic poetry of Tommaso Campanella, himself an exemplary victim of religious persecution:

> Black robes befit our age. Once they were white,
> Next many-hued; now dark as Afric's Moor,
> Night-black, infernal, traitorous, obscure,
> Horrid with ignorance and sick with fright.
> For very shame we shun all colours bright,
> Who mourn our end – the tyrants we endure,
> The chains, the noose, the lead, the snares, the lure – Our dismal heroes, our souls Sunk in the night.[88]

Women followed Spanish constrictive fashions just as well. We have already mentioned Vecellio's description of the exaggerated fastening of Neapolitan ladies' bosoms. Apparently, they did not show much of their legs either, if we are to believe the marquis Giovan Battista del Tufo, who described them as 'light, lovely and slim under their farthingales (*verdocati*) or their skirts'.[89] We can further deduce the vast spread of farthingales from a legal document, issued by the viceroy the Duke of Alcalà in 1559, which was generally meant to ban luxurious garments, but permitted women to wear the bulky skirts within certain limits.[90] The self-effacing Spanish feminine cover also seems to be popular according to Vecellio: 'modern Neapolitan noblewomen … wear outdoors a very thin, black silk mantilla'.[91] An especially telling testimony is given by the Genoese diplomat Giovan Vincenzo Imperiale describing a young Neapolitan widow, wearing her mourning clothes. These were those modest and sober garments, whose main purpose was to expunge any hints of sexuality, matching the conduct expected from ideal ladies, especially if they were widows. However, Imperiale saw right through

them, 'because, as the flames on earth are more resplendent in the midst of night's obscurities, so the rays of that face shone more vehemently between the black of those clothes'.[92] In a half-adulatory, half-malicious tone, he describes her humble clothes, which made her beauty only more evident as it was more concealed, as well as her derivative attitude. 'That gravity of pace ... that modesty of the eyes, that bashfulness of glance, that perfect deportment in conversation, that ostentation of self-disparagement' deserved all the praise. That is 'if only she could be absolved from the suspicion of which Tasso spoke: "Her careless manners are artifices." '[93] In sum, even Imperiale's relatively sympathetic comment opens a window on the standard male perspective of women in the era – the ever-lurking temptress, whose camouflage in rigorous clothes and a chaste attitude made her all the more dangerous.

This trend continued until the first decades of the seventeenth century, when 'the French fashion arrives to subvert everything that had been in use in a long season of Spanish influences'.[94] Who was responsible for making sure that the 'Spanish season' continued? More importantly, how could this be achieved? Giovanni Muto has accurately pointed out that the viceregal court of Naples functioned not just as 'a mere vehicle of power' but also as an institution that embodied a delegated and distant sovereignty.[95] One of the principal vehicles whereby this delegated court had in its power to represent the monarchy was through ostentatious dress, worn on the occasion of meticulously arranged events of pageantry. In the next few pages, I will present a few telling examples, which will illustrate this symbolical form of political behaviour.

Let us start with a banquet organized by the viceroy the Duke of Osuna (1616–20) and his wife in 1617. Twelve noble girls from the highest ranks of the Neapolitan nobility were chosen by the viceregal couple to be dressed at their expense. The entire outfit included some of the classic elements of Spanish fashion for women, although extremely luxurious in essence. These were: a white satin farthingale with golden trims, a long matching jerkin, a veil made of thin silver cloth, a crown made of white feathers, and a pair of Spanish slippers (*chinelas*). It is safe to assume that the predominant white colour of the garments was intended to symbolize the premarital, virginal, candid-white status of these youngsters. Each of these ensembles had cost the considerable amount of 600 *ducati*, and was donated to the girls. No less revealing than this direct top-down fashion influence was the reaction of the viceroy when two girls from the Carafa family declined the invitation. The enraged Osuna banned the entire family from entering the palace.[96] His generous offer was one that could not be refused.

Another example of 'sartorial patronage' on behalf of Osuna can be demonstrated by his initiative during the Carnival of 1617. Not only did he ordain that anyone could wear whatever one pleased, according to the customary norm on these festive occasions,[97] but he also promised prizes for 'new and ridiculous inventions'. He gave an example by appearing in Turkish garb, and a big turban.[98] Osuna relied on a Spanish tradition, dating back to the war of liberation against the Moors in the late fifteenth century, in which his co-nationals masqueraded in Muslim costumes. Its penetration

into Naples was conveyed through Spanish-sponsored tournaments of Arabic origin, such as the reed spear tournament, performed in traditional Arabic costumes.[99] However, the choice of the viceroy's costume also had a clear political meaning. As the chief commander of the kingdom's army one of his primary military goals was to defend Naples from the Turkish menace lurking around the Italian shores. Therefore, using Carnival's meaning of temporarily turning the world upside down, Osuna's costume really meant to represent him, in the real world, as the complete opposite of his costume, namely the sheer personification of the anti-Turk.

Like Osuna, Neapolitans found in Muslim costumes an appealing carnivalesque option, probably because of that element of subterfuge. Perhaps it is not a coincidence, then, that the fishermen – one of the more wretched groups of Neapolitan society, from whom came the famous Neapolitan rebel Masaniello – had long worn it.[100] Finally, another interesting example on this subject can be found, in 1686, when the viceroy the Marquis of Carpio launched a series of festivities giving thanks for the seizure of Buda from Turkish hands by the imperial forces. The programme of the celebrations included a mock battle between the Muslim defenders and the Christian liberators.[101] It was something like the pan-Iberian folkloristic re-enactment of the expulsion of the Moors from Granada, with the difference that Spaniards keep the tradition alive up to this very day.

In 1696 the Viceroy chose to celebrate the restoration of Charles II's health by organizing a parade of masquerades, which aimed to produce a *tour de force* that would camouflage the fragile state of the monarchy. The highlight of the parade included fourteen nobles on horseback, each one representing one of the Spanish realms throughout the world. Each one wore the colours and the insignia of the realm he represented.[102] Apparently, the idea was borrowed from similar displays used at royal funerals. There, instead of knights parading the arms of the various kingdoms, the coats of arms were raised upon banners that were exhibited around the mausoleum. But the idea was the same – to show the continuity of the dynastic power in the various possessions.[103] Unfortunately, the background chosen for the 1696 representation was an ephemeral construction of a big volcano belching out fire and making horrific noises through the air that looked more like a 'written message on the wall' than a festive machine. If the sponsor's intention was to show the endurance of the monarchy despite the many blows it suffered, then the audience missed it. The diarist Domenico Confuorto comments that many thought 'a more merry fabrication could have been made, when relating to the reigns represented and the restored health of His Majesty, God save him'.[104] But even God could not do a thing for a chronically ill and infertile king, and, shortly after, 'the volcano' closed on the dynasty of Spanish Habsburgs.

It would be a mistake to think that only emblematic representations of Spain and the monarchy had a place in the festivities organized by the viceroy. I have already shown how, in the cavalcades, Neapolitan nobles, army officers, and rich middle-class officials fully participated alongside the Spaniards. Here, restricting the focus to sartorial issues,

I will limit myself to emphasizing the telling example of the Representatives of the City, who paraded, on certain occasions, in typical Neapolitan civic attire. José Raneo, the punctilious 'master of ceremonies', gave the precise identity of the functions at which these officials used to parade: 'In the acts of joy or entrances of kings in this city as new rulers, marriages of kings, birth of natural princes and the other *infantes* or some victory or notable enterprise'.[105] In other words, these are precisely those celebrations that are of most interest to this study, since they are organized to celebrate a casual event in relation to the rulers. The Representatives of the City saw it as an honour to participate, but they carried their own colours. They dressed in the ducal style, clothed in drapes of crimson and gold, with robes of yellow brocade, and big round golden bonnets.[106] According to Carlo Celano, the contemporary author of the most distinguished guide to Naples, the red and yellow colours that symbolized the city through the dress of the representatives had an ancient origin that descended from pre-Christian times. When the Emperor Constantine visited the city with his mother, he was greeted with two banners of red and yellow brocade representing the divinities of the sun and the moon, metaphorically personified by the imperial guests. According to local tradition, at the request of Constantine, these colours became the official insignia of the city.[107] Less important than the credibility of this story is the fact that this civic costume stayed more or less the same through the centuries. It is a classic example of what fashion theorist Malcom Barnard calls anti-fashion – a ceremonial dress that means to stress continuity, and the maintenance of the status quo.[108] To be more concrete, just as the Catholic Church tried to project an image of eternalness by means of the unchanging ceremonial dress of the popes, the city of Naples lingered on in its golden and crimson attire, allegedly untouched by external factors.

As previously hinted, the hegemony of Spanish dress in Naples found a serious challenger in France. Before assessing the consequences in Naples of this war of fashion between Spain and France, it is necessary to describe some general aspects of the phenomenon. The decline of Spanish fashion was met by the direct ascendancy of France. Part of the reason was economic. Philip III, who favoured dogmatic ideology over economic welfare, expelled the forcibly converted Muslims of Spain, the *moriscos*, in 1609–14, because their alleged relapse to Islam threatened the integrity of the Catholic faith.[109] By doing so, he doomed to failure the national textile industry, which depended largely on their weaving craftsmanship. Similarly, as already stated, morally oriented considerations on the part of the Habsburgs brought about the ban on typical Spanish attires in their own country, especially during the reign of Philip IV, when national items of fashion such as the ruff, the veil, and the farthingale were declared to be illegal. The ruff was also abandoned because of its costly maintenance, but the motivations behind the banning of the veil and the farthingale were purely moralistic. Women resisted the bans, and the garments lingered on. Nevertheless, the conceptual vacuum that was created by the prohibition of these fashions created a lot of room for alternative French styles to grow.

France, on the other hand, especially under the supervision of Colbert, Louis XIV's skilful minister, expanded and encouraged its textile industry.[110] Some of his policies played on a zero-sum logic, which implied that the reinvigoration of France had to be done at the direct expense of Spain. For example, he craftily coopted artisan elements that were attracted from the Spanish provinces of Italy to the expanding industries of France.[111] Consequently, France's success was felt throughout the continent. After the middle of the seventeenth century, the celebrated English diarist John Evelyn watched with a suspicious eye – not to say xenophobic zeal – how France had turned its fashions into a flourishing business in the English capital: 'It is plainly in their interest and they gain by it. Believe it, La Mode de France is one of the best returns they make, and feeds as many bellies as it clothes backs; or else, we should not hear of such armies, and swarmes of them, as this one City alone maintains.'[112]

However, France's success cannot be explained by negative Spanish policies alone. It was its qualitative input, the ability to create a distinctive 'look' – one that had nothing to do with the sombre and grave Spanish vogue – that seized the European imagination. In the second decade of the seventeenth century, the Spanish physician Carlos García published an essay titled *La oposición y conjunción de los dos luminares de la tierra o Antipatia de Franceses y Españoles* (*The Opposition and Conjunctions of the Two Planets of Earth or Antipathy of French and Spaniards*). Generally speaking, this is a collection of stereotypes, with a thesis that may seem very implausible to the twenty-first-century reader, even if pursued with great rhetorical skills and a delightfully amusing style, which argues for the absolute contrariety between the two nations in every possible aspect of life. So much so that 'in order to define a French there is no more proper way … to say that he is a reversed Spaniard, because the Spaniard ends where the French begins'.[113] Nevertheless, when he speaks about cultural phenomena such as dress or gesture, we walk on safer ground. I allow myself to quote him at length, because I believe his spirited tone captures well the differences of taste and style.

> If we ask a Spaniard what he thinks of French clothes, and fancy, he will not only hold them to be ill favoured, but will be scandalized at something that causes such joy and lifts the heart; for to see a troop of French upon a festive day dressed in such variety of colours, with a thousand variations of feathers and cameos, embroideries, fringes, ornaments, and gold laces, with so many hundreds of jewels, diamonds, pearls, rubies, emeralds, and topazes, that one would think the entire India was landed on them, all of which gives the appearance of a garden enamelled and interlaced with wonderful artifice of various flowers, or a beautiful field full of daisies, lilies, and violets, whose fair show wakens the senses, keeps the mind in suspense and enamours the very soul. Yet the Spaniard will say that it is the greatest folly in the world. And I am not surprised at this because in Spain the grave style is so much in use and the coloured habit so abhorred, that they force the hangman to wear a red or yellow livery to mark his shame and infamy. And if we hear the judgement of a Frenchman concerning the dress and style of a Spaniard, he will say that to go always in black is a sign of despair,

the mark of a widow, or of a person gone bankrupt, even though black is one of the most honourable colours and argues modesty, reputation, authority, and understanding.[114]

Incredible as it may sound, this antithetic nature of Spaniards and French was an accepted topos in the literature of the era. For instance, the Italian anti-Spanish publicist Traiano Boccalini explained the inclination of Spanish bureaucrats to procrastinate stately affairs as if it were the will of God, who had created the character of the French totally opposite to Spaniards. Hence, while the French were precipitous in their negotiations, Spaniards were slow and inconclusive.[115] An occasional merging of the two poles was seen as just the exception that reinforced the rule. In his autobiography, the Spanish Duke of Estrada described his friendship with a Frenchman as an unbelievable sight for whoever witnessed it. Because 'it is a rare and admirable thing to find so much love in people so different in their ages, their status, their qualities, and their nations!'[116]

Even fashion theorist John Harvey believes that an actual black and white divide existed between the two, although not ordained by divine nature or satanic intervention, as some of the supporters of the 'oppositional paradigm' would have us believe, but rather as a result of deliberate choice. 'A rising nation needs to look distinctive: and France not only wanted, but must have felt it needed, to look different from Spain.' To reach that effect, 'France, and its monarchy, made a large use of white.'[117] Various instances of French royal visitors to northern Italy, during the late sixteenth century, show clearly that white cloth played the principal role in their outfits.[118] Later on, light and colourful hues predominated in Versailles, and when in the late seventeenth century France chose a uniform for its army, the coats were white as well.[119]

This opposition between a white or colourful court and a dark and gloomy one also resulted from conscious choices based on different visions of the proper image for kingship. We have already talked about the juxtaposition of the Spanish tradition of 'private kingship' with the French one of 'public kingship'. Let us return to that point, emphasizing the element of personal appearance. From Charles V onwards, especially under his successor Philip II, the king had become a remote and exclusive figure, whose accessibility was highly restricted. This is in complete contrast with the elaborate French style of display, so masterly crafted in the hands of Louis XIV.[120] Recent commentators on European courtly life explain the motivations behind the voluntary withdrawal of the Spanish monarchy as the intention to obtain an image of omnipresence. They claim that one of the profound meanings of Velazquez' masterpiece *Las Meninas*, 'is exactly that of the hidden, yet all seeing monarchy' as the royal couple is merely glimpsed as a reflection in a mirror, craftily devised by the artist, who is being watched at a distance.[121] Apparently, the idea of 'Big Brother' was born long before the celebrated dystopia of George Orwell, *Nineteen Eighty-Four*. This same motivation, coupled with a belief in the divinely ordained ascendancy of Spain to the world's supremacy, is reflected in the Habsburgs' official portraits.[122] According to John Elliott, their strong sense of confidence prevented them from fleshing out any visible signs of royalty such as an

official throne, a sceptre, or a crown, which had to be displayed by lesser rulers. Hence, 'where, as in Habsburg Spain, the supremacy of the king is taken for granted, political imagery can be studiously understated, and . . . may well represent the ultimate in political sophistication'.[123] As a result, four generations of Spanish monarchs, from Charles V to Philip IV, usually posed for their portraits wearing nothing more than black clothes, a white ruff (later substituted by a *golilla*), and a single jewel – a neckpiece with the insignia of the Burgundian *Order of the Golden Fleece*.[124] Contrarily, in France where the purpose was to turn the general attention onto the king's persona, iconography played on the theme of the monarch as a resplendent sun, an outshining ray of light illuminating an amorphous mass of nobles.[125] Eventually, like a self-fulfilling prophecy, the image projected by the Spanish kings turned against themselves as seventeenth-century Habsburgs sank into political obscurity, while Louis XIV will always be remembered as 'the sun king'. Posed in these terms, the opposition between extroverted French and introverted Spaniards, as it is generally presented in García's narrative, can be explained as a social construction of reality that was created at court by the respective ideal types of royalty.

How did these contrasting characters affect seventeenth-century Naples? During the revolt of 1647–48, the Duke of Andria explained the difficulty involved in convincing the Neapolitan nobility to accept French protection as a problem of incompatibility. 'The Spanish humour is more apt to ours, the French being too merry and too amiable for serious and jealous people as we naturally are.'[126] According to the English traveller John Evelyn, visiting Naples in 1645, this incompatibility also received a clear expression in sartorial taste: 'They [the Neapolitans] have a deadly hatred to the French, so that some of our company were flouted at for wearing red cloakes as the mode then was.'[127] However, the second half of the seventeenth century saw the increasing success of French taste. Apparently, according to Cirillo Mastrocinque, Neapolitans just shifted from the grave Spanish style into the gay and liberating French fashion.[128] But things were not as simple and clear-cut as she would have us believe, in her ahistorical description of the French influences of fashion in Naples. Spanish fashion still lingered there, when in other parts of Europe and Italy it had already disappeared. This was especially true when there were attempts to secure its success from above.

Starting from the 1630s various bans were issued against French imports and the consumption of French fashion.[129] Most times, it also involved banishing all French residents from the realm, emphasizing the hostility even further. The decree issued by the viceroy Don Pedro de Aragón in 1667 made it very clear that the motives for such measures were due to the violation of the Peace of the Pyrenees by the King of France. Accordingly he banned the introduction of any merchandise coming from its states and the sequestration of any merchandise already existing. The decree also ordered that all French nationals leave the realm within twelve days. Exempted were only those men or women married to Neapolitan citizens, or those who had lived in the realm for no less than the last ten years.[130] It is not clear how severely enforced those laws were. From

the testimony of the French diarist and bookseller Antonio Bulifon, who chose to adopt Naples as his own home, it is clear that he did not take any chances. He married a local woman in order to avoid being banned from the realm.[131]

Nevertheless, contemporary testimonies show that Spain's anti-French reaction had some success. In 1667, Fuidoro testifies that 'in Naples there can already be seen those foreigners that used to dress in the French way together with the local inhabitants, [who] now because of the ban [against French fashion] are wearing Spanish or Italian dress'.[132] This was clearly pleasing to him, because at the beginning of the decade he expressed his clear criticism of French fashions. 'The dress used is insensate because in the midst of the winter transparent socks of silk … and thin shoes are worn, the sleeves are open and large … and wigs'.[133] In fact, one of the main arguments against French fashion was its effeminacy in men's dress. For example, Carlo Celano writes in his satirical *Gli avanzi delle poste*: 'so many jolly colours … so many ribbons on the arms, and the neck … I truly believe that a newly wed bride would be ashamed to wear them, to avoid being called immodest. They shave the face in a way that they all look like boys, although in this they are somewhat right … [because] aiming to look like women, they must not be hairy'.[134] Curiously enough, despite the evident opposite trend present in Spanish fashion, Hispanophobic Italians used the same lines of argument against it in the previous century.[135] Opponents of foreign fashions could always rely on the consensual fear of subverting categories.[136]

An episode during the harsh plague of 1656 can illustrate the relationship between dress, national identity, and phobias. Parrino tells about a rumour, one among many in those hysterical days, according to which the city was being infected by poisonous powders disseminated by foreigners. 'It was enough to have the dress, the shoes, the hat, the cape; or something else different from the common style of the citizens, to risk one's own life.'[137] Accordingly, an unfortunate Burgundian soldier had his skull fractured, after being approached by a gang of plebeians and questioned if he had 'powders'; he admitted having some, thinking they were referring to gunpowder.[138] In like manner, when the plague hit Milan earlier in that century (1630), a local woman accused a man wearing a French hat of disseminating the disease.[139] An opposite example is provided by Carlos García, whose insistence on wearing his Spanish clothes on a visit to France cost him dearly, as it invited a constant Hispanophobic persecution. So much so, that eventually he was forced to change his national clothes for French attire.[140] Following these persecutions based on garments alone one can understand the detrimental effects of the discriminatory badges used to mark disparaged categories of peoples, on which I will expand in the next section.

From Bulifon's report it is clear that the Spanish reaction was still successful in 1670, the year of his arrival in the city. The entry in his diary in the last days of 1670 begins with four words that supply nothing less than an exquisite treat for costume historians: 'The fashion this year.'[141] I dare to assume that such an introduction, which sounds as if it were extracted from a modern fashion catalogue, could have only come

from a Frenchman's lips, accustomed to a high pace of change in dress style. The rest is up to expectation: 'Nobles and burgesses mostly in the Spanish way ... with the *golilla* on their neck ... wigs in the Spanish fashion, made of long hair split over the forehead; very small straw hats ... covered with black taffeta, called Peñaranda style' (after the previous viceroy).[142] The latter is a suggestion that viceroys had the ability to influence fashion by their personal appearance – a point that will be explored shortly. Apparently, even the French chronicler took to the current fashion: 'This dress I had worn for a few months myself, but, as I felt like a voluntary prisoner in such discomfort, I made haste to free myself'.[143] It can be conjectured that his complaints were mostly directed towards the *golilla* – the notorious creation of Philip IV, which was even tighter and more uncomfortable than the ruff was.[144] Bulifon's further description of women shows the long survival of the veil, worn over their dresses, attached from behind as a gown. Just like the Spanish *tapadas*, 'they see through the aforesaid thin veil, and are not seen'.[145] This unique snapshot of a still dominant Spanish style, which might have only been a relapse into the old costume because of the anti-French bans, is doomed to an end by the early 1670s. By then, the green light for French fashion was given even in the last stronghold of Spanish dress – the court of Madrid.[146]

I have already mentioned the power of kings, such as Charles V or Louis XIV, to dictate the fashion through their personal deportment, not only to the limited realm of their own court but to much larger areas of influence. How successful were the viceroys in achieving this? Researchers dealing with the history of costume usually work with two major sources: visual images and written evidence. Unfortunately, we have very few remaining iconographic testimonies of viceroys. Contemporary written sources tell that the famous Neapolitan artist Massimo Stanzione received a commission from the viceroy, the Count of Oñate to portray all the viceroys, starting from the first, Gonzalo de Córdoba, and up to his day. Once they were completed, these were exhibited in one of the rooms of the Royal Palace.[147] These reports only serve to tease our imagination, as none of the portraits have survived to our time. We can only conjecture what was present in those canvases from engravings and prints left from the seventeenth century.

The most important of these sources is the illustrated version of Parrino's *Teatro eroico*, which adds woodcuts of visual portraits for each of its biographical sketches of viceroys.[148] Unfortunately, the fact that the authorship of these woodcuts is not mentioned by Parrino challenges their validity as visual sources in general. Nevertheless, it seems that they hold a high degree of reliability once we corroborate them with verbal descriptions of the viceroys' appearance. Moreover, the changes in fashion that transpire from these portraits are completely consistent with the information provided by the professional literature on costume concerning the advances of fashion in the period. Accordingly, the following analysis is partly based on this visual evidence and partly on supporting literature.

At the beginning of the seventeenth century, just before its abandonment, the ruff had reached unprecedented proportions, as can clearly be seen in the portraits of the

Count of Lemos (1601–3) (Figure 1) and the Count of Benavente (1603–10) (Figure 2). One typical feature present in all the portraits from the Duke of Alcalá (1629–31) (Figure 3) to the Marquis of Los Vélez (1675–83) (Figure 4) is the disappearance of the ruff in favour of Philip IV's *golilla*. Another significant change is the return of long coiffures. The normal length limit seems to be the shoulder, but with the advancement of the century the length grew further. Beards also lost favour and they were limited to the chin. Many of the viceroys wore their moustaches long and curved upwards (Figures 5–7). Critics of this style compared them to two big question marks.[149] It is hard to tell the colour of the dress from a black and white print, but it is quite clear that their robes bore a dark shade. In fact, these changes were quite mild in comparison to those that swept European fashion during the third quarter of the century emulating the French model, and they well reflect those few that had already been accepted at the court of Madrid by the conservative Philip IV. In fact, in the last portraits of this king, he appears with these very same criteria of dress.

Despite this sketchy description, as appears in the prints, or in the aforementioned bans against French fashions issued during those years, not all viceroys rejected French fashion until the 1680s. For example, when a Genoese officer came to visit the viceroy the Count of Peñaranda in 1660, although he was 'dressed in the French way, as it has become customary in Italy', he was received by the viceroy with all terms of courtesy'.[150] Written testimonies signal the Marquis of Astorga (1672–75) as wearing military dress, which was synonymous with the French masculine outfit. It consisted of a long jacket, known in Naples as *giamberga*, with a small neck and conspicuous cuffs, a waistcoat and tight knee-length breeches. All was accompanied with lace and trimmings of gold and extravagant adornments.[151] Moreover, Astorga encouraged the nobles who accompanied him to the famous promenade at Posillipo to wear the same dress.[152] Later viceroys seem to have done much the same. According to Fuidoro, Astorga's successor, the viceroy Los Vélez, chose an eventful day as Holy Saturday to put on a wig; an action that prompted the chronicler to predict that 'it will be seen as an example to confirm whoever wore it before him and it will also create a desire to wear it for someone who did not wish to do so'.[153] This is confirmed by the visual evidence produced in the festival book of Charles II's first marriage in 1680, where Los Vélez's equestrian portrait depicts him in the French military habit with a wig on his head (see Figure 4).

The political thinker Paolo Mattia Doria dates a complete turnabout in favour of French fashion to the government of the Marquis of Carpio (1683–87), who, according to Doria, did not indulge like his predecessors in keeping up the Spanish ways.[154] In fact, like the previous viceroy, Carpio has been described as wearing the French military habit.[155] Doria claimed that this trend continued even more vigorously with Carpio's successor, the Count of Santisteban (1687–96), speculating that the viceroy expected a French dynastic succession after the imminent death of the childless Charles II. Accordingly, it was essential to 'extirpate from the hearts of the

Figure 1 *Portrait of Viceroy Count of Lemos*

Figure 2 *Portrait of Viceroy Count of Benavente*

Figure 3 *Portrait of Viceroy Duke of Alcalá*

Figure 4 *Equestrian portrait of Viceroy Marquis of Los Vélez*

Figure 5 *Portrait of Viceroy Count of Monterrey*

Figure 6 *Portrait of Viceroy Duke of Arcos*

Figure 7 *Portrait of Viceroy Pedro Antonio de Aragón*

Figure 8 *Portrait of Don Antonio Miroballo*

monarchy's peoples that old hatred towards the French nation, which has been planted meticulously by the very same Spaniards'.[156] One should not take Doria's words at face value, especially given his marked anti-Spanish bias, but there is evidence that seems to support this view. In 1691, Santisteban received alarming reports from the silk traders, who complained about a sharp decline in their business because of the mass introduction of the *giamberga*. This outfit was made of woollen cloth that obviously displaced

Figure 9 *Portrait of Don Cesare Michel Angiolo D'Avalos, Marquis of Pescara*

materials such as silk and taffeta, which had a primary role in Spanish dress.[157] The iconographic evidence seems to support Doria's view, as well. For example, in the frontispiece of the funerary book of Don Antonio Miroballo, published during Santiste-ban's rule (1695), the deceased wears the French *giamberga*. In addition, he is neatly

shaved and he wears a full-curly wig, in plain French style. And maybe most significantly, his neck is adorned with a cravat and not the famous *golilla* (Figure 8). Similarly,
Raffaele Filamondo's book, *Il genio bellicoso di Napoli* (*Naples' Warlike Character*), also
published during Santisteban's rule (1694), contains the portraits of many contemporary Neapolitan noblemen who have fully adopted the French fashion, as exemplified in
the portrait of Don Cesare Michel Angiolo D'Avalos, Marquis of Pescara, to whom the
book is dedicated (Figure 9). If, indeed, as Doria claims, Santisteban had consciously
planned the rapprochement with France, his bet was right because Philip V of Bourbon
succeeded to the Spanish throne.

With the visit of the new king, Philip V, in 1702, we may close the chapter on
Spanish dress with an anecdotal event. Representatives of the Neapolitan association
of solicitors asked the king for permission to wear French clothes, and most importantly to be able to abandon the *golilla*, when presenting a case at the courts of justice.
Not that there existed any law constraining them to appear in any way whatsoever, but
they were afraid of being ill regarded by the judges had they abandoned the conventional dress. The motion was granted, although informally, since no previous formal
rules applied.[158]

In sum, the iconography and the written reports reveal that there was a connection between the personal taste of the viceroys and the introduction of French fashion,
or rather the relinquishment of the Spanish. After the 1670s viceroys fought the French
imports by issuing ineffective decrees against them, while wearing the forbidden attire
themselves and encouraging the Neapolitan nobility to do same.

Governing appearance and luxury

As already shown, sumptuary laws were a common feature of early modern Europe,
and Naples made no exception. These laws have recently been defined as the regulation
either of personal appearance, mainly through rules relating to dress or jewellery, or
of other forms of conspicuous consumption.[159] The motivations behind them can be of
a social, economic or moral nature, or a combination of any of those. Here, the focus
will be on the policies implemented by the Spanish government in order to distinguish
between particular members and groups of society. It will be shown that rather than
promoting the Hispanic style of dress, the sumptuary laws issued by the authorities in
Naples were illustrative of Spanish biases and moral concerns.[160] The key question here
is: to what extent did Neapolitans share the social, moral, and religious values of their
Spanish rulers? This will be assessed according to the degree of compliance or resistance that the local population displayed towards the sumptuary ordinances.

In Spain, as in other Mediterranean countries, various regulations were produced
against certain minority groups of different religious faiths.[161] Spain's religiously
motivated racial policies towards Muslims and Jews, and later towards *moriscos* and

conversos, had their roots in the time of the *Reconquista*. The establishment of the Inquisition and the expulsion of Spanish Jewry mark the high points of the hard-line religious policies of the Catholic monarchs Ferdinand and Isabella, which would deeply affect the future of Spain and its colonies.[162] As already noted, these Spanish racial anxieties received a boost in Italy from the Tridentine Reformation, which endorsed a hypercritical attitude towards groups who did not fit the newly reformed Catholic ethic. Chiefly heretics, but also categories of 'out-groups' that were better tolerated before the Reformation, like Muslims, Jews, and prostitutes, were singled out as socially dangerous menaces. Each of these groups, when not completely expelled, was meticulously ghettoized in restricted areas of the city, isolated from the 'community of believers', and distinguished by conspicuous marks of infamy that were imposed by sumptuary laws. Most of these discriminating measures were not new. The novelty lay in the harshness and the zeal with which they were implemented upon all of the groups at once, especially in the Italian territories controlled by the vanguard forces of the Counter-Reformation – Spain and the papacy.[163]

Out of these groups, the Jews were the first who had to face the consequences of Spanish intolerance.[164] Already at the end of 1492, the same year as the expulsion of Spanish Jewry, King Ferdinand banished the Jews from his Sicilian and Sardinian possessions. Curiously, many found refuge in Aragonese Naples, where Ferdinand's cousin, Ferrante I, was willing to protect them.[165] Naples did not prove to be a safe harbour for long, and Jews were expelled in two consecutive waves, respectively dating from 1510 and 1541. The twitches and turns of Spain's Jewish policy in Naples until 1541, the year of their final expulsion, are less important for us, what matters is that in the final count, all the Jews where Spain ruled were expelled.[166] In the light of this evidence, historians trying to explain the radical worsening of Jews' conditions in sixteenth-century Italy find in Spain a consistent anti-Jewish factor, which eagerly promoted this general turnabout.[167] Bonazzoli goes as far as claiming that the assimilation, on behalf of the Neapolitan population, of the anti-Judaic sentiments promoted by the Spanish authorities, may not be clearly translated as a 'Castilianization', although it certainly may be considered as a strong influence that determined the 'original character' of the Italian Mezzogiorno.[168] Most interesting for this study is to examine this Spanish dissemination of anti-Jewish values through the imposition of marks of infamy on Jews.[169]

'The signs' (*segni*), as defamatory marks were called in Italy, had been ordinarily issued by Italian communes since the end of the fourteenth century, mostly because of the pressure of Franciscan preachers, although without generally being enforced. Quite often, Jews paid the fine for infraction in advance, or simply kept the distinguishing badge covered under their clothes as if it were an identification document to keep in the pocket.[170] However, during the sixteenth century, with the enforcement of the yellow or red headgear, Jews became a definite, uniform, and easily recognizable group, which, according to Roberto Bonfil, 'made the Christians feel threatened and reinforced their fear – the fear of a Jew'.[171] In 1506, Ferdinand the Catholic, aware of this stigmatizing

effect, ordered Neapolitan Jews to wear a red mark of infamy on the chest, preparing the public climate for the expulsion.[172] Not surprisingly, then, the ban was reissued in 1509, just one year before the first expulsion was carried out.[173] According to Bonazzoli, these preliminary measures and the actual delay in the expulsion resulted from internal resistance. The indigenous forces of the kingdom still did not share, at that point, the vivid anti-Jewish feelings and biases held by Spaniards, and preferred to benefit from the economic advantages created by the Jewish presence. Ferdinand's special exemption from expulsion for 200 affluent Jewish families adds support for this interpretation.[174]

The second expulsion followed a similar pattern. A decree was sent directly from Madrid in 1539, signed by Charles V. According to its letter, Jews were to be expelled. However, as a prelude to that, until the final execution of the ban, they were to be physically segregated from Christians in properly designated parts of all urban centres of the realm. In addition, men would have to wear a red or yellow barrette and women a band of the same colour.[175] Why bother to ghettoize and mark the Jews if they were to be expelled anyway? Perhaps Charles V felt the need, like his predecessor, to treat the expulsion with caution, starting with some discriminating measures to test local public opinion. A more plausible explanation is that he was just being consistent with the Spanish obsession with 'purity of blood' (*limpieza de sangre*).[176] This can be supported by Charles' arguments to implement this policy, as we will see below, which were in complete contrast to his previous proclamation, according to which the Jews of the Kingdom of Naples would not have to carry any sign, considering the great injuries that were inflicted upon them because of it.[177] However, following his visit to the Kingdom of Naples he commented to the viceroy Pedro of Toledo that the Jews there were acting with great impudence owing to their being unmarked, thus abusing the privileges he had granted them. Accordingly, perfectly adhering to the principle of *limpieza de sangre*, his greatest concern was that not only were Jews mingling freely with Christians, but they were also having amorous relationships with Christian girls, thus risking to 'infect' with their blood the whole of Christianity.[178]

The ultimate example of Spanish Judeo-phobic decrees can be found in 1572. In a practically Jewish-free Kingdom of Naples, the viceroy the Cardinal de Granvelle issued a ban against those Jews who legally entered the kingdom as pedlars in fairs. 'To avoid the many inconveniences, scandals, and bad examples given by the Jews, who relate with Christian men and women' he ordered the Jewish pedlars to wear a yellow headgear, or else face the punishment of five years in the galleys.[179] Besides the usual Spanish biases, one should take into consideration that this ban was issued at one of the most militant stages of the Counter-Reformation. Accordingly, there were instances where more extreme measures were taken than mere legislation. A year earlier, in 1571, the same year that will see the victory of Lepanto, a group of twelve Catalan women were brought to the cathedral of Naples where they supplied the subject for a 'tremendous spectacle'. Accused of having 'secretly lived in the Jewish way for many years and committing many excesses', they were displayed on a stage, wearing habits of yellow

cloth with a red cross, where they publicly repudiated their Jewish faith.[180] Two of them, not wanting to reform, were sent to Rome to be burnt at the stake. Naples was spared the burden of the Spanish Inquisition, but the above 'spectacle', even if not called that, was nothing more and nothing less than a traditional Spanish *auto-da-fé*, including the notorious penitential habit imposed on the condemned – the *San Benito*.[181] Not surprisingly, under the same viceroy, some blatant ordinances were issued for Muslims as well, as we will now turn to describe.

Muslims were not destined to be expelled from Naples, simply because their considerable numbers in the city – as many as 12,000 in the seventeenth century – comprised mostly slaves, apart from a negligible number of free people, either working as servants in their masters' mansions, or as rowers in the galleys.[182] As elsewhere in the Christian world, despite being legally defined as 'property' their souls were doctrinally perceived as vehicles of salvation and, therefore, worthy targets for conversion. Following the Tridentine pronouncements, these efforts to reform and discipline marginal groups increased. Accordingly, the viceroy promulgated in 1572 a ban whose major concern was to prevent those Muslim inhabitants who had converted to the Christian faith from relapsing back to Islam. To reach this end any relationship between Muslims and converts was forbidden. Besides, obviously, cohabitation, the ban explicitly forbade all human interaction under any pretext – business affairs, friendship, or family ties – and all possible actions – eating, drinking, sleeping, and talking. It went so far as to forbid anything more than a short exchange of words in a casual encounter. In addition, Muslims were forbidden to relate to converts in negative terms, such as physical or verbal abuse, because of their conversion. The most interesting part for us is that in order not to cause any misunderstandings on either part, all unconverted Muslims had to wear a conspicuous mark of infamy – a large yellow band on their garments.[183] Obviously, the ban not only protected those who had converted, but also aimed to push into the arms of Christianity those who had not, by means of social isolation and symbolic censure. Reading between the lines of the ordinance, one can conjecture that Muslims enjoyed considerable amounts of freedom, despite their legal position. However, the enforcement of such a ban would have certainly put a halt to that. To be effective, it needed to enjoy local support, but it is hard to know to what extent Neapolitans shared the intensity of their rulers' anti-Muslim biases.[184] At any rate, to issue it in 1572, a year after the victory of Lepanto, was certainly a good moment to build on fresh anti-Muslim sentiments.

However, from a later anti-Muslim ordinance of this kind, dating from 1657, it is clear that some Muslims tried to integrate themselves into Neapolitan society without encountering a local resistance. The ban astutely picked a common 'Turkish' distinguishing sign, a lock of hair in the centre of the head, and ordained it to be compulsory. As in the Jewish case, the letter of the ordinance clearly pronounced that the greatest Spanish concern was the ability of Muslims to pass unrecognized, abusing their anonymity to deceive women.[185] It is unclear if these regulations were based on

a substantial number of such 'deceptions', or if they were simply issued to appease Spanish anxieties. Be that as it may, the following story told by Domenico Confuorto, in the summer of 1685, might as well represent the worst Spanish nightmare, when Neapolitan deputies of the law ganged up with a Muslim slave precisely in order to trick women.

> On Friday, 6 July, some police officers were sent to jail ... because with devilish astuteness they used to dress a white slave as a noble with a wig and elegant clothes, and they would send him to a house of p— [prostitutes; the word is censored in the original], as if he wished to engage in carnal commerce with them, and then, they would arrive as if to make an inspection ... showing surprise at finding the disguised slave there, they would expose him, by taking off his wig and revealing the flock of hair, which slaves must carry [as a defamatory sign] in the middle of the scalp: after which they would threaten to incarcerate the p— for copulating with the slave and thus transgressing the laws forbidding such instances ... so she, in order not be imprisoned and shamed, would have to compensate them with a sum of money, clothes, or something similar.[186]

This story presents a hilarious vignette of a world turned upside down, where the law is the villain, the slave is a noble, and the treacherous temptress is the one being tricked. But mostly it laughs in the face of the legislators' intentions, on behalf of those who are responsible for enforcing their decrees.

This total disrespect towards Spanish sensibilities conforms well to Croce's shrewd suggestion that the racial policies of Spain backfired, denigrating their own image in the eyes of Italians. Paradoxically, Spaniards came to be associated with an imperfect religious orthodoxy. The harsh repression of the Spanish Inquisition brought the Italians to the logical conclusion that such measures, necessary in the Iberian Peninsula but not in Italy, established Spanish blameworthiness.[187] The greatest irony was that, outside Spain, Spaniards were referred to as *marrani* (pigs) – the Spanish derogatory word for converted Jews. An extreme example is provided by the Neapolitan pope, Paul IV, a severe foe of Spain, who used to call them 'heretics, schismatics, and cursed by God, semen of Jews and *marrani*, dregs of the world'.[188] Poor Spaniards! Having to go through all that trouble and for what? To end up being regarded by the head of the Church as no better than the object of their persecution – poetic justice can hardly be manifested better than this. Yet, set in a proper context, Paul IV's aversion diminishes when it is weighed against the intensive Dutch and English Hispanophobe propaganda, which built on the negative image of Spanish religious orthodoxy to inflict irreparable damage to the Habsburg Empire via the international diffusion of the so-called Black Legend.[189]

Let us leap forward to explore the sumptuary intervention in the case of other groups, starting with the Spanish army, by itself an important agent of diffusion of Spanish fashion in Naples. First, it is important to note that decrees in Spain encouraged a sumptuous style of martial dress. Already in 1499, the Catholic monarchs issued

a decree permitting the usage of silks for the cavalry. During Charles V's reign, various laws were passed to restrict and regulate conspicuous consumption among all the status groups of society.[190] Exempt were only the royal family and nobles in military service. The decrees were explicit about the limits of these exemptions: 'we order that this will be valid while actually being at war and not in festivities and tournaments'.[191] Ruth Matilda Anderson has suggested a functional explanation for these concessions. 'Conspicuous luxury served as insurance for fighters. A well-dressed man on the losing side hoped to become a target for ransom instead of slaughter.'[192] If that was the reason, it did not help scores of French nobles in Pavia (1525) – or any other army after the massive introduction of gunpowder in warfare – who were decimated by distant and efficient gunfire from the Spanish infantry. True enough, superb attire might have served to distinguish officers from simple soldiers in a period that preceded the introduction of uniforms. But the importance of this distinction must have been more symbolic than functional. It may have served to elevate and rehabilitate the status of noble knights and chivalric values, whose prestige waned following the introduction of popular infantries and firearms to early modern warfare.[193]

Whatever the motivations, the same rules applied to the Kingdom of Naples, where viceroys issued similar ordinances during the sixteenth century.[194] For example, in the sumptuary law issued in 1560, soldiers and captains of infantry were exempted from all restrictions.[195] Similarly, the sumptuary law issued by the viceroy the Count of Olivares declared that 'only the soldiers from either the cavalry or the infantry shall be exempted'.[196] The same exemptions were reissued in the seventeenth century.[197] Neapolitan nobles serving in the Spanish army complied with an exuberant display. Among other things, they exhibited stupendous brocade outfits, capes with satin lining, feathered bonnets, arms encrusted with jewellery, and pedigree horses wearing covers with their coats of arms. In addition, every single noble brought an entire army of liverymen, pages, and servants, all displaying a rich livery.[198]

Eventually, the influence of such display permeated to the lower ranks of the army. This is evident in the narratives of Spanish soldiers who served in Naples. Estrada described his galleon as a 'forest of feathers, because everyone had them … and with so many colours that we resembled a big cage of parrots'.[199] Apparently, Estrada's description matches a return of a colourful style, after a generally gloomy adoption of dark fabrics even among the military, following the Counter-Reformation's spirit during the second half of the sixteenth century. According to Raffaele Puddu this was imposed from above since the high expense of war pushed Philip II to issue harsh sumptuary laws that included the military orders.[200] A contemporary testimony lamented such changes, and indulged in nostalgic reminiscences of past military fashions: 'All the soldiers in the past used to wear colourful clothes … and it is very clear, that ten thousand armed soldiers wearing colourful clothes make a bulge, and cause more fear than twenty thousand, especially if they are wearing black. In no sort of people is it worse to alter than in the case of the military, by losing what our ancestors have left for us as a legacy.'[201]

The sumptuary law of 1562 issued in Naples by the viceroy the Duke of Alcalá (1559–71) brings further evidence for Puddu's claim concerning the attempt to reform the sumptuary expenditures of Spanish soldiers during Philip II reign. One of the restrictions addressed the excessive padding of breeches, 'considering the … abuse … in consuming and using so much cloth and silk' in them. This expenditure was alleged to 'cause great poverty among soldiers and commoners'. In addition, it was claimed that this fashion was 'useless and restricting for all men, especially to horsemen and soldiers, be they Spanish or Italian'.[202] This preoccupation with the impoverishment of the troops has a distinct ring of hypocrisy. The economic strain on the Spanish army derived much more from the administration's notorious policy of withholding the troops' salaries than from soldiers' personal indulgence in luxuries. Noting their misery, Fuidoro testified sympathetically that 'these people of the *Armada* find themselves mistreated by [the delay of] thirteen salaries … and they see the delicacies but do not have the money to taste them'.[203] Similarly, Bulifon tells of thirteen Spanish soldiers, who were caught in their attempt to desert in September 1670, 'and it was not to their avail to say that they were running away for not being paid, and that they were starving'.[204] These descriptions represent well a gloomy situation, as it is often reported in the testimonies of Spanish soldiers, true of the entire span of Spanish rule.[205]

The reverse of the coin is the great expenditure on military parades. The viceroys' understanding of the necessity to appear well aided him putting aside any concerns for the soldiers' conspicuous consumption, and forgetting about the increasing debts and economic constraints of the Spanish Empire during the seventeenth century. One telling example is the military parade organized by the Duke of Alba, following the Mantuan war of succession (1627–29).[206] According to José Raneo, the Duke of Alba found an 'extremely important solution' whereby to minimize any damages that might have been caused to the Kingdom of Naples owing to the general unrest caused by the war – a majestic display of power to 'terrorize' the enemies of the monarchy. Cavalry, infantry, and troops in reserve, dispersed throughout the kingdom, were all summoned to take part in the event. In order to put on a great gala display, large sums of money were released, to be spent on sumptuous dress and on gunpowder to use on that day. In order to cover the expenses, an ephemeral construction around the designated arena of the event was erected for paying spectators, 'each seat costing a lot of money'.[207] Here is the description of some of the forces present in the parade: 'The reserve troops … with many sumptuous outfits, bands, feathers, and plaques, each one having the possibility to appear very elegant, since His Excellency ordered the release of funds for the matter. There were also many princes and titled nobles and particular knights … with very … expensive horses, their persons loaded with jewels, the splendour of which dazzled the eye.'[208] The supreme leader gave an appropriate example: 'His Excellency arrived, and mounted on a vigorous, richly decorated horse, with his baton of command in his hand and a collar at his neck and so elegant … that he was envied by many.'[209] Summing up,

Raneo ensured that 'this notable action gave a lot to see and fear to the envious enemies of the Sacred and Royal Crown of Spain'.[210]

Despite the organizers' intentions, actions like these also gave excellent opportunities for critics and satirists. The Genoese diplomat Gian Vincenzo Imperiale describing a similar parade a few years later seemed to be much more amused than impressed. For example, invoking the stereotype of Spanish measured and impassive movements, he described a company of halberdiers as 'marching without marching … at such a moderate pace that it is clear that although they are dressed in the German style, their manner is Spanish'.[211]

Analogously, exploiting Spanish stereotypes while gazing with sarcasm at the gallantry of Spanish and Neapolitan troops, Italian playwrights re-invented the comic type of the Spanish braggart soldier, following the Ancient Roman type of *miles gloriosus* who became popular in theatrical representations from the middle of the sixteenth century onwards.[212] In his *Galateo*, Monsignor Giovanni della Casa portrayed Spanish military costumes as a serious threat to Italian urban values. 'These same feathers which the Neapolitanes and the Spaniardes be wont to weare, and braveries and embroideries; have but ill place amongst grave gowned men, & the attires that Citizens doe weare. But their Armour and weapons become suche place a greate deal worse.'[213] For instance, if they were to visit Venice, 'all begarded, and huffing in feathers, & warlike fellowes, would not doe well, in this Noble Citie so peacefull & Civil. Suche kinde of people be rather, in maner, like nettles and burres, amongst good and sweete garden flowers.'[214] As a matter of fact, 'bad weeds' died hard, and men pursuing military careers, besides the temporary parenthesis of Philip II's reign, did not moderate their styles. On the contrary, in the seventeenth century, with the introduction of French fashions, the appearance of fighters would reach a new climax, as would the criticisms.

The date 6 November 1683 marks a milestone in viceregal intervention concerning the army's dress. On that day, honouring the birthday of Charles II, formal uniforms were created. Unfortunately, we do not have a description of the garments other than the colours: yellow for halberdiers, red for the Spanish infantry, turquoise for the Italian infantry, and purple for the cavalry. These changes were enforced by means of a decree that forbade the usage of colours other than those designated.[215] Does this mean that uniforms, which usually function as a levelling factor, put a stop to the previously noted extravagance? From the general conduct of the Neapolitan nobility in matters of luxury and precedence, the imposition of a standardized appearance within the purple group might only have amplified a stronger need for personal ostentation. If this could not be achieved within the military world, there were plenty of other opportunities in the civic Neapolitan environment, as we will demonstrate.[216]

Let us look more closely at the measures taken by the viceregal court to limit luxury.[217] According to Rosita Levi Pisetzky, the sumptuary laws issued in Naples during the second half of the sixteenth century were extremely tolerant in comparison with the other Italian states. This is because 'the brilliant Southern taste' had been taken into

consideration by the authorities. For example, pearls and precious stones on bonnets were permitted while elsewhere they had been absolutely forbidden. Men and women could wear jewellery made with gold, pearls, and precious stones of any worth, provided that they limited them to precisely foreordained areas in their attires.[218] At the same time, the bans expanded and encompassed more and more items of consumption. The viceroy the Duke of Alcalà added to the limitation on clothes some restrictions on household furnishings, and others on the expenses and excesses that were customary at funerals.[219] After the first quarter of the seventeenth century, the Duke of Alba and the Count of Monterrey further restricted the numbers of servants and carriages.[220]

Despite their relative moderation, it is clear that the laws were met with resistance. For example, in 1560 a new decree was issued in order to enforce the ordinances of the previous year, because they 'had been very badly observed so far'.[221] Similarly, the chronicler Scipione Guerra described the decree issued by the Duke of Alba, on June 1625 concerning the dress of nobles and their servants, but he added with dismissal that 'it has never been observed'.[222] The comment of the agent of the Duke of Urbino is even more cynical and revealing. He describes the enthusiastic zeal of the new viceroy, the Cardinal Borja (1620), who issues 'every day new bans and decrees … and every day we will hear new ones; until he too will accommodate himself to the customs of the country'.[223] It is most probable that Neapolitans were unimpressed by the decrees because of the general tendency of sumptuary law not to be enforced.[224]

The evidence is provided by the Neapolitan local chronicles used for this study, or rather by its absence. Thousands of examples, on a daily basis, report petty crimes and big crimes, vast law enforcement and the administration of justice over men and women from all social strata. However, I have found only a few instances of enforcement of sumptuary laws.[225] Confuorto tells of three merchants who were incarcerated in 1687 because they had spoken against the viceroy, in relation to his latest prohibition of cloth of silver.[226] Even this report has a dubious value, as it would seem that the punishment had been inflicted more to preserve the viceroy's honour than to show a real concern for any violation of the law – a fact which was not even at issue. The same Confuorto, always very informative on issues concerning rank and precedence, tells of the offence taken by the viceroy the Marquis of Carpio in July 1685 when the Marquis of Cucugliudi presented himself in a luxurious craft at the common regatta. The viceroy withdrew his vessel and his presence from the event claiming that the marquis had violated the law with his exaggerated ostentation. Despite the formal allegation, my impression, again, is that the issue was not the infringement of the law *per se* as much as the viceroy's personal concern for his honour. He just refused to be outshone by a lesser noble. Paradoxically, this time, when the law had allegedly been broken, the only measure taken against the perpetrator was to admonish him against a similar infringement in the future.[227] It is of no wonder, then, that under the same viceroy, the Duke of Mataloni showed little concern towards his superior's reaction when he aimed to display a magnificent craft of his own. Only this time, Carpio, who

caught wind of the duke's intentions, succeeded in preventing the ship from setting sail.[228]

If indeed sumptuary law was not enforced then why bother in the first place? As already suggested, the idea behind sumptuary law was not its effectiveness but its mere existence as some sort of ideal moral agenda. This theory applies well to the measures that were taken against prostitutes.[229] Time after time the same decrees were issued in order to 'distinguish the good women from the evil'.[230] Following in the footsteps of the Count of Miranda (1586–95), for more than a hundred years courtesans were prohibited from being transported in a portable chair (a sort of Neapolitan rickshaw), nor in a carriage around the city.[231] The Count of Lemos also forbade them from entering vessels on the Posillipo promenade.[232] In addition, at times, depending on the climate of religious intolerance, they were restricted from living in particular quarters of the city.[233] It is clear that by these means prostitution was legally acknowledged, while repressed at only a very superficial level. It is also very significant that often noble ladies were those initiating anti-vice campaigns. For example, the Duke of Arcos issued the same old ban, after a group of noblewomen excused themselves for not being able to attend the promenade with the viceroy's wife, because 'it was full of courtesans'.[234] The only time that serious action was taken on this matter, during the seventeenth century, at least to the best of my knowledge, was the issue of a decree to deport a limited number of specific prostitutes. Again, the initiative came from the ladies. The specific group of high-rank prostitutes (or rather courtesans) was singled out for being easily mistaken as noblewomen, 'because they used to travel in elegant carriages with pages and servants'. The accusers also claimed 'that with their whorish ways they had impoverished many noble houses'. However, most of the courtesans stayed in Naples 'thinking that when things cool down they will not have to leave'. Eventually, as a matter of fact, they were allowed to stay.[235]

The fact that in a paternalistic and hierarchic society like the one we are dealing with the authorities were moved to action from below – as women were regarded despite their social status – pinpoints the mere formality of the matter. In reality, women of all ranks had very limited power to check their husbands' extramarital passions. The common script worked the other way around: the husband killed his wife for any small suspicion of infidelity. Maria d'Avalos, Princess of Venosa, Giulia Orsino, Princess of Bisignano, and Ippolita Carafa of Stigliano are just three examples of noblewomen of the highest ranks who were 'executed' by their families for adultery.[236] Similarly, the Prince of Caserta was instantly killed by seven shots, fired at him by anonymous assassins 'for coveting the wives of others'.[237] Usually, the killers were left unpunished. As often happens, the authorities were ready to look the other way when society found a consensual form of justice, however crude and cruel it might have been.

Some of the records show that there were other, less sanguinary, informal ways of social control in play. For example, on different occasions, social groups that aspired to more than the social status in which they were born were restrained through ridicule.

A relevant example, related to sartorial issues, was the fate of the participants in a parade organized by the Count of Lemos in 1615, intended for the opening of a scientific academy. Lawyers, medical doctors, and theologians each paraded in a distinctive livery, bearing the colours that were used by those same groups in Spain. But the proud procession was maimed by dames watching from their windows who 'could not contain their laughter, because these ladies felt they were gazing more at a masquerade, than at a procession of doctors'. If that was not enough, the function was completely ruined when once arrived at the academy the intellectuals began to fight over precedence. Of course, such fights were the essence of noble life, and as such they were regarded with all seriousness, but to see this coming from social inferiors was interpreted as a colossal joke. The viceroy, the ladies, and the common people present all shared 'so much laughter and with so much vigour, that these ... were forced to run away and take off their clothes, aware ... of being universally scorned'.[238] Similarly, one rich parvenu wanting to celebrate his social accession to the rank of marquis made a huge celebration inviting all the cream of society, 'spending many thousands of ducats'. His new peers 'after having filled their stomachs ... and taking pleasure from the sights, the tastes, and the sounds, started to mock and deride the solemn madness of the new marquis'.[239]

An opposite example is given by the stir that arose after the public humiliation of a noble by the viceroy the Duke of Osuna (1582–86). Well aware of the importance of appearance among Neapolitan nobility, he inflicted a peculiar punishment on Carlo Tocco, Count of Monte Miletto, for having violated his ordained exile. The count was placed in an open carriage, in order to allow a public view, with a chain on his leg. Thus he was driven through the noble quarters of the city. The effect wished for was well achieved, since the mortification of the count, 'for being exposed in that manner around Naples like a bandit', drove him to attempt suicide on the spot with a knife seized from the hands of a deputy. This time, nobles did not find the incident hilarious at all, claiming that 'a person of such quality should have not received such a punishment'. In addition to their condemnation, they tried to bring the matter to the king himself, openly challenging the viceroy's authority and judgement, but the viceroy was able to prevent the motion.[240] The nobility knew how to look after its own kind, even when it meant defying the viceroy, just as it knew how to keep away those who did not belong to its ranks.

It goes without saying that most of the time the Spanish administration and the nobility worked in close cooperation. Their common goal was to make sure that the social hierarchy remained stable, a fact symbolized by the acceptance of their sartorial pre-eminence by the lower social groups. When in 1647 their hegemonic grasp failed, Masaniello, a young fisherman, barefoot and wearing rags, took the reins of command. It is interesting to note the comment of Fuidoro about the suspicion of there being someone behind Masaniello, who 'used to appear barefoot, with cloth breeches and a blouse, and a white cloth barrette, giving instantaneous orders and issuing decrees to the people'.[241] It is remarkable that despite Masaniello's meteoric success he did not

abandon his simple clothes. He made only two exceptions. The first time, he wore a silver-white outfit in order to meet the viceroy and reach a settlement. The second time, he wore the same dress to attend to the ceremonial signature of concessions made by Spain to the people of Naples, which were forced by the revolt.[242] Even then, it appears that he agreed to wear the ceremonial attire only after the solicitations of Cardinal Filomarino.[243] Moreover, according to the Grand Duke of Tuscany's agent, the costume had been worn with some physical difficulty because Masaniello refused to take his own clothes off and insisted on wearing it over them.[244]

Why did he make such a fuss about keeping his fisherman's clothes? After having turned the world on its head, striking the monarchy and the nobility as no one of his social position had ever dared to do, why stop short before a sumptuous dress? Maybe too much had changed in the few days of his success and he found comfort in his old appearance. Perhaps the reason was not psychological but social. Maybe he was trying to succeed on his own terms, trying to offer an alternative image to hegemonic rule. Giuseppe Donzelli, who presents one of the few contemporary versions of the revolt which is favourable towards the popular masses, often puts in the fisherman's mouth comments of status pride that support this hypothesis. For example, in an incident when Masaniello saw a group of curious nobles assembled under the window of his house, trying to have a glimpse of the new popular leader, he admonished them: 'Gentlemen, leave here, otherwise I will have your heads chopped off, because I want no other company than simple barefoot people, like myself.'[245] When the viceroy tried to give him a golden chain he refused it saying: 'I thank his Excellency, but this is not a thing for me, because, once this business is over I want to go back to selling fish.'[246] If we are to believe the veracity of these words, such moral integrity and naiveté clearly presented an alternative model of deportment.

Contrary to Donzelli's interpretation, Fuidoro claims that at a certain point Masaniello 'started to forget himself'. Wanting to show his greatness, he ordered all his neighbours to evacuate their homes because he wanted to construct a royal palace for himself.[247] Donzelli's version of the facts was that Masaniello indeed cleared his neighbours' houses but out of concern for his life. The space was destined to assure a secure zone around his home.[248] Masaniello's frequent attacks of paranoia, which eventually proved to be well founded since he was assassinated only ten days after his rise to power, seem to support Donzelli's version. It is debatable if Masaniello remained faithful to himself until the end, but it is clear that he tried very hard to do so.

His example was not emulated. The disruption of the social order received a clear expression through dress. Fuidoro tells about Spanish officers who arrived in Naples during the revolt. On their first tour of the city they met the various officials of the people and greeted them respectfully, mistaking them for local nobles. With a manifest antipathy towards social climbers, Fuidoro explains that these were nothing but pedlars and fishermen wearing 'elegant drapes, scarlet capes, sleeves of brocade … feathered hats, earned by their looting and burning'.[249] Needless to say, these acts of

plunder were perpetrated against the nobility and rich parvenus. As a reaction, a reverse phenomenon could be seen. In a topsy-turvy world of a surrealistically unlimited carnivalesque subversion of social categories, nobles furtively walked the streets 'in very vile clothes, wearing a clerical habit in order not to be easily recognized, exchanging their elegant and luxurious clothes'.[250] Ironically, even if it was not intended as such, the pressure from below had achieved in an instant the control of luxury that sumptuary laws had been advocating, unsuccessfully, for centuries.

Notes

This chapter is an updated version of my article, 'Regulation of Appearances during the Catholic Reformation: Dress and Morality in Spain and Italy', in *Les deux réformes chrétiennes. Propagation et difussion*, ed. Myriam Yardeni and Ilana Zinguer (Leiden, 2004), 492–510.

1   Daniel Roche, *A History of Everyday Things: The Birth of Consumption in France, 1600–1800*, trans. Brian Pearce (Cambridge, 2000), 194. For a comprehensive historical account, with a general appeal despite his French focus, see by the same, *The Culture of Clothing: Dress and Fashion in the 'Ancien Régime'*, trans. Jean Birrell (Cambridge, 1994).

2   Roche, *A History of Everyday Things*, 195.

3   For a recent comprehensive institutional study of fashion in Naples see Sonia Scognamiglio Cestaro, *Le Istituzioni della moda. Economia, magistrature e scambio politico nella Napoli moderna* (Benevento, 2008). I would like to thank Dr Scognamiglio for making her book available to me.

4   Fernand Braudel, *Civilization and Capitalism: 15th–18th Century*, vol. 1: *The Structures of Everyday Life: The Limits of the Possible*, trans. Miriam Kochan (London, 1981), 312, 315–20; Alice Mackrell, *An Illustrated History of Fashion: 500 Years of Fashion Illustration* (London, 1997), 30.

5   Carmen Bernis, *Indumentaria española en tiempos de Carlos V* (Madrid, 1962), 32.

6   Michael and Ariane Batterberry, *Fashion: The Mirror of History* (2nd edn, London, 1982), 94–5.

7   *Ibid.*, *Indumentaria española*, 41.

8   *Ibid.*, 32–3; James Laver, *Costume and Fashion: A Concise History* (rev. edn, London, 1995), 90; Brian Reade, *Costume of the Western World: The Dominance of Spain, 1550–1660* (London, 1951), 5–14.

9   José Luis González Novalín, 'La inquisicion española', in *Historia de la Iglesia en España*, vol. 3.2: *La Iglesia en la España de los siglos XV y XVI*, ed. José Luis González Novalín (Madrid, 1980), 249–53.

10 For a concise description of the popes in this period see Eamon Duffy, *Saints and Sinners: A History of the Popes* (New Haven, 1996), 169–73. For detailed biographies of individual popes during the period see Ludwig Pastor, *The History of the Popes*, trans. E. F. Peeler (40 vols., London, 1891–1953).

11 Sarah F. Matthews Grieco, 'The Body, Appearance, and Sexuality', in *A History of Women in the West*, vol. 3: *Renaissance and Enlightenment Paradoxes*, ed. Natalie Zemon Davies and Arlette Farge (Cambridge, Mass., 1993), 46–7; Mary Elizabeth Perry, 'Magdalens and Jezebels in Counter Reformation Spain', in *Culture and Control in Counter Reformation Spain*, ed. Anne J. Cruz and Mary Elizabeth Perry (Oxford and Minneapolis, 1992), 124–44. On some of the disciplinary elements inside the family after Trent see Angelo Turchini, 'Dalla disciplina alla "creanza" del matrimonio all'indomani del concilio di Trento', in *Donna, disciplina, creanza cristiana dal XV al XVII secolo*, ed. Gabriella Zarri (Rome, 1996), 205–14.

12 For sumptuary law in Italy, including valuable information on prostitutes' marks of infamy, see Maria Giuseppina Muzzarelli, 'Le leggi suntuarie', in *La moda. Storia d'Italia. Annali 19*, ed. Carlo Marco Belfanti and Fabio Giusberti (Turin, 2003), 185–220; Diane Owen Hughes,

'Sumptuary Law and Social Relations in Renaissance Italy', in *Disputes and Settlements: Law and Human Relations in the West*, ed. John Bossy (Cambridge, 1983), 69–100; and Paola Venturelli, 'La moda come status symbol. Legislazioni suntuarie e "segnali" di identificazione sociale', in *Storia della moda*, ed. Ranieri Varese and Grazietta Butazzi (Bologna, 1995), 28–52. For Naples see Salvatore di Giacomo, *La prostituzione in Napoli nei secoli XV, XVI e XVII. Documenti inediti* (Naples, 1899); Silvana Musella Guida, 'Il Regno del lusso. Leggi suntuarie e società. Un percorso di lungo periodo nella Napoli medievale e moderna (1290–1784)', in *Proceedings of L'économie du luxe en France et en Italie. Journées d'étude organisées par le Comité franco-italien d'histoire économique (AFHE-SISE) Lille, Ifresi 4–5 mai 2007*, 1–23, http://lodel.ehess.fr/afhe/docannexe.php?id=446; and in *ibid.* see Sonia Scognamiglio Cestaro, 'Leggi "scomode", clientele e fedeltà. Aspetti socio-istituzionali ed economici della legislazione suntuaria del Regno di Napoli in Età moderna', 1–29, http://lodel.ehess.fr/afhe/docannexe.php?id=445. For Rome see Tessa Storey, 'Clothing Courtesans: Fabrics, Signals, and Experiences', in *Clothing Culture: 1350–1650*, ed. Catherine Richardson (Aldershot, 2004), 95–107. For the Papal States see Alessandro Mordenti, 'Vita quotidiana e modelli di cultura in una periferia dello stato pontificio nei secoli XVI–XVII', in *La famiglia e la vita quotidiana in Europa dal '400 al '600. Fonti e problemi* (Rome, 1986), 401–2. For Venice see Margaret F. Rosenthal, *The Honest Courtesan: Veronica Franco Citizen and Writer in Sixteenth-Century Venice* (Chicago and London, 1992), 68–9. For Spain see Juan Sempere y Guarinos, *Historia del luxo y de las leyes suntuarias de España* (2 vols., Madrid, 1788), II, 124–5; Martin Hume, 'A Fight Against Finery', in his *The Year After the Armada and Other Historical Studies* (London, 1896), 251; and Mercè Aventin, 'Le leggi suntuarie in Spagna. Stato della questione', in *Disciplinare il lusso. La legislazione suntuaria in Italia e in Europa tra Medioevo ed Età moderna*, ed. Maria Giuseppina Muzzarelli and Antonella Campanini (Rome, 2003), 109–20.

13 On the discipline of youngsters during the Counter Reformation see Ottavia Niccoli, 'Creanza e disciplina. Buone maniere per i fanciulli nell'Italia della controriforma', in *Disciplina dell'anima, disciplina del corpo e disciplina della società tra medioevo ed età moderna*, ed. Paolo Prodi, *Annali dell'Istituto storico italo-germanico*, Quaderno 40 (Bologna, 1994), 929–63. For the transmission of monastic values to the secular realm in Catholic countries see in *ibid.* Dilwyn Knox, 'Disciplina. Le origini monastiche e clericali del buon comportamento nell'Europa cattolica del Cinquecento e del primo Seicento', 63–99.

14 Quoted in Niccoli, 'Creanza e disciplina', 954.

15 Quoted in Maria Franca Mellano, 'La donna nell'opera riformatrice di S. Carlo', in *San Carlo e il suo tempo. Atti del Convegno Internazionale nel IV centenario della morte (Milano, 21–26 maggio 1984)* (2 vols., Rome, 1986), II, 1092.

16 Niccoli, 'Creanza e disciplina', 955.

17 On the importance of Vives' manual and its diffusion in Italy through the plagiarism of Lodovico Dolce see Rudolph M. Bell, *How to Do It: Guides to Good Living for Renaissance Italians* (Chicago and London, 1999), 216–19, 265.

18 Margaret L. King, 'The Woman of the Renaissance', in *Renaissance Characters*, ed. Eugenio Garin, trans. Lydia G. Cochrane (Chicago and London, 1991), 237.

19 Juan Luis Vives, *Formación de la mujer Cristiana*, in *Obras Completas*, ed. Lorenzo Riber (2 vols., Madrid, 1947). On proper clothes: for young ladies see I, 1015–26; for married women, I, 1116–20; for widows, I, 1169–71.

20 Erasmus is quoted in the introduction by Lorenzo Riber, 'Juan Luis Vives, Valenciano. Ensayo bibliografico', in *ibid.*, 173.

21 For the medieval phase see Diane Owen Hughes, 'Regulating Women's Fashion', in *A History of Women in the West*, vol. 2: *Silences of the Middle Ages*, ed. Christiane Klapisch-Zuber (Cambridge, Mass., 1992), 136–58; and Maria Giuseppina Muzzarelli, ' "Contra mundanas vanitates et pompas". Aspetti della lotta contro i lussi nell'Italia del XV secolo', *Rivista di Storia della Chiesa in Italia*, 40:2 (1986), 371–90. See also by the same, *Gli inganni delle apparenze. Disciplina di vesti e ornamenti alla fine del medioevo* (Turin, 1996), 155–210; and *Guardaroba medievale. Vesti e società dal XIII al XVI secolo* (Bologna, 1999), 324–47.

22 Quoted in Alan Hunt, *Governance of the Consuming Passions: A History of Sumptuary Law* (London, 1996), 234.

23 On Counter-Reformation art and models of conduct for women in Italy see Sarah F. Matthews Grieco, 'Modelli di santità femminile nell'Italia del Rinascimento e della Controriforma', in *Donne e Fede. Santità e vita religiosa in Italia*, ed. Lucetta Scaraffia and Gabriella Zarri (Rome and Bari, 1994), 303–25; and by the same, 'Pedagogical Prints: Moralizing Broadsheets and Wayward Women in Counter Reformation Italy', in *Picturing Women in Renaissance and Baroque Italy*, ed. Geraldine A. Johnson and Sarah F. Matthews Grieco (Cambridge, 1997), 61–87. For the same subject in Spain see Alba Ribero, 'Imagenes de maternidád en la pintura Barroca', *in Las mujeres en el Antiguo Regimen. Imagen y realidad (s. XVI–XVIII)* (Barcelona, 1994).

24 For example, see the influence of friars on Florentine sumptuary laws in Ronald Rainey, 'Dressing Down the Dressed-Up: Reproving Feminine Attire in Renaissance Florence', in *Renaissance Society and Culture: Essays in Honor of Eugene F. Rice Jr.*, ed. John Monfasani and Ronald G. Musto (New York, 1991), 228–37.

25 José Deleito y Piñuela, *La mujer, la casa y la moda* (2nd edn, Madrid, 1954), 276.

26 Rainey, 'Dressing Down', 218–19.

27 Catherine Kovesi Killerby, 'Practical Problems in the Enforcement of Italian Sumptuary Law, 1200–1500', in *Crime, Society and the Law in Renaissance Italy*, ed. Trevor Dean (Cambridge, 1994), 109.

28 For the denial of privileged dress and other sumptuary sanctions against prostitutes see Giustiniani, 'De meretricibus', in *Nuova collezione*, vol. 7, 221–39. For the encouragement of prohibited garments among courtesans in Spain see Hume, 'Against Finery', 251; Sempere y Guarinos, *Historia del luxo*, II, 124–5.

29 Kovesi Killerby, 'Practical Problems', 118–19. The author mentions the problems of enforcement in Italy, but her explanations are valid for sumptuary laws in general.

30 Hunt, *Governance of the Consuming Passions*, 356.

31 Hughes, 'Sumptuary Law', 71.

32 Quoted in María Cruz García de Enterría, 'El cuerpo entre predicadores y copleros', in *Le corps dans la société espagnole des XVIe et XVIIe siècles*, ed. Augustin Redondo (Paris, 1990), 235–6.

33 Burke, 'Presenting and Re-presenting Charles V', 409.

34 Rosita Levi Pisetzky, 'Moda e costume', in *Storia d'Italia*, vol. 5.1, ed. Ruggiero Romano and Corrado Vivanti (Turin, 1973), 962–3.

35 Black J. Anderson and Madge Garland, *A History of Fashion* (2nd rev. edn, London, 1980), 110–16.

36 Rosita Levi Pisetzky, *Storia del costume in Italia* (5 vols., Milan, 1964–69), III, 37.

37 *Ibid.*, 17; Grazietta Butazzi, 'Vesti di "molta fattura": Reflections on Spanish-Influenced Fashion in the Second Half of the Sixteenth Century', in *Velluti e moda. Tra XV e XVII secolo*, ed. Annalisa Zanni (Milan, 1999), 171; Levi Pisetzky, 'Moda e costume', 962–3.

38 On women's constrictive clothes in that period see Marianne Thesander, *The Feminine Ideal*, trans. Nicholas Hill (London, 1997), 55–67; Butazzi, 'Vesti di "molta fattura" ', 169–70.

39 Anderson and Garland, *History of Fashion*, 120.

40 Bernis, *Indumentaria española*, 42.

41 Levi Pisetzky, *Storia del costume*, III, 387.

42 Deleito y Piñuela, *La mujer*, 163 ff.

43 John H. Elliott, 'Power and Propaganda in the Spain of Philip IV', in his *Spain and its World*, 169.

44 John Harvey, *Men in Black* (London, 1995), 77.

45 *Ibid.*, 156.

46 *Ibid.*, 72; Redworth and Checa, 'The Kingdoms of Spain', 59.

47 Baldassare Castiglione, *Il libro del Cortegiano*, ed. Luigi Preti (Turin, 1965), book II, ch. 27.

48 Aileen Ribeiro, *Dress and Morality* (London, 1986), 68. Ribeiro's book gives an extensive survey of ideas of dress and morality in early modern Britain.

49 Burke, 'Presenting and Re-presenting Charles V', 409; Harvey, *Men in Black*, 66–9.

50 Levi Pisetzky, *Storia del costume*, III, 108–19.

51 Harvey, *Men in Black*, 55.
52 BNN, MS. XV. G. 23, *Le Pompe Funebri celebrate in Napoli per la morte del Re Cattolico Filippo IV d'Austria Dal Card. D. Pasquale d'Aragóna Viceré nel dì 18 Febr.° 1666*, fol. 174v.
53 Burke, 'Conspicuous Consumption', in his *The Historical Anthropology*, 140; Levi Pisetzky, *Storia del costume*, III, 307–11.
54 Laver, *Costume*, 93.
55 Malcolm Barnard, *Fashion as Communication* (London and New York, 1996), 174.
56 Peter Burke, 'The Presentation of Self in the Renaissance Portrait', in his *The Historical Anthropology*, 154; Elliott, 'Court of the Spanish Habsburgs', in his *Spain and its World*, 150.
57 Quoted in Díez Borque, *La sociedad española*, 80.
58 For a thorough description of the carefully veiled *tapadas*, see Deleito y Piñuela, *La mujer*, 63–6.
59 Quoted in Díez Borque, *La sociedad española*, 107.
60 Mellano, 'La donna', 1091.
61 Levi Pistzky, *Storia del costume*, III, 37. For the influence of black in male dress see Amedeo Quondam, 'Tutti i colori del nero. Moda "alla spagnola" e "migliore forma italiana" ', in *Giovan Battista Moroni. Il cavaliere in nero. Immagine del gentiluomo nel Cinquecento*, ed. Annalisa Zanni and Andrea di Lorenzo (Milan, 2005), 25–45. In *ibid.*, see also Grazietta Butazzi, 'Intorno al "Cavaliere in nero". Note sulla moda maschile tra Cinque e Seicento', 47–55.
62 Cesare Vecellio, *Habiti antichi et moderni di tutto il mondo* (Paris, 1859), 22.
63 For the farthingale in Genoa see L. T. Belgrano, *Della vita privata dei genovesi* (2ⁿᵈ ed., Genoa, 1875), 268–71; Levi Pisetzky, *Storia del costume*, III, 387.
64 Rosita Levi Pisetzky, 'Il gusto Barocco nel costume italiano del Seicento', *Studi Secenteschi*, 2 (1961), 78.
65 For both quotations see Cirillo Mastrocinque, 'Cinquecento napoletano', 558.
66 Pompeo Gherardo Molmenti, *La storia di Venezia nella vita privata. Dalle origini alla caduta della republica* (2ⁿᵈ ed., Turin, 1880), 274.
67 Giulio Bistort, *Il magistrato alle pompe nella repubblica di Venezia. Studio storico* (Venice, 1912), 167–8.
68 Moderata Fonte (Modesta Pozzo), *The Worth of Women: Wherein is Clearly Revealed Their Nobility and Their Superiority to Men*, ed. and trans. Virginia Cox (Chicago, 1997), 234. The book was written in 1592 and published posthumously in 1600.
69 *Ibid.*, 234–7; Lucrezia Marinella, *The Nobility and Excellence of Women and the Defects and Vices of Men*, ed. and trans. Anne Dunhill (Chicago, 1999), 166–8; Arcangela Tarabotti, *Antisatira*, in *Satira e antisatira*, ed. Elissa Weiser (Rome, 1998), especially 67–91, 95–100.
70 Both quotations are from Sempere y Guarinos, *Historia del luxo*, II, 94.
71 Néstor Luján, *La vida cotidiana en el Siglo de Oro español* (Barcelona, 1988), 76–9.
72 Hume, 'Against Finery', 244.
73 Hunt, *Governance of the Consuming Passions*, 223.
74 Bistort, *Il magistrato alle pompe*, 232.
75 Belgrano, *Vita privata*, 270.
76 Quoted in Hume, 'Against Finery', 251.
77 Ariodante Fabretti, *Statuti e ordinamenti suntuari intorno al vestire degli uomini e delle donne in Perugia dall'anno 1266 al 1536*, in *Memorie della Reale Accademia delle Scienze di Torino*, Serie II, vol. 38 (1888), 188.
78 Quoted in Joaquín Pérez Villanueva, 'Sor María de Agreda y Felipe IV. Un epistolario en su tiempo', in *Historia de la Iglesia en España*, vol. 4: *La Iglesia en la España de los siglos XVII y XVIII*, ed. Antonio Mestre Sanchis (Madrid, 1980), 402.
79 Adelaide Cirillo Mastrocinque, *Usi e costumi popolari a Napoli nel Seicento* (Rome, 1978), 117.
80 See Ruth Matilda Anderson, 'The Golilla: A Spanish Collar of the Seventeenth Century', *Waffen und Kostümkunde,* 11 (1969), 1–19; and Deleito y Piñuela, *La mujer*, 214.
81 Sempere y Guarinos, *Historia del luxo*, II, 122–4. Generally for male attire in this period see Deleito y Piñuela, *La mujer*, 215–33; on sumptuary laws, 275 ff.

82 Henry Kamen, 'Nudité et contre-réforme en Espagne', in *Le corps dans la société espagnole des XVIe et XVIIe siècles*, ed. Augustin Redondo (Paris, 1990), 301; García de Enterría, 'El cuerpo', 241.

83 Levi Pisetzky, *Storia del costume*, III, 442. For wigs see *ibid.*, 407–14; for general sumptuary laws, *ibid.*, 458 ff.

84 Fabriciano Ferrero, 'Mentalità teologica e mentalità scientifica sulla moda femminile del secolo XVII', *Ricerche per la Storia Religiosa di Roma*, 1 (1977), 231–56.

85 *Ibid.*, 251.

86 Cirillo Mastrocinque, 'Cinquecento napoletano', 545.

87 Silvana Musella Guida and Sonia Scognamiglio Cestaro, 'Le origini della moda napoletana', in *Proceedings of the XIII International Congress TICCIH: Industrial Heritage and Urban Landscape, Terni-Rome, 14–18 September 2006*, 1–28, www.ticcihcongress2006.net/paper/Paper%209/Musella_Scognamiglio%209.pdf.

88 Quoted and translated in Batterberry and Batterberry, *Fashion*, 119.

89 Giovan Battista del Tufo, *Ritratto o modello delle grandezze, delitie e meraviglie, Della nobilissima Città di Napoli*, ed. Calogero Tagliareni (Naples, 1959), 144.

90 Giustiniani, 'Lex sumptuaria', in *Nuova collezione*, vol. 7, 26.

91 Vecellio, *Habiti*, 224.

92 Imperiale, 'De' giornali', 364.

93 'Se però foss'ella stata assolta del sospetto, del quale parlò il Tasso: "Le negligenze sue sono artefici." *Ibid.*

94 Cirillo Mastrocinque, 'Cinquecento napoletano', 550.

95 Muto, 'I segni d'honore', 188.

96 Zazzera, *Narrazioni*, 517–18.

97 See for example the dispensations given on 14 September 1686 for the celebrations of Buda's recovery from the Turks in Confuorto, *Giornali*, I, 159: 'In detto giorno Sua Eccellenza diede licenza, con banno publico e con viglietti mandati a' capitani dell'ottine della città, che si potessero fare da ogni qualità di persone maschere all'uso carnavalesco, dispenzando alli mascherati la pramatica del vestire, e ciò in tre giorni disegnati, cioè a' 15, 21 e 22 del detto mese di settembre.'

98 Zazzera, *Narrazioni*, 501–2.

99 Croce, *La Spagna*, 43. Neapolitans had a chance to see a real Muslim ruler and escorting court, with the visit of the Tunisian king in 1543, enabled by Charles V's invasion of North Africa. See *Il meraviglioso Honore fatto dal Vicerè e signori Napolitani al Re di Tunisi per la sua venuta a Napoli con l'ordine de l'entrata sua in detta città e il numero dei suoi cavalli, & i presenti magnifici che si sono fatti, dove s'intende che la gran quantità de dinari portati da esso Re per soldare gente Italiana* (Venice, 1543).

100 See Bulifon, *Giornali*, 245.

101 Confuorto, *Giornali*, I, 161.

102 *Ibid.*, II, 244.

103 A detailed example can be seen in the recording of the Neapolitan obsequies for the death of Queen Margaret of Austria in 1612. See Ottavio Caputi, *Relatione della pompa funerale che si celebrò in Napoli, nella morte della Serenissima Reina Margherita d'Austria* (Naples, 1612), 65–81.

104 Confuorto, *Giornali*, II, 244.

105 Raneo, *Etiquetas*, 19.

106 Celano, *Notizie*, I, 18.

107 *Ibid.*, 22.

108 Barnard, *Fashion*, 13.

109 For a recent contribution on the subject see Már Jónsson, 'The Expulsion of the Moriscos from Spain in 1609–1614: The Destruction of an Islamic Periphery', *Journal of Global History*, 2:2 (2007), 195–212.

110 Mackrell, *History of Fashion*, 30.

111 Levi Pisetzky, *Storia del costume*, III, 307.

112 John Evelyn, *Tyrannus or The Mode*, ed. J. L. Nevison (Oxford, 1951), 6.

113 Carlos García, *La oposición y conjunción de los dos luminares de la tierra o Antipatía de Franceses y Españoles*, ed. Michel Bareau (Edmonton, 1979), 222.

114 *Ibid.*, 200–2.

115 Traiano Boccalini, 'Ragguaglio XXVII', in *Ragguagli di Parnaso*, ed. Luigi Firpo (3 vols., Bari, 1948), III, 86–7.

116 Estrada, *Comentarios*, 380.

117 Harvey, *Men in Black*, 121.

118 Levi Pisetzky, *Storia del costume*, III, 240–3.

119 Harvey, *Men in Black*, 121.

120 Elliott, 'Court of the Spanish Habsburgs', in his *Spain and its World*, 149–50; Checa Cremades, 'Monarchic Liturgies', especially 97–100.

121 Redworth and Checa, 'The Kingdoms of Spain', 59.

122 See *ibid.*, and Checa Cremades, 'Monarchic Liturgies'.

123 Elliott, 'Power and Propaganda', in his *Spain and its World*, 167.

124 Harvey, *Men in Black*, 72; Checa Cremades, 'Monarchic Liturgies', 95 ff.

125 Chaline, 'The Kingdoms of France', 88. For a fundamental study of royal representation in France see Peter Burke, *The Fabrication of Louis XIV* (New Haven, *1992*). For an earlier period see Nicole Hochner, *Louis XII. Les dérèglements de l'image royale* (Paris, 2006).

126 Quoted in Muto, 'I segni d'honore', 174.

127 Evelyn, *John Evelyn in Naples*, 56.

128 Cirillo Mastrocinque, *Usi e costumi*, 117.

129 The protectionary laws against France were issued as follows: 20 June 1635; 18 February 1636; 8 August 1667; 24 August 1667; 25 August 1672; 12 December 1673; 13 January 1676; 28 February 1679; 30 December 1683; 31 January 1684; 6 June 1689; 25 November 1689; 31 March 1690; 21 July 1690. For each of these see respectively Giustiniani, 'De expulsione gallorum', in *Nuova collezione*, vol. 4, 77–8, 78–9, 79–81, 81–2, 82–4, 84–6, 86, 86–7, 87–8, 88–9, 89–90, 90–1, 91–3, 93–5. See also Alessio De Sariis, *Libro secondo. Del diritto pubblico. De' trattati di pace e di commercio esteriore colle potenze straniere*, in *Codice delle leggi del Regno di Napoli* [hereafter *Codice*] (Naples, 1794), II, 24 ff.

130 Giustiniani, 'De expulsione gallorum', in *Nuova collezione,* vol. 4, 78–81.

131 See the editor's introduction in Bulifon, *Giornali*, ix.

132 Fuidoro, Giornali, II, 54.

133 Quoted in Levi Pisetzky, *Storia del costume*, III, 325.

134 Carlo Celano, *Degli avanzi delle poste* (2 vols., Naples, 1676–81), I, 11.

135 Daniel C. Boughner, *The Braggart in Renaissance Comedy: A Study in Comparative Drama from Aristophanes to Shakespeare* (Minneapolis, 1954), 24.

136 Hunt, *Governance of the Consuming Passions*, 13–14.

137 Parrino, *Teatro*, in *Raccolta*, vol. 10, 195.

138 *Ibid.*

139 Levi Pisetzky, *Storia del costume*, III, 318.

140 García, *La oposición*, 208–18.

141 Bulifon, *Giornali*, 188.

142 *Ibid.*

143 *Ibid.*

144 See Anderson, 'Golilla'.

145 Bulifon, *Giornali*, 188.

146 Braudel, *The Structures of Everyday Life*, 317–18.

147 Vincenzo Pacelli, 'L'ideologia del potere nella rittrattistica napoletana del Seicento', *Bollettino del Centro di Studi Vichiani*, 16 (1986), 212.

148 The illustrated version, utilized for some of the images in this book, is different from the one used so far. It was issued in three volumes by the *Nuova stampa del Parrino e del Muti* in 1692–94.

149 Levi Pisetzky, *Storia del costume*, III, 332.

150 Fuidoro, *Giornali*, I, 47.

151 Di Giacomo, *La prostituzione*, 170.

152 Bulifon, *Giornali*, 192.

153 Fuidoro, *Giornali*, IV, 257.

154 Paolo Mattia Doria, *Massime del governo spagnolo a Napoli*, ed. Vittorio Conti (Naples, 1973), 45.

155 Confuorto, *Giornali*, I, 95.

156 Doria, *Massime*, 47.

157 Levi Pisetzky, *Storia del costume*, III, 378.

158 See Galasso, *Napoli spagnola*, II, 647.

159 Hunt, *Governance of the Consuming Passions*, 7.

160 During the Habsburg rule eighteen sumptuary laws were documented in Giustiniani's collection: 27 July 1559; 28 September 1560; 13 November 1560; 30 April 1561; 12 January 1564; 12 February 1569; 30 April 1569, with an amendment issued on 28 February 1603; 16 June 1625; 29 August 1636; 17 January 1639; 17 November 1639; 20 October 1640; 3 August 1684; 2 February 1685; 22 September 1689; 7 January 1690; 16 June 1690; 12 June 1696. For each law see respectively Giustiniani, 'Lex sumptuaria', in *Nuova collezione*, vol. 7, 25–9, 29–35, 35–6, 36–7, 37–9, 39, 39–44, 44–5, 45–6, 46–7, 47–8, 48–9, 49–52, 52–3, 53–4, 54–6, 56, 56–8.

161 For the relations between different religious and ethnic groups in the Mediterranean countries during our period see David Abulafia, *Mediterranean Encounters, Economic, Religious, Political, 1100–1550* (Aldershot, 2000); *Jews, Christians and Muslims in the Mediterranean World after 1492*, ed. Alisa Meyuhas Ginio (London, 1992); and Bernard Lewis, *Christians, Muslims, and Jews in the Age of Discovery* (New York and Oxford, 1995).

162 On the effects of Spanish racial policies on its national consciousness see Helmut G. Koenigsberger, 'National Consciousness in Early Modern Spain', in his *Politicians and Virtuosi: Essays in Early Modern History* (London and Ronceverte, 1986), 126–30. For a fundamental thesis concerning the effects of Islam and Judaism on Spanish history see Américo Castro, *España en su historia. Cristianos, Moros y Judios* (Buenos Aires, 1948).

163 For sumptuary law in Italy see note 12 of this chapter.

164 Essential are the two recent volumes of *Storia d'Italia* concerning different interesting aspects of Italian Jewry, authored by the best experts in the field. Of greater relevance to our period is the first volume *Gli ebrei in Italia. I: Dall'alto Medioevo all'età dei ghetti*, ed. Corrado Vivanti, *Storia d'Italia. Annali 11* (Turin, 1996). For the persecution of Jews in Italy see the proceedings of the conference, *L'Inquisizione e gli ebrei in Italia*, ed. Michele Luzzati and Albano Biondi (Rome and Bari, 1994). A cultural analysis of Italian Jewry during the period in question is provided by Roberto Bonfil, *Jewish Life in Renaissance Italy*, trans. Anthony Oldcorn (Berkeley and London, 1994). For the period after the Spanish conquest, see Viviana Bonazzoli, 'Gli ebrei del Regno di Napoli all'epoca della loro espulsione', II: 'Il periodo spagnolo (1501–1541)', *Archivio Storico Italiano*, 139 (1981), 179–287. For the most updated and critical review of Jewry in the Kingdom of Naples see David Abulafia, 'Il Mezzogiorno peninsulare dai bizantini all'espulsione (1541)', in *Gli ebrei in Italia*, ed. Vivanti, 4–44.

165 Abulafia, 'Il Mezzogiorno peninsulare', 36–7.

166 Last to follow Naples was the latest acquisition of Spain, the Duchy of Milan, from which the Jews were expelled in 1597.

167 Bonfil, *Jewish Life*, 63.

168 Bonazzoli, 'Gli ebrei', 287.

169 On sumptuary laws and marks of infamy for Jews see Diane Owen Hughes, 'Distinguishing Signs: Ear-rings, Jews, and Franciscan Rhetoric in the Italian Renaissance City', *Past and Present*, 112 (1986), 3–59; Ariel Toaf, 'La Prammatica degli ebrei e per gli ebrei', in *Disciplinare il lusso*, ed. Muzzarelli and Campanini, 91–108; also by the same, 'La vita materiale', in *Gli ebrei in Italia*, ed. Vivanti, 245–8, 257–60; Bonfil, *Jewish Life*, 104–11, 244–5. See also by the same, 'Società cristiana e società ebraica nell'Italia medievale e rinascimentale', in *ebrei e cristiani*

nell'Italia medievale e moderna. Conversioni, scambi, contrasti, ed. Michele Luzzati, Michele Olivari, and Alessandra Veronese (Rome, 1988), 257–60.

170 Toaf, 'La vita', 260.

171 Bonfil, Jewish Life, 245.

172 Della Morte, Cronica, 294.

173 De Sariis, Libro primo. Delle ragion ecclesiastica, e sue pertinenze, in Codice, I, 6.

174 Bonazzoli, 'Gli ebrei', 187–92. The verses written by the Neapolitan noble Giovan Battista del Tufo towards the end of the sixteenth century might indicate a change of heart. See his Ritratto, 329: Perfido, ingrato e reo, / malvagio, empio Giudeo / che non conosci e vedi, / i propri danni o le tue infami colpe […] / Deh ciechi a miglior via, / che l'aspettar non giova altro Messia / Che quel, che ad alta voce / Voi scelerati lo poneste in croce.

175 De Sariis, Libro primo, in Codice, I, 6–7.

176 See for example Henry Kamen, 'Una crisis de conciencia en la Edad de Oro en España. Inquisición contra limpieza de sangre', Bulletin Hispanique, 88 (1986), 321–56.

177 See G. Paladino, 'Privilegi concessi agli ebrei dal viceré D. Pedro di Toledo (1535–1536)', ASPN, 38 (1913), 632. See also Bonazzoli, 'Gli ebrei', 266–70.

178 Bonazzoli, 'Gli ebrei', 274.

179 De Sariis, Libro primo, in Codice, I, 7.

180 Bulifon, Giornali, 44.

181 About the San Benito see Batterberry and Batterberry, Fashion, 117–18.

182 Cirillo Mastrocinque, Usi e costumi, 109.

183 De Sariis, Libro Primo, in Codice, I, 3–4.

184 For Spanish anti-Muslim biases see Antonio Domínguez Ortis and Bernard Vincent, Historia de los moriscos. Vida y tragedia de una minoría (Madrid, 1978).

185 De Sariis, Libro primo, in Codice, I, 4.

186 Confuorto, Giornali, I, 128.

187 Croce, La Spagna, 210–13. See also Giovanni Romeo, 'La suggestione dell'ebraismo tra i napoletani del tardo Cinquecento', in L'inquisizione e gli ebrei in Italia, ed. Michele Luzzati (Rome and Bari, 1994), 179–95. The author describes a curious attraction of particular Neapolitan Christians towards the Jewish faith in the late sixteenth century when the physical absence of Jews transformed Judaism into a fascinating quasi-mythical object of interest.

188 This is according to the testimony of the Venetian ambassador Bernardo Navagero, quoted in Croce, La Spagna, 210.

189 For a thorough review of Spain's Black Legend see Ricardo García Cárcel, La leyenda negra. Historia y opinión (Madrid, 1993). Also of relevance is Jocelyn Nigel Hillgarth, The Mirror of Spain, 1500–1700: The Formation of a Myth (Ann Arbor, Mich., 2000), which supplies an excellent survey of European public opinion on Spain during the early modern era.

190 Bernis, Indumentaria española, 14–15.

191 Quoted in ibid., 15.

192 Ruth Matilda Anderson, Hispanic Costume, 1480–1530 (New York, 1979), 17.

193 For a suggestive study of the values of the Spanish army during the pinnacle of Spain's military might see Puddu, Il soldato gentiluomo. For the strains between the nobility and the infantry see especially 69–92.

194 Parrino, Teatro, in Raccolta, vol. 9, 330, 392.

195 Giustiniani, 'Lex sumptuaria', in Nuova collezione, vol. 7, 33.

196 Ibid., 43.

197 See for example the sumptuary law issued in 1684 by the viceroy the Marquis of Carpio, ibid., 51. On this issue see also Scognamiglio Cestaro, 'Leggi "scomode"', 9–10.

198 Cirillo Mastrocinque, 'Cinquecento napoletano', 536–7.

199 Estrada, Comentarios, 319.

200 Puddu, Il soldato gentiluomo, 190–1.

201 Quoted in ibid., 218.

202 The quotations appear in Giustiniani, 'Lex sumptuaria', in Nuova collezione, vol. 7, 37.

203 Fuidoro, *Giornali*, III, 229–30.

204 Bulifon, *Giornali*, 186.

205 Besides the aforementioned autobiographies of Estrada and Contreras, see the others in the compilation *Autobiografías de soldados*, ed. José Cossio; and Raffaele Filamondo, *Il genio bellicoso di Napoli. Memorie istoriche d'alcuni capitani celebri napoletani, c'han militato per la fede, per lo Re, per la Patria nel secolo corrente* (2 vols., Naples, 1694). See also Benedetto Croce, 'Scene della vita dei soldati spagnuoli a Napoli', in *Uomini e cose della vecchia Italia*, 109–32; and Margarita Levisi, 'Golden Age Autobiography: The Soldiers', in *Autobiography in Early Modern Spain*, ed. Nicholas Spadaccini and Jenaro Talens (Minneapolis, 1988), 97–117.

206 The narration of the parade appears in Raneo, *Etiquetas*, 186–9.

207 *Ibid.*, 187.

208 *Ibid.*, 188.

209 *Ibid.*, 189.

210 *Ibid.*

211 Imperiale, 'De' giornali', 328–9.

212 Boughner, *Braggart*, 26.

213 Giovanni della Casa, *A Renaissance Courtesy-Book: Galateo: Of Manners and Behaviours*, trans. Robert Peterson (Boston, 1914), 106.

214 *Ibid.*, 106–7.

215 Confuorto, *Giornali*, II, 110. Previous to the display of the uniforms, the viceroy the Marquis of Carpio issued a ban forbidding the use of these colours for nobles' ensembles and servants' liveries. See De Sariis, *Libro settimo. Della ragion militare*, in *Codice*, VII, 37.

216 Sumptuous martial apparel played a central part in tournaments in viceregal Naples. Here is a short sample of seventeenth-century festival books, where these clothes are described in great detail: Valentini, *Sontuoso torneo*; Fellecchia, *Viaggio*, especially 53–6; and Cirino, *Feste*, especially 68–82, 102–13.

217 See Giustiniani, 'Lex sumptuaria', in *Nuova collezione*, vol. 7, 25–58; and De Sariis, *Libro decimo. Delle scienze, e dell'arti*, in *Codice*, X, 189–93.

218 Lev Pisetzky, *Storia del costume*, III, 277.

219 Giustiniani, 'Lex sumptuaria', in *Nuova collezione*, vol. 7, 25–37.

220 See, respectively, *ibid.*, 44–5, 45–6.

221 *Ibid.*, 29.

222 Guerra, *Diurnali*, 168.

223 'Documenti che riguardano in ispecie la storia economica e finanziera del Regno, levati dal carteggio degli Agenti del Duca di Urbino in Napoli', ed. Francesco Palermo, *Archivio Storico Italiano*, 9 (1846), 236–7.

224 On this issue see Hunt, *Governance of the Consuming Passions*, 325–56.

225 The absence of evidence is also emphasized by Sonia Scognamiglio Cestaro in her unsuccessful search for potential court cases prosecuting infringers of sumptuary law. See her 'Leggi "scomode"', 12.

226 Confuorto, *Giornali*, I, 174.

227 *Ibid.*, 128.

228 ASNA, *Sei libri di cerimoniale*, part II, fols. 88v–89r.

229 See De Sariis, *Libro duodecimo. De' delitti privati, e pubblici, e delle pene*, in *Codice*, XII, 168–84.

230 Guerra, *Diurnali*, 86.

231 De Sariis, *Libro duodecimo*, 168.

232 *Ibid.*, 170.

233 See for example *ibid.*, 169: 'S'ordina, e comanda, che tutte le meretrici, le quali abitano per la strada di Toledo dal regio Palazzo fino alla Porta Reale sfrattino, e vadino ad abitare in altri luoghi, sotto pena della frusta.'

234 'Documenti sulla storia civile', 342.

235 For the entire incident see Confuorto, *Giornali*, I, 4–5.

236 A manuscript conserved at the National Library of Naples witnesses the tragic conclusion of

the illicit liaison of Maria d'Avalos, Princess of Venosa, and Fabrizio Carafa, Duke of Andria. When the husband finds out about his wife's treachery he plots to wash his honour with blood. Pretending to leave for a hunting expedition he returns in the early hours of the morning with three accomplices, surprises the lovers in his wife's bed, and kills them on the spot. See BNN, MS. XV G23, *Successo Tragico degl'amori di D. Maria d'Avalos Principessa di Venosa, e D. Fabrizio Carafa, Duca d'Andria; coll'Informazione pigliata dalla G. C. della Vic.a per la miserabil morte nel dì 19 8bre 1590*, fols. 118r–135v.

237 BNN, MS. XV G30, *Diario ossia Giornale Istorico di quanto piu curioso e memorabile è accaduto in Napoli dall'anno 1700 per tutto l'anno 1701 in cui accadde il tumulto*, fol. 15v.

238 Guerra, *Diurnali*, 92–3.

239 Confuorto, *Giornali*, I, 369–70.

240 Guerra, *Diurnali*, 41–2.

241 Innocenzo Fuidoro, *Successi historici raccolti dalla sollevatione di Napoli dell'anno 1647*, ed. Anna Maria Giraldi and Marina Raffaeli (Milan, 1994), 27.

242 *Ibid.*, 59.

243 'Documenti diversi sulle novità accadute in Napoli l'anno 1647', ed. Francesco Palermo, *Archivio Storico Italiano* 9 (1846), 385.

244 *Ibid.*, 345.

245 Donzelli, *Partenope*, 74.

246 *Ibid.*, 83–4.

247 Fuidoro, *Successi historici*, 55.

248 Donzelli, *Partenope*, 80.

249 Fuidoro, *Successi historici*, 176.

250 *Ibid.*, 232.

5

Political utilization of *imprese* in viceregal Naples

Recent research, resulting from the renewed interest in early modern courts, has shown how extensive state sponsorship of various forms of art, used in princely public displays, served to construct the image of the ideal ruler. The use of visual media in festive displays stemmed from a philosophy which believed that truth could be conveyed through images, in which the rhetorical principle of *persuasio* played an important part. They were based upon a vast tract of literature that included 'how to do it' books of emblems, *imprese*, and mythological manuals.[1] Even though unfamiliar to most twenty-first-century readers – and until very recently treated as marginal in traditional historical studies, or as ancillary for art historians – emblem books were a flourishing form of literature throughout Europe in the sixteenth and seventeenth centuries. It has been calculated that from 1531, with the publication of the *Emblematum Liber* of the celebrated humanist Andrea Alciati, considered as the founding book of the genre, to the end of the sixteenth century alone there were published no fewer than 4,000 different editions of 1,400 authors.[2]

With the advent of the Enlightenment and its rejection of esoteric forms of knowledge, the genre started to wane dramatically.[3] Only in recent years have 'emblem studies' regained interest among the academic community, due among other things to their multimedia appeal, linked to the cybernetic revolution that involves all forms of knowledge. A vivid testimony of this is provided by the various projects for the digitization of emblem books on the Internet, which are at the forefront of parallel research efforts done on other kinds of historical records.[4] Concomitantly, an unprecedented number of seminars and congresses on the subject have developed many topical and theoretical discussions. The following chapter is based on evidence found in Neapolitan festival books, except that the highlight, instead of the aforementioned festive and ludic elements, is exclusively on the various allegorical pictograms that were produced on the spot for the different state occasions – entries, processions/cavalcades, tournaments, and funerals – aggrandizing their objects of adulation in their distinct metaphorical language. In this respect, my contention is that the Neapolitan emblematic pictograms, pretty much like the festival books in which they appear, displayed a particularly

complex, rich, and expensive variation of a widely diffused European phenomenon. Also, as already demonstrated with festivals, this testifies to the high importance attributed to persuasive forms of propaganda in such a turbulent city as early modern Naples.

The uses of *imprese* in tournaments

So far I have avoided the use of one specific term for the subject of this chapter. This requires a clarification. Contemporary experts in the field held lengthy discussions, each offered in an aspiring 'decisive' treatise, about the proper definition of the various emblematic terms. The two more important are emblems and *imprese*. Supposedly it is easy to distinguish one from the other because they differ in form. Theoretically, an emblem is constituted of three parts: an image – belonging to the natural world, to history, or to mythology – a motto – mostly in Latin, but occasionally also in vernaculars – and an explanatory verse; whereas the *impresa*, by definition, consists of only a picture and a motto, also defined by some authors as 'body and soul', indicating the interdependence of the two parts in communicating the meaning of the idea. However, since the verse was not regarded as an essential component (some even dismissed the necessity of a motto) its absence did not automatically mean that the object at issue was an *impresa* and not an emblem. Moreover, there are tripartite *imprese*, just as there are bipartite emblems. Despite disputes and dissension around etymology, historical origins, proper objects to portray and subjects to discuss, and even the desired number of images in each of the two, there was a general agreement about their distinctive functions and purposes. As a rule the *impresa* was supposed to be more ingenious and enigmatic, aspiring to express an individual message from the aristocrat or king who used it. The emblem, on the other hand, was supposed to be more intelligible, as it had a broader social and didactic scope. However, quite often the definitions were not binding – as is testified by scores of obscure and enigmatic emblems and a great variety of moral *imprese* – and the two terms have become interchangeable.[5] The admonition of Emanuele Tesauro, considered one of the more thorough contemporary exponents of emblematics, reflects well the fusion and confusion of the genres: 'If you want to convey your heroic private thought, which is the scope of the *impresa*, and you use a natural property in the image but in the inscription you end up producing a moral document that is proper to the emblem ... you will have made an *Emblematic Impresa*, or an *Impresary Emblem*.'[6] In the following pages, regardless of their adherence to the rules, we will use exclusively the designation *imprese*, simply because these were unanimously chosen by the authors of the Neapolitan festival books where they appear.

Moreover, this seems to be congruent with their wider application. 'For monarchs, *imprese* became an essential expression of their ideals; they were used in the decoration of their palaces and public buildings and even on the most menial items of their everyday life – book-bindings, fabrics, silver, glass and costume.'[7] According to the

somewhat hypocritical lamentations of the Tuscan humanist Angelo Poliziano (1454–94), the demand for such symbolically loaded items was not restricted to sovereigns alone. 'This one wants a motto for the sword's pommel and for the ring's emblem: the other one [wants] a verse to put on the bed's head or private room, this one wants an *impresa*, and not for his silverware, but for ordinary cutlery. And everyone rushes immediately to Poliziano! So much so that I have found myself filling all the walls of the houses with epitaphs.'[8] Likewise, Bulifon tells about a seventeenth-century Neapolitan called Cesare Fanelli, a teacher of philosophy, theology, and civic and canonical law, as also a 'poet in Latin and standard Italian' who was so prolific in improvising Latin epigrams and verses for *imprese* that he produced 'hundreds a day, that is as many as he is ordered'.[9]

Even though these testimonies point towards what would seem an overwhelming 'inflation' of the practice, one has to bear in mind that we are talking mostly of elite circles, or as it had been ably dubbed by Giuseppina Ledda, a kind of 'communication by exclusion'.[10] Customarily, the origin of the *impresa* was identified as the distinctive badge of military nobles.[11] They could be found on the battlefield, on the knight's jerkin, shield or helmet as well as in 'tournaments, parades, in masquerades, in comedies, or on other such occasions', as testified by Girolamo Ruscelli in his *Le imprese illustri* (*The Illustrious Imprese*).[12] Accordingly, Castiglione highly recommended the ideal courtier to wear *imprese* containing 'appropriate mottoes, and ingenious inventions, so to attract the eyes of all those surrounding him as a magnet does to iron'.[13] The interest displayed in the *imprese* worn by Henry VIII, for the birth of his son, surpassed by far the effect recommended by Castiglione. Abusing his invitation to pick off the golden letters and devices that adorned his clothes, a crowd of common spectators reduced the king to nothing more than doublet and hose.[14]

This kind of aristocratic personal *impresa* fits well within the supercilious, riotous, and highly individual character of early modern nobility. Some examples could reach the apex of defiance. For example, the Count of Villamediana, the secret lover of the queen, posing as a living *impresa* in a parade in Madrid at the beginning of the seventeenth century, wore an outfit made of coins, completed with the motto 'Mis Amores Son Reales'. This could either mean, 'my love is for money' if *Real* is interpreted as Spanish currency, but also 'my love affairs are regal', boldly alluding to his outrageous liaison.[15] However, the latter is a relatively extreme example. When nobles displayed their *imprese* in a tournament they usually tried to outdo each other in a competition of wit. According to Tesauro: 'they fought with their ingenuity no less than with their hands: sometimes even inflicting a deeper wound with the acumen of their wit than with the sword'.[16] Actually, the entry of the knights onto the field was considered as a very important part of the tournament, as can be discerned from the disproportional space that contemporary authors of festival books dedicated to it, compared to the description of the combat.[17] Moreover, it was regarded as an integral, officially recognized part of the contest alongside the actual battle. Just to mention a typical example,

the advertisement for a Neapolitan tournament to be held in honour of the marriage between the crowns of Spain and France (1612) promised prizes not only for the best exhibitions with the sword or the pike, but also for the most elegant knight, for the most inventive *apparato* that each knight displayed in his entry, and, of course, for the best *impresa*.[18]

On that same occasion, as usually was the case, the *imprese* displayed a blend of amorous intentions and heroic virility and chauvinism. For example, Don Antonio de Mendoza wore an *impresa* portraying an explosive device laid at the gate of a fortress with a motto in Spanish, 'Mas Fuerça Á Mas Resistencia' (More force to more resistance). In the guise of an emblem, even though the author calls it clearly an *impresa*, there was also a Spanish verse:

> Efecto de la paciencia,
> Y milagro del amor,
> Es mostrar contra il rigor,
> Mas fuerça á mas resistencia.[19]
> (Effect of patience
> And miracle of love,
> Is to show against rigour
> More force to more resistance.)

It is unclear if the *impresa* referred to a specific romantic conquest of its carrier, but the crude message clearly advocates an aggressive pursuit of love, by means of patience and persistence, but shall it not suffice then by sheer force, resembling the conquest of women to the seizure of fortresses.

For the tournaments in Naples for the marriage of Charles II with Marie of Orléans (1680), we find the local nobility exhibiting *imprese* with an even more pronounced cocksure spirit, and a unanimous attempt at self-glorification. 'Vaglio Per Sette' (I am worth seven times over) declared boastfully the motto of an *impresa*, whose picture was the menacing seven-headed Hydra.[20] Adopting a threatening strategy, the motto of another one promised to reply to rays of sun with bolts of lightning.[21] To represent his perpetual aloofness in every situation, and his uniqueness, Don Domenico Capece chose the image of a diamond placed on an anvil, enduring immutably the blows of a hammer.[22] Paradoxically, even a call for self-restraint was done ostentatiously. Don Antonio Pignatello, nominated the 'knight of modesty', displayed an *impresa* with the image of a hidden and yet very ardent furnace, with the motto 'Arde Più Se Splende Meno' (It burns more vehemently if it is less resplendent).[23] Quite consciously, such an *impresa* employed a reverse logic, criticizing the vainglory of his rivals, even though the scope remains the same one of self-exaltation.

Four examples brought by Andrea Rubino for a *gioco dei caroselli* celebrated in 1658 exhibit the exact same spirit:

> One had painted a beating drum and the motto was Con le Percosse Piu mi Invigorisco (Beatings reinvigorate me more). Another had painted a rock hit by

waves and the motto was L'Onda s'Infrange et Io Resisto Immoto (While the wave breaks I remain unmoved). Another had painted a sun that attracted with its rays the smell of aromatic herbs and flowers, and the motto was Altri Idol Non Incensan Gl'Odor Miei (Other idols don't incense my smells). Another had painted a lit torch next to a moth with the motto Mi Consumo e Son Felice (I am consumed and I am happy).[24]

A more interesting and creative use of the *impresa* took place at royal funerals or obsequies. Unlike the chauvinistic and one-dimensional aristocratic *imprese* employed in tournaments, the funerary ones were at the heart of a complex artistic production which combined them with other artistic elements such as statues, epigrams, and various adornments, which were scattered around the church where the obsequies took place, as I will now turn to describe.

Neapolitan *imprese* for the obsequies of the Habsburg monarchs

The following section will emphasize the way in which funerary *imprese* functioned as conveyors of royal political messages in a particular historical situation, relatively neglected so far – the obsequies of Spanish monarchs in Naples under Habsburg rule.[25] I will deal particularly with the funerary honours of three royal persons held in Naples between 1599 and 1666: Philip II (1599), Margarita of Austria (1612), and Philip IV (1666).[26] The omission of those for Charles V, Philip III, and Charles II, other queen consorts, or heirs to the throne who died before their time (*principes jurados*), has been dictated by the lack of detailed chronicles of their respective obsequies.

On the other hand, those that we have present an excellent example of magnificent accounts compared with their Spanish and Italian counterparts, describing the artistic programme that adorned the solemnities.[27] The book for Philip II, despite its lack of illustrations, is packed with detailed information. In the case of Margarita of Austria's funeral book and even more so with the one of Philip IV – judged by Víctor Mínguez as one of the most impressive examples of its kind during the seventeenth century[28] – the texts are embellished with numerous elegant engravings, replicating the emblematic adornments that constructed the iconographic programme of the ceremony. With the exception only of the Palermitan obsequies for Marie-Louis of Bourbon,[29] parallel accounts in the Spanish-controlled cities of Milan, Palermo, or Messina exhibited far more modest editorial efforts, offering shorter narratives and usually no illustrations. The same is true for close Spanish allies like Florence and Rome, which incurred great expense for the obsequies, although their sumptuous *apparati* were not aptly reflected by the relatively moderate editorial productions of the events.[30]

The various territories under Spanish domination competed among themselves to show their allegiance to the Spanish monarchy.[31] Part of this zeal was encouraged by the royal orders issued by the very same Spanish monarchs. Nevertheless, some of

the Spanish representatives responsible for arranging the obsequies took the success of such events as a personal badge of honour. For example, the celebration of the obsequies for Isabelle of Bourbon in 1645, in Naples, arranged by the viceroy Juan Alfonso de Cabrera, Great Admiral of Castile (1644–46), moved the Spanish ambassador in Rome, the Count of Siruela, to organize something that would surpass the Neapolitan effort. Thus, 'he ordered that in competition with those made in Naples it should be shown to the world that … [he] had such a magnanimous spirit that knew how to surpass whomever presumed to top his rare talents'.[32]

The question is how we can compare the grades of magnificence in the various obsequies, given the fact that the customary superlatives present in each chronicle described every specific event in absolute, rather than relative, terms.[33] One possibility is to concentrate on the *pièce de résistance* of the obsequies – the catafalque. In Milan, for the funeral honours of Charles V, the chronicler of the event compared the Milanese obsequies to the 'official' ceremony staged by Philip II: 'these obsequies were really grandiose and can be equated to those made in Brussels'. According to him, the measuring rod was unmistakably 'the great catafalque of Milan, which is able to match the marvellous ship of Brussels'.[34] However, after the erection of a mausoleum for Carlo Borromeo in 1610, the subsequent Milanese catafalques had to move backward from the tallest space within the Milanese cathedral, right under the cupola, in a way that decreased their capacity. The chronicler of Margarita of Austria's obsequies, which were the first to be thus affected, apologizes that the new impediment caused the catafalque's size to be less than desired. Unfortunately, he does not mention the exact measurements.[35]

Actually, it is not customary to relate the precise measurements in the official narration, perhaps to avoid punctilious criticism that would judge the quality of the catafalque by its volume alone. Accordingly, let us cite just a few examples where the measurements are available. The catafalques raised at the official Spanish obsequies for Philip II and Margarita of Austria, which were erected at the church of San Jerónimo, were both about 25 square feet in plan (27 *pies quadrados*) and 65 feet tall (71 *pies*). Comparatively, the catafalque of Philip IV, which was designed for the less capacious church of the royal monastery of La Encarnación, measured only 18.3 feet at the square base (20 *pies quadrados*) and rose to a height of 54 feet (59 *pies*).[36]

Returning to the Italian orbit, in Rome, the catafalque of Philip IV was 34.4 square feet at the base (50 *palmi quadrati*) and 55 feet of height (80 *palmi*). The contemporary chronicler was obviously impressed by the sheer size of it since he commented that 'the volume was more than massive in its proportion'.[37] However, the Neapolitan catafalques seem to outdo them all. The Neapolitan catafalque of Philip II, built by the royal engineer Domenico Fontana at the cathedral, had a square base of 27.6 feet (40 *palmi quadrati*) and a height of 64.6 feet (94 *palmi*).[38] In the absence of Fontana, Margarita of Austria's catafalque was designed by his deputy Bartolomeo Picchiati. It was round, with a diameter of 34.4 feet (50 *palmi*) and a height of 64 feet (93

palmi). Although slightly lower than its predecessor, it was elevated upon a platform that enhanced its height by approximately 6.5 additional feet.[39] Finally, the catafalque for Philip IV, erected by Francesco Antonio Picchiati, had an octagonal base, with the same diameter recorded in Margarita's obsequies, and a record height of 87.2 feet (127 *palmi*) – 33.2 feet higher than the catafalque of La Encarnación. According to the chronicler Marcello Marciano this was the maximum possible height that could be achieved inside the church.[40] The different shapes chosen for the bases of the catafalques – a square for Philip II, a circle for Margarita, and an octagon for Philip IV – also show the inventive spirit of the architects in Naples, unlike most of their Spanish and Italian counterparts who regularly chose the octagonal base during the seventeenth century.[41]

The spirit of competition was extended further at the organizational level. The various sponsors of the obsequies sometimes opted to announce a poetical contest among the various local talents, for the composition of eulogies and *imprese*. For example, Margarita's obsequies in Rome welcomed the participation of several doctors, a licentiate, the poet Margherita Sartocchi, and some Jesuits.[42] For the same occasion in Naples, although the works were commissioned by the viceroy directly from the most erudite groups of intellectuals without a formal competition, their respective compositions were distributed in the church according to a hierarchical logic that ranked the importance attributed to each group. Those of the Jesuits occupied the privileged part in the central nave, those of the *Academici Otiosi* the right side of the crossing, and those of the *Academici Sileni*, whose academy had only recently been founded, the less prestigious left side of the crossing and the choir.[43] The primacy given to the Jesuit fathers was the result of their universally proven ability to forge communicative messages of pedagogical value throughout the Catholic world.[44] As for the members of the Neapolitan academies, the chronicler Ottavio Caputi vouches for their erudition, stating that they were 'religious persons, and secular nobles, trained in human letters and in major studies, giving great examples of virtue'.[45]

Caputi himself, author of both of the funerary books for Philip II and Margarita of Austria, was an *Academico Sileno*, also responsible for the composition of some of the *imprese* and epigrams at these services. Besides a skilful interpretation of the emblematic messages, his competence is proved by his infallible citation of the authorities behind the Latin mottoes that complement the images – usually belonging to the classical tradition such as Vergil, Tacitus, Tertullian, Horace, Claudian, Pliny, etc., and seldom to modern authors such as Torquato Tasso. Unfortunately, apart from a single citation from Alciati,[46] he fails to indicate other sources in contemporary emblem books, although examples from the same Alciati abound, together with borrowings from Girolamo Ruscelli, Paolo Giovio, Giulio Cesare Capaccio, Cesare Ripa, and others (see below). Another deficiency of both of his accounts is the lack of synthesis. The reader is lost in the details of his meticulous description, missing the central idea at the core of the programme. A pronounced difference can be sensed reading the account of Marcello Marciano, the chronicler of Philip IV's obsequies. Marciano was a fiscal lawyer at the

office of the Royal Patrimony, who, like Caputi, was selected by the viceregal administration to be one of the organizers of the obsequies. Written in a typically baroque style,
full of pathos and adorned with elaborate *concetti*, the book is an appropriate companion
to the complicated adornment of the church, which addresses a highly refined audience.

Without further delay, let us examine the *apparati* of the three obsequies under
discussion, putting a special emphasis on their emblematic messages. All three shared
similar constitutive elements: the adornment of the church with black cloth, effigies
of skulls or entire skeletons, and the arms of the house of Austria; a massive catafalque
placed in the nave; and a great variety of paintings, statues, and *imprese*, usually accompanied by Latin, Spanish, and Italian poetic and rhetorical compositions, scattered all
around the church's aisles, and also filling the catafalque, in a way that transformed it
into rather a broad statement of the Baroque's *horror vacui*. In the following analysis
emphasis will be given to the pictorial representations that were drawn for these solemn
occasions. Wishing to avoid the aforementioned debate on the proper terminology for
the various emblematic genres, I will simply refer to these as *imprese*, following the term
chosen by Caputi and Marciano.

In the absence of an openly declared iconographical programme at the obsequies
of Philip II and Margarita of Austria, a general topic emerges: the spiritual virtues of
the deceased triumph over death. According to Steven Orso and Adita Allo Manero this
is the most recurrent theme that dominated royal obsequies throughout the Spanish
world.[47] Accordingly, the *imprese* subdivide into two or three main categories that convey
this message in a sequential logic. First usually appears a series of *imprese* that deals with
the behaviour of the royal person in life, intended to present him or her as a paragon of
comportment. Seldom is there a specific historical reference, but most often the *impresa*
represents a virtue of the deceased. The next category is concerned with the royal
person's afterlife, always assuring the mourners of her or his assured celestial transcendence. The third category is usually restricted to male obsequies, as the 'triumph over
death' has to overcome the concern for dynastic succession. Thus, the respective *imprese*
primarily defend the legitimacy of the successor.[48]

At the obsequies of Philip II, the *imprese* were distributed in two main locations:
inside the catafalque, and around the church. In both cases, the mottoes were written
with golden letters causing a dazzling effect as 'the entire church was covered with black,
and resplendent with the finest gold'.[49] The *imprese* also covered the same three themes
stated above, and they were produced mainly by Jesuits, except for a few examples
created by Ottavio Caputi and other academy members. However, those inside the
catafalque are of greater interest because they interacted with the statues and adornments within the construction, thus creating a coherent ensemble.

The catafalque had a square base, it was shaped like a temple, with an internal
octagonal construction, surmounted by a cupola. Four statues, one at each corner
of the catafalque, represented the angels of the apocalypse that will call humanity to
universal judgement. Eight more statues of angels were seated on the pediments of the

four temple's doors, each holding a laurel crown to symbolize the territorial conquests of the Spanish king. Inside the catafalque were four statues of women in mourning representing the four continents then known, Europe, Asia, Africa, and America, through all of which the Habsburg possessions extended.[50] Finally, sixteen additional standing statues, representing the king's virtues, surrounded the entire structure. Thus, the various sets of statues implicitly traced the path of Philip II's itinerary from this world to the next. In other words, they showed that through his triumphs and virtues in life, he would gain the Kingdom of Heaven on the day of the universal judgement.[51]

The catafalque's *imprese* accurately delivered the very same message. Four sets, each containing six *imprese*, were placed respectively on each of the four sides of the temple. Every set was located between four of the statues representing the various virtues. The first set was placed among Magnanimity, Liberality, Christian Religion, and Justice, and dealt with the biography and personal attributes of Philip II. Caputi does not mention the authors of the *imprese*, yet he notes that they were not original inventions, but *imprese* that had been used by the very same Philip II during his lifetime. Not coincidentally, some of them evoke images and classical myths that were an oblig-atory reference in the Habsburgs' iconography. The first *impresa* depicted Hercules carrying the world on his back, with the motto 'Ut Quiescat Atlas' (Let Atlas take a rest), alluding to the abdication of Charles V, exhausted at carrying the government of the world on his shoulders, passing it over to his son, the new Hercules. Viewed as one of the ancestors of the kings of Spain, regarded as the ultimate example of virtue by contemporary humanists, and carrying a vast potential of worthy paragons within the myths of his heroic labours, Hercules came to be the most exploited ancient hero in the Habsburgs' imagery.[52] A relevant example to our subject is the personal *impresa* of Charles V – the two columns of Hercules, and the motto 'Plus Ultra' (More beyond) – denoting the vastness of the Habsburg Empire that surpassed the bounda-ries of the ancient world, and by association the transcendence of the breach opened by Hercules, by his successor Charles V.[53] Next in the series, there is the carriage of Apollo, rising luminous from the east, with the motto 'Iam Illustrabit Omnia' (Now he will illuminate everything), illustrating the glorious beginning of Philip's reign, making his virtues evident, once he took power.[54] As already mentioned, this analogy between the sun and the ruler is one that had been stressed frequently by early modern monar-chical propaganda. This analogy becomes all the more vivid within the global dimen-sions of the Spanish monarchy, and will be widely stressed in the books of political emblematists like Saavedra Fajardo (1640), Solórzano (1651), Mendo (1657) and in the emblems drawn for various celebrations throughout the Spanish world.[55] In the third *impresa*, Philip II is compared to a compass, with one arm firm in the centre, making a perfect circle, with the motto 'Circuit Immotus' (It made the circle without moving), meaning that although he was usually stationary in Spain, through his mighty empire he had had the world circled. Next, was an *impresa* showing a pair of scales in equal balance, with the motto 'Nec Spe, Nec Metu' (Without hope, without fear).

Lauding the stoic virtue of constancy, it signified that Philip's spirit was immutable, never losing his equilibrium, whatever the circumstances. This *impresa* may as well have served any other of the Habsburg monarchs as impassibility, gravity, and aloofness were qualities that they zealously cherished, and passed from one generation to the other, creating a proverbial image of self-control.[56] Next, a horse jumping out of a circle, with the motto 'Non Sufficit Orbis' (The world is not enough), was equated to Philip II, whose greatness of spirit could not leave him contented with just one world. Last in this series, borrowed from the emblem book of Paolo Giovio,[57] was the image of the Gordian Knot, and a hand armed with a sword in the act of cutting it, with the motto, already used by the Catholic monarchs, 'Tanto Monta' (It amounts so much). According to Caputi, Philip had brought this *impresa* with him to Portugal, wanting to show that he would use sheer force to conquer it, if it would not be rendered to him by his right of succession.[58]

When Caputi mentions the exact placement of the *impresa* in respect to a statue, a thing he does only sporadically, there is a complementary relationship between the two. Thus, the *impresa* with a compass is strategically placed near the statue of liberality, which also carries a compass in her right hand and coins in her left, to show that to be really virtuous, munificence should be done with measure. Similarly, above the statue of justice – represented by a woman carrying a pair of scales, a book of laws, and a sword – was situated the *impresa* with the scales, and below it, the one with the sword cutting the Gordian Knot. So Caputi seems once more to have failed to expose the full programmatic intentions and sophistication of the *apparato* to the reader.

The second and the third sets are interrelated, as they both deal with the king's death, except that the first emphasized his fame and illustrious legacy left on earth, and the next his passage to the afterlife. Hence, the second set of *imprese* situated among Vigilance, Docility, Temperance, and Strength seemed to claim that death had not affected the memory of the king, or the stability of his empire.[59] For this purpose, the Jesuit fathers chose to play on a variety of planetary images, most especially the afore-mentioned solar metaphor. This included *imprese* such as an image of the eighth sphere, full of stars (the king's good deeds), whose light is communicated from the sun (Philip II) and could not be shaded by the earth (his death); and a serene sky full of stars, with the sun just finishing its setting. Two other *imprese* were drawn from the world of nature, showing that the king's virtues became more evident after his death. One was the tree of balsam, which produced its aromatic resin after its trunk had been cut down, and the other a bird of paradise, which is said to be able to change its old feathers into a set of beautiful new ones after its death.[60]

Similar comparisons were also the inspiration of most of the *imprese* of the next set, which were situated amid Mercy, Peace, Prudence, and Faith.[61] The bird of paradise, hanging in a pure air, high above the earth, and a bird breaking the net that had it imprisoned, and flying away, all had a comforting purpose – to assure the mourners of the king's safe arrival in Heaven. As noted by Julian Gallego, the emotional mood of the

participants at the obsequies was a strange mixture of sadness and rejoicing precisely because of this consolatory message.[62]

Last but not least for its political importance was the fourth set of *imprese* situated between the statues of Wisdom, Maturity, Christian Charity, and Hope, representing the theme of succession.[63] The need to convey the message to as many spectators as possible is evident from the clarity of the images, whose significance can be grasped without even having to read the Latin motto. Following are some examples: a sun, setting in the west, leaving a second sun in the middle of the sky; a small phoenix, standing on a great mountain of ashes, showing that it was reborn from the ashes of its mother; an adult eagle flying to the sky, and leaving behind a young eagle, already able to fly on its own; a huge oak tree, which consumed by its old age has fallen to the ground, next to which grows a young, middle-sized descendant, bearing green leaves and fruits; and finally, a dying lion lying on the ground, next to which is a lion cub prepared to fight a dragon standing in front. Besides clarifying the issue of succession, some of the images chosen were universally acknowledged synonyms of royalty, like the sun, the lion, and the eagle. As for the phoenix and the oak tree, they were well-known symbols of eternal endurance. Implicitly, they refer back to the previous theme of celestial transcendence, echoing the celebrated French cry: 'Le roi ne meurt jamais!' ('The king never dies!').[64]

Compared with Philip II's obsequies, those of Margarita of Austria, wife of Philip III, had a more pronounced theatrical quality. Perhaps this was motivated by her tragic death at the young age of twenty-seven, after giving birth to the *infante* Alonso.[65] For example, at the entrance of the church hung various poems inviting the mourners to visit the obsequies of Margarita, as if they were about to attend some sort of theatrical representation. It is worth quoting one particular passage, that draws an unmistakable analogy between the funerary rite and a tragedy played on stage.

> Lugubri imprese, e dolorose insegne.
> Fan di Morte un Teatro, ove n'insegne,
> Quasi in Tragica Scena, human pensiero,
> Che le glorie mortali, ombre del vero,
> Spettator l'Universo ammiri, e sdegne.[66]

> (Mournful *imprese*, and grief-laden insignia
> Make of Death a Theatre, that shows,
> Almost in a Tragic Scene, the human thought,
> That the mortal glories, shadows of truth,
> The Spectator Universe should admire, and disdain.)

The *imprese* covered the entire place, being much more abundant than those produced for Philip II's obsequies. Accordingly, this time, instead of twenty-four *imprese*, the catafalque contained sixty-one. A few images shall suffice. This ephemeral edifice had a circular base, and sixteen surrounding columns, in four groups of four, creating four doors, at the entrance of which stood four statues of angels: Michael, Gabriel, Raphael, and the Guardian Angel. Under each of the four lay a Latin motto and an epigram,

describing their reception of Margarita in Heaven.[67] Eight statues surrounded the catafalque, placed above the sixteen columns of the base. They portrayed angels representing some of the queen's virtues: Love of God, Religion, Divine Grace, Oration, Charity, Compassion towards the Church, Simplicity, and Conjugal Love.[68] Just as in the case of Philip II, the angels and the virtues combined to glorify Margarita for her deeds in life, and to elevate her to beatification after her death. Not coincidentally, the messages of the *imprese* worked in tandem with them.

The first series of *imprese* that adorned the catafalque, composed by the *Academici Otiosi*, started with references to the queen's life and her virtuous conduct, placed in a chronological sequence. Under this category we may place the first thirty-seven *imprese*.[69] The first represented the birth of Margarita (Figure 10), whose name means pearl in Latin, by means of a mother of pearl receiving the celestial dew from which pearls were believed to be created.[70]

This specific *impresa* is a good example to illustrate the fancifulness of some beliefs conveyed through emblems and *imprese* concerning the natural world. It mattered little to the producers of *imprese* if the ideas brought forward were based on scientific truths or mere fantasy, as long as they contained a pedagogic value.[71] The pearl metaphor will appear in many other *imprese* in this account, as was widely exploited in other parallel obsequies for the death of Margarita.[72] According to Caputi 'these *imprese* of pearls were estimated as especially beautiful; because without the need for a metaphor, or some other poetic image, they stood on their own for the name Margarita'.[73] This comment, in which the simplicity of the *impresa* is highly appreciated, perhaps following Ruscelli's prescription, shows the striking shift in taste that will be made evident in the *imprese*

Figure 10 *Impresa signaling the birth of Queen Margarita*

Figure 11 *Impresa showing Queen Margarita's fecundity*

devised for Philip IV.[74] There follow three *imprese* respectively describing a splendid pearl, a virtuous stone, and mother of pearl, representing Margarita's beauty.[75] They allude to a natural and spiritual beauty, not to feminine attractiveness enhanced by the aforementioned external artifices that are allegedly used to tempt the flesh as criticized during the Catholic Reformation.

Next, we find Margarita performing a sequence of 'ideal' gender tasks. First, she is portrayed as Hesperos, the most luminous of stars, which is always close to the sun, alluding to her relation to her husband, Philip III.[76] The importance of her role as loyal wife was by far surpassed because she was a mother, and, even more, because she had assured the Habsburg succession. Not coincidentally a series of *imprese* was dedicated to it. First, to emphasize her fecundity, she appears as a plant of prickly pears bearing fruits (Figure 11).[77] Next, in a replica of an Alciatine emblem,[78] her fecundity and selfless love for her children is represented through the image of a dove that prepares a nest for her nestling from her own feathers, and consequently dies of cold with the arrival of winter (Figure 12).[79] This is also a hint at the circumstances of her premature death. Nevertheless, the last episode of her life receives an even more explicit emblematization – in a subsequent *impresa* Margarita appears as a dying cocoon out of which emerges a butterfly representing the newborn *infante* (Figure 13).[80]

The next group of *imprese* may be characterized as representations of Margarita's spiritual virtues. These fall under a few rubrics. First, to denote that her religious devotion was a source of inspiration, appeared such *imprese* as a phoenix flying to the east, followed by other birds; or a resplendent feather attached to a tree that serves as a guide to travellers at night.[81] The following were intended to emphasize her religious

Figure 12 *Impresa showing Queen Margarita's devoted maternity*

piety: an elephant adoring the moon, while holding a branch of palm in his trunk; a singing phoenix, turned to the east, just before sunrise, showing the queen's vigilance and devotion by starting to say her prayers even before dawn.[82] Her charity was noted through *imprese* such as that of the River Nile with its crocodiles, with the motto 'Secreto De Fonte' (From an unknown source), meaning that just as the River Nile,

Figure 13 *Impresa signaling the death of Queen Margarita and the birth of the Infante*

whose source is unknown, fertilizes Egypt, so Margarita used to give to charity anony-
mously, as ordered by Christ.[83] *Imprese* such as a deer running away from a snake, or a
fish avoiding a net, symbolized her prudence and unequivocal avoidance of sin.[84] The
rest of the *imprese* denoted her humility, temperance, and internal fortitude. Unfortunately, Caputi still fails to show the spatial correspondence of the *imprese* to the
respective statues of the various virtues, although they were all arranged in a neat and
coherent ensemble.

The *imprese* chosen to describe Margarita's life embody in a nutshell, or in her
case one should rather say in a mother of pearl shell, the Counter-Reformation's vision
of the ideal woman. Her salient virtues are necessarily attached to the spiritual world
and not to the political realm, so that her aspirations in life are limited to that of the
obedient wife, the devoted mother, and the pious Christian.[85] In this sense, her public
image stands in stark contrast with the triumphant representation of Philip II, and
his virile attributes. However, when we proceed to the *imprese* describing her celestial transcendence we find almost identical motifs, except that they are adapted to a
feminine imagery. Just to cite a couple of examples, instead of the eclipsed sun that
symbolized the death of the king, Margarita was represented with one of the most
common funerary metaphors for queens – an eclipsed moon – with the motto 'Mox
Splendidior' (Soon to be more splendid) (Figure 14).

The allusion was that just as the moon will shine more brightly after escaping the
shade of earth, so the queen would not be obscured by death, but will be illuminated
by her rise to Heaven.[86] Similarly, instead of the aforementioned perfumed balsam tree,
representing Philip II, Margarita was depicted as a bush of roses, with the Spanish
motto 'Transpuesta Mas Olorosa' (Better smelling when transplanted), implying that

Figure 14 *Lunar emblematization of Queen Margarita*

the passage to Heaven has made the queen's virtues to be even more evident.[87] Since the Spanish succession was based upon a patrilineal principle, and Margarita had left behind a legacy of living male heirs, her death did not cause any related problems. Accordingly, *imprese* dealing with this theme were absent from her funerary honours.

With the obsequies of Philip IV, we face a very different kind of artistic programme. This is not just because of the scale of the material investment, as the entire *apparato* reaches an unprecedented extravagance, increased by the decision to commission the celebrated artist Luca Giordano. Marciano affectedly claims that 'the desire for glory alone moved him to undertake such a great enterprise', despite the great cost.[88] What makes this programme so special is the peculiar tension between the attempt to synthesize and harmonize the various parts of the whole, and the tendency to create complex ideas that verge on the cryptic. Fortunately, Marciano is the right person to explain it all, because unlike Caputi he is very well aware of the idea behind the ensemble, being the one responsible for the 'invention and the compositions'.[89] As he neatly explains at the beginning of the chronicle, the title of the book, *Pompe Funebri dell'Universo (Funeral Ceremonies of the Universe)*, hints at the artistic programme of the obsequies. Namely, the entire universe constituted by the earth, the four elements, the rivers, and so forth, together with the celestial realm made up of the various constellations, is summoned to these obsequies to deplore the king's death.[90] With more precision he says that the readers should not be confounded by the various parts of the *apparato*, which should not be regarded as merely 'accidents united by coincidence, but [as] integral substances of one whole'.[91] A detailed analysis of the three parts of the *apparato*, constituted by the atrium, the church's interior, and the catafalque, has benefited from the excellent scholarship of Víctor Mínguez.[92] Therefore, I will concentrate exclusively on the interpretation of some of the unexplored emblematic compositions of the programme.

This time, rather than being situated in the catafalque as in the previous cases, the principal emblematic compositions were hanging from a black cloth in the church's nave. They represented the sixty constellations of the universe, which like all the other elements present in the programme lamented the death of the monarch at the age of sixty. Especially interesting are the last twelve constellations, which are those discovered in the New World, and were obviously not known to the Ancients. As acknowledged by Marciano in the introduction, those named here are the constellations introduced by Johan Bayer in his seminal book *Uranometria* (1603), the first to treat the entire skies, including the Southern Hemisphere.[93] These constellations can hardly be labelled *imprese*, as their intricate and unusual format included the name and the allegorical image of the constellation, two sides of a medal representing a Habsburg ancestor of the deceased, and two *imprese* – one for the ancestor and one for Philip IV. Finally, a Latin eulogy for Philip IV combined some of the elements present in each respective constellation and gave some sense to the whole. Needless to say, quite often the correspondence between the various parts is equivocal, and the composers have to force

Figure 15 *Constellation of Perseus*

down the pieces in order to complete the jigsaw. Nevertheless, the intellectual effort is laudable. On this occasion I will limit myself to sampling two of these constellations, chosen because of their allusion to the problematic relationship between Naples and the Spanish monarchy after the Neapolitan revolt of 1647 – a relationship that I think had an affect on the exuberance of the programme's format.

The first is the constellation of Perseus, surmounted by a figure of the Greek hero (Figure 15). The Habsburg ancestor chosen to fill one side of the medal was the Emperor Rudolph I, known also as The Victorious for his successes in the battlefield – aptly corresponding to Medusa's vanquisher. On the other side of the medal was Perseus crowned with laurel and the inscription 'Victoria Nobilis' (Noble victory). The *impresa* of Rudolph contained a hand holding a branch of olive and a club with the motto 'Utrum Lubet' (Whichever you please). That of Philip IV contained the winged legs of Perseus, with the motto 'Gemino Commercia Mundo' (Exchange between two worlds), meaning that just as Philip IV has opened commercial exchanges between two worlds in his life, in his death he has opened an exchange of his kingdoms with Heaven. The eulogy used the myth of Perseus to make a comparison with Philip IV. Its relevant part was that, like Perseus, Philip IV had overcome the 'blind Gorgons', so to speak, of the rebellions in Naples, Messina, and Catalonia.[94]

The second constellation – Equus Minor – was marked with a little horse (Figure 16). On one side of the medal appeared the unfortunate son of Philip IV, Prince Baltassar Carlos, who died at the young age of sixteen in 1646. On the reverse of the medal was the inscription 'Generosa Indoles' (Noble character). On the prince's *impresa* was depicted a horse with a bridle, with the motto 'Paret Lentis Animosus' (Furious seems peaceful). According to Marciano, the allusion was to the Neapolitan horse, 'which despite being vigorous and warlike, obsequiously submitted to the most delicate Austrian bridle'.[95] The *impresa* of Philip IV included a horse standing next to a tomb, with the motto 'Domini Consistit In [H]Ora Iacentis (He stands still in the hour when his master is lying down).[96] It meant that the (Neapolitan) horse showed his endless loyalty to his master, the king, even after his death. The eulogy played on the comparison of the bridled horse with Naples. It suggested that it should not be called the little horse, but the great, because it surpassed all the other Habsburg subjects in its docility, loyalty, and now sadness. Hence, it received with happiness the new bridle of the heir Charles II, and showed its deep mourning with the dimness of the four stars of the constellation, which also symbolized the four deceased Habsburg monarchs of Naples (Charles V, Philip II, Philip III, and Philip IV).[97]

Both of these allusions to Naples – one explicitly censuring the revolt of 1647, and the second trying to compensate for the former by exaggerating the allegiance of Naples to the Spanish crown – reinforce Mínguez's claims of the existence of an overstated sadness for the king's disappearance, in a way that exceeds the usual expressions of grief present in the genre, as if trying to make up for the past treachery.[98] This counterbalancing tendency, combined with a lavish baroque style, succeeded in

Figure 16 *Constellation of Little Horse*

bringing about one of the most original and splendid obsequies ever celebrated for a Spanish king.[99] When we add it to the other two examples examined, although the latter are less idiosyncratic and blend well within their contemporary European context, we receive a picture of a rich cultural legacy that vindicates the underrated importance of Naples within the history of Spanish civilization. Moreover, the unusually expensive and elaborated obsequies staged in Naples show us, as I have already demonstrated on other festive occurrences, a characteristic strategy of concealing the conflictive nature of the city with grand public displays of civic solidarity.

Notes

The section 'Neapolitan *imprese*' is an expanded and updated version of my paper published as 'Pictorial Representations for Neapolitan Obsequies of the Spanish Habsburgs', in *Florilegio de estudios de Emblemática: A Florilegium of Studies on Emblematics: Proceedings of the Sixth International Conference of The Society for Emblem Studies: A Coruña, 2002*, ed. Sagrario López Poza (Ferrol, 2004), 425–30.

1　Here is just a sample of some of the books that were relevant to this study: Andrea Alciato, *Los emblemas de Alciato traducidos en rhimas españolas* (Lyon, 1549); Paolo Giovio, *Dialogo dell'Imprese Militari e Amorose* (Rome, 1555); Luca Contile, *Ragionamento sopra la proprietà delle imprese* (Pavia, 1574); Girolamo Ruscelli, *Le imprese illustri* (Venice, 1580); Scipione Bargagli, *Dell'imprese* (Venice, 1594); Giulio Cesare Capaccio, *Delle imprese* (Naples, 1592); Cesare Ripa, *Iconologia* (Rome, 1593). I used Ripa's English translation by Pierce Tempest (London, 1709). Diego Saavedra Fajardo, *Idea de un principe politico christiano, representada en cien empresas* (Munich, 1640); Juan de Solórzano Pereira, *Emblemas regios-politicos* (Valencia, 1658); Emanuele Tesauro, *Il cannocchiale aristotelico* (Turin, 1670); Juan de Borja, *Impresas morales* (Brussel, 1680).

2　The figures are in Giuseppina Ledda, *Contributo allo studio di letteratura emblematica in Spagna (1549–1613)* (Pisa, 1970), 23.

3　See Carlo Ginzburg, 'The High and the Low: The Themes of Forbidden Knowledge in the Sixteenth and Seventeenth Centuries', *Past and Present*, 73 (1976), 28–41.

4　Just to mention a few of the projects, see the various research schemes at the University of Glasgow, www.emblems.arts.gla.ac.uk/; *The English Emblem Book Project*, coordinated by people at The Pennsylvania State University, http://emblem.libraries.psu.edu/home.htm; *German Emblem Books*, by the University of Illinois at Urbana Champaign, http://images.library.uiuc.edu/projects/emblems/; and finally, of most relevance for us is the digitized project of Spanish emblem books, at the University of La Coruña, http://rosalia.dc.fi.udc.es/emblematica/.

5　For a European perspective see John Manning, 'Renaissance and Baroque Symbol Theory: Some Introductory Questions and Problems', in *Aspects of Renaissance and Baroque Symbol Theory 1500–1700*, ed. Peter Daly and John Manning (New York, 1999), xiii–xv. For a Spanish definition of the problem see in *ibid.*, Pedro F. Campa, 'Terms for Emblem in the Spanish Tradition', 13–26. Of fundamental importance for any discussion on Spanish emblems is Julian Gallego, *Visión y simbolos en la pintura Española del Siglo de Oro* (Madrid, 1984). For issues of definition see especially 25 ff.

6　Tesauro, *Cannocchiale*, 706.

7　Strong, *Art and Power*, 25–6.

8　Quoted in Ledda, *Letteratura emblematica*, 19.

9　Bulifon, *Giornali*, 287.

10　Ledda, *Letteratura emblematica*, 18.

11　Fernando R. de la Flor, 'Los contornos del emblema. Del escudo heráldico a la divisa y la

empresa', in *Actas del I simposio internacional de embelmatica, Teruel, 1 y 2 de octubre 1991* (Teruel, 1994), 27–58.

12   See the edition published in Venice, 1580, 10.

13   See Castiglione, *Cortigiano*, book II, ch. 8.

14   Anderson, *Hispanic Costume*, 51.

15   Flor, 'Contornos del emblema', 48.

16   Tesauro, *Cannocchiale*, 626.

17   For example, thirty-one pages are dedicated to the entry in the case of Valentini, *Sontuoso torneo*, 12–40, and only three to the combat, 40–2.

18   *Ibid.*, 9.

19   *Ibid.*, 15–16.

20   Castaldi, *Tributi Ossequiosi*, 76.

21   *Ibid.*, 84.

22   *Ibid.*, 82.

23   *Ibid.*, 80.

24   See SNSP, MS. XXIII. D. 15, *Notitia*, fol. 16.

25   For a rare exception see Víctor Mínguez, 'Exequias de Felipe IV en Nápoles. La exaltación dinástica a través de un programa astrológico', *Ars Longa*, 2 (1991), 53–62.

26   For each of the obsequies see respectively, Ottavio Caputi, *La pompa funeraria fatta in Napoli nell'essequie del catholico Re Filippo II. di Austria* (Naples, 1599); by the same, *Relatione*; and Marcello Marciano, *Pompe Funebri dell'Universo Nella Morte di Filippo Quarto il Grande Re delle Spagne Celebrate dal Eminentissimo Cardinale Aragóna, Arcivescovo di Toleto, Viceré e Capitan Generale del Regno di Napoli* (Naples, 1666).

27   Spanish royal obsequies in Italy have been largely neglected so far; nevertheless, they have started to arouse some interest in recent years. The only comparative work that I know, covering the various states of the Italian peninsula, is by Montserrat Moli Frigola, 'Donne, candele, lacrime, e morte. Funerali di regine spagnole nell'Italia del Seicento', in *Barocco romano e barocco italiano. Il teatro, l'effimero, l'allegoria*, ed. Marcello Fagiolo and Maria Luisa Madonna (Rome, 1985), 135–58. A synthesis of the various Milanese obsequies during Spanish rule is provided by Sonia G. Grandis, 'Teatri di sontuosissima e orrida maestà. Trionfo della morte e trionfo del re nelle pompe funebri regali', in *La scena della gloria. Drammaturgia e spettacolo a Milano in età spagnola*, ed. Annamaria Cascetta and Roberta Carpani (Milan, 1995), 659–715. For Florence see the proceedings of the exhibition *La morte e la gloria. Apparati funebri medicei per Filippo II e Margherita d'Austria*, ed. Monica Bietti (Leghorn, 1999). For Naples see Mancini, *Feste*, 127–38.

28   Mínguez, 'Exequias', 53.

29   Francisco de Montalbo, *Noticias funebres de las magestosas exequias, que hizo la felicissima Ciudad de Palermo, Cabeça Coronada de Sicilia, En la muerte de Maria Luysa de Borbon, nuestra Señora Reyna de Las Españas* (Palermo, 1689).

30   For two relatively costly examples see Vincentio Pitti, *Essequie della Sacra Cattolica Real Maestà del Re di Spagna D. Filippo II d'Austria. Celebrate dal Serenissimo D. Fernando Medici Gran Duca di Toscana nella Città di Firenze* (Florence, 1598); and Antonio Pérez de Rua, *Funeral hecho en Roma en la Yglesia de Santiago de los Españoles a 18 de Diciembre de 1665 a la gloriosa memoria del Rei Catolico de las Españas nuestro señor D. Felipe Quarto el Grande* (Rome, 1666).

31   Carlos M. N. Eire describes how ritual rivalry manifested itself in parallel obsequies throughout the Spanish world, in his *From Madrid to Purgatory: The Arts and Crafts of Dying in Sixteenth-Century Spain* (New York, 1995), 295–6.

32   Quoted in Moli Frigola, 'Donne', 153.

33   For a survey of celebratory books as a genre in early modern Europe see Watanabe-O'Kelly, 'Festivals Books'.

34   Quoted in Grandis, 'Teatri', 665. For the obsequies of Charles V in Brussels and their subsequent influence on Italy see Jaynie Anderson, ' "Le roi ne meurt jamais": Charles V's Obsequies

in Italy', in *El Cardenal Albornoz y el Colegio de Espana*, V (Bologna, 1979), 379–99.

35 Gio. Battista Piccaglia, *Relatione del funerale et esequie fatte in Milano, Per ordine della Cat. Maestà del Potentis. Rè di Spagna Don Filippo Terzo Nostro Signore, Alla Serenissima Regina Donna Marghe- rita d'Austria Sua moglie, li 22 di Decembre 1611* (Milan, 1612), 15.

36 Steven N. Orso, *Art and Death at the Spanish Habsburg Court: The Royal Exequies for Philip IV* (Columbia, 1989), 65.

37 Fagiolo dell'Arco, *Festa barocca*, 430.

38 Caputi, *Pompa funeraria*, 6–9.

39 Caputi, *Relatione*, 10, 57.

40 Marciano, *Pompe Funebri*, 125.

41 Moli Frigola, 'Donne', 144–5.

42 *Ibid.*, 142–3.

43 Caputi, *Relatione*, 100.

44 See Giuseppina Ledda, 'Estrategias y procedimientos comunicativos en la emblemática aplicada (fiestas y celebraciones, siglo XVII)', in *Emblemata aurea. La emblemática en el arte y la literatura del Siglo de Oro*, ed. Rafael Zafra and José Javier Azanza (Madrid, 2000), 251–62.

45 Caputi, *Relatione*, 7.

46 *Ibid.*, 23–4.

47 See Orso, *Art and Death*, 71–81; and Adita Allo Manero, 'Iconografia funeraria de las honras de Felipe IV en España e Hispanoamerica', *Quadernos de Investigacion Historica*, 7 (1981), 81.

48 Orso, *Art and Death*, 76–7. For the same themes in various obsequies for Philip IV, see Allo Manero, 'Iconografia funeraria', 81–91.

49 Caputi, *Pompa funeraria*, 107.

50 Unambiguously, they follow Ripa's guidebook of mythical iconology. In Ripa, *Iconologia*, see for Europe, fig. 185, 47; Asia, fig. 210, 53; Africa, fig. 209, 53; America, fig. 212, 53.

51 See Caputi, *Pompa funeraria*, 6–10.

52 For the political uses of Hercules by various early modern dynasties see Friedrich Polleross, 'From the *Exemplum Virtutis* to the Apotheosis: Hercules as an Identification Figure in Portrai- ture: An Example of the Adoption of Classical Forms of Representation', in *Iconography*, ed. Ellenius, 37–72.

53 For a thorough survey of this imagery see Fernando Checa Cremades, 'The Image of Charles V', in *Charles V*, ed. Soly, 486–9, and in *ibid.*, Burke, 'Presenting and Re-presenting Charles V', 422–5.

54 This appears also in Ruscelli, *Le imprese illustri*, 191.

55 On this issue see Víctor Mínguez, 'Los emblemas solares, la imagen del príncipe y los programas astrológicos en el arte efímero', in *Actas del I simposio internacional de emblemática*, 209–53; González Enciso, 'Del rey ausente', 4; and Santiago Sebastián, *Emblemática e historia del arte* (Madrid, 1995), 207–9.

56 Burke, 'Presenting and Re-presenting Charles V', 409–10. Here is a specific reference concerning Philip IV by the seventeenth-century French traveller Antoine de Brunel, quoted in *La sociedad española*, ed. Díez Borque, 166–7: 'Va acompañado de tanta gravedad, que obra y se mueve con el aire de una estatua animada. Los que se le han aproximado aseguran que cuando le han hablado jamás le han visto cambiar de asiento ni de postura: que les recibía, les escuchaba y les respondía con una misma cara, no moviéndose en todo su cuerpo más que los labios y la lengua.'

57 Giovio, *Dialogo dell'Imprese*, 15–16.

58 For this set of *imprese* see Caputi, *Pompa funeraria*, 12–15.

59 See Caputi, *Pompa funeraria*, 16–18.

60 Birds of paradise were probably first introduced to the attention of Europeans by Antonio Pigafetta, a member of Magellan's crew during the famous circumnavigation of the world (completed on 6 September 1522), who saw the birds in the Moluccas. See his *Primo viaggio intorno al globo terracqueo*, ed. Carlo Amoretti (Milan, 1800), 156. In this *impresa* the birds'

ability to grow feathers after their death is part of the aforementioned tendency of some *imprese* writers to mix myth with reality, as long as it supported their pedagogical messages.

61 *Ibid.*, 19–21.
62 Julian Gallego, 'Aspectos emblemáticos en las reales exequias españolas de la casa de Austria', *Goya*, 187/8 (1985), 120–1.
63 Caputi, *Pompa funeraria*, 23–4.
64 See the classical study of Ralph E. Giesey, *The Royal Funeral Ceremony in Renaissance France* (Geneva, 1960), 177–92.
65 Javier Varela, *La muerte del rey. El ceremonial funerario de la monarquía española, 1500–1885* (Madrid, 1990), 63–4.
66 Caputi, *Relatione*, 8.
67 For a description and a woodcut of each of the angels see *ibid.*, 11–19.
68 These are described in *ibid.*, 54–6.
69 *Ibid.*, 19–40.
70 *Ibid.*, 20.
71 See a good discussion of the topic in José Julio García Arranz, 'Image and Moral Teaching through Emblematic Animals', in *Aspects*, ed. Daly and Manning, 93–108.
72 See for example Grandis, 'Teatri', 672; and Anna Maria Testaverde, 'Margherita d'Austria, regina e "perla" di virtù', in *La morte e la gloria*, ed. Bietti, 132–3.
73 Caputi, *Relatione*, 87.
74 For a thorough discussion of the contemporary debate on the ideal way of producing *imprese* see José Julio García Arranz and Francisco Javier Pizarro Gómez, 'Teoría y práctica de la imagen de las "imprese" en los Siglos XVI y XVII', in *Emblemata aurea*, ed. Zafra and Azanza, 189–207.
75 Caputi, *Relatione*, 21–2.
76 *Ibid.*, 22.
77 *Ibid.*, 23.
78 Alciato, *Emblemas*, 66.
79 Caputi, *Relatione*, 23.
80 *Ibid.*, 24.
81 *Ibid.*, respectively 27, 28.
82 *Ibid.*, respectively, 30, 31.
83 *Ibid.*, 36.
84 *Ibid.*, respectively, 39, 40.
85 For the study of the image of the Spanish queens in Hispanic America see Víctor Mínguez, *Los reyes distantes. Imágenes del poder en el México virreinal* (Castellón, 1995), 109–21. For the image of Spanish queens see Teresa Zapata Fernández de la Hoz, 'La emblemática al servicio de la imagen publica de la reina. Los jeroglíficos de la entada en la corte de Maria Ana de Neoburgo', in *Del libro de emblemas a la ciudad simbolica. Actas del III Simposio Internacional de Emblemática Hispánica*, ed. Víctor Mínguez (2 vols., Castellón, 2000), II, 671–704. In *ibid.*, for the emblematic representation of women in general, see Reyes Escalera Pérez, 'Monjas, madres, doncellas y prostitutas. La mujer en la emblemática', II, 769–91.
86 Caputi, *Relatione*, 42–3. As explained by Mínguez, the moon was the most privileged metaphor to represent the queen, especially for royal honours. Besides the self-evident correspondence of the sun and the moon to the royal couple, the moon lent itself swiftly to represent the metaphor of regency, by substituting 'the sun' during its nightly absence. See his *Reyes distantes*, 113.
87 Caputi, *Relatione*, 43.
88 Marciano, *Pompe Funebri*, 7.
89 *Ibid.*, 5.
90 *Ibid.*, 6.
91 *Ibid.*, 7.

92 Mínguez, 'Exequias', 53–62.
93 The full reference is Johan Bayer, *Uranometria* (Augsburg, 1603).
94 Marciano, *Pompe Funebri*, 41.
95 *Ibid.*, 55.
96 The inscription should probably read 'Hora' instead of 'Ora'.
97 Marciano, *Pompe Funebri*, 55.
98 Mínguez, 'Exequias', 61.
99 See Víctor Mínguez, 'Arte efímero y alegorías. La *Iconología* de Ripa en las exequias romanas de Felipe IV', *Ars Longa*, 1 (1990), 89–96; Allo Manero, 'Iconografía funeraria'; and Orso, *Art and Death*.

Conclusion

The main objective of this book was the exploration of the communication of power of the Spanish viceregal court in Naples and its reception by the citizens of Naples. Accordingly, the emphasis was on the cultural projection of Spain and its values, especially during the seventeenth century, when the princely courts of Europe refined the arts of self-representation and propaganda to unprecedented zeniths of splendour. This was done via the direct visual representations of power of the viceregal court, or by means of the public policies and actions that fostered these attitudes – such as ceremonial and etiquette, state festivities and celebrations, fashion and sumptuary laws, and *imprese*. The response of Neapolitans in all of these instances shows that the viceregal success in achieving its goals was curbed by various degrees of local resistance coming from different social groups, depending on the situation. Indeed, the viceregal limitations of both concrete and symbolic power, best portrayed by the viceroys' attempts to boost their public image and to win over Neapolitan citizens by way of these various forms of political communication, which often proved to be abortive or ineffective, is the leitmotif running through this book.

As soon as this inquiry started it became evident that the political status of the Kingdom of Naples as a state belonging to the Spanish crown, yet governed by an appointed king's stand-in, would complicate any inquiry concerning the representation of the government's power. Whose power was being represented, the king's or the viceroy's? Were these two compatible? And perhaps, more importantly, was the God-given royal charisma a transferable trait that could be simply delegated from one viceroy to the next? The need to ask such questions signalled the peculiarity of the Neapolitan court compared to the great dynastic courts of Spain, France, and England, and of no less interest, the immediate geographical context of Italian principalities. All of these displayed different degrees of pomp and diverse styles of kingship, and achieved various effects of success. None of these, though, had to face the difficulties that were inherent in the viceregal office.

The powers that kings transferred to viceroys conveyed a message of ambiguity. Despite the entrustment of a vast range of authority and jurisdiction over most areas

of government, which placed the viceroys at the top of the city's political hierarchy, the Spanish Habsburgs made sure that their substitutes were placed under binding constrictions. Perhaps the most problematic factor was their election to an initial term of three years, which admittedly could be extended without a specified limit by the king, as testified by Charles V's confidence in Pedro de Toledo, during thirty-one years of government (1532–53). However, the average regency period of viceroys stands at approximately four years. In fact, more often than not, their term was either not extended, or truncated at some point if it was. Viceroys who wanted to assure longevity to their office depended on a myriad of factors. Foremost, their performance had to satisfy the king, who was generally content to extend the term as long as his Neapolitan subjects gave positive feedback concerning the viceroy. Paradoxically, the pressure exerted from Madrid to increase the taxation and mobilization of resources in all the Spanish realms, in order to feed the wars that afflicted the Habsburg Empire during most of the seventeenth century, conspired against the viceroys' popularity. In addition to being subject to a regressive economic policy, Naples was afflicted with chronic forms of social distress such as overpopulation, unemployment, and a high rate of delinquency, and with deep cleavages running between the nobility and *popolo*, in a way that conceding privileges to one status group meant almost automatically earning the resentment of the others. Accordingly, the viceroys' opportunities to objectively satisfy the needs of Neapolitan citizens, and win their sympathy, were almost negligible. To add to the viceroys' objective difficulty to hold on to their offices one should also take into consideration factors beyond their direct control such as the intrigues and machinations between various factions in the court of Madrid that could influence the political decisions taken by the king, or his favourite.

All these obstacles and complications related to the viceroys' concrete exertion of power bore a direct effect on their ritual and representative power. Admittedly, the ceremonial and etiquette that revolved around the Spanish viceroys elevated them above every other person or institution in the realm. The same mechanisms of ceremonial adulation used in European courts, which included grand gestures and situational exaltation to communicate the leader's superiority, were used at the court of Naples. Nevertheless, given the impediments of the office, the public image of viceroys did not benefit from these artificial mechanisms, whose effectiveness depended on concrete sources of legitimization.

Accordingly, the viceroys of Naples usually resembled a bizarre hybrid between a Machiavellian prince and a ruling modern democratic leader running for re-election. Those viceroys who cared more about staying in office rather than emptying the state coffers and fleeing, aimed at the hearts of Neapolitans, always putting a strong emphasis on the external display of their actions. On the positive side, they showed affability towards all their subjects, giving frequent audiences, and mingling and merry-making with both nobility and *popolo*. At the beginning of their term, as if embodying the classical syndrome of 'a new broom sweeps clean', they always showed a strong political

and juridical activism, that faded away after a while, to be resumed towards the end of the term with a strong lobbying and courtship of influential Neapolitans, backed by promises for political jobs, if they were to put in a good word for their reappointment.

What was the result of the combined effect of ceremonial elevation, and a relatively demotic attitude towards the Neapolitan subjects? Compared with the degree of respect achieved by the 'real thing', the King of Spain, the viceroys ranked low indeed. Very often the Neapolitan nobility questioned the conduct and policies of viceroys, protesting against such things as were perceived as ritual affronts to their status, the excessive punishment of their peers, or the advancement of popular issues at their expense. When formal protest did not achieve the desired results, they sent special envoys to the king to ask him to be the final arbiter, or even demanded the viceroy's deposition from office. Similarly, the populist policies of viceroys yielded ambivalent results among the lower strata of the *popolo*. Received as heroes and saviours on their arrival, they often departed with the combined sound of saluting cannons fired from the Spanish fortresses, and the curses and cries of good riddance from the plebeians.

Times of deep crisis even invited episodes of direct challenge and outrageous disrespect of the plebs towards viceroys. Such instances were quite rare, although the unprecedented and solitary violent revolt that was unleashed in July 1647 was enough to expose the total bankruptcy of the viceregal image, diametrically opposed to that of the Spanish king. During the first phase of the revolt, the rebels explained the uprising as a legitimate act against a tyrannical 'bad government', represented by the viceroy and his administration, which misrepresented the godly ordained Spanish monarchs and misinterpreted their will.

In sum, the viceregal court ultimately functioned as a mediator between the king and his Neapolitan subjects, often absorbing the shocks of abrupt exchanges. Paradoxically, the paucity of social revolts in such a problematic city could be the result of the perennial illusion that the present 'bad government', perceived as the cause of all troubles, was only temporary, and that it would soon be supplanted by a better one; a fiction that allowed king and subjects to keep a relatively cordial relationship. In other words, the Spanish ceremonial that served to elevate the viceroy did not suffice to transfer to him the royal charisma, and probably it was never intended to do so. To the detriment of the viceroys, it was all too clear that only the legitimate King of Spain possessed it.

Nevertheless, it would be highly misleading to conclude that the viceregal court exerted no cultural influence on the various forms of self and group representations. After all it functioned as the most available model of a court, and the viceroy was the immediate arbiter concerning issues of ceremony and precedence, and as such it won various degrees of success. For example, the viceregal guidance and maintenance of order was much needed in such socio-political measuring rods as the civic cavalcades. At dozens of these cavalcades every year, celebrating religious and secular events, various social groups paraded, displayed in a hierarchical order. The role of the viceroy in these

exhibitions of power, besides parading at the most privileged spot of the cavalcade, was to regulate any disputes over precedence. As it happens, the apparent covenant of a preordained structure was a fiction, since every so often conflicts arose between different groups, usually between representatives of the *popolo* and nobles, all trying to impose their position. This even happened inside one group, invariably the nobility, in which some nobles claimed a better place, more appropriate to their rank. The usual acceptance of the ruling of the viceroy by the various contestants showed that Neapolitans respected him as a sort of imposing master of ceremonies. Nevertheless, the presence of a royal person in such ceremonial instances threatened to destabilize the entire power structure of the cavalcade and could undermine the viceroy's ability to control the disintegration of its order, as was painfully clarified in the controversial entry of Queen Maria of Austria into Naples in 1630. The failure of the viceroy, the Duke of Alcalá, to prevent and resolve the quarrels of precedence for that entry, cost him his office. This outcome testifies to the importance given to ceremonial issues.

The hierarchical order in cavalcades also reveals deeper layers of meaning related to the relations of power in Neapolitan society as a whole. So far, scholars of Naples have assumed that the order of the groups in the cavalcade was self-explanatory for both contemporary spectators and modern readers. However, a closer look showed that some of the groups were not social groups, as such, but holders of political offices. Hence, the following cardinal questions have not been addressed so far: what was the relationship of social status to these offices? And, was the concrete political power exerted in these offices reflected in the place allocated in the cavalcade?

A few general conclusions emerge from this investigation. First, the conventional assumption of Neapolitanists maintaining that civic processions reproduced the same static and undisputable hierarchy present in the urban social stratification is erroneous. Quite to the contrary, the ceremonial variability of the procession coheres with the constantly growing changeability and social mobility of early modern Naples. This was promoted by the monarchical project of 'divide and rule', which included the political promotion of social groups from the *popolo* and the lower nobility at the expense of the higher nobility. In this respect, the cavalcade reflected a horizontal mobility that took place in society, especially in the various tribunals, as members of lower social groups simply replaced those political posts previously occupied by nobles. Yet, a vertical accession of political groups as such did not occur, and in this sense one may even say that the Neapolitan civic procession during Habsburg rule exhibited a 'false' political hierarchy, because it downplayed the location of the tribunals and the organs of the central government, while the position of the higher nobility remained exaggeratedly exalted. In effect, it appears that the procession exhibited an archaic order that repre-sented a past model of the city's power structure when the affinity between social and political status was greater.

This development may be explained by the different attitude towards honorific issues on behalf of the nobility and the *popolo* – a fact which re-emerged at various

occasions in this investigation. The nobility's general concern for ceremonial appearances claimed the 'lion's share' in the civic procession by retaining the central stage, and by bitterly fighting over every challenge on their individual or corporative position, very much like individual aristocrats would do at every possible contest of precedence which would present itself in daily life. As for the *popolo*'s attitude, it eventually acknowledged the traditional privileges of the higher nobility, as long as it kept clear from the political arena. This seems to be the case even for those commoners who saw the nobility as a 'reference group', as it looked for ennoblement. In fact, there is abundant evidence showing social arrivistes of ignoble origins, promoted and ennobled by the crown, who could not, or would not, integrate into the cultural world of the old nobility. They chose either to decline competitions of conspicuous consumption with their peers of older lineage, or to present alternative models of self-representation. This is most evident in the artistic portraiture of power in early modern Naples. On the one hand, the arrivistes competed with the old nobility to secure chapels across the city to immortalize their deceased family members. On the other hand, the traditional aristocratic model of a martial and chauvinistic warrior, portrayed or sculpted with his armour, sword, and coat of arms, was supplanted with that of a long robed man surrounded with his books, symbolizing the learned means which brought about his ascendance in the world.[1]

As for the third political contender, the monarchy, which had the practical power of actually imposing ceremonial changes in the cavalcade, it is clear that it had no interest in 'rocking the boat'. Although it strove to debilitate the titled nobility's political power, it did not undercut its hegemonic social status – one that remained generally stable throughout our period. In addition, the Spanish crown had a way of compensating the nobility for its loss of political power with honorific privileges – such as grants of chivalric orders, titles, ceremonial duties – that ensured its loyalty to the crown.[2] Similarly, the ranking of the groups within the civic cavalcades might be regarded as part of this conciliatory-honorific practice. Moreover, in Naples as in other courtly environments, the crown and the nobility reinforced and supported each other in the various representations of power. The prominent position of the titled nobility in the cavalcade enhanced the one occupied by the monarchy, and vice versa. This is exemplified by the centrality of the viceroy, with the noble 'mayor' at his side, and preceded by the Seven Great Officers of the Realm, who at the same time represented the nobility and the monarchy. Montesquieu's famous maxim, 'no monarch, no nobility; no nobility, no monarch',[3] rings very true in this case.

The partial success and limitations of the viceregal court are also evident in the celebrations that were initiated, sponsored, and organized by the court. During the early modern period civic celebrations were perceived by the rulers as important tools of propaganda. Accordingly, the viceroy diverted a lot of energy and resources to commemorating with maximal splendour every possible event that involved the house of Habsburg. Obviously, in such a poverty-stricken city as Naples, the plebs' demand for splendid illusions, and Gargantuan largesse of food in the form of cockaignes, surpassed

the ability of supply. Similarly, the Neapolitan nobility, like most aristocratic societies of the time, embraced with pleasure any chance of frolicsome entertainment and personal ostentation. Only a vociferous minority among the more productive elements of the *popolo*, not coincidentally those who paid most of the taxes, voiced their displeasure at the extravagance involved in those manifestations.

On the contrary, the appreciation of public festivals was so great among all the social classes of Naples that when the viceroys tried to follow the lead of other European courts, around the middle of the seventeenth century, by diverting most of the festivals from the public sphere to exclusive aristocratic domains, they had to withdraw owing to public objections. If so, how should we interpret the evidence of contemporary chronicles that showed viceregal attempts at control and the coercion of nobility and *popolo* to active participation in the sponsorship of the spectacles? Since there is also ample evidence to show to the contrary, that there was a general voluntary and generous inclination to invest, we should probably attribute it to the basic insecurity of viceroys, who were afraid of a blow to their reputation if the results did not match the expectations.

One of the more surprising findings in this research was to discover that contrary to the opinion of Neapolitanists researching local festivals, the success of Spanish tournaments, had a great resonance. The evidence shows that carousels, reed spear tournaments and bullfights – three Spanish tournaments *par excellence* – won great attendance from all the Neapolitan citizens who crowded the public arenas, or filled piazzas and special constructions built for the occasion. Moreover, in the case of the bullfight, participation was not limited to nobles fighting the bull on horseback, but, as in Spain, bold elements of the *popolo* took an active part in tormenting the beasts on foot, opening the way for the style of combat of the modern *corrida*. The explanation for the lacunae mentioned here is partly the failure of these scholars to consult Neapolitan festival books where some of the evidence is provided, and partly their failure to put the evidence in context. When other princely courts adopted the French model of tournament, the horse ballet, after the middle of the seventeenth century, Naples, like Spain, stuck to its traditional Spanish heritage.

Another form of Spanish culture that enjoyed great success in Naples was Spanish fashion. Costume research has shown the connection, albeit feebly, between the success of Spanish fashion in Europe and the advent of the Catholic Reformation. In deeper pursuit of this argument I have tried to connect ideas of morality and appearance voiced by religious personalities during the Catholic Reformation and the application of these ideas in the garments of the Spaniards, who carried the banner of the religious movement. The evidence shows that the austere, dark, and constrictive Spanish garments succeeded mostly where the political hegemony of Spain and the Counter-Reformist reaction were more pronounced.

Thus, focusing on the Italian peninsula, places like Naples, Milan, Palermo, and Rome where both of these tendencies prevailed displayed the fashion of Spain, whereas

Venice, which evaded the Spanish clasp, managed to display a more distinctive and liberating style. Not coincidentally, the saviour from Spanish constrictive fashions was its great continental enemy, France. Nor was it a coincidence that the avalanche of sumptuary laws in Spain and Italy, which limited French fashions or tried to superimpose Spanish styles, increased towards the Peace of Westphalia (1648), which has been marked by traditional historiography as the end of the Counter-Reformation. However, these reactionary laws were the 'swan song' of Spanish fashion, which was simply effaced from the earth by the last two decades of the seventeenth century.

The issuing of similar sumptuary laws in Naples during the 1670s revealed the discrepancy between the grave taste and the will of Philip IV to ban French fashions, and the personal style of the viceroys henceforth. The iconography displaying the attire of viceroys and the written reports reveal that during these times the viceroys fought the French imports by issuing toothless decrees against them, while giving their implicit consent by wearing the forbidden attire themselves. A meagre effect was also achieved when the viceroys tried to generally limit luxury. The supercilious nobility was simply not ready to relinquish or even to diminish its exterior signs of superiority, and neither did other categories that were targeted. In fairness it should be noted that sumptuary laws had a very limited amount of success almost everywhere they were issued, if their achievement is measured in terms of following their letter. The idea, more than actually enforcing the notions of class, gender, and morality that imbued the sumptuary impulse, was to make a value judgement on behalf of the ruling elite. In this sense the sumptuary laws issued in Naples, especially those that were used to denigrate Jews and Muslims, or those that tried to prevent women from wearing 'immodest' clothes, reflected well the concern and biases of the Spanish ethos: all values that were obviously not shared by Neapolitans, as their resistance to these laws clearly testifies.

The last chapter of this book dealt with something that may simply be regarded as uncharted territory in terms of Neapolitan research, although Naples was no exception in its enthusiasm for these effective tools of propaganda, which were amply used in public festivals throughout early modern Europe. Moreover, the splendid festival and funeral books issued in Naples display abundant images of these pictogrammes, giving even a relative edge to the Neapolitan productions over Italian or Spanish counterparts. Their most effective application was in the obsequies for Spanish kings and queens. A close analysis of the splendid artistic programmes that were produced in Naples for the Spanish royal deceased vindicates the importance that has been given here to these propagandistic displays. As in other occurrences in this book, this is another testimony of the court's need to assert itself vis-à-vis a particularly volatile society.

Finally, this investigation shows that despite all the cultural differences and disagreements arising between the Spanish court and Neapolitans from various social backgrounds, the Spanish hegemony was generally maintained. The unrivalled international strength and prestige of Spain during most of the Habsburg dominion of southern Italy made it an undisputed cultural model for Naples, until the politically

ascending France could present an attractive alternative at Spain's expense, after the middle of the seventeenth century. Naples' initial emulation of Spain as a model of courtly culture and its later transformation into the French style shows its alignment with general European trends, and reveals that external events had a stronger impact than any possible internal evolution or viceregal attempts at steering and direction.

Notes

1   See Pacelli, 'L'ideologia del potere', 230–1.
2   See Spagnoletti, *Principi italiani e Spagna*, especially 51–128.
3   Montesquieu, *The Spirit of the Laws*, 18.

Bibliography

Printed sources

Advertencias y reglas para torear a caballo (Siglos XVII y XVIII) (Madrid, 1947).

Alciato, Andrea, *Los emblemas de Alciato traducidos en rhimas españolas*, trans. Bernandino Daza Pinciano (Lyon, 1549).

Ammirato, Scipione, *Il Rota, o vero delle imprese. Dialogo* (Naples, 1562).

—— *Delle famiglie nobili napolitane* (Florence, 1580).

—— *Gli opuscoli* (3 vols., Florence, 1637–42).

Bacco Alemanno, Henrico, *Il Regno di Napoli in dodici province* (Naples, 1609).

Bargagli, Scipione, *Dell'imprese* (Venice, 1594).

Bayer, Johan, *Uranometria* (Augsburg, 1603).

Beltrano, Ottavio, *Descrittione del Regno di Napoli diviso in dodeci provincie* (Bologna, 1969).

Bevilacqua, Ferdinando, *Racconto della festa fatta nel Reale Palazzo di Napoli dalli gentil-huomini della corte dell'Eccelentissimo Signor Conte di Ognatte Viceré. Per il felice arrivo in Milano della Sposa Reale del Cattolico, e Gran Ré Filippo Quarto Nostro Signore* (Naples, 1649).

Boccalini, Traiano, *Ragguagli di Parnaso*, ed. Luigi Firpo (3 vols., Bari, 1948).

Borja, Juan de, *Impresas morales* (Brussels, 1680).

Botero, Giovanni, *Delle Relazioni Universali*, Part V: *Spagna*, in *La vita e le opere di Giovanni Botero*, vol. 3, ed. Carlo Gioda (Milan, 1895).

Bouchard, Jean-Jacques, *Journal*, vol. 2: *Voyage dans le Royaume de Naples. Voyage dans le campagne de Rome*, ed. Emanuele Kanceff (2 vols., Turin, 1976).

Breve Ragguaglio delle feste celebrate in Napoli per la ricuperazione di Barzellona fatta dalle armi di S. M. C. (Rome, 1653).

Breve Relatione della Cavalcata Reale, Seguita in questa fedelissima Città di Napoli il dì 14. Gennaro 1680. Per le Feste delle Nozze Reali del Rè N.S. che Dio guardi (Naples, 1680).

Bucca, Ferrante, 'Aggionta alli Diurnali di Scipione Guerra', ed. G. de Blasiis, *ASPN*, 36 (1911), 124–205, 329–82, 507–80, 751–8, and *ASPN*, 37 (1912), 120–45, 272–312.

Bulifon, Antonio, (ed.), *Lettere memorabili, istoriche, politiche, ed erudite* (4 vols., Naples, 1693–97)

——— *Funerali nella morte del Signor D. Antonio Miroballo celebrati nella Real Chiesa di S. Gio. A Carbonara* (Naples, 1695).

——— *Lettera scritta da A.B. a un suo amico in Francia. Dove gli da ragguaglio delle Feste fatte in Napoli coll'occasione della pubblica entrata fatta in essa Città da Filippo V, Monarca delle Spagne* (Naples, 1702).

——— *Altra lettera scritta da A. B. a un suo amico. Nella quale gli da ragguaglio della Seconda Cavalcata fatta a napoli per la solenne entrata dell'Eminentissimo Sig. Cardinal Carlo Barberini, mandato da Sua Santità in qualità di suo Legato a latere a Filippo V monarca delle Spagne* (Naples, 1702).

——— *Distinta, e sincera relazione della regal cavalcata fatta per il publico ingresso in questa fedelissima città di Napoli del gloriosissimo Nostro monarca Filippo Quinto dà Titolati, cavalieri, e Baroni di questo Regno, trà quali tre cardinali, molti Principi, e Signori Romani* (Naples, 1702).

——— *Giornale del Viaggio d'Italia Dell'Invittissimo e gloriosissimo Monarca Filippo V Re delle Spagne, e di Napoli, etc. Nel quale si da ragguaglio delle cose dalla M.S. in Italia adoperate dal dì di 6 d'Aprile, nel quale approdò in Napoli, infin'al dì 16 di Novembre 1702 in cui s'imbarcò in Genova, per far ritorno in Ispagna* (Naples, 1703).

——— *Giornali di Napoli dal MDXLVII al MDCCVI*, ed. Nino Cortese (Naples, 1932).

Campanella, Tommaso, *Della monarchia di Spagna*, in *Opere di Tommaso Campanella*, vol. 2, ed. Alessandro D'Ancona (Turin, 1854).

——— *La monarchia delle nazioni* in *Fra' Tommaso Campanella ne' castelli di Napoli*, ed. Luigi Amabile (Naples, 1887), 299–347.

Capaccio, Giulio Cesare, *Delle imprese* (Naples, 1592).

——— *Mergellina. Egloghe piscatorie* (Venice, 1598).

——— *Pomposa Allegrezza fatta in Napoli per le Reali Nozze tra i Sereniss. Filippo d'Austria con Crisitina di Borbone, e Ludovico XIII Re di Francia con Anna d'Austria, ordinata dall'Eccellenza di Don Pietro di Castro Viceré in questo Regno* (Naples, 1616).

——— *Apparato della festività del glorioso S. Giovan Battista fatto dal Fedelissimo Popolo Napolitano nella venuta dell'Eccellenza del Signor D. Antonio Alvarez di Toledo, Viceré del Regno* (Naples, 1623).

——— *Apparato della festività del glorioso S. Giovan Battista fatto dal Fedelissimo Popolo Napolitano à 24 di Giugno 1624, all'Eccellenza del Signor D. Antonio Alvarez di Toledo Duca d'Alba, Viceré del Regno* (Naples, 1624).

——— *Apparato della festività del glorioso S. Gio. Battista fatto dal Fedelissimo Popolo Napolitano à XXIII di Giugno MDCXXVI, all'Eccellenza del Signor D. Antonio Alvarez di Toledo Duca d'Alba, Viceré del Regno di Napoli* (Naples, 1626).

——— *Apparato della festività del glorioso S. Gio. Battista fatto dal Fedelissimo Popolo Napolitano à XXIII di Giugno MDCXXVII, all'Eccellenza del Signor D. Antonio Alvarez di Toledo, Duca d'Alva, Viceré nel Regno* (Naples, 1627).

——— *Il forastiero. Dialoghi* (Naples, 1634).

Capecelatro, Francesco, *Degli annali della città di Napoli 1631–1640* (Naples, 1849).

Caputi, Ottavio, *La pompa funeraria fatta in Napoli nell'essequie del catholico Re Filippo II. di Austria* (Naples, 1599).

——— *Relatione della pompa funerale che si celebrò in Napoli, nella morte della Serenissima Reina Margherita d'Austria* (Naples, 1612).

Carafa, Ferrante, *Memorie*, appendix in Raffaele Ajello, *Una Società anomala. Il programma e la sconfitta della nobiltà napoletana in due memoriali cinquecenteschi* (Naples, 1996), 411–37.

Castaldi, Giuseppe, *Tributi Ossequiosi della Fedelissima Città di Napoli, Per li Applausi Festivi delle Nozze Reali del Cattolico Monarca Carlo Secondo, Ré delle Spagne con la Serenissima Signora Maria Luisa Borbone. Sotto la direttione dell'Eccellentissimo Signor Marchese de Los Velez Viceré di Napoli* (Naples, 1680).

Castaldo, Antonino, *Dell'istoria … libri quattro. Ne'quali si descrivono gli avvenimenti piu memorabili succeduti nel Regno di Napoli sotto il governo del viceré don Pietro di Toledo e dei viceré suoi sucessori fino al cardinal Granvela*, in *Raccolta di tutti i più rinomati scrittori dell'istoria generale del Regno di Napoli*, vol. 6, ed. Giovanni Gravier (25 vols., Naples, 1769–77).

Castaldo, Salvatore, *Relatione delle famosissime luminarie Fatte nella Città di Napoli nella Festa del gran Patriarca miracoloso B. Gaetano Thiene … nelli giorni 5, 6, e 7 d'Agosto dell'anno 1654* (Naples, 1654).

Castiglione, Baldassare, *Il libro del Cortegiano*, ed. Luigi Preti (Turin, 1965).

Castro, Miguel de, *Libro que comenzó en Malta Miguel de Castro de su nacimiento y demás razones de su familia, segun la que tenia y unas memorias que llevo a España …*, in *Autobiografías de soldados (siglo XVII)*, ed. José Cossio, *Biblioteca de autores españoles*, vol. 90 (Madrid, 1956).

Catalogo delle risoluzioni prese dall'Illustrissima Deputazione della Salute Di questa Fedelissima Città di Napoli (Naples, 1656).

Celano, Carlo, *Degli avanzi delle poste* (2 vols., Naples, 1676–81).

—— *Notizie del bello, dell'antico e del curioso della città di Napoli. Divise dall'autore in dieci giornate per guida e comodo de' viaggiatori*, ed. Atanasio Mozzillo, Alfredo Profeta, and Francesco Paolo Macchia (3 vols., Naples, 1970).

Cherchi, Paolo (ed.), 'Juan de Garnica. Un memoriale sul cerimoniale della corte napoletana', *ASPN*, 13 (1975), 213–24.

Cirino, Andrea, *Feste celebrate in Napoli per la nascita del serenis.*^mo *Prencipe di Spagna Nostro Signore dall'ecc.*^mo *Sig.*^r *Conte di Castriglio, Viceré e Lungotenente e Capitan Generale nel Regno di Napoli* (Naples, 1658).

Confuorto, Domenico, *Giornali di Napoli dal MDCLXXIX al MDCIC*, ed. Nicola Nicolini (2 vols., Naples, 1930–31).

Coniglio, Giuseppe, *Declino del viceregno di Napoli (1599–1689)* (4 vols., Naples, 1990–91).

Contile, Luca, *Ragionamento sopra la proprietà delle imprese* (Pavia, 1574).

Contreras, Alonso de, *Discurso de mi vida. Desde que sali a servir al Rey a la edad de catorce anos, en el año de 1595, hasta fin del año 1630, el 1 de octubre, en que comence esta relacion*, in *Autobiografías de soldados (siglo XVII)*, ed. José Cossio, *Biblioteca de autores españoles*, vol. 90 (Madrid, 1956).

Da Fabriano, Mambrino Roseo, *Del compendio dell'historia del Regno di Napoli*, in *Raccolta di tutti i più rinomati scrittori dell'istoria generale del Regno di Napoli*, vols. 13–14, ed. Giovanni Gravier (25 vols., Naples, 1769–77).

D'Andrea, Francesco, 'Avvertimenti ai nipoti', *ASPN*, 44–6 (1919–21).

De Calamo, Biagio, *I giorni festivi fatti per la presa di Buda dall'Arme Austriache nella*

Fedelissima Città di Napoli Dall'Eccelentissimo Signor Marchese del Carpio, Viceré e Capitan Generale della detta e da'suoi Cittadini l'anno 1686 (Naples, 1687).

De Leonardis, Gio. Francesco, *Prattica degli officiali del Regno di Napoli* (Naples, 1599).

Della Casa, Giovanni, *A Renaissance Courtesy-Book: Galateo: Of Manners and Behaviours*, trans. Robert Peterson (Boston, 1914).

Della Morte, Giacomo (Notar Giacomo), *Cronica di Napoli*, ed. Paolo Garzilli (Naples, 1845).

De Santis, Tommaso, *Istoria del tumulto di Napoli … nella quale si contengono tutte le cose accorte nella città, e nel regno fino al 6 d'Aprile 1648*, in *Raccolta di tutti i più rinomati scrittori dell'istoria generale del Regno di Napoli*, vol. 7, ed. Giovanni Gravier (25 vols., Naples, 1769–77).

De Sariis, Alessio (ed.), *Codice delle leggi del Regno di Napoli* (9 vols., Naples, 1792–97).

De Tarsia, Pablo Antonio, *Tumultos de la ciudad y Reyno de Nápoles en el año de 1647* (Lyon, 1670).

Del Tufo, Giovan Battista, *Ritratto o modello delle grandezze, delitie e meraviglie, Della nobilissima Città di Napoli*, ed. Calogero Tagliareni (Naples, 1959).

Díez Borque, José María (ed.), *La sociedad española y los viajeros del siglo XVII* (Madrid, 1975).

'Documenti che riguardano in ispecie la storia economica e finanziera del Regno, levati dal carteggio degli Agenti del Duca di Urbino in Napoli', ed. Francesco Palermo, *Archivio Storico Italiano*, 9 (1846), 203–41.

'Documenti diversi sulle novità accadute in Napoli l'anno 1647', ed. Francesco Palermo, *Archivio Storico Italiano*, 9 (1846), 357–401.

'Documenti sulla storia civile ed economica del regno, cavati dal Carteggio degli Agenti del Granduca di Toscana in Napoli', ed. Francesco Palermo, *Archivio Storico Italiano*, 9 (1846), 245–353.

Donzelli, Giuseppe, *Partenope liberata* (Naples, 1970).

Doria, Paolo Mattia, *Massime del governo spagnolo a Napoli*, ed. Vittorio Conti (Naples, 1973).

Estrada, Don Diego Duque de, *Comentarios del desengañado de si mismo, prueba de todos estados y eleccion del mejor de ellos, o sea Vida del mesmo autor, que lo es Don Diego Duque de Estrada*, in *Autobiografias de soldados (siglo XVII)*, ed. José Cossio, *Biblioteca de autores españoles*, vol. 90 (Madrid, 1956).

Evelyn, John, *John Evelyn in Naples, 1645*, ed. H. Maynard Smith (Oxford, 1914).

—— *Tyrannus or The Mode*, ed. J. L. Nevison (Oxford, 1951).

Fellecchia, Alessandro, *Viaggio della Maestà della Regina di Bohemia e d'Ungheria da Madrid sino a Napoli. Con la descrittione di Pausillipo, e di molte Dame Napoletane* (Naples, 1630).

Ferraro, Pirro Antonio, *Cavallo frenato …* (Naples, 1602).

Figueroa, Cristóbal Suárez de, *El Pasajero, advertencias utilísimas a la vida humana* (Madrid, 1617).

—— *Pusílipo, Ratos de conversácion, en lo que dura el paseo* (Naples, 1629).

Filamondo, Raffaele, *Il genio bellicoso di Napoli. Memorie istoriche d'alcuni capitani celebri napoletani, c'han militato per la fede, per lo Re, per la Patria nel secolo corrente* (2 vols., Naples, 1694).

Fonte, Moderata (Modesta Pozzo), *The Worth of Women:Wherein is Clearly Revealed Their Nobility and Their Superiority to Men*, ed. and trans. Virginia Cox (Chicago, 1997).

Fuidoro, Innocenzo, *Successi del governo del conte d'Oñatte, MXCXLVIII–MDCLIII*, ed. Alfredo Parente (Naples, 1932).

——— *Giornali di Napoli dal MDCLX al MDCLXXX* (4 vols., Naples, 1934–39).

——— *Successi historici raccolti dalla sollevatione di Napoli dell'anno 1647*, ed. Anna Maria Giraldi and Marina Raffaeli (Milan, 1994).

García, Carlos, *La oposición y conjunción de los dos luminares de la tierra o Antipatía de Franceses y Españoles*, ed. Michel Bareau (Edmonton, 1979).

García Mercadal, José (ed.), *Viajes de extranjeros por España y Portugal. Desde los tiempos más remotos, hasta fines del siglo XVI* (3 vols., Madrid, 1952).

Giannone, Pietro, *Istoria civile del Regno di Napoli* (3rd edn, 4 vols., Naples, 1762).

Giovio, Paolo, *Dialogo dell'imprese militari e amorose* (Rome, 1555).

Giraffi, Alessandro, *Le rivoluzioni di Napoli* (Venice, 1732).

Giuliani, Gio. Bernardino, *Descrittione dell'Apparato di san Giovanni fatto dal fedelissimo popolo Napolitano All'Illustrissimo, & Eccelentissimo Sig. Duca D'Alba l'anno M.DC. XXVIII* (Naples, 1628).

——— *Descrittione dell'Apparato fatto nella Festa di S. Giovanni dal fedelissimo popolo Napolitano all'Illustrissimo et Eccelentissimo Sig. D. Emanuel de Zunica et Fonseca, Conte di Monterrey,Vicere di Napoli l'anno M.DC.XXXI* (Naples, 1631).

Giustinani, Lorenzo (ed.), *Nuova collezione delle prammatiche del Regno di Napoli* (15 vols., Naples, 1803–8).

Grisone, Federico, *Ordini di cavalcare, et modi di conoscere le nature de' cavalli, emendar i vitii loro, et ammaestrargli per l'uso della Guerra commodita de gli huomini* (Venice, 1553).

Gualterotti, Raffaele, *Feste nelle nozze del Serenissimo D. Francesco Medici Gran Duca di Toscana, e della Sereniss. sua Consorte la Signora Bianca Cappello. Con particolar Descrizione della Sbarra ...* (Florence, 1579).

Guerra, Scipione, *Diurnali di Scipione Guerra*, ed. Giuseppe De Montemayor (Naples, 1891).

Il meraviglioso Honore fatto dal Viceré e signori Napolitani al Re di Tunisi per la sua venuta a Napoli con l'ordine de l'entrata sua in detta città e il numero dei suoi cavalli, & i presenti magnifici che si sono fatti, dove s'intende che la gran quantità de dinari portati da esso Re per soldare gente Italiana (Venice, 1543).

Imperiale, Gian Vincenzo, 'De' giornali', ed. Anton Giulio Barrili, in *Atti della Società Ligure di Storia Patria*. vol. 29 (Genoa, 1908), 5–739.

Mandurio, Pietro Roseo da, *Breve relatione della solenne processione e de' ricchi, e nobili apparati, fatti nella festa del Glorioso Padre San Thomaso d'Aquino, del Sacro Ordine de Predicatori, celebrata nella città di Napoli alli 20 del mese di gennaio, dell'Anno MDCV* (Naples, 1605).

Marciano, Marcello, *Pompe Funebri dell'Universo Nella Morte di Filippo Quarto il Grande Re delle Spagne Celebrate dal Eminentissimo Cardinale Aragóna, Arcivescovo di Toleto, Viceré e Capitan Generale del Regno di Napoli* (Naples, 1666).

Marinella, Lucrezia, *The Nobility and Excellence of Women and the Defects and Vices of Men*, ed. and trans. Anne Dunhill (Chicago, 1999).

Martinez de Herrera, Pedro, *Principe advertido y declaracion de las Epigramas De Napoles*

la Vispera de S. Juan (Naples, 1631).

Mazzella, Scipione, *Descrittione del Regno di Napoli. Del signore S. M. napoletano. Aumentata in molti parti dal proprio autore* (Naples, 1601).

Montalbo, Francisco de, *Noticias funebres de las magestosas exequias, que hizo la felicissima Cuidad de Palermo, Cabeça Coronada de Sicilia, En la muerte de Maria Luysa de Borbon, nuestra Señora Reyna de Las Españas* (Palermo, 1689).

Montesquieu, Charles de Secondat, Baron de, *The Spirit of the Laws*, trans. and ed. Anne M. Cohler, Basia Carolyn Miller, and Harold Samuel Stone (Cambridge, 1989).

'Nuovi documenti francesi sulla impresa di Carlo VIII', *ASPN*, 24 (1938), 183–257.

Orilla, Francesco, *Il zodiaco over idea di perfetione di Prencipi, Formata Dall' Heroiche Virtù dell' illustriss. … D. Antonio Alvaros di Toledo Duca D'Alba Viceré di Napoli dal fidelissimo Popolo Napoletano … Nella Pomposissima Festa di San Gio. Battista, celebrato a 23 di Giugno 1629, per il settimo anno del suo Governo* (Naples, 1630).

Paladino, G., 'Privilegi concessi agli ebrei dal viceré D. Pedro di Toledo (1535–1536)', *ASPN*, 38 (1913).

Parrino, Domenico Antonio, *Ossequio Tributario della Fedelissima Città di Napoli per le Dimostranze Giulive nei Regii Sponsali del Cattolico, e Invittissimo Monarca Carlo Secondo colla Serenissima Principessa Maria Anna di Neoburgo, Palatina del Reno, Sotto i Felicissimi Auspicii dell'Eccelentissimo Signor D. Francesco de Benavides, Conte di S. Stefano, Viceré, e capitan Generale nel Regno di Napoli. Ragguaglio Historico* (Naples, 1690).

—— *Napoli città nobilissima, antica e fedelissima, esposta agli occhi et alla mente de' curiosi, divisa in due parti…* (2 vols., Naples, 1700).

—— *Teatro eroico e politico de' governi de' vicerè del Regno di Napoli, dal tempo di Ferdinando il Cattolico fino al presente*, in *Raccolta di tutti i più rinomati scrittori dell'istoria generale del Regno di Napoli*, vols. 9–10, ed. Giovanni Gravier (25 vols., Naples, 1769–77).

Passero, Giovanni, *Storie in forme di Giornali* (Naples, 1785).

Pérez de Rua, Antonio, *Funeral hecho en Roma en la Yglesia de Santiago de los Españoles a 18 de Diciembre de 1665 a la gloriosa memoria del Rei Catolico de las Españas nuestro señor D. Felipe Quarto el Grande* (Rome, 1666).

Piccaglia, Gio. Battista, *Relatione del funerale et esequie fatte in Milano, Per ordine della Cat. Maestà del Potentis. Rè di Spagna Don Filippo Terzo Nostro Signore, Alla Serenissima Regina Donna Margherita d'Austria Sua moglie, li 22 di Decembre 1611* (Milan, 1612).

Pigafetta, Antonio, *Primo viaggio intorno al globo terracqueo*, ed. Carlo Amoretti (Milan, 1800).

Pitti, Vincentio, *Essequie della Sacra Cattolica Real Maestà del Re di Spagna D. Filippo II d'Austria. Celebrate dal Serenissimo D. Fernando Medici Gran Duca di Toscana nella Città di Firenze* (Florence, 1598).

Porzio, Camillo, *Relazione del Regno di Napoli al marchese di Mondesciar viceré di Napoli di Camillo Porzio tra il 1577 e 1579*, in *La congiura de' Baroni del Regno di Napoli contro il re Ferdinando primo e gli altri scritti*, ed. Ernesto Pontieri (Naples, 1958), 343–76.

Raneo, José, *Etiquetas de la corte de Nápoles (1634)*, ed. Antonio Paz y Mélia, *Revue Hispanique*, 27 (1912), 16–284.

Relacion del hazimiento de gracias, que hizo el Supremo Consejo de Italia en Madrid, por el buen Sucesso de Nápoles, por tres dias sucessivos, que fueron a 8, 9, y 10 de Mayo de 1648 (Madrid and Naples, 1648).

Relazione della famosissima Festa Nel giorno della Gloriosa S. Anna a 26. di Luglio 1699. Per solennizare il Nome, che ne porta la Maestà della Regina Nostra Signora, M. Anna di Neoburgo. Fatta celebrare nella Riviera di Chiaja, e nello Scoglio di Mergellina dall Eccelentissimo Signore D. Luigi dela Cerda e d'Aragóna, Duca di Medina Celi, d'Alcalà, e Viceré, e Capitan Generale in questo Regno (Naples, 1699).

Relazione della solenne Festa de'Tori e de'Fuochi Artifiziati fattasi nel mare di Napoli il giorno di S. Anna, del presente Anno 1685. Ordinata da quel Viceré Marchese del Carpio. Per solennizare il nome della Maestà della Regina Madre N.S. (Milan, 1685).

Ripa, Caesar, *Iconologia*, trans. Pierce Tempest (London, 1709).

Rodriguez de Monforte, Pedro, *Descripcion de las honras qve se hicieron ala Catholica Mag.^{d} de D. Phelippe quarto Rey de las Españas y del Nuevo Mundo en el Real Convento de la Encarnacion* (Madrid, 1666).

Rosso, Gregorio, *Istoria delle cose di Napoli sotto l'imperio di Carlo V cominciando dall'anno 1526 per insino all'anno 1537. Scritta per modo di giornali*, in *Raccolta di tutti i più rinomati scrittori dell'istoria generale del Regno di Napoli*, vol. 8, ed. Giovanni Gravier (25 vols., Naples, 1769–77).

Ruscelli, Girolamo, *Le imprese illustri* (Venice, 1580).

Saavedra Fajardo, Diego, *Idea de un principe politico christiano, representada en cien empresas* (Munich, 1640).

Sandys, George, *A Relation of a Journey Begun Ann: Dom: 1610* (3rd edn, London, 1627).

Sarnelli, Pompeo, *Guida de' Forestieri, Curiosi di vedere, e d'intendere le cose più notabili della Regal Città di Napoli, e del suo amenisimo Distretto* (Naples, 1688).

Sempere y Guarinos, Juan, *Historia del luxo y de las leyes suntuarias de España* (2 vols., Madrid, 1788).

Solórzano Pereira, Juan de, *Emblemas regios-politicos* (Valencia, 1658).

Tarabotti, Arcangela, *Antisatira*, in *Satira e antisatira*, ed. Elissa Weiser (Rome, 1998).

Tarcagnota, Giovanni, *La città di Napoli dopo la rivoluzione urbanistica di Pedro di Toledo*, ed. Franco Strazzullo (Rome, 1988).

Tesauro, Emanuele, *Il cannocchiale aristotelico* (Turin, 1670).

Tutini, Camillo, *Dell'origine e fundation de'seggi di Napoli* (Naples, 1644).

—— *Discorsi de sette officii ovvero de sette grandi del Regno di Napoli* (Rome, 1666).

—— *Memorie della vita, miracoli, e culto di San Gianuario Martire, Vescovo di Benevento e Principal Protettore della Città di Napoli* (3rd ed., Naples, 1703).

Valentini, Francesco, *Descrittione del sontuoso torneo fatto nella fidelissima città di Napoli l'anno MDCXII. Con la relazione di molt'altre feste Per allegrezza delli Regij accasamenti seguiti fra le Potentissime Corone Spagna, e Francia* (Naples, 1612).

Vecellio, Cesare, *Habiti antichi et moderni di tutto il mondo* (Paris, 1859).

Vives, Juan Luis, *Formación de la mujer Cristiana*, in *Obras Completas*, ed. Lorenzo Riber (2 vols., Madrid, 1947).

Zazzera, Francesco, *Narrazioni tratte dai giornali del governo di Don Pietro Girone duca d'Ossuna viceré di Napoli*, ed. Francesco Palermo, *Archivio Storico Italiano*, 9 (1846), 473–617.

Secondary sources

Abulafia, David, 'Il Mezzogiorno peninsulare dai bizantini all'espulsione (1541)', in *Gli ebrei in Italia. I: Dall'alto Medioevo all'età dei ghetti*, ed. Corrado Vivanti, *Storia d'Italia. Annali 11* (Turin, 1996), 4–44.

—— *Mediterranean Encounters, Economic, Religious, Political, 1100–1550* (Aldershot, 2000).

Adamson, John, 'The Making of the Ancien-Régime Court 1500–1700', in *The Princely Courts of Europe: Ritual, Politics and Culture under the Ancien Régime, 1500–1750*, ed. John Adamson (London, 1999), 7–41.

Aercke, Kristiaan P., *Gods of Play: Baroque Festive Performances as Rhetorical Discourse* (Albany, NY, 1994).

Ajello, Raffaele, *Una società anomala. Il programma e la sconfitta della nobiltà napoletana in due memoriali cinquecenteschi* (Naples, 1996).

Allo Manero, Adita, 'Iconografia funeraria de las honras de Felipe IV en España e Hispanoamerica', *Quadernos de Investigacion Historica*, 7 (1981), 73–90.

—— 'Organización y definición de los programas iconográficos en las exequias reales de la Casa de Austria', in *El Rostro y el Discurso de la Fiesta*, ed. Manuel Nuñez Rodríguez (Santiago de Compostela, 1994), 224–35.

Anatra, Bruno, 'L'affermazione dell'egemonia spagnola e gli stati italiani', in *Storia della società italiana*, vol. 10: *Il tramonto del Rinascimento*, ed. Giovanni Cherubini, Franco Della Peruta, Ettore Lepore (Milan, 1989), 63–101.

Anderson, Black J. and Madge Garland, *A History of Fashion* (2nd rev. edn, London, 1980).

Anderson, Jaynie, ' "Le roi ne meurt jamais": Charles V's Obsequies in Italy', in *El Cardenal Albornoz y el Colegio de Espana*, V (Bologna, 1979), 379–99.

Anderson, Ruth Matilda, 'The Golilla: A Spanish Collar of the Seventeenth Century', *Waffen und Kostümkunde*, 11 (1969), 1–19.

—— *Hispanic Costume, 1480–1530* (New York, 1979).

Ashley, Kathleen and Wim Husken (eds.), *Moving Subjects: Processional Performances in the Middle Ages and the Renaissance* (Amsterdam and Atlanta, Ga., 2001).

Astarita, Tommaso, *The Continuity of Feudal Power: The Caracciolo of Brienza in Spanish Naples* (Cambridge, 1992).

Aventin, Mercè, 'Le leggi suntuarie in Spagna. Stato della questione', in *Disciplinare il lusso. La legislazione suntuaria in Italia e in Europa tra Medioevo ed. Età moderna*, ed. Maria Giuseppina Muzzarelli and Antonella Campanini (Rome, 2003), 109–20.

Bakhtin, Mikhail, *Rabelais and his World*, trans. Hélène Iswolsky (Bloomington, Ind., 1984).

Barletta, Laura, 'Un esempio di festa. Il Carnevale', in *Capolavori in festa. Effimero barocco a Largo di Palazzo (1683–1759)*, ed. Giuseppe Zampino (Naples, 1997), 91–104.

—— *Fra regola e licenza. Chiesa e vita religiosa, feste e beneficenza a Napoli e in Campania (secoli XVIII–XX)* (Naples, 2003).

Barnard, Malcolm, *Fashion as Communication* (London and New York, 1996).

Batterberry, Michael and Ariane Batterberry, *Fashion: The Mirror of History* (2nd edn, London, 1982).

Belenguer Cebría, Ernest (ed.), *Felipe II y el Mediterráneo* (4 vols., Barcelona, 1999).

Belgrano, L.T., *Della vita privata dei genovesi* (2nd edn, Genoa, 1875).

Bell, Rudolph M., *How to Do It: Guides to Good Living for Renaissance Italians* (Chicago and London, 1999).

Belli, Carolina, 'Cerimonie e feste d'antaño. Schegge d'archivio', in *Capolavori in festa. Effimero barocco a Largo di Palazzo (1683–1759)*, ed. Giuseppe Zampino (Naples, 1997), 105–9.

Benigno, Francesco, 'Conflitto politico e conflitto sociale nell'Italia spagnola', in *Nel sistema imperiale. L'Italia spagnola*, ed. Aurelio Musi (Naples, 1994), 115–46.

Bennassar, Bartolomé, *The Spanish Character: Attitudes and Mentalities from the Sixteenth to the Eighteenth Century*, trans. Benjamin Keen (Berkeley, 1979).

—— *Historia de los Españoles*, vol. I: *Siglos VI–XVII* (Barcelona, 1989).

Bernis, Carmen, *Indumentaria española en tiempos de Carlos V* (Madrid, 1962).

Bertelli, Sergio, 'Il Cinquecento', in *La storiografia italiana degli ultimi vent'anni*, vol. 2: *Età moderna*, ed. Luigi De Rosa (3 vols., Rome and Bari, 1989).

—— *Il corpo del re. Sacralità e potere nell'Europa medievale e moderna* (Florence, 1990).

—— and Giulia Calvi, 'Rituale, cerimoniale, etichetta nelle corti italiane', in *Rituale, cerimoniale, etichetta*, ed. Sergio Bertelli and Giuliano Crifò (Milan, 1986), 11–27.

—— Franco Cardini, Elivira Garbero Zorzi, *Italian Renaissance Courts* (London, 1986).

Bistort, Giulio, *Il magistrato alle pompe nella repubblica di Venezia. Studio storico* (Venice, 1912).

Boiteux, Martine, 'Chasse aux taureaux et jeux romains de la Renaissance', in *Les Jeux à la Renaissance*, ed. Philippe Ariès and Jean-Claude Margolin (Paris, 1982), 32–53.

Bonazzoli, Viviana, 'Gli ebrei del Regno di Napoli all'epoca della loro espulsione', II: 'Il periodo spagnolo (1501–1541)', *Archivio Storico Italiano*, 139 (1981), 179–287.

Bonfil, Roberto, 'Società cristiana e società ebraica nell'Italia medievale e rinascimentale', in *ebrei e cristiani nell'Italia medievale e moderna. Conversioni, scambi, contrasti*, ed. Michele Luzzati, Michele Olivari, and Alessandra Veronese (Rome, 1988).

—— *Jewish Life in Renaissance Italy*, trans. Anthony Oldcorn (Berkeley and London, 1994).

Boughner, Daniel C., *The Braggart in Renaissance Comedy: A Study in Comparative Drama from Aristophanes to Shakespeare* (Minneapolis, 1954).

Braudel, Fernand, *Civilization and Capitalism: 15th–18th Century*, vol. 1: *The Structures of Everyday Life: The Limits of the Possible*, trans. Miriam Kochan (London, 1981).

Breen, Michael P., 'Addressing La Ville des Dieux: Entry Ceremonies and Urban Audiences in Seventeenth-Century Dijon', *Journal of Social History*, 38:2 (2004), 341–64.

Breward, Christopher, *The Culture of Fashion: A New History of Fashionable Dress* (Manchester, 1995).

Burke, Peter, *Popular Culture in Early Modern Europe* (London, 1978).

—— *The Historical Anthropology of Early Modern Italy: Essays on Perception and Communication* (Cambridge, 1987).

—— 'Masaniello: A Response', *Past and Present*, 114 (1987), 197–9.

—— 'The Virgin of the Carmine and the Revolt of Masaniello', in *The Historical Anthropology of Early Modern Italy: Essays on Perception and Communication* (Cambridge, 1987), 191–206.

—— *The Fabrication* of *Louis XIV* (New Haven, 1992).

—— *History and Social Theory* (Cambridge, 1992).

—— *The Art of Conversation* (Cambridge, 1993).

—— 'State-Making, King-Making and Image-Making from Renaissance to Baroque: Scandinavia in a European Context', *Scandinavian Journal of History*, 22:1 (1997), 1–8.

—— 'Presenting and Re-presenting Charles V', in *Charles V, 1500–1558, and his Time*, ed. Hugo Soly (Antwerp, 1999), 393–475.

Butazzi, Grazietta, 'Il modello spagnolo nella moda europea', in *Le trame della moda*, ed. Anna Giulia Cavagna and Grazietta Butazzi (Rome, 1995), 80–94.

—— '*Vesti di "molta fattura"*: Reflections on Spanish-Influenced Fashion in the Second Half of the Sixteenth Century', in *Velluti e moda. Tra XV e XVII secolo*, ed. Annalisa Zanni (Milan, 1999), 169–75.

—— 'Intorno al "Cavaliere in nero". Note sulla moda maschile tra Cinque e Seicento', in *Giovan Battista Moroni. Il cavaliere in nero. Immagine del gentiluomo nel Cinquecento*, ed. Annalisa Zanni and Andrea di Lorenzo (Milan, 2005), 47–55.

Calabria, Antonio, *The Cost of Empire: The Finances of the Kingdom of Naples in the Time of Spanish Rule* (Cambridge, 1992).

—— and John A. Marino (eds.), *Good Government in Spanish Naples* (New York, 1990).

Campa, Pedro F., 'Terms for Emblem in the Spanish Tradition', in *Aspects of Renaissance and Baroque Symbol Theory 1500–1700*, ed. Peter Daly and John Manning (New York, 1999), 13–26.

Cañeque, Alejandro, *The King's Living Image: The Culture and Politics of Viceregal Power in Colonial Mexico* (New York, 2004).

Cannadine, David, 'Introduction: Divine Rites of Kings', in *Rituals of Royalty: Power and Ceremonial in Traditional Societies*, ed. David Cannadine and Simon Price (Cambridge, 1992), 1–19.

Cantù, Francesca (ed.), *Las cortes virreinales de la monarquía española. América e Italia* (Rome, 2008).

Carrasco Urgoiti, María Soledad, *El moro reatdor y el moro amigo. Estudios sobre fiestas y comedias de moros y cristianos* (Granada, 1996).

Carrió-Invernizzi, Diana, 'Entre Nápoles y España. Cultura política y mecenazgo artístico de los virreyes Pascual y Pedro Antonio de Aragón (1611–1672)' (PhD dissertation, Universitat de Barcelona, 2006).

—— *El gobierno de las imágenes. Ceremonial y mecenazgo en la Italia española del siglo XVII* (Madrid, 2008).

Castro, Américo, *España en su historia. Cristianos, Moros y Judios* (Buenos Aires, 1948).

Chabod, Federico, *Storia di Milano nell'epoca di Carlo V* (Turin, 1961).

Chaline, Olivier, 'The Kingdoms of France and Navarre: The Valois and Bourbon Courts, c. 1515–1750', in *The Princely Courts of Europe: Ritual, Politics and Culture under the Ancien Régime, 1500–1750*, ed. John Adamson (London, 1999), 67–93.

Checa Cremades, Fernando, 'Monarchic Liturgies and the "Hidden King": The Function and Meaning of Spanish Royal Portraiture in the Sixteenth and Seventeenth Centuries', in *Iconography, Propaganda, and Legitimation*, ed. Allan Ellenius (Oxford, 1998), 89–104.

—— 'The Image of Charles V', in *Charles V, 1500–1558, and his Time*, ed. Soly (Antwerp, 1999), 477–99.

Checa Cremades, José Luis, *Madrid en la prosa de viaje (siglos XV, XVI, XVII)*, (Madrid, 1992).

Choné, Paulette, 'Triomphes, entrées, feux d'artifice et fêtes religieuses en Italie', in *Spectaculum Europaeum: Theatre and Spectacle in Europe (1580–1750)*, ed. Helen Watanabe-O'Kelly and Pierre Béhar (Wiesbaden, 1999), 644–61.

Cirillo Mastrocinque, Adelaide, 'Moda e costume', in *Storia di Napoli*, vol. 6.2, ed. Ernesto Pontieri (Naples, 1970), 769–807.

—— 'Cinquecento napoletano', in *Storia di Napoli*, vol. 4, ed. Ernesto Pontieri (2nd edn, Naples, 1976), 515–75.

—— *Usi e costumi popolari a Napoli nel Seicento* (Rome, 1978).

Cochrane, Eric, 'southern Italy in the Age of the Spanish Viceroys: Some Recent Titles', *Journal of Modern History*, 58 (1986), 194–217.

—— *Italy, 1530–1630*, ed. Julius Kirshner (London and New York, 1988).

Comparato, Vittor Ivo, *Uffici e società a Napoli (1600–1647). Aspetti dell'ideologia del magistrato nell'Età moderna* (Florence, 1974).

Coniglio, Giuseppe, *I viceré spagnoli di Napoli* (Naples, 1967).

Cortese, Nino, *I ricordi di un avvocato napoletano del Seicento. Francesco d'Andrea* (Naples, 1923).

Croce, Benedetto, *Saggi sulla letteratura Italiana del Seicento* (Bari, 1911).

—— *La Spagna nella vita italiana durante la Rinascenza* (Bari, 1917).

—— *Uomini e cose della vecchia Italia* (2 vols., Bari, 1927).

—— *Storia della età Barocca in Italia* (Bari, 1929).

—— *History of the Kingdom of Naples*, trans. Frances Frenaye (Chicago, 1970).

D'Agostino, Guido, 'Il governo spagnolo nell'Italia meridionale (1503–1580)', in *Storia di Napoli*, vol. 5.1: *Il viceregno*, ed. Ernesto Pontieri (Naples, 1970), 3–132.

D'Alessio, Silvana, *Contagi. La rivolta napoletana del 1647–48. Linguaggio e potere politico* (Florence, 2003).

—— *Masaniello. La sua vita e il mito in Europa* (Rome and Salerno, 2007).

Dandelet, Thomas, *Spanish Rome, 1500–1700* (New Haven and London, 2001).

—— and John A. Marino (eds.), *Spain in Italy: Politics, Society, and Religion 1500–1700* (Leiden, 2006).

Darnton, Robert, *The Great Cat Massacre and Other Episodes in French Cultural History* (London, 1984).

Davis, Kingsley and Wilbert Moore, 'Some Principles of Stratification', *American Sociological Review*, 10 (1945), 242–9.

Dean, Trevor, 'The Courts', in *The Origins of the State in Italy, 1300–1600*, ed. Julius Kirshner (Chicago and London, 1996).

De Cavi, Sabina, 'Spain in Naples: Building, Sculpture and Painting under the Viceroys (1585–1621)' (PhD dissertation, Columbia University, 2007).

—— 'Il palazzo reale di Napoli (1600–1607). Un edificio "spagnolo"?', in *Napoli è tutto il mondo. Neapolitan Art and Culture from Humanism to the Enlightenment*, ed. Livio Pestilli, Ingrid D. Rowland, and Sebastian Schütze (Pisa and Rome, 2008), 147–71.

—— *Architecture and Royal Presence: Domenico and Giulio Cesare Fontana in Spanish Naples*

(1592–1627) (Newcastle, 2009).

D'Elia, Renata, *Vita popolare nella Napoli spagnuola* (Naples, 1971).

Defourneaux, Marcelin, *Daily Life in Spain in the Golden Age*, trans. Newton Branch (London, 1970).

Deleito y Piñuela, José, *La mujer, la casa y la moda* (2nd edn, Madrid, 1954).

—— *...También se divierte el pueblo* (2nd edn, Madrid, 1954).

—— *El rey se divierte. Recuerdos de hace tres siglos* (2nd edn, Madrid, 1964).

De Renzi, Salvatore, *Napoli nell'anno 1656* (Naples, 1968).

De Seta, Cesare, *Napoli* (Rome and Bari, 1981).

—— *Napoli fra Rinascimento e Illuminismo* (Naples, 1991).

Díez Borque, José María, 'Relaciones de teatro y fiesta en el Barroco español', in *Teatro y fiesta en el Barroco. España e Iberoamerica*, ed. José María Díez Borque (Barcelona, 1986), 11–40.

—— *La vida española en el Siglo de Oro según los extranjeros* (Barcelona, 1990).

—— and K. F. Rudolf (eds.), *Barroco español y austríaco. Fiesta y teatro en la corte* (Madrid, 1994).

Di Giacomo, Salvatore, *La prostituzione in Napoli nei secoli XV, XVI e XVII. Documenti inediti* (Naples, 1899).

Domínguez Ortis, Antonio and Bernard Vincent, *Historia de los moriscos. Vida y tragedia de una minoría* (Madrid, 1978).

Donati, Claudio, *L'idea di nobiltà in Italia. Secoli XIV–XVIII* (Bari, 1988).

Doria, Gino, 'I soldati napoletani nelle guerre del Brasile contro gli olandesi (1625–1641)', *ASPN*, 57 (1932), 224–50.

Duffy, Eamon, *Saints and Sinners: A History of the Popes* (New Haven, 1996).

Duindam, Jeroen, *Myths of Power: Norbert Elias and the Early Modern European Court* (Amsterdam, 1999).

—— *Vienna and Versailles: The Courts of Europe's Dynastic Rivals, 1550–1780* (Cambridge, 2003).

Durkheim, Émile, *The Division of Labour in Society*, trans. George Simpson (New York, 1933).

Eire, Carlos M. N., *From Madrid to Purgatory: The Arts and Crafts of Dying in Sixteenth-Century Spain* (New York, 1995).

Elias, Norbert, *The Civilizing Process*, trans. Edmund Jephcott (2 vols., Oxford, 1978–82).

—— *The Court Society*, trans. Edmund Jephcott (Oxford, 1983).

Elliott, John H., *Imperial Spain, 1469–1716* (London, 1963).

—— 'Philip IV of Spain: Prisoner of Ceremony', in *The Courts of Europe: Politics, Patronage, and Royalty 1400–1800*, ed. A. G. Dickens (London, 1977), 169–90.

—— *Spain and its World: Collected Essays* (New Haven and London, 1989).

—— 'A Europe of Composite Monarchies', *Past and Present*, 137 (1992), 48–71.

—— and Jonathan Brown, *A Palace for a King: The Buen Retiro and the Court of Philip IV* (New Haven and London, 1980).

Enciso Alonso-Muñumer, Isabel, *Nobleza, poder y mecenazgo en tiempos de Felipe III. Nápoles y el Conde de Lemos* (Madrid, 2007).

Erspamer, Francesco, *La biblioteca di Don Ferrante. Duello e onore nella cultura del Cinquecento* (Rome, 1982).

Escalera Pérez, Reyes, 'Monjas, madres, doncellas y prostitutas. La mujer en la emblemática', in *Del libro de emblemas a la ciudad simbolica. Actas del III simposio internacional de emblemática hispánica*, ed. Víctor Mínguez (2 vols., Castellón, 2000), II, 769–91.

Fabretti, Ariodante, *Statuti e ordinamenti suntuarii intorno al vestire degli uomini e delle donne in Perugia dall'anno 1266 al 1536*, in *Memorie della Reale Accademia delle Scienze di Torino*, Serie II, vol. 38 (1888), 137–232.

Fabris, Dinko, 'Musical Festivals at a Capital without a Court: Spanish Naples from Charles V (1535) to Philip V (1702)', in *Court Festivals of the European Renaissance: Art, Politics and Performance*, ed. J. R. Mulryne and Elizabeth Goldring (Aldershot and Burlington, Vt., 2002).

Fagiolo dell'Arco, Maurizio, *La festa barocca* (Rome, 1997).

Fantoni, Marcello, 'The Grand Duchy of Tuscany: The Courts of the Medici, 1532–1737', in *The Princely Courts of Europe: Ritual, Politics and Culture under the Ancien Régime, 1500–1750*, ed. John Adamson (London, 2000), 255–74.

Farinelli, Arturo, *Italia e Spagna* (2 vols., Turin, 1929).

Ferrero, Fabriciano, 'Mentalità teologica e mentalità scientifica sulla moda femminile del secolo XVII', *Ricerche per la Storia Religiosa di Roma*, 1 (1977), 231–56.

Fiorentino, Katia, 'La rivolta di Masaniello del 1647', in *Civiltà del Seicento a Napoli* (2 vols., Naples, 1984), II, 43–9.

Flor, Fernando R. de la, 'Los contornos del emblema. Del escudo heráldico a la divisa y la empresa', in *Actas del I simposio internacional de emblemática, Teruel, 1 y 2 de octubre de 1991* (Teruel, 1994), 27–58.

Forgione, Mario, *I Viceré. 1503–1707. Cronache irriverenti di due secoli di dominazione spagnola a Napoli* (Naples, 1998).

Frangito, Gigliola, 'Cardinals' Courts in Sixteenth-Century Rome', *The Journal of Modern History*, 65:1 (1993), 26–56.

Fusco, Fara, 'La "legislazione" sulla stampa nella Napoli del Seicento', in *Civiltà del Seicento a Napoli* (2 vols., Naples, 1984), I, 459–80.

Galasso, Giuseppe, *Economia e società nella Calabria del Cinquecento* (Naples, 1967).

—— 'La festa', in his *L'altra Europa. Per un antropologia storica del Mezzogiorno d'Italia* (Milan, 1982), 121–42.

—— 'Lo stereotipo del napoletano e le sue variazioni regionali', in his *L'altra Europa. Per un antropologia storica del Mezzogiorno d'Italia* (Milan, 1982), 143–90

—— *Napoli spagnola dopo Masaniello. Politica, cultura, società* (2 vols., Florence, 1982).

—— *Alla periferia dell'impero. Il Regno di Napoli nel periodo spagnolo (secoli XVI–XVII)* (Turin, 1994).

—— 'Da "Napoli gentile" a "Napoli fedelissima"', in his *Napoli capitale. Identità politica e identità cittadina. Studi e ricerche 1266–1860* (Naples, 2003), 61–110.

—— *Il Regno di Napoli. Il Mezzogiorno spagnolo ed austriaco (1622–1734)* (Turin, 2006).

Gallego, Julian, *Visión y simbolos en la pintura Española del Siglo de Oro* (Madrid, 1984).

—— 'Aspectos emblemáticos en las reales exequias españolas de la casa de Austria', *Goya*, 187/8 (1985), 120–5.

García Arranz, José Julio, 'Image and Moral Teaching through Emblematic Animals', in *Aspects of Renaissance and Baroque Symbol Theory 1500–1700*, ed. Peter Daly and John Manning (New York, 1999), 93–108.

—— and Francisco Javier Pizarro Gómez, 'Teoría y práctica de la imagen de las "imprese" en los Siglos XVI y XVII', in *Emblemata aurea. La emblemática en el arte y la literatura del Siglo de Oro*, ed. Rafael Zafra and José Javier Azanza (Madrid, 2000), 189–207.

García Cárcel, Ricardo, *La leyenda negra. Historia y opinión* (Madrid, 1993).

García de Enterría, María Cruz, 'El cuerpo entre predicadores y copleros', in *Le corps dans la société espagnole des XVIe et XVIIe siècles*, ed. Augustin Redondo (Paris, 1990).

Giesey, Ralph E., *The Royal Funeral Ceremony in Renaissance France* (Geneva, 1960).

Ginzburg, Carlo, 'The High and the Low: The Themes of Forbidden Knowledge in the Sixteenth and Seventeenth Centuries', *Past and Present*, 73 (1976), 28–41.

—— 'Ritual Pillages: A Preface to Research in Progress', in *Microhistory and the Lost Peoples of Europe*, ed. Edward Muir and Guido Ruggiero (Baltimore, 1991), 20–41.

Giura, Vincenzo, *Storie di minoranze. ebrei, greci, albanesi nel Regno di Napoli* (Naples, 1984).

Gleijeses, Vittorio, *Piccola storia del Carnevale* (Naples, 1971).

—— *Feste, farina, e forca* (Naples, 1972).

Goffman, Erving, *Relations in Public: Microstudies of the Public Order* (New York, 1971).

González Enciso, Agustín, 'Del rey ausente al rey distante', in *Imagen del rey, imagen de los reynos. Las ceremonias públicas en la España moderna (1500–1814)*, ed. Agustín González Enciso and Jesús María Usunáriz Garayoa (Pamplona, 1999), 1–18.

González Novalín, José Luis, 'La inquisicion española', in *Historia de la Iglesia en España*, vol. 3.2: *La Iglesia en la España de los siglos XV y XVI*, ed. José Luis González Novalín (Madrid, 1980).

Grandis, Sonia G., 'Teatri di sontuosissima e orrida maestà. Trionfo della morte e trionfo del re nelle pompe funebri regali', in *La scena della gloria. Drammaturgia e spettacolo a Milano in età spagnola*, ed. Annamaria Cascetta and Roberta Carpani (Milan, 1995), 659–715.

Guarino, Gabriel, 'Pictorial Representations for the Neapolitan Obsequies of the Spanish Habsburgs', in *Florilegio de estudios de Emblemática: A Florilegium of Studies on Emblematics: Proceedings of the Sixth International Conference of The Society for Emblem Studies: A Coruña, 2002*, ed. Sagrario López Poza (Ferrol, 2004), 425–30.

—— 'Regulation of Appearances During the Catholic Reformation: Dress and Morality in Spain and Italy', in *Les deux réformes chrétiennes. Propagation et diffusion*, ed. Myriam Yardeni and Ilana Zinguer (Leiden, 2004), 492–510.

—— 'Spanish Celebrations in Seventeenth-Century Naples', *The Sixteenth-Century Journal*, 37:1 (2006), 25–41.

—— ' "Miscebis Sacra Profanis": Viceregal Exaltation in Religious Rites and Ceremonies', in *Images of the Body Politic*, ed. Giuseppe Cascione, Donato Mansueto, and Gabriel Guarino (Milan, 2007), 69–80.

Gunn, Peter, *Naples: A Palimpsest* (London, 1961).

Hale, John, *The Civilization of Europe in the Renaissance* (London, 1993).

Harvey, John, *Men in Black* (London, 1995).

Hernando Sánchez, Carlos José, *Castilla y Nápoles en el siglo XVI. El virrey Pedro de Toledo. Linaje, estado y cultura (1532–1553)* (Valladolid, 1994).

—— 'Nobiltà e potere vicereale a Napoli nella prima metà del '500', in *Nel sistema imperiale. L'Italia spagnola*, ed. Aurelio Musi (Naples, 1994), 147–63.

—— 'La gloria del caballo. Saber ecuestre y cultura caballeresca en el reino de Napoles durante el siglo XVI', in *Felipe II (1527–1598). Europa y la monarquía católica*, ed. José Martínez Millán (4 vols., Madrid, 1998), IV, 277–310.

—— 'El glorioso triumfo de Carlos V en Nápoles y el humanismo de corte entre Italia y España', *ASPN*, 119 (2001), 447–521.

—— *El reino de Nápoles en el imperio de Carlos V. La consolidación de la conquista* (Madrid, 2001).

—— 'Teatro del honor y ceremonial de la ausencia. La corte virreinal de Nápoles en el siglo XVII', in *Calderón de la Barca y la España del Barroco*, ed. José Alcalá Zamora and Ernest Belenguer Cebría (2 vols., Madrid, 2001), I, 591–674.

—— 'Españoles e italianos. Nación y lealtad en el Reino de Nápoles durante Las Guerras de Italia, in *La monarquía de las naciones. Patria, nación, y naturaleza en la Monarquía de España*, ed. Antonio Álvarez Ossorio-Alvariño and Bernardo J. García y García (Madrid, 2004), 423–81.

—— 'Los virreyes de la Monarquía Española en Italia. Evolución y práctica de un oficio de gobierno', *Studia Historica. Historia Moderna*, 26 (2004), 43–73.

Hillgarth, Jocelyn Nigel, *The Mirror of Spain, 1500–1700: The Formation of a Myth* (Ann Arbor, Mich., 2000).

Hochner, Nicole, *Louis XII. Les dérèglements de l'image royale* (Paris, 2006).

Hughes, Diane Owen, 'Sumptuary Law and Social Relations in Renaissance Italy', in *Disputes and Settlements: Law and Human Relations in the West*, ed. John Bossy (Cambridge, 1983), 69–100.

—— 'Distinguishing Signs: Ear-rings, Jews, and Franciscan Rhetoric in the Italian Renaissance City', *Past and Present*, 112 (1986), 3–59.

—— 'Regulating Women's Fashion', in *A History of Women in the West,* vol. 2: *Silences of the Middle Ages*, ed. Christiane Klapisch-Zuber (Cambridge, Mass., 1992), 136–58.

Huizinga, Johan, *Homo Ludens: A Study of the Play-Element in Culture*, trans. R. F. C. Hull (London, 1998).

Hume, Martin, 'A Fight Against Finery', in *The Year After the Armada and Other Historical Studies* (London, 1896), 207–60.

Hunt, Alan, *Governance of the Consuming Passions: A History of Sumptuary Law* (London, 1996).

Iannella, Gina, 'Les fêtes de la Saint-Jean à Naples (1581–1632)', in *Les fêtes urbaines en Italie à l'époque de la Renaissance. Vérone, Florence, Sienne, Naples*, ed. Françoise Decroisette and Michel Plaisance (Paris, 1993), 131–83

Jacquot, Jean (ed.), *Les fêtes de la Renaissance* (3 vols., Paris, 1956–75).

Jónsson, Már, 'The Expulsion of the Moriscos from Spain in 1609–1614: The Destruction of an Islamic Periphery', *Journal of Global History*, 2:2 (2007), 195–212.

Kamen, Henry, 'Una crisis de conciencia en la Edad de Oro en España. Inquisición contra limpieza de sangre', *Bulletin Hispanique*, 88 (1986), 321–56.

—— 'Nudité et contre-réforme en Espagne', in *Le corps dans la société espagnole des XVIᵉ et XVIIᵉ siècles*, ed. Augustin Redondo (Paris, 1990), 297–306.

—— *Early Modern European Society* (London and New York, 2000).

Kanceff, Emanuele and Franco Paloscia (eds.), *Napoli e il regno dei grandi viaggiatori* (Rome, 1994).

Kantorowicz, Ernst H., *The King's Two Bodies: A Study in Medieval Political Theology* (Princeton, 1957).

Kertzer, David, *Ritual, Politics, and Power* (New Haven, 1988).

King, Margaret L., 'The Woman of the Renaissance', in *Renaissance Characters*, ed. Eugenio Garin, trans. Lydia G. Cochrane (Chicago and London, 1991), 207–49.

Kipling, Gordon, *Enter the King: Theatre, Liturgy, and Ritual in the Medieval Civic Triumph* (Oxford, 1998).

Knox, Dilwyn, 'Disciplina. Le origini monastiche e clericali del buon comportamento nell'Europa cattolica del Cinquecento e del primo Seicento', in *Disciplina dell'anima, disciplina del corpo e disciplina della società tra medioevo ed età moderna*, ed. Paolo Prodi, *Annali dell'istituto storico italo-germanico*, Quaderno 40 (Bologna, 1994), 63–99.

Koenigsberger, Helmut G., *The Government of Sicily under Philip II of Spain: A Study in the Practice of Empire* (London, 1951).

—— *The Habsburgs and Europe, 1516–1660* (Ithaca, NY, and London, 1971).

—— *Politicians and Virtuosi: Essays in Early Modern History* (London and Ronceverte, 1986).

Kovesi Killerby, Catherine, 'Practical Problems in the Enforcement of Italian Sumptuary Law, 1200–1500', in *Crime, Society and the Law in Renaissance Italy*, ed. Trevor Dean (Cambridge, 1994), 99–120.

Labrot, Gérard, *Baroni in città. Residenze e comportamenti dell'aristocrazia napoletana, 1530–1734* (Naples, 1979).

—— *Palazzi napoletani. Storie di nobili e corteggiani, 1520–1750* (Naples, 1997).

Ladurie, Emmanuel Leroy, *Carnival in Romans*, trans. Mary Feeny (New York, 1979).

Laver, James, *Costume and Fashion: A Concise History* (rev. edn, London, 1995).

Ledda, Giuseppina, *Contributo allo studio di letteratura emblematica in Spagna (1549–1613)* (Pisa, 1970).

—— 'Estrategias y procedimientos comunicativos en la emblemática aplicada (fiestas y celebraciones, siglo XVII)', in *Emblemata aurea. La emblemática en el arte y la literatura del Siglo de Oro*, ed. Rafael Zafra and José Javier Azanza (Madrid, 2000), 251–62.

Lepre, Aurelio, *Storia del Mezzogiorno d'Italia*, vol. 1: *La lunga durata e la crisi, 1500–1656* (2 vols., Naples, 1986).

Levi Pisetzky, Rosita, 'Il gusto Barocco nel costume italiano del Seicento', *Studi Secenteschi*, 2 (1961), 61–94.

—— *Storia del costume in Italia* (5 vols., Milan, 1964–69).

—— 'Moda e costume', in *Storia d'Italia*, vol. 5.1, ed. Ruggiero Romano and Corrado Vivanti (Turin, 1973), 939–78.

—— *Il costume e la moda nella società italiana* (Turin, 1978).

Levisi, Margarita, 'Golden Age Autobiography: The Soldiers', in *Autobiography in Early Modern Spain*, ed. Nicholas Spadaccini and Jenaro Talens (Minneapolis, 1988), 97–117.

Lewis, Bernard, *Christians, Muslims, and Jews in the Age of Discovery* (New York and Oxford, 1995).

Lisón Tolosana, Carmelo, *La imagen del rey. Monarquía, realeza y poder ritual en la Casa de los Austrias* (Madrid, 1991).

Luján, Néstor, *La vida cotidiana en el Siglo de Oro español* (Barcelona, 1988).

Luzzati, Michele and Albano Biondi (eds.), *L'Inquisizione e gli ebrei in Italia* (Rome and Bari, 1994).

Mackrell, Alice, *An Illustrated History of Fashion: 500 Years of Fashion Illustration* (London, 1997).

Mancini, Franco, *Feste ed apparati civili e religiosi in Napoli dal viceregno alla capitale* (Naples, 1968).

—— 'Feste, apparati e spettacoli teatrali tra il '600 e il '700', in *Storia di Napoli*, vol. 6.1, ed. Ernesto Pontieri (Naples, 1972), 1157–219.

—— ' "L'immaginario di regime". Apparati e scenografie alla corte dei viceré', in *Civiltà del Seicento a Napoli* (2 vols., Naples, 1984), II, 27–35.

Manning, John, 'Renaissance and Baroque Symbol Theory: Some Introductory Questions and Problems', in *Aspects of Renaissance and Baroque Symbol Theory 1500–1700*, ed. Peter Daly and John Manning (New York, 1999), xiii–xv.

Maravall, José Antonio, *Culture of the Baroque: Analysis of a Historical Structure*, trans. Terry Cochran (Manchester, 1986).

Marino, John A., 'Celebrating a Royal Birth in 1639: "The Rape of Europa" in the Neapolitan Viceroy's Court', *Rinascimento*, 43 (2003), 233–47.

—— 'An Anti-Campanellan Vision on the Spanish monarchy and the Crisis of 1595', in *A Renaissance of Conflicts: Visions and Revisions of Law and Society in Italy and Spain*, ed. John A. Marino and Thomas Kuehn (Toronto, 2004), 367–93.

—— 'The Foreigner and the Citizen: A Dialogue on Good Government in Spanish Naples', in *Reason and its Others: Italy, Spain and the New World (1500s–1700s)*, ed. David Castillo and Massimo Lollini (Nashville, 2006), 145–64.

—— 'The Zodiac in the Streets: Inscribing "Buon Governo" in Baroque Naples', in *Embodiments of Power: Building Baroque Cities in Austria and Europe*, ed. Gary B. Cohen and Franz A. J. Szabo (Oxford and New York, 2007), 203–29.

Marvin, Gary, *Bullfight* (Oxford and New York, 1988).

Masson, Georgina, *Courtesans of the Italian Renaissance* (London, 1975).

Matthews Grieco, Sarah F., 'The Body, Appearance, and Sexuality', in *A History of Women in the West*, vol. 3: *Renaissance and Enlightenment Paradoxes*, ed. Natalie Zemon Davies and Arlette Farge (Cambridge, Mass., 1993), 46–84.

—— 'Modelli di santità femminile nell'Italia del Rinascimento e della Controriforma', in *Donne e Fede. Santità e vita religiosa in Italia*, ed. Lucetta Scaraffia and Gabriella Zarri (Rome and Bari, 1994), 303–25.

—— 'Pedagogical Prints: Moralizing Broadsheets and Wayward Women in Counter Reformation Italy', in *Picturing Women in Renaissance and Baroque Italy*, ed. Geraldine A. Johnson and Sarah F. Matthews Grieco (Cambridge, 1997), 61–87.

Megale, Teresa, ' "Sic per te superis gens inimica ruat". L'ingresso trionfale di Carlo V a Napoli (1535)', *ASPN*, 119 (2001), 587–604.

Mellano, Maria Franca, 'La donna nell'opera riformatrice di S. Carlo', in *San Carlo e il suo tempo. Atti del Convegno Internazionale nel IV centenario della morte (Milano, 21–26 maggio 1984)* (2 vols., Rome, 1986).

Meyuhas Ginio, Alisa (ed.), *Jews, Christians and Muslims in the Mediterranean World after 1492* (London, 1992).

Mínguez, Víctor, 'Arte efímero y alegorías. La *Iconología* de Ripa en las exequias romanas de Felipe IV', *Ars Longa*, 1 (1990), 89–96.

—— 'Exequias de Felipe IV en Nápoles. La exaltación dinástica a través de un programa astrológico', *Ars Longa*, 2 (1991), 53–62.

—— 'Los emblemas solares, la imagen del príncipe y los programas astrológicos en el arte efímero', in *Actas del I simposio internacional de emblemática, Teruel, 1 y 2 de octubre de 1991* (Teruel, 1994), 209–53.

—— *Los reyes distantes. Imágenes del poder en el México virreinal* (Castellón, 1995).

Minguito Palomares, Ana, 'Linaje, poder y cultura. El gobierno de Íñigo Vélez de Guevara, VII Conde de Oñate en Nápoles (1648–1653)' (PhD dissertation, Universidad Complutense de Madrid, 2002).

Mitchell, Bonner, *The Majesty of the State: Triumphal Progresses of Foreign Sovereigns in Renaissance Italy (1494–1600)* (Florence, 1986).

Mitchell, Timothy, *Blood Sport: A Social History of Bullfighting* (Philadelphia, 1991).

Moine, Marie-Christine, *Les fêtes à la cour du Roi-Soleil, 1653–1715* (Paris, 1984).

Moli Frigola, Montserrat, 'Donne, candele, lacrime, e morte. Funerali di regine spagnole nell'Italia del Seicento', in *Barocco romano e barocco italiano. Il teatro, l'effimero, l'allegoria*, ed. Marcello Fagiolo and Maria Luisa Madonna (Rome, 1985), 135–58.

Molinié-Bertrand, Annie, Jean-Paul Duviols, and Araceli Guillaume-Alonso (eds.), *Des taureaux et des hommes. Tauromachie et société dans le monde ibérique et ibéro-américain. Actes du colloque international* (Paris, 1999).

Molmenti, Pompeo Gherardo, *La storia di Venezia nella vita privata. Dalle origini alla caduta della republica* (2nd edn, Turin, 1880).

Mordenti, Alessandro, 'Vita quotidiana e modelli di cultura in una periferia dello stato pontificio nei secoli XVI–XVII', in *La famiglia e la vita quotidiana in Europa dal '400 al '600. Fonti e problemi* (Rome, 1986).

Mozzarelli, Cesare, 'Strutture sociali e formazioni statuali a Milano e Napoli tra '500 e '700', *Società e Storia*, 3 (1978), 431–63.

Mozzillo, Atanasio, *Passaggio a Mezzogiorno. Napoli e il Sud nell'immaginario barocco e illuminista europeo* (Milan, 1993).

Muir, Edward, *Mad Blood Stirring: Vendetta and Factions in Friuli during the Renaissance* (Baltimore, 1993).

—— *Ritual in Early Modern Europe* (Cambridge, 1997).

Mulryne, J. R., Helen Watanabe-O'Kelly, and Margaret Shewring (eds.), '*Europa Triumphans': Court and Civic Festivals in Early Modern Europe* (2 vols., Aldershot and Burlington, Vt., 2004).

Musella Guida, Silvana, 'Il Regno del lusso. Leggi suntuarie e società. Un percorso di lungo periodo nella Napoli medievale e moderna (1290–1784)', in *Proceedings of L'économie du luxe en France et en Italie. Journées d'étude organisées par le Comité franco-italien d'histoire économique (AFHE-SISE) Lille, Ifresi 4–5 mai 2007*, 1–23, http://lodel.ehess.fr/afhe/docannexe.php?id=446.

—— 'Don Pedro Alvarez de Toledo. Ritratto di un principe nell'Europa rinascimentale', *Samnium*, 81–2: 21–2 (2008–9), 239–353.

—— and Sonia Scognamiglio Cestaro, 'Le origini della moda napoletana', in *Proceedings*

of the XIII International Congress TICCIH: Industrial Heritage and Urban Landscape, Terni-Rome, 14–18 September 2006, 1–28, www.ticcihcongress2006.net/paper/Paper%209/Musella_Scognamiglio%209.pdf.

Musi, Aurelio, 'La rivolta di Masaniello tra mito, ideologia e scienza storica', *Prospettive Settanta*, 2–3 (1983), 265–80.

—— 'Tra burocrati e notabili. Potere e istituzioni nella Napoli del Seicento', *Bollettino del Centro di Studi Vichiani*, 16 (1986), 157–76.

—— 'La rivolta antispagnola a Napoli e in Sicilia', in *Storia della società italiana*, vol. 11: *La Controriforma e il Seicento*, ed. Giovanni Cherubini, Franco Della Peruta, Ettore Lepore (Milan, 1989), 317–58.

—— *La rivolta di Masaniello nella scena politica barocca* (Naples, 1989).

—— 'L'Italia nel sistema imperiale spagnolo', in *Nel sistema imperiale. L'Italia spagnola*, ed. Aurelio Musi (Naples, 1994), 51–66.

—— *L'Italia dei Viceré. Integrazione e resistenza nel sistema imperiale spagnolo* (Cava de' Tirreni, 2000).

—— 'Il Regno di Napoli, e il sistema imperiale spagnolo', in *L'Italia dei Viceré. Integrazione et resistenza nel sistema imperiale spagnolo* (Cava dei Tirreni, 2000), 23–35.

Muto, Giovanni, 'Il Regno di Napoli sotto la dominazione spagnola', in *Storia della società italiana*, vol. 11: *La Controriforma e il Seicento*, ed. Giovanni Cherubini, Franco Della Peruta, Ettore Lepore (Milan, 1989), 225–316.

—— 'Problemi di stratificazione nobiliare nell'Italia spagnola', in *Dimenticare Croce? Studi e orientamenti di storia del Mezzogiorno*, ed. Aurelio Musi (Naples, 1991), 73–111.

—— ' "I segni d'honore". Rappresentazioni delle dinamiche nobiliari a Napoli in età moderna', in *Signori, patrizi, cavalieri in Italia centro-meridionale nell'età moderna*, ed. Maria Antonietta Visceglia (Rome, 1992), 171–93.

—— 'Spazio urbano e identità sociale. Le feste del popolo napoletano nella prima età moderna', in *Le regole dei mestieri e delle professioni. Secoli XV–XIX*, ed. Marco Meriggi and Alessandro Pastore (Milan, 2001), 305–25.

—— 'A Court without a King: Naples as a Capital City in the First Half of the 16th Century', in *The World of Charles V*, ed. W. Blockmans and N. Mout (Amsterdam, 2004), 129–42.

—— 'Fedeltà e patria nel lessico politico napoletano della prima età moderna', in *Storia Sociale e politica. Omaggio a Rosario Villari*, ed. Alberto Merola, Giovanni Muto, Elena Valeri, and Maria Anonietta Visceglia (Milan, 2006), 495–522.

—— 'Fidelildad, política y conflictos urbanos en el Reino de Nápoles (siglos XVI–XVII)', in *Ciudades en conflicto (siglos XVI–XVII)*, ed. Jose I. Portea and Juan E. Gelabert (Junta de Castilla y León, 2008), 370–95.

Muzzarelli, Maria Giuseppina, ' "Contra mundanas vanitates et pompas". Aspetti della lotta contro i lussi nell'Italia del XV secolo', *Rivista di Storia della Chiesa in Italia*, 40:2 (1986), 371–90.

—— *Gli inganni delle apparenze. Disciplina di vesti e ornamenti alla fine del medioevo* (Turin, 1996).

—— *Guardaroba medievale. Vesti e società dal XIII al XVI secolo* (Bologna, 1999).

—— 'Le leggi suntuarie', in *La moda. Storia d'Italia. Annali 19*, ed. Carlo Marco Belfanti and Fabio Giusberti (Turin, 2003), 185–220.

Nappi, Eduardo, *Aspetti della società ed economia napoletana durante la peste del 1656. Dai documenti dell'archivio storico del banco di Napoli* (Naples, 1980).

Niccoli, Ottavia, 'Creanza e disciplina. Buone maniere per i fanciulli nell'Italia della controriforma', in *Disciplina dell'anima, disciplina del corpo e disciplina della società tra medioevo ed età moderna*, ed. Paolo Prodi, *Annali dell'Istituto storico italo-germanico*, Quaderno 40 (Bologna, 1994), 929–63.

Nicolini, Fausto, *Aspetti della vita italo-spagnuola nel Cinque e Seicento* (Naples, 1934), 127–288.

Nussdorfer, Laurie, 'The Vacant See: Ritual and Protest in Early Modern Rome', *Sixteenth Century Journal*, 18:2 (1987), 173–89.

Orso, Steven N., *Art and Death at the Spanish Habsburg Court: The Royal Exequies for Philip IV* (Columbia, 1989).

Osorio, Alejandra, *Inventing Lima: Baroque Modernity in Peru's South Sea Metropolis* (New York, 2008).

Pacelli, Vincenzo, 'L'ideologia del potere nella rittrattistica napoletana del Seicento', *Bollettino del Centro di Studi Vichiani*, 16 (1986), 197–241.

Palos Peñarroya, Joan Luís, 'Un escenario italiano para los gobernantes españoles. El nuevo palacio de los virreyes de Nápoles (1599–1653)', *Cuadernos de Historia Moderna*, 30 (2005), 125–50.

Paloscia, Francesco (ed.), *Napoli e il regno dei grandi viaggiatori* (Rome, 1994).

Paravicini, Werner, 'The Court of the Dukes of Burgundy: A Model for Europe?', in *Princes, Patronage, and the Nobility: The Court at the Beginning of the Modern Age, c.1450–1650*, ed. Ronald G. Asch and Adolf M. Birke (Oxford, 1991), 69–102.

Park, Katharine, 'The Criminal and the Saintly Body: Autopsy and Dissection in Renaissance Italy', *Renaissance Quarterly*, 47:1 (1994), 1–33.

Parker, Geoffrey and Lesley M. Smith (eds.), *The General Crisis of the Seventeenth Century* (London, 1978).

Pastor, Ludwig, *The History of the Popes*, trans. E. F. Peeler (40 vols., London, 1891–1953).

Paulicelli, Eugenia (ed.), *Moda e moderno. Dal Medioevo al Rinascimento* (Rome, 2006).

Pepe, Gabriele, *Il Mezzogiorno d'Italia sotto gli Spagnoli. La tradizione storiografica* (Florence, 1952).

Pérez Villanueva, Joaquín, 'Sor María de Agreda y Felipe IV. Un epistolario en su tiempo', in *Historia de la Iglesia en España*, vol. 4: *La Iglesia en la España de los siglos XVII y XVIII*, ed. Antonio Mestre Sanchis (Madrid, 1980).

Perry, Mary Elizabeth, 'Magdalens and Jezebels in Counter Reformation Spain', in *Culture and Control in Counter Reformation Spain*, ed. Anne J. Cruz and Mary Elizabeth Perry (Oxford and Minneapolis, 1992), 124–44.

Petito, Luigi, *San Gennaro. Storia, folklore, culto* (Rome and Naples, 1983).

Petrarca, Valerio, *La festa di San Giovanni Battista a Napoli nella prima metà del Seicento. Percorso macchine immagini scritture* (Palermo, 1986).

Picatoste, Felipe, *Estudios sobra la grandeza y decadencia de España. Los españoles en Italia* (Madrid, 1887).

Pinna, Raimondo, *Atlante dei feudi in Sardegna. Il periodo spagnolo 1479–1700* (Cagliari, 1999).

Polleross, Friedrich, 'From the *Exemplum Virtutis* to the Apotheosis: Hercules as an

Identification Figure in Portraiture: An Example of the Adoption of Classical Forms of Representation', in *Iconography, Propaganda, and Legitimation*, ed. Allan Ellenius (Oxford, 1998), 37–72.

Porter, Jeanne, Chenault, 'Reflections of the Golden Age: The Visitor's Account of Naples', in *Parthenope's Splendour: Art of the Golden Age in Naples* (Papers in Art History from The Pennsylvania State University, vol. VII), ed. Jeanne Chenault Porter and Susan Scott Munshower (University Park, Pa., 1993), 11–48.

Prodi, Paolo, *The Papal Prince: One Body and Two Souls: The Papal Monarch in Early Modern Europe*, trans. Susan Haskins (Cambridge, 1987).

Puddu, Raffaele, *Il soldato gentiluomo. Autoritratto di una società guerriera. La Spagna del Cinquecento* (Bologna, 1982).

Quazza, Guido, *La decadenza italiana nella storia europea. Saggi sul Sei-Settecento* (Turin, 1971).

Quondam, Amedeo, 'Tutti i colori del nero. Moda "alla spagnola" e "migliore forma italiana" ', in *Giovan Battista Moroni. Il cavaliere in nero. Immagine del gentiluomo nel Cinquecento*, ed. Annalisa Zanni and Andrea di Lorenzo (Milan, 2005), 25–45.

Rainey, Ronald, 'Dressing Down the Dressed-Up: Reproving Feminine Attire in Renaissance Florence', in *Renaissance Society and Culture: Essays in Honor of Eugene F. Rice Jr.*, ed. John Monfasani and Ronald G. Musto (New York, 1991), 228–37.

Rak, Michele, 'A dismisura d'uomo. Feste e spettacolo del barocco napoletano', in *Gian Lorenzo Bernini e le arti visive*, ed. Marcello Fagiolo (Rome, 1987), 259–312.

—— 'Il sistema delle feste nella Napoli barocca', in *Centri e periferie del Barocco*, vol. 2: *Barocco napoletano*, ed. Gaetana Cantone (Rome, 1992), 301–27.

Reade, Brian, *Costume of the Western World: The Dominance of Spain, 1550–1660* (London, 1951).

Redworth, Glyn and Fernando Checa, 'The Kingdoms of Spain: The Courts of the Spanish Habsburgs 1500–1700', in *The Princely Courts of Europe: Ritual, Politics and Culture under the Ancien Régime, 1500–1750*, ed. John Adamson (London, 1999), 43–65.

Ribeiro, Aileen, *Dress and Morality* (London, 1986).

Ribero, Alba, 'Imagenes de maternidád en la pintura Barroca', in *Las mujeres en el Antiguo Regimen. Imagen y realidad (s. XVI–XVIII)* (Barcelona, 1994).

Ribot García, Luis Antonio and Ernest Belenguer Cebría (eds.), *Las sociedades ibéricas y el mar a fin del siglo XVI* (4 vols., Pabellón de España, 1998).

Roche, Daniel, *The Culture of Clothing: Dress and Fashion in the 'Ancien Régime'*, trans. Jean Birrell (Cambridge, 1994).

—— *A History of Everyday Things: The Birth of Consumption in France, 1600–1800*, trans. Brian Pearce (Cambridge, 2000).

Rodríguez, Manuel Rivero, 'De la separación a la reunión dinástica. La corona de Aragón entre 1504 a 1516', in *La corte de Carlos V*, vol. I: *Corte y gobierno*, ed. José Martínez Millán (Madrid, 2000), 73–101.

Rodríguez Villa, Antonio, 'Etiquetas de la casa de Austria', *Revista Europea*, 5:75 (1875), 161–8.

Romeo, Giovanni, 'La suggestione dell'ebraismo tra i napoletani del tardo Cinquecento', in *L'inquisizione e gli ebrei in Italia*, ed. Michele Luzzati (Rome and Bari, 1994), 179–95.

Roosen, William, 'Early Modern Diplomatic Ceremonial: A Systems Approach', *The*

Journal of Modern History, 52:3 (1980), 452–76.

Rosenthal, Margaret F., *The Honest Courtesan: Veronica Franco Citizen and Writer in Sixteenth-Century Venice* (Chicago and London, 1992).

Rovito, Pier Luigi, *Respublica dei togati. Giuristi e società nella Napoli del Seicento* (Naples, 1981).

Rubin, Miri, *Corpus Christi: The Eucharist in Late Medieval Culture* (Cambridge, 1991).

Ruotolo, Renato, 'Aspetti del collezionismo napoletano del Seicento', in *Civiltà del Seicento a Napoli* (2 vols., Naples, 1984), I, 41–8.

Ryder, Alan, *The Kingdom of Naples Under Alfonso the Magnanimous: The Making of a Modern State* (Oxford, 1976).

Schipa, Michelangelo, *La cosidetta rivolta di Masaniello da memorie contemporanee inedite* (Naples, 1918).

—— *Masaniello* (Bari and Rome, 1925).

Scognamiglio Cestaro, Sonia, 'Leggi "scomode", clientele e fedeltà. Aspetti socio-istituzionali ed economici della legislazione suntuaria del Regno di Napoli in Età moderna', in *Proceedings of L'économie du luxe en France et en Italie. Journées d'étude organisées par le Comité franco-italien d'histoire économique (AFHE-SISE) Lille, Ifresi 4–5 mai 2007*, 1–29, http://lodel.ehess.fr/afhe/docannexe.php?id=445.

—— *Le Istituzioni della moda. Economia, magistrature e scambio politico nella Napoli moderna* (Benevento, 2008).

Sebastián, Santiago, *Emblemática e historia del arte* (Madrid, 1995).

Sebeok, Thomas (ed.), *Carnival!* (Berlin, 1984).

Sella, Domenico, *Italy in the Seventeenth Century* (London, 1997).

Signorotto, Gianvittorio, 'Milano e la Lombardia sotto gli spagnoli', in *Storia della società italiana*, vol. 11: *La Controriforma e il Seicento*, ed. Giovanni Cherubini, Franco Della Peruta, Ettore Lepore (Milan, 1989), 189–223.

—— (ed.), *L'Italia degli Austrias. Monarchia cattolica e domini italiani nei secoli XVI e XVII*, special issue of *Cheiron*, 17–18 (1992).

—— and Maria Antonietta Visceglia (eds.), *La corte di Roma tra Cinque e Seicento. 'Teatro' della politica europea* (Rome, 1998).

Smith, Hannah, 'Court Studies and the Courts of Early Modern Europe', *The Historical Journal*, 49 (2006), 1229–338.

Spagnoletti, Angelantonio, 'La nobiltà napoletana del '500: Tra corte e corti', in *'Famiglia' del principe e famiglia aristocratica*, ed. Cesare Mozzarelli (2 vols., Rome, 1988), II, 375–90.

—— *Principi italiani e Spagna nell'età barocca* (Milan, 1996).

—— 'Grandi famiglie napoletane nel tramonto del sistema imperiale spagnolo', in *Italia 1650. Comparazioni e bilanci*, ed. Giuseppe Galasso and Aurelio Musi (Naples, 2002), 87–100.

—— 'El concepto de naturaleza, nación y patria en Italia y en el Reino de Nápoles con respecto a la Monarquía de los Austrias', in *La monarquía de las naciones. Patria, nación, y naturaleza en la Monarquía de España*, ed. Antonio Álvarez Ossorio-Alvariño and Bernardo J. García y García (Madrid, 2004), 483–503.

Storey, Tessa, 'Clothing Courtesans: Fabrics, Signals, and Experiences', in *Clothing Culture: 1350–1650*, ed. Catherine Richardson (Aldershot, 2004), 95–107.

Strazzullo, Franco, *La peste del 1656 a Napoli* (Naples, 1957).

—— *Edilizia e urbanistica a Napoli dal '500 al '700* (Naples, 1968).

Strong, Roy, *Art and Power: Renaissance Festivals (1450–1650)* (Woodbridge, 1984).

Stumpo, Enrico, 'La crisi del Seicento in Italia', in *La storia. I grandi problemi dal medioevo all'età contemporanea*, vol. 5, ed. Nicola Tranfaglia and Massimo Firpo (Turin, 1986), 313–37.

Tejada, Francisco Elias de, *Nápoles Hispánico* (5 vols., Madrid, 1958–64).

Testaverde, Anna Maria, 'Margherita d'Austria, regina e "perla" di virtù', in *La morte e la gloria. Apparati funebri medicei per Filippo II e Margherita d'Austria*, ed. Monica Bietti (Leghorn, 1999), 132–7.

Thesander, Marianne, *The Feminine Ideal*, trans. Nicholas Hill (London, 1997).

Toaf, Ariel, 'La vita materiale', in *Gli ebrei in Italia. I: Dall'alto Medioevo all'età dei ghetti*, ed. Corrado Vivanti, *Storia d'Italia. Annali 11* (Turin, 1996).

Tuan, Yi-Fu, 'Space and Context', in *By Means of Performance: Intercultural Studies of Theatre and Ritual*, ed. Richard Schechner and Willa Appel (Cambridge, 1990), 236–44.

Turchini, Angelo, 'Dalla disciplina alla "creanza" del matrimonio all'indomani del concilio di Trento', in *Donna, disciplina, creanza cristiana dal XV al XVII secolo*, ed. Gabriella Zarri (Rome, 1996), 205–14.

Van Gennep, Arnold, *The Rites of Passage*, trans. Monika B. Vizedom and Gabrielle L. Caffee (London, 1960).

Varela, Javier, *La muerte del rey. El ceremonial funerario de la monarquía española, 1500–1885* (Madrid, 1990).

Varey, James E., 'Processional Ceremonial of the Spanish Court in the Seventeenth-Century', in *Studia Iberica. Festschrift für Hans Flasche*. ed. Karl-Hermann Körner and Klaus Rühl (Bern, 1973), 643–52.

—— 'The Audience and the Play at Court Spectacles: The Roles of the Kings', *Bulletin of Hispanic Studies*, 61 (1984), 399–406.

Ventura, Piero, 'Mercato delle risorse e identità urbana. Cittadinanza e mestiere a Napoli tra XVI e XVII secolo', in *Le regole dei mestieri e delle professioni. Secoli XV–XIX*, ed. Marco Meriggi and Alessandro Pastore (Milan, 2001), 268–304.

Venturelli, Paola, 'La moda come status symbol. Legislazioni suntuarie e "segnali" di identificazione sociale', in *Storia della moda*, ed. Ranieri Varese and Grazietta Butazzi (Bologna, 1995), 28–52.

Verga, Ettore, 'Le leggi suntuarie e la decadenza dell'industria in Milano, 1565–1750', *Archivio Storico Lombardo*, 27 (1900), 49–116.

Villari, Rosario, 'La Spagna, l'Italia e l'assolutismo', *Studi Storici*, 18 (1977), 5–22.

—— 'Masaniello: Contemporary and Recent Interpretations', *Past and Present*, 103 (1985), 117–32.

—— *The Revolt of Naples*, trans. James Newell and John A. Marino (Cambridge, 1993).

—— *Per il re o per la patria. La fedeltà nel Seicento* (Rome and Bari, 1994).

Vincent, Bernard, 'The *Moriscos* and Circumcision', in *Culture and Control in Counter-Reformation Spain*, ed. Anne J. Cruz and Mary Elizabeth Perry (Minneapolis and Oxford, 1992), 78–92.

Visceglia, Maria Antonietta, *Il bisogno di eternità. I comportamenti aristocratici a Napoli in età moderna* (Naples, 1988).

—— 'Introduction', in *Signori, patrizi, cavalieri in Italia centro-meridionale nell'età moderna*, ed. Maria Antonietta Visceglia (Rome, 1992), v–xxxiii.

—— 'Rituali religiosi e gerarchie politiche a Napoli in età moderna', in *Fra storia e storiografia. Scritti in onore di Pasquale Villani*, ed. Paolo Macry and Angelo Massafra (Bologna, 1994), 587–620.

—— and Catherine Brice (eds.), *Cérémonial et rituel à Rome. XVIe–XIXe siècle* (Rome, 1997).

Vitale, Giuliana, *Ritualità monarchica, cerimonie e pratiche devozionali nella Napoli aragonese* (Salerno, 2006).

Watanabe-O'Kelly, Helen, 'Festivals Books in Europe from Renaissance to Rococo', *The Seventeenth Century Journal*, 3 (1988), 181–201.

—— 'Tournaments in Europe', in *Spectaculum Europaeum: Theatre and Spectacle in Europe (1580–1750)*, ed. Helen Watanabe-O'Kelly and Pierre Béhar (Wiesbaden, 1999), 595–720.

Wilentz, Sean (ed.), *Rites of Power: Symbolism, Ritual, and Politics since the Middle Ages* (Philadelphia, 1985).

Willette, Thomas, 'Bernardo De Dominici e la sua "Vita" di Stanzione', in *Massimo Stanzione. L'opera completa*, by Sebastian Schütze and Thomas Willette (Naples, 1992), 153–62.

Zapata Fernández de la Hoz, Teresa, 'La emblemática al servicio de la imagen publica de la reina. Los jeroglificos de la entada en la corte de Maria Ana de Neoburgo', in *Del libro de emblemas a la ciudad simbolica. Actas del III simposio internacional de emblemática hispánica*, ed. Víctor Mínguez (2 vols., Castellón, 2000), II, 671–704.

Zotta, Silvio, *G. F. De Ponte. Il giurista politico* (Naples, 1987).

Index

Note: 'n.' after a page reference indicates the number of a note on that page.